MAXIMUM SECURITY

FOURTH EDITION

Anonymous

SAMS

201 West 103rd St., Indianapolis, Indiana, 46290 USA

Maximum Security, Fourth Edition

International Standard Book Number: 0-672-32459-8

Library of Congress Catalog Card Number: 2002106456

Printed in the United States of America

First Printing: December 2002

05   04   03   02   4   3   2   1

Trademarks

Warning and Disclaimer

Acquisitions Editor
Jenny L. Watson

Development Editor
Heather Goodell

Managing Editor
Charlotte Clapp

Project Editor
Matthew Purcell

Copy Editors
Chip Gardner
Seth Kerney
Megan Wade

Indexer
Chris Barrick

Proofreader
Leslie Joseph

Technical Editors
Rob Blader
Marc Charney

Team Coordinator
Amy Patton

Multimedia Developer
Dan Scherf

Interior Designer
Gary Adair

Cover Designer
Gary Adair

Page Layout
Julie Parks

Graphics
Tammy Graham
Laura Robbins

Contents at a Glance

Table of Contents

15   Sniffers   281

About the Lead Author

Anonymous is a self-described Unix and Perl fanatic who lives in southern California with his wife Michelle and a half-dozen computers. He currently runs an Internet security consulting company and is at work building one of the world's largest computer security archives. He also moonlights doing contract programming for several Fortune 500 firms.

About the Contributing Authors

Craig Balding is a full-time security practitioner employed by one of the largest banking and finance companies in the world. This role has taken Craig around the world, from Eastern Europe to Asia. In addition to heading up Unix security, he is responsible for IDS strategy, technical e-business security assessments, and penetration testing. Craig has worked with Unix for some eight years in multivendor environments across diverse sectors. He has been at the sharp end, working on high-end, mission-critical Unix servers and multiterrabyte databases. When he's not submerged in geeky stuff, he loses himself in a world of sound synthesis—Craig loves techno.

Billy Barron (bbbarron@delphis.com) is a principal Java/OO consultant for Delphi Consultants, LLC (http://www.delphis.com/). He founded the Java Metroplex User Group (JavaMUG at http://www.javamug.org/) and was the first Webmaster in the Dallas/Fort Worth area. He has coauthored and tech-edited numerous books including *Web Programming Unleashed, Tricks of the Internet Gurus, Maximum Java 1.1, Web Commerce Unleashed, Creating Web Applets with Java,* and *Internet Unleashed.*

Robert Blader has worked for more than 15 years at the Naval Surface Warfare Center. For nearly 3 years he has worked in the Information Systems Security Office, which performs intrusion detection and risk management for systems and networks on the base, as well as security training and forensics. For 10 years prior to that, he worked as a systems administrator for the Trident missile project. He has contributed to SANS GIAC courses and *SysAdmin* magazine. He holds a bachelor's degree in computer science from Long Island University.

Chad Cook is co-founder and chief security architect of Zetari Inc., where he is responsible for product security, software design, and development. Prior to starting Zetari Inc., he was a senior member of the Internet security consulting firm @stake, where he worked in research and development and on client solutions. He has developed new security technologies and published papers on numerous security topics, including secure product design, vulnerability analysis, and encryption. Chad has 10 years of experience in the Internet security field with emphasis on secure product architecture, network and operating system security, and the research and development of new security technologies with companies including BBN, GTE, and Infolibria.

Jonathan Feldman is the author of *Sams Teach Yourself Network Troubleshooting in 24 Hours* and Que's *Network+ Exam Guide*. He is a contributing editor with *Network Computing* magazine, where he writes a column and frequently contributes technical workshops. He enjoys living in Savannah, Georgia, working as chief technical manager for Chatham County, where he handles the practical and political aspects of network security on a daily basis. In his copious spare time, he enjoys running, cooking, and playing the guitar, but not all at the same time. He can be reached at jf@feldman.org.

David Harley (harley@sherpasoft.org.uk) manages security for a major cancer research organization in the United Kingdom. He also works with TruSecure (formerly ICSA), the WildList Organization, and the European Institute for Computer Anti-virus Research. He maintains a number of virus- and security-related information resources at sherpasoft.org.uk and macvirus.com, and a security alert verification service at security-sceptic.org.uk. He writes regularly for *Virus Bulletin* and is a frequent speaker at security conferences. His book *Viruses Revealed* (with Robert Slade and Urs Gattiker) was published in late 2001. He lives in London with his 11-year-old daughter.

Joe Jenkins is a system administrator/security consultant with NoWalls, Inc. (http://www.nowalls.inc). Joe has been dealing with network security since 1993, conducting in-depth security audits and consulting on various aspects of intrusion detection, perimeter defense, and policy. Joe routinely writes for online security magazines, notably *SecurityFocus*, and has also worked as a programmer and hardware engineer.

L.J. Locher began working with mainframe and personal computers in the mid-1980s, and has since been employed as a network administrator, programmer, and security consultant for mainframe systems and PC LANs. Now a full-time author and editor, L.J. has contributed to numerous books and articles for various publishers including Microsoft Press and *Windows 2000* magazine.

Toby Miller is a security engineer for Advanced Systems Development. Toby holds a bachelor's degree in computer information systems and is working toward his master's degree. Toby is a contributing author for *Intrusion Signatures and Analysis* (New Riders). Toby is also the author of many papers published for SecurityFocus.com and the SANS Institute. Toby works as an MCP and a GIAC analyst.

Brooke Paul began working in information technology as a systems and network administrator at the University of California. Due to the loose nature of university security at the time, he experienced several security incidents within his first few months on the job. He quickly learned about the limitations of TCP/IP security and the lack of security in most vendors' default operating system configurations. Taking this as a challenge, he began working on improving the security of the systems and networks under his care. He now works as an information technology and security consultant and frequently publishes articles about security in technology trade magazines.

Nicholas Raba goes by the handle Freaky. Nicholas originally started writing by creating an underground printed publication, and from there created the Web site Freak's Macintosh Archives. Nicholas loves security, and MacOS just so happened to be the niche category he chose to specialize in. He created SecureMac.com and ever since then has been writing security articles covering all aspects of the MacOS for that Web site and various magazines. Nicholas has also given speeches for Defcon 7 and Defcon 8 on Macintosh hacking/security. He says, "Thanks to Rie, who pushed me to contribute to this book." You can reach Nicholas with any questions/comments about Macintosh security at nick@staticusers.net.

Greg Shipley is a native Chicagoan. Greg was introduced to the world of computers through a dangerous fixation with video games and taught himself assembly on his Commodore 64. After spending a number of years studying computer science, Greg moved into the world of network engineering and Internet security. Today, Greg serves as the CTO for Neohapsis, a U.S.-based information security consultancy. When he's not immersed in the seas of corporate security storms, he's busy at work performing product testing in the Neohapsis/Network Computing Chicago lab. Greg would like to send his greetings to the people of Molokai, as they helped him gain some much-needed perspective during the early stages of this book.

Gregory B. White, Ph.D., joined SecureLogix in March 1999. He serves as the Vice President of Professional Services. Before joining SecureLogix, he was the deputy head of the computer science department and an associate professor of computer science at the United States Air Force Academy in Colorado Springs, Colorado. While at the Academy, Dr. White was instrumental in the development of two courses on computer security and information warfare. He also ensured that security was taught throughout the computer science curriculum. During his two tours at the Academy, he authored a number of papers on security and information warfare, and is a coauthor for two textbooks on computer security.

Dr. Cyrus Peikari finished his formal training with honors in electrical engineering from Southern Methodist University in 1991. For eight years Dr. Peikari taught advanced mathematics at the SMU Learning Enhancement Center in Dallas, Texas. He has also worked as a telecommunications software research and development engineer for Alcatel. Dr. Peikari has developed several award-winning security software programs. He also co-founded DallasCon, the largest annual wireless security conference in the Southwest. You can reach him at cyrus@virusmd.com.

Brett L. Neilson is a network and system engineer with a strong background in the wireless industry. Mr. Neilson has previously worked for Verizon Wireless as a Senior Systems Administrator and RF Field Technician. While at Verizon he worked to develop, deploy, and maintain their national infrastructure. Currently Mr. Neilson works for a leading infosec corporation. As an FCC licensed amateur radio operator, he has worked with various government agencies providing communication assistance and coordination. His broad range of computer and RF skills has led him to perform groundbreaking research in practical wireless security. Mr. Neilson also teaches a series of review courses for the Wireless Security Expert Certification (WSEC).

Jim Cooper, MCSE, has over 15 years of information technology experience and specializes in Microsoft Windows Active Directory and Exchange design. He is one of the founders and current Senior Engineer of Micradex Systems, a network and domain outsourcing and design company headquartered in Charlotte, North Carolina. Jim is a frequent contributor of chapters for Pearson Technology Group and has also provided technical editing for numerous other titles.

Greg Vaughn just transitioned into corporate employment at LandSafe, Inc. after eight years as a consultant in Austin and Dallas, Texas, looking to make a positive long-term impact on development and security practices. He's an accomplished conference speaker, and now that his first child has turned two years old, he's finding some time to write. He earned an M.S. degree from Texas Tech University, and during his consulting career has worked on a huge range of devices, from PDAs to enterprise servers.

Dedication

For Danielle. Of my blood, you officially own 6.25%.
Of my heart and soul, oceans more. — Anonymous

Acknowledgments

My deepest thanks to a crack editing team: Mark Taber, Jenny Watson, Dan Scherf, Matt Purcell, Seth Kerney, and Chris Barrick, and my special thanks to the Pearson Education team. It's been a pleasure working with you all.

We Want to Hear from You!

As the reader of this book, *you* are our most important critic and commentator. We value your opinion and want to know what we're doing right, what we could do better, what areas you'd like to see us publish in, and any other words of wisdom you're willing to pass our way.

You can email or write me directly to let me know what you did or didn't like about this book—as well as what we can do to make our books stronger.

Please note that I cannot help you with technical problems related to the topic of this book, and that due to the high volume of mail I receive, I might not be able to reply to every message.

When you write, please be sure to include this book's title and author as well as your name and phone or email address. I will carefully review your comments and share them with the author and editors who worked on the book.

Email: networking@samspublishing.com

Mail: Mark Taber
         Associate Publisher
         Sams Publishing
         201 West 103rd Street
         Indianapolis, IN 46290 USA

Reader Services

For more information about this book or others from Sams Publishing, visit our Web site at http://www.samspublishing.com. Type the ISBN (excluding hyphens) or the title of the book in the Search box to find the book you're looking for.

Introduction

Welcome to *Maximum Security, Fourth Edition*. This introduction covers the following topics:

Why Did We Write This Book?

The *Maximum Security* series, which debuted in 1997, has thus far enjoyed relative success. I use the term "relative success," because security title sales have historically trickled, rather than gushed. For altering this and fostering a new market, the editors at Sams deserve kudos. Their insights have proven providential: Today, *Maximum Security* titles sell in five countries, five languages, and on four continents. Furthermore, the *Maximum Security* series has inspired many fine similar books from seasoned security professionals here and abroad.

The success of the *Maximum Security* series is no mystery. Security has never before been so sensitive an issue, nor an issue so vital to business. Many firms have now evolved well beyond mere Web presences and incorporate sophisticated e-commerce functionality into their systems. These developments have increased the demand for books that help administrators shield their enterprises from crackers, and *Maximum Security* titles have—in varying degrees—satisfied that need.

System Requirements

This section addresses what hardware, software, and documentation you'll need to reap the maximum benefit from this book. I've divided these into four sections:

- Absolute requirements—Things you must have.
- Archiving tools—Tools to unpack source code, archives, and packages that can enhance and secure your servers and network.
- Text and typesetting viewers—Tools that will substantially enhance and widen your knowledge by enabling you to read relevant online documents.
- Programming languages—Tools to use source code, packages, and utilities that enhance your network's security and functionality.

Absolute Requirements

To benefit from this book, you'll need at least the following:

- Unix, Linux, Windows, Amiga, OS/2, or BeOS

- A dedicated box running one of these platforms

- A network or Ethernet connection

Your network or Ethernet connection is not a strict requirement (you can use simple loopback), but without it, you won't be able to exploit some of the examples. However, loopback enables you to simulate many conditions and configurations that would normally exist only on the Internet or in intranet environments. Thus, even a single machine not connected to a network provides you with a microcosmic version of the Internet, and this, for the most part, will suffice.

Archiving Tools

You'll also need document and file utility support. This book points you to many Net-based resources, and even now not all Web sites or researchers provide documents in a standardized format (although Adobe's Portable Document Format (PDF) seems to be rapidly filling that gap).

Also, many utilities, source code, and packages originate from disparate platforms. Some are compressed on Unix, some are packaged on Windows, and so on. Therefore, you will need to have at least the tools mentioned in Table I.1.

TABLE I.1 Popular Archive Utilities

Utility	Platform	Description and Location
Winzip	Windows	Winzip decompresses files compressed to ARC, ARJ, BinHex, gzip, LZH, MIME, TAR, Unix compress, and Uuencode archives. Winzip is available at http://www.winzip.com/.
gunzip	Unix	gunzip unpacks files compressed with gzip or compress.
tar	Unix	tar unpacks tar archives made on Unix systems.
StuffIt	Macintosh	StuffIt decompresses ARC, Arj, BinHex, gzip, Macbinary, StuffIt, Uuencoded, and ZIP archives. StuffIt is available at http://www.aladdinsys.com/expander/index.html.

Text and Typesetting Viewers

Many commercial word processors and editors read and write data to proprietary formats. Plain text viewers seldom read such formats, which often contain control characters, unprintable characters, and sometimes even machine language. Although this situation is changing (because most text and word processors are now migrating to XML), many documents I reference are not backward compatible or don't open cleanly in plain text viewers. Thus, you'll need one or more readers to examine them.

> **NOTE**
>
> *Readers* decode documents written in formats not supported by your native application set. For example, Adobe's free PDF reader enables you to read PDF documents, and Microsoft's Word reader enables users that don't own Word to read Word-encoded documents.

Table I.2 lists several such utilities and their locations.

TABLE I.2 Readers for Popular Word-Processing Formats

Reader	Description and Location
Adobe Acrobat	Adobe Acrobat Reader decodes PDF files. Acrobat Reader is available for DOS, Windows, Windows 95, Windows NT, Unix, Macintosh, and OS/2. Get it at `http://www.adobe.com/supportservice/custsupport/download.html`.
GSView	GSView reads PostScript and GhostScript files. GSView is available for OS/2, Windows, Windows 3.11, Windows NT, and Windows NT. Get it at `http://www.cs.wisc.edu/~ghost/gsview/index.html`.
Word Viewer	Word Viewer reads Microsoft Word files. Word Viewer is available for Windows (16-bit) and Windows 95/NT. You can get either version here: `http://www.asia.microsoft.com/word/internet/viewer/viewer97/default.htm`.
PowerPoint Viewer	PowerPoint Viewer decodes Microsoft PowerPoint presentations. PowerPoint Viewer for Windows 95 is available here: `http://www.gallaudet.edu/~standard/presentation/pptvw32.exe`. PowerPoint Viewer for Windows NT is available here: `http://www.gallaudet.edu/~standard/presentation/pptvw32.exe`.

Programming Languages

Some examples in this book reference source code. To use the source code in this book, you'll need one or more compilers or interpreters.

Table I.3 lists these languages and tools.

TABLE I.3   Compilers and Interpreters

Tool	Description and Location
C and C++	The Free Software Foundation offers freeware C/C++ compilers for both Unix and DOS. The Unix version can be downloaded here: http://www.gnu.org/software/gcc/gcc.html. The DOS version can be downloaded here: http://www.delorie.com/djgpp/. Also, any recently released native or third-party C/C++ compiler will do, including CygWin, Watcom, Borland, and so on.
Perl	The Practical Extraction and Report Language (Perl) is often used in network programming (and especially Common Gateway Interface programming). Perl runs on Unix, Macintosh, and Windows NT, and is freely available here: http://www.perl.com/latest.html.
Java	Java (a Sun Microsystems programming language) is free and available here: http://www.javasoft.com/.
JavaScript	JavaScript is a language embedded in Microsoft Internet Explorer (MSIE), Netscape Navigator, and many other Web clients. To use JavaScript scripts, you should have MSIE, Netscape Navigator, or Netscape Communicator. These are free for noncommercial use and are available at either http://www.microsft.com or http://home.netscape.com.
PHP	PHP, the Hypertext Pre-Processor, is a lightweight but powerful in-line scripting language that interfaces through Web servers to MySQL and other database packages. If you don't already have it, get PHP here: http://www.php.net.
Python	Python is an object-oriented scripting language now commonly used in system administration and CGI work. Like PHP, it also interfaces with Web servers and even low-level operating system administrative utilities. Only a few examples in this book use Python, but to try them, you'll need a Python interpreter. Get one here: http://www.python.org/.
SQL	Structured Query Language (SQL) is for interacting with databases. SQL is not strictly required. However, even a shallow knowledge of SQL might help, as some examples briefly touch on it. For this, you needn't obtain any particular utility, but rather an introductory primer (book, Web site, and so on) for reference purposes.
VBScript	VBScript is a Microsoft scripting language that manipulates Web browser environments. VBScript itself and VBScript documentation are freely available at http://msdn.microsoft.com/scripting/vbscript/default.htm.

NOTE

If the comments on programming languages seem intimidating, have no fear. This book will explain everything necessary to use the examples herein. You needn't be a programmer nor ever write a line of code to use this title.

About Examples in This Book

If you're like me, you buy computer titles for their examples. Often, such examples instruct you to execute a command or compile source code. It is through such examples and exercises—even more than by attending formal classes—that we learn to administrate our systems, achieve competence in various technologies, and write solid code.

Unfortunately, many computer titles contain examples that for one reason or another don't enlighten us, or worse, don't work properly.

Some familiar scenarios:

- Authors sometimes demonstrate a command but include only its abbreviated output. They omit additional output, including unexpected output, errors, and so on. Books that omit such data leave you stranded when things go wrong. You're unfamiliar with the unexpected output, and you don't know how to proceed.

- Authors also sometimes generate examples on custom platforms and configurations, using custom tools. They might use shared libraries, for example, which you haven't yet installed, or libraries that your operating system doesn't natively support. If authors fail to warn you about these conditions, you may encounter unexpected or negative results.

- Other authors, faced with impending deadlines, work in haste and sometimes fail to double-check that their examples work as intended. Although most such authors have excellent technical editors charged with nixing unacceptable code, such errors can still slip through to printed editions. (This is especially so when multiple authors and/or editors work on the same title).

- Finally, many authors assume that their readers have long experience in advanced subjects (such as compilation), and therefore skip details that, when absent, can materially affect your project (or even flatly prevent you from achieving the desired result).

Publishers invariably correct these issues by posting errata and patch code on their Web sites. However, these corrections emerge weeks or months after the title's initial release. In the interim, readers angrily voice their complaints on Amazon, in newsgroups, and in other public places—and rightly so. Computer titles are expensive, after all, and at a minimum, their examples should work as promised.

Hence, starting with *Maximum Linux Security*, I have taken a fastidious approach to examples and program output:

- If an example worked only on exotic configurations, I omitted it.

- If, when testing a program, utility, or configuration, I found that it behaved strangely or in an unintended manner, I omitted it.

- When documenting examples, I often include exhaustive output. This isn't to seed the book with superfluous filler (raising the page count, and therefore the price). Rather, I do it to ensure that what you see is precisely what you'll see when you implement an example. My aim is to show you *exactly* what to expect. If your output differs from mine, an abnormal condition arose. And, more times than not, if you skip ahead a paragraph or two beyond the example, I explain possible alternatives, output, and the likely cause.

This approach guarantees that some examples and their accompanying commentary will seem inordinately verbose. However, it also guarantees that this book will give you a more holistic understanding of security than most others in its class. Indeed, after reading this book, you'll find errors, output, and general system behavior far less perplexing. You'll proceed competently, armed with implacable confidence.

About Links and References in This Book

Like all *Maximum Security* titles, *Maximum Security, Fourth Edition* provides many links to online resources. I (and my coauthors) do this for several reasons. First, no book can impart everything about a given subject. Rather, books at best offer an overview, point you in the proper direction, and give you hands-on experience through examples. But in IT—a rapidly evolving field you must constantly update your skill set— even these generous gifts are insufficient. Today's computer books must do more than merely explain technologies; they must serve as springboards that not only inform you, but also inspire and enable you to conduct further, independent research.

Also, after you ace installation or configuration of a given operating system or application, you're ready to move on. If the application is extensible, you'll want to extend it; if it needs a patch, you'll want to patch it; if other tools collaborate with it, you'll want them, as well.

Finally, today, time *is* money. Each time you spend an hour or more searching for an online tool, advisory, or article, you lose money (not to mention precious minutes of life). In the meantime, you could be doing something else, something *productive*. *Maximum Security* titles provide innumerable pointers at your fingertips and alleviate the need for you to search for anything. This saves you time, money, and aggravation.

So, I always include in my titles long resource lists pertaining to the present subject matter. Thus, my titles serve not merely as treatises, but also references and road maps to detailed information located elsewhere.

Some facts about this book's links:

- I and the Sams editorial team took exhaustive measures to ensure that this book's links were valid at press time. This doesn't mean that every link will be valid, though. The WWW is dynamic, documents move, some Web masters are flaky, and some ISPs fold. Hence, it's likely that a small percentage of the URLs I reference will be invalid by the time you read this. Regrettably, this is beyond our control. For this reason (and to further reduce the likelihood of you drowning in 404 errors), I have provided at least one alternative URL for each link whenever possible.

- Regarding URLs built from CGI strings: These strings can be incredibly long and inconvenient to manually enter. I approached this in two ways. First, if a document resided at such a URL, I used the filename to search for an alternative location, one with a shorter URL. Whenever possible, I provided the alternative URL instead. In cases where the 130-character CGI-based URL was the only source available, I added that URL to `long-urls.html` on the accompanying CD-ROM. Thus, when you surf URLs from this book, if you encounter an impossibly long one, throw in the CD, pull up the file, and click away.

- Regarding commercial, shareware, and freeware products: My coauthors and I point to hundreds (or sometimes, thousands) of applications, tools, and utilities. We often comment on these, too, sometimes praising their functionality and developers. If we mention a product, we do so merely because it's useful or because we generated examples with it (and not because we want to commercially endorse the product). Having related that, we do thank vendors and developers that rendered technical support on their products—their help was indispensable.

A Final Note

In this fourth edition (as with its predecessor), I'm proud to have excellent and highly competent coauthors aboard. I'm indebted to Billy Barron, Brooke Paul, Greg Vaughn, Rob Blader, David Harley, Jim Cooper, Nicholas Raba, Cyrus Peikari, Brett Neilsen, Craig Balding, Greg Shipley, Jonathan Feldman, Chad Cook, L.J. Locher, Joe Jenkins, Toby Miller, and Gregory White for enhancing this edition of *Maximum Security*.

Maximum Security starts with general security issues common to any server and ends with security issues surrounding very specific configurations, operating systems, and technologies. We hope you find it useful.

—Anonymous

PART I
Security Concepts

IN THIS PART

1

Building a Roadmap for Securing Your Enterprise

Any attempt to secure an enterprise must be well thought out and planned. Ad-hoc security measures, although useful, will not lead to an enterprise being truly secure. Proper security is a complex ongoing process. Without proper preparation, any security program is going to fail because it will have gaps in its coverage. This chapter briefly examines essential components of an effective security program.

Reactive Versus Proactive Models

In security, two models or postures exist:

- *Reactive*—The reactive model is a largely historical animal. In it, administrators add security controls as needed, on a case-by-case basis. This model is typically used in response to security incidents, such as attackers cracking a machine because it didn't have network access control.

- *Proactive*—The now preferred proactive model, this is where administrators perform risk analysis, establish stringent controls, and apply those controls enterprise-wide. No machine on this network can have connectivity until it first has network access control.

Reactive policies were once the norm, but changes in the business world rendered them inadequate. A good comparison is a country. As leader of a country, do you wait until you are attacked to have an army to defend yourself? If you decide to have a standing army, do you have training and advanced planning in place? Of course, you need a standing army that has been trained and some planning on how to defend the company in place. The same applies to your computer systems. Thus, your security program *must* be proactive.

To establish such a program, you must, at a minimum

- Understand your enterprise

- Perform risk assessment

- Identify your digital assets

- Protect assets

- Identify and remove vulnerabilities

- Establish and enforce policies

- Educate your personnel

- Constantly repeat these steps

Understanding Your Enterprise

A decade ago, most enterprises weren't wired, or if they were, their networks were closed and had no Internet connectivity. The average security administrator's universe, therefore, was limited. Her network supported few protocols, a limited application set, and known users.

Today this is no longer true. Modern computing has become ubiquitous. By default, every box on every network supports multiple protocols, thousands of applications, and potentially unlimited users, many that are (or can be) anonymous.

To appreciate how profoundly this climate affects an administrator's responsibilities, consider this: Historically, few administrators had to understand workflow patterns or human process models because data rarely traversed networks as pervasively as it does today. Rather, in those golden, olden days, administrators needed only to understand where an enterprise's valued assets were, and the measures to protect them.

Today, *where* is relative, because an organization's data can exist in several places simultaneously. For example, how many times a day do you mail spreadsheets to multiple recipients? Of those recipients, how many are in-house, and how many operate from outside domains? Can you definitively say (at this moment) *where* your data is?

This new climate demands that contemporary security administrators understand more than merely data's static locale and the tools to secure it. Security administrators must now grasp *how* their enterprise operates, and not just in general terms.

To that end, administrators now grapple with issues that once had limited security relevance, including the following:

- Contractor relationships

- Government regulations

- Workflow patterns

Consider, for example, a security administrator at a hospital that falls under the Health Insurance Portability and Accountability Act (commonly called "HIPAA"). HIPAA imposes regulations and restrictions on qualified health care facilities regarding the transmission and storage of confidential patient data.

Two such restrictions are

- Documents must have digital signatures or checksums

- Transmissions must travel encrypted

On their face, such regulations seem straightforward enough. However, bringing a facility into compliance presents security administrators with unique and sometimes difficult problems. The divide between well-intentioned guidelines and practical application can be considerable, because information technology has limitations. To demonstrate this point, I offer two real-life scenarios, one for each of the aforementioned regulations.

Certain data, such as admission information, follow a patient through various hospital departments. Many departments use admission data to derive new documents, and by law, each such new document must carry a checksum. These conditions demand that the hospital administrator understand workflow patterns.

Many health care facilities, for example, now use digital duplicators that transmit pages via IP. That is, you create and scan a document in one office, and the network delivers copies to another (or several). This poses a unique problem, especially if the initiating software interfaces directly with duplicator hardware, and many such programs do.

If the document you broadcast this way is new, how do you derive its checksum and preserve that checksum's relationship to the document? Where in that workflow pattern can you insert a checksum generation routine? Finally, until you do, must you resign yourself to manual checksum generation? What if your professional staff transmits and distributes 1,000 such documents daily?

Next, consider the encryption regulations. The hospital doesn't do its own billing but instead outsources that task to a billing contractor. That contractor demands patient billing information in X12 format (plain text, essentially), and provides a gateway service that receives transmissions electronically over the network.

Even five years ago this scenario presented few concerns, but today HIPAA demands encrypted transmissions. Hence, the administrator must convene with the billing contractor's security staff and establish a mutually acceptable encryption scheme, and until she does, each X12 transmission will violate government regulations. Further, she can't develop and test the new scheme on production systems, for if she does, this activity can interrupt billing (a vital service).

Many enterprises, and not merely those in healthcare, face stringent regulations or policies such as HIPAA. Moreover, even those firms that escape regulatory guidelines face complicated workflow patterns that offer attackers innumerable opportunities.

Your first aim, therefore, is to understand your enterprise's process model, and this may prove more difficult than it first seems. You may discover that no one in your enterprise has ever modeled its workflow patterns before, and you must do so yourself.

Workflow and Security

When we discuss process models and workflow patterns, what do we mean? In software circles, these terms conjure images of application phases, subroutines, stored procedures, and so forth. Most administrators and programmers have experience in these areas. However, a smaller number have never seen or drafted business-oriented process models. Because this issue is vital to your security program, we'll quickly cover it here.

Business-oriented process models illustrate data paths as they relate to tasks vital to business operation. That is, business process models graphically show a given transaction's workflow pattern, the personnel or automated systems that intervene during each phase, the decisions these individuals or systems can make, and every possible result.

For example, suppose your enterprise performs telephone sales. Each day, the database must distribute sales leads to sales personnel. In turn, sales personnel call those leads and make sales (you hope). If sales personnel do make a sale, they record that data somewhere, the system retrieves it, and custom applications track it. Finally, when a purchase order comes due, collectors bill clients and make attempts to collect. If clients pay, the system records this information.

Throughout that process (or, more esoterically, that *life cycle*) many things can happen—humans can make decisions, and upon such decisions, take action. Each decision can trigger different results, and those results can create, affect, transform, or destroy data. Moreover, each phase along the route will expose your enterprise's data to different environments, and often each such environment will expose your data to unique risks.

What you want, in short, is a model showing a data element's entire life cycle as it winds through your enterprise. After you can visualize this path, you'll know what controls to institute and where, when, and how to use them.

In drafting that model, you'll consider many issues, including the following:

- How does a data element come into being?

- Where does that genesis happen?

- From there, where can the data go?

- Along its route, who can access the data and how?

- At what points along the route must you accrue accounting, auditing, or logging statistics?

- At its final destination (presumably, a database), in what form must the data exist? Who can access it there? Who can change it and how?

To ascertain all this, you'll interface with other individuals and departments, and this process can often take time. Don't become discouraged, though. Mapping your firm's process model is the most vital step you'll take.

Risk Assessment: Evaluating Your Enterprise's Security Posture

After you grasp your enterprise's process model, you can perform risk analysis, and you begin by evaluating your firm's security posture.

In doing so, consider the following issues:

- Management awareness

- Employee awareness

- Security policies

- Network security

- Application security

- Prior losses and security incidents

- Incident tracking and response

These inquiries will tell you how vulnerable the enterprise is or was, what risks it faces, and the likelihood of future loss. Armed with this data, you can author a decent security proposal. However, even here, you'll need to get creative.

Traditionally, such proposals revolved around cost-benefit analyses, and from those analyses, management decided what controls to institute. One popular formula was to evaluate annual losses against annual costs of security measures. That is, if real or projected losses did or were likely to exceed a specific security measure's cost, the enterprise should deploy that security measure. Conversely, if the measure's cost exceeded projected losses, the enterprise can survive without it.

These formulas, once staples of risk assessment, are likely outdated. Today, data doesn't always have a concrete, identifiable value. In many cases, the data itself does not have an easily quanitifable valuable, but instead represents competitive advantage, prospective advantage, or other difficult-to-articulate benefits.

Rather, such cost-benefit analysis formulas are today more suited for calculating a firm's disaster recovery costs (replacing hardware, software, and so on) than costs of security breaches.

> **NOTE**
>
> In some situations, such formulas are still appropriate. For example, let's revisit our hospital security administrator. She has certain advantages in evaluating risk. HIPAA regulations assign specific monetary penalties for each violation. Hence, it's easy to attach a concrete dollar value to a given security lapse. Such environments, however, are more exceptions than rules these days.

The key to identifying likely losses and affixing concrete values to them (if you can) is known as digital asset assessment.

Identifying Digital Assets

When pondering the term *asset identification*, most IT folks think of asset management or asset tracking. This is because most (if not all) administrators have received, at one time or another, orders to catalog physical network assets, record serial numbers, and track what employee signed out what laptop and when.

Overt costs in such garden-variety asset tracking are obvious. An e-commerce system can consist of a dozen Web servers, several database servers, a merchant gateway, and supporting infrastructure equipment. Such a setup can run $400,000 in hardware. That's a concrete, easily identifiable cost. Likewise, the software and network devices all have set book values you can easily calculate and depreciate.

A more difficult problem is to identify the costs that a site-wide outage might accrue, but given sufficient time, you can still skillfully juggle the numbers to derive a reasonably accurate forecast. Here, you'll calculate hourly or daily revenue losses, costs of emergency response, technical support costs, and other costs unattached to any physical quantity or commodity.

Some costs are still more difficult to identify, though. Suppose your e-commerce initiative's client records and purchasing trend data reside on a single database server. Again, the server's value is obvious. But what happens when attackers compromise that server? What if they leak your data to the public? This can trigger other, less tangible but still critical costs: damaged consumer confidence, damaged industry reputation, or even legal liability.

Such costs are more difficult (and sometimes impossible) to forecast. Damaged strategic or financial partners, for example, might bring not only contract claims but also tort claims, and today, jury awards are sometimes inequitable, unreasonable, or inexplicable. Similarly, insurance companies may initially agree to defend you, and then midstream through a litigation procedure, refuse to go further, leaving you to bankroll your own defense.

Bookstores carry many asset identification titles that ponder how asset management relates to risk analysis, but few such books offer definitive formulas on forecasting "unforeseeable losses." Instead, authors typically identify key digital assets and classify these as low, medium, and high-value items.

Most authors identify the following assets as high-value:

- Customer data
- Financial reports
- Financial systems
- Marketing strategies
- Miscellaneous proprietary data
- Payroll information
- Research and development data
- Sales information
- Source code

Of these, you must choose what are most valuable, and only you can determine that (and then, only armed with a process model in hand). After you determine their relative values, you must next decide on what means you'll use to protect them.

Protecting Assets

Many organizations begin their analysis at their perimeter and move inward, roughly simulating (what they perceive to be) an attacker's entry point and ultimate trajectory. Organizations that adopt this posture typically identify their perimeter by equating it with a tangible, physical point in space. This point in space, more often than not, is their firewall.

This approach has merit from a network security standpoint, but also has pitfalls. For example:

- Statistics indicate that internal security breaches far outweigh external breaches. For this reason, some administrators prefer to start at an enterprise's core and work outward.

- This "fortress mentality" sometimes concentrates human efforts telescopically on perimeter systems. This leads to an inverse relationship between security and network depth. That is, the deeper you travel into the network's inner core, the less security controls you find. This results in a hard outer shell and a comparatively soft internal posture.

- Not every enterprise operates in an exclusively horizontal environment, where frontal attacks comprise their sole risk. Some enterprises operate in vertical (or even parallel) environments, where frontal attacks take a back seat to other attack methodologies.

- Often there are non-obvious ways to bypass the firewall. A couple of examples are modems and VPNs.

- Finally, some enterprises simply can't rely solely on the fortress posture because their business models depend on open, ubiquitous computing (a P2P file-sharing system, for example, with thousands of anonymous users).

Hence, during this phase, your enterprise's process model plays a starring role. As you examine each possible phase or transformation a data element can traverse, you'll find that data element deposited in widely varying environments. For each such environment that may pose different or unique risks, you must identify a protection scheme that meets its specific demands.

Unless you're using an entirely Web-based solution that centralizes all data and processing, you'll invariably find many environments along the process route that demand solutions for which no existing out-of-the-box cure exists. For this reason, you'll initially benefit more from an education in prevailing security technologies (and schools of thought) than with specific vendor products.

Several reasons necessitate this:

- Security vendors earn their daily bread by exploiting fear. Often, such vendors peddle quality products that nonetheless fail to address your specific needs. By knowing what technologies your network requires, you can cut through marketing smoke.

- It's more important that, at a glance, you have the capability to determine that a specific environment requires a proxy gateway (described in detail in Chapter 10), than that you need this or that commercial firewall product.

- It's vital that you understand *why* you need a given technology. A vendor might well sell you the correct or applicable tool, but as a security administrator, you must know how that product's controls will help you, and what potential risks such a product presents.

When (and only when) you understand the risks inherent in each environment along the process path, you'll next break risks into their respective categories. It's here that you begin identifying solutions that have real relevance. During this process model phase, the data travels from your network to your partner's, and therefore, you must encrypt it. Possible solutions include IPsec, SSH, and RSA, among others.

However, before you make final decisions on solutions, you first narrow your investigation's scope even further. You do this by identifying and removing pre-existing system vulnerabilities, and here's why: Risk management, security, and administration hinge much on efficiency. Commercial security solutions are expensive, and wherever possible, you should exploit pre-existing controls. Your administrative personnel likely already have proven experience with your firm's platforms and their security controls. Exploit their knowledge wherever and whenever possible, because new products sometimes present steep learning curves.

Identifying and Removing Vulnerabilities

The process of identifying and removing vulnerabilities differs from evaluating environmental risks along your process model's route. In examining your process model, you seek to isolate human or business procedures that expose data to external risks (for example, where data must pass from one network to another safely, encrypted and protected against electronic eavesdropping). Such risks aren't attributable to any particular weakness or flaw in your specific underlying system.

In contrast, the process of identifying and removing vulnerabilities focuses on your specific hardware, software, and network equipment. All of these elements likely harbor flaws, and not merely environmental conditions that incidentally expose data to risk. Instead you'll look for software and hardware design errors, security holes, weak encryption algorithms, weak password storage procedures, bad application security policies, and so on.

Here, you seek several objectives:

- Identify and eliminate historical hardware and software security issues to achieve a baseline from which to work (for example, determine which systems are patched, which aren't, and remedy this where necessary).

- Identify and eliminate application security policies that invite security breaches (for example, install proactive password checking so that even at an application level, your security remains proactive).

- Identify weaknesses for which infrastructure vendors have no immediate, viable solution (so you can find or recommend alternatives).

Only after you take these steps can you determine what specific security solutions and products (hardware, software, and so on) you need to harden your enterprise. Like all *Maximum Security* titles, this edition both lists and provides (on the accompanying CD-ROM) many security assessment tools to assist you in this phase.

From all this data (risk assessment, digital assets, your enterprise's process model, risky environments, application security policies, and inherent platform weaknesses), you can generate the two cardinal documents or *roadmap elements*:

- Your security proposal—This is a document describing what your firm must do to achieve baseline security, the costs involved, and what tools, modalities, and, if necessary, services you'll require.

- Your forward-thinking, proactive security plan—This is a document that establishes what tools, policies, procedures, and postures your organization must deploy to sustain security.

Your security proposal will develop dynamically as you conduct your investigation. Your proactive security plan, however, emerges only after you finish your investigation. Its main body will consist of proactive policies, the most important of which focus on internal system standardization. Let's discuss that now.

Standardization and Proactive Policies

A natural by-product of your investigation is a transparent look at what technologies are vital to your enterprise. This will emerge without much effort on your part. As you interface with each department or division in your process model analysis, folks there will tell you (perhaps in more detail than you'd like) what applications they need to satisfy their responsibilities.

This data provides you with a basis on which to classify departments or divisions by their respective functions, and within that framework, identify indispensable technologies for them. After you know this, you can compile an approved application set—that is, you can develop a generic must-have list in topology, platforms, services, protocols, and applications on a department-by-department basis.

This, too, is more complicated than it initially seems, because many firms deploy widely disparate technologies. IT divisions today often commonly support Solaris, Windows NT, NetWare, Linux, HP/UX, AIX, AS/400, and OS/390-based systems, all in the same enterprise, and sometimes, in the same divisions. However, the totality of systems will eventually emerge as a fixed quantity (even if it's wide in scope).

After you have this information, you begin the standardization process and establish the following:

- What topology, platforms, services, protocols, and applications each department needs

- The security issues common to each department

Based on these variables, you next establish standard installation, deployment, policy, security, auditing, and application settings on each respective platform or infrastructure system. This provides you with a template of sorts, and that template should explicitly specify the following:

- Approved applications—These are applications vital to the enterprise. You add applications not on this list (chatting and messaging systems that employees don't deploy except for personal use, for example) to your disapproved applications list.

- Disapproved applications—These are superfluous applications you can neither support nor secure, and which don't contribute to your enterprise's productivity or security.

- Installation options—Most operating systems and service applications now ship with dozens of features your enterprise likely doesn't need (and which invite security breaches). Prohibit such unneeded features.

- Directory, filesystem, and application resource layouts—These are configuration options indispensable to your enterprise. For example, perhaps every user in accounting needs access to the same shared-out volume.

- Account security policies—Certain departments will require specific security policies. For example, divisions that employ part-time, temporary, or consulting-basis personnel have high turnover rates. These departments will probably demand more stringent password lockout, audit, and regeneration policies than anchor divisions.

- Network security policies—Certain network resources are more sensitive than others. For some, you'll deploy deep, stringent, or fanatical logging, auditing, and authentication procedures. For others, you may establish less stringent guidelines.

These templates not only standardize and simplify your security posture enterprise-wide, they also provide you with an immediate upgrade, restoration, or recovery path (or an easy way to duplicate them, such as when you add a station to a given department). Finally, they provide a baseline to which all personnel must adhere, so they eliminate unknown quantities or qualities. This fosters much easier and more efficient security management.

Other issues your proactive security plan's policies should account for are

- Acceptable usage

- Data value classification

- Data disclosure and destruction

- Roles and responsibilities

- Change control

- Business continuity plan

NOTE

Business continuity planning is the process by which you can plan on how to continue running your business if something bad happens, such as a tornado or a terrorist attack. In the past, the term disaster recovery was used to mean the same thing, but it has fallen out of fashion.

You'll naturally need management approval for your plan and policies, and that's why you must document all the aforementioned things scrupulously. You must also incorporate two final features into your proposal: your incident response policy and personnel education.

Incident Response Policy

Incident response policy articulates what steps security personnel must take when a breach occurs. Issues your proposal should cover in this department include the following:

- Taxonomy of security incidents—This articulates all known security breach types.

- Security incident risk classification—This articulates the risk level for each type of security breach.

- Incident team roster—This identifies who (besides yourself) is responsible for responding to security incidents, and who's authorized to direct such activity and make decisions.

- Incident response path—This describes, in general terms, what acts security personnel should undertake in sequence.

- Escalation protocol—This indicates time periods or events after which security personnel take increasingly proactive, hands-on, or critical (emergency) procedures.

- Reporting—This describes how, when, to whom, and in what intervals security personnel provide on-the-scene updates.

Training Users and Administrators

Finally, we reach the issue of personnel education. Here, you'll encounter the most resistance, but you must nonetheless include education in your proposal. You'll doubtless find creative ways to express the need for security education, but ensure that you do the following:

- Inform all employees of security policies (such as AUPs, or Acceptable Use Policies).

- Embark on an awareness campaign. This will help the general user population understand threats and reaffirm that your organization has an information security effort afoot.

- Enlist an executive sponsor willing to publish memos, issue statements, and otherwise support you in establishing and maintaining aggressive security practices.

- Introduce responsibility matrices that identify specific security responsibilities, including those expected of average employees (such as not taping post-it notes with passwords to their monitors).

40,000-Foot Review

Now that we've enumerated all the aforementioned granularly, let's quickly look at the entire process. Figure 1.1 illustrates a fast-track cycle to an effective proactive security plan.

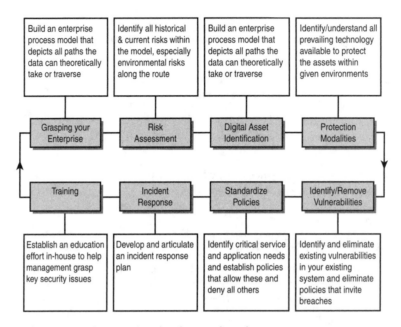

FIGURE 1.1   A proactive security plan fast-track cycle.

We'll proceed hereafter with a very small model, a mere division of an enterprise, in a telephone sales operation. In that operation, a sales department employee's responsibilities and data access are limited to examining and calling on leads and reporting pitch results, as shown in Figure 1.2.

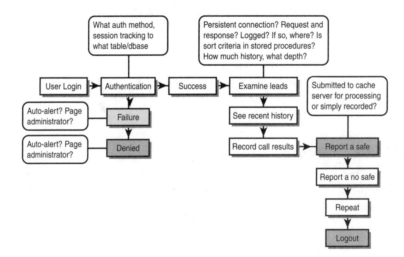

FIGURE 1.2   A sales representative's daily process model.

The sales representative performs his duties from a workstation bay that other sales personnel also use, and this bay is connected to larger system. Hence, even in the salesperson's relatively simple process model, he ties into a superceding life cycle. Your chief objective, then, is to ascertain the environmental risks that exist along that life cycle's route, and where these occur. To do so, you examine all technology systems within that cycle, illustrated in Figure 1.3.

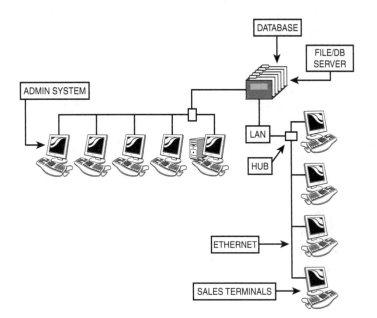

FIGURE 1.3   The life cycle to which a salesperson belongs.

Figure 1.3, even at a glance, reveals several environmental risks.

First, salespeople share bandwidth at adjacent terminals, drawing connectivity from a simple Ethernet strung to a hub. Hence, wily salespersons could install electronic eavesdropping devices to intercept competing sales personnel's leads. Moreover, because the file and database server's connectivity comes from the same source, they can even sniff database traffic. (This probably calls for a switch-based solution coupled with encrypted traffic.)

Next, the system survives on a single database server. Access to this server—for all departments—is direct, and no redundancy exists. One good attack is all it takes: a skilled attacker who had breached the system's security could destroy your database. Here, perhaps you would consider shared-out volumes from a RAID that snapshots hourly, data replication (if your RDBMS supports it), or other measures.

Third, the model as-is doesn't specify what type of network device ties administration into the database. Unknown quantities such as this obstruct your ability to accurately assess risk. Given these facts, you might have to physically go to the network operations center and ascertain that device's type, make, model, and so on.

Additionally, at some point, you must ascertain what protocols users use to access the database. This can be anything (simple Ethernet, SQL*Net, TCP/IP, and so on), but whatever it is will bear on security. Moreover, you must ascertain what authentication methods the database supports. This will give clues as to whether you'll need additional third-party or native authentication support (and so it goes).

Also, by examining such a model, you can identify where your digital assets are, where they go, who can access them, and so forth. Here, you can physically notate your most valuable digital assets, calculate their exposure risk, and determine where you should concentrate your efforts.

After assaying all this, you next turn to determining the system's current vulnerabilities (perhaps with system assessment tools). Concurrent with this, you catalog patch and maintenance histories for all integrated systems, review their security policies, and update or tighten these where necessary.

Based on your findings, you establish your guidelines and policies for each class of station or system, and enforce these policies system-wide. This establishes an across-the-board, baseline security posture.

And finally, you establish an incident response policy based on what risks remain, and institute an education program.

Summary

This chapter is not exhaustive. Instead, it merely offers a bare bones, fast-track route to a proactive security program. For more in-depth information, see Chapter 19, "Network Architecture Considerations," and Chapter 25, "Policies, Procedures, and Enforcement." In the interim, we'll move on to the next chapter, which highlights important risks.

2

The State of the Net: A World at War

Since 1973, Internet sites have been breached on a regular basis. Although it's difficult to compare the Internet of the late 70s and 80s with the network known as the Internet today, it is safe to say that the attack trends are not decreasing. This chapter was designed to give you a tour of some of the chaos that exists on the Internet today, as well as to provide some insight into what could possibly lie ahead. We will examine the fact that every type of organization in existence has been broken into, ranging from educational institutions to corporations to the U.S. Department of Defense (DoD). There is evidence that Internet-based attacks could be used to cripple organizations and government agencies for political purposes. With the worldwide fight against terrorism, these issues are more relevant than ever. The Internet is just one battleground of many. Today, security technologies are complex, but the Internet is still easily cracked. This chapter discusses who can, and has been, broken into and why.

Hacking, Cracking, and Other Malicious Behavior

Although most people have succumbed to using the term *hacked* when they refer to illegal intrusions, the term *cracked* might be more proper. *Cracked* refers to that condition in which the victim network suffers an unauthorized intrusion. There are various degrees of this condition. Here are a few examples:

- The intruder gains access and nothing more (*access* being defined as simple unauthorized entry on a network that requires—at a minimum—a login and password).

- The intruder gains access and destroys, corrupts, or otherwise alters data.

- The intruder gains access and seizes control of a compartmentalized portion of the system or the whole system, perhaps denying access even to privileged users.

- The intruder does not gain access, but instead forges messages from your system. (Folks often do this to send unsolicited mail or spam.)

- The intruder does not gain access, but instead implements malicious procedures that cause the network to fail, reboot, hang, or otherwise manifest an inoperable condition, either permanently or temporarily. These type of attacks are usually classified as denial-of-service (DoS) attacks.

Modern security techniques have made cracking more difficult. However, the distance between the word *difficult* and the word *impossible* is still wide. Today, crackers have access to a wealth of security information, most of which is freely available on the Internet. The balance of knowledge between crackers and bona fide security specialists is not greatly disproportionate. In fact, it is arguable that each side possesses components that the other side lacks, which makes the balance all the more interesting.

This chapter shows that cracking is a common activity—so common that assurances from anyone that the Internet is secure should be viewed with extreme suspicion. To drive that point home, I will begin with governmental entities. After all, defense and intelligence agencies form the basis of our national security infrastructure. They, more than any other group, must be secure.

Governments at War

If I asked you who your friends were, you'd answer without hesitation. That's because human relationships are based on mutual interest and affection, simple qualities that are largely subjective. If I asked you to identify friends of the United States, again, you would answer without hesitation. In that instance, however, your answer would probably be dead wrong.

In diplomatic circles, the word *ally* describes any foreign nation that shares common territorial, ideological, or economic interests with your own. We call this or that foreign state an ally based on various treaties, a handful of assurances, and on occasion, binding contracts.

For example, we count France and Israel as allies. Each occupies a geographical region that we have interest in protecting, and each shares with us a vision of democracy. (The French stood with us against the Nazis, and we have long supported Israel in the repatriation of Jews driven from Soviet Russia.) If these nations are our friends, why are they spying on us? In the last decade, the United States has been the target of widespread technological and industrial espionage, often perpetrated by friends and allies. In 2002, security experts estimated that at least 12 of the top trading partners of the U.S. had systematic spying programs directed at the U.S. This includes the seven largest European Union members, as well as China, Israel, Japan, South Korea, and Taiwan. Most of these countries are considered U.S. allies. More information can be found at `http://www.worldtrademag.com/CDA/ArticleInformation/features/BNP__Features__Item/0,3483,74603,00.html`.

CAUTION

Do you fly Air France? If so, watch what you say on the telephone. Air France has been caught intercepting electronic communications of American tourists in transit to Europe. An article on the subject can be found at `http://www.newsmax.com/showinside.shtml?a=2001/6/14/153545`.

China and Japan have been caught stealing data communications information from Lucent. France targeted Boeing as well. Like most nations spying on us, France employs these generic intelligence-gathering techniques:

- Eavesdropping

- Penetrating computer networks

- Stealing proprietary information

Do you still believe that France is an ally?

You're probably shocked that I would say all this. Let me take a different angle. If you're a French, Israeli, German, or South Korean national, know this: The U.S. government spies on your countrymen 24 hours a day, 7 days a week. In fact, every industrialized country does it. Many non-industrialized countries do it as well. That's simply the way it is; nations have their own economic and political agendas. These agendas naturally—and necessarily—have far greater priority than pacts made with allies. In other words, we can't blame France for trying.

The problem is, times have changed drastically. For 10,000 years, spying, sabotage, and warfare have all required human participation. Indeed, the spy's face has changed little throughout the ages. Whether he was a stealthy infiltrator, an agent of influence, or an agent provocateur, he was still human.

The rules have since changed. Telecommunications and computer technology have made electronic espionage and warfare not simply fanciful notions, but hard realities. Therefore, hostile foreign nations need not send human spies anymore. Instead, they can send packets—and why not? Packets are cheaper. Packets don't drink or smoke (that we know of), they don't gamble, and they cannot be compromised by virtue of reputation, sexual indiscretion, or criminal record. Most importantly, packets are invisible (at least to folks who maintain poor security practices).

From this, it's only a small step to imagine the Internet as a superb espionage tool. Many government sources were slow to recognize this. However, the U.S. government is at least well aware of the problem now and takes it seriously.

Can the Internet Be Used for Espionage?

The better question is, *how often* is the Internet used for espionage? Analysts have hotly debated for quite some time now whether the Internet could be used for spying. They can stop arguing—it is already happening. For example, the Soviet Union's space shuttle program was based on American technology stolen from the Internet. Designs were acquired from various technical universities online. In fact, in his article "How Soviets Stole a Shuttle," Robert Windrem says that:

> So thorough was the online acquisition, the National Security Agency learned, that the Soviets were using two East-West research centers in Vienna and Helsinki as covers to funnel the information to Moscow, where it kept printers going "almost constantly"... Intelligence officials told NBC News that the Soviets had saved billions on their shuttle program by using online spying.

The Soviets have long recognized the Internet as a valid intelligence source. An Internet legend gained international fame by breaking a KGB spy ring that used the Internet to steal American secrets. I refer here to Clifford Stoll, an astronomer then working at a university in Berkeley, California.

Stoll set out to discover the source of a 75-cent accounting error. During his investigation, he learned that someone had broken into the university's computers. Instead of confronting the intruder, Stoll watched the activity. What he saw was disturbing.

The intruder was using Stoll's servers as a launch point. The real targets were military computers, including servers at the Pentagon. The intruder was probing for information on U.S. nuclear preparedness. Stoll recognized this for what it was: spying. He therefore contacted the Federal Bureau of Investigation. However, to Stoll's surprise, FBI agents dismissed the entire incident and refused to offer assistance. Stoll began his own investigation. What followed has since become the most well-known chapter in Internet folklore.

After analyzing chained connections through the telephone system, Stoll traced the spy to Germany. His evidence would ultimately prompt the FBI, the CIA, and the West German secret police to get involved. In March 1989, Clifford Stoll was credited with cracking a German spy ring that stole U.S. secrets from the Net and sold them to the KGB. (An interesting side note: The German spies received not only money, but also large amounts of cocaine for their services.)

Can the Internet Be Used for Terrorism?

The term for this is cyberterrorism. The definition is somewhat vague, and has several different meanings. One is planning physical terrorism by exchanging information on the Internet. Another is damaging the Internet itself. We will look at both kinds.

Intelligence experts have determined that Al-Qaeda used the Internet to plan the attempted bombing of LAX (the Los Angeles airport), and troop movements were also planned over the Internet. In both of these cases, they tried to disguise the conversations in terms of wedding and travel plans. Also, Web sites containing thousands of coded files belonging to the terrorists have been found. There have also been persistent but unconfirmed reports that messages were hidden inside pornographic images on the Internet. This is known as *steganography*, and more information can be found at `http://www.jjtc.com/Steganography`. Finally, defaced Web sites are very common these days, sometimes to further terrorist ends.

NOTE

Find out more about terrorists and the Internet in Chapter 9, "Dispelling Some of the Myths."

Discussions in the U.S. Congress have revealed that the Internet traffic exchange points are relatively few. All the fiber connections between the U.S. and Europe go through New York City. Eighty percent of the United States's Internet traffic goes through just a dozen locations. That means that there are potentially serious physical security issues that need to be addressed to prevent terrorists from taking out the Internet.

The Threat Gets More Personal

Hostile foreign nations are studying how to use the Internet to attack us. The new threat, therefore, is not simply espionage, but all-out Internet warfare. Are we ready? Sort of.

Information warfare has been on the minds of defense officials for years. Recent studies suggest that we'll experience our first real information warfare attack within 20 years. Most hostile foreign nations are already preparing for it:

> Defense officials and information systems security experts believe that over 120 foreign countries are developing information warfare techniques. These techniques enable our enemies to seize control of or harm sensitive defense information systems or public networks, which Defense relies upon for communications...They could infect critical systems, including weapons and command and control systems, with sophisticated computer viruses, potentially causing them to malfunction. They could also prevent our military forces from communicating and disrupt our supply and logistics lines by attacking key Defense systems.
>
> —"Information Security: Computer Attacks at Department of Defense Pose Increasing Risks."
> (Testimony, 05/22/96, GAO/T-AIMD-96-92).

Most information warfare policy papers center on the importance of information warfare in a wartime situation. However, some U.S. information warfare specialists have recognized that we needn't be at war to be attacked:

> The United States should expect that its information systems are vulnerable to attack. It should further expect that attacks, when they come, might come in advance of any formal declaration of hostile intent by an adversary state... This is what we have to look forward to in 2020 or sooner.
>
> —"A Theory of Information Warfare; Preparing For 2020."
> Colonel Richard Szafranski, USAF.

The real question is this: If they attack, what can they do to us? The answer might surprise you.

The President's Commission on Critical Infrastructure Protection (PCCIP, a group studying U.S. vulnerability) has identified key resources that can be attacked via the Internet. Here are a few:

- Information and communications
- Electrical power systems
- Gas and oil transportation and storage
- Banking and finance
- Transportation
- Water supply systems
- Emergency services
- Government services

In 1998, the PCCIP delivered a report with preliminary findings. They, too, concluded that we might be attacked without warning:

> Potentially serious cyber attacks can be conceived and planned without detectable logistic preparation. They can be invisibly reconnoitered, clandestinely rehearsed, and then mounted in a matter of minutes or even seconds without revealing the identity and location of the attacker.

Is the situation that critical?

Who Holds the Cards?

Technology is a strange and wonderful thing. Depending on who's using it, the same technology used to create Godzilla can also be used to create weapons of mass destruction. For this reason, technology transfer has been tightly controlled for almost five decades.

During that time, however, commercial advances have dramatically influenced the distribution of high-grade technology. Thirty years ago, for example, the U.S. government held all the cards; the average U.S. citizen held next to nothing. Today, the average American has access to technology so advanced that it approaches the technology currently possessed by the government.

Encryption technology is a good example. Many Americans use encryption programs to protect their personal data from prying eyes. Some of these encryption programs (such as Pretty Good Privacy) produce military-grade encryption. This is strong enough that U.S. intelligence agencies have a hard time cracking it within a reasonable amount of time, and time is often of the essence.

Encryption has already thwarted several criminal investigations. For example, in the case of famed cracker Kevin Mitnick, the prosecution had a problem: Mitnick encrypted much of his personal data. As reported by David Thomas from Online Journalism:

> The encrypted data still posed a problem for the court. As it stands, government officials are holding the encrypted files and have no idea of their contents. The defense claims that information in those files might prove exculpatory, but revealing their contents to the government would violate Mitnick's Fifth Amendment protection against self-incrimination. Further, prosecutors have indicated that they will not be using the encrypted files against Mitnick, but they refuse to return the evidence because they do not know what information the files hold. Ultimately, the court sided with the prosecution. Judge Pfaelzer described Mitnick as "tremendously clever to put everyone in this position" but indicated that "as long as he (Mitnick) has the keys in his pocket, the court is going to do nothing about it."

Advanced technology has trickled down to the public. In many cases, crackers and hackers have taken this technology and rapidly improved it. Meanwhile, the government moves along more slowly, tied down by restrictive and archaic policies. As a result, the private sector has caught (and in some cases, surpassed) the government in some fields of research.

This is a matter of national concern and has sparked an angry debate. Consider the Mitnick case. Do you believe that the government is entitled to Mitnick's encryption key so it can find out what's inside those files? That's a hard question to answer. If Mitnick has a right to conceal that information, so does everybody else.

In the meantime, there's a more pressing question: How does this technology trickle-down affect our readiness for an Internet attack?

Can the United States Protect the National Information Infrastructure?

From a military standpoint, there's no comparison between the United States and even a gang of third-world nations. The same is not true, however, in respect to information warfare.

In March 1997, a Swedish cracker penetrated and disabled a 911 system in Florida. Eleven counties were affected. The cracker amused himself by connecting 911 operators to one another (or simply denying service altogether).

NOTE

The Swedish case was not the first instance of crackers disrupting 911 service. In Chesterfield, New Jersey, a group dubbed the Legion of Doom was charged with similar crimes. What was their motivation? "[T]o attempt to penetrate 911 computer systems and infect them with viruses to cause havoc."

NOTE

Another disturbing case occurred in March 1997, when a Rutland, Massachusetts, teenager cracked an airport. During the attack, the airport control tower and communication facilities were disabled for six hours. (The airport fire department was also disabled.) It was reported as follows:

"Public health and safety were threatened by the outage which resulted in the loss of telephone service, until approximately 3:30 p.m., to the Federal Aviation Administration Tower at the Worcester Airport, to the Worcester Airport Fire Department, and to other related concerns such as airport security, the weather service, and various private airfreight companies. Further, as a result of the outage, both the main radio transmitter, which is connected to the tower by the loop carrier system, and a circuit which enables aircraft to send an electric signal to activate the runway lights on approach were not operational for this same period of time."

—Transport News, March 1998

NOTE

On April 25, 2002, thieves stole 17 traffic control computers in Santiago, Chile. Traffic was deadlocked for three days. If computers like these were taken out of action while a physical attack was taking place, the result would be heightened confusion and delayed emergency responses.

The introduction of advanced minicomputers has forever changed the balance of power. The average PC processor is more powerful than many mainframes were five years ago. Add to this advances in clustering and distributed processing solutions, and with relatively cheap hardware you can start approaching the processing power that was previously only known by a few government and research institutes.

A third-world nation could theoretically pose a threat to our national information infrastructure. Using advanced microcomputers and some high-speed connections, a third-world nation could wage a successful information warfare campaign against the United States at costs well within its means. In fact, bona fide cyberterrorism will probably emerge in the next few years.

Furthermore, the mere availability of such advanced technology threatens our military future in the "real" world. Nations such as Russia and China have progressed slowly because they lacked access to such technology. Their missiles are less accurate because their technology base was less advanced. U.S. defense programs, however, were sufficiently advanced that even when we appeared to make concessions in the arms race, we really made no concessions at all. Here's an example: The United States only agreed to quit nuclear tests after we developed the technology to perform such tests using computer modeling.

As the United States's perceived enemies obtain more sophisticated computer technology, their weapons will become more sophisticated—but it's not simply weapons that make the difference. It's the combination of weapons, communication, and information. If our enemies can alter our information, or prevent us from accessing it, they can gain a tremendous tactical military advantage. This could make up for shortcomings in other areas. Shane D. Deichman reports the following in his paper "On Information War":

> A key element of the information warfare environment is the participants need not possess superpower status. Any power (even those not considered nation-states) with a modicum of technology can disrupt fragile C2 networks and deny critical information services. Rather than

a Mahanian "information control" strategy that attempts to dominate all segments of the information spectrum, though, a more realistic strategy for U.S. forces is one of "information denial" (that is, the denial of access to truthful information).

Perhaps a question less asked, however, is, should the U.S. government be responsible for protecting all of the U.S. infrastructure? After all, aren't the companies that operate systems like our telephone networks FOR PROFIT? Shouldn't the protection of these systems be one of their primary concerns?

You would think so, wouldn't you? Although the U.S. government has more than its fair share of problems and tasks, organizations turning to the government to make their information security problems go away are missing the point. Information security is everyone's problem—welcome to the party.

What Would an Information Attack Look Like?

There hasn't yet been an all-out information war. The distributed denial-of-service (DDoS) attacks that hit in February 2000 were the closest to this description to date, but it's difficult to say how a full-scale attack would be conducted. Military officials aren't willing to talk specifics. We can speculate, however, as many think tanks do.

TIP

In February 2000, some of the largest sites were knocked off the Internet using distributed denial-of-service tools. The attack made headlines in just about every news publication out there. These attacks are discussed in detail in Chapter 16, "Denial-of-Service Tools."

On September 26, 2001, Michael Vatis, Director of the Institute for Security Technology Studies at Dartmouth College, spoke before a U.S. House Committee on the United States's preparedness against cyberterrorism. (The full report can be found at http://www.ists.dartmouth.edu/ISTS/counterterrorism/preparedness.htm.)

Mr. Vatis stated that an attack would target the Web sites of government agencies as well as private companies. The attack might use worms, viruses, or denial-of-service attacks. Crackers might break in to disrupt systems and networks. Then these actions might be combined with physical terrorism to maximize the damaging effects. This is a fairly accurate picture of what could happen.

The Institute for Security Technology Studies at Dartmouth also prepared a report called "Cyber Attacks During the War on Terrorism: a Predictive Analysis," which is available at http://www.ists.dartmouth.edu/ISTS/counterterrorism/cyber_a1.pdf. What is really interesting about this report is that it points out that there have been at least four physical conflicts that have spilled over into a mini-cyberwar.

The first is the ongoing Kashmir conflict between Pakistan and India. Web deface-ment has been very common, with hundreds of sites being hit, including that of the Indian Parliament. Also, five megabytes of sensitive nuclear research was down-loaded by crackers from the Bhabha Atomic Research Centre.

The next is the Israeli/Palestinian conflict. Pro-Israeli crackers have made sustained DDoS attacks against the Palestinian Authority, Hezbollah, and Hamas. Pro-Palestinian crackers have returned the favor by taking down the sites of the Tel Aviv Stock Exchange, the Bank of Israel, and some divisions of the Israeli government.

The third case occurred during the Kosovo conflict between Yugoslavia and NATO. DDoS attacks were made against NATO Web sites, and American sites were defaced during the same time frame. NATO admitted that it had some serious disruptions in communications, but it did not affect the military campaign.

The final case is the U.S.-China spy plane incident during 2001. About 1,200 U.S. sites were defaced with pro-Chinese images. The planning took place over IRC and Internet postings. It is unknown whether these actions were supported by the Chinese government or not. American hackers supposedly defaced 2,500 Chinese Web sites as well, and possibly made DDoS attacks against a Chinese Web portal.

You would have to believe that if a major world power was directly involved, these kinds of attacks could be much more serious and damaging. Also, these incidents have focused on Web sites—it is highly likely that at some point in the future it will spill over into systems that control people's day-to-day lives. Imagine if a successful attack was made against the electric power grid instead of just Web sites—that would be much more serious.

The State of the Government

Throughout the Internet's history, government sites have been popular targets. One of the primary reasons this happens is because of press coverage that follows such an event. Crackers enjoy media attention, so their philosophy oftentimes is that, if you're going to crack a site, crack one that matters.

Government sites are supposed to have better security than their commercial coun-terparts. Hence, the media reacts more aggressively when a government site is cracked. Likewise, crackers who successfully penetrate a government site gain greater prestige among their fellows (whether it's deserved or not).

NOTE

The Government Accounting Office (GAO) regularly audits the government's computers systems, and they regularly find that the government does not do a good job in securing them. In 1999, their review found that the U.S. Army Corps of Engineers was in very bad shape. In an updated review on June 10, 2002, there was improvement, but still found weak-nesses in such basic things as securing networks and controlling access.

This phenomenon is not new, nor have government officials done much to improve the situation. Indeed, some very high-profile government sites have been cracked in recent years. In 2001, 32 different government agencies reported 155 computers had been cracked. This number is up from 64 in 1998. Of course, this doesn't count how many were cracked and not detected. The General Services Administrator stated that about 75% of the attacks were from foreign sources.

Federal agencies aren't the only targets, either. In July 2001, crackers from China broke into computers owned by the state of Kentucky and sent workers anti-U.S. messages. These attacks are increasing, and so far the availability of advanced security technology has had little impact. Why? It's not the technology; it's the people.

TIP

Although I could go on listing government sites that were hacked until I'm blue in the face, there is already a great, up-to-date site that does it for me. See `http://lists.insecure.org/alldas/` for a massive archive of defaced Web sites. Although defacements are not always as severe as thorough break-ins, they serve as a good tell-tale sign that a site's security is not up to par.

The National Infrastructure Protection Center (NIPC)

In February 1998, Attorney General Janet Reno announced the formation of the National Infrastructure Protection Center (NIPC), an investigative organization populated with personnel from the FBI's Computer Investigations and Infrastructure Threat Assessment Center (CIITAC). The NIPC tracks network intrusions and attempts to develop long-range solutions, including intrusion detection and international cooperation of police agencies.

The NIPC Web site (`http://www.nipc.gov/`) is one of the best on the Internet for getting information. One page there in particular needs to be pointed out. The Cybernotes page (`http://www.nipc.gov/cybernotes/cybernotes.htm`) is of particular interest—it contains bi-weekly updates of the latest security holes, available patches, and trends in viruses.

Summary of Government Vulnerabilities

To date, government security has been largely inadequate, and although the efforts of the PCCIP, NIPC, and CIITAC are doubtless improving the situation, further work is needed.

Until information security officers are properly trained, government sites will be cracked on a regular basis. Reasonable levels of security are obtainable, and if the government cannot obtain them on its own, it must enlist private sector specialists who can. In some places in the government, this is already being done.

The State of the Corporate Sector

It's clear that government servers can be successfully attacked, but what about the private sector? Is American business—big or small—immune to the cyber threat? Hardly. In fact, private sites are taken down with much greater frequency. Virtually every information security survey ever issued has reported a steep rise in incidents, and some security Web sites report hundreds of Web site defacements per month. Worse, although Web site defacements are publicly humiliating, most security experts agree that they are only the tip of the iceberg in terms of total incidents in the field.

Marketers who are anxious to engage in electronic commerce with the public assure us that these incidents are harmless. They point out, for example, that credit card and personal data is perfectly safe. Are they right? No—not by a long shot.

Credit Card Theft Goes Cyber: The StarWave Incident

In July 1997, crackers demonstrated one of the first widely known attacks on Internet credit card data. Their targets weren't small-time firms, either. The credit card numbers of NBA and ESPN site users were captured and distributed.

StarWave was the site responsible for protecting that data. StarWave is a widely known firm that hosts many large commercial sites, including ABC News. However, in July 1997, StarWave officials were apparently unprepared for the security breach.

The cracker or crackers took the credit card numbers and mailed them to NBA and ESPN subscribers to demonstrate to those users that their credit data was unsafe. Included in the mailing was a message. The relevant portion of that message was this:

> Clearly, StarWave doesn't consider the protection of individual credit card numbers a worth-while endeavor. (This is one of the worst implementations of security we've seen.)

StarWave officials responded quickly, explaining that the security breach was minor. They also changed system passwords and have since added an extra level of encryption. However, the fact remains: User credit card data had leaked out.

Credit Card Theft Hits Overdrive

Electronic commerce advocates originally asserted that the StarWave case was an isolated incident. In fact, at the time, many contended that few verified cases of credit card theft existed, and that the threat was relatively small. Time eventually proved them dead wrong.

Consider the case of Carlos Felipe Salgado. Salgado used a sniffer program (you'll learn about these in Chapter 15, "Sniffers") to steal thousands of credit card numbers off the Net. In their affidavit, FBI agents explained:

> Between, on or about May 2, 1997, and May 21, 1997, within the State and Northern District of California, defendant CARLOS FELIPE SALGADO, JR., a.k.a. "Smak," did knowingly, and with intent to defraud, traffic in unauthorized access devices affecting interstate commerce, to wit, over 100,000 stolen credit card numbers, and by such conduct did obtain in excess of $1,000; in violation of Title 18, United States Code, Section 1029(a)(2).

Salgado's method was one well known to crackers:

> While performing routine maintenance on the Internet servers on Friday, March 28, 1997, technicians discovered that the servers had been broken into by an intruder. Investigation by technicians revealed a "packet sniffer" installed on the system. The packet sniffer program was being used to capture user IDs and passwords of the authorized users....the FBI met "Smak" at the appointed hour and place. "Smak" delivered an encrypted CD containing more than 100,000 stolen credit card numbers. After the validity of the credit card information was confirmed through decryption of the data on the CD, "Smak" was taken into custody by the FBI.

Sniffer attacks are probably the most common way to grab credit card data (and usernames and password pairs). They are so common that Jonathan Littman (a renowned author of a best-selling book on hacking) wrote this in response to the Salgado case:

> Fact No. 1: This was an old fashioned attack—and it happens about as often as dogs sniff themselves. The packet sniffer that Carlos Felipe Salgado Jr., a.k.a. Smak, allegedly installed in a San Diego Internet provider's server is something hackers have been doing for years. My provider in Northern California was hacked a couple of months ago and just last week, too. Guess what that hacker was about to install?
>
> —"Take No Solace in This Sting," Jonathan Littman, ZDNET News

Unfortunately, these incidents were only the start. Consider the following cases:

- In January 2000, thieves stole 300,000 credit cards from CD Universe. At the time, this was the largest theft of credit cards to be publicly reported.

- In March 2000, a cracker known as Curador led authorities on a global chase after lifting some 26,000 credit cards from an assortment of e-commerce sites. Curador was caught later that same month.

- In September 2000, Western Union shut down its Web site for five days after crackers stole 15,000 credit card numbers.

- In December 2000, Egghead.com reported that they had suffered a security breach that might have exposed 3.7 million credit card numbers. Egghead later reported that it didn't believe the intruder was able to access the credit cards, but the scare was definitely significant.

- The FBI was investigating 55,000 stolen credit card numbers from CreditCards.com in January 2001. The cracker tried to extort $100,000. When payment did not come, 25,000 of the numbers were posted on the Internet.

- In March 2001, the FBI and NIPC issued a warning that Russian and Ukrainian thieves had stolen more than one million credit cards.

- In late 2001, I personally had a bogus charge from a supposed Web site called Pornotherapy.org on one of my credit cards. The credit card company immediately changed my card number. My best guess is that it was stolen on the Internet. It just goes to show this doesn't just happen to others.

- In November 2001, Playboy.com was cracked. An undisclosed number of credit card numbers were stolen.

- In February 2002, crackers broke into the database of the World Economic Forum. The credit card numbers of 1,400 WEF members were stolen. A few of the cards belonged to Bill Clinton, Bill Gates, Yasser Arafat, and Shimon Peres.

- In September 2002, a Web site owned by Spitfire Ventures received 140,000 credit card submissions in 90 minutes. All were for $5.07. Out of these, 62,477 were approved. It is speculated that this was an attempt to see which numbers were valid.

Notice a trend here? The problem is only getting worse. It should also be noted that the fraud rate for online credit card transactions is about triple the rate for offline transactions. These are just some of the reasons why the Internet is a dangerous place to do business. Unfortunately, the stories are only getting more and more outrageous.

The Trends

Hard statistics on security breaches are difficult to come by. However, there are a few good sources. One is the Computer Security Institute's Computer Crime and Security Survey. The CSI Survey is conducted annually, and the 2002 results are in. You can obtain those results at http://www.gocsi.com/press/20020407.html. Briefly, the 2002 results indicate yet another increase in computer crime. For example, 90% of the respondents reported security breaches in the previous year. Approximately 40% of all respondents suffered hard denial-of-service attacks, and an equal number experienced penetration by remote attackers. Of all respondents, 74% indicated that the Internet was the point of entry for intruders.

The Ernst & Young LLP/ComputerWorld Information Security Survey

If your company has asked you to justify a security plan, you're probably looking around for more statistics. No problem; there's a lot of material out there. One good source is the Ernst & Young LLP/ComputerWorld Information Security Survey, located at

```
http://www.ey.com/global/download.nsf/International/Global_Information_Security_
➥Survey_2002/$file/FF0210.pdf
```

The Ernst & Young survey differs a bit from others mentioned earlier. For a start, it's a survey of human beings. (Actually, it's a survey of 459 information managers.) Respondents were asked a wide variety of questions about Internet security and secure electronic commerce.

One recurring theme throughout the 2002 survey was this: September 11th made IT security a bigger priority than ever. Businesses are getting better about their security planning, but have a long way to go still. Respondents also indicated the following:

- Only 40% feel confident that they could detect an attack.

- Forty percent of the organizations do not investigate security incidents.

- Only 41% of organizations are concerned about internal attacks.

If your company holds similar attitudes about security measures, you need to get busy.

A Warning

Many companies that consider establishing a Web server feel that security is not a significant issue. For example, they might co-locate their boxes, and in doing so might throw both the responsibility and liability to their ISP. After all, ISPs know the lay of the land, and they never get cracked, right? Wrong. ISPs get cracked all the time.

> **TIP**
>
> Do not exclude universities from your sites, either. For example, in December 2000, SecurityFocus ran a report on the University of Washington break-in. Intruders stole more than 5,000 patient records from the University's Medical Center. See a report on this incident at `http://www.securityfocus.com/news/122`.

If you're an information officer and your firm requests Internet connectivity, be sure to cover all the bases. Make it known to all concerned that security is a serious issue. Otherwise, you'll take the blame later. You should also be wary of any ISP that gives you blanket assurances. Today, even firewalls can be cracked, and cracked through the same old methods by which servers are cracked—exploitation of human error.

Summary

We've established that any site can be cracked, including the following types:

- Banks

- Military servers

- Universities

- Internet service providers

Do not expect this climate to change, either. New and more effective cracking methods are surfacing, and the pace is only getting quicker. New cracking tools and viruses are being manufactured every day, and these tools—which were once toys for hackers and crackers—have now become viable weapons. These methods will be used by both hostile foreign nations seeking to destroy other countries' national information infrastructure, as well as kids who are bored and want to take down a popular Web site.

On the information warfare front, there are several key objectives, but these four are particularly prominent:

- Denying the target computer services

- Destroying the target's computer systems

- Stealing data

- Modifying data

Today's denial-of-service attacks and viruses will likely form the basis for tomorrow's information warfare arsenal. Considering that anyone anywhere can obtain these tools, compile them, and deploy them in minutes, the immediate future looks pretty scary.

Additional Information

Internet Resources on Information Warfare

The following papers focus on Internet and information warfare. Most are written by folks now actively engaged in information warfare research.

An Analysis of Security Incidents on the Internet. John D. Howard.
http://www.cert.org/research/JHThesis/index.html

Defensive Information Warfare. David S. Alberts.
http://www.ndu.edu:80/ndu/inss/books/diw/index.html

Foreign Information Warfare Programs and Capabilities. John M. Deutch,
Director of Central Intelligence. http://www.odci.gov/cia/public_affairs/speeches/
archives/1996/dci_testimony_062596.html

From InfoWar to Knowledge Warfare: Preparing for the Paradigm Shift.
Philippe Baumard. http://www.indigo-net.com/annexes/289/baumard.htm

Induced Fragility in Information Age Warfare. Bruce W. Fowler and Donald
R. Peterson. http://lionhrtpub.com/orms/orms-4-97/warfare.html

**Information Security: Computer Attacks at Department of Defense Pose
Increasing Risks.** U.S. Government Accounting Office.
http://www.access.gpo.gov/cgi-bin/getdoc.cgi?dbname=gao&docid=f:ai96084.txt

Information War and the Air Force: Wave of the Future? Current Fad?
Glenn Buchan. http://www.rand.org/publications/IP/IP149/

Information Warfare and International Law. Lawrence T. Greenberg,
Seymour E. Goodman, and Kevin J. Soo Hoo. http://www.dodccrp.org/iwilindex.htm

Information Warfare. Brian C. Lewis.
http://www.fas.org/irp/eprint/snyder/infowarfare.htm

**Intelligence-Based Threat Assessments for Information Networks and
Infrastructures.** Kent Anderson from Global Technology Research, Inc.
http://www.aracnet.com/~kea/Papers/threat_white_paper.shtml

Knowledge-Based Warfare: A Security Strategy for the Next Century.
Lawrence E. Casper, Irving L. Halter, Earl W. Powers, Paul J. Selva, Thomas W.
Steffens, and T. LaMar Willis. http://www.dtic.mil/doctrine/jel/jfq_pubs/1813.pdf

Network-Centric Warfare: Its Origin and Future. Vice Admiral Arthur K.
Cebrowski, U.S. Navy, and John J. Garstka.
http://www.usni.org/Proceedings/Articles98/PROcebrowski.htm

**Political Aspects of Class III Information Warfare: Global Conflict and
Terrorism.** Matthew G. Devost. http://www.mnsinc.com/mdevost/montreal.html

Books on Information Warfare

Information Warfare: Chaos on the Electronic Superhighway. Winn Schwartau. (Engaging infowar title by the owner of http://www.infowar.com.) Thunder's Mouth Press. 1996.

Strategic Information Warfare: A New Face of War. Roger C. Molander, Andrew S. Riddile, and Peter A. Wilson. Rand Corporation. 1996.

Cyberwar: Security, Strategy, and Conflict in the Information Age. R. Thomas Goodden. AFCEA International Press. 1996.

Defensive Information Warfare. David S. Alberts. Diane Publishing. 1996.

The First Information War: The Story of Communications, Computers, and Intelligence Systems in the Persian Gulf War. Alan D. Campen, ed. AFCEA International Press. 1992.

Information Warfare: How Computers Are Fighting the New World Wars. James Adams. 1998.

Introduction to Information Warfare. Edward L. Waltz. 1998.

Netspionage: The Global Threat to Information. W. Boni and G. Kovacich. Butterworth-Heinemann. 2000.

Cyberwar 3.0: Human Factors in Information Operations and Future Conflict. A. Campen and D. Dearth. AFCEA International Press. 2000.

Networks and Netwars: The Future of Terror, Crime and Militancy. J. Arquilla and D. Ronfeldt, eds. Rand Corporation. 2001.

Strategic Warfare in Cyberspace. G. Rattray. MIT Press. 2001.

Global Information Warfare: How Businesses, Governments, and Others Achieve Objectives and Attain Competitive Advantages. A. Jones, G. Kovacich, and P. Luzwick. Auerbach Publishing. 2002.

Information Warfare Principles and Operations. Edward Waltz. Artech House. 2002.

Hackers and Crackers

The purpose of this chapter is to illustrate the methodology and steps a hacker or cracker employs when attacking a network. It also provides an overview of the System Administration Network Security (SANS) Top 20 vulnerabilities that crackers can exploit.

The Difference Between Hackers and Crackers

To understand the methodology of a hacker or cracker, one must understand what a hacker or a cracker is. Internet enthusiasts have argued the difference between hackers and crackers for many years. This chapter contains my contribution to that debate.

If I were forced to define the terms *hacker* and *cracker*, my bottom line would probably be this:

- A *hacker* is a person intensely interested in the arcane and recondite workings of any computer operating system. Hackers are most often programmers. As such, hackers obtain advanced knowledge of operating systems and programming languages. They might discover holes within systems and the reasons for such holes. Hackers constantly seek further knowledge, freely share what they have discovered, and never intentionally damage data.

- A *cracker* is one who breaks into or otherwise violates the system integrity of remote machines with malicious intent. Having gained unauthorized access, crackers destroy vital data, deny legitimate users service, or cause problems for their targets. Crackers can easily be identified because their actions are malicious.

Additionally, it should be mentioned that there are two major types of crackers. The first is fortunately few and far between. They are the expert crackers who discover new security holes and often write programs that exploit them. The second type, the *script kiddie*, only knows how to get these programs and run them. Script kiddies are more numerous, but much easier to stop and detect.

Tools of the Trade

The "tools of the trade" are the means a cracker or hacker might use to penetrate your network. Some of the tools covered are programs, and some of these tools are techniques.

Reconnaissance

When most people hear the word *reconnaissance*, they think of spies and the espionage world. Although that community does indeed use reconnaissance, so does the cracker community. What is reconnaissance, and why do crackers use it? *Reconnaissance* is the process of gathering information about specific target(s). When a good burglar decides to rob a house, he will scope out an area to see how often neighbors, cops, and other traffic passes through. This gives the robber a good idea of the best time of day to attack. The same basic philosophy holds true for a cracker when she wants to attack a network or Web site.

When a cracker decides she wants to attack a network, there are many "recon" tools at her disposal. Let's look at a few of them and see how they work.

Social Engineering

The first and probably the most underrated tool available is social engineering. *Social engineering* involves tricking, conning, or manipulating people into providing information detrimental to a company, organization, or a person. This type of information can be used to help plan, organize, or execute an attack.

NOTE

Ira Winkler's excellent book *Corporate Espionage* (Prima Communications) covers social engineering, along with many other tactics used in obtaining information. It also discusses how to protect yourself against these types of attacks. For more on Ira, you can go to http://www.annonline.com/interviews/970512/. Another good book on social engineering is *The Art of Deception* (John Wiley & Sons) by the famous cracker Kevin Mitnick.

How does social engineering work? A good example is through a help desk. Cracker A wants to attack ABC123 Inc., a computer software company, and therefore wants to find out usernames, passwords, and maybe even some security measures ABC123 has in place. He begins by calling ABC123's main number, explains to the secretary that he is new to the company, works offsite, and needs the help desk number in order to set up his account and password. The secretary provides him with the number. Cracker A then calls up the help desk number, explaining the situation to the person on the phone and asks for a username, a password, and how he can get access to the network from the outside. Help Desk Worker B happily provides this information within seconds, not once questioning his request. (Why not? Most help desk operations I have seen stress customer service—"Remember: Never anger a customer.")

This simple scenario can provide the attacker with enough information to make an attack much easier to pull off without being detected. Other techniques that are related to social engineering are

- Dumpster diving—A person goes through a dumpster or trash can looking for trash that contains information, such as an IP address, old passwords, and quite possibly a map of the network. Although this technique is often a dirty one, it is very effective.

- Impersonations—A cracker pretends to be someone important and uses that authority to obtain the information she is looking for.

These social engineering techniques are effective, and there are many more that are beyond the scope of this book. Keep in mind that people still use these techniques, and they are a threat to both you and your company's security.

Port Scanners and Passive Operating System Identification

This section provides a technical overview of port scanners and sniffers, along with details regarding the art of passive operating system identification.

Port scanners are programs that check a computer's TCP/IP stack for ports that are in the LISTEN state. TCP/IP combines many protocols, enabling communication on the Internet. The TCP/IP protocol suite consists of 65,535 ports. Ports 1–1023 are considered "well-known" and on many computer systems—only users with root/admin privileges can use start processes that listen on these ports. Ports 1024–49151 are called *registered ports*, and ports 49152–65535 are considered dynamic and/or private ports.

TIP

Find the port numbers list online at http://www.iana.org/assignments/port-numbers.

The Transmission Control Protocol is covered by RFC 793, which defines many standards that socket programmers need to follow. It also defines how TCP will react to certain packets (FIN, ACK, and SYN):

If the state is CLOSED (that is, Transmission Control Block does not exist) then all data in the incoming segment is discarded. An incoming segment containing a RESET (RST) is discarded. An incoming segment not containing a RST causes a RST to be sent in response. The acknowledgment and sequence field values are selected to make the reset sequence acceptable to the TCP that sent the offending segment.

If the state is LISTEN then first check for an RST. An incoming RST should be ignored. Second, check for an ACK. Any acknowledgment is bad if it arrives on a connection still in the LISTEN state. An acceptable reset segment should be formed for any arriving ACK-bearing segment. Third, check for a SYN; if the SYN bit is set, check the security. If the security/compartment on the incoming segment does not exactly match the security/compartment in the TCB then send a reset and return.

What this tells us is how listening and closed ports respond to certain TCP flags. Knowing this, programmers can write programs that go out and identify open and closed ports. These programs are considered port scanners.

Let's look at some "famous" port scanners and see what they can and cannot do.

TIP

To find out more information on TCP/IP, see the RFCs online at http://www.ietf.org/rfc/rfc0793.txt?number=793 and http://www.ietf.org/rfc/rfc0791.txt?number=791.

For some great information on TCP/IP fingerprinting, see http://www.insecure.org/nmap/nmap-fingerprinting-article.html.

Nmap

Nmap is probably the most popular port scanner being used and actively developed today. The brainchild of Fyodor (www.insecure.org), Nmap has grown through the active participation of the open source community. Nmap gives the user many options in scanning. Listing 3.1 shows the results of nmap -h. This is a great starting point for Nmap. For more details on Nmap, see the man page at http://www.insecure.org/nmap/data/nmap_manpage.html.

LISTING 3.1   Nmap -h Results

```
Nmap V. 3.10ALPHA3 Usage: nmap [Scan Type(s)] [Options] <host or net list>
Some Common Scan Types ('*' options require root privileges)
* -sS TCP SYN stealth port scan (default if privileged (root))
  -sT TCP connect() port scan (default for unprivileged users)
* -sU UDP port scan
  -sP ping scan (Find any reachable machines)
* -sF,-sX,-sN Stealth FIN, Xmas, or Null scan (experts only)
```

LISTING 3.1   Continued

```
 -sR/-I RPC/Identd scan (use with other scan types)
Some Common Options (none are required, most can be combined):
* -O Use TCP/IP fingerprinting to guess remote operating system
  -p <range> ports to scan.  Example range: '1-1024,1080,6666,31337'
  -F Only scans ports listed in nmap-services
  -v Verbose. Its use is recommended.  Use twice for greater effect.
  -P0 Don't ping hosts (needed to scan www.microsoft.com and others)
* -Ddecoy_host1,decoy2[,...] Hide scan using many decoys
  -6 scans via IPv6 rather than IPv4
  -T <Paranoid|Sneaky|Polite|Normal|Aggressive|Insane> General timing policy
  -n/-R Never do DNS resolution/Always resolve [default: sometimes resolve]
  -oN/-oX/-oG <logfile> Output normal/XML/grepable scan logs to <logfile>
  -iL <inputfile> Get targets from file; Use '-' for stdin
* -S <your_IP>/-e <devicename> Specify source address or network interface
  —interactive Go into interactive mode (then press h for help)
Example: nmap -v -sS -O www.my.com 192.168.0.0/16 '192.88-90.*.*'
SEE THE MAN PAGE FOR MANY MORE OPTIONS, DESCRIPTIONS, AND EXAMPLES
```

Listing 3.1 illustrates how easy Nmap is to configure, and what options are available for scanning. Let's take a look at a few switches, discuss what they do, and how they can be used in reconnaissance.

The -sT switch is probably the *loudest* switch we will cover (not as stealthy as others). This switch tells Nmap to make a complete connection with the targeted computer. This type of scan is easy to detect, and probably won't be used if an attacker is serious about performing reconnaissance on a computer system.

NOTE

In early 2001, a group of SANS analysts put together a book about intrusion detection signatures called *Intrusion Signatures and Analysis* (New Riders). It's a great reference for anyone who wants to dig deeper into intrusion detection and attack signatures.

The -sF switch sends FIN packets to the targeted computer. How does this work? When a computer receives a FIN, it has a few reaction options:

- If the port is in the LISTEN state, the computer will not reply.

- If the port is in the CLOSED state, the computer will respond with a RESET.

- If there has been a connection, the computer will begin breaking the connection. (We won't worry about this option right now.)

The computer's response tells Nmap what ports are open when using the -sF switch. Listing 3.2 shows the results of an -sF scan from a user standpoint.

LISTING 3.2   Nmap -sF User Results

```
Starting nmap V. 3.10ALPHA3 ( www.insecure.org/nmap/ )
Interesting ports on (192.168.1.3):
(The 4000 ports scanned but not shown here are in state: closed)
Port    State    Service
47017/tcp    open    unknown
TCP Sequence Prediction: Class=random positive increments
Difficulty=3980866 (Good luck!)
Remote operating system guess: Linux 2.1.122 - 2.2.16
Nmap run completed — 1 IP address (1 host up) scanned in 5 seconds
```

This scan ran against a Linux machine that had the t0rn rootkit (port 47017 is a dead giveaway) running, and these are the results:

```
20:00:48.813047 > 192.168.1.5.47257 >
➡192.168.1.1.473: F 0:0(0) win 1024 (ttl 48, id 31728)
            4500 0028 7bf0 0000 3006 8b89 c0a8 0105
            c0a8 0101 b899 01d9 0000 0000 0000 0000
            5001 0400 6e1a 0000
20:00:48.813153 > 192.168.1.5.47257 >
➡192.168.1.1.663: F 0:0(0) win 1024 (ttl 48, id 56669)
            4500 0028 dd5d 0000 3006 2a1c c0a8 0105
            c0a8 0101 b899 0297 0000 0000 0000 0000
            5001 0400 6d5c 0000
20:00:48.813188 > 192.168.1.5.47257 >
➡192.168.1.1.1458: F 0:0(0) win 1024 (ttl 48, id 23854)
            4500 0028 5d2e 0000 3006 aa4b c0a8 0105
            c0a8 0101 b899 05b2 0000 0000 0000 0000
            5001 0400 6a41 0000
```

If a person was running a sniffer, he would see this code. What you don't see here are the resets being sent back by the ports being scanned. This technique is used by many crackers to perform reconnaissance against a target. This scan is much harder to detect than the -sT switch.

The -sS switch uses SYN packets to determine whether a port or group of ports is open. This scan is commonly referred to as the *half-open* scan. Why? Well, Nmap sends a SYN packet to a port. If the port is open, it will respond with a SYN|ACK. If Nmap receives the SYN|ACK, it will respond with a RESET. Therefore, if you send half-open packets, your chance of being detected decreases (in theory). Many crackers use this scanning technique to check for open ports, because sometimes this activity is logged. In today's world, though, many firewalls and IDSs do log these attempts.

The final switch is -sX, Nmap's "X-mas tree" packet, in which Nmap sets the FIN, URG, and PUSH flags, as well as others. Under normal conditions, this is not a normal flag combination. Normally, a person would see FIN, URG, and ACK, but not a FIN, URG, and PUSH combination. The reason for this flag combination is simple: Crackers can bypass some firewalls and intrusion detection systems with it.

How does this relate to reconnaissance? Nmap is a great tool for performing reconnaissance. With all the switches and options available, it is difficult for a firewall administrator or IDS analyst to positively identify all the possible scans available with Nmap.

TIP

Dying for more information on Nmap? Direct your browser to http://www.insecure.org.

hping2

Another great port scanner used today for reconnaissance is hping2. This is probably one of my favorite tools to have because it is very configurable. Table 3.1 lists many of the options available with hping2.

TIP

Information on hping2 can be found at http://www.kyuzz.org/antirez/hping2.html.

TABLE 3.1   hping2 Options

Usage	hping2 Host	Options
-h	--help	Show this help
-v	--version	Show version
-c	--count	Packet count
-i	--interval	Wait (uX for *X* microseconds, for example, -i u1000)
-n	--numeric	Numeric output
-q	--quiet	Quiet
-I	--interface	Interface name (otherwise, default routing interface)
-V	--verbose	Verbose mode
-D	--debug	Debugging info
-z	--bind	Bind Ctrl+Z to ttl (default to dst port)
-Z	--unbind	Unbind Ctrl+Z

TABLE 3.1   Continued

Usage	hping2 Host	Options
Modes		
Default	default mode	TCP
-0	--rawip	RAW IP mode
-1	--icmp	ICMP mode
-2	--udp	UDP mode
-9	--listen	Listen mode
IP		
-a	--spoof	Spoof source address
-t	--ttl	ttl (default 64)
-N	--id	id (default random)
-W	--winid	Use win* id byte ordering
-r	--rel	Relativize id field (to estimate host traffic)
-f	--frag	Split packets in more fragments (can pass weak ACL)
-x	--morefrag	Set more fragments flag
-y	--dontfrag	Set don't fragment flag
-g	--fragoff	Set the fragment offset
-m	--mtu	Set virtual mtu; implies --frag if packet size > mtu
-o	--tos	Type of service (default 0x00); try --tos help
-G	--rroute	Include RECORD_ROUTE option and display the route buffer
-H	--ipproto	Set the IP protocol field, only in RAW IP mode
ICMP		
-C	--icmptype	ICMP type (default echo request), try --icmptype help
-K	--icmpcode	ICMP code (default 0)
	--icmp-help	Display help for other ICMP options
UDP/TCP		
-s	--baseport	Base source port (default random)
-p	--destport	[+][+]<port> destination port (default 0) Ctrl+Z increase/decrease
-k	--keep	Keep still source port
-w	--win	Set window size (default 64)
-O	--tcpoff	Set fake TCP data offset (instead of tcphdrlen/4)
-Q	--seqnum	Show only TCP sequence number
-b	--badcksum	Send packets with a bad IP checksum
-M	--setseq	Set TCP sequence number
-L	--setack	Set TCP ack
-F	--fin	Set FIN flag
-S	--syn	Set SYN flag
-R	--rst	Set RST flag
-P	--push	Set PUSH flag

TABLE 3.1   Continued

Usage	hping2 Host	Options
UDP/TCP		
-A	--ack	Set ACK flag
-U	--urg	Set URG flag
-X	--xmas	Set X unused flag (0×40)
-Y	--ymas	Set Y unused flag (0×80)
	--tcpexitcode	Set last `tcp->th_flags` as exit code
TS		
-d	--data	Data size (default is 0)
-E	--file	Data from file
-e	--sign	Add "signature"
-j	--dump	Dump packets in hex
-J	--print	Dump printable characters
-B	--safe	Enable "safe" protocol
-u	--end	Tell you when `--file` reaches EOF and prevent rewind
-T	--traceroute	(Implies `--bind`) traceroute mode

You can see from the help file how configurable hping2 really is. A cracker can modify almost any byte in the TCP/IP header. This enables a cracker to really become creative with her scanning techniques in performing reconnaissance. This tool also enables the cracker to insert crafted data into the packet. This means that the cracker could insert malicious code of any kind—buffer overflows, Trojans, and so on—into a packet and use it to penetrate networks. If you don't have hping2, I recommend downloading it and giving it a test drive. The next version, hping3, will be scriptable and provide better output capabilities.

There are many more great port scanners out there than what we have covered here. Port scanners provide the cracker with a tool that "knocks" on the door of computer networks. This also gives the cracker an idea of what operating system and services the targeted network is running. With this type of information, the cracker can then proceed to her favorite exploit toolkit and proceed to penetrate the targeted network. These tools can and should be used by the computer professional to evaluate systems. By using these tools, a systems administrator can identify vulnerabilities before an attacker does.

Passive Operating System Identification Fingerprinting

Passive OS fingerprinting is a technique that is gaining popularity in both the cracker world as well as in the security world. Passive OS fingerprinting enables a person to identify an operating system by analyzing its TCP/IP stack. This technique is as stealthy as it gets, because all you need is a packet sniffer and some time. An attacker using a sniffer does not have to worry about sending strange packets to determine what OS he is up against.

Almost all operating systems have default settings, including settings for TCP/IP. An example of this is Linux. If you look at /proc/sys/net/ipv4 in Listing 3.3, you'll find a wide range of settings that contain default information that the system uses in its daily tasks. Listing 3.3 shows the TCP/IP parameters in Linux.

LISTING 3.3   /proc/sys/net/ipv4

```
Conf
icmp_destunreach_rate
icmp_echo_ignore_all
icmp_echo_ignore_broadcasts
icmp_echoreply_rate
icmp_ignore_bogus_error_responses
icmp_paramprob_rate
icmp_timeexceed_rate
igmp_max_memberships
ip_always_defrag
ip_autoconfig
ip_default_ttl
ip_dynaddr
ip_forward
ip_local_port_range
ip_masq_debug
ip_no_pmtu_disc
ipfrag_high_thresh
ipfrag_low_thresh
ipfrag_time
neigh
route
tcp_fin_timeout
tcp_keepalive_probes
tcp_keepalive_time
tcp_max_ka_probes
tcp_max_syn_backlog
tcp_retrans_collapse
tcp_retries1
tcp_retries2
tcp_rfc1337
tcp_sack
```

LISTING 3.3   Continued

```
tcp_stdurg
tcp_syn_retries
tcp_syncookies
tcp_timestamps
tcp_window_scaling
```

Let's look at a few of these parameters and determine what they do and how they affect the operating system.

- ip_default-ttl—This parameter sets the default time-to-live value to 64. It can be changed on a Linux box by using echo 128 >> ip_default_ttl.

- ip_forward—Although this parameter does not directly affect passive OS finger-printing, it does have a big effect on OS security. By default, ip_forward is set to 0, which disables IP forwarding. Setting it to 1 enables IP forwarding and also permits the computer to forward packets from one interface to another, which can be a security issue.

- ip_local_port_range—This parameter identifies the default source port range that Linux will use. Normally, this is set to 1024-4999. This is good information to know if you are attempting to determine whether a packet is good or bad.

- tcp_sack—This parameter lets the operating system know whether it supports the Selective Acknowledgment standard (RFC 2883). By default (Linux), this is set to 1 (supporting this standard).

- tcp_timestamps—This parameter lets the operating system know whether it supports the timestamp function. By default (Linux), this is set to 1.

- tcp_window_scaling—This parameter lets the operating system know whether it supports the window scaling function. This option is used to decrease conges-tion. By default (Linux), this is set to 1.

Listing 3.3 shows only the parameters that are related to passive OS fingerprinting. Although we have only covered Linux default settings so far, every OS has its own set of default settings. A good example is the Windows platform: Windows 98, NT, and 2000 all use a default TTL of 128.

TIP

There is, however, a whole world using ICMP. To check this out, go to http://www. sys-security.com. There is an ICMP-based OS fingerprinting program on this site as well.

Let's look at a few other operating systems and their default TCP/IP settings:

- Microsoft (98, NT)

  Packet size (just headers) = 44 bytes (default)

  SYN or SYN|ACK packets = Sets the Don't Fragment (DF) flag and the Maximum Segment Size (mss) flag

  TTL = 128

- Microsoft (2000)

  Packet size (just headers) = 48 bytes (default)

  SYN or SYN|ACK packets = Sets the Don't Fragment (DF) flag, Maximum Segment Size (mss) flag, two nops, and the Selective Acknowledgment flag.

  TTL = 128

- Linux (Red Hat 6.2)

  Packet size (just headers) = 60 bytes (default)

  SYN or SYN|ACK packets = Sets the Don't Fragment (DF) flag, Maximum Segment Size (mss) flag, nops, Selective Acknowledgment flag, Timestamp, Window Scaling (wscale). These hold true for the initial SYN. SYN|ACK Linux responds according to the computer that made the initial SYN.

  TTL = 64 (On a RESET packet, the TTL is 255)

Knowing this, you can identify operating systems by looking at network traffic. One thing to keep in mind is that if a sysadmin or cracker changes any of the parameters, it will throw off your analysis. Therefore, passive OS fingerprinting is not 100% accurate—but then again, nothing is. Listing 5.4 shows two packets that will help you identify an OS using passive fingerprinting.

LISTING 3.4   Identifying Operating Systems

```
15:59:52.533502 > my_isp.net.1100 > 134.11.235.232.www:
➥S 325233392:325233392(0) win 32120
➥<mss 1460,sackOK,timestamp 88950 0,nop,wscale 0> (DF) (ttl 64, id 505)
          4500 003c 01f9 4000 4006 0522 xxxx xxxx
          860b ebe8 044c 0050 1362 aaf0 0000 0000
          a002 7d78 7887 0000 0204 05b4 0402 080a
          0001 5b76 0000 0000 0103 0300

16:00:14.188756 >my_isp.net.1105 >
➥134.11.235.232.www: R 346737591:346737591(0) win 0 (ttl 255, id 544)
```

LISTING 3.4   Continued

```
4500 0028 0220 0000 ff06 860e xxxx xxxx
860b ebe8 0451 0050 14aa cbb7 0000 0000
5004 0000 973c 0000
```

In Listing 3.4, you see two packets. The first is a SYN packet, and the second is a RST packet. Looking at the SYN packet, notice some important indicators:

- The SYN has a TTL of 64.

- The SYN sets its mss, sackOK, nop, and wscale parameters and the DF flag. Also, pay close attention to the header size (3c = 60 bytes).

- Look at the source port as well. Port 1100 falls within the default source port range of 1024–4999.

These indicators point to…Linux. That's right, the OS we were looking at in Listing 3.4 is coming from a Linux machine. Let's take a brief look at the RST packet. First, look at the TTL (255). When Red Hat Linux sends an RST, it will use a default TTL of 255; whereas when it is trying to establish a connection, it uses a TTL of 64. Another characteristic of Linux RST packets is their size. Normally, a Red Hat packet is 60 bytes in length. When setting the RST flag, RH Linux has a packet length of only 40 bytes.

How do OS fingerprinting and Linux tie back into reconnaissance? If a cracker uses any of the previously mentioned techniques, he can obtain very valuable information about a computer network. That type of information includes network mapping, IP addresses, patch levels, and the discovery of different operating systems.

Exploits and the SANS Top 20

In this section, we will cover the exploits run by crackers. We will also look at the SANS 20 Most Critical Internet Security Threats list.

Exploits

Reconnaissance is vital in figuring out what is open and what is closed. The next step for a cracker is to actually break into a computer network. Crackers do this by exploiting weaknesses in operating system services.

There are many exploits out there, and finding the right exploit can be a headache. Not all exploits are created equal. By this, I mean that most exploits are operating system-dependent. Just because there is a line printer exploit for Linux doesn't mean it would work on Solaris, and vice versa.

TIP

If you want to find out about the latest exploits and vulnerabilities, subscribe to the BugTraq mailing list at `http://online.securityfocus.com/cgi-bin/sfonline/subscribe.pl` or look at the archives at `http://online.securityfocus.com/archive/1`.

To help explain what an exploit is and what it looks like when it is being executed, I have included the output from an exploit and some packets involved in the exploit. The exploit we are going to look at is related to the Red Hat line printer daemon, though it has been fixed in the current version of RedHat.

Here are the listings, along with some play-by-play for each:

```
+++ www.netcat.it remote exploit for LPRng/lpd


+++ Exploit information
+++ Victim: 192.168.1.25
+++ Type: 0 - RedHat 7.0 - Guinesss
+++ Eip address: 0xbffff3ec
+++ Shellcode address: 0xbffff7f2
+++ Position: 300
+++ Alignment: 2
+++ Offset 0


+++ Attacking 192.168.1.25 with our format string
+++ Brute force man, relax and enjoy the ride ;>
```

From this output, we know that the exploit is attacking a Red Hat line printer. Want to see how tcpdump views this attack?

```
18:34:19.991789 > 192.168.1.5.2894 >
➥192.168.1.25.printer: S 4221747912:4221747912(0)
➥win 32120 <mss 1460,sackOK,timestamp 4058996 0,nop,wscale 0>
➥(DF) (ttl 64, id 11263)
            4500 003c 2bff 4000 4006 8b4e c0a8 0105
            c0a8 0119 0b4e 0203 fba2 c2c8 0000 0000
            a002 7d78 8bb1 0000 0204 05b4 0402 080a
            003d ef74 0000 0000 0103 0300
18:34:19.993434 < 192.168.1.25.printer >
➥192.168.1.5.2894: S 397480959:397480959(0) ack 4221747913 win 32120
➥<mss 1460,sackOK,timestamp 393475 4058996,nop,wscale 0>
➥(DF) (ttl 64, id 3278)
            4500 003c 0cce 4000 4006 aa7f c0a8 0119
            c0a8 0105 0203 0b4e 17b1 13ff fba2 c2c9
```

```
          a012 7d78 5ee7 0000 0204 05b4 0402 080a
          0006 0103 003d ef74 0103 0300
18:34:19.993514 > 192.168.1.5.2894 > 192.168.1.25.printer: . 1:1(0)
➡ ack 1 win 32120 <nop,nop,timestamp 4058996 393475> (DF)
➡(ttl 64, id 11264)
          4500 0034 2c00 4000 4006 8b55 c0a8 0105
          c0a8 0119 0b4e 0203 fba2 c2c9 17b1 1400
          8010 7d78 8dac 0000 0101 080a 003d ef74
          0006 0103


18:34:19.999662 < 192.168.1.25.printer > 192.168.1.5.2894: P 1:31(30)
➡ack 1 win 32120 <nop,nop,timestamp 393476 4058996> (DF) (ttl 64, id 3279)
          4500 0052 0ccf 4000 4006 aa68 c0a8 0119
          c0a8 0105 0203 0b4e 17b1 1400 fba2 c2c9
          8018 7d78 3e5b 0000 0101 080a 0006 0104
          003d ef74 6c70 643a 203a 204d 616c 666f
          726d 6564 2066 726f 6d20 6164 6472 6573
          730a
18:34:19.999686 > 192.168.1.5.2894 >
➡192.168.1.25.printer: . 1:1(0) ack 31 win 32120
➡<nop,nop,timestamp 4058997 393476> (DF) (ttl 64, id 11265)
          4500 0034 2c01 4000 4006 8b54 c0a8 0105
          c0a8 0119 0b4e 0203 fba2 c2c9 17b1 141e
          8010 7d78 8d8c 0000 0101 080a 003d ef75
          0006 0104
18:34:20.000863 < 192.168.1.25.printer >
➡192.168.1.5.2894: F 31:31(0) ack 1 win 32120
➡<nop,nop,timestamp 393476 4058997> (DF) (ttl 64, id 3280)
          4500 0034 0cd0 4000 4006 aa85 c0a8 0119
          c0a8 0105 0203 0b4e 17b1 141e fba2 c2c9
          8011 7d78 8d8b 0000 0101 080a 0006 0104
          003d ef75
18:34:20.000878 > 192.168.1.5.2894 > 192.168.1.25.printer: . 1:1(0)
➡ack 32 win 32120 <nop,nop,timestamp 4058997 393476> (DF)
➡(ttl 64, id 11266)
          4500 0034 2c02 4000 4006 8b53 c0a8 0105
          c0a8 0119 0b4e 0203 fba2 c2c9 17b1 141f
          8010 7d78 8d8b 0000 0101 080a 003d ef75
          0006 0104
18:34:20.049095 > 192.168.1.5.2894 > 192.168.1.25.printer: P 1:424(423)
➡ ack 32 win 32120 <nop,nop,timestamp 4059002 393476> (DF) (ttl 64,
➡id 11267)
```

```
4500 01db 2c03 4000 4006 89ab c0a8 0105
c0a8 0119 0b4e 0203 fba2 c2c9 17b1 141f
8018 7d78 54c5 0000 0101 080a 003d ef7a
0006 0104 4242 f0ff ffbf f1ff ffbf f2ff
ffbf f3ff ffbf 5858 5858 5858 5858 5858
5858 5858 5858 5858 252e 3137 3675 2533
3030 246e 252e 3133 7525 3330 3124 6e25
2e32 3533 7525 3330 3224 6e25 2e31 3932
```

Let's look at what's happening here. First, we see 192.168.1.5 and 192.168.1.25 attempting to make a connection using the typical TCP three-way handshake. In the next sequence of events, we see 192.168.1.5 attempting to run the exploit against 192.168.1.25. Finally, we see the 192.168.1.5 pushing 423 bytes of data to 192.168.1.25. The exploit continues this for a while until it is able to brute-force the exploit.

When this exploit worked, 192.168.1.25 provided me with a shell running as root, and I could do whatever I wanted.

Exploits are the way crackers break into systems. To protect yourself against them, you will have to update your operating system with patches. (This goes for all systems.)

The SANS Top 20

The SANS Top 20 Most Critical Internet Security Threats is a list of the most common exploits found on computer networks. What makes this list so valuable is that SANS provides a list of the related CVE entries (Common Vulnerabilities and Exposures), so you can do more research if necessary. This list was compiled by SANS with the help of many security experts and the security community.

TIP

The CVE database can be found at http://www.cve.mitre.org/. To read more on the SANS Top 20, visit http://www.sans.org/top20.

The first threat is the default installation of operating systems, which can lead to a number of problems: The system might have default passwords, it probably doesn't have the latest security patches, and it most likely is running unnecessary services that should be turned off to improve security.

The second exploit is the use of weak passwords. Need I say more? In any form of risk assessment, this is one of the most common vulnerabilities I see. When coming up with a password, remember to follow these simple guidelines:

- Make sure that the password is at least eight characters in length.

- Make sure that the password is a combination of numbers, special characters, and alphanumeric characters.

- Pick a password that is not in the dictionary.

It is often useful to enforce the guidelines by configuring the password policy in the operating system or via a third-party product such as Password Bouncer (http://www.passwordbouncer.com). For more information, see Chapter 14, "Password Security."

TIP

For more information on password strengths, visit http://www.cert.org/tech_tips/passwd_file_protection.html.

Failing to keep good, up-to-date backups is the next issue. Backups need to be regularly verified to ensure that they are working, which many companies rarely do.

Another problem is having a large number of open ports. You can think of each port as a way to break into your system. Therefore, it makes sense to only keep open ports that you absolutely need.

The next threat on the SANS list is incorrect packet filtering rules on your firewall. More information can be found in Chapter 10, "Firewalls," and Chapter 23, "Routers, Switches, and Hubs."

SANS also points out that one of the biggest problems is inadequate logging. It is good to do a review of your systems to make sure that you are logging what you need during a security incident. Also, you need to make sure that the logs are getting stored somewhere secure so the cracker won't erase or modify them.

Vulnerable CGI programs are the seventh exploit in the SANS Top 20. These have been around for years, and are the main reason for most of the hack Web sites that receive mainstream attention. This type of vulnerability seems like it won't go away. Even in 2002, after knowing about this problem for years, the Bugzilla program suffered from one. Many of these CGI-BIN programs are vulnerable, especially the samples provided by vendors, and allow a malicious user to obtain root access. When an attacker obtains that level of access, he can do as he pleases (include changing the Web site).

TIP

More information can be found on CGI-BIN attacks at `http://www.cert.org/` `advisories/CA-1997-24.html`, `http://www.cert.org/advisories/CA-1996-11.html`, or `http://www.cert.org/advisories/CA-1997-07.html`. This list is *not* comprehensive; please dig a little further if you think you are vulnerable.

Windows-Specific Exploits

SANS also lists several Windows-specific problems. The first problem is Unicode vulnerabilities. Unicode is a character set, which in some ways is an extended form of ASCII, that allows you to represent the characters of just about every written language on Earth. ASCII, on the other hand, is limited to a subset of European languages. Using this and some tricks, a cracker can break in through your IIS server. The solution is fairly easy, in that you just need to stay current on IIS patches.

Next is the ISAPI extension buffer overflow. Buffer overflows are discussed in detail in Chapter 26, "Secure Application Development, Languages, and Extensions." This bug affects several Microsoft products. Again, the best fix is to make sure you have the latest security patches installed.

The third Microsoft-specific exploit on the list is vulnerable Remote Data Service security holes in IISI. You can prevent this exploit by simply patching your IIS.

TIP

More information can be found on RDS security holes at `http://www.wiretrip.net/rfp/` `p/doc.asp?id=29&iface=2`.

Next is global file sharing using NetBIOS (ports 135–139). This is probably the biggest security problem users have if they are connected to a cable modem or DSL. Most do not understand the concept of file sharing, and leave it enabled. Another problem is Napster. Although Napster is not listed here, it does require people to share directories, and that can lead to sharing more than what is necessary. Preventive measures are given on the SANS sites, but the basic idea is to minimize the number of shares, use passwords, and restrict access.

Consider implementing the `RestrictAnonymous` registry key for Internet-connected hosts in standalone or untrusted domain environments.

The fifth Microsoft-specific problem is anonymous logins. Crackers can connect and get information about systems without having to log in. This problem can be minimized by setting some registry keys, as documented on the SANS site, but cannot be completely eliminated if you have domain controllers.

The next problem is that Windows uses weak encryption by default for backward-compatibility reasons. However, most people do not need this. Unfortunately, the fix is very complex and might require that you get rid of any Windows 9x client machines.

NOTE

The National Security Agency has published many worthwhile guides to securing Windows 2000. They are available at http://nsa2.www.conxion.com/win2k/download.htm.

Unix-Specific Exploits

The first Unix exploit is the use of vulnerable Remote Procedure Calls (RPCs). RPCs enable C programs to make procedure calls on other machines across the network. Most vendors provide patches to help tighten up RPC services. Nevertheless, the best policy regarding this service is if you don't need it, then kill it. You can run `ps-ef|grep rpc`, find the Process ID (PID), and then run `kill -9 PID`. You can also disable RPC services at startup on most Unix operating systems by changing the startup file (located at /etc/rc.d/) from an S (start up) to K (kill). You can find out what RPC programs are running by using `rpcinfo -p`.

TIP

More information can be found on RPC attacks from http://www.cert.org/
incident_notes/IN-99-04.html.

The second Unix exploit is vulnerable sendmail and MIME attacks. These vulnerabilities are related to buffer overflows as well as pipe attacks that enable immediate root compromise. There are a couple of ways to secure these problem areas: The first is to maintain the correct patches for your sendmail/mail servers. The other is that if you do not need to run either of these services, disable them (follow the same procedures as spelled out for RPC).

TIP

More information can be found on sendmail security holes at http://www.cve.mitre.org/
cgi-bin/cvekey.cgi?keyword=sendmail. The latest version of sendmail can always be found
at http://www.sendmail.org/.

The next issue listed in the Top 20 is BIND. BIND is a program used for DNS servers to help resolve names to addresses, and is used throughout the Internet. In the recent years, major holes have been found in many versions of BIND. It is vital for anyone who runs BIND to always keep up on the latest vulnerabilities. If you check the CVE database for BIND, you'll see that, like clockwork, it has a security problem every few months.

The fourth Unix problem described by SANS is the use of r commands. These are commands that bypass normal authentication mechanisms, and should be disabled. More information is available in Chapter 21, "Unix."

SANS also lists the line printer daemon as a threat. By sending enough print jobs, it is possible to either cause a denial-of-service attack or break into a machine. The solution is to keep up-to-date on patches.

The sixth Unix exploit is vulnerable sadmind and mountd. This vulnerability applies to many versions of Unix.

TIP

For more information on the sadmind and mountd security holes, visit
`http://www.cert.org/advisories/CA-99-16-sadmind.html` or `http://www.cert.org/advisories/CA-1998-12.html`.

The final exploit in the SANS Top 20 is Default SNMP community strings set to `"public"` and `"private"`. Along with the weak passwords, this vulnerability can be controlled by basic administration.

TIP

For more information on SNMP and community strings, see `http://www.cisco.com/univercd/cc/td/doc/cisintwk/ito_doc/snmp.htm#xtocid210315`.

Keep in mind that these are not the only vulnerabilities on the Internet. A cracker can use any exploit he has in his bag of tricks against you and your network.

Summary

This chapter covered a variety of topics, including passive OS fingerprinting, social engineering, tools, and the SANS Top 20. Hopefully after reading this chapter you can grasp the thinking and the process a cracker will go through to obtain access to a network. With cybercrime on the rise, protecting yourself and your information will become more challenging. Knowing how a hacker/cracker works can assist you in protecting yourself against these people. As Bruce Schneier of CTO Counterpane Internet Systems says, "Security is a process, not a product." As for the products you do have, remember to apply the latest patches and disable the services you don't need.

4

Mining the Data Monster

Computer security is a constant process, not a product, and not following it can prove disastrous. Generally speaking, the security process goes something like this:

1. After configuring your system as securely as possible with help from the resources discussed in this chapter, you, or some other party, discover a vulnerability.

2. An exploit for that vulnerability becomes public knowledge.

3. Your system's vendor responds, typically with a patch or upgrade.

4. By staying on top of alerts posted by vendors and security organizations, you learn of the exploit, assess its potential impact on your organization, and, if appropriate, download the fix, test it, and install it.

With luck, the fix works without any negative effects, and the process begins anew as you await the discovery of the next vulnerability. The key is that this is an iterative process, and an important part of it is staying current on the information available without suffering information overload.

Information Overload

This chapter offers a laundry list of mailing lists, Web sites, and FTP archives that house security information. That's great, but if you subscribe to any security mailing list, you'll immediately discover that list members are only slightly more courteous than Usenet users. These folks argue like schoolchildren, and they'll do it on your time.

This dissension is a major problem. Your mailbox will be filled with, say, 100 messages daily, when only 12 of them have valuable information. The rest will consist of arguments, "me-too"s, and, sadly, spam.

This might not seem like a serious problem, but it is. If you run a heterogeneous network, you might need to subscribe to several lists. Because the average list generates about 30 messages a day, you might end up receiving between 150 and 300 messages daily.

Here are some suggestions to help you out:

- Before joining a slew of mailing lists, prepare your system to compartmentalize the output. Set up an email box expressly for receiving security-based mail. Allot one email address for each mailing list you join. For example, create accounts `ntsec`, `sunsec`, and `hpuxsec` to receive mail related to NT security, Sun security, and HP-UX security. This will at least separate the material by operating system or subject. (If you don't have a permanent network connection, you can still do this by establishing Web-based mailing addresses. Many companies provide free email accounts to the public. The downside with that, of course, is that many mailing lists will block domains such as `hotmail.com` and `altavista.net`, because these domains are often used for spamming.)

- Subscribe only to digests or moderated groups. Most mailing lists offer a digested or moderated version of their list. These versions generally have a lesser noise-to-signal ratio. In other words, irrelevant posts and messages are edited out prior to distribution. You therefore receive more relevant and pertinent information.

- Choose lists that have searchable archives, such as BugTraq or the others located at `http://www.securityfocus.com`.

It might be worth your time to automate at least the cursory analysis of advisories and mailing list messages. For example, if you maintain a network that runs three or four platforms, the amount of security mail you receive each day will be more than you can humanly read. With the use of Perl scripts, you can develop a primitive but effective method of mining data automatically. It works like this:

1. As suggested previously, structure your directory to reflect the names of various operating systems (`/aix`, `/linux`, and so on) and various security issues (such as `/denial_of_service`).

2. When a mail message arrives, it's examined by subject line and the first six lines of the body. If an operating system name appears in those lines, the mail is redirected to the appropriate directory.

3. Once a day, a Perl script traverses those directories, scanning for original posts.

(In other words, all "Re:" posts are discarded from the list.) Alternatively, if you use an email client such as Outlook or Outlook Express, you can configure a rule to delete posts from the mailing list that have Re: in the subject line.

4. The resulting messages are printed.

This process ensures that you see every original advisory. The obvious problem with this approach, however, is that often meaningful discussion appears in follow-up posts. Most moderated mailing lists enable you to search for a particular "thread" of interest. This way, your time is focused on the few items of importance to you, rather than on several issues that do not affect you.

How Much Security Do You Need?

Do you really need all that information from all those lists? Probably. Most vendors wait until strategically favorable moments to distribute patches on hard media. Therefore, by the time you get a CD-ROM with patches, your system can be 30–100 patches behind. In the interim, your system isn't safe.

Additionally, if you don't keep up with developments on at least a weekly basis, bringing your network up to date might prove to be an overwhelming task.

> **NOTE**
>
> Another irritating factor is that some vendors aren't in any hurry to publicly acknowledge flaws in their software. Microsoft is sometimes guilty of this, denying problems until proof becomes so widespread that they no longer have plausible deniability. Even then, the information often only becomes available in knowledge base articles and exploit Web sites.

Just as a car manufacturer cannot be held responsible if the owner has not maintained the brakes and tires, a computer vendor cannot be responsible for a system that is not configured securely with up-to-date patches. The bottom line is that it's your responsibility to chase down security information. If your network gets cracked, it's you (and not your vendor) who shoulders the blame. You must keep yourself informed on recent developments.

The remainder of this chapter identifies key sources of up-to-date security information. I strongly suggest that you assign someone in your organization to track such information.

General Sources

The following sources have both up-to-the-minute information and legacy information.

The Computer Emergency Response Team (CERT)

Computer Emergency Response Team (CERT) Coordination Center

Software Engineering Institute

Carnegie Mellon University

URL: http://www.cert.org

The Computer Emergency Response Team (CERT) was established in 1988 following the Morris Worm incident. Since then, CERT has issued hundreds of security advisories, and has responded to more than 140,000 reports of Internet break-ins, and more than 7,000 vulnerabilities (see http://www.cert.org/stats/cert_stats. html#incidents).

CERT not only issues advisories whenever a new security vulnerability surfaces, but it also

- Remains on call 24 hours a day to provide vital technical advice to those who have suffered a break-in.

- Uses its Web site to provide valuable security information, both new and old (including papers from the early 1980s).

- Publishes an annual report that can give you great insight into security statistics.

There was a time when CERT did not publish information on a hole (a vulnerability) until after a fix had been developed. Opinion on this stance varied. Some felt it was counterproductive to advertise an exploit until it was fixed. On the other side of the fence were those who believed that by the time the "white hat" community became aware of a vulnerability, the "black hat" cracking community was well aware of it, and probably had been circulating information about it through their channels for some time. By not publishing the information right away, CERT was keeping the ethical hacking community unaware and vulnerable. In October 2000, CERT compromised by adopting a policy whereby it will issue an alert 45 days (in most cases) after its initial report, regardless of vendor action. Complete details on CERT's disclosure policy can be found on its Web site at http://www.cert.org/faq/ cert_faq.html#C9.

CERT advisories generally contain location URLs for patches and vendor-initiated information. From these sites, you can download code or other tools that will help proof your system against the vulnerability. CERT is also a good starting place to check for older vulnerabilities, as the database goes back to 1988.

NOTE

A bit of trivia: The first CERT advisory was issued in December 1988—it concerned a weakness in FTPD.

There are several sources where you can obtain CERT advisories, including the following:

- **The CERT mailing list**—The CERT mailing list distributes CERT advisories and bulletins to members. To subscribe, send email to `majordomo@cert.org` and include `"subscribe cert-advisory"` in the body of the message. For more details about signing up, see `http://www.cert.org/contact_cert/certmaillist.html`.

- **The CERT Web site**—If you don't want to clog your email directory with advisories, you can still obtain them from the CERT Web site. To do so, point your browser to `http://www.cert.org/nav/alerts.html`.

The U.S. Department of Energy Computer Incident Advisory Capability

Computer Incident Advisory Capability (CIAC)

Computer Security Technology Center

Lawrence Livermore National Laboratory

URL: `http://www.ciac.org/ciac`

Computer Incident Advisory Capability (CIAC) was established in 1989. CIAC maintains a database of security-related material intended primarily for the U.S. Department of Energy. However, most information and tools housed at CIAC are available to the public.

The CIAC site is an excellent information source. Here are some CIAC resources available to you:

- **CIAC virus information**—CIAC has links to eight of the major anti-virus corporations' databases (`http://www.ciac.org/ciac/ciac_virus_info.html`).

- **CIAC security bulletins**—CIAC bulletins are very much like CERT advisories. They describe particular vulnerabilities and possible solutions. CIAC has a search engine as well, so you can rake through past bulletins for interesting information.

- **CIAC security documents**—CIAC has an interesting and ever-growing collection of security documents. Some are how-to in nature (for example, how to secure X Window System), whereas others are informational (such as lists of security information links). Most are available in both plain text and PDF formats.

- **CIAC tools**—CIAC has links to excellent security tools, most of which are free. There are tools that support DOS/Windows 9*x*, NT/2000, Unix, and Macintosh. Some are free only to government agencies and their contractors.

CIAC has a searchable archive of advisories and bulletins at `http://www.ciac.org/cgi-bin/index/bulletins`.

The following are some examples of important information provided by CIAC to the public:

- Defense Data Network advisories

- CERT advisories

- NASA advisories

The National Institute of Standards and Technology Computer Security Resource Clearinghouse

Computer Security Resource Clearinghouse (CSRC)

National Institute of Standards and Technology (NIST)

URL: `http://csrc.nist.gov/`

The NIST CSRC Web site offers a sizable list of publications, tools, pointers, organizations, and support services. In particular, the following resources are extremely helpful:

- **NIST Information Technology Laboratory (ITL) computer security bulletins**—Bulletins from ITL cover various topics of current interest. Although ITL documents seldom deal with specific vulnerabilities, they do apprise readers of the latest developments in security technology.

- **CSRC drafts**—CSRC drafts record important security research being conducted at NIST and elsewhere. These documents can help you define security plans and policies. (A sample title is "User Guide for Developing and

Evaluating Security Plans for Unclassified Federal Automated Information Systems.") In particular, CSRC has a multitude of documents that deal with security policy.

- **The CSRC search engine**—CRSC provides a search engine that links information from a wide range of agencies and resources.

The CSRC advisory page has links to other valuable references, including the Federal Computer Incident Response Capability (FedCIRC), CERT, the National Infrastructure Protection Center (NIPC), and the Forum of Incident Response and Security Teams (FIRST). These sources provide up-to-the-minute warnings about various vulnerabilities.

The BugTraq Archives
The BugTraq archives contain all messages sent to the BugTraq mailing list. The majority of these messages describe holes in the Unix operating system. The site is of particular interest because it features a search mechanism that enables you to search based on platform (Sun, Linux, Microsoft) viruses, IDSs, advisories, and other topics.

The BugTraq list is an excellent resource because it isn't inundated with irrelevant information. The majority of posts are short and informative. Chris Chasin, the founder of BugTraq, describes the list as follows:

> This list is for *detailed* discussion of UNIX security holes: what they are, how to exploit, and what to do to fix them. This list is not intended to be about cracking systems or exploiting their vulnerabilities. It is about defining, recognizing, and preventing the use of security holes and risks.

BugTraq is probably the Internet's most valuable resource for online reporting of Unix-based vulnerabilities. There are more than 20 different mailing lists that focus on specific platforms and security issues, including forensics, Microsoft, security basics, VPNs, mobile code, and others. Visit it at http://www.securityfocus.com.

The Forum of Incident Response and Security Teams (FIRST)
FIRST is a coalition of many organizations, both public and private, that work to circulate Internet security information. Some FIRST members are

- DoE Computer Incident Advisory Capability (CIAC)

- NASA Automated Systems Incident Response Capability

- Purdue University Computer Emergency Response Team

- Stanford University Security Team

- IBM Emergency Response Service

- Australian Computer Emergency Response Team

FIRST exercises no centralized control. All members of the organization share information, but no one exercises control over any of the other components. FIRST maintains a list of links to all FIRST member teams with Web servers. Check out FIRST at `http://www.first.org/team-info/`.

Mailing Lists

Table 4.1 identifies key security mailing lists. The majority of these lists issue up-to-the-minute advisories.

TABLE 4.1   Mailing Lists for Holes and Vulnerabilities

List	Description
`http://www.iss.net/security_center/maillists/`	The alert list at Internet Security Systems, features alerts, product announcements, and company information. To subscribe to this and other ISS lists, complete the form at `http://online.securityfocus.com/cgi-bin/sfonline/subscribe.pl`. BugTraq and several other mailing lists are available at `http://www.security focus.com`. This Web page has instructions and an online form for you to pick which mailing lists you want to join. As of this writing, there are 20 lists to choose from. Their Mailing Lists pull-down menu has an Other Lists link with pointers to even more mailing lists hosted by other sites.
`http://honor.icsalabs.com/mailman/ listinfo/firewall-wizards`	The Firewall Wizards mailing list. This list is a moderated forum for advanced firewall administrators.
`https://listman.redhat.com/mailman/listinfo/`	Get information regarding Red Hat mailing lists.
`http://www.checkpoint.com/ services/mailing.html`	The Firewall-1 security list. This list focuses on issues related to CheckPoint's Firewall-1 product.
`http://www.isc.org/services/public/ lists/firewalls.html`	The Firewalls mailing list focuses on firewall `lists/firewalls.html` security (previously known as `firewalls@greatcircle.com`).

TABLE 4.1   Continued

List	Description
`majordomo@toad.com`	The Cyberpunks mailing list. Members discuss issues of personal privacy and cryptography. (If a major cryptographic API is broken, you'll probably hear it here first.) To subscribe, send a message with the command SUBSCRIBE in the body.
`majordomo@uow.edu.au`	The Intrusion Detection Systems list. Members of this list discuss real-time intrusion detection techniques, agents, neural-net development, and so forth. To subscribe, send a message with the command subscribe ids in the body.
`risks-request@csl.sri.com`	The Risks forum—members of this list discuss a wide variety of risks that we are exposed to in an information-based society. Examples are invasion of personal privacy, credit card theft, cracking attacks, and so on. To subscribe, send a message with the command SUBSCRIBE in the body.
`ssl-talk-request@netscape.com`	The Secure Sockets Layer mailing list—members of this list discuss developments in SSL, and potential security issues. To subscribe, send a message with the command SUBSCRIBE in the body.

For a thorough compilation of mailing lists, you can also go to `http://www.security-focus.com`. Select mailing lists from the main page—you will see about 20 lists. To see even more, click Other Lists or go directly to it at `http://www.securityfocus.com/focus/home/menu.html?fm=8,23,0&action=unfold` and explore the lists by category.

Usenet Newsgroups

You can also occasionally collect interesting information that doesn't appear elsewhere from Usenet security groups. Table 4.2 outlines some newsgroups that discuss security holes. Some newsgroups such as `alt.2600` are included so you can get an idea of how the hacker community shares, debates, and brags. The newsgroups are not all intended for everyday reading, but are interesting to visit once in a while. One final note: Newsgroups come and go, and activity might decrease over time. Make use

of a newsgroup search engine such as Google Groups—http://www.google.com/
grphp?hl=en&ie=UTF-8&oe=UTF-8—to find newsgroups that are active and relevant
to you.

TABLE 4.2   Security Newsgroups

Newsgroup	Topics Discussed
alt.2600.crackz	Hacking, cracking. This group focuses mainly on cracks. This is a distribution point for cracks and warez.
alt.2600.hackerz	Hacking, cracking. This group is similar to alt.2600.
alt.computer.security	General computer security. Roughly equivalent to comp.security.misc, described later.
alt.hackers.malicious	DoS, cracking, viruses. These folks focus on causing damage to their targets.
alt.security	Very general security issues. Occasionally, there is some interesting information here. However, this group also carries personal security information, including alarms and pepper spray as well as terrorism and espionage.
alt.security.pgp	Pretty good privacy. This group spawns interesting (and occasionally exhaustive) debates on cryptography.
comp.lang.java.security	The Java programming language. This group has interesting information. Certainly, whenever some major defect is found in Java security, the information will appear here first.
comp.security.firewalls	Firewalls. This group is a slightly more risqué environment than the Firewalls mailing list. The discussion here is definitely noteworthy and worthwhile.
comp.security.misc	General security.
comp.security.unix	Unix security. This group often has worthwhile discussions and up-to-date information. Probably the best overall Unix newsgroup.
comp.os.linux.security	Good Linux security. It contains a broad range of security-related topics, including firewalls (ipchains), networking, and system administration.

Vendor Security Mailing Lists, Patch Depositories, and Resources

Finally, this section identifies vendor sites, patch archives, and lists that house
important security information.

Silicon Graphics Security Headquarters

Silicon Graphics, Inc.

URL: http://www.sgi.com/support/security/

The Silicon Graphics Security Headquarters provides the following services to the public:

- **SGI security advisories**—SGI advisories provide up-to-the-minute information on vulnerabilities in the IRIX operating system. These advisories are available at `http://www.sgi.com/support/security/advisories.html`.

- **SGI security patches**—SGI provides a patch archive. This is a good place to find solutions to older vulnerabilities. SGI patches are located at `http://www.sgi.com/support/security/patches.html`.

- **Q's toolbox of programs**—This is a collection of security-related programs that can help shore up your SGI system's security. (These include scanning tools, logging utilities, and even access control list tools.) Get these programs at `http://www.sgi.com/support/security/toolbox.html`.

- A site with several FAQs, which would be of interest not only to security managers, but also to administrators and developers, is `http://www-viz.tamu.edu/~sgi-faq/faq/html-1/`. A sample tip that can be found here is what to do when you've forgotten the root password.

The Sun Security Bulletin Archive

Sun Microsystems provides up-to-date security bulletins about many of its products. These bulletins and patches are available on the SunSolve server at `http://sunsolve.sun.com/pub-cgi/show.pl?target=security/sec`.

The ISS Security Center

This site (`http://www.iss.net/security_center/`) maintains an excellent vulnerability database. It is searchable by the name of the vulnerability or by system platform. The site also has a newsletter, mailing list and security library with links to dozens of other sites, presentations, and PDF documents for ISS products.

Eugene Spafford's Security Hotlist

Eugene Spafford's site can be summed up in five words: the ultimate security resource page. Of the hundreds of pages devoted to security, this is the most comprehensive collection of links available. In contrast to many link pages whose links expire, these links remain current. Check it out online at `http://www.cerias.purdue.edu/ /hotlist/`.

SANS Institute

The SANS Institute offers free subscriptions to newsletters that do a lot of the data mining for you. SANS pulls news of critical security news from several of the sources mentioned previously (CERT, NIPC, BugTraq, and so on) as well as vendor sources that were not mentioned. SANS also puts together three digests:

- Security Alert Consensus (SAC)—weekly
- SANS NewsBites—weekly
- SANS Windows Security Newsletter—monthly

Particularly noteworthy is the SAC. When subscribing from the SANS Web site, you can specify which platforms you are interested in. This enables you to personalize your newsletter and limit the "noise" you might otherwise have to sift through. Currently, SANS collects news from 72 sources, so you only need to read one. Sign up at http://www.sans.org/sansnews.

International Association of Computer Investigative Specialists (IACIS)

An excellent resource for anyone involved in the investigation of computer crime is IACIS. IACIS is a organization of dedicated volunteers catering to those in law enforcement. They provide training in the legal aspects of search and seizure of computer equipment, forensic analysis of computer evidence, and provide a certification program for forensic examiners called the CFCE (Certified Forensic Computer Examiner). The certification process is vendor-neutral, and starts with a two-week training conference (which can be waived if you have sufficient work experience). Unlike other certification "bootcamps," you are then assigned a mentor to help guide you through the remainder of the process. This includes completion of seven projects and a written exam, all of which must be completed within a year.

Another invaluable resource they provide is the IACIS List-Server. This mailing list enables a world-wide community of law-enforcement professionals to assist one another with questions ranging from how to extract a hard drive from a specific laptop computer to handling legal issues. There is also an FTP site with tools, technical papers, and procedural documents available. For more information, see http://www.cops.org.

Summary

Your key to success is timely access to relevant information. Too much information, and you might not pay enough attention to an important issue that gets lost in the noise. So, before you subscribe to every list you find, keep in mind that there is a fair bit of redundancy and overlap in what many of them cover. Look through the lists' archives/Web sites and see which lists suit you—which go into the level of detail you are comfortable with, and pay attention to issues that are relevant to your environment. This will be time well spent, because the window between vulnerability announcements is becoming shorter and shorter.

5

Internal Security

The most peaceable way for you, if you do take a thief, is to let him show himself what he is, and steal out of your company.

—*William Shakespeare,* Much Ado About Nothing

This chapter focuses on securing your network from the inside, with the assumption that all your external security efforts are in vain if the inside security is a pushover. Secondly, because "inside jobs" are rarely pretty or welcome, this chapter details some practices that avoid—in the best case—and detect and punish—in the worst case—an intruder in your midst.

Internal Security: The Red-Headed Stepchild

It's probably a good bet that your network perimeter is incredibly more secure than the inside of your network; most networks are "crunchy on the outside, chewy on the inside." You can probably blame the "firewalls-fix-everything" mentality of the last several years for this. This means that your *internal* vulnerabilities might very well be the cause of your worst security nightmare.

In fact, although the Computer Security Institute's most recent *Computer Crime and Security Survey* says that 90% of respondents detected security breaches, the report goes on to say that only 40% of the respondents detected breaches from the *outside*. Do the math.

NOTE

You can see the executive summary of the Computer Security Institute's *2002 Computer Crime and Security Survey* at `http://www.gocsi.com/press/20020407.html`

(See the "Resources" section at the end of the chapter for more surveys, articles, and so on.)

The survey goes on to state that 78% of respondents detected unauthorized access by insiders. Clearly, internal security is a *huge* problem. The ICSA (International Computer Security Association) agrees, believing that insiders cause 80% of security problems.

NOTE

Stressing that firewalls are *not* a security panacea, the ICSA outlines some internal security problems in its *Firewall Buyers Guide* at `http://www.icsalabs.com/html/communities/firewalls/buyers_guide/chap_2.shtml`.

Internal Risks: Types of Harm and Vectors

Fine. So breaches of internal security are common. But what's the worst thing that could happen? What are the risks? More to the point, what can you do about these risks?

Many times, assessing an organization's internal risks can point directly to the necessity of implementing particular policies. It's useful to break these risks down into *types of harm* and *vectors*.

Some of the common types of harm that you'll want to consider are:

- Server compromise

- Network infrastructure compromise

- Application-level compromise

- Workstation compromise (Trojans)

- Loss or theft of proprietary data

- Transmission of inappropriate or harmful data to business partners

- Denial of service

When we talk about *vectors*, we're really talking about the human factor—any type of human action that can introduce harm into your network. The human factor is rather complex; it's useful to further break down this factor into *organizational roles* and *type of intent*.

Some types of intent typically are:

- Well-meaning/unwitting—A person accidentally introduces harm into the network

- Scofflaw—A person knowingly bypasses security checkpoints

- Disgruntled/malicious/opportunistic

The types of organizational roles are:

- Members of the public—That is, users of a kiosk, folks who are wandering your building and stumble across an unlocked wire closet, or even people driving by with a wireless network card if you have a wireless network (see Chapter 27, "Wireless Security Auditing.")

- Temporary employees

- Departmental users—Each department should really be considered separately, because each can present a different level of privilege and/or risk.

- Infrastructure, server, or application administrators

To visualize the way that these two factors interact to generate a level of risk, it's useful to set them into a chart where the upper left represents the least amount of risk, and the lower right represents the most risk.

TABLE 5.1 Human Vectors: Degree of Risk

Human Vectors: Degree of Risk	Well-meaning/ Unwitting	Scofflaw	Disgruntled/ Malicious/ Opportunistic
Members of public (kiosk, unlocked wire closet)	Least risk		
Temporary employees		↖	
Departmental users (each considered separately)		↘	
Infrastructure, server, or application administrators			Most risk

Obviously, a malicious administrator is your organization's worst nightmare, but gone are the days when "only" IT professionals could rock the network boat. Today's high-profile security problems, coupled with "script kiddie" exploits and a permissive workstation policy, means that any jerk with an attitude, an IQ of more than 80, and a PC can take advantage of your untended network. To fight back, enact a strong Acceptable Use Policy (AUP); check up on it with auditing and IDS tools; and enforce it. (See Chapter 25, "Policies, Procedures, and Enforcement," for more info on building an AUP.)

Well-meaning/Unwitting Employees

Just about any of your employees could fall into this category under the influence of the hacker strategy of social engineering. *Social engineering* is the act of using interpersonal skills to get people to give away information that they otherwise wouldn't. The implication is not widely understood, but yes, some hackers do have social skills.

Their methods can be quite ingenious. Perhaps a hacker notices on some hobby discussion board that a particular mid- to low-level employee is dialing up from an ISP instead of the usual IP block of your company. The hacker might then call an IT admin in the company pretending to be that worker, and explain that he is telecommuting today, his machine crashed and he's having to reinstall, and he needs to know the VPN (Virtual Private Network) settings. Assuming a large organization and an admin that doesn't know that employee's voice very well, she just might give the information out.

The hacker might follow up by calling the main number of your company pretending to be a vendor and requesting to talk to a high-level manager. If the receptionist tells him that the manager is on vacation today, he can ask to leave a voicemail and try to subvert your phone system to send a voicemail on behalf of that manager. In the voicemail, he could tell a system administrator to create a new user account. With a VPN connection and a user account, he then has practically unfettered access to your systems.

That's just one example. The important thing to take away from this is not the details, but the generalities. Hackers could go on a smoke break by the back door with your employees and sneak inside, then pretend to be a new hire in person. Consider a separate, unpublished phone number for telecommuter tech support. Make sure your phone system is secure. Have photo ID badges for all who are authorized to be in the building—and enforce it. And most importantly, you should train everyone in the company to not give out any information unless they are certain of whom they are talking to, lest they become unwitting victims of social engineering.

Scofflaw Employees

Scofflaw employees—that is, employees who want to bypass your normal security measures for their own convenience—can also be a huge problem.

The classic example of a scofflaw employee is one who ignores policy, bypasses the organization's remote access mechanism, and decides to install a modem and PCAnywhere on her PC—many times without a reasonably good password. All of a sudden, there is an open door from the outside to your internal network—not a good thing.

Other examples include VIP users who do not want their Internet access to be monitored by IT. They therefore bypass corporate firewalls and dial into their own ISPs, which don't necessarily have the same type of security policies as the organization.

> **NOTE**
>
> I knew one VIP user in particular who bypassed his organization's email system—a system that scanned inbound and outbound email for viruses. He decided to use a dial-up account with a local vendor that did *not* have virus protection on the mail gateway.
>
> To make a long story short, his workstation hadn't received the most recent virus pattern update yet, and one of his cronies sent him a virus that messed up his workstation, necessitating an "emergency" call to the help desk. Scofflaws oftentimes shoot themselves in the foot while they're putting the organization at risk.

As workstation-based Trojans become more common, bypassing a site's security checkpoints becomes worse and worse. Consider AOL's recent problem with a workstation-based trojan; hundreds of member accounts were compromised when employees executed an interesting-looking program that arrived by email:

> America Online Inc. acknowledged last week that 200 member accounts were compromised when targeted AOL employees opened infected e-mail attachments. The attachments unleashed a Trojan horse program that created a connection to the employees' machines, allowing intruders to access password and credit card information.
>
> —"AOL Investigates Theft of Account Data," *Computerworld*, Ann Harrison, June 26, 2000

These AOL employees were scofflaws in that they ignored an AOL policy: They opened executable content from untrusted sources because it looked less boring than the work that they were doing. Scofflaw users *will* become more and more of a threat as these types of Trojans proliferate. (See Chapter 18, "Trojans," for more information.)

You can mitigate this risk somewhat by using desktop management tools to "lock down" the desktop—and in some organizations, this can in fact be appropriate—

but in the end, it's a policy problem, not a technology problem. Desktop management is only effective if the politics of an organization allow it to be.

Bottom line: Top-level management wouldn't allow a VIP to erect a ladder on the side of the building to bypass corporate security's checkpoints; it also should not allow *anyone* to bypass network security's checkpoints. If top-level management truly understands the parallel, you have a powerful ally in the battle against scofflaws.

IT Employees

Of course, just because "everybody" is now a potential problem doesn't mean that disgruntled IT workers and coders don't have their own special set of concerns. More potential privileges mean more potential problems, naturally. Case in point is the oft-cited "logic bomb":

> Although the identification of the first software bomb is not certain, a classic example occurred in 1988 when a Texas firm called IRA suffered the deletion of some 168,000 payroll records from a database. This was shown to have been caused by a logic bomb planted by an employee named Burleson which was triggered 6 months after he left the firm.
>
> —*Computer Crime: An Historical Survey*, Richard E. Overill, Defence Systems International 98.
> http://www.kcl.ac.uk/orgs/icsa/Staff/overill.htm

System administrators and network infrastructure administrators can also be part of the problem—but they can also be part of the solution. If you have more than one hand in every pot, it's a *lot* harder for one person to leave back doors, plant subversive code, and so on. That is, collaborative practices mean that systems and code are always subject to someone else's review (see the next section, "Risk Mitigation Policies")—which means that you can nip problems in the bud. (See also Chapter 13, "Logging Tools.")

Risk Mitigation Policies

You'll want to establish clear, written policies in partnership with your organization's management team. This partnership can't be emphasized enough—a policy without teeth might as well never have been written. You'll want to

- Establish good physical security for all infrastructure—no matter how insignificant a piece of infrastructure might seem.

- Get management to build some level of concern for network security into the hiring process.

- Explicitly forbid bypassing security checkpoints (such as firewalls, remote access servers, and so on) in your AUP.

- Establish desktop management policies as they relate to virus/Trojan protection and levels of workstation lockdown.

- Encourage *small* teams of administrators to collaborate. If there's more than one administrator watching the henhouse, it's less attractive to the fox.

- Employ intrusion detection systems (IDSs, see Chapter 12, "Intrusion Detection Systems"), being careful to employ those that can handle high-bandwidth internal networks.

- Audit your systems and procedures periodically. (See Chapter 11, "Vulnerability Assessment Tools (Scanners)," and Chapter 13.

- Maintain current levels of operating systems and applications—vendors usually patch script kiddie exploits rather quickly. (See Part V, "Architecture, Platforms, and Security," for more information on maintaining current levels.)

Physical Security

It's actually pretty easy to practice due diligence with physical security. You've just got to be meticulous and consistent, and take it seriously. Pretend that someone could burglarize you personally if you're not careful. It might help to pretend that you live in New York.

In all seriousness, physical security is where the battle can easily be lost—although it can't be totally won with just physical safeguards. Little things like the capability to reboot a server from a floppy, or finding an unused username on a printout—or even finding a tape with a copy of a security database on it—make an intruder's job easier. Let's make it *hard*.

Here are some "dos" and "don'ts" that will make your job a little easier, an intruder's life a little harder, and your data a little more secure:

- **DO** lock every wiring closet—and keep them locked.

- **DO** use switches rather than hubs, *especially* for LAN segments that have administrative users on them. (They still must be physically secure to ensure that someone can't access the switch and packet sniff via port mirroring.) The price differential between hubs and switches has come down dramatically in recent years.

- **DO** change locks or door passcodes, and passwords to any shared accounts immediately when employees leave.

- **DO** erase hard drives, flash, and so on, when you take them out of service. Nobody's going to remember to do it before the surplus auction, and all sorts of passwords and/or sensitive data might be on them.

- **DO** write nonsense data to magnetic media when you are erasing it. Dropping a partition table is NOT good enough. (Degaussing is okay, though.)

- **DO** use a paper shredder. Don't laugh. Dumpster diving is more common than you think.

- **DO** lock your server cabinets when you're not using them.

- **DO** restrict or forbid the use of modems on desktops; they are the number one method of bypassing your organization's security checkpoints.

- **DO** make sure that any "road" laptop or PDA has appropriate data protection software and hardware installed before deployment.

- **DO** consider whether user access to floppy disks or other removable media make sense for your environment; they constitute a possible bypass of your security checkpoints.

- **DO** consider the use of smart cards/token-based security devices rather than passwords for administrative users or sensitive systems. Many operating systems now support token-based authentication in addition to passwords.

- **DO** remember that your phone PBXs must also be secured.

- **DON'T** send off-site backups to unsecured locations.

- **DON'T** give keys to vendors. Let them in to do their work, and then politely wave bye-bye when they leave.

- **DON'T** allow anyone other than key personnel ad hoc access to the data center.

- **DON'T** share wire closets with user-oriented peripherals such as printers.

- **DON'T** put servers into unsecured areas.

- **DON'T** leave server keys attached to the back of a server. Believe it or not, other people will think of this, too.

- **DON'T** let cleaning people—or other untrusted service people—into secured areas without an escort.

- **DON'T** store any sensitive data on user hard drives—if you must, think about hard drive encryption products.

- **DON'T** discuss passwords or other sensitive information over unsecured channels such as cell phones, cordless phones, 800MHz radios, or instant messaging.

- **DON'T** put consoles, keypads, or administrative workstations near windows.

The Hiring Process

Naturally, J. Random Hacker isn't going to show up and reveal his otherworldly activities at a job interview. And even doing background checks can turn into nothing more than lip service, depending upon who's doing the checks—and whether the individual has been caught in the past.

Still, there are things you can do to minimize your risks during the employment process. Start out by doing a "due diligence" background check—particularly for employees that will be involved in any level of IT. Do your homework and use a reputable agency to do your background checks—as with anything else in computing, "garbage in, garbage out." If you are using an internal HR check or some other check that you don't get invoiced for, communication is the key. Don't *assume* that silence from your background check folks means "Everything is OK." Lack of "NACK" (Negative *ACK*nowledgement) does *not* mean "ACK." It might simply mean that your request form got thrown out with lunch's pizza box. See http://www.nwc.com/1201/1201colfeldman.html for more discussion of the hiring process.

After you've worked with management to establish an Acceptable Use Policy, your next step is to work with HR to integrate it as part of the employment process for *any* employee. You want it integrated for two reasons: First, because it sends a message, and might dissuade an employee from snooping or fiddling where she doesn't belong. Second, if termination or disciplinary action is necessary because of AUP violation, it's definitely a *lot* easier to do if you have an "I-have-read-and-understood-this" AUP to back you up.

Establishing Desktop Lockdown

Lockdown, in the desktop management context, means that you've managed to apply the straps to your users in such a way that they can't hurt themselves—or your network. In the best case, this is done in such a way that the users don't feel constricted or stifled. Having a heart-to-heart with management about the level of lockdown can only be a good thing. Users get extremely irrational about losing *any* amount of autonomy, and you will *definitely* want management to buy into any lockdown that you need to enact.

It should be pointed out that desktop management—*any* desktop management—that resides on a local workstation can be bypassed by a clever user, unless there is serious physical security in place (no floppies, an "unpickable" case lock, and so forth). This, of course, is the type of security that you *must* have if you have public information terminals, kiosks, and so on. The point is that any workstation that isn't physically secured can usually be booted from alternative media, and then the local OS can be modified to a malicious user's heart's content.

Still, desktop management and lockdown for nonpublic users are important due diligence measures, and definitely should not be skipped. The important thing here is to prevent either well-meaning or scofflaw users from hurting themselves and others. Defeating a truly noncasual and malicious user isn't the primary purpose of desktop management.

TIP

As far as manual procedures go, you can see some sample system lockdown checklists at http://www.nswc.navy.mil/ISSEC/Form/index.html.

Virus protection, of course, is a mandatory component to desktop management. Virus protection is (or should be) such second nature to today's IT staff that we mention it here simply to ask one question: Can the user turn off virus protection?

Some virus protection suites let the user do this; others password-protect the entire control panel. You should certainly password-protect the control panel if possible, but you should also enact desktop management policies that check and re-install virus protection if the workstation's otherwise permissive operating system allows its removal.

Good desktop management tools enable you to not only "force" certain applications, but they can also

- Force applications to be configured in a certain way (notably browsers).
- Restrict users from running anything but a certain set of applications.
- Restrict use of removable media.
- Prevent users from modifying system configuration.

Restricting Content

It used to be that IT managers were only worried about what users were able to download; that is, folks were concerned about employee abuse of the Internet. At the time, there wasn't technology to check *what* the actual downloaded content was—so managers contented themselves with blocking sites based upon *where* the user tried to surf. Certain software manufacturers also became service organizations (notably Cyber Patrol, discussed later in this chapter) that maintained a list of URLs in certain categories: adult-oriented, comedy, shopping, news, and so on. As a manager, you could then block various categories with a perimeter device that had access to these lists.

This strategy, however, wasn't complete in and of itself. Objectionable sites surface overnight, and the list didn't always reflect reality. And, filtering outbound URLS does nothing to fight questionable content that *leaves* your site.

Because one of the risks to your organization is the unauthorized disclosure of content (customer lists, intellectual property, and so on), one of the hottest topics in corporate security today is that of *content management* (also called *content filtering*, *content services*, and *content restriction*). Content management works in conjunction with your perimeter security devices. The software can perform lexical analysis, pattern matching—even image recognition. (Yes, *those* images.)

Another risk faced by your organization is the transmission of inappropriate content (pornographic, libelous, or otherwise offensive data) or dangerous content (such as Trojans and viruses) to business partners. You'd have to be nuts to think that *any* tool could totally eliminate the possibility of inappropriate content making it through your checkpoints. But content management tools can limit the possibility. Virus gateway protection software is one example of specialized content management.

Some vendors label their products as content filters, when in fact they are *site filters* or *URL filters*. Again, rather than checking the data stream for objectionable content, they check the Web address against a categorized list of known Web sites. Site filtering has merit. It can definitely decrease the amount of day trading/time-wasting/non-work-related surfing at your organization—but it's not content filtering. It is only as effective as the folks who update the lists. And, site management doesn't do anything for your intranet.

That said, content management tools fall into two categories: those that offer generic content-checking services to the network, and those that operate solely on a specific application.

Those that offer generic content services tend to do it via CheckPoint Software's CVP (Content Vectoring Protocol). CVP accepts a connection from a client, proxies the request to the server, scans the content, and either modifies or denies the request when content does not pass muster.

There is not yet an RFC-based content restriction protocol that has been widely implemented. If you're not using Firewall-1 or another firewall that supports CVP, you might have to purchase individual products that separately monitor Web content (HTTP), email (SMTP), news (NNTP), and FTP.

You'll also probably have to put up with some degree of false positives—yet another thing to administrate. For example, content filters commonly block *Network Computing*'s "Centerfold," a showcase of innovative companies' networks.

Still, content filters can be worthwhile, if you target and configure them correctly. See the section "Products," later in this chapter for a sampling of content-filtering tools. Look for content management to change and grow in the next couple of years; hit the Web or magazines like *Network Computing* for the latest scoop.

Administrative Collaboration

At first, administrative collaboration doesn't seem like much of a security practice. How can teamwork make your internal network a safer place?

First, consider that any illegal or unethical action involving partners automatically means that there are witnesses and possible leads to an investigation. As Benjamin Franklin said, "Three can keep a secret if two of them are dead."

Secondly, take the case where there is no explicit partnership during a questionable activity. The fact that there is another administrator who has responsibility for the system involved means that the system itself is under scrutiny. The fact that there is third-party scrutiny of the system might discourage the perpetrator in the best case, or at least lead to discovery of the questionable activity.

You should be careful, however, to avoid assigning too many hands to any given pot. Not only can this lead to system chaos, but it also can make unethical activity harder to trace, either during an incident or an audit. You definitely want a limited pool of individuals accountable for a given system.

Products

Products change all of the time—you'll want to check the latest industry magazines and Web sites to make sure that you've got the latest options in front of you. The following sections list sample products in various categories so you can get off on the right foot.

Desktop Management

Product: LANDesk

Company: Intel

URL: http://www.intel.com/network/products/landesk/products/ilms/

Description: Platform-agnostic desktop management; works with Win9x, WinNT/Win2K, Netware, and Linux.

Product: Systems Management Server (SMS)

Company: Microsoft

URL: http://www.microsoft.com/smsmgmt/default.asp

Description: Certainly the easiest way to manage the desktops of a Windows network. Works with Win9x and NT with ZAK (Zero Administration Kit) and Win2000's Group Policies.

Product: ZENWorks for Desktops

Company: Novell

URL: http://www.novell.com/products/zenworks/

Description: Desktop management using NDS (Novell Directory Services) as the configuration data store. Scales extremely well.

Laptop/PDA Security

When a portable device walks away, it's not pretty; the loss of the device is nothing compared to the potential loss of sensitive information. Although "password-at-power-up" is popular, it is not a good solution after someone has stolen your device; use real data encryption instead. There are a huge number of options, and it's not our intention here to offer a complete buyer's guide. Rather, this is a starting point. When you're looking to buy portable device security solutions, consider the following points:

- Physical tokens are available—If the device will be used in a public place, there is always the risk of someone "keystroke watching" during password entry, and later stealing the device.

- What type of encryption is used—Some vendors use a proprietary algorithm that hasn't been publicly examined for flaws. Stay well away from these, as well as those algorithms that use "obscuring" tactics like XOR (bit-complement), which are *not* secure.

PDA Security

Product: MemoSafe

Company: DeepNet Technologies

URL: http://deepnettech.com/memosafe.html

Description: MemoSafe uses the public domain SAFER-SK cipher to encrypt your MemoPad memos.

Product: ReadThis!

Company: PixIL

URL: http://www.schachar-levin.net/PixIL/Software/ReadThis/

Description: A module that requires HackMaster, and encrypts arbitrary Palm records. Beware, as the default method is XOR—as stated previously, *not* a secure method. Fortunately, an externally available IDEA encryption module is available. Source is only available for the external module.

Product: Safe

Company: Palmgadget.com

URL: `http://www.palmgadget.com/palmsafe.html`

Description: Triple DES memo pad encryptor; the source code is available for inspection, which is a real plus.

Laptop Security

Product: Invincible Disk

Company: Invincible Data Systems, Inc.

URL: `http://www.incrypt.com/idisk01.html`

Description: Encrypts an entire hard drive using the Blowfish encryption algorithm. Supports physical tokens.

Product: SafeHouse for Windows

Company: PC Dynamics

URL: `http://www.pcdynamics.com/SafeHouse/`

Description: Offers several different encryption options, including Blowfish, and Triple DES; but also includes the not-so-secure DES algorithm, as well as a proprietary algorithm that has not been publicly scrutinized.

NOTE

If you use Unix or Linux on laptops, see the section "Resources" later in this chapter for a paper describing encrypted file systems such as cfs, sfs, cryptfs, and so on.

Physical Security

Product: Barracuda Anti Theft Devices

Company: Barracuda Security Devices International

URL: `http://www.barracudasecurity.com`

Description: Barracuda's flagship product is a PC card that is inserted into an expansion slot; it monitors all computer components. You are paged when any component is tampered with or removed. A terribly shrill alarm goes off as well.

Product: Modem Security Enforcer

Company: IC Engineering, Inc.

URL: `http://www.icengineering.com/mse/mseinfo.html`

Description: Modem Security Enforcer includes callback authentication, password protection, firmware password storage (inaccessible to internal users), nonvolatile memory storage settings, and a completely configurable interface. There is a 9600bps version and a 19,200bps version.

Product: ModemLock for SmartCard Modems

Company: Intertex Data AB

URL: `http://www.algonet.se/~intertex/html/modemlock.html`

Description: Software that restricts incoming or outgoing modem use. Unfortunately, it requires that you use Intertex's brand of smart card modems.

Content Management

Product: eSafe Gateway

Company: Aladdin Knowledge Systems

URL: `http://www.ealaddin.com/esafe/gateway/index.asp`

Description: Filters Web traffic for hostile applets, viruses; can do URL filtering; inspects MIME-encoded mail.

Product: MIMESweeper product family—MAILSweeper, PORNSweeper, WEBSweeper, SECRETSweeper

Company: Re-Soft International, LLC

URL: `http://www.re-soft.com/product/mimesweep.htm`

Description: The kitchen sink, oven, stove, and dust-buster of content management. Filters everything from MIME-encoded email to porn-bearing GIFs.

Product: SuperScout, CyberPatrol, SurfControl

Company: SurfControl

URL: `http://www.surfcontrol.com/`

Description: All products use the same CyberNOT subscription list, and perform varying degrees of site filtering. SuperScout in particular can deny/allow sites based on file types.

Product: Various

Company: CheckPoint

URL: http://www.opsec.com/solutions/sec_content_security.html

Description: List of companies and products that have partnered with CheckPoint, and use CVP (Content Vectoring Protocol) as a central service for content scrutiny.

Resources

Computer Security Institute's 2002 Computer Crime and Security Survey.
http://www.gocsi.com/press/20020407.html

Computer Crime & Security Survey 2002. http://www.deloitte.com.au/
downloads/computercrime_may02.pdf

Computer Crime—An Historical Survey. Richard E. Overill.
http://www.kcl.ac.uk/orgs/icsa/Old/crime.html

Risk Assessment Strategies. Workshop about risk management.
http://www.nwc.com/1121/1121f3.html

How to Fire A System Administrator. M. Ringel and T. Limoncelli.
http://research.lumeta.com/tal/papers/LISA1999/adverse.html

A Contextual Love Letter for You. http://www.nwc.com/1117/1117colfeldman.html

Zero Administration Kit for Windows (Win9*x* and WinNT desktop management). http://www.microsoft.com/windows/zak/

Using Group Policy Scenarios (Win2000 desktop management). http://
www.microsoft.com/windows2000/techinfo/howitworks/management/grouppolicyinfo.asp

Palm Security: Encryption Tools.
http://palmtops.about.com/gadgets/palmtops/library/weekly/aa06182000a.htm

Encrypting Your Disks With Linux. Covers technologies that work on Linux and other Unix derivatives. http://koeln.ccc.de/~drt/crypto/linux-disk.html

Using Win2000's Foolproof Encryption. Uses Win2000's native file encryption technology. http://www.nwc.com/1121/1121ws1.html

Summary

Good internal security amounts to doing the same things you do for external security, and practicing due diligence with regard to self-auditing and policy enforcement. There are tools that can help, such as auditing tools/security scanners, content filtering tools, desktop management, and IDS, but in the final analysis, no tool can replace meticulous and sharp-eyed individuals.

PART II

Hacking 101

IN THIS PART

6

A Brief TCP/IP Primer

In this chapter, you'll learn about various protocols (or methods of data transport) used on the Internet, including Transmission Control Protocol (TCP) and Internet Protocol (IP). This chapter is not an exhaustive treatment of TCP/IP. Instead, it is intended to ensure that you have enough understanding of TCP/IP to get maximum benefit out of the chapters that follow. Throughout this chapter, links are provided to other documents and resources from which you can find more comprehensive information on TCP/IP.

What Is TCP/IP?

TCP/IP refers to two network protocols used on the Internet: Transmission Control Protocol and Internet Protocol. However, TCP and IP are only two protocols belonging to a much larger collection of protocols called the *TCP/IP suite*.

The TCP/IP suite of networking protocols connects various operating systems and network components. It provides a standard method for moving data between systems, and is used both on the Internet as well as in the world of private networking.

Protocols within the TCP/IP suite provide data transport for all services available to today's network user. Some of those services include

- Transmission of electronic mail
- File transfers
- Instant messaging
- Access to the World Wide Web

The Open Systems Interconnection (OSI) Reference Model

The OSI Reference Model was defined to standardize discussion of various technologies involved in networking. Its seven layers represent the architecture for data communication protocols. Each layer in the OSI model specifies a particular network function. The OSI model can be thought of as a stack, with each layer lying on the one below it. The services that a given layer performs are defined by the protocols at that layer. Understanding the OSI model and each layer is very helpful in conceptualizing how the different parts of TCP/IP networks and applications interact. The seven layers of the OSI model stack are

- Layer 7 (Application)—The highest layer of the OSI model. This layer defines the way applications interact with the network and between systems.

- Layer 6 (Presentation)—Contains protocols that are part of the operating system. This layer defines how information is formatted for display. Data encryption and translation can occur at this layer.

- Layer 5 (Session)—Coordinates communication between endpoints. Session state is maintained at this layer for security, logging, and administrative functions.

- Layer 4 (Transport)—Controls the flow of data between systems, defines the structure of data in messages, and performs error checking. Web browser encryption commonly occurs at this layer.

- Layer 3 (Network)—Defines protocols for routing data between systems. This is the layer where endpoint addressing occurs; it makes sure that data arrives at the correct destination.

- Layer 2 (Data-link or Network interface)—Defines the rules for sending and receiving information from one node to another in local network environments (LANs).

- Layer 1 (Physical or Media)—Governs hardware connections and byte-stream encoding for transmission. It is the only layer that involves a physical transfer of information between network nodes.

TCP/IP was created prior to the development of the OSI reference model, and, although TCP/IP fits within the OSI architecture, not all OSI layers are relevant when talking about TCP/IP. With respect to TCP/IP, the most important OSI layers are the application, transport, network, and data-link. Each of these layers has specific protocols associated with them, which we'll examine in detail later in this chapter. Common protocols at these layers are

- Application: Hypertext Transfer Protocol (HTTP)

- Transport: Transmission Control Protocol (TCP)

- Network: Internet Protocol (IP)

- Data-link: Address Resolution Protocol (ARP)

These protocols can be divided into two types, network and application (see Figure 6.1):

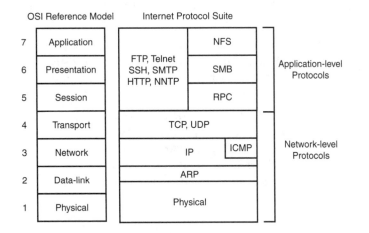

FIGURE 6.1 OSI and IP protocol stacks.

Network-Level Protocols

Network-level protocols manage the mechanics of data transfer, and are typically invisible to the end user. For example, the Internet Protocol (IP) provides packet delivery of information sent between the user and remote machines. It does this based on a variety of data, most notably the IP address of the two machines. Based on the IP address and other information, IP provides a "best-effort" service to route the information to its intended destination. Throughout this process, IP interacts with other network-level protocols engaged in data transport. Short of using network utilities (perhaps a sniffer or other device that reads IP datagrams), the user will never see IP's work on the network.

Application-Level Protocols

Unlike network-level protocols, application-level protocols are visible to the user. For example, Hypertext Transfer Protocol (HTTP) is an interactive protocol; you see the results of your connection and transfer as it's happening. This information is presented in error messages and status reports on the transfer—for example, the number of bytes that have been transferred at any given moment.

The History of TCP/IP

In 1969, the Defense Advanced Research Projects Agency (DARPA) commissioned development of a network for its research centers. The chief concern was this network's capability to withstand a nuclear attack. If the Soviet Union launched a first strike, the network still had to facilitate communication. The design of this network had several other requisites, the most important of which was the capability to operate independently of any centralized control. The prototype for this system (called ARPANET) was based in large part on research done in 1962 and 1963.

The original ARPANET worked well, but was subject to periodic system crashes. Furthermore, long-term expansion of that network proved costly. A search was therefore initiated for a more reliable set of protocols; that search ended in the mid-1970s with the development of TCP/IP.

TCP/IP had two chief advantages over other protocols: It was lightweight and could be implemented at lower cost than the other choices then available. Based on these factors, TCP/IP became exceedingly popular. By 1983, TCP/IP was integrated into release 4.2 of Berkeley Software Distribution (BSD) Unix. Its integration into commercial forms of Unix soon followed, and TCP/IP was established as the Internet standard. It has remained so to this day.

Today, TCP/IP is used for many purposes, not just for Internet communication. For example, intranets are often built using TCP/IP. In such environments, TCP/IP can offer significant advantages over other networking protocols. For example, TCP/IP works on a wide variety of hardware and operating systems. Using TCP/IP, one can quickly and easily create a heterogeneous network that links Macs, IBM compatibles, mainframes, Sun Unix servers, MIPS machines, and so on. Each of these can communicate with its peers using a common protocol suite. For this reason, TCP/IP has remained extremely popular since its introduction.

The RFCs

The protocols of TCP/IP suite are usually defined by documents called *Requests For Comments* (*RFCs*). The RFC approval process is managed by the Internet Engineering Steering Group (IESG) based on recommendations from the Internet Engineering Task Force (IETF). RFCs can be composed and submitted by anyone. In addition, RFCs are unlike many other networking standards in that they are freely available online and are open to comment by anyone.

TIP

For complete information about the Internet Standards Process, see http://www.ietf.org/rfc/rfc2026.txt.

The IETF is primarily responsible for forming working groups focused on strategic TCP/IP issues. Standards RFCs are often the product of many months of discussion within these working groups, which are made up of people interested in a particular aspect of the Internet. The working groups often draft proposed RFCs and make them available for discussion. These discussions typically take place on mailing lists, which welcome input from any interested party. Not all RFCs specify TCP/IP standards. Some RFCs contain background information, some provide documentation and tips for managing a TCP/IP network, some document protocol weaknesses, and some are even completely humorous. The core RFCs that define the standards associated with TCP/IP networking are

- RFC 768: User Datagram Protocol

- RFC 791: Internet Protocol

- RFC 792: Internet Control Message Protocol

- RFC 793: Transmission Control Protocol

- RFC 1122: Requirements for Internet Hosts—Communication Layers

- RFC 1123: Requirements for Internet Hosts—Application and Support.

TIP

For more complete information about Internet protocols and associated RFCs, visit an RFC archive such as that provided by the IETF at `http://www.ietf.org/rfc.html`.

Implementations of TCP/IP

The de facto standard for TCP/IP implementations has been the 4.*x* BSD releases, and this code has been the starting point for many other implementations. There are numerous implementations available, including a number of BSD derivatives such as FreeBSD, OpenBSD, and NetBSD. In addition, the Unix-like operating system GNU/Linux includes source code for a TCP/IP implementation. Source code for non-Unix implementations is also available. Packages for MS-DOS and Windows include WATTCP/WATT-32 and KA9Q.

How Does TCP/IP Work?

As with the OSI model, TCP/IP operates through the use of a *protocol stack*. This stack is the sum total of all protocols necessary to transfer data between two machines, as shown in Figure 6.2. (It is also the path that data takes to get out of one machine and into another.)

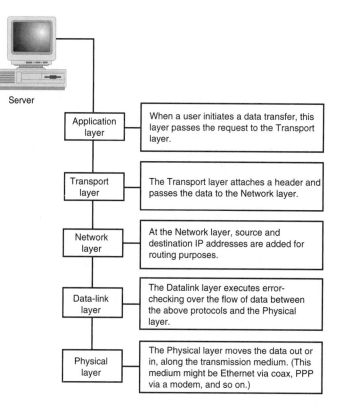

Server

Application layer	When a user initiates a data transfer, this layer passes the request to the Transport layer.
Transport layer	The Transport layer attaches a header and passes the data to the Network layer.
Network layer	At the Network layer, source and destination IP addresses are added for routing purposes.
Data-link layer	The Datalink layer executes error-checking over the flow of data between the above protocols and the Physical layer.
Physical layer	The Physical layer moves the data out or in, along the transmission medium. (This medium might be Ethernet via coax, PPP via a modem, and so on.)

FIGURE 6.2 The TCP/IP protocol stack.

After data passes through the stack, it travels to its destination on another machine or network. There, the process is executed in reverse. (The data first meets the physical layer and subsequently travels its way up the stack.) Throughout this process, a system of error checking is employed both on the originating machine and the destination machine.

Each stack layer can send data to and receive data from its neighbor. Each layer is also associated with multiple protocols. At each tier of the stack, these protocols provide the user with various services. When two applications are communicating over a network, data passes from one application to the other by moving down the stack from the application on the transmitting system and back up the stack of the receiving system to the application running there. As information moves down the stack, information is added to the packet in the form of a header. This header information is like an envelope in which the previous layer's information is wrapped. As the packet goes up the stack, the header is processed and removed before that packet is passed on to the next layer (much like a person opening an envelope to read the letter inside).

The Individual Protocols

Data is transmitted via TCP/IP using the protocol stack. In each layer of the TCP/IP stack, individual protocols provide certain network services. These protocols can be categorized as network-level or application-level, with many individual protocols existing in each level.

Network-Level Protocols

Network-level protocols facilitate the data transport process transparently. They are invisible to the end user, unless that user employs utilities to monitor system processes.

TIP

Sniffers are devices that can monitor network processes. A sniffer is a device—either hardware or software—that can read every packet sent across a network. Sniffers are commonly used to isolate network problems that, although invisible to the end user, are degrading network performance. As such, sniffers can read all activity occurring between network-level protocols. Moreover, sniffers can pose a tremendous security threat. You will examine sniffers in Chapter 15, "Sniffers."

Important TCP/IP network-level protocols include the following:

- Address Resolution Protocol (ARP)
- Internet Control Message Protocol (ICMP)
- Internet Protocol (IP)
- Transmission Control Protocol (TCP)
- User Datagram Protocol (UDP)

We will briefly examine each, ascending up the stack from the data-link layer to the transport layer.

TIP

For more comprehensive information about protocols (or the OSI stack in general), see *TCP/IP Illustrated, Volume 1*, by W. Richard Stevens (Addison Wesley).

The Address Resolution Protocol (ARP)

The Address Resolution Protocol (ARP) serves the critical purpose of mapping Internet addresses into hardware addresses and translating the network layer address (or IP address) to the data-link address. This is vital in routing information between hosts on a local network, and out onto the Internet. Before a message (or other data) is sent, it is packaged into IP packets, or blocks of information suitably formatted for Internet transport. These contain the numeric network IP address of both the originating and destination machines. What remains is to determine the hardware, or the data-link address of the destination machine. This is where ARP makes its entrance.

An ARP request message is broadcast on a local network. If the destination IP address is active on the local network, the destination host will reply with its own hardware address. The originating machine receives this reply, and the transfer process can begin.

If the destination IP address is not active on the local network, the IP packet must be transmitted off the local network and toward the network of the destination system. This is accomplished through a process called IP routing, which we will examine shortly.

TIP

For those readers seeking in-depth information on ARP, see RFC 826 at http://www.ietf. org/rfc/rfc0826.txt.

The Internet Control Message Protocol (ICMP)

The Internet Control Message Protocol provides error and control messages that are passed between two (or more) computers or hosts. It enables those hosts to share information on the state of the network between them. In this respect, ICMP is critical for diagnosis of network problems. ICMP provides helpful messages, such as the following:

- Echo and reply messages to test for network availability

- Redirect messages to enable more efficient routing

- Time-exceeded messages to inform sources that a packet has exceeded its allocated time within the network

An ICMP packet can be of several types. The two most common are the ICMP_ECHO_REQUEST and ICMP_ECHO_REPLY. These packets are used to test network connectivity to make sure a host or network component is active and reachable.

TIP

Perhaps the most widely known ICMP implementation involves a network utility called ping. ping is often used to determine whether a remote machine is alive. ping's method of operation is simple: When the user pings a remote machine, a series of ICMP_ECHO_REQUEST packets are forwarded from the user's machine to the remote host. The remote host replies with

`ICMP_ECHO_REPLY` packets. If no reply packets are received at the user's end, the ping program usually generates an error message, indicating that the remote host is down or unreachable.

TIP

In-depth information about ICMP can be found in RFC 792 at `http://www.ietf.org/rfc/rfc0792.txt`.

The Internet Protocol (IP)

The Internet Protocol provides packet delivery for all protocols within the TCP/IP suite. Thus, IP is the heart of the process by which data traverses the Internet. The IP *datagram*, or packet, is the vehicle for transmission of data on TCP/IP networks. The structure of an IP datagram is shown in Figure 6.3.

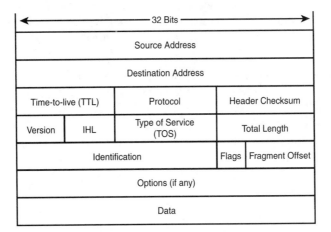

FIGURE 6.3   The IP datagram.

An IP datagram is composed of several parts. The first part, the *header*, is composed of important network information, including source and destination IP addresses. Together, these elements form a complete header. The remaining portion of a datagram contains whatever data is being sent. IP datagrams are often called "packets."

One of the important aspects of IP networking is that it can be used to transmit data using a number of protocols (TCP, UDP, and so on). Each protocol serves a particular function; we'll be looking at some important ones soon. In addition, IP enables the fragmentation and reassembly of data. At the data-link layer, networks can only transmit data in discrete chunks up to a specific size, called the *Maximum*

Transmission Unit (MTU). If the data you want to transmit is larger than the MTU that a network can transmit, the data must be broken into pieces smaller than the MTU, transmitted, and then put back together at the other end. IP provides a mechanism for fragmenting the data, tracking it, and reassembling it. Fragmentation is also important from a security perspective. In some cases, it can be manipulated to work around security measures if security isn't implemented carefully.

An IP datagram also contains a *time-to-live (TTL)* field. A numeric value, the TTL is decremented as the IP datagram traverses the network. When that value finally reaches zero, the datagram is discarded. This ensures that the network doesn't become clogged with datagrams that can't find their destination in a timely fashion. Many other types of packets have time-to-live limitations, and some network utilities (such as Traceroute) use the time-to-live field as a marker in diagnostic routines.

IP Network Addressing   The IP address is a unique identifier for a system on the network. It is 32 bits long and is usually represented as four numbers, each a byte, and separated by decimal points: for example, `32.96.111.130`. Each byte, or *octet*, in an IP address can range from 0 to 255. This representation of an IP address is called *dotted-decimal notation*, and is the most common humanly readable format for working with IP addresses.

A contiguous range of IP addresses defines an IP network. This range of IP addresses is denoted by the combination of an IP address and network mask (or *netmask*). A netmask is a 32-bit value like an IP address that, when combined with the IP address, defines address boundaries of the IP network. This requires conversion of the IP address and netmask to binary format and their combination using binary arithmetic. Note that the first address in a contiguous range of IP addresses indicates the network address. The last address in the contiguous range denotes the network broadcast address.

The network layer in TCP/IP is usually considered to be unicast. *Unicast* indicates that IP communications occur between two endpoints in a point-to-point fashion. This is in contrast to the data-link layer, where ARP operates in a broadcast mode. However, an IP datagram can be addressed to the network broadcast address. This causes the IP datagram to be received and responded to by all nodes on the IP network. Several network based denial-of-service attacks take advantage of this broadcast capability in IP.

IP Routing   IP routing is the process of delivering an IP datagram to its destination when the destination IP address is not on the local network. The first step in routing an IP datagram is to send it to the local network gateway. This gateway is usually a device called a *router*. Routers are responsible for moving IP packets between local networks, and rather than having a single connection to a network, they have connections to multiple networks. Local networks are connected via routers to form larger networks. Large networks like the Internet are really a collection of interconnected local networks.

A key component in making a decision about how to route an IP packet is the IP routing table. Each system on an IP network has an IP routing table that is consulted when determining where to send an IP packet. The routing table is a list of IP networks and associated destination addresses. The system consults the routing table to find the best place to send a given IP packet. The routing table will usually indicate a destination address for all networks that the system or router knows. In the case where a system doesn't know where to send a given IP packet, it sends it to the local network gateway (also known as the default router or gateway of last resort). It is assumed that the local network gateway will have a better idea of where to send the IP packet.

Local network protocols like ARP play a part in moving packets from one router to another. In the case where the destination IP address is not on the local network, an ARP request message is still broadcast, but instead of the ARP request being for the hardware address of the destination machine, the request will be for the local network gateway. If the destination system is attached to a network that the local network gateway is also attached to, the local network gateway delivers the IP packet. Otherwise, it passes the packet on to the next router in the series toward the destination system. This process, much like a bucket brigade, is repeated until the IP packet reaches its destination.

TIP

In-depth information on the Internet Protocol can be found in RFC 760 at http://www.ietf.org/rfc/rfc0760.txt.

The Transmission Control Protocol (TCP)

The Transmission Control Protocol (TCP) is one of the main protocols employed on the Internet. Working at the transport level in the stack, it facilitates such mission-critical tasks as file transfers and remote sessions. TCP accomplishes these tasks through a method called *reliable communication*. In this respect, TCP is more reliable than other protocols within the suite because it includes mechanisms for sequencing and acknowledgment of data transmission.

As with IP, TCP has its own packet structure (see Figure 6.4), composed of source port and destination port numbers that identify services. In addition, important parts of a TCP packet are the sequence number, flags, and checksum. The *sequence number* tracks a TCP connection and the order in which data is sent. The *flags* control the connection state, whether it is being established, in use, or being closed. There are six flags that can be used in combination to describe the state of a TCP connection. The most important for this analysis are SYN, ACK, and FIN. The *checksum* in the TCP packet ensures that the data has not been corrupted during transmission.

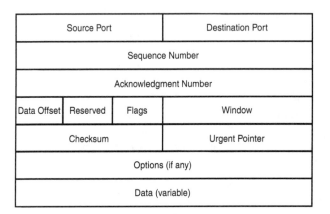

Source Port			Destination Port
Sequence Number			
Acknowledgment Number			
Data Offset	Reserved	Flags	Window
Checksum			Urgent Pointer
Options (if any)			
Data (variable)			

FIGURE 6.4   TCP packet structure.

The TCP system relies on a virtual circuit between the requesting machine (client) and its target (server). This circuit is opened via a three-part process, often referred to as the *three-way handshake.* The process typically follows the pattern illustrated in Figure 6.5.

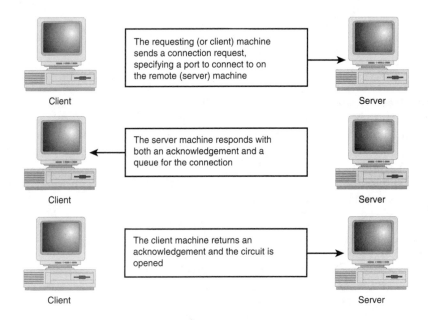

Client — The requesting (or client) machine sends a connection request, specifying a port to connect to on the remote (server) machine → Server

Client ← The server machine responds with both an acknowledgement and a queue for the connection — Server

Client — The client machine returns an acknowledgement and the circuit is opened → Server

FIGURE 6.5   Establishing a TCP connection.

To establish a TCP connection, the three-way handshake must be completed as follows:

1. The client sends a TCP SYN packet to the server that it wants to establish a connection with. This is a TCP packet with only the SYN flag active. The packet also contains an initial sequence number (ISN) that will be used to track the connection.

2. The server responds with a TCP SYN packet with its own ISN. The server also acknowledges the client's TCP SYN by setting the ACK flag on this packet and using the client's ISN plus 1 as the acknowledgment number.

3. The client acknowledges the server's TCP SYN with a TCP ACK using the server's ISN plus 1.

No data is exchanged during this process, but when it is completed, a connection is available for data transfer between the client and server. This connection provides a *full-duplex transmission path*. Full-duplex transmission enables data to travel to both machines at the same time. In this way, while a file transfer (or other remote session) is underway, any errors that arise can be forwarded to the requesting machine.

TCP also provides extensive error-checking capabilities. For each block of data sent, a checksum is calculated, and the sequence number is incremented. The two machines identify each transferred block using the sequence number. For each block successfully transferred, the receiving host sends an ACK message to the sender that the transfer was clean. Conversely, if the transfer is unsuccessful, one of two things might occur:

- The requesting machine receives error information.

- The requesting machine receives nothing.

When an error is received, the data is retransmitted unless the error is fatal, in which case the transmission is usually halted. A typical example of a fatal error would be if the connection was dropped.

Similarly, if no confirmation is received within a specified time period, the information is also retransmitted. This process is repeated as many times as necessary to complete the transfer or remote session.

TCP Connection Termination   As you might expect, because TCP provides a protocol for establishing a connection, it also provides a protocol for terminating a connection. Establishing a TCP connection takes three steps, whereas terminating one takes four steps. Because a TCP connection is bi-directional or full-duplex, transmission in both directions of the connection must be shut down separately. This is done by using the TCP FIN packet, much as the TCP SYN packet is used to create a connection. When a client is finished using a connection, it will issue a TCP FIN packet to the server. The server responds with a TCP ACK to acknowledge that the connection is closing. Because the connection is bi-directional, the server will also issue a TCP FIN to the client. The client will then acknowledge the server's TCP FIN, thus completing the TCP connection termination process.

TCP connections can also be terminated in a less graceful fashion when one of the systems sends a TCP RST (RESET) packet. This causes the connection to be aborted without any negotiation.

> **TIP**
>
> In-depth information about TCP can be found in RFC 793 at http://www.ietf.org/rfc/rfc0793.txt.

User Datagram Protocol (UDP)

The User Datagram Protocol (UDP) is a simple, connectionless transport layer protocol. In fact, it is so simple that the RFC that defines it is only three pages long. Unlike TCP, UDP provides no reliability, and, because it is connectionless, it doesn't have any mechanism for connection establishment or termination. It does provide data integrity checks via a checksum. Although it might seem that UDP is inferior to TCP, it is in fact much better for certain applications because it has very low overhead.

> **TIP**
>
> In-depth information about UDP can be found in RFC 768 at http://www.ietf.org/rfc/rfc0768.txt.

Application-Level Protocols—The Ports

Each time a machine requests services from another, it specifies a particular destination and transport method. The destination is expressed as the Internet (IP) address of the target machine, and the transport method is the transport protocol (that is, TCP or UDP). Further, the requesting machine specifies the application it is trying to reach at the destination by using a system of *ports*.

Just as machines on the Internet have unique IP addresses, each application (FTP or Telnet, for example) is assigned a unique address called a *port*. The port defines the type of service that is being requested or provided. The application in question is bound to that particular port, and, when any connection request is made to that port, the corresponding server application responds.

There are thousands of ports on the average Internet server, although oftentimes most will not be active. For purposes of convenience and efficiency, a standard framework has been developed for port assignments. (In other words, although a system administrator can assign services to the ports of his choice, services are generally assigned to recognized ports commonly referred to as *well-known ports*.) Table 6.1 shows some commonly recognized ports and the applications typically bound to them.

TABLE 6.1   Common Ports and Their Corresponding Services or Applications

Service or Application	Port
Hypertext Transfer Protocol (HTTP)	TCP port 80
Domain Name System (DNS)	UDP and TCP port 53
Telnet	TCP port 23
File Transfer Protocol (FTP)	TCP port 20 and 21
Simple Mail Transfer Protocol (SMTP)	TCP port 25
Secure Shell (SSH)	TCP port 22
HTTP over SSL/TLS (HTTPS)	TCP port 443

Each of the ports described in Table 6.1 are assigned to application-level protocols or services—that is, they are visible to the user, and the user can interact with them. We will examine each of these applications in the following sections.

TIP

For a comprehensive list of all port assignments, visit http://www.iana.org/assignments/port-numbers. This document is extremely informative and exhaustive in its treatment of commonly assigned port numbers.

Hypertext Transfer Protocol (HTTP)

Hypertext Transfer Protocol (HTTP) is perhaps the most renowned protocol of all because it enables users to surf the World Wide Web. Stated briefly in RFC 1945, HTTP is

...an application-level protocol with the lightness and speed necessary for distributed, collaborative, hypermedia information systems. It is a generic, stateless, object-oriented protocol which can be used for many tasks, such as name servers and distributed object management systems, through extension of its request methods (commands). A feature of HTTP is the typing of data representation, enabling systems to be built independently of the data being transferred.

TIP

RFC 1945 has been superseded by RFC 2068, which is available at http://www.ietf.org/
rfc/rfc2068.txt. RFC 2068 is a more recent specification of HTTP, and defines version 1.1 of
the HTTP protocol.

HTTP has forever changed the nature of the Internet, primarily by bringing the
Internet to the masses. Using a common browser such as Netscape Navigator or
Microsoft Internet Explorer, you can monitor the process of HTTP as it occurs.
Depending upon the version of HTTP the server supports, your browser will contact
the server for each data element (text, graphic, sound) on a WWW page. Thus, it will
first grab text, then a graphic, then a sound file, and so on. In the lower-left corner
of your browser's screen is a status bar. Watch it for a few moments while it is
loading a page. You will see this request/response activity occur, often at a very
high speed.

HTTP typically runs on port 80 using TCP. HTTP does little to protect the confidentiality of data because documents are transmitted without encryption or authentication. Some security can be added by using HTTPS, which is HTTP transmitted over
Secure Sockets Layer (SSL) or Transport Layer Security (TLS). SSL/TLS provides the
capability to encrypt data and authenticate both the client and server involved in an
HTTPS session. HTTPS typically runs on port 443 using TCP.

Domain Name System (DNS)

The Domain Name System (DNS) provides services that translate host names to IP
addresses and back again. Much as Address Resolution Protocol provides a mechanism for translating addresses between the data-link and network layers (hardware
address to IP address), DNS translates addresses between the network layer and the
application layer (IP address to hostnames). Because IP addresses aren't exactly
human-friendly, the Domain Name System was developed to allow people to use
human-friendly naming for systems. For example, when you enter **www.fbi.gov** into
your Web browser, the name needs to be translated from that friendly format into an
IP address that can be used by the network layer.

DNS has two modes of operation. The first mode is primarily for communications to
clients that need names resolved to addresses. Because this is a small, easy task,
transport for this mode is provided by UDP. DNS servers also must transfer large
blocks of DNS records so that the workload and administration involved with resolving names to and from IP addresses can be distributed. These larger transfers (called
DNS zone transfers) occur via TCP.

DNS is a very active area of discussion, and numerous Internet drafts and RFCs have
been created to add functionality and security to DNS.

TIP

The core RFCs for DNS are 1034 and 1035. You can find them at http://www.ietf.org/rfc/rfc1034.txt and http://www.ietf.org/rfc/rfc1035.txt.

All modern operating systems that run TCP/IP come with a DNS client (called a *resolver*) as part of the OS. A client program that enables a user to query DNS directly is often included. On Unix and Microsoft Windows NT or 2000, the program nslookup is provided. This DNS client lets you interactively connect to a DNS server and perform various queries of the DNS data.

The most widely used DNS server is the Berkeley Internet Name Domain (BIND) DNS server. Developed and supported by the Internet Software Consortium, BIND is available for most Unix systems as well as for Microsoft Windows NT. DNS typically runs on port 53 using UDP and TCP.

Telnet

Telnet is best described in RFC 854, the Telnet protocol specification:

> The purpose of the Telnet protocol is to provide a fairly general, bi-directional, eight-bit byte-oriented communications facility. Its primary goal is to allow a standard method of interfacing terminal devices and terminal-oriented processes to each other.

Telnet not only enables the user to log in to a remote host, it also lets that user execute commands on the host. Thus, an individual in Los Angeles can telnet to a machine in New York and begin running programs on the New York machine just as though she were in New York.

For those of you who are unfamiliar with Telnet, it operates much like the interface of a bulletin board system (BBS). Telnet is an excellent application for providing a terminal-based front-end to databases. For example, many university library catalogs can be accessed via Telnet or tn3270 (a variation that emulates an IBM 3270 terminal). Figure 6.6 shows an example of a Telnet library catalog screen.

Even though GUI applications have taken the world by storm, Telnet—which is essentially a text-based application—is still incredibly popular. Telnet enables you to perform a variety of functions (retrieving mail, for example) at a minimal cost in network resources.

To use Telnet, the user issues whatever command necessary to start his Telnet client, followed by the name (or numeric IP address) of the target host. In Unix, this is done as follows:

```
% telnet www.fbi.gov
```

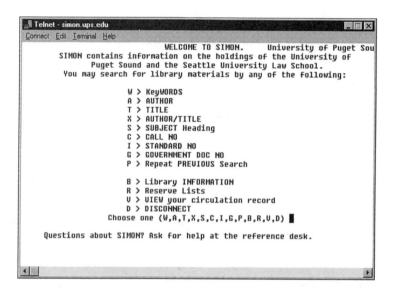

FIGURE 6.6   A sample Telnet session.

This command launches a Telnet session, contacts www.fbi.gov, and requests a TCP connection on port 23. That connection request will either be honored or denied, depending on the configuration at the target host. In Unix, the telnet command has long been a native one. In addition, Telnet has been included with Microsoft Windows distributions for more than a decade.

Telnet is a simple protocol, and offers very little in the way of security. All data transmitted during a Telnet session, including the login ID and password, are sent unencrypted. Anyone with access to a sniffer and the network between the client and server could capture critical data including your password.

Secure Shell (examined later in this chapter) provides services similar to Telnet, but adds security by encrypting the data between client and server.

Telnet typically runs on port 23 via TCP.

File Transfer Protocol (FTP)

File Transfer Protocol (FTP) is a standard method of transferring files from one system to another. Its purpose is set forth in RFC 0765 as follows:

> The objectives of FTP are 1) to promote sharing of files (computer programs and/or data), 2) to encourage indirect or implicit (via programs) use of remote computers, 3) to shield a user from variations in file storage systems among Hosts, and 4) to transfer data reliably and efficiently. FTP, though usable directly by a user at a terminal, is designed mainly for use by programs.

For more than two decades, researchers have investigated a wide variety of file-transfer methods. The development of FTP has undergone many changes in that time. Its first definition occurred in April 1971, and the most recent full specification can be read in RFC 959.

TIP

RFC 114 contains the first definition of FTP, but the most recent specification is documented in RFC 959. RFC 959 can be found at `http://www.ietf.org/rfc/rfc0959.txt`.

Mechanical Operation of FTP   File transfers using FTP can be accomplished using any suitable FTP client. Table 6.2 defines some common FTP clients, by operating system.

TABLE 6.2 FTP Clients for Various Operating Systems

Operating System	Clients
Unix/Linux/Mac OS X	Native, LLNLXDIR2.0, FTPtool, NCFTP
Microsoft Windows	Native, WS_FTP, Netload, Cute-FTP, Leap FTP, SDFTP, FTP Explorer
Macintosh	Anarchie, Fetch, Freetp

FTP file transfers occur in a client/server environment. The requesting machine starts one of the clients named in Table 6.2. This generates a request that is forwarded to the targeted FTP server (usually a host on another network). Typically, the request is sent by the client to port 21. For a connection to be established, the targeted file server must be running an FTP server.

FTPD: An FTP Server Daemon   FTPD is the standard FTP server daemon for Unix. Its function is simple: to reply to connect requests received and to satisfy those requests for file transfers. An FTP daemon comes standard on most distributions of Unix (for other operating systems, see Table 6.3).

TABLE 6.3 FTP Servers for Various Operating Systems

Operating System	Servers
Unix/Linux/Mac OS X	Native (FTPD), WUFTD, NCFTPD
Microsoft Windows 98	WFTPD, Microsoft FrontPage, WAR FTP Daemon, Vermilion
Microsoft Windows NT/2000/XP	Microsoft Internet Information Server, Serv-U, OmniFSPD
Macintosh	Netpresenz, FTPd

FTPD waits for a connection request. When such a request is received, FTPD requests the user login. The user must either provide her valid user login and password or log in anonymously (if the server allows anonymous sessions).

When logged in, the user can download files. In certain instances and if security on the server allows, the user can also upload files.

As with Telnet, FTP is an insecure protocol. It does nothing to encrypt the user ID, password, or any of the files being transferred. Secure Shell provides a more secure method of file transfer via either Secure Copy (SCP) or Secure FTP (SFTP). FTP uses ports 20 and 21 via TCP.

Simple Mail Transfer Protocol (SMTP)

SMTP is the protocol responsible for email transmission between servers, and the sending of email from clients to servers. Its purpose is stated concisely in RFC 821:

> The objective of Simple Mail Transfer Protocol (SMTP) is to transfer mail reliably and efficiently.

SMTP is an extremely lightweight protocol. Running any SMTP-compliant client, the user sends a request to an SMTP server. The client forwards a series of instructions, indicating that it wants to send mail to a recipient somewhere on the Internet. If the SMTP allows this operation, an affirmative acknowledgment is sent back to the client machine. At that point, the session begins. The client might then forward the recipient's identity, his IP address, and the message (in text) to be sent.

Despite the simple character of SMTP, mail service has been the source of countless security holes. The configuration of an SMTP server can be complex, depending upon the options an administrator needs to support. A combination of SMTP server application bugs, and difficulty in configuration have led to numerous security holes. These security issues are covered in detail later in this book.

Most networked operating systems have SMTP servers available for use. STMP server support is included as sendmail for most Unix distributions, or part of Internet Information Services for Microsoft Windows. SMTP typically runs on port 25 via TCP.

TIP

Further information on SMTP is available in RFC 821 `http://www.ietf.org/rfc/rfc0821.txt`.

Secure Shell Protocol (SSH)

The Secure Shell protocol (SSH) is relatively new to the TCP/IP suite of protocols. Unlike the application protocols we've examined already, SSH was widely implemented without completing the RFC process. This is largely because of the vast demand for a more secure method of providing services similar to Telnet and FTP.

There are two versions of the SSH protocol, and a number of implementations. The first widely used version of the protocol was SSH1, which was defined in an Internet draft (a pre-RFC document) in 1995. There is an Internet Engineering Task Force working group responsible for developing the SSH protocol. They have produced a second generation of the SSH protocol called SSH2. Based upon that group's Internet drafts, a number of SSH2 implementations have been completed.

TIP

Draft RFCs for SSH are being written by the IETF SSH working group. The latest Internet drafts, as well as other SSH-related information can be found at http://www.ietf.org/html.charters/secsh-charter.html and http://www.ssh.org/.

SSH allows you to log in to another computer over a network, to execute commands in a remote machine (like Telnet), and to move files from one machine to another (like FTP). It provides for strong authentication and secure, encrypted communications over otherwise insecure networks. It is intended as a replacement for Telnet and other remote access protocols like rlogin, rsh, and rcp. In SSH2, there is a replacement for FTP as well, called sftp.

Secure Shell client implementations exist for a variety of platforms, as shown in Table 6.4.

TABLE 6.4   SSH Clients for Various Operating Systems

Operating System	Clients
Unix/Linux/Mac OS X	Native, OpenSSH, F-Secure, SSH Communications
Microsoft Windows	PuTTY, SSH Communications, F-Secure, TeraTerm, FiSSH, SecureCRT, MindTerm
Macintosh	MacSSH, F-Secure, NiftyTelnet 1.1 SSH, MindTerm

Secure Shell server implementations are also available, although not on as many platforms as for clients (see Table 6.5).

TABLE 6.5   SSH Servers for Various Operating Systems

Operating System	Servers
Unix/Linux/Mac OS X	Native, OpenSSH, SSH Communications, F-Secure,
Microsoft Windows	SSH Communications, F-Secure, Cygwin32

IPsec, IPv6, VPNs, and Looking Ahead

The Internet Protocol discussed in this chapter is version 4 (IPv4). It was developed many years ago, and although it has delivered amazing potential and growth, it really wasn't designed to provide many of the services that we expect from the Internet today. Some of the limitations of IPv4 that need to be addressed are

- **Limitations on addressing**—Because of the explosive growth of the Internet, there is a critical shortage of available IP addresses. As the Internet continues to grow and more devices become Internet-enabled, there will be an increased demand for new IP addresses.

- **Lack of prioritization**—There is currently no method to prioritize particular kinds of traffic on the Internet. For example, a packet stream that provides real-time audio or video gets the same priority as a packet containing an email message. If packets are a few seconds late delivering real-time audio or video, it is very noticeable. If a few packets arrive later for a non-real-time service such as email, no one will notice.

- **Lack of security**—The current version of IP doesn't provide for the authentication or the privacy of data transmitted.

Actions have been taken over the past few years to address these issues. The lack of available IPv4 addresses has been temporarily alleviated through the use of address translation techniques, but this will only suffice for a time before addresses are completely used up. In addition, address translation is known to break certain protocols that expect valid, non-changing IP addresses on datagrams.

Prioritization technologies are available for use with IPv4, but are limited to use in local networks. These technologies will not work in the Internet environment, where a central authority is not available to manage the flow of data.

Finally, security needs to be added to the Internet if we expect to transmit confidential data (bank accounts, medical records, personal data, and so on) with the confidence that no one will break into our home and business systems connected to the Internet.

A great deal of effort has been put forth in the area of IPv4 security. SSL/TLS can be used to address some of the challenges. In addition, IP Security (IPsec) has been developed to offer security services at the IP layer. IPsec provides methods for authentication and encryption of data at the network layer, but they are not universally available. IPsec can be used to establish Virtual Private Networks (VPNs), which are logical private networks created over the Internet. However, these extensions are not normally available to the average Internet user. In addition, the successes of IPsec extensions do not yet address some of the more unusual aspects of IPv4, such as address translation.

> **TIP**
>
> Information on IP Security can be found in RFC 2401 at `http://www.ietf.org/rfc/rfc2401.txt`. You can also visit the IP Security working group's Web site at `http://www.ietf.org/html.charters/ipsec-charter.html`.

Fortunately, planning has been going on for quite some time to develop the next generation of the Internet Protocol. Enter Internet Protocol version 6 (IPv6)! IPv6 has been a very active area of discussion at the Internet Engineering Task Force, and has generated numerous RFCs over the past few years as planning for the next phase of Internet growth and services continues.

IPv6 promises to alleviate the limitation on IP addresses, add proper flow control and data prioritization, and provide security at the network layer. In addition, IPv6 will provide nice services such as the auto-configuration of networked systems, simplification of datagrams, improved performance, and greater capability for expansion. However, IPv6 is not currently widely deployed, and it is still evolving. IPv6 has been in the works for almost a decade now, and it will likely be a number of years before the standards are solidified. It will be several years beyond that when Internet providers base their services upon IPv6. IPv4 will be with us for the foreseeable future.

> **TIP**
>
> Information on IPv6 (previously called IPng for "next generation") can be found in RFC 2460 (`http://www.ietf.org/rfc/rfc2460.txt`) and by visiting the IPv6 working group's Web site, `http://www.ietf.org/html.charters/ipv6-charter.html` and `http://playground.sun.com/pub/ipng/html/ipng-main.html`.

Summary

TCP/IP makes up the Internet itself. It is a complex collection of hundreds of protocols, and many more are being developed each year. Many of the primary protocols in use on the Internet have been found to have one or more security problems.

In this chapter, you learned about these relevant points about the TCP/IP protocol suite:

- The TCP/IP suite contains all protocols necessary to facilitate data transfer over the Internet.

- The TCP/IP suite provides quick, reliable networking without consuming heavy network resources.

- TCP/IP is implemented on almost all computing platforms.

- Security is lacking in IPv4.

Now that you know a little bit about TCP/IP, let's move ahead to a more exciting subject: hackers and crackers.

7

Spoofing Attacks

In this chapter you'll learn about spoofing attacks—how they are performed, and how you can prevent them.

What Is Spoofing?

The secret to creativity is knowing how to hide your sources.

—*Albert Einstein*

Spoofing can be summed up in a single sentence: It's a sophisticated technique of authenticating one machine to another by forging packets from a trusted source address.

From that definition, you can safely conclude that spoofing is a complicated process. However, by this chapter's end, you'll have a clear understanding of spoofing and how to prevent it.

Internet Security Fundamentals

There are two recurring themes in Internet security:

- Trust

- Authentication

Trust is the relationship between machines that are authorized to connect to one another. *Authentication* is the process those machines use to identify each other.

Trust and authentication generally have an inverse relationship. Thus, if a high level of trust exists between machines, stringent authentication is not required to make a connection. On the other hand, if little or no trust exists between machines, more rigorous authentication is required.

If you think about it, humans exercise similar rules. For example, if your best friend came to your front door, you'd let him right in. Why not? You trust him. However, if a total stranger came knocking, you would demand that he identify himself.

Methods of Authentication

Although you might not realize it, you are constantly being authenticated. For example, you might have to provide a username and password to use any of the following services:

- Your Internet connection

- FTP sites

- Telnet services and shell accounts

- Web sites

- Applications

In fact, today most subscription-based Web sites require a username and password. You're subjected to high levels of authentication every day. Do you know what that means? The Internet simply doesn't trust you!

Authenticating humans, therefore, involves a password scheme. Some models employ a simple username/password scheme, whereas others can be more complex, such as challenge-response systems based on one-time passwords. The end result is the same, though—the user either has the correct password or she does not.

Machines can be authenticated in other ways, depending on their trust relationship. For example, a machine can be authenticated by its host name or an IP source address. Using RHOSTS entries is a common procedure in the Unix world for setting this up.

RHOSTS

The RHOSTS system can be used to establish a relationship of trust between machines. It's described in the Solaris Manual Page:

> The /etc/hosts.equiv and .rhosts files provide the "remote authentication" database for rlogin(1), rsh(1), rcp(1), and rcmd(3N). The files specify remote hosts and users that are considered "trusted." Trusted users are allowed to access the local system without supplying a password.

NOTE

hosts.equiv files are essentially .rhosts configuration files for the entire system. These are set by root and apply hostwide. In contrast, .rhosts files are user-based and apply only to particular users and directories. (This is why users should be restricted from making their own .rhosts files. These open smaller holes all over the system.)

A sample .rhosts file might look like this:

```
node1.sams.hacker.net hickory
node2.sams.hacker.net dickory
```

This file specifies that the user hickory on node1 and user dickory on node2 are now trusted. These users can access the local machine through the r services without being subjected to password authentication. No other users from these nodes are trusted, however.

To complete the process (and create a two-way trust relationship), all four of the machines must also maintain rhost entries.

NOTE

The r services consist of the following applications:

rlogin—Remote login. This works in a very similar fashion to Telnet, and offers a remote login session.

rsh—Remote shell. This enables users to run shell commands on the remote box.

rcp—Remote file copy. This enables users to copy files from local to remote machines, and vice versa.

rcmd—Remote command. This enables privileged users to execute commands on remote hosts.

All four r services use the /etc/hosts.equiv or .rhosts allow/deny schemes for trust purposes. No trust exists if these files are empty or don't exist, and therefore a spoofing attack (of this variety) cannot occur.

The authentication that occurs at connection time, then, is based solely on the IP source address. This is known to be a flawed model, as Steve M. Bellovin explains in his paper "Security Problems in the TCP/IP Protocol Suite":

> If available, the easiest mechanism to abuse is IP source routing. Assume that the target host uses the reverse of the source route provided in a TCP open request for return traffic. Such behavior is utterly reasonable; if the originator of the connection wishes to specify a particular

path for some reason—say, because the automatic route is dead—replies may not reach the originator if a different path is followed.

The attacker can then pick any IP source address desired, including that of a trusted machine on the target's local network. Any facilities available to such machines become available to the attacker.

TIP

"Security Problems in the TCP/IP Protocol Suite" by Steve M. Bellovin can be found on the Web at `http://www.deter.com/unix/papers/tcpip_problems_bellovin.pdf`.

The following points have been established for now:

1. Trust and authentication have an inverse relationship; more trust results in less stringent authentication.

2. Initial authentication is based on the source address in trust relationships.

3. IP source address authentication is unreliable because IP addresses (and most fields of an IP header) can be forged.

4. A trust relationship of some kind must exist for a spoofing attack to work.

From this, you can surmise one of the reasons why IP spoofing has achieved cult status in the cracker community. Most cracking attacks have historically relied on password schemes; crackers would steal the /etc/passwd file and crack it. They would do their dirty work after obtaining the root password (and at least one user login/password). In spoofing, however, neither a username nor a password is passed during the attack. The security breach occurs at a very discrete level.

Another reason IP spoofing has gained much notoriety is that it can be used as a key element in other forms of attack. One example of this is known as *"session hijacking,"* which is described in the next section.

The Mechanics of a Spoofing Attack

The mere fact that source address authentication is flawed does not in itself make IP spoofing possible. Here's why: The connection process requires more than just the right IP address. It requires a complete, sustained dialog between machines.

You can more easily understand the process in steps:

- IP is responsible for packet transport. Packet transport performed by IP is unreliable, meaning that there is no absolute guarantee that packets will arrive unscathed and intact. (For example, packets can be lost, corrupted, and so forth.) The main point is this: IP merely routes the packets from Point A to Point B. Therefore, the first step of initiating a connection is for the packets to arrive intact to the proper host.

- After the packets arrive, TCP takes over. TCP is more reliable, and has facilities to check that packets are intact and are being transported properly. Each one is subjected to verification. For example, TCP first acknowledges receipt of a packet and then sends a message verifying that it was received and processed correctly.

TCP's process of packet error checking is done sequentially. If five packets are sent, Packets 1, 2, 3, 4, and 5 are dealt with in the order they were received. Each packet is assigned a number as an identifying index. Both hosts use this number for error checking and reporting.

In his article "Sequence Number Attacks," Rik Farrow explains the sequence number process used in the attack on Tsutomu Shimomura's computer by Kevin Mitnick:

> The sequence number is used to acknowledge receipt of data. At the beginning of a TCP connection, the client sends a TCP packet with an initial sequence number, but no acknowledgment (there can't be one yet). If there is a server application running at the other end of the connection, the server sends back a TCP packet with its own initial sequence number, and an acknowledgment: the initial sequence number from the client's packet plus one. When the client system receives this packet, it must send back its own acknowledgment: the server's initial sequence number plus one. Thus, it takes three packets to establish a TCP connection....

TIP

Find "Sequence Number Attacks" by Rik Farrow online at http://www.nwc.com/unixworld/security/001.txt.html.

The attacker's problem is thus twofold: First, he must forge the source address, and second, he must maintain a sequence dialog with the target. It is this second task that makes the attack complex. Here's why: The sequence dialog is not arbitrary. The target sets the initial sequence number, and the attacker must counter with the correct response.

This further complicates the attack: The attacker must guess the correct sequence response because he never actually receives packets from the target. In his article "A Weakness in the 4.2BSD UNIX TCP/IP Software," Robert Morris explains:

4.2BSD maintains a global initial sequence number, which is incremented by 128 each second and by 64 after each connection is started; each new connection starts off with this number. When a SYN packet with a forged source is sent from a host, the destination host will send the reply to the presumed source host, not the forging host. The forging host must discover or guess what the sequence number in that lost packet was, in order to acknowledge it and put the destination TCP port in the ESTABLISHED state.

TIP

Find Morris's article online at `http://www.pdos.lcs.mit.edu/~rtm/papers/117-abstract.html`.

That might sound confusing, so let me illustrate the concept more clearly. Assume the following:

- The cracker knows that the hosts `207.171.0.111` and `199.171.190.9` have a trust relationship.

- He intends to penetrate `207.171.0.111`.

- To do so, he must impersonate `199.171.190.9`.

- To impersonate `199.171.190.9`, he forges that address.

The problem is that all responses from `207.171.0.111` are actually routed to `199.171.190.9` (and not the cracker's machine). Because of this, the cracker cannot see the packet traffic. He is driving blind. It is because of this inability to see the responses that this method of spoofing is known as *blind spoofing*. *Non-blind spoofing* occurs when the responses can be seen because the traffic occurs along a network segment that the attacker can watch.

The blind spoofing situation presents an even more serious obstacle. What if `199.171.190.9` responds to packets from the target while the cracker is conducting his attack? This blows the entire operation by throwing off the expected sequence numbers. Therefore, the cracker must perform one last additional step prior to actually conducting the attack: He must either attempt the spoof when `199.171.190.9` is not running or put `199.171.190.9` to sleep.

NOTE

Killing `199.171.190.9` is simple. To do so, the cracker exposes `199.171.190.9` to a syn-flood attack. This floods the connection queues of `199.171.190.9`, temporarily rendering that machine unable to process incoming connection requests. This works because of the way connection requests are processed. Each time a connection request is received, the target attempts to complete the three-way handshake. Eventually, the target times out on that request and attempts to process the next one. All connection requests are handled in the order they're received. Thus, if the target is flooded with hundreds of such requests, considerable time will pass before the flooded host can again process connection requests.

At this point, let's recap everything presented until now.

The Ingredients of a Successful Spoofing Attack

These are the essential steps that must be taken in a spoofing attack:

1. The cracker must identify his targets.

2. He must anesthetize the host he intends to impersonate.

3. He must forge the address of the host he's impersonating.

4. He must connect to the target, masquerading as the anesthetized host.

5. He must accurately guess the correct sequence number requested by the target.

The first four steps are easy. The difficult part is guessing the correct sequence number. To do so, the cracker must execute a trial run:

- He contacts the intended target requesting connection.

- The target responds with a flurry of sequence numbers.

- The cracker logs these sequence numbers and cuts the connection.

The cracker next examines the logs of sequence numbers received from the target. In his analysis, he seeks to identify a pattern. He knows, for example, that these sequence numbers are incremented uniformly by an algorithm designed specially for this purpose. His job is to determine that algorithm, or at least determine the numeric values by which the numbers are incremented. When he knows this, he can reliably predict what sequence numbers are required for authentication.

He is now ready to perform the spoofing attack. In all, spoofing is an extraordinary technique. However, what's even more extraordinary is this: Since 1985, the security community has known that spoofing was possible.

Opening a More Suitable Hole

When the connection and authentication procedures are complete, the cracker must create a more suitable hole through which to compromise the system. (He should not be forced to spoof each time he wants to connect.) He therefore fashions a custom hole. The easiest method is to rewrite the .rhosts file so that the now-compromised system accepts connections from any source without requiring additional authentication.

Having done this, the cracker shuts down the connection and reconnects. He can now log in without a password and has control of the system.

Who Can Be Spoofed?

IP spoofing can only be implemented against certain machines running certain services. Many flavors of Unix are viable targets. (This shouldn't give you the impression that non-Unix systems are invulnerable to spoofing attacks. There's more on that later in this chapter.)

The following are some of the configurations and services are known to be vulnerable:

- Any device running Sun RPC
- Any network service that uses IP address authentication
- The X Window System from MIT
- The r services

To put that in perspective, consider this: Most network services use IP-based authentication, and although RPC, X Window System, and the r services have problems inherent to Unix-based operating systems, other operating systems are not immune.

Windows NT and even Windows 2000, for example, are vulnerable to sequence number attacks. Sessions can be hijacked via TCP sequence number guessing. At its heart, the problem is a spoofing issue. It affects a multitude of network services, not just RPC. In fact, it even affects NetBIOS and SMB connections. Exploit code for the attack can be found at `http://www.engarde.com/software/seqnumsrc.c`.

TIP

Sun RPC refers to Sun Microsystems' standard of *Remote Procedure Calls*, which enable users to issue system calls that work transparently over networks. The RFC that addresses RPC, titled "RPC: Remote Procedure Call Protocol Specification," can be found at `http://www.netsys.com/rfc/rfc1057.txt`.

How Common Are Spoofing Attacks?

Spoofing attacks used to be rare. However, they became far more common after January 1995. Consider this Defense Data Network advisory from July 1995:

ASSIST has received information about numerous recent IP spoofing attacks directed against Internet sites internationally. A large number of the systems targeted in the IP spoofing attacks are name servers, routers, and other network operation systems, and the attacks have been largely successful.

TIP

To view the DDN bulletin online, visit `http://csrc.ncsl.nist.gov/secalert/ddn/1995/sec-9532.txt`.

Prior to 1995, spoofing was a very grass-roots attack. Anyone trying to spoof had to have a very strong background in TCP/IP, sockets, and network programming in general. This is no longer true.

After it was demonstrated that spoofing actually worked (it was previously a theoretical notion), spoofing code immediately began surfacing. Today, prefabbed spoofing utilities are widely available. The following sections present some useful spoofing utilities.

Spoofing/Hijacking Utilities

1644

Author: V. Vasim

Language: C

Build Platform: FreeBSD

Target Platform: Unix

Requirements: C compiler, IP header files, FreeBSD

URL: `http://www.insecure.org/sploits/ttcp.spoofing.problem.html`

Hunt

Author: Pavel Krauz

Language: C

Build Platform: Linux

Target Platform: Linux

Requirements: C compiler, Linux

URL: `http://lin.fsid.cvut.cz/~kra/index.html`

ipspoof

Author: Unknown

Language: C

Build Platform: Unix

Target Platform: Unix

Requirements: C compiler, IP Header Files, Unix

URL: `http://www.psyon.org/archive/source_code/c/ipspoof.c`

Juggernaut

Author: route

Language: C

Build Platform: Unix

Target Platform: Unix

Requirements: C compiler, IP Header Files, Unix

URL: `http://staff.washington.edu/dittrich/talks/qsm-sec/P50-06.txt`

rbone

Author: Unknown

Language: C

Build Platform: Linux

Target Platform: Unix

Requirements: C compiler, IP header files, Linux

URL: `http://packetstorm.decepticons.org/Exploit_Code_`
`Archive/rbone.tar.gz`

Spoofit

Author: Brecht Claerhout

Language: C

Build Platform: Linux

Target Platform: Unix

Requirements: C compiler, IP header files, Linux 1.3 or later

URL: `http://packetstormsecurity.nl/spoof/spoofit/`

synk4.c (Syn Flooder by Zakath)

> Author: Zakath with Ultima
>
> Language: C
>
> Build Platform: Linux
>
> Target Platform: Unix
>
> Requirements: C compiler, IP header files, Linux
>
> URL: `http://packetstormsecurity.nl/Exploit_Code_Archive/synk4.c`

NOTE

There's also a UDP spoofing utility available. To try it, download it from `http://www.deter.com/unix/software/arnudp.c`.

Documents Related Specifically to IP Spoofing

There are many documents online that address IP spoofing. Here are a few good ones:

> *"A Weakness in the 4.2BSD UNIX TCP/IP Software."* Robert T. Morris. Technical Report, AT&T Bell Laboratories. `http://www.pdos.lcs.mit.edu/~rtm/papers/117-abstract.html`
>
> *"Sequence Number Attacks."* Rik Farrow. (UnixWorld.) `http://www.nwc.com/unixworld/security/001.txt.html`
>
> *"Security Problems in the TCP/IP Protocol Suite."* Steve Bellovin.
> `http://www.deter.com/unix/papers/tcpip_problems_bellovin.pdf`
>
> *"Defending Against Sequence Number Attacks."* S. Bellovin; RFC 1948. AT&T Research. May 1996. `http://andrew2.andrew.cmu.edu/rfc/rfc1948.html`
>
> *"A Short Overview of IP Spoofing."* Brecht Claerhout. `http://www.nmrc.org/files/unix/ip-exploit.txt` (An excellent freelance treatment of the subject)
>
> *"Internet Holes—Eliminating IP Address Forgery."* Management Analytics.
> `http://all.net/journal/netsec/9606.html`
>
> *"Ask Woody about Spoofing Attacks."* Bill Woodcock from Zocalo Engineering.
> `http://www.netsurf.com/nsf/v01/01/local/spoof.html`
>
> *"IP-Spoofing Demystified Trust-Relationship Exploitation."* `route@infonexus.com` (Michael Schiffman). `http://www.phrack.com/show.php?p=48&a=14`

How Do I Prevent IP Spoofing Attacks?

Configuring your network to reject packets from the Net that claim to originate from a local address can thwart IP spoofing attacks. This is done at the router level. Conversely, it is also generally a good policy to reject packets originating from inside your network that claim to come from a host on the inside.

> **NOTE**
>
> Although routers are a solution to the general spoofing problem, they too operate by examining the source address. Thus, they can only protect against incoming packets that purport to originate from within your internal network. If your network (for some inexplicable reason) trusts foreign hosts, routers will not protect against a spoofing attack that purports to originate from those hosts.

There are several products that incorporate anti-spoofing technology into their general design. Here are a couple:

- **NetVision Synchronicity for Windows NT.** The Synchronicity product line incorporates concurrent management of NDS and NT objects and systems. Anti-spoofing support is built in. Check it out at
  http://www.netvision.com/products/synchronicity.html.

- **Cisco PIX Firewall.** PIX is Cisco's premier Internet security product. This is a full-fledged firewall with built-in anti-spoofing capabilities.
  http://www.cisco.com/warp/public/cc/pd/fw/sqfw500

Certain products can also test your network for vulnerability to IP spoofing. (Check Chapter 11, "Vulnerability Assessment Tools," for scanners that perform this diagnostic.)

> **CAUTION**
>
> If you're running a firewall, it does not automatically protect you from spoofing attacks. If you allow internal addresses access through the outside portion of the firewall, you're still vulnerable. Moreover, if your firewall runs proxies, and those proxies perform their authentication based on the IP source address, you have a problem. (Essentially, this type of authentication is no different from any other form of IP-based authentication.)

Closely monitoring your network is another preventative measure. Try identifying packets that purport to originate within your network, but attempt to gain entrance at the firewall or first network interface that they encounter on your wire. The following paragraph is excerpted from Defense Information System Network Security Bulletin #95-32. This bulletin can be found online at http://csrc.ncsl.nist.gov/secalert/ddn/1995/sec-9532.txt.

There are several classes of packets that you could watch for. The most basic is any TCP packet where the network portion (Class A, B, or C or a prefix and length as specified by the Classless Inter-Domain Routing (CIDR) specification) of the source and destination addresses are the same but neither are from your local network. These packets would not normally go outside the source network unless there is a routing problem worthy of additional investigation, or the packets actually originated outside your network. The latter can occur with mobile IP testing, but an attacker spoofing the source address is a more likely cause.

As a closing note, if you can afford the resource overhead, you can also detect spoofing through logging procedures (even in real-time). Running a comparison on connections between trusted hosts is a good start. For example, assume that trusted hosts A and B have a live session. Both will show processes indicating that the session is underway. If one of them doesn't indicate activity, a spoofing attack is afoot.

Other Strange and Offbeat Spoofing Attacks

IP spoofing is only one form of spoofing. Other spoofing techniques exist, including ARP, DNS, and Web spoofing. Let's examine each.

ARP Spoofing

ARP spoofing is a technique that alters the ARP cache. Here's how it works: The ARP cache contains hardware-to-IP mapping information. The key is to keep your hardware address, but to assume the IP address of a trusted host. This information is simultaneously sent to the target and the cache. From that point on, packets from the target are routed to your hardware address. (The target now "believes" that your machine is the trusted host.)

There are severe limitations to this type of attack. One is that the ruse might fail when crossing intelligent hubs and some routers. Therefore, ARP cache spoofing is reliable only under certain conditions, and even then it might be restricted to the local network segment. Moreover, cache entries expire pretty quickly. Thus, you still have to backtrack periodically and update the cache entries while implementing the attack.

Can ARP spoofing be defeated? Absolutely. There are several things that you can do. One is to write your address mappings in stone. This can, however, be an irritating prospect. Paul Buis explains in his paper "Names and Addresses":

> Many operating systems do however have provisions for making entries in the ARP cache "static" so they do not time out every few minutes. I recommend using this feature to prevent ARP spoofing, but it requires updating the cache manually every time a hardware address changes.

TIP

Get Paul Buis's paper from `http://www.cs.bsu.edu/homepages/peb/cs637/nameadd/`.

Another choice is to use ARPWATCH. ARPWATCH is a utility that watches changes in your IP/Ethernet mappings. If changes are detected, you are alerted via email. (Also, the information will be logged, which helps track down the offender.) Get ARPWATCH at `ftp://ftp.ee.lbl.gov/arpwatch.tar.gz`.

NOTE

To use ARPWATCH, you need Unix, C, and awk. (The distribution comes in source only.)

DNS Spoofing

In *DNS spoofing*, the cracker compromises the DNS server and explicitly alters the hostname-IP address tables. These changes are written into the translation table databases on the DNS server. Thus, when a client requests a lookup, she is given a bogus address; this address is the IP address of a machine that is completely under the cracker's control.

DNS spoofing has now been automated, at least on some platforms. A utility called Jizz, written by Nimrood (and based on code written by Johannes Erdfelt), does this. To try it out, download it from `http://packetstormsecurity.org/Exploit_Code_Archive/jizz.c`.

DNS spoofing is fairly easy to detect, however. If you suspect one of the DNS servers, poll the other authoritative DNS servers on the network. Unless the originally-affected server has been compromised for some time, evidence will immediately surface that it has been spoofed. Other authoritative servers will report results that vary from those given by the cracked DNS server.

Polling might not be sufficient if the originally-spoofed server has been compromised for some time. Bogus address-host name tables might have been passed to other DNS servers on the network. If you are noticing abnormalities in name resolution, you might want to employ a script utility called DOC (domain obscenity control). As articulated in the utility's documentation:

> DOC (domain obscenity control) is a program which diagnoses misbehaving domains by sending queries off to the appropriate domain name servers and performing a series of analyses on the output of these queries.

TIP

DOC is available online at `ftp://coast.cs.purdue.edu/pub/tools/unix/sysutils/doc/doc.2.0.tar.Z`.

Other techniques that defeat DNS spoofing attacks include the use of reverse DNS schemes. Under these schemes, sometimes referred to as *tests of your forwards*, the service attempts to reconcile the forward lookup with the reverse. This technique might have limited value. In all likelihood, the cracker has altered both the forward and reverse tables. For more information on configuring your DNS server, see the following sites:

`http://www.dns.net/dnsrd/`

`http://www.cert.org/advisories/CA-1999-14.html`

Web Spoofing

Quite a few sites on the Internet these days require a paid membership to access their content. Often, when you pay for membership at one site, you also get access to other paid content as well. There are several ways this can be implemented. It is easy, however, to implement a setup that is easy to spoof.

Our examples feature a paid membership site called Music By Gus (`http://members.musicbygus.com/`). All the members of Gus's site also get free access to the site Music by Alice (`http://members.musicbyalice.com/`). It should be stressed that you can easily find examples of each of the following setups on the Internet, as they're all common.

The Partner Password Setup

Alice and Gus first agree that Gus will publish a user ID and password to Alice's site in his membership area. This user ID/password combination is the same for all of Gus's users. Needless to say, over time this password leaks out to nonmembers on the Internet.

Alice learns about this, so she and Gus decide to change the password every day. This greatly improves the situation. However, what they don't know is that there are dozens of underground hacker sites and IRC channels on the Internet that find and publish passwords in a matter of minutes.

Alice decides that this approach is not going to work. She talks to some Web experts and comes up with a more advanced system.

The Referrer Setup

When you connect to a Web page, your browser reports what site you were on when you clicked the link to go to the current page. This piece of information is known as a *referral*, and Alice decides to make use of it. If the Referrer field tells her Web site that the user came from Gus's membership site (for example, `http://members.musicby-gus.com/partners.html`), she'll allow them into her Web site without asking for a user ID and password. This is a trust relationship, and in many ways similar to the RHOSTS approach we discussed earlier.

Remember all the steps we had to go through to spoof IP packets? By comparison, spoofing the referral is a piece of cake. For one thing, the source code for Mozilla is open source. It wouldn't be hard for a programmer to build a Mozilla that lies about the Referral field. Also, Windows offers APIs that allow you to take control of Internet Explorer (IE).

However, it doesn't even require this much trouble: Hacker tools, most of which are based on the IE APIs, are available that are so easy to use that computer novices can referral spoof to their heart's content. Novices can also find files containing spoofs of thousands of Web sites, which can be loaded into these tools. The most famous of these tools is ZSpoof, which is available at `http://www.securityadvise.de/deny/hosted/wm/`.

The Session-Specific URL Setup

Alice learned that the referral setup didn't work either. The Web experts next recommend that Gus and Alice agree on some session-specific URLs that time out. Basically, Gus's site will generate URLs that look like `http://members.musicbyalice.com/ab38383afe39393/music.html`. The string of characters in the middle is the session key. This session key is based on an algorithm, and times out after a while.

In the end, the problem ends up being the same as the temporary passwords we discussed earlier. Hackers will quickly post these URLs up on sites and via IRC.

A Solution

Now Alice fires her Web experts. She hires some new ones who tell her the problem all along was that she was using trust relationships, and trust relationships by their nature allow spoofing attacks. They recommend that she must authenticate Gus's users. This means one of two setups.

The first is that Gus sends all new accounts to Alice, and she creates the user accounts as well. Users must now log in twice: first to Gus's site, and then again to access Alice's site if they come through the link.

The other option is that Alice and Gus share a common authentication realm so that users only need to log in once. However, this couples their Web sites closer together, and could make severing the partnership difficult.

Summary

Spoofing is popular, and when done from the outside, leaves relatively little evidence. At a minimum, you should block apparent local requests that originate outside your network, and as always, you should employ logging utilities. Finally, I recommend keeping up with the latest advisories—particularly from your router vendor. New spoofing attacks tend to emerge every few months or so.

8

Personal Privacy

Many tools are available to you if you are looking to protect your data. The list is almost endless: digital certificates, packet filters, strong encryption, firewalls, virus utilities, virtual private networks, network appliances, and a dozen other tools. Each can offer some assurance that your Internet site and network is safe. What about more basic issues? For example, what steps can you take to secure your privacy while surfing online? As with data protection, there are also several methods available for protecting your personal privacy on the Internet. This chapter looks at these methods.

Degrees of Exposure

Unless you take steps to prevent it, your identity will eventually be exposed if you surf the Internet. That exposure will manifest in different forms and degrees depending on many factors, including

- Your network connection
- Your browser
- Your public traffic
- The plug-ins and applications you support

These variables expose you to two different types of intelligence:

- Human intelligence
- Network intelligence

Let's examine each in turn.

Human Intelligence

Human beings can spy on you. Through such spying, they can discover your identity, track your movements, or even catch you in a criminal act. Of all forms of intelligence, human intelligence is the oldest. (In fact, spies often muse that human intelligence is the world's oldest profession.)

Human intelligence comes in two flavors, collective and penetrative:

- *Collective intelligence* has as its chief objective to collect information without necessarily establishing direct contact.

- *Penetrative intelligence* has as its chief objective to establish direct contact, gain the contacted person's trust, and obtain information on an ongoing basis.

The Internet is a superb tool for collective intelligence. For example, consider your posts to Usenet. These are available to the public, to persons known and unknown. Others can track your messages closely and can learn a great deal about you by doing so. Naturally, this presents law-enforcement agencies with a unique opportunity. Simply by using search engines, they can conduct collective intelligence at a whim.

This is completely different from the situation 25 years ago. To illustrate how different, let me take you back to the early 1970s. Here in America, the '70s were filled with political turmoil. Many radical organizations emerged, and some advocated violent overthrow of the government. U.S. intelligence agencies responded by conducting collective and penetrative operations. These operations were carried out by human beings. For example, to identify supporters of the Students for a Democratic Society, the FBI would send agents on foot. (These agents might have been employed by the FBI or they might have been civilian informers. It didn't really matter.) Such agents would mix with the crowds at political rallies and record license plate numbers or gather names. Later, field agents would connect faces, fingerprints, and addresses to those names by running license plate files, retrieving criminal records, or questioning still other informants.

Those methods are no longer necessary. Instead, the Internet enables intelligence agencies to monitor public sentiment from the comfort of their own offices. Furthermore, they can do this without violating any law. No search warrant is required to study someone's activity on the Internet. This means any agency can freely utilize tools and software available on the Internet to collect data on anyone. Likewise, no warrant is required before using the Internet to compile lists of people who might be involved in illegal or seditious activity. A warrant is only required when the data needed resides on private systems, such as an ISP. After obtaining a subpoena, an intelligence agency can then gain access to ISP log files, any email traffic (if available), and any other digital data pertaining to the individual.

If you harbor radical political views, you should keep them to yourself. (Either that or gain a decent education in cryptography.) Here's why: Today's search engines can be used to isolate all Usenet traffic between a particular class of individuals (militia members, for example). You can bet your last dollar that Kirk Lyons (a white supremacist lawyer whose clients have been a "Who's Who" of the radical right) has been monitored closely by the FBI.

Be forewarned: Usenet is not a forum to exercise your right to free speech. Instead, it's a place where you are exposed, naked to the world. Usenet is just the beginning. Six out of every ten Web sites you visit track your movements. (Probably eight out of ten big commercial sites try to.) Advances in digital snooping make it possible for nearly anyone with a computer to become an electronic Peeping Tom.

In 2000, the FBI introduced DCS1000, a system that, when plugged into a computer network, captures and tracks all network communication through that system. DCS1000, formerly known as Carnivore, has created a large controversy with privacy advocates. One of the biggest reasons for this is simply that DCS1000 is not designed to monitor just a single individual (or select individuals) whom the FBI might be legally wiretapping. It captures all communications on the systems that the investigators plug it into. With the help of the Freedom of Information Act, about 600 documents relating to DCS1000 were released. From this information, SecurityFocus.com has put together an interesting overview:

> Newly declassified documents obtained by Electronic Privacy Information Center (EPIC) under the Freedom of Information Act reveal that DCS1000 can monitor all of a target user's Internet traffic, and in conjunction with other FBI tools, can reconstruct Web pages exactly as a surveillance target saw them while surfing the Web.

This is fine for tracking and monitoring illegal activities of people suspected of criminal activity, but what about all the innocent users that have unknowingly had their privacy violated? The FBI doesn't let the public know what it does with the data gathered from DCS1000.

Beyond DCS1000, the FBI has been working on another system called Magic Lantern. Magic Lantern is known as a keyboard sniffer that logs every keystroke. What is not known is how it gets on the suspect's computer. Some rumors say it is a virus, whereas others say that the FBI can get a court order to install it on a machine by entering a home without the owner's knowledge. In either case, it's a scary proposition that the FBI could be watching your every computer action without your knowledge.

Web Browsing and Invasion of Privacy

Before Web browsers existed, you could only access the Internet from a command-line interface. This interface was bare bones and intimidating to most people. Browsers changed that by turning the Internet into a point-and-click paradise; anyone with a mouse could easily navigate the World Wide Web. The results were phenomenal. Indeed, practically overnight, millions of users flocked to the Web.

When humanity rushed to the Web, marketing agencies took notice. This question was immediately posed: How can we use the Internet to make a buck? Companies came up with various answers, including electronic commerce. (In electronic commerce, consumers buy products or services over the Web, right from their own homes.)

From the start, there was a strong drive to develop methods of tracking not only consumer purchases, but also consumer interests. Many such methods emerged by 1993, and today there are more than a dozen. In the following pages, you'll learn how your identity is ferreted out, bit by bit, by persons known and unknown.

Internet Architecture and Privacy

I'll begin by making a blanket statement and one you should never forget: The Internet's architecture was not designed with personal privacy in mind. In fact, there are many standard Internet utilities designed specifically for tracing and identifying users.

In a moment we'll examine some and how they work. First, however, we need to cover how user information is stored on servers.

How User Information Is Stored on Servers

There are two universal forms of identification on the Internet: your email address and your IP address. Both reveal your identity. At a minimum, both serve as good starting places for a spy.

Your email address in particular can reveal your real name. Here's why: Even if your Internet service provider uses Windows to host a few Web sites, almost all ISPs use Unix as their base platform. That's because Unix (coupled with a protocol called RADIUS) makes management of dial-up accounts very easy. (It also provides better mail support than Windows if you are dealing with hundreds or even thousands of accounts.)

On the Unix system, user information is often stored in a file called `passwd`, which is located in the `/etc` directory. This file contains user login names, usernames, and occasionally, user passwords (although only in encrypted form). An entry from the `passwd` file looks like this:

```
jdoe:x:65536:1:John Doe:/export/home/jdoe:/sbin/sh
```

If you examine the entry closely, you'll see that the fields are colon-delimited. Here you should be concerned with fields 1, 5, and 6. Using the entry as an example, those fields are as follows:

- `jdoe`   Your username

- `John Doe`   Your real name

- `/export/home/jdoe`   Your home directory

This information is vital, and Unix uses it for many tasks. For example, this information is double-checked each time you log in, each time you receive mail, and each time you log out. Unfortunately, the information is also usually available to the general public through a utility called finger.

finger

finger is a service common to Unix systems. Its purpose is to provide user information to remote hosts, and like all TCP/IP services, finger is based on the client/server model.

When a Unix system first boots, it loads nearly a dozen remote services (for example, a Web server, an FTP server, a Telnet server, and so forth). The finger server is called `fingerd` and is commonly referred to as the *finger daemon*.

The finger daemon listens for local or remote requests for user information. When it receives such a request, it forwards whatever information is currently available on the target. (The target in this case is you.)

On Unix, a finger request can be issued from a command prompt. The results from the finger server are then printed to the local terminal. Here's what a command-prompt finger request looks like:

```
$finger -l jdoe@john-doe.com
```

The command translates into plain English like this: "Look up `jdoe` and tell me everything you can about him." When a user issues such a request, the finger daemon at `john-doe.com` is contacted. It searches through the system for `jdoe`, and ultimately, it returns this information:

```
Login name: jdoe                         In real life: John Doe
Directory: /                             Shell: /sbin/sh
Last login Tue May 18 19:53 on pts/22
New mail received Mon May 18 04:05:58 1997;
   unread since Mon May 18 03:20:43 1997
No Plan.
```

For years, this information was available only to Unix and VAX/VMS users. Not any more. Today, there are *finger clients* (programs that perform finger lookups) for all platforms. Windows NT/2000/XP has one built in that can be accessed from a DOS window. Table 8.1 lists a few.

TABLE 8.1   finger Clients for Non-Unix, Non-Windows NT Users

Client	Platform	Location
Total Finger	Windows	`http://www.mrfrosty.co.uk/files/tfinger.exe`
IPNetMonitor	Mac OS	`http://www.sustworks.com/site/prod_ipmonitor.html`

NOTE

To finger someone with the built-in finger client from an NT box, simply open a command prompt window and type `finger_target@host.com`.

These days, most system administrators deny remote finger requests to their networks, even internally. When network finger requests are allowed, they are often unrestricted and unregulated. This permits remote users to identify not only you, but also everyone on the system. To do so, remote users issue the following command:

`finger @my_target_host.com`

The @ symbol works precisely as an asterisk does in regular expression searches. In plain English, the command says this: "Tell me about all users currently logged on."

When writing this chapter, I wanted to give you an example, so I fingered all users at Reed College in Portland, Oregon. Here is the result from that query:

```
finger @reed.edu
[reed.edu]
Login       Name               TTY Idle    When          Office
copeland D. Jeremy Copeland   *p1   12 Tue 19:24 Box 169    775 6945
boothbyl Lawrence E. Boothby   p3 121d Sun 09:05
mab      Mark Bedau            p4      Tue 19:32
copeland D. Jeremy Copeland    p6    4 Tue 19:29 Box 169    775 6945
slam     Greg (don't call me   p7  13d Wed 08:36 Box 470    or Coleman
slam     Greg (don't call me   p8  18d Fri 07:29 Box 470    or Coleman
mayer    Ray Mayer            *p9   2d Mon 16:59 (fac)
mcclellj Joshua J McClellan    pf   4d Fri 14:45 (813)
slam     Greg (don't call me   pe   6d Wed 08:19 Box 470    or Coleman
mcclellj Joshua J McClellan    q0   4d Fri 16:12 (813)
moored   Dustin B Moore        q2 6:32 Tue 13:05 (1172)
obonfim  Osiel Bonfim          q3 3:02 Mon 16:07
```

```
rahkolar Rahua Rahkola        q6    46 Tue 18:34
obonfim  Osiel Bonfim         q9  2:59 Tue 09:45
mcclellj Joshua J McClellan   qb    4d Fri 15:00   (813)
jwitte   John Witte          *qc  4:00 Tue 15:14
lillieb  Ben Lillie           r3    58 Tue 13:11   P04
szutst   Tobi A. Szuts       *r7     5 Tue 14:51   (819)
mcclard  Ron McClard         *re  1:22 Mon 10:55   (x218)
queue    Print Queue Display  qd    8d Mon 15:42
jimfix   James D. Fix        *qf    32 Tue 13:04
mcclellj Joshua J McClellan   r6  3:50 Mon 10:47   (813)
```

It doesn't look like these folks have much privacy, does it? Well, here's a fact: 99% of listings I checked around the Internet revealed the users' real names. If you think that listing only your company name will hide your identity, think again. Take a look at the first line of the preceding output:

```
copeland D. Jeremy Copeland   *p1   12 Tue 19:24  Box 169     775 6945
```

Here, as you can see, we already have this person's full name, his login name, email address (copeland@reed.edu), and a phone number. Using Google (http://www.google.com), I found his personal Web site at Reed College. I can also safely assume from the location of the college that he is in Portland, Oregon. A search on WorldPages (http://www.worldpages.com) gave me four individuals matching this person, all with home phone numbers and personal addresses. Not a lot of personal privacy here, is there?

In many cases, by starting with finger and ending with WorldPages, you can find someone's home address (along with a map for directions) in fewer than 30 seconds. If someone tells you that finger doesn't present a privacy issue, give her a copy of this book. finger can bring a total stranger right to your doorstep.

Solutions for the finger Problem

There are solutions for the finger problem. But, before you bother, you should check to see whether you are a viable target.

NOTE

If you use America Online, know that AOL does not allow finger requests on their users.

There are two ways to determine whether you are a viable finger target:

- Perform a finger query on yourself.

- Check the /etc/passwd file on your ISP's server.

To check from a shell prompt, issue one of the following commands:

```
grep your_username /etc/passwd
```

```
ypcat passwd || cat /etc/passwd | grep your_username
```

```
niscat passwd.org_dir | grep your username
```

These commands will print the information in the server's `/etc/passwd` file. The output will look like this:

```
jdoe:x:65536:1:John Doe:/export/home/jdoe:/sbin/sh
```

If you are a viable finger target, there are several things you can do to minimize your exposure:

- Use the utility `chfn` to alter the finger information available to outsiders.

- If `chfn` is not available, request that the system administrator change your information.

- Cancel your current account and start a new one.

NOTE

You might be puzzled why I suggest canceling your account. Here's why: It was you who provided the information in the `/etc/passwd` account. You provided that information when you signed up. If you can't access `chfn` and your sysadmin refuses to change this information, it will remain there until you cancel your account. If you cancel your account and create a new one, you can dictate what information the server has on you.

On the other hand, if you don't care about getting fingered, but you simply want to know who's doing it, you need MasterPlan.

MasterPlan

MasterPlan (written by Laurion Burchall) takes a more aggressive approach by identifying who is trying to finger you. Each time a finger query is detected, MasterPlan captures the hostname and user ID of the fingering party. This information is stored in a file called `finger_log`. MasterPlan also determines how often you are fingered, so you can detect whether someone is trying to clock you. (In *clocking*, user A attempts to discern the habits of user B via various network utilities, including finger and the r commands.)

In clocking, the snooping party uses an automated script to finger his target every x number of minutes or hours. Reasons for such probing can be diverse. One is to build a profile of the target: When does the user log in? How often does the user check mail? From where does the user usually log in? From these queries, a nosy party can determine other possible points on the network where you can be found.

Here's an example: A cracker I know wanted to intercept the email of a nationally renowned female journalist who covers hacking stories. This journalist had several accounts and frequently logged in to one from another. (In other words, she *chained* her connections. In this way, she was trying to keep her private email address a secret.)

By running a clocking script on the journalist, the cracker was able to identify her private, unpublished email address. He was also able to compromise her network and ultimately capture her mail. The mail consisted of discussions between the journalist and a software engineer in England. The subject matter concerned a high-profile cracking case in the news. (That mail was later distributed to crackers' groups across the Internet.)

MasterPlan can identify clocking patterns, at least with respect to finger queries. The utility is small and easy to configure. The C source is included, and the distribution is known to compile cleanly on most Unix systems. One nice amenity for Linux users is that a precompiled binary comes with most distributions. The standard distribution of MasterPlan is available at the following address:

```
ftp://ftp.netspace.org/pub/Software/Unix/masterplan.tar.Z
```

The Linux-compiled version is available at this address:

```
ftp://ftp.netspace.org/pub/Software/Unix/masterplan-linux.tar.Z
```

After you shield yourself against finger queries, you might feel that your name is safe from prying eyes. Wrong again. finger is just the beginning. There are a dozen other ways your email address and your name reveal information about you.

Beyond finger

Even if your provider forbids finger requests, your name is still easy to obtain. When snoops try to finger you and discover finger isn't running, they turn to your mail server. In most cases, servers accept Telnet connections to port 25 (the port that sendmail runs on). Such a connection looks like this:

```
220 shell. Sendmail SMI-8.6/SMI-SVR4 ready at Wed, 19 Feb 1997
➥07:17:18 -0800
```

If outsiders can reach the prompt, they can quickly obtain your name by issuing the following command:

```
expn username
```

The `expn` command expands usernames into email addresses and real names. The response will typically look like this:

```
username <username@target_of_probe.com> Real Name
```

The first field will report your username or user ID, followed by your email address, and finally, your "real" name.

System administrators can disable the `expn` function. If the `expn` function is operable, nosy individuals can still get your real name, if it is available. Again, the best policy is to remove your real name from the `passwd` file.

NOTE

Unfortunately, even if the `expn` function has been disabled, the snooping party can sometimes still verify the existence of your account using the `vrfy` function (if your server supports it).

As you can see, finger poses a unique privacy problem—but that's just the beginning.

Browser Security

With the rise of electronic commerce, various methods to track your movements have been developed. Three key methods are implemented through your Web browser:

- IP address and cache snooping
- Cookies
- Banner ads and Web bugs

By themselves, these techniques seem harmless enough. However, if you want to remain anonymous, you must take steps to safeguard yourself against them. Let's examine each in turn.

IP Address and Cache Snooping

Each time you visit a Web server, you leave behind a trail. This trail is recorded in different ways on different servers, but it is always recorded. A typical log entry on Unix (running Apache) looks like this:

```
153.35.38.245 [01/May/1998:18:12:10 -0700] "GET / HTTP/1.1" 401 362
```

Note the first entry (the IP address). All Web server packages are capable of recording visitor IP addresses. However, most Web servers can also record other information, including your hostname and even your username. To see what a Web server can tell about you, visit this site:

```
http://www.anonymizer.com/snoop/test_ip.shtml
```

This site will do a seven-part analysis on your vulnerability. It can detect your IP address, the last Web site you visited, how many Web sites you have visited, where you are physically, your browser type, OS, and even possibly grab your clipboard if you are using IE.

Using these logs and scripts, Webmasters can precisely pinpoint where you are, what your network address is, and where you've been. Are you uncomfortable yet? Now quickly examine cookies.

Cookies

Cookies. The word might sound inviting to you, but not to me—I value my privacy very much. In the past, many reporters have written articles about cookies, attempting to allay the public's fears. In such articles, they minimize the influence of cookies, dismissing them as harmless. Are cookies harmless? Not in my opinion.

Cookies (which Netscape calls Persistent Client State HTTP Cookies) are used to store information about you as you browse a Web page. The folks at Netscape explain it this way:

> This simple mechanism provides a powerful new tool that enables a host of new types of applications to be written for Web-based environments. Shopping applications can now store information about the currently selected items; for fee services can send back registration information and free the client from retyping a user-id on next connection; sites can store per-user preferences on the client and have the client supply those preferences every time that site is connected to.

TIP

The article from which the previous quote is excerpted, "Persistent Client State HTTP Cookies," can be found at http://wp.netscape.com/newsref/std/cookie_spec.html.

The cookie concept is like getting your hand stamped at a dance club that serves cocktails. You can roam the club, have some drinks, dance the floor, and even go outside for a few minutes. As long as the stamp is on your hand, you will not have to pay again, nor will your access be restricted. Similarly, cookies enable Web servers to "remember" you, your password, your interests, and so on. That way, when you return, this information is automatically retrieved. The issue concerning cookies, though, isn't that the information is retrieved. The controversy is about where the information is retrieved from—your hard disk drive.

The process works like this: When you visit a Web page, the server writes a cookie to your hard disk drive. This cookie is stored in a special file.

NOTE

Windows users can find the cookies file in varying places, depending on their browser type and their version of Windows. In older distributions cookies are kept in a file called cookies.txt. In newer distributions (and with Microsoft Internet Explorer), cookies are stored individually in the directory cookies, which is usually stored along with your user profile. (On Macintosh systems, the file is called MagicCookie.)

Here are some typical entries from a cookie file:

```
www.webspan.net    FALSE    /~frys    FALSE    859881600    worldohackf
➡   2.netscape.com    TRUE    /    FALSE    946684799
➡NETSCAPE_ID
1000e010,107ea15f.adobe.com    TRUE    /    FALSE    946684799    INTERSE
➡207.171.18.182 6852855142083822www.ictnet.com    FALSE    /    FALSE
➡946684799    Apache    pm3a-4326561855491810745.microsoft.com    TRUE
➡    /    FALSE    937422000    MC1
➡GUID=260218f482a111d0889e08002bb74f65.msn.com    TRUE    /    FALSE
➡937396800    MC1    ID=260218f482a111d0889e08002bb74f65comsecltd.com
➡FALSE    /    FALSE    1293753600    EGSOFT_ID
➡207.171.18.176-3577227984.29104071
.amazon.com    TRUE    /    FALSE    858672000    session-id-time
➡855894626.amazon.com    TRUE    /    FALSE    858672000
➡    session-id    0738-6510633-772498
```

This cookie file is a real one, pulled from an associate's hard disk drive. You will see that under the GUID (field number 6), the leading numbers are an IP address. (I have added a space between the IP address and the remaining portion of the string so that you can easily identify the IP. In practice, however, the string is unbroken.) From this, you can see that setting a cookie generally involves recording your IP address.

Advocates of cookies insist that they are harmless, cannot assist in identifying the user, and are therefore benign. That is not true, as explained by D. Kristol and L. Montulli in RFC 2109:

> An origin server could create a Set-Cookie header to track the path of a user through the server. Users may object to this behavior as an intrusive accumulation of information, even if their identity is not evident. (Identity might become evident if a user subsequently fills out a form that contains identifying information.)

Today, cookies are routinely used for user authentication. This is disturbing and was immediately recognized as a problem. As expressed in RFC 2109:

> User agents should allow the user to control cookie destruction. An infrequently used cookie may function as a "preferences file" for network applications, and a user may wish to keep it even if it is the least-recently-used cookie. One possible implementation would be an interface that allows the permanent storage of a cookie through a checkbox (or conversely, its immediate destruction).

Despite these early warnings about cookies, mainstream Web browsers still ship with the Accept Cookies option enabled. Worse still, although most browsers have an option that warns you before accepting a cookie, this option is also disabled by default. Netscape Communicator 4, for example, ships this way. If you use Netscape Communicator, take a moment to go to the Edit menu and choose Preferences. After you have the Preference option window open, click Advanced. In Netscape 6 and higher, as well as Mozilla, the settings can be found in the menu File, Preferences, Privacy & Security, Cookies. Microsoft Internet Explorer ships in basically the same state. To disable cookies in Internet Explorer, click Tools, and then select Internet Options from the list. A new window will open. Click the Security tab. You can change the security level to High, or click Custom Level, where you will find the options to disable cookies in Internet Explorer.

Think about that for a moment: How many new computer owners are aware that cookies exist? Shouldn't they at least be informed that such intelligence gathering is going on? I think so.

Combating Cookies

Cookies can easily be managed and defeated using *cookie cutters*. These are programs that give you control over cookies (such as viewing them, deleting them, or conditionally refusing them). The easiest solution is to use Netscape 7 or Mozilla as your browser, because the cookie-cutting functionality is built into the browser. Table 8.2 provides names and locations of several cookie cutters that are useful with other browsers.

TABLE 8.2   Cookies Cutters, Their Platforms, and Their Locations

Cutter	Platform	Location
Cookie Pal	Windows	`http://www.kburra.com/downloads/cp1setup.exe`
Cookie Cruncher	Windows	`http://www.rbaworld.com/Programs/CookieCruncher/`
NoMoreCookies	Mac OS	`http://downloads.zdnet.co.uk/downloads/detail/` `1002-2271-880008.html`
ScapeGoat	Mac OS	`http://www.zdnet.com.au/downloads/mac/swinfo/` `0,2000036795,899153,00.htm`

NOTE

Windows and Mac OS users can also make the cookies file or directory read-only. This will prevent any cookies from being written to the drive. Unix users should delete the `cookies.txt` file and place a symbolic link there that points to `/dev/null`.

If you want to learn more about cookies, check out some of the following articles:

- "A Cookies Monster?" Stephen T. Maher, *Law Products* Magazine. `http://www.usual.com/article6.htm`.

- Cookies and Privacy FAQ. `http://www.cookiecentral.com/n_cookie_faq.htm`.

- "Are Cookie Files Public Record?" Dan Goodin, CNET. `http://www.news.com/News/Item/0,4,17170,00.html`.

- "How Web Servers' Cookies Threaten Your Privacy." Junkbusters. `http://www.junkbusters.com/ht/en/cookies.html`.

- HTTP State Management Mechanism (RFC 2109, a document discussing the technical aspects of the cookie mechanism.) `http://www.ics.uci.edu/pub/ietf/http/rfc2109.txt`.

You should also know this: Cookies and the `test-cgi` script are not the only ways that Webmasters grab information about you. Other, less conspicuous techniques exist. Many JavaScript and Perl scripts can "get" your IP address. This type of code also can get your browser type, your operating system, and so forth. The following is an example in JavaScript:

```
<script language=javascript>
   function Get_Browser() {
```

```
    var appName = navigator.appName;
    var appVersion = navigator.appVersion;
    document.write(appName + " " + appVersion.substring
➡(0,appVersion.indexOf(" ")));
    }
</script>
```

JavaScript will get the browser and its version. Scripts like this are used at thousands of sites across the Internet. A very popular one is the "Book 'em, Dan-O" script. This script (written in the Perl programming language) will get the time you accessed the page, your browser type and version, and your IP address.

> **TIP**
>
> The "Book 'em, Dan-O" script was written by an individual named Spider. It is currently available for download at Matt's Script Archive at `http://worldwidemart.com/scripts/dano.shtml`.

Similar programs are available in a wide range of programming languages, including Java. You will find a Java program designed specifically for this purpose here:

`http://www.teklasoft.com/java/applets/connect/socket.html`

Ads and Web Bugs

You've no doubt visited plenty of Web sites with advertisements. The Internet has become a marketing executive's dream come true, with nearly unlimited methods of tracking and recording information on consumers. Today, nearly every popular Web site is littered with annoying banner ads, pop-up ads, Web bugs, and targeted marketing. The only cost is your own personal privacy. Whenever ads are mentioned in this section, it is referring to both banner ads and popup ads. The major difference is that pop-ups are more annoying. Ads are a necessary evil of the Internet economy, but did you know that these innocent images can also be used to track users and transmit demographics back to the advertising companies responsible for them?

The methods vary, but it generally works like this: A user visits a popular Web site with an ad that has the capability to track. As the page loads, it will grab the required image directly off of a Web server run by the advertising company. Every time this happens, the ad server has the capability to log a great deal of information about who is loading that image. Using cookies, sophisticated JavaScript, and CGI, the unwitting visitor might be sending nothing more that her IP or every piece of personal information she might have previously submitted to another Web site. It is also possible for the remote ad server to set a cookie on the user's computer to help it track that person in better detail.

The latest trend in violating your Web-surfing privacy comes from Web bugs. A Web bug is usually a small, transparent .gif, 1×1 pixels in size, that works in a similar manner to a tracking ad. When the page loads, the invisible Web bug also loads, triggering the same transfer of information that the ads can send. The biggest difference is simply stealth. You can't see or detect a Web bug, unless you look at the source for that particular Web page. Take a look at this example from the ZDNet Web site:

```
<img src="http://ads3.zdnet.com/i/g=r001&c=a56998&idx=2001.01.04.21.48.58/
http://images.zdnet.com/adverts/imp/dotclear.gif">
```

This is the HTML code to display an image on the ZDNet Web page. This, however, is no ordinary image. It's a Web bug used to track people visiting the Web site. Notice the height and width parameters, and the lack of a border or an ALT entry. This invisible image, when loaded, triggers the ad server at ZDNet to record whatever information they programmed it to retrieve. ZDNet is not alone in this behavior. I simply loaded the first Web site that came to mind and found this Web bug.

TIP

There are several good articles online about the proliferation of Web bugs and banner ads with tracking capabilities. Be sure to check out "Nearly Undetectable Tracking Device Raises Concerns" by Stefanie Olsen at http://news.cnet.com/news//0-1007-200-2247960.html.

What do these companies need this information for? Why do they violate your privacy without your permission or consent? Marketing. Marketing and selling products to consumers requires detailed demographics and statistics. With this information, the advertising companies are better able to target a specific group to sell them something. If you visit a lot of Web sites related to computers, for instance, you will notice that the ads you see will be designed to get you to buy computer-related products and services. Also, a high-traffic Web site can make a good sum of money by enabling advertisers to post ads and Web bugs on their pages.

TIP

If you want to see if Web bugs are being used on Web pages you are visiting, take a look at Bugnosis (http://www.bugnosis.org/). Bugnosis integrates into Internet Explorer version 5 or higher. It will highlight and explain Web bugs.

Protecting Yourself from Ads and Web Bugs

Thankfully, there are many solutions for combating intrusive cookies, ads, and Web bugs. Today, there are several software programs that you can proxy your Web browser traffic through to block this material. A proxy is a type of software that acts as a sort of middleman between you and the Internet. Your Internet traffic flows through it, and depending on the proxy's functionality, it is sped up, filtered, or redirected. My personal favorite is the Internet Junkbuster. Junkbuster's developers have also recently released a consumer version of Junkbuster called Guidescope, which is aimed at the general public and is easy to install and use. Guidescope offers the same level of protection as Junkbuster, but it is designed to be a lot more user friendly and easier to install and maintain.

Internet Junkbuster acts as a proxy server for all your Web surfing traffic. As you load Web pages, it inspects the incoming code for common patterns used by banner ads and Web bugs. Before this code ever reaches your Web browser, it is stripped from the HTML, effectively sterilizing the privacy-invading banners and bugs. Not only does this help safeguard your privacy, but blocking banner advertisements also significantly speeds up Web browsing, and you will find it is a lot easier to concentrate on the information you came to see, rather than flashy obnoxious Web advertising. Internet Junkbuster and Guidescope can also be configured to block cookies.

NOTE

If your privacy is important, you should take a few minutes to take a look at the Junkbuster Web site. They provide a great deal of information on proactively protecting yourself from invasive advertising in email, postal mail, telemarketing, and other means.

More information on Internet Junkbuster and Guidescope can be found at http://www.junkbusters.com and http://www.guidescope.com.

Another option is to install your own local proxy server. The Proxomitron (http://proxomitron.org/) is an excellent one. Some of its features include blocking banner ads, lying about the type of browser you have, and removing JavaScripts.

If you just want to get rid of pop-up ads, software is available for that as well. The first anti-pop-up measure is to use Netscape 7 or Mozilla as your browser. To eliminate pop-ups, go to Edit, Preferences, Advanced, Scripts & Windows. In that menu, uncheck Open Unrequested Windows (also known as pop-ups). For good measure, while you're there, uncheck Move or Resize Existing Windows and Raise or Lower Windows. If you are using IE or an old version of Netscape, you can eliminate pop-ups using a software such as Popup Ad Filter (http://www.meaya.com/?xfx) instead.

It should be noted that some companies (for example, http://www.anti-leech.com) are trying to sell products to Webmasters that are geared toward eliminating your privacy. These products try to detect that you are blocking their ads, and if so, refuse to let you look at their site. My advice is not to use those sites and let the Webmaster know that.

Spyware

The newest trend in Internet privacy invasion is spyware, also known as adware. Spyware is software that is usually included in some free software you have downloaded. The spyware component monitors your computer activity and periodically sends reports back to an advertiser about your behavior, so they can target their ads better to you. It's obvious, in theory, that the spyware could read your private email or do anything else it wants on your system.

If you have loaded software such as RealPlayer, Kazaa, or GoZilla, you might have spyware on your computer. The good news is that you can do something about it.

The first strategy is to become knowledgeable about what you have loaded that might be spyware. A couple of Web sites can help you: SpyChecker (http://www.spychecker.com/) and SpyWare List (http://www.tom-cat.com/spybase/spylist.html). Both sites have lists of spyware. However, it makes sense to check both. SpyChecker says the RealPlayer 7 is not spyware, whereas SpyWare List says it is.

If you would prefer a program that can search your computer for spyware, try Ad-aware from http://www.lavasoftusa.com/. Ad-aware is a little more advanced. Most programs that include spyware buy their components from a handful of vendors. Ad-aware will search your computer (much like an antivirus program) and detect what spyware components are loaded on your machine. It then gives you the option of removal. You can also register Ad-aware, and when you do, you get a program called Ad-watch, which watches your computer in real-time and lets you know when some spyware has been installed on your machine.

By having Ad-aware remove the spyware, the programs that included the spyware might not work any longer. Likewise, if you find the package you are using on the lists mentioned previously, you might be faced with a tough choice. The good news is that it is almost always possible to find a similar free package that does not include spyware. The Ad-aware people have a partial list at http://www.lavasoftusa.com/more.html.

Although I'm not sure of the legalities, there is another option if you want to use your favorite software without the spyware. Some hackers out on the Internet grab spyware-enabled programs and then disable the spyware components. One prime example is Kazaalite (http://www.kazaalite.com), which is Kazaa with the spyware removed.

Personal firewall software, such as ZoneAlarm (http://www.zonealarm.com) can help as well. Most personal firewall packages can be configured to block the outgoing messages from spyware. In some cases, it may break the spyware-enabled program.

Finally, there is my personal favorite. The Kazzalite site also has a special hosts file in which you can add to the hosts file on your machine. This hosts file contains the domain names for many spyware and banner ad tracking sites. However, instead of containing their correct IP address, every IP address is set to 127.0.0.1, which means the local computer. Therefore, whenever the spyware tries to contact the spyware site with your information, it will fail. Also, after loading this file, you'll notice error messages and block images on some Web pages as well, because banner ads and Web bugs are failing.

Your Email Address and Usenet

Earlier in this chapter, I claimed that your email address could expose you to spying on Usenet. In this section, I will prove it.

Your email address is like any other text string. If it appears on (or within the source code of) a Web page, it is reachable by search engines. When a spy has your email address, it's all over but the screaming. In fact, perhaps most disturbing of all, your email address and name (after they are paired) can reveal other accounts that you might have.

To provide you with a practical example, I pondered a possible target. I was looking for someone who changed email addresses frequently and routinely used others as fronts. *Fronts* are third parties who post information for you. By using a front, you avoid being pinned down, because it's the front's email address that appears, not your own.

I decided to do a bit of research on a controversial person, Kirk D. Lyons of the Southern Legal Resource Center (SLRC). This name might not be too familiar to many people right away. Mr. Lyons is an outspoken attorney with a history of defending right-wing and extremist groups. He has also been a prominent voice and an active participant in several newsworthy incidents, especially in the past 10 years. Mr. Lyons has been directly involved with issues relating to the Oklahoma federal building bombing and Timothy McVeigh, the Ruby Ridge incident with Randy Weaver, and the Waco stand-off, to name a few.

NOTE

The following exercise is not an invasion of Mr. Lyons' privacy. All information was obtained from publicly available databases on the Internet. Instead, this exercise is very similar to the results of a June 1997 *Time* magazine article about Internet privacy. In that article, a *Time* reporter tracked California Senator Dianne Feinstein. The reporter did an extraordinary job and even managed to ascertain Senator Feinstein's Social Security number. The article, "My Week as an Internet Gumshoe," is by Noah Robischon. At the time of this writing, it is available online at http://www.pathfinder.com/time/magazine/1997/dom/970602/technology.my_wek.html.

The first step in tracking an individual is to capture their email addresses. To find Kirk D. Lyons's email address, any garden-variety search engine will do, although AltaVista and Google have the most malleable designs. That's where I started. (Remember that I have never met Mr. Lyons and know very little about him.)

I began my search with AltaVista (`http://www.altavista.com`). AltaVista is one of the most powerful search engines available on the Internet and is provided as a public service by CMGI, Inc. It accepts various types of queries that can be directed toward WWW pages (HTML), images and video, and other forms of digital media. I followed up using Google (`http://www.google.com`).

I chose AltaVista for one reason: It performs case-sensitive, exact-match regular expression searches. That means that it will match precisely what you search for. (In other words, there are no "close" matches when you request such a search. This feature enables you to narrow your results to a single page out of millions.)

To force such a precise search, you must enclose your search string in double-quotation marks. I began by searching the Web for this string:

```
"Kirk D. Lyons"
```

This search returned nearly 200 matches, and I started sorting them looking for anything interesting. Most of what I found were various articles and publications either about Mr. Lyons or written by him. I was able to discover an older, shared email address used by Mr. Lyons and one of his colleagues, `unreconfed@cheta.net`. Searching for just this email address yielded very little, so I turned to Usenet postings. Using `http://groups.google.com/`, I was able to search thousands of postings. I came across some by Kirk himself using the previous email address. What was interesting here was that the email header information was left intact, which gives quite a bit of information:

```
Return-Path: unreconfed@cheta.net
Received: from lexington.ioa.net
  (IDENT:root@lexington.ioa.net [208.131.128.7])
  by mail.hal-pc.org (8.9.1/8.9.0) with ESMTP id DAA09388
for <abnrngrs@hal-pc.org>; Thu, 4 Nov 1999 03:23:08 -0559 (CST)
  Received: from 1861 (ppp227.arden.dialup.ioa.com [205.138.38.236])
  by lexington.ioa.net (8.9.3/8.9.3) with SMTP id EAA29654;
Thu, 4 Nov 1999 04:19:27 -0500
Message-ID: <1bed01bf26a5$a5ea0560$cb268acd@1861>
To: <Undisclosed.Recipients@lexington.ioa.net>
From: "Kirk D. Lyons or Dr. Neill H. Payne" <unreconfed@cheta.net> Subject: HELP
```

From this, it is possible to determine who is using this address, and where they were connecting from and which service provider they were using to send the message. I can also determine that this is a dial-up account, possibly a home user account in Arden, North Carolina. Further investigation helped me discover that this individual is heavily involved in Civil War re-enactment. This led me to discover Mr. Lyons's sideline business, Different Drummer, including more detailed information including the address, phone number, fax number, and email for this business.

This might not seem like much information, but, in reality, it is enough that I could easily start pulling up business and tax records, property information, and other public data on Mr. Lyons. There is very little limit on how far this investigation could be taken. In just a few minutes using freely available Internet Web site-based searching, I was able to gather a considerable amount of information about Mr. Lyons.

That might not initially seem very important. You are probably thinking, "So what?" However, think back to what I wrote at the beginning of this chapter. Twenty years ago, the FBI would have spent thousands of dollars (and secured a dozen wiretaps) to discover the same information.

Usenet is a superb tool for building models of human networks. (These are groups of people who think alike.) If you belong to such a group (and maintain controversial or unpopular views), do not post those views to Usenet.

Even though you can prevent your Usenet posts from being archived by making `x-no-archive: yes` the first line of your post, you cannot prevent others from copying the post and storing it on a Web server. By posting unpopular political views to Usenet (and inviting others of like mind to respond), you are inadvertently revealing your associations to the world. If your posts are archived, they might be available for all eternity, thanks to the folks at `http://groups.google.com`.

Google Groups

The DejaNews search engine was a specialized tool designed solely to search Usenet. In early 2001, Google purchased the DejaNews service and renamed it Google Groups. The archive goes back to 1981 and contains 700 million messages.

DejaNews has advanced indexing functions as well. For example, you can automatically build a profile on the author of a Usenet article. (That is, the engine will produce a list of newsgroups that the target has posted to recently.) In this way, others can instantly identify your interests. Worse still, they can actually find you.

To recap, assume that although your real name does not appear on Usenet postings, it does appear in the `/etc/passwd` file on the Unix server that you use as a gateway to the Internet. Here are the steps someone must take to find you:

1. The snooping party sees your post to Usenet. Your email address is in plain view, but your name is not.

2. The snooping party tries to finger your address, but as it happens, your provider prohibits finger requests.

3. The snooping party telnets to port 25 of your server. There, he issues the `expn` command and obtains your real name.

Having gotten that information, the snooping party next needs to find the state you live in. For this, he turns to the WHOIS service.

The WHOIS Service

The WHOIS service contains domain registration records of all American, nonmilitary Internet sites. This registration information contains detailed information on each Internet site, including domain name, server addresses, technical contacts, the telephone number, and the address. In the past, the WHOIS information was all in one database, but since there are now multiple domain registrars, it is distributed.

The first thing you'll need is a WHOIS client. If you are on Unix, it mostly likely will already be available to you. If you are on Windows, you'll need to download one such as WHOIS for Windows (`http://www.compulink.co.uk/~net-services/spam/whois.htm`). On the Mac, you can use WhatRoute (`http://www.mac.org/internet/whatroute/`).

I am going to show you how to use WHOIS by looking at the ISP Netcom. First, you'll need to go to the WHOIS page at InterNIC (`http://www.internic.net/whois.html`) with your Web browser. Enter the domain name (that is, `netcom.com`) and submit. One of the fields you will see is the Whois Server. In this case, it is `whois.networksolutions.com`.

Now you'll use your WHOIS client to query `whois.networksolutions.com` for `netcom.com`. If you are using the Unix WHOIS, type **whois -h whois.networksolutions.com netcom.com**. You will get the following response:

```
Registrant:
NETCOM On-Line Communication Services, Inc (NETCOM-DOM)
    1430 West Peachtree St
    Suite 400
    Atlanta, GA 30309

    Domain Name: NETCOM.COM

    Administrative Contact:
        MindSpring Abuse  (MA127-ORG)          abuse@MINDSPRING.COM
        MindSpring Enterprises
```

```
    1430 West Peachtree St NW
    Atlanta, GA 30309
    US
    404-815-0770
    Fax- - 404-815-8805
Technical Contact:
    Hostmaster  (HOS272-ORG)          hostmaster@MINDSPRING.NET
    MindSpring Enterprises, Inc.
    1430 West Peachtree Street NE
    Suite 400
    Atlanta, GA 30309
    US
    404-815-0770
    Fax- 404-815-8805


Record expires on 03-Feb-2003.
Record created on 01-Feb-1991.
Database last updated on 15-Sep-2002 09:19:12 EDT.


Domain servers in listed order:

SPEAKEASY.EARTHLINK.NET      207.69.188.200
HEARSAY.EARTHLINK.NET        207.69.188.201
```

Take a good look at the Netcom WHOIS information. From this, the snooping party discovers that Netcom is in Georgia. (Note the location at the top of the WHOIS return listing, as well as the telephone points of contact for the technical personnel.)

Armed with this information, the snooping party proceeds to http://www.worldpages. com/. WorldPages is a massive database that houses the names, email addresses, and telephone numbers of several million Internet users.

At WorldPages, the snooping party uses your real name as a search string, specifying California as your state. Instantly, he is confronted with several matches that provide name, address, and telephone number. Here, he might run into some trouble, depending on how common your name is. If your name is John Smith, the snooping party will have to do further research. However, assume that your name is not John Smith—that your name is common, but not that common. The snooping party uncovers three addresses, each in a different California city: One is in Atlanta, one is in Athens, and one is in Plains. How does he determine which one is really you? He proceeds to the host utility.

The host utility will list all machines on a given network and their relative locations. With large networks, it is common for a provider to have machines sprinkled at various locations throughout a state. The host command can identify which workstations are located where. In other words, it is generally trivial to obtain a listing of workstations by city. These workstations are sometimes even named for the cities in which they are deposited. Therefore, you might see an entry such as the following:

```
chatsworth1.target_provider.com
```

Chatsworth is a city in northwest Georgia. From this entry, we can assume that `chatsworth1.target_provider.com` is located within the city of Chatsworth. What remains for the snooper is to re-examine your Usenet post.

By examining the source code of your Usenet post, he can view the path the message took. That path will look something like this:

```
news2.cais.com!in1.nntp.cais.net!feed1.news.erols.com!howland.erols.net!
➥ix.netcom.com!news
```

By examining this path, the snooping party can now determine which server was used to post the article. This information is then coupled with the value for the NNTP posting host:

```
grc-ny4-20.ix.netcom.com
```

The snooping party extracts the name of the posting server (the first entry along the path). This is almost always expressed in its name state and not by its IP address. For the snooping party to complete the process, the IP address is needed. Therefore, he telnets to the posting host. When the Telnet session is initiated, the hard, numeric IP is retrieved from DNS and printed to STDOUT. The snooping party now has the IP address of the machine that accepted the original posting. This IP address is then run against the outfile obtained by the host query. This operation reveals the city in which the machine resides.

TIP

If this information does not exactly match, the snooping party can employ other methods. One technique is to issue a `traceroute` request. When tracing the route to a machine that exists in another city, the route must invariably take a path through certain gateways. These are main switching points through which all traffic passes when going in or out of a city. Usually, these are high-level points, operated by telecommunication companies such as MCI, Sprint, and so forth. Most have city names within their addresses. Bloomington and Los Angeles are two well-known points. Thus, even if the reconciliation of the posting machine's name fails against the host outfile, a `traceroute` will reveal the approximate location of the machine.

Having obtained this information (and having now differentiated you from the other names), the snooping party returns to WorldPages and chooses your name. Within seconds, a graphical map of your neighborhood appears. The exact location of your home is marked on the map by a circle. The snooping party now knows exactly where you live and how to get there. From this point, he can begin to gather more interesting information about you. For example:

- The snooping party can determine your status as a registered voter and your political affiliations. He obtains this information at `http://www.wdia.com/lycos/voter-records.htm`.

- From federal election records online, he can determine which candidates you support and how much you have contributed. He gets this information from `http://www.tray.com/cgi-win/indexhtml.exe?MBF=pr_info`.

- He can also get your Social Security number and date of birth. This information is available at `http://kadima.com/`.

- He might be able to determine the value of your house, what company has your mortgage, and the amount of property tax you have paid every year. Many counties now have their property records available for free over the Web.

Many people minimize the seriousness of this. Their prevailing attitude is that all such information is available through other sources anyway. The problem is that the Internet brings these sources of information together. Integration of such information allows this activity to be conducted on a wholesale basis, and that's where the trouble begins.

As a side note, complete anonymity on the Internet is possible, but usually not achievable by legal means. Given enough time, for example, authorities could trace a message posted via anonymous remailer. (Although, if that message were chained through several remailers, the task would be far more complex.) The problem is in the design of the Internet itself. As Ralf Hauser and Gene Tsudik note in their article, "On Shopping Incognito:"

> From the outset, the nature of current network protocols and applications runs counter to privacy. The vast majority have one thing in common: They faithfully communicate end-point identification information. "End-point" in this context can denote a user (with a unique ID), a network address, or an organization name. For example, electronic mail routinely communicates sender's [sic] address in the header. File transfer (for example, FTP), remote login (for example, Telnet), and hypertext browsers (for example, WWW) expose addresses, host names, and IDs of their users.

Then there is the question of whether users are entitled to anonymity. I believe they are. Certainly, there are plenty of legitimate reasons for allowing anonymity on the Internet. The following is excerpted from *Anonymity for Fun and Deception: The Other Side of "Community"* by Richard Seltzer:

> Some communities require anonymity for them to be effective, because without it members would not participate. This case with Alcoholics Anonymous, AIDS support groups, drug addiction support, and other mutual help organizations, particularly when there is some risk of social ostracism or even legal consequences should the identity of the members be revealed.

This is a recurring theme in the now-heated battle over Internet anonymity. Even many members of the "establishment" recognize that anonymity is an important element that might preserve free speech on the Internet—not just here, but abroad. This issue has received increased attention in legal circles. A. Michael Froomkin, a lawyer and prominent professor, wrote an excellent paper on the subject. In "Anonymity and Its Enmities," Froomkin writes

> Persons who wish to criticize a repressive government or foment a revolution against it may find remailers invaluable. Indeed, given the ability to broadcast messages widely using the Internet, anonymous email may become the modern replacement of the anonymous handbill. Other examples include corporate whistle-blowers, people criticizing a religious cult or other movement from which they might fear retaliation, and persons posting requests for information to a public bulletin board about matters too personal to discuss if there were any chance that the message might be traced back to its origin.

TIP

"Anonymity and Its Enmities" by Professor Froomkin is an excellent source for links to legal analysis of Internet anonymity. The paper is an incredible resource, especially for journalists. It can be found on the Web at `http://www.wm.edu/law/publications/jol/95_96/` `froomkin.html`.

However, not everyone feels that anonymity is a good thing. Some people believe that if anonymity is available on the Internet, it amounts to nothing but anarchy. A rather ironic quote, considering the source, is found in *Computer Anarchy: A Plea for Internet Laws to Protect the Innocent*, by Martha Seigel:

> People need safety and order in cyberspace just as they do in their homes and on the streets. The current state of the Internet makes it abundantly clear that general anarchy isn't working. If recognized governments don't find a way to bring order to the growing and changing Internet, chaos may soon dictate that the party is over.

You might or might not know why this quote is so incredibly ironic. The author, Martha Seigel, is no stranger to "computer anarchy." In her time, she has been placed on the Internet Blacklist of Advertisers for violating network policies against spamming the Usenet news network. The Internet Blacklist of Advertisers, now defunct, was intended to curb inappropriate advertising on Usenet newsgroups and via junk email. It worked by describing offenders and their offensive behavior, expecting that people who read it will punish the offenders in one way or another. The following is quoted from the docket listing on that Blacklist in regards to Cantor & Seigel, Ms. Seigel's law firm:

> The famous greencard lawyers. In 1994, they repeatedly sent out a message offering their services in helping to enter the U.S. greencard lottery to almost all Usenet newsgroups. (Note in passing: They charged $100 for their service, while participating in the greencard lottery is free and consists merely of sending a letter with your personal information at the right time to the right place.) When the incoming mail bombs forced their access provider to terminate their account, they threatened to sue him until he finally agreed to forward all responses to them.

However, all this is academic. As we move toward a cashless society, anonymity might be built in to the process. In this respect, at least, list brokers (and other unsavory information collectors) had better do all their collecting now. Analysis of consumer-buying habits will likely become a thing of the past, at least with relation to the Internet. The majority of electronic payment services being developed (or already available) on the Internet include anonymity as an inherent part of their design.

TIP

Several digital electronic payment systems exist today. A lot of research has been done in this area. A couple of companies with currently deployed systems are

- PayPal (`http://www.paypal.com`), which is now owned by eBay.
- VeriSign Payment Processing (`http://www.verisign.com/products/payment.html`), formerly CyberCash.

What I have a hard time understanding is how these systems can provide anonymous transactions. The reason I bring this up is simply that records must be maintained, log files generated, transactions authorized, and people involved to ensure the system works. Therefore, these "anonymous" transactions really aren't—and that brings you to my warning.

At Work

When you are at work, you need to assume that you have no privacy at all. Companies search email messages for employees who are looking for another job, giving out company secrets, and the like. It is also likely that your email messages have been recorded to a backup tape somewhere and could be around for years. Even Bill Gates has suffered from this problem when the government got a hold of these email messages via court order and presented them in court proceedings.

However, it does not stop at just email. Companies often monitor Web browsing in the same way. If you go to Web sites that are not work-related, you could be fired.

To make matters worse, some even go an extra step. If you view your Hotmail or Yahoo! Mail accounts from work, they can capture your email messages to monitor you even more.

If you don't like this, what can you do? To be honest, the best options are either to find a position at a less paranoid company or just never do any nonwork-related Internet use from the office. If neither of these are an option, the best I can suggest is to use one of the anonymous surfing services given at the end of the chapter, which enable you to use SSL to encrypt your traffic. Unfortunately, there are no guarantees even in that case.

A Warning

Technology is rapidly changing our society, and personal privacy is disappearing in the process. The Internet will only further facilitate that process.

Already, many banks are using biometrics for customer identification. The process is bone chilling. To withdraw your money, you must surrender your retina or thumbprint to a scanner that authenticates you. This technology is already being marketed for personal computers, and the sales pitch sounds enticing. After all, aren't you tired of having to enter a password every time you boot your machine or log on to the Net?

Soon, biometric authentication will be used in online electronic commerce. Before you close this book, I ask you to consider this very carefully: Imagine the climate a decade from now. Each user will have a unique, digital ID based on a cryptographic value. That value will be a 32-bit or 64-bit number derived from the physical characteristics of your face or your right hand. Without that number, you will not be able to buy or sell anything. When that time comes, remember that you read it here first.

Internet Resources

Finally, here are some good sources concerning privacy on the Internet.

Privacy & Anonymity on the Internet FAQ

Author: L. Detweiler

Content: Many sources on privacy and anonymity on the Internet; a must for users new to identity issues on the Net.

URL: `http://www.prz.tu-berlin.de/~derek/internet/sources/privacy.faq.02.html`

Anonymous Remailer FAQ

Author: Andre Bacard

Content: A not-too-technical description of anonymous remailers, how they work, and where they can be found. Bacard is also the author of *Computer Privacy Handbook* ("The Scariest Computer Book of the Year").

URL: `http://www.astalavista.com/privacy/library/remailer/remailer.shtml`

Anonymity on the Internet

Author: William Knowles

Content: Locations of anonymous remailers on the Internet as well as related topics.

URL: `http://www.sendfakemail.com/~raph/remailer-list.html`

How-To Chain Remailers with PGP Encryption

Author: Anonymous

Content: A no-nonsense tutorial on how to chain remailers, and in doing so, send a totally anonymous message with encryption.

URL: `http://www.email.about.com/internet/email/library/weekly/aa042400a.htm`

Privacy on the Internet

Authors: David M. Goldschlag, Michael G. Reed, and Paul F. Syverson, Naval Research Laboratory Center for High Assurance Computer Systems

Content: A good primer that covers all the aspects discussed in this chapter.

URL: `http://www.itd.nrl.navy.mil/ITD/5540/projects/onion-routing/inet97/index.htm`

Anonymous Connections and Onion Routing

Author: David M. Goldschlag, Michael G. Reed, and Paul F. Syverson, Naval Research Laboratory Center For High Assurance Computer Systems

Content: PostScript presented in the proceedings of the Symposium on Security and Privacy in Oakland, CA, May 1997. A detailed analysis of anonymous connections and their resistance to tracing and traffic analysis. (Also discusses vulnerabilities of such systems; a must read.)

URL: `http://www.itd.nrl.navy.mil/ITD/5540/projects/onion-routing/OAKLAND_97.ps`

The Electronic Frontier Foundation

Author: N/A

Content: Comprehensive sources on electronic privacy.

Location: `http://www.eff.org/`

The Electronic Privacy Information Center (EPIC)

Author: N/A

Content: Civil liberties issues; this site is indispensable in getting legal information on privacy and anonymity on the Internet and elsewhere.

URL: `http://epic.org/`

Computer Professionals for Social Responsibility (CPSR)

Author: N/A

Content: A group devoted to discussion about ethics in computer use.

URL: `http://www.cpsr.org/`

The Anonymizer

Author: N/A

Content: A site that offers free anonymous surfing. The application acts as a middle-man between you and the sites you surf. Basically, it is a more complex proxying service. It allows chaining as well, and your IP is stripped from their logs.

URL: `http://www.anonymizer.com/`

MegaProxy

Author: N/A

Content: A site that offers free anonymous surfing. It makes money from banner ads, however. It is recommended that their Advertising FAQ be read before use.

URL: `http://www.megaproxy.com/`

The Cloak

Author: N/A

Content: A site that offers free and paid anonymous surfing. The free service has bandwidth caps.

URL: `http://www.the-cloak.com/`

Safe Proxy

Author: N/A

Content: A site that offers free and paid anonymous surfing. The disadvantage of the free version is that logs are kept for two days and there is a 2MB file-size cap.

URL: `http://www.safeproxy.org/`

Articles and Papers and Related Web Sites

"Data Spills in Banner Ads." Richard M. Smith. February 14, 2000. `http://www.computerbytesman.com/privacy/banads.htm`.

"Nameless in Cyberspace: Anonymity on the Internet." Jonathan D. Wallace, 1996. `http://www.cato.org/pubs/briefs/bp-054es.html`.

"The Anonymous E-mail Conversation." Ceki Gulcu. Technical Report, Eurecom Institute. June 1995.

"E-Mail Security." Dr. John A. Line. UKERNA Computer Security Workshop, 15/16. November 1994. `ftp://ftp.cert.dfn.de/pub/pem/docs/UKERNA-email-security.ps.gz`.

"How Companies Track Your Movements on the Internet." `http://www.privacy.net/track/` provided by privacy.net.

"Electronic Fingerprints: Computer Evidence Comes of Age." M.R. Anderson, *Government Technology Magazine*. November 1996.

"Achieving Electronic Privacy." David Chaum. *Scientific American*, pp. 96-101. August 1992.

"Erased Files Often Aren't." M.R. Anderson, *Government Technology Magazine*. January 1997.

"The FBI's Magic Lantern: Ashcroft Can Be in Your Computer." Nat Hentoff. The Village Voice. May 24, 2002. `http://www.villagevoice.com/issues/0222/hentoff.php`.

"Reality check: Does adware work?" Rachel Konrad, CNET News.com. June 26, 2002. `http://news.com.com/2009-1023-938263.html?tag=rn`.

9
Dispelling Some of the Myths

The explosive growth of the Internet has thrust the topic of computer security directly in the face of everyone, whether they work with computers or not. Everywhere we read about viruses, system break-ins, malicious software, and a myriad of other threats. It really comes as no surprise that there is also a rising number of hoaxes, myths, and exaggerations about the risks you might face every time your computer is turned on and connected to the Internet. Although you should definitely be concerned about those risks, it is just as important to realize when someone is trying to con you or exaggerate the truth.

The movie *The Net* draws viewers into a world in which a group of crackers erase the identity of an innocent person to protect themselves. By using the Internet, they are nearly able to destroy the victim's life without much more than a mouse click or a keystroke. What many might not realize is that this scenario is extremely implausible in today's networked world. Hollywood has turned the black art of cracking into a glamorous place where anyone can control nearly every aspect of the human experience from a desktop computer. Nothing could be further from the truth.

In this chapter, I will help you understand when and where you might be vulnerable, who is actually perpetrating the attacks, why they are doing it, and what risks you might actually face.

When Can Attacks Occur?

I've heard it said many times: "The only secure computer is the one that is left turned off and unplugged." This is actually not far from the truth. The moment a computer system comes online and connects to any network, it becomes a potential target. This doesn't mean that the minute you connect to the Internet, you are immediately being attacked. There are several important factors that come into play. I'll cover some of these first.

How Do I Become a Hacker's Target?

The minute you link up to the Internet, you are unwittingly opening yourself up for an attack. To become a target, you first have to be discovered or selected by the cracker as his victim. In some cases, you might be attacked at random when someone runs software that randomly selects addresses and launches an attack. Random selection is less common than discovery or targeting.

In the case of discovery, the methods used to find out who and where you are, and how vulnerable you might be, are often the same. An attacker runs a port scanner, such as Nmap, feeding it a large block of IP addresses to check. The program will then report back to the end user what computers it has found in that range of addresses, what ports are open, and in the case of Nmap, what operating system the remote system is running. Using this information, the attacker now has several potential targets to choose from. With the information he received on the remote operating system and open ports, he can now narrow the scope of the attack to target known vulnerabilities within the remote system or service. This type of probe is often carried out before any actual cracking attempt is made.

The following shows the output from Nmap when scanning one of my own workstations. It also shows just how easy it is to get a lot of information about a single machine:

```
[root@server user]# nmap -vO 10.0.0.15
Starting nmap V. 2.53 by fyodor@insecure.org ( www.insecure.org/nmap/ )
No tcp,udp, or ICMP scantype specified, assuming vanilla tcp connect() scan.
Use -sP if you really don't want to portscan (and just want to
  see what hosts are up).

Host  (10.0.0.15) appears to be up ... good.
Initiating TCP connect() scan against  (10.0.0.15)
Adding TCP port 554 (state open).
Adding TCP port 5900 (state open).
Adding TCP port 1433 (state open).
Adding TCP port 445 (state open).
Adding TCP port 1025 (state open).
Adding TCP port 427 (state open).
Adding TCP port 139 (state open).
Adding TCP port 135 (state open).
```

```
Adding TCP port 25 (state open).
Adding TCP port 5800 (state open).
The TCP connect scan took 1 second to scan 1523 ports.
For OSScan assuming that port 25 is open and port 1 is closed and neither are
firewalled
Interesting ports on  (10.0.0.15):
(The 1513 ports scanned but not shown below are in state: closed)
Port        State       Service
25/tcp      open        smtp
135/tcp     open        loc-srv
139/tcp     open        netbios-ssn
427/tcp     open        svrloc
445/tcp     open        microsoft-ds
554/tcp     open        rtsp
1025/tcp    open        listen
1433/tcp    open        ms-sql-s
5800/tcp    open        vnc
5900/tcp    open        vnc

TCP Sequence Prediction: Class=random positive increments
                        Difficulty=9491 (Worthy challenge)
Sequence numbers: B896EAF2 B897E041 B8988355 B89936FB B89A1722 B89B1A0A
Remote operating system guess: Windows 2000 RC1 through final release
Nmap run completed — 1 IP address (1 host up) scanned in 43 seconds
[root@server user]#
```

You can see that this machine is running Windows 2000, a Microsoft SQL database server, an email server, and many other services. With this information, it becomes easy for the would-be cracker to do a little research online about vulnerabilities and exploits for your specific system or software. Often, this information also includes code or examples of methods used to exploit the weakness, making the job of the cracker that much easier. Even if the person probing your system is an unskilled cracker (also called a *script kiddie*), he can improve his attack by employing some of the software programs freely available on the Internet. These programs will test any remote system for hundreds of known vulnerabilities automatically.

The best thing you can do to prevent being selected this way is to install a firewall. A properly configured firewall will reduce the number of open ports you expose to the outside world. In that case, it is possible that the cracker will never even see a potential target like the Microsoft SQL server in the previous example.

An attacker can also be someone who has preselected you as his victim. The reasons for this are varied, but they include notoriety, contempt, theft of information, or financial gain. In this scenario, the attacker doesn't need to waste any time searching large network IP blocks to find a victim; he's already got one in mind. Depending on his motivation, he will most likely do a considerable amount of research before actually engaging in any malicious activity. The type of victim you are will determine the amount of caution or stealth employed by the cracker to avoid detection. For example, if the computers you work on belong to the Central Intelligence Agency, a great deal of time and ingenuity will be used by any attacker crazy enough to attempt to penetrate the systems to begin with.

Who you are, or for whom you work, also plays an important part in why or how often you might be targeted. A home or small office user is unlikely to be specifically targeted unless there is something worth the time and effort to be gained from doing so. If you happen to be the system administrator for Microsoft, things are very different indeed. Companies such as Microsoft typically log thousands of unsuccessful attack attempts every day. There are some fairly obvious reasons for this. The first one is simply name recognition. Just about anyone to ever operate a computer knows of Microsoft. Launching a successful attack against Microsoft would bring a cracker or group of crackers some considerable bragging rights. Microsoft is also one of the wealthiest computer software companies on the planet. The monetary and intellectual worth of source code and design documentation, financial data, and business information housed on the systems at Microsoft are, no doubt, very high indeed. Some of the more shady competitors of Microsoft would likely pay a good deal of money to get their hands on information like that.

TIP

In October 2000, Microsoft fell victim to crackers via the Internet. Apparently, an employee opened an email that had an attached Trojan, which was then used by the attacker to gain entry into Microsoft's corporate network. Although Microsoft denies any damage was done, it is rumored that source code and other proprietary information was leaked and made public. You can read all about it at `http://www.abcnews.go.com/sections/tech/DailyNews/microsoft_hacked001027.html`.

It should also be mentioned that it is possible to make yourself a target just by participating in the use of a popular network service, such as IRC (Internet Relay Chat). IRC is often the home base and the battlefield for many cracking groups, large and small. IRC network operators often must go to great lengths to keep abuse on their systems to a minimum. In retaliation, the attackers target the IRC service providers and innocent users of the service. As of late, the IRC network Undernet, one of the largest free IRC services worldwide, has been the victim of continual assaults. These have escalated to the point that the service operators are ready to pull the plug permanently.

TIP

More information about the January 2001 Undernet IRC attacks can be found at `http://www.` `newsfactor.com/perl/story/6655.html`.

Dial-Up Versus Persistent Connections

How you make your connection to the Internet plays a significant role in how easy it is to find and target you, and there are trade-offs for each method. The most popular connection methods include dial-up connections, modems or ISDN, or persistent "always-on" connections, such as a cable modem, leased line, or any type of digital subscriber line (DSL).

When you use a modem to connect to an Internet service provider (ISP), you typically dial into a modem bank at the ISP, and its systems pick an IP address for you from a pool of addresses assigned to it. This address is required to make a TCP/IP connection and is unique for every host connecting to the Internet. The immediate benefit of this is that, every time you dial up and connect to the Internet, you have a different IP address, and this makes specifically targeting you a lot more difficult. On the downside, a dial-up connection is slow, unreliable, and in most cases, extremely vulnerable to denial-of-service attacks, as you will see later in this chapter.

Dial-up connections are becoming less common. With cable modems, DSL, and other high-speed Internet access technologies, anyone from almost anywhere can enjoy a very fast and considerably stable Internet connection. In most cases, these connections are considered "always-on," which indicates that every time your computer is turned on, it is connected to the Internet. This is great for end-user convenience. I certainly enjoy being able to sit down and get to work online immediately. This also puts you at considerable risk for an Internet attacker to target you and attempt to break into your machine or take it offline. Some always-on connections assign you a static IP address. This is really nice for people who need to be able to connect to their computer remotely, but it also makes it really easy for your machine to be found on the Internet. It also helps make it easy to find you again later on, if the attacker decides she isn't through with you. Even if you don't have a static IP address, an always-on connection usually does not change its address often enough to be hard to find.

Which Computer Operating Systems Are Vulnerable?

Everyone that uses a computer for anything will eventually find an operating system that they are most comfortable with and that they most enjoy using. The average computer user rarely uses system security as a basis from which to make this choice. These users are typically drawn to a particular interface or by the available applications for the operating system. Even when security is an issue, many people are led to believe that their OS of choice is somehow more secure than another. The truth is simply that every operating system is vulnerable in one way or another. Computer users will stubbornly defend their OS over another and most often bash the other systems available, especially where it concerns system security. It doesn't matter whether you run Windows, Linux, or any other operating system. You are potentially vulnerable.

There are operating systems that are designed to be secure. For example, OpenBSD is an operating system built from the ground up to be the most secure operating system available. OpenBSD has had relatively few remote exploits. Even with this record, it has had several locally exploitable vulnerabilities.

Windows users are often the target of verbal abuse and ridicule by security professionals, script kiddies, and crackers alike. Many Windows users have been driven into some sort of security paranoia, believing that people can connect to their computers, get inside, and wreak all kinds of havoc. In most cases, this is simply not true.

Before the Windows users break out the champagne, let me bring you back down to earth. As soon as you set up any type of network connection under Windows, you are throwing the doors wide open. Windows will install several unnecessary components, along with a network adapter or a dial-up configuration. Services such as file and print sharing, and in some cases, Internet connection sharing, are activated without the end user being made aware of it. Some may argue whether these services are needed, but for a standalone Internet connection, they just aren't needed.

Windows users also suffer from other glaring security problems that don't even exist on other systems. Viruses, malicious scripts, Trojans, and back doors, plus a weak TCP/IP stack implementation, make Windows extremely vulnerable to a wide variety of attacks. Also, Windows often installs file and print sharing over TCP/IP and NetBIOS along with its other networking components, even when you are only a dial-up user. In a normal network environment, this allows Windows users to share files and printers with other people on the same network. Many people might never use or need this feature, and they don't disable it. This can be an open door for anyone on the Internet to access the system and do his dirty work.

Some people might not consider Unix variants such as Linux, FreeBSD, NetBSD, OpenBSD—operating systems more commonly found in servers—as desktop operating systems, but they are gaining acceptance rapidly in this area. Out of the box, Unix systems come with all sorts of services installed, such as Telnet, FTP, and httpd (Web server service), including easily exploitable legacy daemons. It is up to you as an end user to assess security after the installation and make necessary changes.

Macintosh and the Mac OS are not as popular as they were back in the mid-1980s, but they are still widely used, and Mac users are just as stubborn when defending the Mac OS. The Mac OS has grown up into a very robust and powerful operating system, especially since OS X is a version of Unix. Of course, it, too, has its vulnerabilities. Macs can fall victim to viruses just as easily as any Windows system. Depending on your version of the Mac OS, you can also be targeted because of weaknesses in Apple's Web sharing and file sharing. Unless absolutely needed, these features should be permanently disabled.

My Firewall Will Stop the Pesky Crackers!

The biggest craze in protection from attack has got to be the firewall. A hardware firewall is a device that sits between your computer(s) and another network, such as the Internet, and can be configured to block access to services and data inside the firewall. A personal (software) firewall runs on your computer and protects only your computer by blocking access. A properly configured firewall is a great tool for defending your assets from remote attack. It is not, however, the end-all solution. A firewall also allows traffic to come through, and because of this, the hole is not completely plugged. Many firewalls also give you the option of setting up service proxies, which gives the user the ability to allow a dangerous service through, but only through a *protected* proxy.

Recently, I did a security audit for clients who were using a high-end commercial grade firewall. They had left a Telnet proxy service running, and through it, I was able to penetrate and map their entire network, using the firewall as my point of access. This service allows people to use a simple network Telnet client to pass directly though the firewall without authentication. The people using the system had not correctly configured the firewall, and by doing so, made it easy for anyone outside to get in. Most people don't realize that proper security requires more than just a fancy firewall. With the increase of email–based viruses, Trojans, and malicious scripts, firewalls are becoming less effective. The ffirewall would correctly permit the email traffic to come in, but by the time anything dangerous is detected, it could be too late. For more information, see Chapter 10, "Firewalls."

What Kinds of Attackers Exist?

There are as many definitions out there for network attackers as there are for attacks. Most commonly, you will hear people refer to these individuals as hackers, crackers, script kiddies, black and white hats, and many other names. I will touch on the most common types here.

Script Kiddies—Your Biggest Threat?

The most common and prolific type of attacker today is the script kiddie. These people get their name from the simple fact that they are most often young, unskilled crackers who find and use scripts and utilities other skilled attackers have written and released free to anyone on the Internet. Mom and Dad got the kiddies an AOL account, and the first keyword they went looking for on a search engine was *hacking*. With all the glorification of hacking in the media and on the Internet, and the relative safety of perpetrating this type of crime, young people are easily lured to this dark underworld. There are thousands of Web sites with material and information to get the young, enterprising cracker started.

Often, many of the attacks proliferated by script kiddies are unsuccessful, or perhaps just mildly annoying to the victim. However, because of their relentless persistence, they will and often do eventually find systems they can break into, damage, and use to attack other computers. There is no love in the security community for this type of cracker. Script kiddies are more likely to attack systems and maliciously damage data than any other type of cracker. Even professional crackers speak about this group with ill will.

Black Hats—"The Dark Side"

Black hats are generally considered "The Dark Side" of the hacking community. These people are generally highly skilled with computers, programming, and network security and administration. They are the crackers who rarely get caught, who take their time and target specific systems for specific reasons. Often, these are the people who discover the vulnerabilities you and I read about, and they often will code the exploit that allows the system to be attacked or penetrated (which eventually fall into the hands of the script kiddies, who use them against other unsuspecting victims).

Black hat crackers do not often talk about or boast about their skills or activities. They are generally secretive in nature. I have heard some people refer to them as the Ninja of the Internet. Black hat groups often hold cracking conferences, such as DEFCON, where they get together to share and learn from each other. A lot of security professionals love to attend these conferences also, as does the FBI. Not surprisingly, the crackers don't use their real names at these events.

White Hats—The Good Guys

On the other end of the spectrum are the white hat hackers. These are often security professionals who work very hard to help test and make available security patches, information, and software to the user community to help users become more secure. Often, companies call on white hats to help test and implement security or to help improve it. Some white hats got their start in the security community as black hat crackers. For whatever reason, they decided to put their skills to use to help others with system security. A lot of these people have started and continue to run professional security companies.

Operating Systems Used by Crackers

As I mentioned earlier, everyone that uses computers will most likely develop a preference for a particular operating system. In my opinion, you should use what works best for you. There are arguments good and bad for any system you might be interested in using. Here, I will explain why crackers choose to use a particular operating system. In Part V, "Architecture, Platforms, and Security," you will learn more about specific platform vulnerabilities.

Windows Operating Systems

Windows is the most popular operating system available these days. It is easy to use and is installed on the majority of systems shipped in the world. Windows has been translated to multiple languages and is run by users all over the world. It certainly doesn't appeal to most users as a cracker OS, but it does get used in this arena. In most cases, script kiddie crackers use the Windows operating system. There are many cracking utilities and such written for the Windows environment. These prepackaged apps generally are not powerful enough to penetrate most systems. Most of these utilities are for mail bombing, denial of service, port scanning, and IRC (Internet Relay Chat) user attacks. Windows is of limited use to intelligent attackers, and therefore, I only reference it briefly.

Linux/NetBSD/FreeBSD

The open source software movement has given the Internet community and computer users everywhere a plethora of robust and reliable operating systems. The most common ones you will hear of or use are Linux, FreeBSD, or NetBSD, which are popular with both the cracking underground and security professionals alike.

Open source operating systems are very popular simply because they are open source. This means that the end user has full access to the source code of the entire operating system. This allows the user to learn and understand how the system works, how to make it secure, and how to exploit its weaknesses on other computers. Another benefit of open source is the speed of patch releases. In most cases, the moment a security issue is released relating to an open source operating system, it will typically be fixed and patched within an hour or less of the initial announcement. This allows the end user to maintain every aspect of system security, including the ability to patch the operating system when necessary. Most crackers using open source operating systems such as Linux learned security exploitation techniques while securing and maintaining their own systems.

Another benefit of an open source OS is that the cracker has full access to the network protocol stacks and can manipulate packets easily and efficiently when required. This allows the user to craft very specific exploits that rely on very specific weaknesses in other systems. Most open source operating systems come with a free compiler such as gcc, which allows users to write their own code, compile it, and distribute it all over the Internet. gcc is one of the most powerful C/C++ compilers out there, and it is completely free and has been ported to several platforms.

Many of the best utilities exist and are available free for open source operating systems. Tools for scanning, packet capture and analysis, security auditing, and other related programs have been written directly for these operating systems and are not available in most cases for Windows- or Macintosh-based operating systems.

Another attraction in using open source operating systems is attitude and the perception of others. People who have never become familiar with a POSIX-compliant operating system, such as Linux or FreeBSD, are often intimidated by their complexity. Computer users taking the initiative to learn a powerful operating system such as Linux are usually looked on with respect by those afraid to venture into this territory.

OpenBSD

OpenBSD is billed as the most secure operating system freely available to anyone outside of government agencies. OpenBSD is a BSD-based (Berkeley Software Design), free, and secure version of the Unix operating system. As I mentioned earlier, this OS has a long history of excellent security, and because of this, makes an ideal operating system for a cracker. Any cracker worth his salt in the cracking community also needs to maintain his own high system security. What better operating system to use than the one with best record of security? Also, OpenBSD is completely open source, giving the same benefits I listed for Linux, NetBSD, and FreeBSD. The same utilities for those operating systems compile and run just fine in OpenBSD as well. OpenBSD will also run Linux, FreeBSD, and NetBSD software, if the need arises. If you want to be as secure as possible, out-of-the-box OpenBSD wins hands down.

Is There a Typical Attack?

When it comes to being a victim of a network attack, I don't think any one incident can be described as typical. No matter the scale of the attack, being a cracker's victim is a very infuriating experience. It can feel as much of a violation as having your home broken into and robbed. There are several common attacks that anyone can experience at any time. Attacks that an average user is most likely to face in everyday computer use include denial-of-service, viruses, malicious scripts or Trojans, or Web site defacement. We'll explore each of these in the following sections. (You'll also learn more about these types of attacks in Part IV, "Weapons of Mass Destruction.") We'll also briefly look at insider attacks.

Denial-of-Service Attacks

A denial-of-service attack is the intentional overload of a network service or connection with excessive or disruptive data that causes the connection or service to fail. In the late 1990s and early 2000s, many well-known, Web-based companies and services fell victim to this type of attack. The attackers used what is now termed *distributed denial-of-service (DDoS) attacks*, wherein multiple coordinated machines are used in tandem to launch a denial-of-service attack against a host or network.

Depending on the speed of your Internet connection, you might be more susceptible than others. Because a denial-of-service attack relies on overloading the remote network connection, the slower the victim's connection, the more likely it is that it can be taken offline. For example, a 56Kbs modem is an easy target for denial of service. When enough data is slammed against such a weak connection, normal network traffic cannot flow properly, often causing serious connection lag and finally disconnection.

One of the biggest problems with this type of attack is the difficulty in tracking and stopping the people perpetrating them. In the case of a DDoS attack, it becomes infinitely harder to determine who is attacking you as the number of machines in the attack multiply. Also, there currently aren't many solutions to warding off this type of attack. Most companies with Internet access only host one route of access to the Internet. When enough data is thrown against this connection for an extended period of time, eventually the connection or the system hosting the connection will fail.

Usually, this type of attack does not direct damage to the affected systems. However, if this is successful against a company that relies on customers visiting its site from the Internet, there is the obvious possibility of financial loss because of downtime, customer and staff frustration, and recovery costs.

Viruses, Trojans, and Malicious Scripts or Web Content

Almost everyone knows about computer viruses. They have been in existence nearly as long as computers and operating systems. A *virus* is a small piece of software that is designed to replicate and spread itself from one system to the next. Most known viruses are not malicious in nature. They are generally more annoying than malicious. There are some very dangerous computer viruses in existence, but you are not as likely to come across many of these. In fact, the name *virus* is now being used to categorize malicious scripts, also.

These scripts, often coded in Microsoft Visual Basic, propagate from machine to machine via email, or they are sometimes embedded in a Web site. When the unsuspecting visitor loads the page, the script loads and installs somewhere on the host machine without the user knowing. From there, it will usually replicate, drop its payload, and then try to email everyone in your email address book. Many of these viruses will automatically send everyone listed there a copy of the virus without your control or knowledge. The person receiving this will think it came legitimately from someone they know and trust, open the attachment, and start the process all over again.

In the Internet age, email is the primary distribution method for malicious viruses and scripts. Outlook and Outlook Express (Microsoft email clients) are the systems most vulnerable to this type of virus or script transmission mechanism. The best practice is to use a safe email client and be suspicious of *any* email attachment.

Back Orifice is a Trojan (for more on Trojan programs, see Chapter 18, "Trojans") that has created quite a bit of controversy around the Net. Written and maintained by the Cult of the Dead Cow cracking group, Back Orifice demonstrated the weaknesses of Microsoft operating systems security. When it is installed on a machine, it hides itself and its process so that the host has no idea it is running there. When it is running, the attacker just needs to run the client program and connect to the affected machine to have complete control and access to everything on the machine. You can easily see the problems that this would present. Back Orifice is often designed to seem like an innocuous piece of friendly software that a computer user could download from the Internet or receive as an email attachment. Thinking it is safe to run, the user executes the program, and it installs Back Orifice (or some other Trojan) quietly in the background while the user is distracted by some sort of cute or interesting front end.

NOTE

Most known viruses and Trojans only affect Windows or Macintosh operating systems. This is due mostly to the nature of these systems. Security is often an afterthought in most consumer operating systems. Consumer operating systems like Windows 98 and Me do not employ filesystem- and kernel-level process security, so a virus or a Trojan can easily run freely through the system, doing anything it wants.

Web Defacement/"Tagging"

Web defacement is the electronic equivalent of spray-painted graffiti. Although this type of attack isn't usually damaging, it can be frustrating and embarrassing. If you run a high traffic Web site, and a cracker comes along and "tags" it with erroneous, belittling, or socially unacceptable content, people visiting your site will see the tag, too. If you are running a business at the site, your customers might question the integrity of your systems and go somewhere else. Obviously this could constitute a considerable loss to the business that is targeted by this attack.

Web defacement is growing in popularity, especially by small groups or cliques of crackers. It is very similar to gang behavior in most modern cities, except instead of guns and spray paint, crackers use security exploits and Web tagging to harass victims. Many times, the tag left is a greeting to fellow crackers, friends, and often a note to the system administrator telling him to tighten security. I have even seen defacements where the attacker leaves his email address, inviting the admin to contact him to discuss the weakness in his systems.

Also, political activists (often called *hacktivists*) have gotten into the act as well. They will deface the site of their main opponent in many cases. The most recent well-known example was against the RIAA (Recording Industry Association of American) in August 2002. You can see the defacement at `http://defaced.alldas.org/mirror/2002/08/28/www.riaa.org/storymain.html`.

TIP

If you are interested in seeing more examples of Web site defacement, you can check out `http://zone-h.org/en/defacements`. This site includes the actual defacement and the operating system of the affected Web server.

Attacks from the Inside

Most people, especially home Internet users, will never experience or need to worry about internal attack. However, it occurs more commonly than any successful remote exploit that exists. This is often simply because the person responsible already has access, either physically or from across your network, to the targets she has chosen to attack.

Also, it takes a lot less work to perpetrate an internal attack. The attacker already knows plenty about the systems and software in place, making it that much easier to thwart security and cause problems. This method is obviously most common in an office or corporate environment. For whatever reasons, most administrators in this type of environment fail to realize the dangers or take precautions against this all too common scenario.

Who Gets Targeted Most Frequently?

As mentioned before, there is nothing typical when it comes to having network security compromised and being attacked. With the large number of systems on the Internet, there is no end of potential targets or victims available. There are, however, computers or systems more likely to be attacked than others, and the methods and motivation vary greatly. We'll take a look at motivation later in this chapter. Let's examine the most commonly attacked Internet targets. Hopefully, as we go along, it will become clearer to you why these targets are singled out.

Home and Small Business Internet Users

Home and small business users are just as vulnerable as any large scale dot-com. The biggest difference is that they are more likely to suffer from denial-of-service or virus-type attacks.

The number of home and small business users with always-on connections has increased exponentially in recent years, adding to the probability of attack. Also, for this group of users, Internet or system security is routinely not an issue. Most small businesses do not employ a system administrator, nor can they afford to hire a security professional to address these issues. Home users generally fall into the casual computer users category, with little or no experience in computer security issues. Most home users feel relatively safe running an outdated virus scanner or installing a personal firewall, which seems to be all the rage lately.

Larger Businesses and Corporations

In recent history, are several prominent companies have had their system security attacked in one way or another. Companies such as Yahoo!, eBay, Nike, and Microsoft have been victimized by intrusions, denial of service, Web defacement, and theft of customer and credit card information. If companies like these are vulnerable, why do so many of us believe we are somehow immune? Several well-known network security companies have also been attacked, with varying degrees of success. Almost every day, you can read about another company falling prey to crackers.

Government and Military Institutions

Believe it or not, the computer systems of government and military institutions—no matter what nationality—are some of the most popular cracker targets anywhere. These are high profile systems, and because of that, any attacker going after them faces considerable risk in doing so. In the United States, it is a federal crime to tamper with or attempt to access information systems of the U.S. government or military. Also, these are some of the best-protected systems on the planet. The U.S. Department of Defense logs thousands of attacks on its systems daily. Interestingly, some such attacks actually are successful and undetected, and in some cases, classified material has been stolen, or government Web sites have been defaced. Many attacks against government computers often originate from another country, making it more difficult to find and prosecute anyone involved.

The governments and militaries of various countries pay crackers to attack the sites of other countries. The famous book *Cuckoo's Egg* by Clifford Stoll (Pocket Books) documents the story of tracking down crackers who were being paid by the KGB to crack and steal information.

Financial Institutions

When it comes to picking a target, selecting a financial institution makes more sense to me than most any other objective. I can understand someone wanting to profit from their cracking work a lot more than I can make any sense of someone wanting to cause a remote user to disconnect.

It should be noted right off that banks and other financial institutions often employ some of the best network security in the world. Financial institutions rely heavily on computer equipment and networks to manage finance and transfer money electronically from one institution to the next. Security can never be an afterthought. When someone's money is at stake, as well as the institution's reputation, banks spare no expense making sure that everything is as safe and cracker-proof as possible. This doesn't mean that they have not fallen victim; they certainly have on several occasions. Financial institutions realized the need for expert security long before computers and networks came along. It is no surprise then that they work so hard to protect the financial assets of their customers.

NOTE

The majority of cracks against banks and other financial institutions are inside jobs. Because of the amount of security in place, these too are rarely successful, and the crook ends up vacationing in a federal prison.

What Is the Motivation Behind Attacks?

By now, you might be asking yourself why people do these things to begin with. What is the motivation? As with any form of crime, the attacker is meeting his own needs, for whatever reason, and the motivation varies. There are no doubt thrills associated with breaking into and gaining complete access to others' computer systems. Those who get caught often state that this rush alone is motivation enough. For now, we will take a look at the following motivations:

- Notoriety
- Maliciousness or destruction
- Making a political statement
- Financial gain and theft
- Knowledge

Notoriety, or the "Elite" Factor

Probably more common than any other motivating factor for cyber attacks is simply becoming notorious in the cracking community. This is most common with script kiddies and unskilled crackers who want to be the next Kevin Mitnick. Unfortunately, it seems that even with all the publicity of the consequences, crackers still can't seem to stop cracking into vulnerable systems. For whatever reason, they seek fame from perpetrating some of the most ridiculous and pointless computer crimes known today. In most cases, you can find these people hanging out in obscure channels on IRC bragging to other script kiddies about how elite they are ("3l33t" in script kiddy parlance). Most of these individuals are young teenage boys with a computer, an Internet connection, and far too much free time on their hands.

On a positive note, many of them are skilled computer users, and they eventually grow out of being pranksters to become excellent security professionals in the white hat community. As you probably already guessed, those drawn to "The Dark Side" end up very differently indeed. Notoriety or hacker "brand-name" recognition only take you so far.

TIP

Kevin Mitnick is a well-known cracker who, in the early 1990s, was charged with 25 counts of federal computer and wire fraud violations. He spent nearly five years in federal prison, is not allowed to use a computer until January 20, 2003, and has amassed quite a following around the world. For more information, check out http://www.kevinmitnick.com. However, please note that this site is pro-Kevin Mitnick. Most people I know feel that he got what he deserved.

Maliciousness and Destruction

Most people would assume that the majority of cracking attempts are destructive in nature, but this is rarely accurate. Depending on the degree of the damage, it might be merely annoying or a complete loss. We'll take a look at a couple of common examples.

Destructive Pranks or Lack of Cause

Some people are just outright malicious. Some crackers are this way, too. They enjoy damaging or destroying things that do not belong to them. They could be best related to someone who randomly throws rocks through windows or sets buildings on fire. Often, the reasons don't make sense, or there is no obvious cause-and-effect relationship. The attacker was merely venting his anger, rage, or frustration on someone completely innocent. When similar attackers gain access to a computer, they will plant destructive viruses, delete important system files or personal documents, or just completely wipe the system's hard drive clean, rendering it useless. If the owner doesn't routinely back up his data, the loss can be severe.

Disgruntled Employees

Another type of person you don't want to confront at all is a disgruntled employee. Although most people deal with on-the-job anger and frustration in a constructive and mature manner, there are those people who only know how to lash out when they are set off. If the company they work for relies heavily on computers, the computers likely will be used to vent the angry employee's frustration. I already covered insider attacks briefly in this chapter, but it gets much worse when the attacker also has a personal vendetta against the company for which she works. This can result in considerable loss for the company. These days, most companies using computers also have a security policy in place, which outlines the consequences employees might face if they violate system security in any manner. Employees are routinely required to sign and agree to such policies as a condition of their employment. When anger is present, these policies naturally slip the mind of the angry worker as he systematically goes about destroying the data of his employer. I'll also revisit this charming individual in a moment when I discuss financial motivations for attacks.

Making a Political Statement

Earlier we looked at any government being a potential target for computer attack. In many cases, the reason is simply political. Often these attacks come from outside the country that is being victimized, but they also originate quite frequently from citizens of that country. Recently, many small countries in Europe and in third-world areas have been targeted over the Internet in a rash of political attacks on various governments, leaders, and military forces. During the war in Serbia, several small groups from all over the world launched cracking attacks on Serbian computer networks. Most of these failed, largely because the communication systems of that country were quickly cut off as a result of the fighting. Israel and Palestine hacktivists have been engaging each other in a long "cyber battle" for several months. China has also fallen victim to computer crackers, mostly because of its stance on human rights issues. Chinese hacktivists struck back in 2001 by defacing U.S. Web sites after the spy plane incident. Al-Qaeda was training people for cyber warfare as well, though little seems to have come of it. The new soldier is a computer with an Internet connection, and the new battlefield is cyberspace. Wars are being fought there that could potentially become as serious as a real war, if a country's infrastructure is targeted.

Financial Gain

Everybody wants more money, right? Why should crackers be any different? The digital thieves of the twenty-first century are quickly becoming the most elusive and daunting criminals in the world. The world's vast computer network is synonymous to the wild west enterprises of nineteenth century North America. With so much electronic wealth flowing from one computer to the next, it was only a matter of time before shady characters started finding ways to dip their greedy fingers into the Internet goldmine.

As stated earlier, companies dealing with finance or money in any way rely heavily on computer systems to remain in the business. Now, their customers expect that they can also access this same data from the comfort of their home via the Internet. Most banks now allow full account control from a Web browser over the Internet.

Thousands of companies have moved their ordering and inventory systems online so that anyone can purchase these products with nothing more than a computer, an Internet connection, and a credit card number. All of this has come into existence only within the last few years, and as such, the technology and standards driving e-commerce are far from mature or secure. It really is a cracker's goldmine out there, if he knows where to look. The following sections look at the most common issues.

Theft or Unauthorized Transfer of Funds

Money zips all over the world electronically 24 hours a day. The digital economy is booming, but it's also fragile and prone to criminals, just as any bank would be. It also seems a lot easier and safer to rob a bank with a computer than with a gun. Before the Internet existed, stealing from the electronic money stream did happen, most often by an employee with access to the proper systems. In nearly every case I have ever read about, the thief simply set up some sort of dummy account and set up a process to transfer a portion of the e-money into the dummy account. After doing this for some period of time, the money would be withdrawn or transferred again to an accessible account. This type of theft has been very successful in many cases. Depending on how it is perpetrated, the victims often don't detect the loss of funds for some time, and usually by then it is too late. The banks have to cover such losses through insurance, the cost of which eventually trickles down to honest consumers. With the Internet, a whole new set of possibilities for theft exists. There have been cases of these illegal transfers taking place across international borders, making it difficult to ever recover the stolen funds or prosecute the crook responsible.

TIP

Read more about "How to Hack a Bank" by David H. Freedman at http://www.forbes.com/asap/2000/0403/056.html. Mr. Freedman cites a noteworthy example of a 24-year-old programmer in Russia who nailed Citibank for $10 million electronically. He is now serving time in the United States.

Theft of Intellectual Property and Corporate Espionage

A more common, and often undetected, crime occurs every day at companies around the world. With so much money invested in storing important company data on computers, it's easy to see why eventually stealing it and selling it to the competition has become big business. Employees of the target company generally commit this type of computer crime. In some cases, the competition will employ shady characters to penetrate and steal vital trade secrets and other company data. Using this information, they can beat their competition and possibly make a lot of money in the process. With everyone being networked over the Internet these days, imagine how much easier this is. Because most company data is now stored in digital form, all it takes is a simple file transfer or an email, and that company's hard-earned intellectual property has been smuggled undetected to the outside world.

Software companies are particularly susceptible to this. Many software companies put millions of dollars into designing top-of-the-line software packages for other companies to buy. These packages often cost anywhere from a few hundred to several hundred thousand dollars to purchase. More often than not, however, someone inside leaks the software out to the Internet *warez* (pirated software) community, and within a few hours, it can spread around the world. Although most of the people that pirate this software do not profit from its use or trade, it often ends up being used at companies where no legitimate license is owned. By this, the company can potentially make money using a product it never paid for, which takes money from the pockets of the software company that initially publishes it.

The Internet piracy community spans the globe. One merely has to enter *warez* in one's favorite search engine and click on some of the results. WARNING: Several of these sites contain nothing more than banner ads to pornography Web sites and other offensive material.

TIP

The Internet is littered with warez groups, Web sites, and pirated software. Read more about piracy and how it might affect the Internet economy at
`http://www.findarticles.com/m0NEW/2000_April_6/61411395/p1/article.jhtml`.

Financial data kept by a company can also be worth the criminal act of stealing it and transferring it. Most notably, stock information, customer databases, and other financial records can be very valuable to the right people.

Credit Card Theft and "Carding"
Most everyone now uses the Internet as a place to buy and sell goods and services of every description. Most often, the transaction is paid for with a credit card. The company selling the products or services receives this credit card information and stores it somewhere electronically in order to maintain records and fulfill the customer's order. Most Web sites offering credit card transactions do so over SSL (Secure Sockets Layer.) This only encrypts the information being transferred between

the customer and the company. After the data is in the hands of the company, they can store it in any number of ways. Most often, this information is not stored securely and is compromised by crackers or criminal employees.

There have been a lot of credit card database thefts in the news lately. In a few cases, the company that had the credit card numbers stolen was storing them unencrypted on the Web server that they used to take the orders from! All the thief had to do was break in and steal a simple text file with all this customer information. It doesn't matter who you are, either. Bill Gates of Microsoft had his number pilfered on two separate occasions.

You might be wondering what good these credit card numbers are to someone other than the card owner. What many people don't understand is that credit card fraud is simple, it's easy, and it's very hard to catch the crook responsible. With the Internet, it has become a great deal easier to commit credit card fraud. Most businesses that accept credit cards numbers for payment do not require any type of verification that the person using the card number is who they say they are. All the thief needs to do is set up some sort of drop, go shopping, and then meet the deliveries at his drop and collect the goods.

With the Internet being so open and anonymous, it's not hard to take someone's number and go shopping in relative safety. Credit card companies are struggling to catch their breath with the rampant explosion of Internet fraud cases they endure daily. Most people also have credit cards that allow money withdrawals and transfer of funds, creating even more ways for a criminal to take advantage of them. Some people also pay criminals good money for credit card numbers, making it more lucrative than ever to commit fraud.

Cracking for Knowledge

We've covered a lot of reasons someone might be motivated to break into or crack computer systems. One reason that doesn't come up often is the simple pursuit of knowledge. Many crackers are driven by the challenge of figuring out how a system works, how to break into it, and how to make it more secure. For these individuals, it is not about being destructive or gaining notoriety—it is the thrill of the game. Breaking into a well-protected computer system is like an intense game of chess. It requires intelligence, a lot of abstract and forward thinking, and patience. Often, this type of cracker uses what he learns to be a better administrator or a better programmer. The things he can learn will often be shared with others in the community, furthering the collective knowledge base that is so critical to those that work in the field of information security.

There are also crackers who use the knowledge they gain to proliferate more attacks on other systems, for whatever reason. The information they glean from penetrating the barriers of other networks is often shared with like-minded people over the

Internet, thus propagating the problem. It is almost like a continuous game, one side against the other, trying to remain one step ahead of each other.

Breaking In to Break In

Right off, the phrase "breaking in to break in" might not make any sense to you at all, but it will. Many attackers crack systems for the sole purpose of having a compromised system from which to launch other attacks. This is beneficial in many ways, especially if the cracker has several systems through which she can chain connections, one machine to the next. Think of it as stringing popcorn on fishing line. If each piece of popcorn represents a compromised system, and the line is the network connection from one machine to the next, it is easy to visualize the benefits. The farther away the attacker is from his own home base, and the more machines he's running through to achieve this, the harder it will be for anyone to ever discover his true identity. Each machine the connection is chained through adds another degree of complexity when security managers try to backtrack to find the culprit. If the machines are in different countries, and if the connections cross international borders, traversing political and language barriers, it probably isn't even worth trying to track the cracker down at all. The most skilled attackers use methods such as this to keep their identity a complete secret. This helps keep them protected, and at the very least, buys them some time should anyone come looking for them.

Summary

This chapter explained in what ways and to whom you might be vulnerable as it pertains to network security. Obviously, there are countless variations and methods that can be used against you, but there are also technical limitations on how far and in what direction a security attack can go. This is the age of digital paranoia, and because of that, there are many doomsayers in the world. Whether it is for attention, or money, or both, many people that don't know what they are talking about spout ridiculous rumors and myths about using computers and the Internet.

As you have read, there are plenty of ways that you can be a victim of Internet security issues. You can be targeted. You can suffer frustration or data/financial loss. Your personal privacy can easily be violated.

You are also completely capable of defending yourself. The most important thing you can do is educate yourself on the risks and the steps that are necessary to combat the hackers and crackers effectively. It is just as important to know what threats don't concern you or your personal or system security and also when someone is trying to con you.

As with any other problem in the world, ignoring security issues will not make them go away. Using a computer now carries with it some personal responsibility. You are the only one who can take these matters into your own hands to protect yourself. This doesn't mean you need to mortgage your house to buy a top-of-the-line firewall to protect your cable modem or DSL line. By taking a proactive stance about your computer security and remaining current on the latest issues, you can stay one step ahead of those who might want to do you harm.

PART III

A Defender's Toolkit

IN THIS PART

10

Firewalls

Security is a process, not a product.

—Bruce Schneier, Counterpane Labs

Firewalls have been around for years, and now serve as pillars for the information security strategies of most organizations. Although firewalls are fundamentally very important, any organization that relies entirely upon a firewall to fulfill its security needs does so foolishly. Firewalls are not bulletproof. In fact, recently many of the most popular firewall platforms have fallen victim to some of the problems that have long plagued operating systems and applications. Buyers, beware!

Although parts of this chapter will be familiar territory to veteran administrators, some of the material presented here might be new ground. We will investigate what firewalls are, what they do, and more importantly, what they do *not* do. At the end of this chapter, you'll understand the basics of firewalling, where and why it can be useful, how to do further research on the subject, and where the "We have a firewall—we are safe" philosophy falls flat on its face.

What Is a Firewall?

A *firewall* is any device used as a network-level access control mechanism for a particular network or set of networks. In most cases, firewalls are used to prevent outsiders from accessing an internal network. However, firewalls can also be used to create more secure pockets within internal LANs for highly sensitive functions such as payroll, payment processing, and R&D systems. They are not limited to perimeter use exclusively. The firewall devices themselves are typically standalone computers, routers, or firewall "appliances." Firewall appliances are usually proprietary hardware devices, often running a custom or proprietary OS. The Cisco PIX series is a good example of a firewall appliance.

Firewalls are designed to serve as control points to and from your network. They evaluate connection requests as they are received. Firewalls check whether or not the network traffic should be allowed, based on a predefined set of rules or "policies." Only connection requests from authorized hosts to authorized destinations are processed; the remaining connection requests are discarded.

NOTE

As high-speed residential Internet service continues to make its way into the world, organizations will be forced to face the growing issues surrounding the remote user. Security officers should begin looking at the adoption of "personal firewalls" now, to help address this growing threat. Although they are relatively new, products by McAfee, InfoExpress, F-Secure, and other vendors will become more critical in defending external assets. VPN access is another choice for remote users.

Most firewalls accomplish this by screening the source and destination addresses along with port numbers. For example, if you don't want folks from `www.samspublishing.com` connecting to your FTP site (via FTP), you can bar their access by blocking connection requests from `206.246.131.227` to your FTP site's address (`ftp.yoursite.example`) on port 21. On their end, the `samspublishing.com` folks see a message that reports "Connection Refused" or something similar (or they might receive no notice at all; their connection attempts might simply be blocked).

Other Features Found in Firewall Products

Firewalls can analyze incoming packets of various protocols. Based upon that analysis, a firewall can undertake various actions. Firewalls are therefore capable of performing conditional evaluations ("If this type of packet is encountered, I will do this").

These conditional constructs are called *rules*. Generally, when you erect a firewall, you furnish it with rules that mirror access policies in your own organization. For example, suppose you had both accounting and sales departments. Company policy demands that only the sales department should have access to your FTP site. To enforce this policy, you provide your firewall with a rule; in this case, the rule is that connection requests from the accounting department to your FTP site are denied.

In this respect, firewalls are to networks what user privilege schemes are to operating systems. For example, Windows NT enables you to specify which users can access a given file or directory. This is discretionary access control at the operating-system level. Similarly, firewalls enable you to apply such access control to your networked workstations and your Web site.

However, access screening is only a part of what modern firewalls can do. In recent years, firewall vendors have begun implementing the "kitchen sink" approach to feature development—that is, many vendors have been tossing every feature BUT the kitchen sink into their firewall offerings. Some of the added features include

- Content filtering—Some organizations want to stop their users from browsing particular Web sites: Web-based email sites, "underground" sites, day trading gateways, sites with pornography, and so on. Content filtering features and services can help block these sites, as well as protect against some types of ActiveX and Java-based hostile code and applets. Finally, content filtering can do some antivirus screening, though it's still a good idea to have an antivirus product on PCs and email servers.

- Virtual Private Networking (VPN)—VPNs are used to tunnel traffic securely from Point A to Point B, usually over hostile networks (such as the Internet). Although there is a wide range of dedicated VPN appliances on the market today, vendors such as Checkpoint and Cisco have rolled VPN services into their firewall offerings. Many firewall products now offer both client-to-enterprise VPN functionality, as well as LAN-to-LAN functionality.

- Network Address Translation (NAT)—Network address translation is often used for mapping illegal or reserved address blocks (see RFC 1918) to valid ones (for example, mapping `10.0.100.3` to `206.246.131.227`). Although NAT isn't necessarily a security feature, the first NAT devices to show up in corporate environments are usually firewall products.

- Load balancing—More of a generic term then anything else, load balancing is the art of segmenting traffic in a distributed manner. Although firewall load balancing is one thing, some firewall products are now supporting features that will help you direct Web and FTP traffic in a distributed manner.

- Fault tolerance—Some of the higher-end firewalls like the Cisco PIX and the Nokia/Checkpoint combination support some fairly intricate fail-over features. Often referred to as High-Availability (HA) functionality, advanced fault-tolerance features often allow firewalls to be run in pairs, with one device functioning as a "hot standby" should the other one fail.

- Intrusion detection—The term *intrusion detection* can mean many things, but in this case, some vendors are beginning to integrate an entirely different product type with their firewall offering. Although this doesn't create a problem in itself, people should be wary of the kind of workload this might impose on their firewall. Also, it creates a single point of failure from a security point of view.

Although the thought of managing all these features from within a single box or product can be appealing, one should approach the kitchen sink mentality with a fair amount of skepticism. Firewalls have always been viewed as playing pivotal roles in organizational security models. Borrowing from the KISS (Keep It Simple, Stupid) principle that is held so dear in the network administration world, we could suggest that going the route of feature bloat might not be the smartest thing to do when it comes to a security product. But we need not speculate on this—the latest round of firewall vulnerabilities have confirmed our suspicions for us. Read on.

Firewalls Are Not Bulletproof

Although vendors like to think their firewall products are immune to the problems that plague operating system and application developers, the fact of the matter is that they are every bit as vulnerable. Consider a sample of some of the issues that have crept up in firewall products:

- July 2000: During the Black Hat briefings, two well-known security researchers, John McDonald and Thomas Lopatic, reported a number of vulnerabilities they found in Checkpoint's Firewall-1 product. (See it at `http://www.dataprotect.com/bh2000/blackhat-fw1.html`.) This was significant, as Checkpoint's product is one of the most widely deployed firewalls in the world.

- June 2001: Cisco IOS was found to have a security hole whereby a cracker could execute privileged commands via the built-in HHTP server. Read more at `http://www.cisco.com/warp/public/707/IOS-httplevel-pub.html`.

- July 2001: Check Point Firewall-1 and VPN-1 had a vulnerability in which crackers could pass their traffic into and out of networks when they should not have been able to. Find out more at `http://www.computerworld.com/security-topics/security/firewall/story/0,10801,62218,00.html`.

- October 2001: Cisco had to replace many PIX firewalls at customer sites because they would hang or shutdown because of hardware flaws. Have a look at `http://www.computerworld.com/securitytopics/security/firewall/story/0,10801,65363,00.html`.

- August 2002: Symantec's Raptor firewall had a problem in which a cracker could hijack sessions passing through the firewall. Read more about it at `http://www.eweek.com/article2/0,3959,436818,00.asp`.

This list is by no means conclusive—it's simply a taste of some of the recent problems discovered in today's firewall products. Also, consider that the some of these issues are *directly* related to non-core functionalities found in firewall products that the vendors have added: content filtering and encapsulation (for VPN use).

It remains to be seen whether the firewall vendors will treat security considerations equally with that of feature additions. However, to the vendors' credit, they claim that most of their clients aren't asking for more security, but rather more features. I present the question to the reader: What do you think is more important in your firewall? Do us all a favor—let your vendor know how you feel.

A Look Under the Hood of Firewalling Products

In the esoteric sense, components of a firewall exist in the mind of the person constructing them. A firewall, at its inception, is a concept rather than a product; it's the idea surrounding the access control mechanism that enables traffic to and from your network.

In the more general sense, a firewall consists of software and hardware. The software can be proprietary, shareware, or freeware. The hardware can be any hardware that supports the software.

Firewall technologies can generally be classified into one of three categories:

- Packet filter-based (usually routers, Cisco IOS, and so on)
- Stateful packet filter-based (Checkpoint FW-1, PIX, and so on)
- Proxy-based

Let's briefly examine each.

Packet Filter-Based Firewalls

Packet filtering firewalls are typically routers with packet-filtering capabilities. Using a basic packet-filtering router, you can grant or deny access to your site based on several variables, including

- Source address
- Destination address
- Protocol
- Port number

Router-based firewalls are popular because they're easily implemented. (You simply plug one in, provide an access control list, and you're done.) Moreover, routers offer an integrated solution. If your network is permanently connected to the Internet, you'll need a router anyway. So, why not kill two birds with one stone?

On the other hand, router-based firewalls have several deficiencies. First, they usually aren't prepared to handle certain types of denial-of-service attacks. Many of the denial-of-service tactics used on the Internet today are based on packet mangling, SYN flooding, or forcing other TCP/IP-based anomalies. Basic routers aren't designed for handling these types of attacks, though enterprise class routers can usually deal with them. Second, some low-end routers can't keep track of session state data though that is discussed more in the stateful section below. Administrators are then forced to keep all ports above 1024 open to handle TCP sessions and session negotiations properly. It's not generally a good practice to leave unused ports open to the outside.

Finally, using ACLs (access control lists) on high-end routers that are supporting extremely busy networks can contribute to performance degradation and higher CPU load. However, for most low-speed connections (such as T1 circuits) on lower-end routers (such as Cisco 2500 series routers), normal packet filtering will not tax the router to any significant degree.

NOTE

For a long time, it was believed that putting ACLs on routers would greatly degrade their performance. Although sticking a 100-rule ACL on a Cisco 7000 supporting a dozen ATM connections might not be the best of ideas, placing basic ACLs on routers supporting low-speed (10Mbps or lower) connections doesn't usually degrade their performance noticeably. Two members of the underground, rfp and NightAxis, published some basic findings on this subject that can be found at `http://packetstormsecurity.nl/papers/contest/RFP.txt`. Since then, other studies have also been performed (your mileage may vary). Remember, even the low-end Cisco 2500 series routers were based on Motorola 68030 and 68040 chip sets, and the newer ones are using even more advanced RISC-based chips. Routers are more powerful than many people give them credit for. Test it yourself—see what you find.

TIP

Many network administrators will use ACLs on their perimeter routers in conjunction with a more advanced firewall to create a multi-tier approach to network access control.

Personal Firewalls

Another type of packet filter firewall that has become popular over the past couple of years is the personal firewall. The personal firewall protects only one machine instead of a whole network. This makes it appropriate for home use, or even corporate environments, where certain machines need added security.

Personal firewalls are loaded on whatever computer is being protected, and the personal firewall software will then monitor all incoming connections. It will accept, reject, or ask the user to decide what to do.

Stateful Packet Filter-Based Firewalls

Stateful packet filtering builds on the packet filtering concept and takes it a few steps further. Firewalls built on this model keep track of sessions and connections in internal state tables, and can therefore react accordingly. These firewalls can detect anomalous situations that violate protocol standards that a plain packet filter cannot. This allows the stateful firewall to block attacks that a packet filter might miss. Because of this, stateful packet filtering-based products are more flexible than their pure packet filtering counterparts. In addition, most stateful packet filtering-based products are designed to protect against certain types of DoS attacks, and to add protection for SMTP-based mail and an assortment of other security-specific features.

Checkpoint pioneered the technique called *stateful inspection (SI)*, which takes stateful packet filtering up one notch. SI enables administrators to build firewall rules to examine the actual data payload, rather than just the addresses and ports.

> **NOTE**
>
> Because stateful packet filtering-based firewalls track session states, they can keep the ports above 1024 closed by default and only open the high ports on an as-needed basis. As simple as this might sound, this is why most administrators consider stateful packet filtering to be the minimum technology they will implement for their firewall solutions.

Proxy-Based Firewalls

Another type of firewall is the *proxy-based* firewall (sometimes referred to as an application gateway or application-proxy). When a remote user contacts a network running a proxy-based firewall, the firewall proxies the connection. With this technique, IP packets are not forwarded directly to the internal network. Instead, a type of translation occurs, with the firewall acting as the conduit and interpreter.

How does this differ from stateful packet filtering and generic packet filtering, you ask? Good question—and one that many people ask. Both packet filters and stateful filtering processes examine incoming and outgoing packets at the network levels (see Chapter 6, "A Brief TCP/IP Primer"). They examine IP source and destination addresses along with ports and status flags, compare them to their rulesets and table information, and then decide whether the packet should be forwarded. Proxy-based firewalls, on the other hand, inspect traffic at the application level in addition to lower levels. A packet comes into the firewall and is handed off to an application-specific proxy, which inspects the validity of the packet and application-level request itself. For example, if a Web request (HTTP) comes into a proxy-based firewall, the data payload containing the HTTP request will be handed to an HTTP-proxy process. An FTP request would be handed to an FTP-proxy process, Telnet to a Telnet proxy process, and so on.

This concept of a protocol-by-protocol approach is more secure then stateful and generic packet filtering because the firewall understands the application protocols themselves (HTTP, FTP, SMTP, POP, and so on). The firewall will reject anything that does not match the protocol specs. It's more difficult for intruders to sneak past something that is watching more than just the ports and IP addresses. However, notice that I used the word *concept* in reference to it being more secure. The truth of the matter is that in real-world applications, this approach has had its fair share of problems.

Proxy-based firewalls have always been slower than stateful packet-filtering-based ones. Now, for most networks (10Mbps or slower), this difference is moot. However, for heavily loaded networks (T3s at 45Mbps, multiple T3s approaching 100Mbps, and so on), this becomes a much larger issue. As technology improves, the gap might close, but for now the use of pure proxy-based technology is still a concern for high-volume networks.

In addition to the performance problem, the proxy-based solution also has some adaptability issues. Suppose for example that a new protocol is invented to manage your coffeemakers at home. We'll call this protocol the Percolation Control System, or PCS for short. Now, let's also assume that PCS uses TCP and runs over port 666. Administrators of stateful packet filtering-based firewalls will simply have to build a new rule into their firewall allowing traffic over TCP on port 666, and it's a done deal. Administrators of proxy-based firewalls, however, have a new problem: They don't have a proxy (yet) for PCS. It's a brand-new protocol. Although some proxy-based firewalls have a generic proxy for such problems, now we're back to basic packet filtering, which defeats the purpose of having a proxy to begin with.

However, taking this example one step further, let's say the proxy-based firewall vendor eventually writes a PCS proxy, and all is well in Coffeeville. Soon after, some mischievous helpdesk contractors resurrect their old copies of network *Doom*, which also runs over port 666, and they start abusing an old addiction. Low and behold, network *Doom* won't make it through the proxy-based firewall, but it will through the stateful packet filtering-based one.

We will cover how this can be used maliciously a little later on, but suffice it to say that the proxy-based approach is a little more secure from a theoretical standpoint—but the products based on this approach can also be a big pain in the butt.

Programmers Bypassing the Firewall

Many corporate programmers have been tasked with exchanging data with partners and customers. In the old days before firewalls were common, they might have just written socket-based programs that made a direct connection. With firewalls in place, they are unable to do this. Therefore, they figured out ways to bypass the firewall by using HTTP as their new transport protocol.

You might think that HTTP is harmless because it's just serving up documents, right? Wrong—protocols such as SOAP (Simple Object Access Protocol) enable remote access to function calls via HTTP. The Web page `http://www.xmlhack.com/read.php?item=630` contains an excellent discussion of SOAP's "firewall-penetrating" abilities.

Security firewalls that deal with SOAP and other such technologies are brand-new. One such solution is Quadrasis' SOAP Content Inspector, which can be found at `http://www.quadrasis.com/solutions/products/easi_product_packages/easi_soap.htm`. The integration of this kind of technology into traditional firewalls is at least a couple of years down the road.

Pitfalls of Firewalling

One pitfall in the world of firewalls is that security can be configured so stringently that it can actually impair the process of networking. For example, some studies suggest that the use of a firewall is impractical in environments where users critically depend on distributed applications. Because firewalls can implement such strict security policies, these environments can become bogged down. What they gain in security, they lose in functionality. To some, this might be viewed simply as an inconvenience. However, the problem can bring about long-term effects that are far more damaging. For example, inevitably all administrators face the classic square-off between user X who needs to do Y, and the security problems that surround her request. Although the dilemma touches on a number of information security principles, one of the largest being policy definition, it can also cross some organizational boundaries as well. If, for example, the technical staff loses its battle to block service Y, they run the risk of having an organization-wide precedent set. This can lead to the security personnel getting crushed by the business people, and sooner or later something is opened up on the firewall that really shouldn't be. On the other hand, smart organizations know to examine these situations on a case-by-case basis and act accordingly. Unfortunately, we don't all work for "smart" organizations....

Firewalls can help create sticky situations. The solution is to know how to avoid these situations, and what to do when you do lose a battle. For example, if some bonehead VP gets the approval to allow third-party access to the payroll system through the Internet, rather then lose sleep over it, consider ways of controlling the damage. Segment the payroll systems onto a separate subnet, look to implement stronger system-level audit logs, work at getting an intrusion detection system (IDS) implemented on the questioned segment, and so on. Many times, perceived losses can be turned into long-term victories, if you play your cards right.

TIP

Although users might seem more like pesky annoyances than necessary evils, it's important to remind yourself that the network is there for one reason: connectivity. Although security is an important part of an administrator's responsibility, so is basic usability. At the end of the day, if the users can't do their job, we're all going to be in trouble. Good administrators know which battles to fight, and which ones to work on from another angle...

Another more serious issue is that of a perceived and false sense of security. Administrators who are content that their firewalls will protect them from all evils are setting themselves up for a rude awakening. Part of the challenge of deploying a firewall is to help build a feeling of safety without overdoing it. Fun challenge, huh? The reason why this balance is so important is that without secondary levels of defense, you are placing all your eggs in one basket. If your firewall is broken, your internal networks can easily be destroyed. Firewalls are *part* of a security model; they shouldn't be *the* security model, because they have their own set of downfalls. Remember, tiered security models are your friend.

There is hope. Five years ago, we were fighting battles with the CIOs to get firewalls in the first place. Now we're fighting battles trying to convince them that just a firewall isn't enough. Hey, at least we're making progress.

Firewall Appliances

The word *appliance* became all the rage in late 1999 as the term appeared to be universally adopted by marketing departments across the globe. The concept of an appliance is a simple and arguably quite appealing one: a turnkey, integrated hardware/software solution that comes ready to run, securely, out of the box.

Since that time, the firewall appliance has really caught on in the small networking environment. Dozens of vendors have firewall appliance boxes on the market. They tend to be easy to configure and easy to deploy, especially for people who are less than security experts. The default configuration often forbids inbound connections, but allows any outbound connections. This is what most home users want and need.

Should you move to a firewall appliance? It really depends on what your needs are. Some people like the capability to use standard Unix commands on their firewalls for examining logs, parsing tables, and so on, so using an appliance might stymie them a bit. However, by using a standard OS such as Microsoft Windows NT or Sun Solaris, you increase the risk of an oversight or misconfiguration. These problems can allow the firewall machine itself to become a vulnerable target. For some, the appliance approach is a little more bulletproof, and appliance performance figures will soon match that of most Sparc-based firewalls, if they haven't already. For others, having the mainstream OS under the hood might be an advantage.

NOTE

The term *solid state* originally came from the world of electrical engineering. The term was used in reference to the move from vacuum tubes to transistors. However, the term has recently been bastardized by vendors and marketing departments alike, and is now commonly used to convey the concept of "no moving parts."

Building Firewalls in the Real World

"Okay," you ask, "So, what's the best firewall, and what's the best way to deploy it?" Ah, if only life were so simple. The short answer is that there is no single, best solution. However, there are some good tips and guidelines that can help you come to a strong decision, and I will do my best here to get you started down the right road.

Let's begin with a few prepurchase guidelines:

1. Understand that firewall platforms change—there is no superior firewall platform. For example, Vendor X might have its head in the clouds for a few revisions, and then get its act together for the next version of the product. By the same token, Vendor Y and Vendor Z might have great products one year, and deep-six them the following year after all their lead developers die bungee-jumping in Kazakhstan. Keep up with the testing done by magazines like *Network Computing* and *InfoWorld*, talk to your peers, and, above all else, *test the products if you can*. Think of a firewall as a new car: If you don't like how it feels, you don't want to be driving it for the next few years.

2. Understand and document your requirements. Do you need your firewall to support token ring, or just Ethernet? Do you need your firewall to support Network Address Translation (NAT)? How many interfaces do you need? Does the firewall need to run on a particular platform? All too often, people get caught up in extreme benchmarking numbers and massive feature lists. But if you don't need your firewall to manage your toasters, and you don't have 15 OC12 links coming into your DMZ, you might not need the fastest and the shiniest. Remember what your firewall is primarily going to be used for: controlling access into and out of your network.

3. Know your limitations. If you are primarily a Windows NT shop with no Unix expertise, going out and purchasing a Unix-based firewall that requires a lot of command-line interaction might not be the best of ideas. Keep in mind that a good portion of firewall failures are because of "pilot error"—that is, the firewall does not fail, the person administering it does. Know your limits. If you or your staff don't understand how to use it, or if the technology is way over your head, that is only going to come back to haunt you. Don't choose the firewall with the prettiest GUI, but don't pick one that takes a Ph.D. to administer, either.

4. Go with a product that has been at least ICSA certified, and preferably something that has a respectable installed base of users. Just because it says "firewall" in the product literature doesn't mean it's secure. Go with something that has been proven on the battlefield.

NOTE

One of my employer's clients (a Fortune 100 company) contracted our team to take a look at a new firewall "appliance" that they were thinking of migrating to. This client was looking at purchasing these units in bulk, but wanted a third-party evaluation done before jumping ship from their main firewall vendor. Within three days of our team banging on the units, we discovered that, not only were we able to format the entire box through the Web administration interface, but the units that the vendor had shipped us had pirated copies of a popular graphics package stored on the hard drive. (Whoops.) Sometimes "too good to be true," is, well, too good to be true.

Before you buy a firewall, you should seriously research your own network, your users, and their needs. You should also generate a visual representation of the connections that will be traveling through your firewall and document those findings. Not only will this help you with your requirement gathering, it will leave a paper trail detailing why certain openings were made, and what processes and people were behind those openings. Should anything come into question years from now, you (or your successor) will have something to turn to for help.

There are five primary steps you must take when building a firewall:

1. Identify your topology, application, and protocol needs.

2. Analyze trust relationships and communication paths in your organization.

3. Evaluate and choose a firewall product.

4. Plan and deploy the firewall correctly.

5. Test your firewall policies stringently.

Identifying Topology, Application, and Protocol Needs

Your first step is to identify your topology, application, and protocol needs. This step is more difficult than it sounds, depending on the size and composition of your network. If you run one of the few homogenous networks in existence and only need to support basic protocols (SMTP, HTTP, FTP, and so on)—you are in luck. The task ahead of you is pretty easy.

But if you are like the majority of the organizations out there, you need to support a mix of platforms, protocols, and applications. Although this might appear to be easy, it can quickly get messy. For example, your application developers might say, "We just need access to the Lotus Notes servers from the Internet." Sounds simple enough, right? Well, let's dig a bit deeper. What kind of access? "Well, we need to replicate data to our suppliers, and we need to be able to use the Lotus Notes clients remotely."

Whoa! That's a little more in-depth then just "accessing Notes." It sounds as though we might need to support the ports related to the Notes clients (TCP port 1352). We will need to support the ports relating to the replication process, if the developers want to access anything via the Web interface. Plus, we'll need to support HTTP (usually over port 80), and what about remote management?

"Oh yeah, we'll be using PCAnywhere to manage the servers remotely."

Yuck! Okay, you see where I'm going with this: Simple requests can turn out to be more complex than they initially seem and might defeat the purpose of the firewall to begin with. Plan accordingly! You will need to *dig deep* into your organization, and make sure you talk to everyone who will be using/depending on this firewall.

> **TIP**
>
> Although it smells like a CYA (Cover Your Ass) move, when going through requirement-gathering phases, it's a good idea to be as loud and as encompassing as possible within your organization. That way, if a user or project team approaches you after the firewall deployment with some bizarre need or functionality requirement, you have some room to stand your ground on why the function wasn't built into the deployed model. "Why didn't you inform me of this during my requirement-gathering phase?" You might be surprised at how much room this tactic can give you to breathe.

Companies focused on e-commerce sometimes separate their product network from that of their internal LAN-based network services. For example, let's say that you're building a new e-commerce site selling the new integrated PCS-enabled toaster/coffeemaker combos. You'll want 24×7 Web server farms, 24×7 payment processing gateways (often called *merchant gateways*), possible email servers, and needed support systems (application servers, database servers, and so on). Now, you will most likely want to separate these mission-critical 24×7 systems from less critical day-to-day internal systems, such as the internal email SMTP gateway, the internal FTP sites, the proxy servers, and so on. This quickly becomes a topology issue: How many interfaces will your firewall need to support this configuration? Better yet, how many firewalls will you need? Do you need hot-standby functionality? Will your firewall need to support extended high-availability (HA) protocols such as HSRP and VRRP?

Better to ask these questions beforehand than to get stuck with a solution that won't scale.

Analyze Trust Relationships and Communication Paths in Your Organization

Just as it's important to understand applications and protocols heading outbound from your organization, you also need to take the time to understand inbound processes as well. This is important for a number of reasons. First, in the end, the applications you are supporting have to work. If you move the middle-tier (the application servers) of your three-tier e-commerce solution to your firewalled segment, and the servers become cut off from their database counterparts, you'll have a lot of angry users on your hands (and a broken application). At the same time, if a server that is "Internet exposed" has free, unrestricted access to your internal networks and infrastructure, you have a potential security nightmare on your hands if that machine is ever compromised by a hostile intruder.

Again, this is more up-front investigative work you need to perform. This might involve discussions with individual departments. Certain network segments might need to access one another's resources. To prevent total disruption of your current system, it's wise to perform a detailed analysis of these relationships first.

TIP

Throughout this process, use considerable tact. You might encounter users or managers who insist, "We've been doing it this way for 10 years now." You have to work with these people. It's not necessary that they understand the process in full. However, if your security practices are going to heavily affect their work environment, you should explain why. This is also an area where up-front policy creation helps—if there are defined, ratified policies in place before going into potential conflicts, your chances of coming out of meetings unscarred greatly increase. Managers tend to avoid monkeying with policies that have been ratified "from above."

Evaluate and Choose a Firewall Product

Next, based on what you discover about your network and those who use it, you need to evaluate and decide on a firewall product. Before conducting purchasing research, you should generate a list of must-haves. You'll ultimately base your purchasing decision on this list. Now, the preferred way of handling the next step is to get your top firewall choices into a lab and do some testing. However, not everyone has a test lab and a few extra weeks to play with cool security products. If you do, enjoy it for those of us who don't!

The next best thing is to get a product demo, visit someone who does have a lab, or ask your vendor for suggestions on how you can see the product in a live environment. If your vendor is good, they'll most likely be able to help you out. Common criteria most people use in deciding on a firewall include the following:

- Capacity—Can the firewall support the throughput that you estimate? Does it have room to scale? Typically, if you are talking speeds of T3 (45Mbps) or slower, almost any firewall will work.

- Features—Although we talked about the problems of feature bloat earlier, features still count. Make sure your firewall can do what you need it to do. However, be realistic with what you are going to use it for. If you aren't going to manage your toaster with it, you don't really need that feature. Also, logging is an important detail. If it gives you too little or the wrong information, you may have trouble handling incidents.

- Administrative interface—You've got to live with this thing. If you aren't comfortable with the interface, or if you don't understand the interface, chances are you might mess it up. Avoid pilot error—go with something you like.

- Price—Okay, who are we kidding? This is always a factor. Although many people have traditionally opted to go the route of CheckPoint FW-1, oftentimes even a basic deployment of FW-1 is intense on the pocketbook, costing five to ten times as much as other products. Take a look at all your options; sometimes the second-best will still secure you for a lot cheaper.

- Reputation—Has the vendor typically been responsive to product vulnerabilities? What's the product's track record? Does it have a deployed user base, or is it a recent addition to the scene?

Also, consider looking at independent testing labs and respected technical, testing-oriented trade magazines for other sources of information.

TIP

Network Computing magazine tests firewall products a few times a year, and usually does a fairly good job in their reviews. Check out `http://www.nwc.com` for more information.

Deploying and Testing Your Firewall

Finally, after you've purchased your firewall, you'll put your research to good use by implementing your firewall and its supporting ruleset(s). First, make sure that the firewall itself is secured. If the unit is an appliance, chances are there is little outside of changing default passwords that you'll need to do to harden the unit. However, if it is an NT- or Unix-based firewall, make sure that the OS on which you deploy the firewall software is properly hardened. (See Chapter 20, "Microsoft;" Chapter 21, "Unix;" and Chapter 22, "Novell NetWare," for more information).

The next step is to put your new firewall into your production environment. If this is planned properly, and in the right environment, you might even be able to transition the firewall into the production environment by moving one server at a time behind it. However, oftentimes it is not this easy. Expect at least a few problems, and also budget some time for network down time. (Also, be prepared to field some fairly angry users.) It is extremely unlikely that you'll get it right the first time—unless your network environment is extremely simple, or you are a ruleset wizard. If you get it right on the first try, congratulations—you are one of the few! Otherwise, join the ranks of the rest of us, and don't be too hard on yourself. This stuff isn't rocket science, but it's not tinker toy construction, either.

Finally, you'll need to test your rulesets. For this, I recommend extensive test runs. There are really two phases:

1. Testing the ruleset from the outside

2. Testing the ruleset from the inside

Consider using the Nmap tool, available from `http://www.nmap.org`, to take snapshots of your network from an internal perspective (inside the firewall), and from an external perspective (outside the firewall). Make sure the external view is in line with what you expect.

Above all else, remember—DEFAULT DENY should be your mindset. If you don't know what it is, don't allow it through your firewall. Better to struggle through learning about protocols and application dependencies than to unknowingly open huge holes into your enterprise. Think minimalist.

TIP

People often make the mistake of "firing and forgetting" with their firewalls. They deploy them, they test them, and then they forget about them. One of the top things you should look to implement *after* your firewall deployment is a process for reviewing your firewall logs. Not only will this help you identify potential problems and trends with your configuration, it will help you get an advanced warning of who is at your doorstep. If any potential intruders come around to rattle your doorknobs, your firewall logs will be the first place where you'll spot them. Use your logs—they are your friend. Additionally, it's a good idea to periodically review the rulesets on the firewall to make sure they're meeting current requirements.

Sample Failures of Firewall Technology

Let me first start by saying that this section is not designed to be an all-encompassing view of how firewalls can be circumvented. In fact, quite the opposite. My goal is to simply provide you with clear, simple examples of how firewalls can fail you.

I would also argue that these aren't even failures of the firewalls themselves, but rather of their deployers and the expectations placed on them.

I assume here that you are familiar with the tool netcat, a network testing tool. More information on netcat can be found in Chapter 21.

The "Whoops, Where Did My Web Server Go?" Problem

Picture this: You have a stateful packet filtering-based firewall that allows inbound traffic through port 80 to a single NT-based Web server. That NT Web server is behind the firewall, with most of the more trivial services shut down. (Workstation service, server service, FTP service, Gopher service—all are disabled.) Your perimeter router is secured, and let us also assume that the firewall itself is properly configured and secured.

But somehow, using this configuration, an intruder is able to get administrative shell access, via Telnet, to your protected NT Web server in under two minutes. How is this possible?

Microsoft's Internet Information Server (IIS is the Web server used natively on NT and 2000) installs a number of nasty sample scripts by default. Combine this with the RDS/MDAC problem (see Chapter 20 for further explanation), and intruders can not only execute commands remotely on the NT server (via standard HTTP requests), they can build FTP scripts. Using RFP's `msadc.pl` Perl exploit script on a vulnerable Windows NT/IIS installation, combined with netcat and the `echo` command, an intruder can:

1. Create an FTP script that will retrieve a copy of netcat.

2. Execute that FTP script using `msadc.pl` and `FTP -s -a <scriptname>`.

3. Create a script to shut down the Web server, and bind netcat to port 80 using `nc -l -p 80 -e cmd.exe`.

4. Telnet into the Web server (`telnet 10.0.0.2 80`) over port 80 to connect to an active copy of netcat (see Figure 10.1).

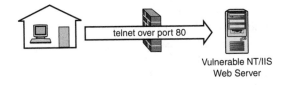

Vulnerable NT/IIS
Web Server

FIGURE 10.1   Firewall only allowing inbound data through port 80.

So although the configuration appears to be solid, the intruder is sitting there with an administrative shell on your NT machine. What went wrong? Firewalls are not a substitute for end-node security. Even if you deploy the tightest configuration possible on the firewall (short of disconnecting the network), a single open vulnerability on a single end-node can blow your whole model.

Now, a proxy-based firewall would have blocked the netcat shell, because the Telnet traffic over port 80 would not have been viewed as valid HTTP requests. However, proxy-based firewalls would not have stopped the RDS/MSADC. It *is* valid traffic, and the attacker could have altered his attack accordingly.

NOTE

There is another point to be made here: Blocking types of outbound traffic can be a good thing, although few administrators consider doing this. During one penetration test, we ran into a savvy admin who had blocked outbound FTP access from his Internet-exposed Web servers. Even though we were able to execute commands on the target machines by manipulating faulty CGI scripts, we were unable to fetch our intrusion tools (such as netcat) via FTP. This slowed us down quite a bit.

Using SSH to Bypass RuleSets

This scenario is a bit different. Let's say that our network policy prohibits the use of unencrypted POP from outside of the organization because it passes clear-text passwords. Let's assume that using our proxy-based firewall we've blocked external POP access to the organization's POP mail server, which inhibits external users from checking their mail while at home. Let us also assume that we enable the use of SSH outbound.

We discover one day that one of our more clever users is checking his mail from home, using POP remotely. Worse, we soon discover that he is doing so across the Internet via his cable-modem attachment. His POP password is now being sent across the Internet in the clear, validating our original concern. So how could this happen with us blocking inbound POP at the firewall?

There is a neat little feature found in most SSH clients called *tunneling*. Tunneling enables you to seamlessly transport other types of connections through established SSH sessions. In our scenario, this user would initiate an outbound SSH session from within the organization from the Unix server running POP. He would connect to a server at his ISP, and set up a listening tunnel on the ISP's server on port 1828 that would redirect a session back to the POP server. This tunnel would then enable him to connect to the internal POP server from home, after he modified his POP client to connect on port 1828 (rather than 110) on his ISP's machine. As long as the SSH session remained active, the tunnel would work (see Figure 10.2).

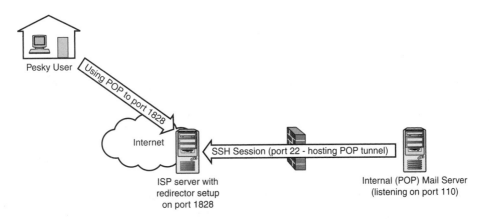

FIGURE 10.2   Firewall blocking POP (port 110) inbound.

The clever user has effectively bypassed our ruleset. Although the POP request comes in encrypted from the ISP's machine (because it's over the SSH session), its path to the ISP machine is still out in the open. So where did we go wrong? Well, combine the fact that proxy-based firewalls can't "peek" inside of encrypted traffic with the rather useful tunneling feature of SSH, and you have the makings of our little problem. Although naive administrators might be tempted to blame the firewall for this problem, the simple fact of the matter is that firewalls have their weaknesses—blocking SSH inbound tunnels is one of them.

These are just two examples. Trust me, there are many more.

NOTE

The inability to eavesdrop on encrypted tunnels applies to SSL and VPNs, as well. In fact, during one of our team's engagements, we found ourselves cut off from email because of the client's restrictive proxy. This proxy, however, allowed outbound SSL. Just for fun, one of our team members took putty, an open-source SSH client, and modified it to tunnel SSH through SSL. Voilà—we had our email connection, and the firewall admin was none the wiser. Encryption will continue to be both a blessing and a curse to security administrators in years to come.

Commercial Firewalls

This next section provides details on firewall vendors, their products, and any special characteristics their firewall might have. I am not recommending these firewalls, but rather simply providing this list as a resource.

BlackICE

Firewall Type: Packet filter-based (personal firewall)

Manufacturer: ISS

Supported Platform: Windows 98 and up

Further Information:

`http://www.iss.net/products_services/hsoffice_protection/index.php`

BorderManager

BorderManager is the premier firewall for Novell environments, but it will also protect Unix- and NT-based systems. The product offers centralized management, strong filtering, and high-speed, real-time analysis of network traffic. Also, BorderManager offers the capability to create "mini-firewalls" within your organization to prevent internal attacks from departments or local networks.

Firewall Type: Stateful packet filter-based

Manufacturer: Novell Inc.

Supported Platform: Novell NetWare

Further Information:

`http://www.novell.com/products/bordermanager/index.html`

FireBOX

Firewall Type: Stateful packet filter-based

Manufacturer: Watchguard

Supported Platform: Unix

Further Information: `http://www.watchguard.com`

Firewall-1

Checkpoint's Firewall-1 is one of the most frequently deployed firewalls in the industry today. The product features packet filtering, strong content screening, integrated protection against spoofing, VPN options, real-time scanning for viruses, and a wide assortment of other features. It is one of the most feature-rich firewalls out there, but is also one of the most expensive.

Firewall Type: Stateful inspection-based

Manufacturer: Check Point Software Technologies Ltd.

Supported Platforms: Windows NT and Unix

Further Information: http://www.checkpoint.com/

FireWall Server

Firewall Type: Proxy-based

Manufacturer: BorderWare

Supported Platforms: Custom (proprietary OS running on Intel hardware)

Further Information: http://www.borderware.com

GNAT Box Firewall

GNAT is a firewall appliance. You can manage the GNAT box with either a command-line or Web-based interface. GNAT filters incoming traffic based on IP source address, destination address, port, network interface, and protocol.

Firewall Type: Stateful packet filter-based

Manufacturer: Global Technology Associates

Supported Platforms: N/A (appliance)

Further Information: http://www.gnatbox.com/

Guardian

Guardian is an NT-based firewall.

Firewall Type: Stateful packet filter-based

Manufacturer: NetGuard Inc.

Supported Platform: Windows NT

Further Information: http://www.netguard.com

NetScreen

NetScreen is a firewall appliance that supports IPsec, DES, and Triple DES encryption.

Firewall Type: Stateful packet filter-based

Manufacturer: NetScreen Technologies Inc.

Supported Platforms: N/A (Appliance)

Further Information: http://www.netscreen.com/

PIX Firewall

The PIX, along with Firewall-1, are the two most widely deployed firewall products today. The PIX is a firewall appliance that is devoid of any moving parts. It supports IPsec, and can be administered through Telnet or SSH sessions, or through the Cisco Security Policy Manager (CSPM) framework product.

Firewall Type: Stateful packet filter-based

Manufacturer: Cisco Systems Inc.

Supported Platforms: N/A (Appliance)

Further Information: http://www.cisco.com/warp/public/cc/pd/fw/sqfw500/index.shtml

SideWinder

Firewall Type: Proxy-based

Manufacturer: Secure Computing

Supported Platform: Unix (custom build, however, ships with the product)

Further Information: http://www.securecomputing.com

Sonicwall

Firewall Type: Stateful packet filter-based

Manufacturer: SonicSystems

Supported Platforms: N/A (appliance)

Further Information: http://www.sonicwall.com

Symantec Enterprise Firewall

Symantec also has other related firewall products.

Firewall Type: Proxy-based

Manufacturer: Axent

Supported Platforms: Solaris and Windows NT

Further Information: http://enterprisesecurity.symantec.com/default.cfm?EID=0&PID=na

Tiny Personal Firewall

Firewall Type: Packet filter-based (personal firewall)

Manufacturer: Tiny Software

Supported Platforms: Windows 98 and up

Further Information: `http://www.tinysoftware.com/home/tiny2?la=EN`

ZoneAlarm Pro

Firewall Type: Packet filter-based (personal firewall)

Manufacturer: Zone Labs

Supported Platforms: Windows 98 and up

Further Information: `http://www.zonelabs.com/store/content/home.jsp`

Summary

Firewalls are not bulletproof. Anyone relying on them for the majority of their security is setting themselves up for a nasty fall. However, in many cases, firewalls are quite necessary and can prove to be very useful. A firewall's success depends on the proper utilization of feature sets, proper configuration, and proper monitoring. As with any security product, testing it before purchasing it is key. If you can test them yourself, great; otherwise, look to third parties and industry-recognized security sources for further information.

Books and Publications

Internet Firewalls and Network Security, Second Edition. Chris Hare and Karanjit Siyan. (New Riders) ISBN: 1-56205-632-8. 1996.

Internet Firewalls. Scott Fuller and Kevin Pagan. (Ventana Communications Group Inc.) ISBN: 1-56604-506-1. 1997.

Building Internet Firewalls. D. Brent Chapman and Elizabeth D. Zwicky. (O'Reilly & Associates) ISBN: 1-56592-124-0. 1995.

Firewalls and Internet Security: Repelling the Wily Hacker. William R. Cheswick and Steven M. Bellovin. (Addison-Wesley) ISBN: 0-201-63357-4. 1994.

Actually Useful Internet Security Techniques. Larry J. Hughes, Jr. (New Riders) ISBN 1-56205-508-9. 1995.

Internet Security Resource Library: Internet Firewalls and Network Security, Internet Security Techniques, Implementing Internet Security. (New Riders) ISBN: 1-56205-506-2. 1995.

"Network Firewalls." Steven M. Bellovin and William R. Cheswick. IEEECM, 32(9), pp. 50–57, September 1994.

"Session-Layer Encryption." Matt Blaze and Steve Bellovin. Proceedings of the Usenix Security Workshop, June 1995.

"IP v6 Release and Firewalls." Uwe Ellermann. 14th Worldwide Congress on Computer and Communications Security. Protection, pp. 341–354, June 1996.

Internet Resources

Firewalls FAQ. http://www.faqs.org/faqs/firewalls-faq

"There Be Dragons." Steven M. Bellovin. Proceedings of the Third Usenix UNIX Security Symposium, Baltimore, September 1992. AT&T Bell Laboratories, Murray Hill, NJ. August 15, 1992. http://www.deter.com/unix/papers/dragons_bellovin.ps.gz

"Keeping Your Site Comfortably Secure: An Introduction to Internet Firewalls." John P. Wack and Lisa J. Carnahan. National Institute of Standards and Technology. http://csrc. nist.gov/nistpubs/800-10/

"Covert Channels in the TCP/IP Protocol Suite." Craig Rowland. Rotherwick & Psionics Software Systems Inc. http://www.psionic.com/papers/whitep03.html

"A Network Perimeter with Secure External Access." Frederick M. Avolio and Marcus J. Ranum. A paper that details the implementation of a firewall purportedly at the White House. http://www.alw.nih.gov/Security/FIRST/papers/firewall/isoc94.ps

"Packets Found on an Internet." Steven M. Bellovin. Lambda. Interesting analysis of packets appearing at the application gateway of AT&T. ftp://ftp.research.att.com/dist/smb/packets.ps

"X Through the Firewall, and Other Application Relays." Treese/Wolman. Digital Equipment Corp. Cambridge Research Lab. ftp://crl.dec.com/pub/DEC/CRL/tech-reports/93.10.ps.Z

"Benchmarking Methodology for Network Interconnect Devices (RFC 1944)." S. Bradner and J. McQuaid. http://archives.neohapsis.com/archives/rfcs/rfc1944.txt

"SOAP Could Slip Up Security." John Leyden. http://www.vnunet.com/News/1103805

11

Vulnerability Assessment Tools (Scanners)

With vulnerability announcements being released at a dizzying pace, most organizations face an uphill battle when it comes to hunting down the security holes that reside on their systems. In an attempt to aid organizations in this ongoing quest, a number of commercial and open source efforts have risen to automate the process of vulnerability discovery. These vulnerability assessment tools, or *scanners*, come in many shapes and sizes, with varying degrees of accuracy. This chapter will outline some of the pros and cons of using these tools, as well as identify where their use can be helpful. We will also shed some light on what's important when selecting such a tool to aid in the never-ending war to keep your environment secure.

The History of Vulnerability Scanners

Turn back the calendar to the early 1990s. The Internet is off the ground and running in universities. CERT is up and operational. The World Wide Web is more or less an experiment that is creeping into Gopher's territory. Vendors are vehemently denying most security bugs, and Unix administrators are just beginning to feel the wrath of clever attackers. Internet security practices as we know them today are in their infancy, but the blueprints for modern day tool sets are being drawn up.

In 1992, a computer science student named Chris Klaus was experimenting with Internet security concepts. He created a scanning tool called Internet Security Scanner (ISS) that could be used to remotely probe Unix systems for a set of common vulnerabilities. In Chris's words:

> ISS is a project that I started as I became interested in security. As I heard about crackers and hackers breaking into NASA and universities around the world, I wanted to find out the deep secrets of security and how these people were able to gain access to expensive machines that I would think were secure. I searched [the] Internet for relative information, such as Phrack and CERT advisories.
>
> Most information was vague and did not explain how intruders were able to gain access to most systems. At most the information told administrators to make password security tighter and to apply the vendor's security patches. They lacked real information on how an intruder would look at a site to try to gain access. Having talked with security experts and reading CERT advisories, I started trying to look for various security holes within my domain.
>
> To my surprise, I noticed that many of machines were adequately secured, but within a domain there remained enough machines with obvious holes that anyone wanted into any machine could attack the weak 'trusted' machine and from there could gain access to the rest of the domain.
>
> —Chris Klaus (ISS v1.0 readme file, 1993).

Although the cynic in me is inclined to ask what has changed since then (many of Chris's observations still ring true today), ISS was one of the early, if not the first, remote vulnerability assessment scanners to be deployed en masse on the Internet. ISS looked for a few dozen common security holes and flagged them as issues to be resolved. Although a few people were nervous about the tool's obvious power in the wrong hands, most administrators welcomed it with open arms.

A few years later, Dan Farmer (of COPS fame) and Wietse Venema (of TCP_Wrapper fame) authored a similar tool called SATAN (Security Administrator Tool for Analyzing Networks). SATAN essentially did the same thing as ISS, but had some advancements: a more mature scanning engine, a Web-based interface, and a wider assortment of checks. Unlike ISS, however, the pending release of SATAN became a media-crazed event. So hyped was its release that in April 1995 (the month it was officially released), *Time* magazine published an article on it and Dan Farmer. CERT even issued an advisory on its abilities (CA-1995-06). Many people feared that the release of SATAN would bring about total chaos on the Internet.

Obviously this was not the case, as SATAN's release did little more than cause some extra traffic for a few days as people downloaded it, but this does show how the public's attitude toward the Internet had changed in the intervening years. By 1995, commerce had begun in earnest and the real risk of monetary losses due to security became apparent.

NOTE

Oddly enough, although Farmer lost his job at SGI over SATAN, Klaus managed to use ISS to build a multimillion dollar security products juggernaut—Internet Security Systems (ISS).

Since then, the vulnerability assessment scene has continued to grow and mature. Today, there are more than a dozen scanners in circulation, each with its own set of strengths and weaknesses. The fundamental concepts, however, have not changed much since the early days of ISS and SATAN.

How Vulnerability Scanners Work

As you'll see in both the Microsoft and Unix chapters, vulnerabilities come in many flavors. However, there are primarily two classifications for operating system vulnerabilities: ones that are local exposure points (host-level), and ones that are remote exposure points (remote-level).

In addressing remote exposure points, there are a number of methods one can use to approach the task of automated vulnerability scanning. For example, one approach might involve using a port-scanning tool such as Nmap, identifying the operating system, and then logging all the listening ports. The user would then be given a list of ports (21, 25, 53, 80, and so on) and an OS type (Linux Kernel 2.2). This approach has a few problems, however, as the user is left with a ton of data (port information) and no details as to what services are actually vulnerable. The user is simply given a blueprint of the system. Identifying what those listening services are, and whether they are vulnerable, is an exercise left to the user. For example, if my data set tells me that machine X is running the Linux 2.2 Kernel and has a service listening at port 21, I still have very little idea as to whether I am vulnerable to the any of the wu-ftpd buffer-overflow bugs. In fact, I don't even know whether this particular system is running wu-ftpd—it might be running ProFTPd or glftpd, instead. So even when hunting down a single port, I still need to

A. Identify what is listening at that port,

B. Identify what version that service is,

C. Research whether there are any known vulnerabilities associated with that service and version number.

Although this approach might be feasible for a dozen machines or so, it obviously won't work in mid- to large-sized organizations where thousands of machines are present. The task at hand then moves from difficult to impossible.

A more practical approach would be to build on the previous model of port scanning and OS identification, and then add some mechanism to identify the listening service types and versions. You would then have another piece of the puzzle completed. Going back to the wu-ftpd buffer overflow example, by identifying the service version, you would now know

A. That the server is Linux Kernel 2.2-based,

B. That port 21 is listening,

C. What the service type and version is.

Let's say that your service query process informs you that you are using wu-ftpd v2.4.2. This gets you even closer, as now you simply need to research whether wu-ftpd v2.4.2 has any known vulnerabilities.

NOTE

You should note the difference between *port scanning* and *vulnerability scanning*. Although most vulnerability scanners do indeed scan for open TCP and UDP ports, this is only one of their many features. In contrast, although port scanners like Nmap are capable of performing some interesting feats (such as OS fingerprinting), they rarely contain any sort of vulnerability database. In short, most vulnerability scanners take port scanning a few steps farther.

The last remaining component to this process is research—knowing what versions of what services are vulnerable. In many ways, this ties into what attackers do: scan, query, research, and exploit. In this case, it turns out that wu-ftpd v2.4.2 is indeed vulnerable to a known attack type.

Based on the sheer number of known product vulnerabilities (estimated between 2,000–3,000 to date), creating a thorough system to properly identify and track *all* these product vulnerabilities is a fairly daunting task. The mining and managing of this vulnerability data presents the biggest challenge and the biggest argument for using an automated tool.

Although implementation details vary, based on these examples, you can deduce that there are a number of common components throughout most scanning approaches:

• The vulnerability data—Vulnerability assessment scanners have internal databases of vulnerability information that help them accurately identify remote system exposure points.

• The scanning mechanism—The technical guts of the scanner lie in its capability to properly identify services, subsystems, and vulnerabilities. Depending on how the scanner was written, it might not be efficient at scanning large ranges of machines.

- The reporting mechanism—Finding a problem is one thing; adequately reporting on it is something entirely different. Some products are stronger than others when it comes to clearly stating what they've discovered.

Some scanners will break this mold, but they are more often the exception than the rule.

NOTE

A more thorough—and definitely more dangerous—approach is to create a tool that looks for vulnerabilities and actually attempts to *exploit* them. SNI started going down this path with its original Ballista product. In theory, this would definitively end the problems associated with misdiagnosed vulnerabilities (also referred to as *false positives*). However, it could also bring about some serious chaos. For example, exploiting vulnerabilities such as the BIND NXT bug crashes the DNS server. If this particular exploit were implemented, all DNS servers running vulnerable versions of BIND would be disabled during every scan!

What to Look For When Choosing a Scanner

Like any product-purchasing decision, before answering the question of which product is right, you first need to decide your specific requirements. For example, if plotting vulnerability-remediation progress over time is something you want automated, then a product's capability to log and plot multiple scan sets is a feature you need to look for. If you have a large NetWare environment, you might want to make sure that the scanner has NetWare-specific checks. If you have to scan 50–100 hosts, efficiency might not be an issue. However, if you need to scan thousands at a time, you'll want to make sure the scanner can scale to that range. Again, many of these issues are specific to what you'll need your vulnerability scanner to do.

There are also some common areas of concern that all products need to address. A few of the issues that you will come into contact with in choosing a vulnerability scanner include the following:

- Completeness of the vulnerability checks—I don't recommend falling into the trap of playing the numbers game when picking a scanner. However, the number of vulnerabilities a scanner looks for is still important. At a bare minimum, scanners should look for the known critical vulnerabilities that allow for root/administrator-level compromises.

- Accuracy of the vulnerability checks—It's important that scanners have a good set of vulnerability checks. However, a scanner's capability to accurately identify those vulnerabilities is also important. Missing a bunch of holes is as undesirable as being forced to sift through a report identifying hundreds of nonexistent vulnerabilities. Like intrusion detection systems, some scanning products still have problems with false positives.

- Scope of the vulnerability checks—It should be noted that most vulnerability scanners are designed to discover remote vulnerabilities, not local (host-level) vulnerabilities. However, a few products like ISS and Webtrends have system-level agents that will also look for local vulnerabilities—vulnerabilities that would otherwise be undetectable by remote scans. Although these system agents often address a greater range of vulnerabilities, they also require installation, making them a management nightmare for large environments.

- Timely updates—Although scanners will always be one step behind the vulnerability announcements, they should be updated at a fairly regular (once per month or more) interval. You'll want to look for a scanner that has a significant R&D team behind it that is consistently updating the product.

- Reporting capabilities—Finding vulnerabilities is important, but properly describing the problems and their subsequent fixes is also important—and so is the accurate ranking of the vulnerabilities. This is of particular concern for larger organizations because they usually rely on system administrators to remediate the discovered problem. Some scanners are now offering an autofix capability to download and install the needed patches through the application. PatchLink is one of the most advanced in this area.

- Licensing and pricing issues—Some of these products are licensed per node; some per server scanned; and some are free. Some of them have an easy licensing system (like NAI); others (like ISS) require a convoluted key-cutting system. Attempting to provide accurate prices and licensing information in this book would be an exercise in futility, as the vendors are constantly changing the terms. However, it should be noted that licensing issues should be thoroughly investigated before purchasing decisions are made, as some of these pricing schemes are just downright obnoxious. When in doubt, however, there is always Nessus, which is free.

No scanner that I know of has addressed all these issues well, but Nessus and Internet Security Scanner come pretty close.

TIP

In February 2002, *Network World Fusion* magazine released a fairly comprehensive analysis of these tools. Based on their requirements, eEye's Retina won *NWF's* Blue Ribbon Award. Harris Security Threat Avoidance Technology (STAT) was a close second. Nessus and IIS made a good showing, but were listed in the second tier because of their speed. You can find the story at http://www.nwfusion.com/reviews/2002/0204bgrev.html.

Fundamental Shortcomings

Just about every security tool discussed in this book has had a set of fundamental problems, and vulnerability scanners are no different. Knowing their limitations is as important as knowing their strengths.

The major shortcomings of these products can be grouped into three categories: completeness, timeliness, and accuracy. First, reviews of these products have shown that many of them catch a fairly high number of known vulnerabilities, but none of them are equipped to identify all of them.

TIP

You can view the SANS Top 20 list of common vulnerabilities at http://www.sans.org/top20.htm. Although not a definitive list by a long shot, it does list some of the more common holes found on machines today. They also compare how well scanners find them at http://www.sans.org/top20/tools.pdf.

Second, none of these products can be completely up to date. From the time a new vulnerability becomes known, it takes time to incorporate it into the product and release a new version. Some products are released on an as needed basis, or a fixed regular schedule—some as long as once per quarter. If a vulnerability is announced in January, your scanner might not be equipped to detect that vulnerability until March. That leaves you with two months to fend for yourself when it comes to scanning. Now, your internal threat identification effort should be on top of this problem anyway, but the point is that these scanners should not be your primary method of defense when it comes to hunting down remotely exploitable exposures. When you really get down to the fundamentals, these products can do nothing that a well-informed security specialist can't do manually.

Another problem is that most modern-day scanners are simply implementing "banner-grabbing" techniques to identify service versions. This technique is arguably sufficient for most environments; however, it can create some interesting scenarios. For example, by simply telnetting to port 25 (SMTP mail) and port 21 (FTP), you can identify versions of these two services.

Note that these two machines appear to be running Microsoft Exchange 5.5 and version 4.0 of the Microsoft FTP server. However, many services such as BIND, sendmail, and wu-ftpd are now allowing administrators to change these banners in their configuration files. Although this is not a security threat, changing a default wu-ftpd banner to "Fabio's favorite FTP Server v1.0" will completely confuse most vulnerability scanning tools. The strange and disturbing moral of this story is that if you want your scanners to be effective, don't change your default banners.

In addition to changed-banner confusion, some companies choose to run well-known services on ports other than the standard port (HTTP servers on port 8080, for example). This can cause some scanners to fail. Some address this issue and test the type of service running on each port rather than making assumptions about standards. If your organization uses nonstandard ports, be certain that the product you choose has this feature.

Finally, these products still struggle with false positives. Frequently on large and diverse networks, vulnerability scanners will misfire and report on vulnerabilities that simply do not exist. Although it's better to be safe than sorry, this does create some overhead as personnel then have to run around trying to hunt down phantom vulnerabilities.

Top Vulnerability Scanners

In an ideal world, technology-purchasing decisions would be backed by proper requirement gathering, proper testing, and realistic budgeting. However, I've grown to realize that people rarely have the luxury of doing things the right way. It is for this very reason that I've picked what I consider to be the top vulnerability scanners on the market today, and listed them here. This is not to say that the other products won't do a sufficient job—these are just my personal favorites based on my field experiences and testing. I still encourage the reader to perform a thorough investigation when choosing a product to adopt, but the list of products in the following sections should get you started.

Retina

eEye's Retina is a relative newcomer to the field of vulnerability scanners; however, it has quickly moved near the top of the ranks because of its easy user interface, the speed of its scans, and its daily updates. You can set the application to check for and download the latest vulnerability definitions from eEye's Web site with each run.

Retina does not make assumptions about the service protocols running on standard ports, but analyzes the traffic to determine what services are running. It also offers a scheduling function to run at given intervals. As it is minimally intrusive on the systems being scanned, it might make sense in your organization to automate scans.

eEye has a strong R&D department that has offered initial advisories about some new vulnerabilities. Plus, it's added a feature called CHAM (Common Hacker Attack Methods), which attempts to find unknown vulnerabilities through AI-based heuristics. Personally, I don't expect a whole lot from this feature, but it certainly can't hurt.

> Vendor: eEye Digital Security
>
> Platform: Windows
>
> URL: http://www.eeye.com

NetRecon

NetRecon complements Symantec's existing line of firewall and intrusion detection suites. NetRecon's strengths are its interface, strong reporting abilities, moderately sized vulnerability database, and its capability to perform what is often referred to as secondary exploitation—using knowledge gained from one server to assess another. Although it's rare that I've found this last feature useful, it is something not seen in many other products.

NetRecon has traditionally not been as thorough as Nessus, Cybercop Scanner, or ISS, but it is still a fairly comprehensive scanning tool that can be quite useful. It can also report into Enterprise Security Manager (ESM), which can be used for more general risk assessment efforts.

> Vendor: Symantec (formerly Axent)
>
> Platform: Windows
>
> URL: http://enterprisesecurity.symantec.com/

ISS Internet Scanner

ISS initially built its company on Internet Scanner, and it has historically been regarded as the de facto standard in the industry for vulnerability scanning. Internet Scanner has a strong reporting back end, and a comprehensive set of vulnerability checks. ISS has obviously spent as much time polishing the product as they have on the back end scanning engine itself. For example, the scanner provides a significant amount of background data on each vulnerability check.

Internet Scanner uses a Microsoft ODBC–based back end to store its scan data, which can be used later for doing long-term trending. As in NetRecon's integration with ESM, Internet Scanner integrates with the ISS Decisions product. Combined with scanner data, ISS Decisions can be used in conjunction with other security products (firewalls, intrusion detection systems, and so on) to paint a more global picture of vulnerability and threat points.

Although Internet Scanner traditionally hasn't had as many problems with false positives as other products, it does still lag behind on the update front. The other negative point worth mentioning is that in my experience, Internet Scanner appears to have become less stable in the 6.x series of releases. I've had numerous problems with it crashing during large scans, and occasionally I'll have to clear out its internal database and start again clean before it will cooperate. It has always been recoverable, however.

It should be noted that ISS also makes two other scanning products, System Scanner and Database Scanner, although both are agent-based and incapable of scanning remote systems.

Vendor: Internet Security Systems, Inc.

Platform: Windows NT Workstation v4.0

URL: http://www.iss.net

Cybercop Scanner

Cybercop Scanner's roots come from NAI's (Network Associates, Inc.) acquisition of SNI (Secure Networks, Inc.) and their Ballista product. Although Cybercop Scanner has an impressive number of vulnerability checks and moderate reporting abilities, it also comes with a number of surprisingly useful tools. Two of the tools that are of particular interest are CASL and the SMB grinder. CASL enables the GUI-based construction of IP packets, whereas the SMB grinder is similar to the password-cracking capabilities of L0phtCrack.

Cybercop's primary downsides are its lack of some fundamentally important vulnerability checks, and its bizarre licensing scheme. NAI usually tries to sell Cybercop on a per-node basis, as opposed to a per-number-of-servers-scanned basis. This can create some horrendously high pricing schemes, depending on the alignment of the stars and the salesperson's current commission plan.

Vendor: Network Associates, Inc.

Platform: Windows NT and Unix

URL: http://www.nai.com

The Open Source Nessus Project

Nessus was written by Renaud Deraison, an open source author living in Paris, France. Renaud discovered Linux at age 16 and has been hacking it ever since. In 1996, Renaud began attending 2600 meetings and subsequently developed a strong interest in security. This spawned a partnership between Renaud and two other programmers, and together they wrote their first auditing tool in 1997. After tackling that project, Renaud conceived Nessus in early 1998.

Nessus is quickly becoming the Linux of the vulnerability-scanning field. Driven by the open source movement, Nessus wasn't much to speak of a few years ago, but is now gaining ground on—and sometimes surpassing—its commercial counterparts. Nessus employs an extensible plug-in model that enables the security community to add scanning modules at will. This gives Nessus a development edge, because any check that it doesn't have can be created by anyone with some time and coding abilities on their hands.

Nessus uses a console-engine model, and the console can reside on the same computer as the scanning engine. This distributed architecture allows for some interesting flexibility, as you don't need to be anywhere close to the scanning engine to control it.

At the time of this writing, Nessus had more than 500 vulnerability checks, some of which still aren't available in the commercial scanning tools. Depending on how the development efforts continue to progress, Nessus could surpass commercial scanners in overall thoroughness in the near future.

Platform: Unix (Windows console available)

URL: `http://www.nessus.org`

Whisker

Whisker was written by a hacker by the name of rain forest puppy (rfp), who has carved out a niche for himself discovering Web-based vulnerabilities. Whisker doesn't fit the general definition of a vulnerability scanner, as it is specifically focused on scanning for known vulnerable CGI scripts. In fact, the *only* things it looks for are vulnerable CGI scripts. However, its list of CGI checks is more comprehensive than all the commercial scanners combined. Because of this, I highly recommend you use Whisker in addition to a mainstream scanner.

Vendor: Open source—rfp labs

Platform: Windows and Unix

URL: `http://www.wiretrip.net/rfp/`

Other Vulnerability Scanners

The following is a list of scanners that are up-and-coming (although this is not as comprehensive a list as the previous one). I encourage the reader to continue to monitor the progress of these products, and test them whenever possible.

HackerShield

Vendor: BindView

Platform: Windows

URL: `http://www.bindview.com`

Update

Vendor: PatchLink Corporation

Platform: Windows

URL: `http://www.patchlink.com/`

Cisco Scanner

Vendor: Cisco Systems

Platform: Windows

URL: http://www.cisco.com

SAINT

Vendor: SAINT Corporation

Platform: Unix

URL: http://www.wwdsi.com

SARA, TARA, and WebMon

Vendor: Advanced Research Corporation (open source)

Platform: Unix

URL: http://www-arc.com

STAT

Vendor: Harris

Platform: Windows and Unix

URL: http://www.statonline.com/

Security Analyzer

Vendor: NetIQ CorporationPlatform: Windows and Unix

URL: http://www.netiq.com

Summary

Although vulnerability scanners are by no means an all-encompassing solution to identifying vulnerabilities and locking down systems, they can still be extremely valuable tools. As with any security tool, however, one should be aware of the weaknesses these tools exhibit. They are consistently behind when it comes to vulnerability announcements, they do not always report information accurately, they have false positives, and they are not exhaustive when it comes to the depth of their vulnerability data. Using a scanner in conjunction with a solid vulnerability identification effort and a solid set of system lockdown procedures, however, will result in a strong strategy for combating the overall problem.

12

Intrusion Detection Systems

Intrusion detection is one of the hottest areas in the information security landscape, with International Data Corporation (IDC) stating that the market has grown enormously the past couple of years (http://www.mindbranch. com/listing/product/R104-10352.html). Although the promise of technology that automatically detects, alerts, and possibly stops hostile intruders is extremely attractive, the technology is also fairly young. This chapter provides the reader with a guide to intrusion detection system (IDS) products and introduces some of the ins and outs of implementing IDS solutions. The chapter also sheds some light on how to select the best IDS for your environment and your needs and gives you a realistic review of what these systems can and cannot do.

An Introduction to Intrusion Detection

The term *intrusion detection* means many things to many people; however, for the sake of clarity, we're going to define it as the act of detecting a hostile user or intruder who is attempting to gain unauthorized access. Assuming this definition, a number of popular methods are used to detect intruders—for example, inspecting system, Web, application, firewall, and router logs for hostile or unusual activity. Some system administrators implement binary integrity checkers such as AIDE or Tripwire in hopes of catching successful attackers when they deposit Trojan code on compromised servers. (Chapter 21, "Unix," has further details on Tripwire.) Other administrators simply monitor event logs looking for failed user login attempts.

Although all these methods are helpful, they become difficult, if not impossible, to perform on a daily basis.

Introduce a few hundred machines, and the task becomes downright overwhelming. Enter the intrusion detection system.

The roots of modern-day intrusion detection systems lie in the Intrusion Detection Expert System (IDES) and Distributed Intrusion Detection System (DIDS) models developed by the U.S. Department of Defense (DOD) back in the late 80s and early 90s. These were some of the first automated systems deployed. Today, most intrusion detection (ID) systems are designed with the same goal in mind: to help automate the process of looking for intruders. This can be as simple as the real-time parsing of firewall logs looking for port scans or as complex as applying inspection routines to raw network traffic looking for buffer overflow attempts.

Traditional IDS classification schemes put most systems into two distinct camps: misuse detection models and anomaly-based detection models. This chapter focuses on two implementations of the misuse detection (also called *signature-based detection*) model: network-based intrusion detection systems (NIDSs) and host-based intrusion detection systems (HIDSs). Readers should note that many other intrusion detection models do exist, but most of them are less popular. However, most modern-day IDS implementations can be grouped into one of these categories:

- Network-based IDS—In their current form, NIDS devices are raw packet-parsing engines—glorified sniffers on steroids. They capture network traffic and compare the traffic with a set of known attack patterns or signatures. NIDS devices compare these signatures with every single packet that they see, in hopes of catching intruders in the act. NIDS devices can be deployed passively without requiring major modifications to systems or networks.

- Host-based IDS—These systems vary from vendor to vendor, but they are usually system centric in their analysis. Most host-based IDSs have components that parse system logs and watch user logins and processes. Some of the more advanced systems even have built-in capabilities to catch Trojan code deployments. Host-based systems are agent based—that is, they require the installation of a program on the systems they protect. This allows them to be more thorough on some levels but also more of a headache to deploy and administer.

- Anomaly-based IDS—Anomaly-based systems are a bit more obscure and are oftentimes referred to as more of a "concept" than an actual model. The philosophy behind anomaly-based approaches is to understand the patterns of users and traffic on the network and find deviations in those patterns. For example, a user who normally logs in Monday through Friday but is now logging in at 3 a.m. on a Sunday might be flagged as a potential problem by an anomaly IDS. In theory, an anomaly-based IDS could detect that something was wrong without knowing the specific source of the problem.

The most common IDS types, both commercial and deployed, are HIDS and NIDS models. Anomaly-based IDSs are fairly new in the marketplace and are usually part of a Hybrid IDS that is part NIDS or HIDS and part anomaly-based.

NOTE

Many people unfamiliar with the intrusion detection system field confuse the technology with access control devices such as firewalls. Most intrusion detection systems, in their current form, do not serve as a method of access control. A number of them can be configured to interact with firewalls, but this is not their primary purpose. Beginners should think of an intrusion detection system as a type of burglar alarm and not as a lock or door.

Who Should Be Using an IDS

Although IDS technology is certainly attractive, before sinking any time into IDS research, you should first ask whether an IDS makes sense for your organization. If, for example, an organization is lacking basic security fundamentals such as firewalls, system/OS lockdown procedures, or virus protection, an IDS deployment shouldn't take priority over those efforts. An IDS should be installed only after other facets of the information security strategy have already been initiated (see Chapter 1, "Building a Roadmap for Securing Your Enterprise") or to solve specific situations or shortcomings. For example, if a new e-commerce initiative is launched that you simply cannot secure adequately, an IDS might help you keep a sharper eye on it. In addition, some people use IDSs as validation tools for their firewall rulesets. But if your network is a chaotic collage of vulnerabilities, an IDS will simply help you become the master of the obvious. You'll already have problems that an IDS certainly won't fix. Remember, modern-day IDSs are still, for the most part, reactive devices (although they are starting to block attacks as well). They won't fix your problems.

However, if deploying an IDS is in your future, the following sections should guide you to making informed product decisions.

Network-Based IDSs

Essentially, network-based IDSs are designed to inspect network traffic and look for known attack patterns, or *signatures*. They perform this task by examining each and every packet that traverses the monitored network segment. This is usually accomplished by putting the network interface card (NIC) in "promiscuous" mode and passing every frame to the running IDS process for analysis.

One of the most appealing aspects of the NIDS model is that NIDS devices are passive. In most cases, the rest of the systems don't even know the NIDS devices are there. Even better, deploying NIDS devices doesn't require the involvement of system administrators—a resource that becomes a stumbling point for large HIDS deployments.

Although the NIDS design is moderately effective, it brings with it a few interesting issues. For starters, the attack signatures are based on *known* attack types. This means that most attacks for which the devices have not been programmed will pass by unnoticed. This places the users of these systems one step behind in a game that most are already losing. For example, when the BIND NXT bug hit the Internet in 1999, no NIDS product on the market was capable of detecting the exploitation of the hole. Why? Because it was a new vulnerability and IDS programmers hadn't built a check for it into their signature libraries yet. One by one, vendors began creating signatures for the attack, but most of these updates occurred weeks, sometimes months, after the attack was widespread.

TIP

For a description of the BIND NXT vulnerability, along with other BIND vulnerabilities, see `http://www.isc.org/products/BIND/bind-security-19991108.html`.

In short, if the IDS is not updated on a constant basis, it will be unable to help identify new attacks and trends—much like vulnerability assessment (VA) scanners. (See Chapter 11, "Vulnerability Assessment Tools (Scanners).") Unfortunately, even when vendors and administrators alike work to keep NIDS devices up-to-date, they will still be one step behind.

Another issue that plagues the NIDS model is the widespread deployment of switched environments. Switches, by their very nature, reduce the amount of traffic that is sniffable. NIDS devices rely on their capability to view all network traffic, so if the NIDS devices can't see the traffic, they can't inspect it.

NIDS devices are also traffic sensitive. Although some of the higher-end NIDS systems are currently pushing the gigabit boundaries, some NIDS devices struggle in high-bandwidth environments.

Finally, IDS evasion via packet-mangling techniques and other clever tricks are big problems. Several papers and studies have been released detailing methods of fooling intrusion detection devices. These techniques revolve around resequencing attacks, fragmenting attacks, and performing other techniques that could be used to confuse NIDS devices. Vendors have responded to many of these issues, but evasion techniques will continue to be a problem for many NIDS solutions.

TIP

Security experts Timothy Newsham and Thomas Ptacek published one of the more famous IDS evasion papers in 1998. It continues to be referenced years later, because many vendors have failed to address the problems Newsham and Ptacek pointed out. You can find it at `http://www.robertgraham.com/mirror/Ptacek-Newsham-Evasion-98.html`.

Host-Based ID Systems

The host-based model varies from the NIDS model on a number of fronts. First and foremost, the host model is a more intrusive one. Whereas NIDS devices are passive, host-based systems require agents to be installed on all monitored systems. This isn't usually a problem on a few dozen machines, but placing agents on a few hundred—or worse, a few thousand—machines is no small chore. The potential overhead in deploying and managing a large number of agents has led many organizations to install the host-based models on critical machines and to use NIDS devices for the rest of the enterprise.

NOTE

Don't assume that you are stuck with choosing between the host and network models. Most vendors agree that the ideal IDS deployment consists of an integrated approach, incorporating both host-based and network-based detection. In fact, this holistic model has been adopted by most vendors.

Some of the host-based models are more full-featured than others. For example, most products monitor system logs for basic events such as failed login attempts, the creation of new user accounts, or access violations. Some monitor kernel messages for certain types of activity that might be interpreted as hostile, and more advanced HIDS agents watch for the installation of Trojan code and back-door programs and even terminate rogue processes.

Although all these features sound cool, and can be quite useful, the host-based model is not without its problems. For example, HIDS agents are still limited by the same factors that plague the NIDS model: They primarily look for known problems. If a HIDS agent is programmed to spot Back Orifice (a well-known Trojan), it will most likely be successful in performing that task. When a new next-generation Trojan hits the scene, however, there is a good chance the HIDS agent will miss it until a product update/revision is released.

Another problem, albeit minor for most environments, is that of CPU load. HIDS agents are active processes and consume CPU cycles. On underutilized machines, this is a moot point. However, for machines that are squeezed for every single CPU cycle, a busy HIDS agent might be the straw that breaks the camel's back.

Despite these shortcomings, one of the primary benefits of deploying host-based IDSs is the fact that they centralize and parse your system logs. This alone is a huge benefit because most organizations do not review their system logs until something goes wrong.

Anomaly-Based IDSs

The other types of IDS are based on knowing the attack signatures that crackers use to attempt to break in. The underlying assumption of anomaly-based IDS is that your network has regular patterns of usage.

However, if you do not have regular patterns of usage, the anomaly-based IDS has a hard time functioning. An example of a network that would be a bad choice for an anomaly-based IDS is a university network where it is almost unpredictable what kinds of legitimate usage occurs on the network.

The way most anomaly-based IDSs work is that you have to put the IDS in training mode for a while for it to learn your network. Then, you switch it to detection mode. Every time it sees a new behavior on the network, you have to tell it whether that behavior is normal or not. Getting an anomaly-based IDS up and running is a very time-consuming process in the beginning and requires more personnel hours than other IDSs.

One of the better papers on the anomaly-based IDS appears in Phrack, of all places, and is available at `http://www.phrack.com/phrack/56/p56-0x0b`.

What to Look for When Choosing an IDS

You should note two points above all others when reading this section. First, there is no "one size fits all" IDS solution on the market today, and I highly doubt there will be one anytime soon. The IDS product landscape is a diverse one. Products such as ISS RealSecure are easy to install and have a wide range of features, but they often fall over in high-bandwidth environments. Enterasys Dragon performs well and is liked by most Unix-savvy individuals, but its user interface and the learning curve associated with the product turn away most Windows-focused administrators. BlackICE's raw power and simplicity might tempt some small organizations, but when you need to manage hundreds of thousands of events, Cisco's IDS with the Cisco Secure Policy Manager (CSPM) is a much more manageable solution. In short, organizations need to understand what their parameters are and adopt a product that best serves those requirements.

Second, the product balances change almost yearly. For example, in one year, Cisco went from having one of the worst user interfaces (an HP OpenView hack) in the market to one of the best (CSPM). In three years' time, the product known as ID-track from the company called Internet Tools was acquired by Axent, expanded upon, relabeled as NetProwler, and later acquired by Symantec when Axent and Symantec merged. NFR Security, Inc. (NFR) was way ahead of the IDS technology curve at one point and within three years was considered by most to be somewhat behind. The bottom line is this: Consider the comments in this text, the reviews that are published in magazines, and anything else you might find on the Internet, but be conscious of the age of the information. The issues will stay somewhat constant, but who and how they are addressed could change in as short a time as six months. Although products such as firewalls are fairly mature and are now mostly differentiated by features, speed, and price, the IDS market is anything but mature. The only thing that you can be sure of on the IDS front is that nothing will remain the same.

Common Evaluation Criteria

When choosing an intrusion detection system, understand that you are choosing two things: a) a product, and b) a partner (vendor) who will be updating that product. Although the vendor (or team, in the case of open-source solutions) behind the product is always a consideration, it becomes even more critical in the intrusion detection market. Because IDSs are so time-sensitive and dependent on product updates, a good system will become increasingly less useful if it is not attended to properly and regularly. Evaluating the vendor's track record in regard to product updates is a worthy effort.

On the product side, several issues and features can be found in one IDS but not in another. However, many of the bells and whistles of these products are just that—cute features. Make sure that you evaluate the core components first, and then examine the bonus features. The following is a list of core components you should evaluate when making IDS selection decisions:

- Depth of coverage—One of the more important components of an intrusion detection system is its capability to detect a wide array of attacks. Although a great back-end engine, diverse customization options, and a slick management interface are all strong selling points, if the product is incapable of detecting more than a handful of attacks, it will do little good. Be sure that any NIDS solution you examine is bundled with a healthy set of attack signatures. On the HIDS front, be sure that the product does more than inspect a few log files for a handful of events, and make sure that the product supports all the platforms you need to monitor. If, for example, the HIDS agents support only Windows NT but you have both Solaris and Linux machines, you are going to come up short in regard to overall coverage.

- Accuracy of coverage—This is a hard factor to determine without thorough testing, but it should be noted that not all signatures have been created equal. False positives are a big problem with most NIDS solutions, and in large environments, these misfires can jeopardize the overall effectiveness of the intrusion detection effort. Products designed with the reduction of false positives in mind are always more desirable.

- Robust architecture—There are multiple components to an intrusion detection solution, and it is important that both the engines and the IDS framework itself have been designed with strength in mind. On the engine/agent side, products should be capable of withstanding both attacks and basic evasion techniques. Although evasion has traditionally been a problem that has plagued NIDS devices, and will most likely continue to trouble them for some time, insightful vendors have continued their attempts at addressing these issues. Less insightful vendors have chosen to ignore them, which not only reduces product effectiveness, but also reduces confidence among security professionals.

- Scalability—Multiple components affect IDSs on the "scaling" front, but the two biggest are in the areas of high-bandwidth monitoring and data management. The bandwidth issues apply to NIDS devices in that many products have problems monitoring high-bandwidth, high-session environments. On the management front, some products struggle with monitoring, storing, and presenting large volumes of alert data. For example, if you deploy a few dozen sensors (host- or network-based) on a high-traffic/high-alert network, they will be pumping a lot of data back to the centralized databases and consoles. Some back-end systems will crumble under such loads, or worse, the volume of data will make it incredibly hard for the security officers to sort through the alerts. However, it should be noted that these issues are not relevant in all environments. For example, if you are looking to place a few ID devices to watch over a few T1 connections, you aren't likely to run into bandwidth and data storage issues.

- Management framework—Being able to detect attacks is crucial for an IDS, but equally important is the capability to clearly and efficiently present the data related to those attacks. If security officers are unable to access attack and alert data easily, the overall usefulness of the IDS is limited. When evaluating intrusion detection systems, be sure to use the management console in a live environment. Also, be sure you are comfortable with a system's management framework, and make sure it allows you to easily access the information you want. In short, the management framework used to control and monitor the devices is almost as important as the HIDS and NIDS devices themselves.

- Timely updates—Much like in the vulnerability assessment (VA) and antivirus product fields, as new attacks continue to surface, the need for timely IDS product updates becomes critical. Operating an outdated IDS is analogous to operating an airport without radar. Although updates are a bigger issue in regard to NIDS products, the issue is still relevant to all IDS models.

- Customizability—Some intrusion detection products allow for a diverse range of customization, whereas others are fairly static and inflexible. For some organizations, customization features will not be a big issue, because they will be operating IDS solutions with out-of-the-box configurations. For others, customization is a must. However, when choosing an IDS vendor, you should evaluate your needs now, as well as in the future. Although you might not require the capability to write a custom signature today, you might need that functionality in the future.

- Skill set requirements—Intrusion detection devices should be treated like any other component of enterprise IT—properly trained staff should operate the solution. Unfortunately, the one thing both administrators and managers alike seem to cast aside are the issues surrounding IDS upkeep.

Snort and Other Open Source IDS Solutions

Several open source IDS solutions in the community are worth investigating. The most popular is Snort, created by Marty Roesch. Snort is often considered to be the Linux of the intrusion detection field. It touts a very active development community, a wide set of signatures, and a large base of deployed users. Snort uses an NIDS model and has a fairly extensive set of plug-ins and supporting applications. For example, the Carnegie Mellon CERT team has created a front-end Web interface for Snort called Analysis Console for Intrusion Databases (ACID). ACID provides administrators and security officers a more user-friendly view of Snort output, which is natively quite raw. Snort is actively being developed on Unix, although Windows ports of the application exist.

> **TIP**
>
> Snort's home page: `http://www.snort.org`
>
> ACID's home page: `http://www.cert.org/kb/acid/`

Two other popular open source IDS tools are SNARE and SHADOW—both are Unix based. SNARE (`http://www.intersectalliance.com/projects/Snare/`) is an HIDS, and SHADOW (`http://www.nswc.navy.mil/ISSEC/CID/`) has long been a favorite among government and military personnel.

> **TIP**
>
> You can find a good list of HIDS and NIDS tools at `http://www-rnks.informatik.tu-cottbus.de/~sobirey/ids.html`.

Although some components of open source IDS tools are a bit behind those of their commercial counterparts, portions of programs such as Snort are quite advanced. In the coming years, it will be interesting to see whether the successes of open source initiatives like the FreeBSD and Linux projects will be shared by the open source intrusion detection community.

Intrusion Detection Product Listing

The following is a list of some of the more common intrusion detection products on the market today. I've attempted to list all the major players, but please remember that the IDS industry is still quite young, with new vendors popping up periodically and others fading away or being bought and sold. Use this section as a guide, but be sure you do some online research when investigating IDS solutions.

Cisco Secure IDS

Cisco is very active in the IDS market; it has a host sensor product as well as the NIDS products it has had for a few years. Its HIDS product runs on Solaris, Windows NT, and Windows 2000. Cisco is selling its NIDS as appliances—the idea is that you buy a fully contained box and drop it onto your network with a minimum of installation effort. Cisco is also one of the few vendors that sells an enterprise class as well as low levels for small shops. The NIDSs also support anomaly detection.

> Vendor: Cisco Systems
>
> Platform: Appliance, Solaris, Windows
>
> Product: Cisco IDS
>
> URL: http://www.cisco.com/warp/public/cc/pd/sqsw/sqidsz/index.shtml

Computer Associates eTrust Intrusion Detection

Computer Associates bought the eTrust Intrusion Detection System, as well as the whole company, from Platinum. It also has several unusual features such as URL blocking to keep your employees from viewing Web pages they shouldn't. The marketing for this product is definitely overboard; it has language like "complete protection" and "isolates, contains, and extinguishes all enterprise threats." Needless to say, this is not really true. Discussions on the Net mention that it is very resource intensive.

> Vendor: Computer Associates
>
> Platform: Windows
>
> Product: eTrust Intrusion Detection
>
> URL: http://www.ca.com

Enterasys Dragon IDS

Enterasys acquired the Dragon IDS with its acquisition of Network Security Wizards in 2000. Dragon is a Unix-based system that was built for easy monitoring of high-bandwidth environments. Dragon has traditionally been less polished than most IDS offerings, but it's far more robust. Organizations with Unix expertise that require a highly customizable and extremely powerful NIDS solution will probably like Dragon a great deal. Those that have lower requirements or primarily Windows-based operations might be more comfortable with other offerings. Enterasys also offers a HIDS agent that ties into the Dragon framework.

Vendor: Enterasys Networks, Inc.

Platform: Appliance and Unix

Product: Dragon

URL: http://www.enterasys.com

Intrusion SecureNet NID/SecureHost HID

Intrusion has an interesting history. It was originally known as ODS and provided network hardware. At the end of 1998, it got into the IDS business. In 2000, it changed its name to Intrusion.com, and then after the dotcom crash in late 2001, it became just Intrusion. Its product lines are the SecureNet NIDS appliances and SecureHost HIDS for Windows.

Vendor: Intrusion, Inc.

Platform: Appliance and Windows

Product: SecureNet and SecureHost

URL: http://www.intrusion.com/default.asp

IntruVert IntruShield

IntruVert is a relatively new player in the IDS game with the company founded in October 2000. IntruVert is focused on the high end of the market with products that can handle high-bandwidth enterprise class operations. It is a combination of an NIDS and an anomaly-based system.

Vendor: IntruVert

Platform: Appliance

Product: IntruShield

URL: http://www.intruvert.com

ISS RealSecure

ISS was one of the first vendors to completely integrate its host-based and network-based offerings into a unified management framework. ISS RealSecure has one of the easiest management consoles to use, and its server and network sensors have matured greatly over the years. RealSecure runs on an assortment of platforms, including Windows and many versions of Unix, and has one of the broadest sets of attack signatures in the industry today. ISS seems to be making real progress: It recently certified its RealSecure product at gigabit speeds and now has a HIDS product as well.

Vendor: Internet Security Systems, Inc.

Platform: Windows NT, Windows 2000, Solaris, HP/UX, AIX

Product: RealSecure

URL: http://www.iss.net

ISS BlackICE

ISS took over this product originally from Network ICE. It is a Windows-based solution that boasts a substantial signature base with an easy-to-use interface. BlackICE is also a favorite among home users, because watching all the attacks that come in through cable and DSL connections can be an enjoyable pastime. BlackICE's biggest weakness has traditionally been in relation to its centralized console and management features. Running a single instance of BlackICE is easy; running a few dozen has traditionally been painful. It is a nice low-end product, though.

Vendor: ISS

Platform: Windows NT

Product: BlackICE

URL: http://blackice.iss.net

NFR Security Intrusion Detection System

NFR has long been acknowledged as one of the first vendors to address many of the well-known NIDS evasion techniques. NFR's Network Intrusion Detection System is a NIDS-based product that allows a high degree of customization through the use of ncode, a scripting language NFR developed. NFR's product has traditionally been enjoyed by experienced IDS veterans. Although the product is capable of handling various types of packet-mangling attacks, it tends not to hold up in high-bandwidth situations. NFR has also added the NFS Host Intrusion Detection System to its product line.

Vendor: NFR Security, Inc.

Platform: Appliance

Product: NFR IDS

URL: http://www.nfr.com

nSecure Software nPatrol

nPatrol tries to do it all: It's a NIDS and a HIDS with anomaly detection. It is a relatively new company, founded in February 2000.

Vendor: nSecure

Platform: Linux

Product: nPatrol

URL: http://www.nsecure.net

Symantec NetProwler and Intruder Alert

Symantec's IDS strategy integrates its host-based system (Intruder Alert) with its network-based system (NetProwler). Although the two can be tied together using a common management platform, their similarities end there. NetProwler has traditionally possessed some interesting features not found in other IDSs, but it lacks some of the back-end support to handle many NIDS evasion techniques. NetProwler runs only on Windows NT, except for the Console which will also run on 2000, and a new version hasn't been released in two years. In contrast, the HIDS Intruder Alert has one of the broadest offerings on the market in terms of supported operating systems.

Vendor: Axent/Symantec

Platform: Windows, various Unix versions

Product: NetProwler, Intruder Alert

URL: http://enterprisesecurity.symantec.com/products/products.cfm?ProductID=50

Summary

Intrusion detection technology can be a powerful ally. If organizations lack the capability to detect and respond to attacks, malicious users have a higher chance of successfully hurting these organizations. However, intrusion detection is far from a mature technology. Organizations looking to adopt IDSs should carefully gather their requirements, document their needs, and be prepared to support another operational system in moving forward. IDSs are not silver-bullet solutions, but their usefulness can be realized through intelligent deployment efforts.

The IDS Frequently Asked Question (FAQ) list. This is a great place for beginners: http://www.ticm.com/kb/faq/idsfaq.html. The ARACHNIDS database is an interesting open-source effort for community-driven IDS signature development: http://www.whitehats.com/ids/index.html.

International Symposium on Recent Advances in Intrusion Detection. A conference Web site of the yearly conference on intrusion detection. The papers are on this site, so it lets you keep up with the latest developments: http://www.raid-symposium.org/.

Talisker's IDS page. Talisker keeps good track of all the latest IDS products and round-ups. If it's an IDS product, he'll have it listed: http://www.networkintrusion.co.uk/.

Two very informative mailing lists for in-depth IDS discussions are the Security Focus IDS list (Focus-IDS) and the IDS list run from the University of Australia. HTML archives can be found at http://archives.neohapsis.com/archives/sf/ids/ or http://archives.neohapsis.com/archives/ids/.

Intrusion Detection. Rebecca Bace. Macmillan Technical Publishing. ISBN: 1-57870-185-6. 2000. (Bace provides some of the best insight and history of the intrusion detection scene, complete with insights into different models and theories.)

Intrusion Signatures and Analysis. Cooper, Northcutt, Fearnow, Frederick. New Riders. ISBN: 0-7357-1063-5. (This is another outstanding IDS application.)

The Practical Intrusion Detection Handbook. Paul Proctor. Prentice Hall. ISBN: 0-13-025960-8. 2001. (This is one of the best IDS application books I've seen.)

13

Logging Tools

This chapter explains why logs are important, how to create a logging strategy, and how to avoid some of the common pitfalls associated with logging and auditing. We will introduce the tools and techniques that will help you get the most from your logs without losing your mind.

Why Log?

Logs are another set of double-edged swords that lie quietly behind the scenes. They can completely save your butt, or completely overwhelm you, depending on the situation. Their importance, however, is frequently under-estimated.

Logs are useful for a number of things. They can help you troubleshoot problems. They can be used for tracking down network anomalies. They can help trace an intruder's steps, or help solidify your case in a court of law. However, if you don't have a logging strategy, rest assured you will eventually come to regret it.

Logs from a Cracking Perspective

If your operating system already supports logging, you might be tempted to forgo additional logging tools. Try to resist that temptation. You can't always trust your logs. In fact, altering logs to cover one's tracks is one of the first things crackers learn. The practice has become so common that there are tools that automate the process. A list of the many available tools can be found at `http://www.apocalypseonline.com/security/tools/tools.asp?exp_category=Log%20Cleaners`, but here are a few of the more well-known ones:

- **UTClean**—UTClean is a utility that erases any evidence of your presence in wtmp, wtmpx, utmp, utmpx, and lastlog. Check out UTClean at http://www.kyuzz.org/jaromil/files/exploits/utclean.c.

- **remove**—remove will clean utmp, wtmp, and lastlog, erasing any evidence of your presence. Check out remove at http://www.kyuzz.org/jaromil/files/exploits/remove.c.

- **marry**—marry is a tool for editing utmp, wtmp, and lastlog entries. Check out marry at http://www.apocalypseonline.com/security/tools/redirect.asp?red_tool=marry.c.

NOTE

On many Unix systems, wtmp, wtmpx, utmpx, and lastlog record and report user information, including what time a particular user accessed the system. For example, grepping for a last entry on root will produce output like this:

```
root      console   Fri Jun 19 17:01 - down    (00:01)
root      console   Fri Jun 12 12:26 - down    (4+02:16)
root      console   Tue May 19 10:45 - down    (01:50)
root      console   Fri May  1 11:23 - down    (00:02)
root      console   Fri Apr 24 09:56 - 09:56   (00:00)
root      console   Mon Mar 23 02:53 - down    (00:01)
root      console   Mon Mar 23 02:43 - down    (00:01)
```

When an intrusion occurs, system administrators turn to these logs to determine who accessed the machine and when.

TIP

It should also be noted that "rootkits," packages designed to cover an intruder's tracks and provide back doors into the system, usually contain log cleansers as well. One of the largest collections of rootkits I've seen can be found at http://packetstorm.decepticons.org/UNIX/penetration/rootkits/.

Forming a Logging Strategy

To hedge your bets against crackers tampering with your log entries, you should create a logging strategy that's difficult to circumvent. The easiest way to achieve this is to write your logs to a one-way write-once device, or to copy your logs to a secured logging server. Some administrators have their Unix machines write their logs to a serial port that is attached to a standalone machine. Although this is certainly quite secure, the model doesn't scale very well.

One model that is a little more scalable revolves around using the syslog protocol. syslog is a native service on almost every Unix platform, and recently add-on products have made it available on other platforms (such as Windows NT) as well. Although there are more secure alternatives to syslog, it is now common across most router and firewall products. This ubiquity gives administrators a common denominator with which to centralize all logging. For example, administrators can configure all hosts to log to a protected and centralized syslog-based logging server—giving security teams a single point at which to coordinate log data (see Figure 13.1).

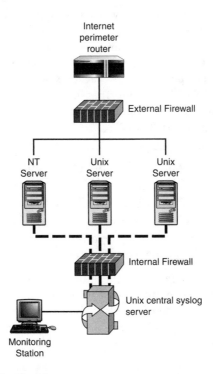

FIGURE 13.1   Centralizing logging.

When configured properly, the only traffic allowed to the syslog server is traffic destined for UDP port 514 (the syslog port). By sending system logs to a separate, secure machine, you make it a LOT more difficult for intruders to clean their tracks.

TIP

Adiscon makes a great Windows NT/2000-based utility called Event Reporter that enables you to send the Windows event logs to a syslog-based server. See http://www.eventreporter. com for more information.

TIP

A couple of years ago a program called SRS (Secure Remote Streaming) came onto the scene. SRS was written to replace syslog with security at the core of its design. It's not as frequently adopted as syslog, but it is certainly worth checking out as a more secure alternative: `http://packetstormsecurity.nl/groups/w00w00/SRS/`. Another alternative worth checking out that can encrypt data is nsyslogd, available at `http://cheops.anu.edu.au/~avalon/nsyslog.html`.

In addition to centralizing your logs, you might want to consider using at least one third-party logging or parsing tool. This approach has several advantages. First, although the cracker community is familiar with operating system-based logs, few crackers have the knowledge or the means to circumvent third-party logging software. Second, good third-party software packages derive their logs independently of the operating system logs. You'll know that intruders have penetrated your system when you compare this information and discover a discrepancy between your third-party logs and your regular logs.

This is especially true if you insulate your third-party logs. For example, suppose you use a third-party logging tool to later verify the integrity of operating system-based logs. Although expensive, writing those third-party logs to write-once media guarantees you one set of reliable logs, and reliability is everything.

Using third-party products is prudent in case your out-of-the-box logging utilities fail. For example, on some versions of Solaris, the `tmpx` file will truncate incoming hostnames, rendering any data obtained via `last` erroneous and incomplete.

Coming at this from a different angle, it's now a pretty common procedure for crackers to kill your logging capabilities prior to launching a real attack. If the target is running an unpatched version of Solaris 2.5.*x*, for instance, you can kill `syslogd` simply by sending it an external message from a nonexistent IP address. Similarly, if `syslogd` accepts remote messages, anyone can make a false entry in the log.

You should consider an alternative logging system for all these reasons. The next section briefly covers several good ones.

Network Monitoring and Data Collection

The following tools not only report data from logs, they also collect data from diverse sources. Note that some of these tools are starting to tread pretty close to the intrusion detection space, which we covered in detail in Chapter 12, "Intrusion Detection Systems." It will be interesting to see whether the two types of utilities will interoperate over time.

SWATCH (The System Watcher)

The authors wrote SWATCH to supplement the logging capabilities of out-of-the-box Unix systems. SWATCH, consequently, has logging capabilities that far exceed your run-of-the-mill syslog. SWATCH provides real-time monitoring, logging, and reporting. Because SWATCH is written in Perl, it's both portable and extensible.

SWATCH has several unique features:

- A "backfinger" utility that attempts to grab finger information from an attacking host.

- Support for instant paging so you can receive up-to-the-minute reports.

- Conditional execution of commands. (If this condition is found in a log file, do this.)

Lastly, SWATCH relies on local configuration files. Conveniently, multiple configuration files can exist on the same machine. Therefore, although originally intended only for system administrators, any local user with adequate privileges can use SWATCH.

Author: Stephen E. Hansen and E. Todd Atkins

Platform: Unix (Perl is required)

URL: http://www.oit.ucsb.edu/~eta/swatch/

Watcher

Kenneth Ingham developed Watcher while at the University of New Mexico Computing Center. He explains that the Computing Center was being expanded at the time, so the logging process they were using was no longer adequate. Ingham was looking for a way to automate log scanning, and Watcher was the result of his labors.

Watcher analyzes various logs and processes, looking for radically abnormal activity. The author sufficiently fine-tuned this process so that Watcher can interpret the widely variable output of commands such as ps without setting off alarms.

Watcher runs on Unix systems and requires a C compiler.

Author: Kenneth Ingham

Email: ingham@i-pi.com

URL: http://www.i-pi.com/watcher.html

lsof (List Open Files)

lsof version 4 traces not only open files (including network connections, pipes, streams, and so on), but the processes that own them. lsof runs on many Unix systems, including but not limited to the following:

- AIX

- BSDI BSD/OS

- NetBSD 1.[23] for Intel and SPARC-based systems

- FreeBSD

- Digital Unix (DEC OSF/1)

- HP-UX

- IRIX

- Linux

- NEXTSTEP 3.1 for NEXTSTEP architectures

- SCO UnixWare

- Solaris and SUN OS

    Author: Vic Abell

    Platform: Unix

    URL: `ftp://vic.cc.purdue.edu/pub/tools/unix/lsof/`

Private-I

Private-I has two primary functions. First, it serves as a back-end log archiver for Cisco IOS-based routers, PIX and Checkpoint firewalls, and SonicWall VPN devices. Second, it is capable of generating real-time alerts based on known firewall and IOS event codes. Because Private-I has been designed to process the vendor-specific event codes piped to it via syslog, it can alert administrators of problems in real-time, as well as produce informative reports.

    OpenSystems.com

    URL: `http://www.opensystems.com`

WebSense

Though WebSense is best known for its screening capabilities, the product also has powerful logging capabilities. (These have recently been enhanced, as the product has been designed to work closely with firewalls from many vendors.)

WebSense, Inc.

Email: `info@websense.com`

URL: `http://www.websense.com/`

Win-Log version 1

Win-Log is a very simple utility for Windows NT. It logs when, how often, and how long Windows NT is used. You can use this utility to ascertain whether someone has been rebooting your box, even if they somehow circumvent Event Logger.

iNFINITY Software

Email: `jcross@griffin.co.uk`

URL: `http://www.crossj.pwp.blueyonder.co.uk/winlog.html`

SNIPS

SNIPS is a network and system monitoring package. It allows administrators to quickly find out whether there is something wrong with their systems.

URL: `http://www.netplex-tech.com/software/snips/`

Tools for Analyzing Log Files

The following tools examine log files, extract the data, and generate reports.

NetTracker

NetTracker analyzes both wall and proxy files. It has extensive filtering and reporting, and can export data to Excel and Access file formats. NetTracker can also analyze general access logs and format custom reports suitable for graphing. NetTracker runs on Windows; a 30-day evaluation is available on the Web.

Sane Solutions, LLC

Email: `info@sane.com`

URL: `http://www.sane.com/products/NetTracker/`

LogSurfer

LogSurfer is a comprehensive log analysis tool. The program examines plain text log files and can perform various actions based on what it finds (and the rules you provide). These might include creating an alert, executing an external program, or even taking portions of the log data and feeding that to external commands or processes. LogSurfer requires a C compiler.

Univ. of Hamburg, Dept. of Computer Science

DFN-CERT

URL: `ftp://ftp.cert.dfn.de/pub/tools/audit/logsurfer/`

WebTrends for Firewalls and VPNs

WebTrends for Firewalls and VPNs combines Web link, usage, and traffic analysis with log analysis for more than 20 firewalls.

WebTrends can pull some very impressive statistics, and writes to a wide variety of database report formats. (This product runs on Windows.)

NetIQ

URL: `http://www.netiq.com/webtrends/default.asp`

Analog

Analog is probably the only truly cross-platform log file analyzer. Analog currently runs on most operating systems.

Not only is Analog cross-platform, it also has built-in support for a wide variety of languages, including English, Portuguese, French, German, Swedish, Czech, Slovak, Slovene, Romanian, and Hungarian.

Analog also does reverse DNS lookups (slowly), has a built-in scripting language (similar to the shell languages), and has at least minimal support for AppleScript.

Lastly, Analog supports most of the well-known Web server log formats, including Apache, NCSA, WebStar, IIS, W3 Extended, Netscape/iPlanet, and Netpresenz.

Author: Stephen Turner

URL: `http://www.analog.cx/`

Summary

Never underestimate the importance of keeping detailed logs. Not only are logs essential when you're investigating a network intrusion, they're also a requisite for bringing charges against an attacker. Sparse logs simply won't do.

In recent years, many criminal cracking cases have ended in plea bargains. One of the primary reasons for this is because perpetrators were often kids—kids who were just "having a little fun." However, plea bargains are becoming less prevalent as real criminal elements migrate to the Net. Real criminals know that proving a case before a judge or jury is very difficult (especially if the prosecution has little Internet experience). When judges and jurors are asked to send a human being to prison, they need substantial proof. The only way you can offer substantial proof is by having several fail-safe methods of logging.

Crimes perpetrated over the Internet are unlike most other crimes. For example, in a robbery case, crooks are placed in a lineup so the victim can identify the culprit. In burglary cases, fingerprints will generally reveal the identity of the perpetrator. On the Internet, however, you have neither a physical description nor fingerprints. Therefore, without logs, making a case against a cracker is almost impossible.

14

Password Security

This chapter examines password crackers and other programs designed to circumvent password security. Although password cracking is a core skill of most intruders, it is also important for system and network administrators to understand the ins and outs of password security. Comprehending where and why passwords can fail is paramount in maintaining enterprise security; many times, passwords are the first, and unfortunately only, line of defense. This chapter explains how passwords are stored, how they can be stolen, how they are cracked, and what you can do to minimize the risks associated with using passwords.

An Introduction to Password Cracking

Passwords and "pass phrases" are used for everything ranging from logging into terminals, checking email accounts, and protecting Excel spreadsheets to securing the encryption keys for PKI-enabled enterprise networks. Their use in enterprise is widespread, to say the least.

Password crackers are programs that aid in the discovery of protected passwords, usually through some method of automated guessing. Although some applications and poorly designed infrastructure equipment will encrypt or encode passwords, most modern day operating systems and devices create a *hash* of the password instead. I will go into the differences between hashing and encrypting in the next section, but for now simply note that they are two different methods of storing password information.

Although some poor encryption mechanisms can be easily reversed, modern day hashing methods are *one-way*—that is, they cannot be reversed, and therefore decryption is not an option. Although the use of one-way algorithms can sound like a rock-solid solution, it simply makes the task at hand a little more time-consuming. To circumvent the challenges created by hashing, password crackers simply employ the same algorithm used to encrypt the original password. The tools perform comparative analysis (a process explained later in this chapter), and simply try to match their guesses with the original encrypted phrase or password hash.

Many password crackers are nothing but guessing engines—programs that try word after word, often at high speeds. These programs rely on the theory that eventually you will encounter the right word or phrase. This theory is sound, because humans are lazy creatures. They rarely take the trouble to create strong passwords. However, this shortcoming is not always the user's fault:

> Users are rarely, if ever, educated as to what are wise choices for passwords. If a password is in the dictionary, it is extremely vulnerable to being cracked, and users are simply not coached as to "safe" choices for passwords. Of those users who are so educated, many think that simply because their password is not in /usr/dict/words, it is safe from detection. Many users also say that because they do not have private files online, they are not concerned with the security of their account, little realizing that by providing an entry point to the system they allow damage to be wrought on their entire system by a malicious cracker.
>
> —*A Survey of, and Improvements to, Password Security.*
> Daniel V. Klein, Software Engineering Institute,
> Carnegie-Mellon University, Pennsylvania.
> (PostScript creation date reported: February 22, 1991.)

It should be noted, however, that the raw "It's-not-in-the-dictionary" approach is now somewhat misleading as well. Password-cracking dictionaries now contain hundreds of thousands of popular names, characters, musical bands, slang, expletives, and an assortment of culturally popular terms that might or might not be in a classic dictionary. We'll explore the depth and versatility of password guessing later on, but the new rule of thumb is to avoid any kind of word all together. For example, "808state" is easily guessed by most password crackers, not only because it's based on a word (state) and a number (808), but also because it's the name of a popular band out of Manchester, England. Stronger passwords can be created by using a combination of letters, numbers, and extended characters. Acronyms work wonderfully, for example, "I'm trying to learn information security techniques quickly!" could be translated to "IT2LISTQ!". This is a MUCH harder password to guess, but is not all that difficult to remember.

The simple password problem is a persistent one, despite the fact that it is easy to provide password-security education. It's puzzling how such a critical security issue (which can easily be addressed) is often overlooked. The issue goes to the very core of security:

Exploiting ill-chosen and poorly-protected passwords is one of the most common attacks on system security used by crackers. Almost every multiuser system uses passwords to protect against unauthorized logons, but comparatively few installations use them properly. The problem is universal in nature, not system-specific; and the solutions are simple, inexpensive, and applicable to any computer, regardless of operating system or hardware. They can be understood by anyone, and it doesn't take an administrator or a systems programmer to implement them.

—"Understanding Password Security for Users On and Offline."
K. Coady. *New England Telecommuting Newsletter*, 1991.

TIP

One additional password pitfall that is frequently overlooked is the password overload scenario. If users have a multitude of passwords to remember, there is a greater chance that they will write them down, use weaker passwords, or introduce an assortment of other insecure password practices into your environment. This is where centralized authentication systems, directory services, and single-sign on solutions can help you. Not only do they reduce operating costs and complexity, they ultimately help you with your overall security posture.

Password Cryptography 101

The etymological root of the word *cryptography* is instructive. The word *crypto* stems from the Greek word *kryptos*. *Kryptos* describes anything that is hidden, obscured, veiled, secret, or mysterious. The word *graph* is derived from *graphia*, which means *writing*. Thus, *cryptography* is the art of secret writing. Yaman Akdeniz, in his paper *Cryptography and Encryption*, gives an excellent and concise definition of cryptography:

Cryptography, defined as "the science and study of secret writing," concerns the ways in which communications and data can be encoded to prevent disclosure of their contents through eavesdropping or message interception, using codes, ciphers, and other methods, so that only certain people can see the real message.

—"Cryptography and Encryption."
Yaman Akdeniz. Cyber-Rights & Cyber-Liberties (UK), August 1996,
at http://www.cyber-rights.org/crypto/cryptog.htm.
Criminal Justice Studies of the Law Faculty of University of Leeds.

To illustrate the process of cryptography, I'll reduce it to its most fundamental parts. Imagine that you've created your own code, in which each letter of the alphabet corresponds to a number (see Figure 14.1).

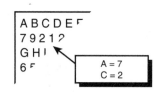

FIGURE 14.1   A primitive example of a code.

Figure 14.1 shows part of a *table*, or *legend*. Below each letter is a corresponding number. A = 7, B = 9, and so forth. This is a code of sorts. If you write a message using these rules, only you and the recipient will know what the message really says.

Unfortunately, such a code can be easily broken. For example, if each letter has a fixed numeric counterpart, you will only use 26 different numbers (perhaps 1 through 26, although you could choose arbitrary numbers). Lexical analysis would reveal your code within a few seconds. (Some software programs perform such analysis at high speed, searching for patterns common to your language.)

ROT-13

Another slightly more complex method is to make each letter become another letter, based on a standard incremental or decremental operation. One system that works this way is ROT-13 encoding. In ROT-13, a substitute letter is used. Moving 13 letters ahead (see Figure 14.2) in the chosen alphabet derives the substitute letter.

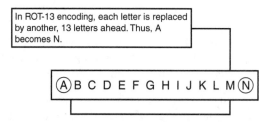

FIGURE 14.2   The ROT-13 system of letter substitution.

This, too, is an ineffective method of encoding or encrypting a message (although it worked in Roman times for Caesar, who used a shift-by-three formula). Some programs quickly identify this pattern. However, this doesn't mean that techniques such as ROT-13 are useless. I will illustrate why, and in the process, I can demonstrate the first important point about encryption:

> Any form of encryption can be useful, given particular circumstances. These circumstances might depend upon time, the sensitivity of the information, and from whom you want to hide data.

In other words, techniques such as ROT-13 can be quite useful under the right circumstances. Here's an example: Suppose a cracker wants to post a new cracking technique to Usenet. He's found a hole and wants to publicize it while it's still exploitable. To prevent security specialists from discovering that hole as quickly as the crackers, the cracker uses ROT-13 to encode his message.

There are a number of organizations that download Usenet traffic on a wholesale basis. In this way, they gather information about the cracker community. Some organizations even use popular search engines to ferret out cracker techniques. These search engines employ *regex* (regular expression) searches (that is, they search by word or phrase). For example, the searching party enters a combination of words such as

- crack

- hack

- vulnerability

- exploit

When this combination of words is entered correctly, a wealth of information emerges. However, if the cracker uses ROT-13, search engines will miss the post. For example, the message

```
Guvf zrffntr jnf rapbqrq va EBG-13 pbqvat. Obl, qvq vg ybbx fperjl hagvy jr
haeniryrq vg!
```

is beyond the reach of the average search engine. What it really looks like is this:

```
This message was encoded in ROT-13 coding. Boy, did it look screwy until we
unraveled it!
```

Most modern mail and newsreaders support ROT-13 encoding and decoding (Outlook Express by Microsoft is one; Netscape Communicator's Mail package is another). Again, this is a rudimentary form of encoding something, but it demonstrates the concept. Now, let's get a bit more specific.

DES and Crypt

Today, Internet information servers run many different operating systems. However, for many years, Unix was the only game in town. The greater number of password crackers were designed to crack Unix passwords. Let's start with Unix, then, and work our way forward.

On most Unix systems, all user login IDs and passwords are centrally stored in either one of two files: the passwd file, usually found in the /etc directory, or a file called shadow, also located in the /etc directory. These files contain various fields. Of those, we are concerned with two: the login ID and the hashed password.

TIP

Using "shadow passwords" is the preferred way of storing password hashes. The /etc/shadow file is only accessible by the root account and system services, as opposed to /etc/passwd, which is readable by everyone. If you have any systems that are still storing password hashes in /etc/passwd, either upgrade them to shadow passwords, or remove them from your environment as soon as possible.

The login ID is stored in plain text, or human-readable English. The password is stored in encrypted form. The encryption process is performed using Crypt(3), a program based on the Data Encryption Standard (DES).

IBM developed the earliest version of DES; today, it is used on all Unix platforms for password encryption. DES is endorsed jointly by the National Bureau of Standards and the National Security Agency. In fact, since 1977, DES has been the generally accepted method for safeguarding sensitive data. Figure 14.3 contains a brief timeline of DES development.

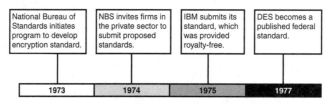

Brief Timeline of the Data Encryption Standard Development

FIGURE 14.3   A brief timeline of the development of DES.

DES was developed to protect certain nonclassified information that might exist in federal offices, as set forth in Federal Information Processing Standards Publication 74, *Guidelines for Implementing and Using the NBS Data Encryption Standard*:

> Because of the unavailability of general cryptographic technology outside the national security arena, and because security provisions, including encryption, were needed in unclassified applications involving Federal Government computer systems, NBS initiated a computer security program in 1973 that included the development of a standard for computer data encryption. Because Federal standards impact on the private sector, NBS solicited the interest and cooperation of industry and user communities in this work.

Information about the original mechanical development of DES is scarce. Reportedly, at the National Security Agency's request, IBM made certain documents classified. However, the source code for Crypt(3) (the current implementation of DES in Unix) is widely available. This is significant, because in all the years that source has been available for Crypt, no one has yet found a way to easily reverse-encode information encrypted with it.

There are several versions of Crypt, and they work slightly differently. In general, however, the process is as follows:

1. Your password is taken in plain text (or, in cryptographic jargon, *clear text*).

2. Your password is used as a key to encrypt a series of zeros (64 in all). The resulting encoded text is thereafter referred to as *cipher text*, the unreadable code that results after plain text is encrypted. This cipher text is sometimes referred to as a *hash*, as well, but the term only loosely fits in this case.

NOTE

One-way hash functions are frequently used as an alternative to actually encrypting passwords. By using hashing algorithms such as MD5 (Message Digest 5) or SHA-1 (Secure Hashing Algorithm 1), a digital footprint can be created of the password that doesn't contain the actual password itself. This varies from the process of encryption because the output does not contain the original input in any form, and it is therefore impossible to derive the original input from the output. Many modern Unix systems are moving towards the use of MD5, SHA-1, or SSHA (Salted Secure Hashing Algorithm) hashes instead of relying on the crypt/DES process. If you are interested in one-way hashing techniques, or cryptography in general, Bruce Schneier's *Applied Cryptography* (John Wiley & Sons, ISBN 0-471-12845-7) is a must-have.

Certain versions of Crypt, notably Crypt(3), take additional steps. For example, after going through this process, the encrypted text is again encrypted, numerous times, using the password as a key. This is a fairly strong method of encryption; it is extremely difficult to break. It is estimated, for example, that the same password can be encoded in 4,096 different ways. The average user, without any knowledge of the system, could probably spend her entire life trying to crack DES and never be successful. To get that in proper perspective, here's an estimate from the National Institute of Standards and Technology:

> The cryptographic algorithm [DES] transforms a 64-bit binary value into a unique 64-bit binary value based on a 56-bit variable. If the complete 64-bit input is used (i.e., none of the input bits should be predetermined from block to block) and if the 56-bit variable is randomly chosen, no technique other than trying all possible keys using known input and output for the DES will guarantee finding the chosen key. As there are more than 70,000,000,000,000,000

(seventy quadrillion) possible keys of 56 bits, the feasibility of deriving a particular key in this way is extremely unlikely in typical threat environments.

—"Data Encryption Standard (DES),"
Federal Information Processing Standards Publication 46-2,
NIST, December 30, 1993.
`http://csrc.nist.gov/fips/fips46-2.txt.`

One might think that DES is entirely infallible. It isn't. Although the information cannot be reverse-encoded, passwords encrypted via DES can be revealed through a comparative process. The process works as follows:

1. You obtain a *dictionary file*, which is really no more than a flat file (plain text) list of words (commonly referred to as *wordlists*).

2. These words are encrypted using DES.

3. Each encrypted word is compared to the target password. If a match occurs, there is a 98% chance that the password was cracked.

The process itself is both simple and brainless, yet quite effective. However, password-cracking programs made for this purpose are often times a little more clever. For example, such cracking programs often subject each word to a list of rules.

NOTE

Because DES is a rather old algorithm and is limited by its 56-bit key, most people are of the opinion that is it at the end of its useful life. The first improvement to DES was Triple DES (3DES), which is three DES operations with three 56-bit keys. This leads to an effective key size of 168 bits.

3DES is partially just a stopgap, but is going to remain a government approved standard for a while. The U.S. government went through a selection process for their replacement for DES, which they are calling Advanced Encryption Standard (AES). The algorithm selected was originally called Rijndael. Provided no unexpected holes are found, Rijndael is trillions of times stronger than DES.

A *rule* could be anything, any manner in which a word might appear. Typical rules might include the following:

• Alternate uppercase and lowercase lettering.

• Spell the word forward and then backward and then fuse the two results (for example, can becomes cannac).

• Add the number 1 to the beginning or end of each word.

Naturally, the more rules you apply, the longer the cracking process takes. However, more rules also guarantee a higher likelihood of success for a number of reasons:

- The Unix file system is case sensitive (WORKSTATION is interpreted differently than Workstation or workstation is).

- Alternating letters and numbers in passwords is a common practice.

Password crackers have had a tremendous impact on Internet security, chiefly because they are so effective:

> Crypt uses the resistance of DES to known plain text attack and make [*sic*] it computationally unfeasible to determine the original password that produced a given encrypted password by exhaustive search. The only publicly known technique that can reveal certain passwords is password guessing: passing large wordlists through the crypt function to see whether any match the encrypted password entries in an /etc/passwd file. Our experience is that this type of attack is successful unless explicit steps are taken to thwart it. Generally we find 30 percent of the passwords on previously unsecured systems.
>
> —*UNIX Password Security—Ten Years Later.*
> David Feldmeier and Philip R. Karn. (Bellcore)

Password-cracking programs are improving in their effectiveness, too. The newer programs incorporate more extensive rules and diverse wordlists. Most wordlists are plain text files with one word per line. These files range in size from 1MB to more than 20MB. Many wordlists are available on the Internet; they come in a wide variety of languages (so an English-speaking American cracker can crack an Italian machine, and vice versa). In fact, the new password-cracking programs are so effective that one site with 5,000 users ran the L0phtcrack cracking program and had broken 90% of the users' passwords within two hours.

TIP

There are several popular wordlist collections. Some are simply dictionaries, and others contain hyphenated words, uppercase and lowercase, and so on. One of the best sites for wordlists is http://www.cotse.com/tools/wordlists2.htm.

The Password-Cracking Process

If you're new to system administration, you're probably wondering how you can benefit from password crackers. Password crackers can help you identify weak passwords on your network.

Ideally, you should run a password cracker once a month. If your network supports several platforms, you might need a wide range of password-cracking utilities. Although password crackers such as John the Ripper can crack both Windows NT-based password files and Unix-based ones, most password crackers are designed to crack only a single type of password.

To crack passwords, you need the following elements:

- Sufficient hardware (a Pentium III-based machine will do nicely)

- A password cracker (such as John the Ripper, Crack, L0phtCrack, and so on)

- A password file (/etc/shadow, the NT SAM file, and so on)

I discuss methods of grabbing password files (like the Unix shadow file, or the Windows NT SAM file) throughout this book, and we will examine the password-cracking programs themselves in the next section. On the hardware front, however, you need only really know one thing: More is better.

Cracking passwords is a CPU- and memory-intensive task. It can take seconds, minutes, days, weeks, months, or even years depending on the strength of the password and the algorithms used. To crack passwords effectively, you need suitable hardware. The more powerful the hardware, the faster you will be able to crack even relatively strong passwords.

For cracking common password files, like those found on Unix and Windows NT systems, I have found that to comfortably handle large password files, you should have the following resources:

- A 400MHz Pentium II or better

- 64MB of RAM or better

A single-processor Pentium II-based system dedicated to password cracking can chew through most NT SAM (password) files in under 48 hours. Dual-processor, Pentium III-based systems will work even faster.

There are techniques, however, for overcoming hardware restrictions. One is the parlor trick of *distributed cracking*. In distributed cracking, you run the cracking program simultaneously on separate processors. There are a few ways to do this. One is to break the password file into pieces and crack those pieces on separate machines. In this way, the job is distributed among a series of workstations, thus cutting resource drain and the time it takes to crack the entire file.

The problem with distributed cracking is that it makes a lot of noise. Remember the Randal Schwartz case? Mr. Schwartz probably would never have been discovered if he were not distributing the CPU load. Another system administrator noticed the heavy processor power being eaten. (He also noted that one process had been running for more than a day.) Distributed cracking really isn't viable for a cracker unless he is the administrator of a site or he has a network at home (which is not so unusual these days; I have a network at home that consists of Windows 95, Windows NT, Linux, Sun, and Novell boxes).

The Password Crackers

Most of the remainder of this chapter is devoted to individual password crackers. Some tools are made for cracking Unix `passwd` and `shadow` files, some are for cracking NT SAM files, and some work across applications and services you might not have even heard of. Some of the tools here are not even password crackers; instead, they are auxiliary utilities that can be used in conjunction with existing password-related tools.

Password Crackers for Windows

Windows NT keeps password hashes in a protected portion of the Registry called the *SAM*. However, there are a number of ways to get these hashes. The easiest method is to use the `rdisk` command to create a backup of the SAM, and then copy that file to a password-cracking machine. `rdisk /s-` will create a compressed SAM image in the `repair` directory of the `%systemroot%` (usually `c:\winnt\repair`).

Another trick is to sniff the password hashes off of the wire. L0phtCrack, for example, has this feature built in. Regardless of how you get the NT password hashes themselves, the following utilities can be used to aid your Windows NT-based cracking efforts.

L0phtCrack/LC4

L0phtCrack is the most celebrated NT password-cracking tool to date, primarily because it uses a two-prong approach, as explained by its authors:

> Passwords are computed using 2 different methods. The first, a dictionary lookup, called dictionary-cracking, uses a user supplied dictionary file. The password hashes for all the words in the dictionary file are computed and compared against all the password hashes for the users. When there is a match the password is known. This method is extremely fast. Thousands of users can be checked with a 100,000-word dictionary file in just a few minutes on a PPro 200. The drawback to this method is that it only finds very simple passwords....
> The second method is the brute-force computation. This method uses a particular character set such as A–Z or A–Z plus 0–9 and computes the hash for every possible password made up of those characters.

When L0phtCrack was released, it caused considerable debate, especially because the program's authors pointed out that Microsoft's password algorithm was "intrinsically flawed." Microsoft officials hotly disputed that claim, but their efforts were for naught. L0phtCrack works very well, and it is now an accepted fact that Windows NT's password-hashing techniques are flawed from a security standpoint.

To effectively use L0phtCrack, you need the password hashes.

LC4, the most recent version of L0phtCrack, is located at `http://www.atstake.com/research/lc/`.

John the Ripper by Solar Designer

John the Ripper is one of the most diverse password crackers in circulation today. John runs on both DOS and Windows platforms, as well as on most flavors of Unix. The binary distribution was released in December 1996, and the package has continued to be updated ever since.

John's real strength lies in its diversity. John can crack Unix files natively and Windows NT SAM files with the use of Pwdump. Modules have been created to attack other platforms, such as LDAP and Kerberos as well. John can also perform true brute-forcing of password files—that is, password cracking going beyond basic dictionary-based guessing. It is extremely resource intensive, and has only become practical in recent years by the rapid advances in processing power.

Penetration testers and crackers alike love John because they can perform cross-platform password cracking on a single, centralized machine. John is maintained by Solar Designer, and its home page is `http://www.openwall.com/john/`.

If you are cracking SHA-based passwords on an LDAP server, a patch is available to make John the Ripper work with that as well. It is available at `http://www.bastard.net/~dos/john-sha`.

NTCrack

NTCrack is a curious utility. As its authors explain, it isn't really intended for cracking passwords in a practical sense. However, it does demonstrate that a brute-force cracker can work against Windows NT. The program's purpose is to perform high-speed, brute-force attacks against an NT box. As reported by the folks at Somarsoft, the original maintainers of the program:

> The program below [NTCrack] does about 1000 logins per minute, when run on a client 486DX-33 with 16MB of RAM, a server 486DX2-66 with 32MB of RAM, and a 10 MBps Ethernet. This is equivalent to testing 1,152,000 passwords per day. By comparison, there are perhaps 100,000 common words in the English language.

To prevent such attacks, it is suggested that you enable account lockout, rename the Administrator account, disable network logins for Administrator, and disable SMB over TCP/IP (if appropriate). You can read more about passfilt and securing Windows NT servers in Chapter 20, "Microsoft."

You can find NTCrack at `http://www.wiretrip.net/na/NTCrack.zip`.

NT Accessories
The NT accessories listed in Table 11.1 are indispensable.

TABLE 11.1   Accessories for Use in Cracking NT Passwords

Application	Description and Location
Samdump	Samdump is a utility that automates the process of dumping NT password hashes. It dumps these values from the SAM file located either in the Registry on an emergency repair disk or off the hard disk drive. Samdump is available at `http://www.multimania.com/toopert/samdump.zip`.
Pwdump2	Pwdump2 is similar to Samdump. It dumps NT usernames and passwords, and it can dump Active Directory as well. (Fortunately, Pwdump2 requires Administrator privileges.) Pwdump2 is available at `http://razor.bindview.com/tools/desc/pwdump2_readme.html`.
NTFSDOS (Pro)	NTFSDOS and NTFSDOS Pro are tools that enable you to mount NTFS volumes and view them as though they were FAT32. You can use these tools to extract SAM password information from a NTFS drive. The older, free NTFSDOS is available at `http://www.sysinternals.com/ntw2k/freeware/NTFSDOS.shtml`. There is also a more advanced Professional version available at `http://www.winternals.com/products/repairandrecovery/ntfsdospro.asp`.

Notes on NT Password Security
Rather than simply use the utilities described here, you might want to investigate exactly what factors led to such poor password security in NT in the first place. The following documents are excellent resources:

- A L0phtCrack Technical Rant. A detailed analysis (really, the gory details) of NT password weaknesses. Authored by mudge@l0pht.com. `http://packetstormsecurity.nl/Crackers/NT/l0phtcrack/l0phtcrack.rant.nt.passwd.txt`

- "On NT Password Security." Jos Visser. An excellent paper that discusses both the mechanical and theoretical problems with the NT password scheme. The author also discusses how to perform an attack against Windows NT password dumps. `http://ihide.virtualave.net/archive/pwsec.html`

- NT Cryptographic Password Attacks and Defences FAQ. Alan Ramsbottom. This document provides information on why certain Microsoft fixes didn't work, as

well as perspective on the weakness in Microsoft's implementation of DES.
`http://www.ntbugtraq.com/default.asp?sid=1&pid=47&aid=17`

Unix Password Cracking

This next section discusses the issues surrounding Unix password cracking. Most of
these programs were designed for Unix as the hosting platform, but some of them
will run on other platforms such as DOS and Windows 95. All of them are, however,
designed to crack Unix passwords.

About Unix Password Security

Unix password security, when implemented correctly, is fairly reliable. The main
problem is that people continue to pick weak passwords. Unfortunately, because
Unix is a multiuser system, every user with a weak password represents a risk to the
remaining users. This is a problem that must be addressed:

> It is of utmost importance that all users on a system choose a password that is not easy to
> guess. The security of each individual user is important to the security of the whole system.
> Users often have no idea how a multiuser system works and don't realize that they, by choos-
> ing an easy-to-remember password, indirectly make it possible for an outsider to manipulate
> the entire system.
>
> —"UNIX Password Security." Walter Belgers. December 6, 1993.

TIP

The paper "UNIX Password Security" gives an excellent overview of exactly how DES works
into the Unix password scheme. It includes a schematic that shows the actual process of
encryption using DES. For users new to security, this paper is an excellent starting point. You
can find "UNIX Password Security" at `http://www.het.brown.edu/guide/UNIX-password-security.txt`.

What are weak passwords? Characteristically, they are anything that might occur in a
dictionary. Moreover, proper names are poor choices for passwords. However, there is
no need to theorize on what passwords are easily cracked. It's safe to say that if the
password appears in a password-cracking wordlist available on the Internet, the password is no good.

TIP

Start your search for wordlists at `http://www.cotse.com/tools/wordlists2.htm`.

By regularly checking the strength of the passwords on your network, you can ensure that crackers cannot penetrate it (at least not through exploiting bad password choices). Such a regimen can greatly improve your system security. In fact, many ISPs and other sites now employ tools that check a user's password when it is first created. This basically implements the philosophy that

> ...the best solution to the problem of having easily guessed passwords on a system is to prevent them from getting on the system in the first place. If a program such as a password cracker reacts by guessing detectable passwords already in place, then although the security hole is found, the hole existed for as long as the program took to detect it.... If however, the program that changes users' passwords...checks for the safety and guessability before that password is associated with the user's account, then the security hole is never put in place.

> —"Improving System Security Via Proactive Password Checking."
> Matthew Bishop, UC Davis, California, and Daniel Klein, LoneWolf Systems Inc.
> *Computers and Security* [14, pp. 233–249], 1995.

TIP

The paper "Improving System Security Via Proactive Password Checking" is probably one of the best case studies and treatments of easily guessable passwords. It treats the subject in depth, illustrating real-life examples of various passwords that you might think are secure but actually are not. You can find "Improving System Security Via Proactive Password Checking" at http://seclab.cs.ucdavis.edu/papers/bk95.ps.

Crack

Crack is the de facto standard for Unix password cracking. It was written by Alec D. E. Muffett, a Unix software engineer in Wales. In the documentation, Muffett concisely articulated the program's purpose:

> Crack is a freely available program designed to find standard Unix eight-character DES encrypted passwords by standard guessing techniques.... It is written to be flexible, configurable and fast, and to be able to make use of several networked hosts via the Berkeley rsh program (or similar), where possible.

Crack runs on Unix only. It comes as a tarred, gzipped file, and is available at http://www.users.dircon.co.uk/~crypto/.

To get Crack up and running, set the root directory. You assign this variable (Crack_Home) in the configuration files. The Crack_Home variable tells the Crack program where Crack's resources reside. To set this variable, edit the shell script Crack. After you do that, you can begin.

You begin your Crack session by starting the program and providing the name of the file to crack (as well as any command-line arguments, including specifications for using multiple workstations). A bare command line looks like this:

```
Crack my_password_file
```

What follows is difficult to describe, so I ran a sample Crack session. Crack started the process and wrote the progress of the operation to files with an out prefix. In this case, the file was called outSamsHack300. The following is an excerpt from that file:

```
1: pwc: Jan 30 19:26:49 Crack v4.1f: The Password Cracker,
➥(c) Alec D.E. Muffett, 1992
2: pwc: Jan 30 19:26:49 Loading Data, host=SamsHack pid=300
3: pwc: Jan 30 19:26:49 Loaded 2 password entries with 2 different
➥(salts: 100%
4: pwc: Jan 30 19:26:49 Loaded 240 rules from 'Scripts/dicts.rules'.
5: pwc: Jan 30 19:26:49 Loaded 74 rules from 'Scripts/gecos.rules'.
6: pwc: Jan 30 19:26:49 Starting pass 1 - password information
7: pwc: Jan 30 19:26:49 FeedBack: 0 users done, 2 users left to crack.
8: pwc: Jan 30 19:26:49 Starting pass 2 - dictionary words
9: pwc: Jan 30 19:26:49 Applying rule '!?Al' to file 'Dicts/bigdict'
10: pwc: Jan 30 19:26:50 Rejected 12492 words on loading, 89160 words
➥(left to sort
11: pwc: Jan 30 19:26:51 Sort discarded 947 words; FINAL DICTIONARY
➥(SIZE: 88213
12: pwc: Jan 30 19:27:41 Guessed ROOT PASSWORD root (/bin/bash
➥(in my_password_file) [laura] EYFu7c842Bcus
13: pwc: Jan 30 19:27:41 Closing feedback file.
```

Crack guessed the correct password for root in just under a minute. Line 1 reveals the time at which the process was initiated (Jan 30 19:26:49); line 12 reveals that the password—Laura—was cracked at 19:27:41. This session occurred on a 133MHz processor with 32MB of RAM.

Because the password file I used was small, neither time nor resources were an issue. In practice, however, if you crack a file with hundreds of entries, Crack will eat resources voraciously. This hunger is especially evident if you use multiple wordlists that are in compressed form. (Crack automatically identifies them as compressed files and decompresses them.)

As mentioned earlier, you can get around this resource drain. Crack can distribute the work to different workstations of different architectures. You can use Crack on an IBM compatible running Linux, a RS/6000 running AIX, and a Macintosh running A/UX.

Crack is extremely lightweight and one of the best password crackers available.

TIP

To perform a networked cracking session, you must build a network.conf file. This file identi-fies which hosts to include, their architecture, and several other key variables. You can also specify what command-line options are invoked as Crack is unleashed on each machine. In other words, each member machine can run Crack with different command-line options.

John the Ripper by Solar Designer

John was discussed in the NT section, so I will only briefly touch on it here. Although John can crack both NT- and Unix-based passwords, the one thing that is unique about John on the Unix side of the fence is its capability to do raw brute-forcing. Performing a raw brute-force attack (trying every possible combination of characters) was impractical on hardware of a few years ago, but is a reality today. If you want to get medieval on a Unix password file, John is the tool for you.

PaceCrack95 (pacemkr@bluemoon.net)

PaceCrack95 runs on Windows 95 in console mode or in a shell window. Its author reports that the development of PaceCrack95 was prompted by deficiencies in other DOS-based crackers. He writes

> Well you might be wondering why I have written a program like this when there already is[sic] many out there that do the same thing. There are many reasons, I wanted to challenge myself and this was a useful way to do it. Also there was this guy (Borris) that kept bugging me to make this for him because Cracker Jack (By Jackal) doesn't run in Win95/NT because of the weird way it uses the memory. What was needed was a program that runs in Win95 and the speed of the cracking was up there with Cracker Jack.

To the author's credit, he created a program that does just that. It is fast, compact, and efficient.

You can find PaceCrack95 at http://www.securityadvise.de/deny/files/BruteForce/pacecrack.zip.

Star Cracker by the Sorcerer

Star Cracker, which was designed to work under the DOS4GW environment, is a complete password-cracking suite. Some of its more interesting advantages are

- A fail-safe power outage provision—If a blackout in your city shuts down your computer, your work is not lost. Upon reboot, Star Cracker recovers all work previously done (up until the point of the power outage) and keeps right on going.

- Time-release operation—You can establish time windows when the program does its work. That means you could specify, "Crack this file for 11 hours. When the 11 hours are up, wait 3 hours more. After the 3 hours, start again."

Star Cracker really makes the password-cracking process painless.

You can find Star Cracker at http://www.kontek.net/pi/pass_crack/sc10b1.zip.

Cracking Cisco, Application, and Other Password Types

Although you can certainly use password crackers for devious activities, there are plenty of legitimate reasons for needing to access data that might be password protected. For example, if an employee forgets the password to a protected-access database, or if someone leaves the company without passing on the pass phrase for a zip file, an organization might have legitimate needs to get at that data.

The following section goes over some of the password crackers for less common (not OS-related) applications. I encourage the reader to note the diverse assortment of password crackers listed. Hopefully this list will help dispel the myth that application-level passwords are inherently secure. The truth of the matter is that rarely do application vendors create secure password-protection mechanisms—most are easily broken.

Cracking Cisco IOS Passwords

Cisco stores encrypted login, username, and "enable" passwords in standard IOS configuration files. If these configuration files are not protected, they can be run through decryption scripts that will reveal the passwords in clear text. We will talk more about securing Cisco equipment in Chapter 23, "Routers, Switches and Hubs," but, for now, know that protecting your configuration files is extremely important.

Many scripts exist for decrypting standard Cisco passwords. One such script can be found at http://www.alcrypto.co.uk/cisco/perl/ios7decrypt.pl. GetPass is a Windows-based program that does the same thing, and it can be found at http://www.boson.com/promo/utilities/getpass/getpass_utility.htm.

TIP

A neat tool for auditing Cisco router configuration files can be found at `http://packetstorm-security.nl/cisco/CiscoAuditingTool-v1.tar.gz`. Cisco administrators would be wise to check this one out.

Commercial Application Password Crackers

There are a number of companies that provide commercial password-cracking services and tools. A couple of the fairly well-known ones are

- PWD Service, Inc. `http://www.pwdservice.com`

- Password Crackers, Inc. `http://www.pwcrack.com`

Here is just a sample list of some of the applications these organizations offer password-cracking software for:

- Microsoft Word

- Microsoft Excel

- Microsoft Access

- Microsoft Outlook

- Microsoft Project

- Microsoft Backup

- Microsoft Money

- Lotus 1-2-3

- Lotus Word Pro

- Quickbooks

- ACT

- Paradox

- M.Y.O.B

- Quicken

- Peachtree Accounting

- PKZIP

- WordPerfect

It's important to note that many of these password crackers do their cracking in less than a few seconds. Although I am not a password or cryptography expert, I think it's safe to draw the conclusion that most application-based password protection schemes are little more than an annoyance for intruders. If you can crack them with a $30 piece of software in a few seconds, realize that anyone else can, too.

ZipCrack by Michael A. Quinlan

ZipCrack does just what you think it would: It is designed to brute-force crack passwords that have been applied to files with a `*.zip` extension. (In other words, it cracks the password on files generated with PKZIP.)

No documentation is included in the distribution (at least, not the few files that I have examined), but I am not sure there is any need for documentation. The program is straightforward. You simply provide the target file, and the program does the rest.

The program was written in Turbo Pascal, and the source code is included with the distribution. ZipCrack works on any IBM compatible that is a 286 or higher. The file description reports that ZipCrack cracks all the passwords generated by PKZIP 2.0. The author also warns that, although you can crack short passwords within a reasonable length of time, long passwords can take "centuries." Nevertheless, I sincerely doubt that many individuals provide passwords longer than five characters. ZipCrack is a useful utility for the average toolbox. It's one of those utilities you think you will never need, and later, at 3:00 in the morning, you swear bitterly because you don't have it.

ZipCrack can be found at `http://packetstormsecurity.org/crypt/msdos/ZIPCRACK.ZIP`.

AMI Decode (Author Unknown)

AMI Decode is designed expressly to grab the CMOS password from any machine using an American Megatrends BIOS. Before you search for this utility, however, you might use the factory default CMOS password. It is, oddly enough, `AMI`. In any event, the program works, and that is what counts.

AMI Decode can be found at `http://packetstormsecurity.org/Crackers/bios/amidecod.zip`.

> **NOTE**
>
> Many BIOS chips have backdoor passwords built into them. One list of these passwords can be found at `http://www.freelabs.com/~whitis/security/backdoor.html`.

PGPCrack by Mark Miller

Before readers who use PGP get all worked up about PGPCrack, a bit of background information is in order. Pretty Good Privacy (PGP) is one of the strongest and most reliable encryption utility available to the public sector. Its author, Phil Zimmermann, summed it up as follows:

> PGP uses public-key encryption to protect email and data files. Communicate securely with people you've never met, with no secure channels needed for prior exchange of keys. PGP is well featured and fast, with sophisticated key management, digital signatures, data compression, and good ergonomic design.

PGP can apply a series of encryption techniques. One of these, which is discussed in Chapter 15, "Sniffers," is IDEA. To hint about how difficult IDEA is to crack, here is an excerpt from the PGP Attack FAQ, authored by Route (an authority on encryption and the editor of *Phrack* magazine):

> If you had 1,000,000,000 machines that could try 1,000,000,000 keys/sec, it would still take all these machines longer than the universe as we know it has existed and then some, to find the key. IDEA, as far as present technology is concerned, is not vulnerable to brute-force attack, pure and simple.

In essence, a message encrypted using a 1,024-bit key generated with a healthy and long pass phrase is, for all purposes, unbreakable. Why did Mr. Miller author this interesting tool? Pass phrases can be poorly chosen, and if you are going to crack a PGP-encrypted message, the pass phrase is a good place to start. Miller reports

> On a 486/66DX, I found that it takes about seven seconds to read in a 1.2 megabyte passphrase file and try to decrypt the file using every passphrase. Considering the fact that the NSA, other government agencies, and large corporations have an incredible amount of computing power, the benefit of using a large, random passphrase is quite obvious.

Is this utility of any use? It is quite promising. Miller includes the source with the distribution as well as a file of possible pass phrases. (I have found that at least one of those pass phrases is one I have used.) The program is written in C and runs in DOS, Unix, and OS/2 environments.

You can find PGPCrack at http://packetstormsecurity.org/crypt/pgp/pgpcrack99.tgz.

Improving Your Site's Passwords

All is not hopeless in the fight against crackers breaking your passwords. First, you should develop a strong password policy. This is discussed in Chapter 25, "Policies,

Procedures, and Enforcement." This should give your users some guidance in picking a good password.

As was mentioned earlier, you can run these password cracker programs periodically against your site. However, this is quite a bit of work and requires you to block accounts when the passwords are cracked. A class of products now exist that automatically enforce your password policy by not allowing users to enter bad passwords to begin with.

The way these programs work is by screening the user's password when she tries to change it. The program has a set of rules that the password must match. If the password does not match these guidelines, the password change request fails, and the user is told why.

Windows NT/2000

Windows NT has a DLL called `passfilt.dll` from Microsoft that can be installed. The rules it enforces are very minimal. They stipulate that the password must be at least six characters in length, a mix of different types of characters must be used, and passwords can't match part of your username or full name. More information can be found at `http://support.microsoft.com/default.aspx?scid=KB;EN-US;Q161990&`.

In Windows 2000, `passfilt.dll` is built in. To enable it, you have to run the appropriate management tools, such as Local Security Policy, Domain Security Policy, or Domain Controller Security Policy. Within these programs, you will find the available settings in Security Settings, Account Policies, Password Policy.

If you are a programmer, it's possible to write your own version of `passfilt.dll` and install it on the system. However, care should be taken when doing so.

Passfilt Pro

`passfilt.dll` is pretty weak, so it is not surprising to find companies out there offering improved replacements. Passfilt Pro is a commercial upgraded version of `passfilt.dll`. Passfilt Pro adds about a dozen more rules, and a check against a dictionary as well. More information is available at `http://www.altusnet.com/passfilt/overview.htm`.

Password Bouncer

Remember the administrator we discussed earlier that could break 90% of his users' passwords in two hours? He installed the Password Bouncer product from Avatier. After installing it with a minimal product configuration and making his users change their password, he ran l0phtCrack again. This time it took three days to crack 12% of his passwords. With even more configuration, it might be possible to improve those numbers.

Password Bouncer is similar to Passfilt Pro, except that it has even more features and rules that can be set within the product, allowing the user even more control over the password policy. Finally, Password Bouncer can be integrated into Avatier's other management products, Trusted Enterprise Manager and PasswordStation.Net. Password Bouncer can be found at `http://www.passwordbouncer.com`.

Unix

Each of the major Unix versions has some type of password policy system built into them. HP-UX, Linux, and Solaris are all very similar. They each have a couple of configuration files that control the password policy rules. For example, on Solaris, these are `/etc/shadow` and `/etc/default/passwd`. They all use PAM (Pluggable Authentication Modules), which provide hooks for administrators and programmers into the password system so they can greatly customize password policy.

AIX has a very advanced password policy system, but does not use PAM. It has the most rules of any OS system, and it also has a documented API for programming additional rules.

LDAP Servers

Some LDAP servers have a minimal set of password policies built in as well. For example, the Sun ONE Directory Server can check the password length, a password history, and whether or not the password matches certain attributes of the user's data in the LDAP server.

Other Resources

This section contains a list of sources for further education. Some of these documents are not available on the Internet. However, you can obtain some articles through various online services (perhaps Uncover), or at your local library through interlibrary loan or microfiche. You might have to search more aggressively for some of these papers, perhaps using the Library of Congress (`http://www.loc.gov`), or perhaps an even more effective tool such as WorldCat (`http://www.oclc.org`).

> **NOTE**
>
> Many of the files for papers have `.ps` extensions. This signifies a PostScript file. PostScript is a language and method of preparing documents. It was created by Adobe, the makers of Acrobat and Photoshop.
>
> To read a PostScript file, you need a viewer. One good viewer is Ghostscript, which is shareware available at `http://www.cs.wisc.edu/~ghost/`.
>
> Another good package (and a little more lightweight) is a utility called Rops. Rops is available for Windows, and is located at `http://www.rops.org/`.

Internet Resources

Observing Reusable Password Choices. Purdue Technical Report CSD-TR 92-049, Eugene H. Spafford, Department of Computer Sciences, Purdue University, July 3, 1992. Search string: `Observe.ps`

Password Security: A Case History. Robert Morris and Ken Thompson, Bell Laboratories. Date: Unknown. Search string: `pwstudy.ps`

Opus: Preventing Weak Password Choices. Purdue Technical Report CSD-TR 92-028, Eugene H. Spafford, Department of Computer Sciences, Purdue University, June 1991. Search string: `opus.PS.gz`

Federal Information Processing Standards Publication 181. Announcing the Standard for Automated Password Generator. October 5, 1993. `http://www.alw.nih.gov/Security/FIRST/papers/password/fips181.txt`

Augmented Encrypted Key Exchange: A Password-Based Protocol Secure Against Dictionary Attacks and Password File Compromise. Steven M. Bellovin and Michael Merrit, AT&T Bell Laboratories. Date: Unknown. Search string: `aeke.ps`

A High-Speed Software Implementation of DES. David C. Feldmeier, Computer Communication Research Group, Bellcore, June 1989. Search string: `des.ps`

Using Content Addressable Search Engines to Encrypt and Break DES. Peter C. Wayner, Computer Science Department, Cornell University. Date: Unknown. Search string: `desbreak.ps`

Encrypted Key Exchange: Password-Based Protocols Secure Against Dictionary Attacks. Steven M. Bellovin and Michael Merrit, AT&T Bell Laboratories. Date: Unknown. Search string: `neke.ps`

Computer Break-Ins: A Case Study. Leendert Van Doorn, Vrije Universiteit, The Netherlands, January 21, 1993. Search string: `holland_case.ps`

Security Breaches: Five Recent Incidents at Columbia University. Fuat Baran, Howard Kaye, and Margarita Suarez, Center for Computing Activities, Columbia University, June 27, 1990. Search string: `columbia_incidents.ps`

Optimal Authentication Protocols Resistant to Password Guessing Attacks. Li Gong, Stanford Research Institute, Computer Science Laboratory, Men Park, CA. Date: Unknown. Search string: `optimal-pass.dvi` or `optimal-pass.ps`

Publications and Reports

"Undetectable Online Password Guessing Attacks." Yun Ding and Patrick Horster, *OSR*, 29(4), pp. 77–86. October 1995.

"A Password Authentication Scheme Based on Discrete Logarithms." Tzong Chen Wu and Chin Chen Chang, *International Journal of Computational Mathematics*; Vol. 41, Number 1-2, pp. 31–37. 1991.

"Differential Cryptanalysis of DES-Like Cryptosystems." Eli Biham and Adi Shamir, *Journal of Cryptology*, 4(1), pp. 3–72. 1990.

"A Proposed Mode for Triple-DES Encryption." Don Coppersmith, Don B. Johnson, and Stephen M. Matyas. *IBM Journal of Research and Development*, 40(2), pp. 253–262. March 1996.

"An Experiment on DES Statistical Cryptanalysis." Serve Vaudenay, Conference on Computer and Communications Security, pp. 139–147. ACM Press. March 1996

Department of Defense Password Management Guideline. If you want to gain a more historical perspective regarding password security, start with the *Department of Defense Password Management Guideline*. This document was produced by the Department of Defense Computer Security Center at Fort Meade, Maryland.

Checklist: Create Strong Passwords. `http://www.microsoft.com/security/articles/password.asp`

"Psst...I Know Your Password." Robert Lemos, *ZDNet News*, May 22, 2002. `http://zdnet.com.com/2100-1105-920092.html`

"Military Computers Easily Cracked, Experts Say." Andy Sullivan, Reuters, August 16, 2002. `http://www.reuters.com/news_article.jhtml?type=technologynews&StoryID=1340741`

"You're Only as Good as Your Password." Jim Kerstetter, *Business Week*, August 23, 2000.
`http://www.businessweek.com/smallbiz/content/aug2002/sb20020823_5482.htm`

TIP

You can find the *Department of Defense Password Management Guideline* at `http://www.alw.nih.gov/Security/FIRST/papers/password/dodpwman.txt`.

Summary

Password crackers provide a valuable service to system administrators by alerting them of weak passwords on the network. The problem is not that password crackers exist; the problem is that they aren't used frequently enough by the good guys. Administrators should take the time to build password cracking into their monthly routines. By doing so, they can proactively pursue any weaknesses in their enterprise that result from weak passwords. However, administrators should also take care to ensure that both the raw password files and the results of their cracking efforts be deleted after their cracking sessions. Leftover password files can create issues that are worse than bad passwords themselves.

Finally, although the days of passwords serving as a primary means of authentication might be numbered, their overall use is not. Pass phrases will be used for some time to come for protecting keys, certificates, and a varying assortment of protected data. The technology might become more complex, but the solution to the surrounding problems will not. Education is key—use it.

15

Sniffers

Sniffers are devices that capture network packets. Their legitimate purpose is to analyze network traffic and identify potential areas of concern. For example, suppose that one segment of your network is performing poorly: packet delivery seems incredibly slow, or machines inexplicably lock up on a network boot. You can use a sniffer to determine the precise cause.

NOTE

The term *sniffer* is derived from a product, called the Sniffer, originally manufactured by Network General Corporation. As Network General dominated the market, this term became popular, and protocol analyzers have since then generally been referred to as such.

Sniffers vary greatly in functionality and design. Some analyze only one protocol, whereas others can analyze hundreds. As a general rule, most modern sniffers will analyze at least the following protocols:

- Standard Ethernet
- TCP/IP
- NetBIOS

Proprietary sniffers are expensive (vendors often package them on special computers that are "optimized" for sniffing). Freeware sniffers, on the other hand, are cheap, but offer no support.

In this chapter, we'll examine sniffers as both security risks and network administration tools.

Sniffers as Security Risks

Sniffers differ greatly from keystroke-capture programs. Key-capture programs save, or *capture*, keystrokes entered at a terminal. Sniffers, on the other hand, capture actual network packets. Sniffers do this by placing the network interface—an Ethernet adapter, for example—into promiscuous mode. Sniffers also differ in one key aspect from other attack methods—sniffers are passive, only listening to the network traffic.

A sniffer always functions in a promiscuous mode. Normally, a system's network card will only grab packets destined for that system. In promiscuous mode, however, instead of ignoring all other packets, the system captures every packet that it sees on the network. To further understand how promiscuous mode works, you must first understand how local area networks are designed.

Local Area Networks and Data Traffic

Local area networks (LANs) are small networks connected (generally) via ethernet. Data is transmitted from one machine to another via cable.

Data travels along the cable in small units called *frames*. These frames are constructed in sections, and each section carries specialized information. For example, the first 12 bytes of an ethernet frame carry both the destination and source MAC address. These values tell the network where the data came from and where it's going. Other portions of an ethernet frame carry actual user data, TCP/IP headers, IPX headers, and so forth.

Frames are packaged for transport by special software called a *network driver*. The frames are then passed from your machine to cable via your Network Interface Card (NIC). From there, they travel to their destination. At that point, the process is executed in reverse: The recipient machine's NIC picks up the frames, tells the operating system that frames have arrived, and passes those frames on for processing.

Sniffers pose a security risk because of the way frames are transported and delivered. Let's briefly look at that process.

Packet Transport and Delivery

Each workstation in a LAN has its own hardware address or Media Access Control (MAC) address. This address uniquely identifies that machine from all others on the network. (This is similar to the Internet address system.) When you send a message across the LAN, your packets are sent to all connected machines.

Under normal circumstances, all machines on the network can "hear" that traffic going by, but will only respond to data addressed specifically to them. In other words, Workstation A will not capture data intended for Workstation B. Instead, Workstation A will simply ignore that data.

If a workstation's network interface is in promiscuous mode, however, it can capture all packets and frames on the network. A workstation configured in this way (and the software on it) is a sniffer.

What Level of Risk Do Sniffers Represent?

Sniffers represent a high level of risk. Here's why:

- Sniffers can capture account names and passwords.

- Sniffers can capture confidential or proprietary information.

- Sniffers can be used to breach the security of neighboring networks, or to gain leveraged access.

In fact, the existence of an unauthorized sniffer on your network might indicate that your system is already compromised.

Has Anyone Actually Seen a Sniffer Attack?

Sniffer attacks are common, particularly on the Internet. A well-placed sniffer can capture not just a few passwords, but thousands. In 1994, for example, a massive sniffer attack was discovered, leading a naval research center to post the following advisory:

> In February 1994, an unidentified person installed a network sniffer on numerous hosts and backbone elements collecting over 100,000 valid user names and passwords via the Internet and Milnet. Any computer host allowing FTP, Telnet or remote log in to the system should be considered at risk...All networked hosts running a Unix derivative operating system should check for the particular promiscuous device driver that allows the sniffer to be installed.
>
> —Naval Computer and Telecommunications Area Master Station LANT advisory

The attack on Milnet was so serious that the issue was brought before the Subcommittee on Science, Space, and Technology at the U.S. House of Representatives. F. Lynn McNulty, Associate Director for Computer Security at the National Institute of Standards and Technology, gave this testimony:

> The recent incident involved the discovery of "password sniffer" programs on hundreds of systems throughout the Internet...The serious impact of the recent incident should be recognized; log-in information (i.e., account numbers and passwords) for potentially thousands of host system user accounts appear to have been compromised. It is clear that this incident had a negative impact on the operational missions of some Government agencies. Moreover, this should be viewed as [an] ongoing incident, not an incident that has happened and been dealt

with. Indeed, administrators of systems throughout the Internet were advised, in turn, to direct their users to change their passwords. This is, indeed, very significant, and we may be seeing its effects for some time to come. Not only is it difficult, if not impossible, to identify and notify every user whose log-in information might have been compromised, it is unlikely that everyone, even if notified, will change his or her passwords.

TIP

You can access McNulty's full testimony at `http://www-swiss.ai.mit.edu/6.805/articles/ mcnulty-internet-security.txt`.

The Department of Defense, in particular, has experienced numerous attacks and been victimized by sniffers on its networks. In one of the more interesting incidents on February 1998, intruders installed sniffers on DoD and university systems, compromising numerous user accounts. This incident is referred to as Solar Sunrise by DoD officials, involved two teenagers from California and their mentor in Israel.

TIP

Numerous discussions on this incident can be found online, including `http://www.sans.org/ newlook/resources/IDFAQ/solar_sunrise.htm`.

What Information Do Sniffers Capture?

Sniffers will capture all packets on the network, but in practice, an attacker has to be choosier. A sniffer attack is not as easy as it sounds. It requires some knowledge of networking. Simply setting up a sniffer and leaving it will lead to problems, because even a five-station network transmits thousands of packets an hour. Within a short time, a sniffer's outfile could easily fill a hard disk drive to capacity (if you logged every packet).

To circumvent this problem, crackers generally sniff only the first 200–300 bytes of each packet. The username and password are contained within this portion, which is really all most crackers want. However, it is true that you could sniff all the packets on a given interface; if you have the storage media to handle that kind of volume, you would probably find some interesting things.

Authentication information is one of the most common targets for sniffer activity. In particular, information sent to ports 23 (Telnet), 80 (HTTP), and 21 (FTP) are valuable, because authentication information (such as usernames and passwords) is sent in clear text in these protocols. Port 513 (rlogin) is also useful when trust relationships don't exist. (If a trust relationship does exist, then no username or password is required, but the system becomes a potential target for spoofing.)

TIP

The authentication information from encrypted connections are generally not vulnerable to sniffer attacks. By switching from an unencrypted protocol to an encrypted one, you can improve your security. For example, use SSL (Secure Socket Layer) to encrypt Web traffic, or SSH (Secure Shell) to encrypt remote shell instead of Telnet or rlogin. We'll cover more on this subject later in the chapter.

Where Is One Likely to Find a Sniffer?

You are likely to find a sniffer almost anywhere. However, there are some strategic points that a cracker might favor. One of those points is anywhere adjacent to a machine or network that receives many passwords. This is especially true if the targeted machine is a gateway to the outside world. If so, the cracker will want to capture authentication procedures between your network and other networks. This could exponentially expand the cracker's sphere of activity.

NOTE

I do not believe that, in practice, any sniffer can catch absolutely all traffic on a network. This is because, as the number of packets increase, the chance of lost packets is high. If you examine technical reports on sniffers, you will discover that at high speeds and in highly traf-ficked networks, a significant amount of data can be lost. (Commercial sniffers, which tend to have better designs, are far less likely to suffer packet loss.) This suggests that sniffers might be vulnerable to attacks themselves. In other words, just how many packets-per-second can a sniffer take before it fails in its fundamental mission? That is a subject worth investigating.

Security technology has evolved considerably. Some operating systems now employ encryption at the packet level, and therefore, even though a sniffer attack can yield valuable data, that data is encrypted. This presents an additional obstacle likely to be passed only by those with deeper knowledge of security, encryption, and networking. An example of this is the Windows NT/2000 authentication mechanism.

TIP

More information about Windows authentication can be found at `http://www.windowsitlibrary.com/Content/617/06/toc.html`.

Where Can I Get a Sniffer?

Sniffers come in two basic flavors: commercial and freeware. If you're just learning about networking, I recommend getting a freeware sniffer. On the other hand, if you manage a large network, your company should purchase at least one commercial sniffer. They are invaluable when you're trying to diagnose a network problem.

Commercial Sniffers

The sniffers in this section are commercial, but many of these companies offer demo versions. Prices range from $200 to $2,000.

Sniffer Technologies and Products from Network Associates

Network Associates has a whole line of Sniffer-related products, divided into three types. The first is the Distributed Environment line, which are permanently installed at fixed locations on the network. The second is the Portable line, which are designed for carrying around to hotspots on the network for diagnostic purposes. Finally, there's a Wireless product line for troubleshooting problems with wireless equipment. To give you an idea of how advanced the Sniffer line is, it can decode more than 450 different protocols. Also, it can handle many different types of network media and systems. One of the strengths of the Sniffer line has always been that it is a good real-time and historical reporting product at the same time. Of course, all this power means the units are fairly expensive.

> Network Associates, Inc.
>
> Sniffer Technologies
>
> URL: http://www.networkassociates.com/

Finisar-Systems Surveyor

Finisar-Systems LAN Analyzers are heavy-duty hardware/software solutions that support 10/100Mbps and gigabit Ethernet. The systems work with both Ethernet and token ring networks and offer real-time reporting. Surveyor operates on Windows. Finisar also offers a plug-in module for Surveyor, which provides Quality of Service analysis for factors important to voice-over IP applications.

> Shomiti Systems, Inc.
>
> Email: enterprise-sales@finisar.com
>
> URL: http://www.finisar.com

PacketView by Klos Technologies

PacketView is a DOS-based packet sniffer designed for use in Ethernet, token ring, and FDDI environments. It runs about $299. You can try before you buy by downloading a demo version located at www.klos.com/get.pvdemo.html.

> Klos Technologies, Inc.
>
> Email: sales@klos.com
>
> URL: http://www.klos.com/

Ranger Network Probe from Network Communications

Network Communications produces several network analyzers, including the Ranger Network Probe. The Ranger Network Probe is designed for use on WANs, and supports a large number of protocols.

Network Communications Corporation

Email: sales@netcommcorp.com

URL: http://www.netcommcorp.com

LANWatch by Precision Guesswork

LANWatch is a software-based sniffer solution for Windows. It will monitor packets from the following protocols: TCP, UDP, IP, IPv6, NFS, NetWare, SNA, AppleTalk, VINES, ARP, NetBIOS, and some 50 others. LANWatch monitors traffic in real-time, and can display a wide range of usable statistics. A demo version is located at www.guesswork.com/demo.html.

Precision Guesswork

Email: info@precision.guesswork.com

URL: http://www.guesswork.com

EtherPeek and AiroPeek from WildPackets Inc.

EtherPeek and AiroPeek are available for Windows. EtherPeek is for Ethernet networks, and AiroPeek is for wireless. Both support all the major protocol suites.

WildPackets, Inc.

Email: info@wildpackets.com

URL: http://www.wildpackets.com/

NetMinder Ethernet by Neon Software

NetMinder Ethernet is a Macintosh-based protocol analyzer that can produce automatically-updated HTML output reports. Not only does it support Ethernet, it supports wireless as well. These reports are updated in real-time, allowing system administrators to access their latest network analysis statistics from anywhere in the world and from any platform. (Naturally, the application also provides real-time analysis in the standard GUI environment.) A demo version is available at http://www.neon.com/demos_goodies.html.

Neon Software

Email: info@neon.com

URL: http://www.neon.com

LinkView Classic Network Analyzer by Acterna

LinkView Classic Network Analyzer supports token ring, Ethernet, and fast Ethernet, but it's designed chiefly for protocol analysis on internetworks. It therefore automatically segregates IP-reporting statistics from other protocol statistics. LinkView Classic runs on Windows. LinkView Classic is a software-only LAN analyzer that works with most third-party network cards.

> Acterna, Inc.
>
> URL: `http://www.linkview.com`

ProConvert from WildPackets, Inc.

ProConvert is not a sniffer, but is instead a tool for integrating data from disparate sniffers. This allows data from different vendors' formats to be converted into a single format, enabling the user to view packets on a platform separate from the one on which the packets were captured. ProConvert decodes (and provides universal translation between) 20 different sniffer file formats, including EtherPeek, Fireberd500, Internet Advisor LAN, LAN900, LANalyzer for Windows, LANWatch, Network Monitor, NetXRay, LinkView, and TCPDUMP formats. In other words, ProConvert is the Rosetta stone for sniffer logs. It can save you many, many hours of work.

> WildPackets, Inc.
>
> Email: `info@wildpackets.com`
>
> URL: `http://www.wildpackets.com/`

LANdecoder32 by Triticom

LANdecoder32 is a popular sniffer for use on Windows. It has advanced reporting capabilities, and can be used to analyze frame content. Other features include remote monitoring (requiring RMON on the remote system), ASCII filtering (filter by string), and real-time reporting. Demonstration versions can be obtained by contacting Triticom.

> Triticom
>
> Email: `info@triticom.com`
>
> URL: `http://www.triticom.com/`

Vericept

Vericept is an unusual sniffer product. Instead of being designed to troubleshoot your networks, it is designed to help you monitor your employees for policy violations.

> Vericept
>
> URL: `http://www.vericept.com`

Freely Available Sniffers

Many freeware and shareware sniffers are also available. These are perfect if you want to learn about network traffic without spending any money. Unfortunately, some are architecture-specific, and the majority are designed for Unix.

Snoop

Solaris ships with a packet sniffer called Snoop. It has very nice output formats compared to many of the Unix sniffers. To find out more, type `man snoop` on a Solaris system.

Esniff

Esniff is a standard, Unix-based sniffer. It was one of the first sniffers, and was originally released in *Phrack* Magazine (an online hacker zine). Esniff is a very small C program that requires a C compiler and IP include files. A modified version for Solaris 2.X called solsniffer.c also exists. Esniff is available at `http://www.netsw.org/net/ip/audit/sniffer/esniff/`.

TCPDUMP

TCPDUMP is one of the most popular tools for network diagnostics and analysis. TCPDUMP can be used to monitor and decode all IP, TCP, UDP, and ICMP headers. The user can vary the amount of the packet that is grabbed, but the default is 64 bytes. TCPDUMP was loosely based on Sun's etherfind, and was designed to aid in ongoing research to improve TCP and Internet gateway performance. TCPDUMP is a Unix-based program, but a Windows version known as WINDUMP exists. TCPDUMP can be obtained at `http://www.tcpdump.org/`.

WINDUMP can be found at `http://netgroup-serv.polito.it/windump/`.

LinSniff

LinSniff is a password sniffer. To compile it, you need all the necessary network include files (`tcp.h`, `ip.h`, `inet.h`, `if_ther.h`, and so on) on a Linux system. It is available at `http://www.pdaconsulting.com/Cracker%20Tools/linsniff.c`.

Defeating Sniffer Attacks

Now that you understand how sniffers work and the dangers they pose, you are probably wondering how to defeat sniffer attacks. Get ready for some bad news: Defeating sniffer attacks is not easy. You can take two approaches:

- Detect and eliminate sniffers
- Shield your data from sniffers

Let's briefly look at the pros and cons of each method.

Detecting and Eliminating Sniffers

Sniffers are extremely difficult to detect because they are passive programs. They don't generate an audit trail, and unless their owner is very stupid, they use up no network resources. Some operating systems provide a mechanism to determine whether a network interface has been placed in promiscuous mode, which can aid greatly in determining if a sniffer is running on a specific host.

On a single machine, it is theoretically feasible to determine whether a sniffer has been installed. For example, you could rely on the MD5 algorithm (see Chapter 18, "Trojans," for more on MD5), provided you have a decent database of original installation files (or a running database of installed files). If you intend to use MD5 and search by checksum, you should obtain md5check, an awk script that automates the process. md5check was originally distributed by CERT and works well for SunOS. md5check can be found at `http://lvl.sourceforge.net/md5check.php`. Another alternative is Tripwire (`http://www.tripwire.org`), or see Chapter 21, "Unix," for more on Tripwire.

Certainly, searching by checksum on a single box is effective enough. However, finding a sniffer on a large network is difficult. The question of detecting sniffers on diverse architecture is a bitter debate in the security community. (You can see folks arguing this issue for weeks at a time without resolution.) However, there are several tools that can help—if you have the right architecture:

- Snifftest—Written by "Beavis and Butthead," Snifftest will detect a sniffer on SunOS and Solaris. It will detect a sniffer even if the network interface isn't in promiscuous mode, so it's especially useful. It works solely for Sun, and requires a C compiler and TCP/IP header files. It is located at `http://packetstorm.decepticons.org/Exploit_Code_Archive/snifftest.c`.

- Nitwit—Nitwit runs as a NIT (Network Interface Tap) and can detect sniffers, even if the network interface is not in promiscuous mode. It is similar to Snifftest in that regard. Nitwit is available at `http://www.cotse.com/sw/sniffers/nitwit.c`.

- Promisc—Written by `blind@xmission.com`, Promisc will detect sniffers on Linux. (There are some reports of this program working on Sun, but these have not been verified.) Promisc is available at `http://www.cotse.com/sw/sniffers/promisc.c`.

- PromiScan—A Windows 2000/XP promiscuous mode detector, PromiScan is available at `http://www.securityfriday.com/ToolDownload/PromiScan/promiscan_doc.html`.

- PromiscDetect—A Windows NT/2000/XP promiscuous mode detector, this can be found at `http://ntsecurity.nu/toolbox/promiscdetect/`.

- Sentinel—A remote promiscuous mode detector for Linux- and BSD-based Unix versions. It can be downloaded from `http://www.packetfactory.net/Projects/sentinel/`.

Detecting a sniffer in heterogeneous networks is more difficult—difficult, that is, without physically checking each machine. For example, suppose your network is made up exclusively of AIX systems. Suppose further that someone goes into an empty office, unplugs a RS/6000, and hooks up a PC laptop, which they use as a sniffer. This is difficult to detect unless you are using *network topology maps* (tools that red-flag any change in topology) and check them daily. Otherwise, the network appears just as it did, with no indication of trouble. After all, the PC has the same IP as the RS/6000 did. Unless you run daily scans, you would probably never detect the PC.

A more complicated situation occurs when intruders attach physical devices that sniff. (For example, they can splice themselves in at points not visible to the naked eye. I've seen offices that run their coax wire overhead, in the space above the ceiling. This allows anyone in an adjacent office to snag the wire and patch themselves in.) Other than physically checking each wire lead throughout the network, there is no easy way to identify a spliced connection. (Although, again, network topology mapping tools would warn that an extra IP had been added to your subnet. Unfortunately, however, most small businesses can't afford such tools.)

At day's end, however, proactive solutions are difficult and expensive. Instead, you should take more defensive measures. There are two chief defenses against sniffers:

- Safe topology
- Encrypted sessions

Let's quickly cover both defenses.

Safe Topology

Sniffers can only capture data on the instant network segment. This means that the tighter you compartmentalize your network, the less information a sniffer can gather. This used to be expensive, but switches have dropped in price so much that a low-end switch does not cost much more than a hub. There are three network interfaces that a sniffer cannot easily cross:

- Switches
- Routers
- Bridges

You can create tighter network segments by strategically placing these devices on the network. You could possibly compartmentalize 20 workstations at a crack—this seems like a reasonable number. Once a month you could physically check each segment (and, also perhaps once a month, you could run MD5 checks on random segments). It should be noted that programs such as macof have been developed to flood switches in the hope that they would fail open. This would then eliminate the protection that switching might otherwise have provided.

Encrypted Sessions

Encrypted sessions provide a different solution. Instead of worrying about data being sniffed, you simply scramble the data portion of the packet beyond recognition. The advantages to this approach are obvious: Even if an attacker sniffs data, it will be useless to him. However, the disadvantages are weighty. There are two chief problems with encryption. One is a technical problem, and the other is a human problem.

Technical issues include whether the encryption is strong enough, and whether it's supported. For example, 40-bit encryption might be insufficient, and not all applications have integrated encryption support. Furthermore, cross-platform encryption solutions used to be rare and typically available only in specialized applications. Recently, cross-platform and generalized encryption services are becoming more common and will continue to do so.

Moreover, human users can resist using encryption. They might find it too troublesome. (For example, can you imagine forcing Macintosh users to use S/Key every time they logged in to the server? These folks are accustomed to ease-of-use, not generating one-time passwords for every new session.) Users might initially agree to such policies, but they rarely adhere to them.

In short, you must find a happy medium—applications that support strong, two-way encryption and also support some level of user-friendliness. That's why I like Secure Shell.

Secure Shell (SSH) provides secure communications in an application environment like Telnet. SSH binds to port 22, and connections are negotiated using RSA. All subsequent traffic is encrypted using IDEA after authentication is complete. This is strong encryption, and is suitable for just about any nonsecret, nonclassified communication.

Secure Shell is a perfect example of an application that meets user and administrative standards.

Versions of SSH and OpenSSH (a free version of SSH) exist for just about all of the major operating systems. Check out Secure Shell at http://www.ssh.com/ or http://www.openssh.com.

Summary

Sniffers represent a significant security risk, mainly because they are not easily detected. You would benefit tremendously by learning how to use a sniffer, and understanding how others can employ them against you. The best defenses against sniffing are secure topology and strong encryption.

Further Reading on Sniffers

The following documents offer further information about sniffers and the threats they pose:

- Sniffing (network wiretap, sniffer) FAQ. Robert Graham.
  http://www.robertgraham.com/pubs/sniffing-faq.html

- Tik-76.115 Functional Specification. (Specification for a sniffer application used in visualization of TCP/IP traffic.) http://mordor.cs.hut.fi/tik-76.115/ kesa-96/palautukset/Sniffers/pt/tm/FM_3.0.html

- "Sniffers: What They Are and How to Protect Yourself." Matthew Tanase.
  http://online.securityfocus.com/infocus/1549

- "Privacy and Security on the Internet." Lawrence E. Widman, M.D., Ph.D., University of Texas Health Science Center.
  http://www.med-edu.com/internet-security.html

PART IV

Weapons of Mass Destruction

IN THIS PART

16

Denial-of-Service Attacks

In this chapter you'll learn about denial-of-service (DoS) attacks, how they work, their history, targets, and programs used to launch them.

What Is Denial of Service?

Denial of service is the category of attacks that cause a loss of service or an inability to function. They come in many forms and strike many different targets. The results can last for minutes, hours, or days, and can impact network performance, data integrity, and system operation.

The first DoS attack of significance was the Morris Worm, estimated to have taken some 5,000 machines out of commission for several hours. At the time (November 1988), it was a disaster for academic and research centers, but had little impact on the rest of the world. Today, comparable DoS attacks, such as those against Yahoo!, Amazon, and other major Web sites in February 2000, have resulted in millions of dollars in lost business and revenue. The frequency of DoS attacks is increasing at an alarming rate, due in part to the prevalence of tools written for this purpose. The complexity of the attacks is also being taken to new levels, which mandates the need for stringent security practices and the implementation of new protection mechanisms.

Many denial-of-service tools are written as proof-of-concept code. The purpose is to demonstrate insecurities within common operating systems, such as Windows, Linux, Solaris, and the BSD-derived Unixes. The Morris Worm was an experiment in distributed computing, albeit a little forcefully done. Poor development practices and a failure to introduce security early into new applications and operating systems cause many of these exploitable problems to exist. The growing complexity of network design and organization pushes the limits of current technology and exacerbates new vulnerabilities. The presence of denial-of-service attacks is a double-edged sword. On the one hand, it is unfortunate that conditions exist that allow denial-of-service techniques to proliferate. On the other, its presence is part of the technology evolution that generates higher-security products and applications.

The standard for security has risen greatly, and this is apparent with the reaction to DoS attacks. Only recently have we seen legislation that deals with this form of attack. It is no longer considered a silly prank when revenue is lost in our Internet-driven economy.

NOTE

It should be noted that sometimes denial of service is not the result of an attack. On September 11, 2001, most of the major news sites, such as CNN, were unavailable. The reason was that they simply had too many people trying to read the news—the sites did not have the resources available to handle such an unexpectedly heavy load.

How Denial of Service Works

Denial-of-service attacks are generally pulled off by exploiting programming flaws in software and by writing specialized programs whose purpose is to perform attacks. DoS attacks generally work in one of the following ways:

- Bandwidth consumption

- Resource saturation

- System and application crash

Bandwidth consumption is an attack against network resources, and refers to the complete use of available network bandwidth by an attacking computer or computers. This makes network response slow or stops the server completely while the attack is ongoing, and causes an inability to reach services such as Web sites, email, and files. *Resource saturation* targets specific computer systems that provide services such as Web access, email, DNS, and FTP, and causes them to slow or halt. System and application crashes result in denial of service, as the particular system or software freezes or crashes.

Bandwidth Consumption

Each network can support only a finite amount of network traffic at one time, and this amount is dependent upon a few factors: network speed, equipment types, and their performance. Common communication types of links from an ISP to an organization are ISDN, DSL, broadband (using cable modems), T1, and T3. These link types also reflect different bandwidth capabilities. Common Local Area Network (LAN) topologies use 10BASE-T and 100BASE-T. For further information about network bandwidth and speeds, see http://www.speedguide.net/Cable_modems/bandwidth.shtml.

Denial of service by bandwidth consumption occurs when the entire capacity of the network link is used. When the network bandwidth capacity is reached, new network data cannot be sent. This means new connections to the Internet, file servers, Web servers, email servers, or any other function that requires network communication will not work. Connections that are already established will slow to a crawl, freeze, or be disconnected.

Attacks against bandwidth can occur via specialized attack programs and the misconfiguration of network equipment. The programs used to cause denial of service are discussed later in this chapter in the section "Recent DoS Attacks." Misconfiguration of network equipment includes any device that connects to the network, such as computer systems, routers, switches, and other devices.

Bandwidth attacks are active; the denial of service occurs only as long as the bandwidth is used fully. As soon as the attacking program stops sending data, or the device is configured properly, bandwidth again becomes available. Most network functionality will return to normal, except for a few connections that might need restarting.

Common attacks include protocol-based exploits that consume network bandwidth by sending crafted network data. The access device, such as a router, can fail as it becomes inundated with more traffic than it can process. Another form of bandwidth attack relies on the reaction of network-connected systems and devices to specific network data. Many or all of the computers on the target network can be made to respond simultaneously to network traffic, such as IP broadcasts (IP packets that are sent to the broadcast address of a network instead of to a specific machine), thereby consuming all of the available bandwidth. The "Smurf" attack is one popular example of this form of attack. This and other forms are outlined in the section "Recent DoS Attacks."

Resource Saturation

Like a network, each computer system also has a finite set of resources, including memory, storage, and processor capacities. *Resource saturation* is when all of one or more of these resources is used up, which leaves nothing for other applications. The SYN flood is a popular example of an attack that uses all the available networking resources on a system.

Each operating system that supports TCP/IP network connectivity has limitations on the number of connections that can be maintained at one time. The SYN flood exploits the three-way handshake of a TCP connection, which is outlined in Chapter 6, "A Brief TCP/IP Primer." The SYN flood succeeds by creating "half-open" connections on the port on the target server. Half-open connections are those in which the three-way handshake is not completed. Normally, the handshake completes or times out, causing the connection to be deleted. Each port can only support a finite number of half-open connections, and when this number is exceeded, no other new connections can be made. By sending only the first packet of the TCP handshake with invalid or spoofed source addresses, the server responds to the SYN packet with an acknowledgment. Because this acknowledgment goes to a falsified address, the response to it never arrives. This causes a backlog of half-open connections that are waiting to be completed, preventing new connections from being accepted.

The Web server is a good sample target for a denial-of-service attack, although any network service can be targeted. As we have all probably experienced, a busy Web server tends to respond more slowly to our requests. A bit of knowledge about TCP/IP and the Hypertext Transfer Protocol (HTTP) is needed to understand how these attacks work. A single HTTP request and connection is made when the browser connects to the Web server. This request asks the server for a particular file; the server then sends the file, and the connection is closed. Under these circumstances, a Web server can handle a large number of requests because the requests usually take a very short time to complete, and they arrive one after another. As the server receives more simultaneous requests, the application becomes loaded as it processes all of these connections at the same time. Even with this slowdown, the Web server can still function.

To cause the Web server to stop functioning, the attacker needs to increase the time needed to handle these connections, or increase the processing power needed to handle each one. A SYN flood against a Web server makes the server unable to accept new connections by exceeding the maximum number of connections for the port it uses. The SYN flood is difficult to defend against. If the attacker forges packets to look as if they are coming from an unreachable system, the server has no way of knowing that they are not typical traffic. The server then responds as it would to any other connection, and waits for a timeout to occur before it realizes it should close the connection. As outlined in the SYN flood description above, the denial of service occurs when the Web server receives a large number of these forged packets—so many that it cannot handle any more new connections—and is inevitably stuck waiting for these falsified connections to timeout before it can continue processing. Similar attacks are the ICMP flood and the UDP flood, which use other protocols to achieve the same effect.

Another example of resource saturation can occur with the use of external programs such as Common Gateway Interface (CGI) programs with the Web server. Programs that store data in files on the Web server can be exploited to fill the hard disk on the server. The server operating system uses files for much of its normal functionality, and when full, it can often fail to function. Similarly, applications that allocate a lot of memory or require a lot of processing power for complex computations can be exploited to use all of those resources, preventing new processes and applications from functioning. These attacks are not exploitable only via the Web server—any access to the system might allow an attack to succeed. The email bomb discussed in the "Exploitation and Denial of Service" section is a good example of this.

System and Application Crash

System and application crashes are fast and easy approaches to denial of service, wherein a programming flaw is exploitable and causes the application or operating system to crash. A well-known example of these crashes is the "Ping of Death" attack, which uses oversized ICMP echo requests. The target machine crashes due to improperly implemented handling of this type of network data.

These attacks are also commonly directed against network access devices such as IP routers, cable routers, managed Ethernet switches, VPNs, and other application-specific devices. These devices often support some form of management interface including a Command Line Interface (CLI) and a Web management interface. Through various methods, including a large number of simultaneous connections, buffer overflows in user input routines, and improper data validation, these devices have been made to crash. A denial-of-service attack on an access device has a wider influence than an attack on a single machine, because these devices are typically gateways to multiple networks.

Many of these attacks can be prevented by the safe configuration of the network device. This includes changing factory-set default passwords, setting IP filtering, and configuring the device to allow management from only a select group of machines.

Exploitation and Denial of Service

This section outlines common attacks through the denial-of-service methods outlined in the previous section:

- Email bomb resource attacks
- Protocol attacks

Email Bomb Resource Attacks

Email bombs are insidious attack methods that make up for simplicity with their effects. A traditional *email bomb* is simply a series of messages (perhaps thousands) sent to your mailbox. The attacker's objective is to fill your mailbox with junk, or to fill the hard disk or file system on which the mail server runs with junk. If mailbox quotas are used, the receiver of an email bomb cannot receive new messages until the mailbox is cleaned up. If the file system of the mail server is full, no other users can receive new messages. Email bombs lead to the loss of important data, along with increased bandwidth and resource usage, which can translate into higher network charges. If you use a dial-up connection, this can also translate into increased connection charges and wasted time.

Email Bomb Packages

Email bomb packages are programs that automate the process of email-bombing someone. System administrators should be aware of these packages and the file-names associated with them. (Although this knowledge will not prevent your system from being attacked, it might prevent your users from attacking other systems.)

Table 16.1 lists the most popular email bomb packages and filenames associated with them. If you run a network with multiple users, you should scan your drives for those filenames.

TABLE 16.1   Common Email Bomb Packages and Associated Filenames

Bombing Package	Filenames
Aenima	`aenima17.zip, aenima20.zip`
Avalanche	`alanch3.zip, alanch35b.zip, ava.zip, avalance.zip`
Euthanasia	`euthan15.zip, et15.zip`
Gatemail	`gatemail.c`
Ghost Mail	`gm51.zip`
HakTek	`hatetuk.zip`
Kaboom	`kaboom3.zip, kab3.zip`
Serpent (Linux)	`serpent.zip`
The Unabomber	`unabomb.zip, unz.zip`
UNIX Mailbomber	`mailbomb.c`
Up Yours	`upyours3.zip, up4beta3.zip`
The Windows Email Bomber	`bomb02b.zip`

Many of these files can be found at `http://home.cyberarmy.com/hackshock/bomber.htm`.

Dealing with Email Bombs

Kill files, exclusionary schemes, or mail filters are all cures for an email bomb. Using these tools, you can automatically reject mail sent from the source address. There are various ways to implement such an exclusionary scheme. Unix users can find a variety of sources online.

If you use Windows or Mac OS instead, I would recommend any of the mail filter applications listed in Table 16.2. Many of these are shareware, so you can try them before you buy them.

TABLE 16.2 Popular Mail Server Filter Applications and Their Locations

Filter Package	Location
EIMS(MacOS)	http://www.eudora.com/
E-Mail Chomper (Win95/98/NT)	http://www.sarum.com/echomp.html
Mail Siphon (MacOS)	http://www.maliasoft.com/siphon/
Musashi (PPC, MacOS)	http://www.sonosoft.com/
SIMS (MacOS)	http://www.stalker.com/
Spam Buster (Win 9x/ME/NT/2000/XP)	http://www.contactplus.com/
SpamKiller (Win 9x/NT/ME/2000/XP)	http://www.spamkiller.com/

In addition to these packages, you can use the filtering capabilities built into most of the major email packages. You can add filters based on keywords such as "Viagra" that appear in a lot of spam, or you can reject particular senders.

If someone starts bombing you, you can also try a human approach by contacting the attacker's postmaster. This is generally effective; the user will be counseled that this behavior is unnecessary and will not be tolerated. In most cases, this proves to be a sufficient deterrent. Some providers have strong appropriate usage policies and will immediately terminate the user's account if it is used inappropriately.

Lastly, know this: Not all ISPs are responsible. Some of them might not care whether their users are email-bombing others. If you encounter this situation, you don't have many choices. The easiest cure is to disallow any traffic from their entire domain.

Email Bombs as Security Risks

In many circumstances, email bombs can result in denial of service. For example, one individual bombed Monmouth University in New Jersey so aggressively that the mail server temporarily died. This resulted in an FBI investigation, and the young man was arrested.

NOTE

Most mail packages will die given the right circumstances on the right platform. For example, one of my clients found that directing a 40MB mail message to mailserv on UnixWare will kill the entire box. The freeze is unrecoverable except via reboot, and reboot is no recovery at all. There is no fix for this.

If you experience this level of attack, you should contact the authorities, especially when the attacker varies his origin, thus bypassing mail filters or exclusionary schemes at the router level. Chances are, if the attack is that persistent, your only remedy is to bring in the police.

Email Bombing Viruses

The recent trend towards email-based viruses also presents a denial-of-service condition. The automation and integration of newer applications allows greater flexibility and increased functionality, but also presents security risks if not used appropriately. Windows-based macro and Visual Basic Script (VBS) viruses demonstrate this clearly. The VBS.LoveLetter, "I Love You" and "Anna Kournikova" viruses, and the Klez and VBS.SST worms show the fine line between viruses and denial of service. All of these viruses exploit the capabilities of Microsoft's Outlook mail client to automatically execute executable code contained in messages. The virus code replicates and sends itself to many other recipients, magnifying the problem and resulting in widespread infection and loss of service as files are deleted and mail servers cease functioning. Disabling Windows Scripting Host can help alleviate the problem of automatic execution. See `http://www.sophos.com/support/faqs/wsh.html` for further information.

NIMDA AND KLEZ

We will look at two of these email-based viruses in detail. The first is the Nimda (*Admin* spelled backwards) worm. Out of all of the viruses I have seen over the years, Nimda has caused the most damage by far—some estimates put the damage at two billion dollars. Last fall at a previous employer, I went into work one day a little bit late. When I got there, many of our Windows-based servers and workstations were having serious problems. The worst part was that our administrator would clean up one machine, and then a few minutes later it would be infected again. Nimda wasn't just an ordinary mail-bombing virus. It also attacked IIS, would infect Web pages so that IE users could be infected, and infect via file sharing. Once a machine was infected, it would basically make huge security holes in the machine and consume a large amount of resources.

In the end, each machine that was infected had to be removed from the network, cleaned, and then put back on the network to prevent re-infection. One machine never fully recovered from the damage, and the OS was later reloaded on it. My Windows 2000 machine was one of the few that avoided Nimda in our office. A large part of the reason is that I purposely do not run Outlook and IE because of their history of security-related problems. You can find an excellent report on the effects of Nimda at `http://www.incidents.org/react/nimda.pdf`. The charts alone showing the traffic spike on the Internet due to Nimda are very interesting.

The other notable virus is Klez. For the past few months, I have been receiving copies of Klez every day. In fact, I have received more copies of Klez than all the other viruses combined. Klez has at least nine different variants; eight of them are mass-mailers. Though the variants work slightly differently, the basic premise is that Klez uses holes in Outlook, forges email to other people, and then attacks, damaging files on the system. The forgery part is very interesting. The very first copy of Klez I got claimed to be from a good friend who does not use Outlook. I thought that was strange and started looking at the mail headers. It didn't come from him. What that particular variant does is look at the Outlook address book and use it to fill in the To: and From: fields in the email. I've tried to figure out a way to write a mail filter for Klez, and the only commonality I can find in the email messages I get it from is that there is an attachment about 120K in size. An article on the virus is available at http://www.wired.com/news/technology/0,1282,52174,00.html.

List Linking

List-linking attacks have similar effects to email bombs, but their appearance is more inconspicuously malignant. In *list linking*, the target subscribes you to dozens of mailing lists, which can fill your mailbox and possibly the mail server with data.

NOTE

Mailing lists distribute mail messages collected from various sources. These messages typically concentrate on a special interest subject. These mail servers (sometimes called *list servers*) collect such messages and mail them to members of the list on a daily, weekly, or monthly basis. Members can subscribe to such a list in several ways, though most commonly through email.

Mail-bombing packages automate the process of list linking. For example, Kaboom and Avalanche are two well-known email bomb packages that offer point-and-click list linking. The results of such linking can be disastrous. Most mailing lists generate at least 50 mail messages daily, and some of those include binary attachments. If the attacker links you to 100 lists, you will receive 5,000 email messages per day. Furthermore, you must manually unsubscribe from each mailing list once you are linked. Moreover, attackers often choose times when you are known to be away, such as when you are on vacation. Thus, while you are absent, thousands of messages accrue in your mailbox. This can amount to a denial-of-service attack, particularly if your system administrator puts quotas on mailboxes.

List linking is particularly insidious because a simple mail filter doesn't really solve the problem—it just sweeps it under the rug. Here's why: The mail keeps coming until you unsubscribe from the lists. In fact, it will generally keep coming for a minimum of six months. Some mailing lists request that you renew your member-ship every six months or after some other specified period of time. This typically entails sending a confirmation message to the list server. In such a message, you request an additional six months of membership. Naturally, if you fail to provide such a confirmation message, you will eventually be taken off the list. However, in this scenario, your first opportunity to get off the list will not occur for six months. Therefore, no matter how irritating it might be, you should always deal with list linking immediately.

The cure for list linking is to unsubscribe from all lists you have been linked to. Doing this is more difficult than it sounds for a variety of reasons. One reason is that new lists seldom include instructions to unsubscribe. Therefore, you might be forced to trace down that information on the Web. If so, expect several hours of downtime.

TIP

To help fight against list linking, most mailing list administration software requires confirmation of subscriptions and also provides passwords for list members. These passwords are used to modify the user's subscription information and provide authentication. It is useful to keep copies of the initial subscription messages after signing on to a mailing list. These informational messages are invaluable, and often contain the pertinent information needed to unsubscribe and maintain list membership.

Your ability to quickly and effectively unsubscribe from all lists will also depend largely on your email package. If your email client has powerful search functions that allow you to scan subject and sender headings, you can gather the list server addresses very quickly. However, if you use an email client that has no extended search functions, you are facing an uphill battle. If you are currently in this situation and have been list linked, communication with the maintainer of the list is often useful. Most mailing lists function by programs that automate most of the functionality the list provides. Contact with a real person is vital in the event of list linking. Should all attempts to unsubscribe fail, the user can implement permanent mail filtering, or, in the worst case scenario, a new email address might be warranted.

A Word About Mail Relay

Another issue related to mail bombing and list linking, as well as the overall presence of unsolicited commercial email (UCE) or spam, is the capability of the attacker to relay mail. In order to obscure their identity, most mail bombs arrive from fictitious users. The attacker's capability to falsify his identity arises from the configuration of various ISPs' mail servers. Mail relaying allows a mail server to be used to send mail to foreign networks.

As part of the transaction for sending a mail message, the software used to send mail connects to the mail server. The recipient's address and the sender's address are specified, and the message is then transmitted. Mail relaying occurs when either the sender's address or the system from which the sender connects to the server is not on the same network as the server. Mail servers that are configured to allow relaying allow foreign users and systems to send mail to any other user. Servers that are configured to disallow relaying will not allow messages with sender addresses on unknown networks, or from systems on those networks.

In general, mail relaying is seen as a security risk and is disabled. For those systems that allow relaying, little can be done to prevent its misuse. Filtering packages are incapable of supplying the needed security. Filtering by domain name or IP addresses might disallow legitimate email from being sent—this is not the desired outcome. For example, filtering to stop UCE from AOL will likely disallow millions of users' email from being delivered.

The issue of mail relaying is complex, because messages such as mail bombs and UCE are syntactically the same as legitimate mail messages. Therefore, it is important to be aware of this issue as it relates to denial of service because it is one piece of the prevention puzzle.

Mail Relaying Blocking Lists

A variety of mail relaying blocking systems exist. Distributed Sender Boycott List (DSBL, `http://dsbl.org/`, formerly ORBZ), Mail Abuse Prevention System (MAPS, `http://www.mail-abuse.org/`), Relay Stop List (RSL, `http://relays.visi.com/`), and Open Relay DataBase (ORDB, `http://www.ordb.org/`) are a few. They work by compiling a list of sites they believe spammers can use to relay mail. They then recommend that you block any email coming from these sites to stop spam.

Unfortunately, this is a case where the solution may be just as bad or worse than the original problem. First of all, some of the lists have been called "personal vendetta lists." Apparently, some sites have been listed that should not have been, and some of these sites have even sued (see `http://www.stoporbs.org/` for more information). Also, take a look at the FAQs for a couple of blocking lists: `http://relays.osiru-soft.com/faq.html` and `http://www.dorkslayers.com/faq.html`. Honestly, after reading these, there is no way I'd trust these lists as being rational in their decisions.

BLACKLISTS: A HIDDEN DOS ATTACK?

At one place where I used to work, all of a sudden we could no longer receive emails from some of our customers. After investigating, we discovered that our ISP implemented one of these blocking lists without telling us. If our salespeople hadn't been diligent in following up with potential customers, we might have lost some business. We got the ISP to remove it. Then a few months later, our system administrator changed our email server package and made a configuration error. Boom, we were blacklisted, and the next thing we knew, outgoing mail was bouncing. If the list had just sent us an email saying that we had 24 hours to fix the problem before being blacklisted, that would have been fine, but they didn't. The moral of the story is that blacklists cause more problems than they solve.

Although these lists' purpose is to prevent denial of service from spammers, they create a whole new denial of service where you can't get mail to and from legitimate contacts. Businesses need to be especially careful in using such a list, because when their customers can no longer send them email, they are likely to take their business elsewhere. Crackers who want to cause problems for an entire site can work at getting the site listed on one of these lists.

Protocol Attacks

Attacks against network protocols make up a large portion of the DoS attacks that occur. Protocol attacks result in bandwidth consumption, system crashes, and resource saturation, causing denial-of-service conditions. These attacks are very threatening, and can stop network connectivity and system functionality for an indeterminate amount of time. Prevention of protocol attacks also requires considerably more advanced and complex procedures and countermeasures.

Protocol attacks strike at the heart of IP implementations. Hence, they can crop up on any platform. Worse still, because IP implementations are not drastically different from platform to platform, a single DoS attack might well work on several target operating systems. A well-known example of this is the LAND attack, which could incapacitate almost two dozen different operating systems, including Windows NT and a slew of Unix flavors. Other examples include the previously mentioned SYN, UDP, and ICMP flood attacks.

Furthermore, analysis of DoS code releases consistently shows that when a new attack is out, it will eventually work on nearly all platforms, even if it doesn't initially. New strains of DoS attacks are released about every two weeks or so. Such releases are typically written on a single build platform (Linux, for example) to attack a single target platform (Windows NT, for example). After such code is released, it is examined by the hacker and cracker communities. Within days, someone releases a modified version (a *mutation*) that can incapacitate a wider variety of operating systems.

The "Ping of Death," SYN flood, and some other attacks should sound familiar by now. These protocol attacks rely on the continued existence and use of these common protocols. Their effects are widespread because of the prevalence of vulnerable operating systems and network equipment. New methods to prevent and defend against exploitation at this basic level have arisen. These methods are outlined in the DoS attack index that follows.

Denial-of-Service Attack Index

Here is a comprehensive index of recent and old DoS attacks; each is fully documented. The fields provided and their significance are as follows:

- Filename—The filename provided is the one by which the attack is most well-known. However, as folks distribute *exploit code* (programs that make an attack), different people name the file different things. There are various reasons for this, but the most common is to obscure the exploit code from system administrators. Since system administrators generally know the filenames of such tools, crackers rename them.

- Author—In this field, you often see aliases or email addresses instead of real names. In the index, I have made every good faith effort to obtain the name, email address, or alias of each program's original author. If you authored one of the following programs and credit has erroneously been given to some other party, please contact Sams and let them know.

- Location—This is the location of the source code for the exploit code. From this URL, you can download the source code and test it on your own machine.

- Background—The Background field denotes locations where further documentation can be found. This usually points to an article or mailing list posting that details the attack's chief characteristics.

- Build Operating System—This field indicates either what platform the attack code was written on, or which operating system will successfully run the code.

- Target Operating System—This field indicates what platform can be successfully attacked using the source code found at the Location.

- Impact—This field briefly describes the effect of an attack using the source code.

- Fix—This field points to URLs that hold patches or workarounds.

Recent DoS Attacks

If you want to stay up-to-date with the latest attacks, go to `http://www.packetstormsecurity.com/` and look at the "last 20 exploits" list.

BIND

Filename: `bind_nuke.txt`

Author: Artur Swakina

Location: `http://packetstorm.decepticons.org/Exploit_Code_Archive/bind_nuke.txt`

Background: Crashes BIND (DNS)

Build Operating System: Unix with BASH shell

Target Operating System: Any system that runs BIND 8.1

Impact: Crashes DNS.

Fix: Upgrade BIND.

Additional Note: There are many more BIND exploits that can be found at `http://www.packetstormsecurity.com`.

Smurf

Filename: `smurf.c`

Author: TFreak

Location: `http://www.packetstormsecurity.com` and search for "smurf"

Background: `http://www.cert.org/advisories/CA-1998-01.html`

Build Operating System: Unix

Target Operating System: Any system that responds to ICMP data.

Impact: Causes denial of service via spoofed ICMP echo requests to a network broadcast address.

Fix: Disable IP directed broadcasts on the router and configure operating systems not to respond to packets sent to IP broadcast addresses.

Fraggle

Filename: `fraggle.c`

Author: TFreak

Location: `http://www.packetstormsecurity.com` and search for "fraggle"

Background: Smurf with a UDP twist; see the previous entry

Build Operating System: Unix

Target Operating System: Any system that responds to UDP data.

Impact: Causes denial of service by making systems send UDP network data to a spoofed target.

Fix: Disallow unused ports on the firewall and configure network equipment and operating systems not to respond to UDP broadcasts.

The following flood attacks are general mechanisms that are still common today, although the technology has been available for quite some time.

ICMP Flood

Filename: `pingflood.c`

Author: Various

Location: `http://www.packetstormsecurity.com` and search for "pingflood"

Background: `http://www.rycom.ca/solutions/whitepapers/toplayer/dos_attacks.htm`

Build Operating System: Unix

Target Operating System: Various

Impact: Denial of service via network bandwidth overutilization.

Fix: Block ICMP traffic at the firewall and at the operating system. Monitor the network for attack signatures.

SYN Flood

Filename: `synflood.c`

Author: Various

Location: `http://www.packetstormsecurity.com` and search for "synflood"

Background: `http://www.rycom.ca/solutions/whitepapers/toplayer/dos_attacks.htm` and `http://www.niksula.cs.hut.fi/~dforsber/synflood/result.html`

Build Operating System: Unix

Target Operating System: Various

Impact: Denial of service as the target system exceeds its maximum number of half-open/queued connections.

Fix: Configure the operating system to allow a higher number of open connections. Monitor the network for attack signatures.

UDP Flood

Filename: `udpflood.tgz`

Author: Various

Location: `http://www.packetstormsecurity.com` and search for "udpflood"

Background: `http://www.rycom.ca/solutions/whitepapers/toplayer/dos_attacks.htm`

Build Operating System: Unix

Target Operating System: Various

Impact: Denial of service as the target system receives more traffic than it is capable of handling at one time.

Fix: Disallow UDP traffic and services on the firewall and operating systems. Monitor the network for attack signatures.

Historical List of Well-Known DoS Attacks

The following attacks are early, well-known and well-documented DoS attacks. The vulnerabilities allowing most of these attacks to succeed have been solved in newer versions of operating systems, but many organizations still have older and unpatched systems around. If you are responsible for securing a network, make sure you cover these bases. Fixes are available for all of these attacks, and should be understood and implemented. Take a moment now to run through the following attacks to see if you're vulnerable. Most are easily fixed.

For more information about past and present DoS attacks organized by operating system, software and device, see "The DoS Database" at http://www.attrition.org/security/denial/.

Teardrop

Filename: teardrop.c

Author: Route@infonexus.com

Location: http://www.packetstormsecurity.com and search for "teardrop"

Background: See the source code and comments

Build Operating System: Unix

Target Operating System: Windows 95 and Windows NT

Impact: IP fragment attack will lock up the target.

Fix: Search for "teardrop" in the knowledge base at http://support.microsoft.com/.

Teardrop was an early DoS attack that spawned several variants. This set the stage for many new DoS attacks and approaches to DoS tool creation.

Bonk/Boink Attacks

Filename: bonk.c, boink.c

Author: The people at Rootshell.com

Location: http://www.packetstormsecurity.com/ and search for "bonk" or "boink"

Background: See source code

Build Operating System: Unix

Target Operating System: Windows 95 and Windows NT. Patched and later versions are unaffected.

Impact: This utility will crash any Windows 95 or NT box, and it is basically a modified version of code previously written by route@infonexus.com. The malformed packet has a fragment offset that is greater than the header length.

Jolt2

Filename: jolt2.c, jolt2_v1_2.zip

Author: Phonix (phonix@moocow.org)

Location: http://www.packetstormsecurity.com and search for "jolt2"

Background: `http://www.packetstormsecurity.com` and search for "jolt2.c-analysis.txt"

Build Operating System: Unix

Target Operating System: Windows 98/NTsp5/NTsp6/2000/XP.

Impact: 100% CPU utilization.

Fix: `http://support.microsoft.com/`

LAND

Filename: `land.c`

Author: The people formerly at `http://www.rootshell.com` (site is now down)

Location: `http://www.packetstormsecurity.com` and search for "land.c"

Background: `http://www.cisco.com/warp/public/770/land-pub.shtml`

Build Operating System: Unix

Target Operating System: Many networked operating systems, including older versions of BSD, Linux, Solaris, Digital Unix, HP-UX and Windows 95, Cisco IOS.

Impact: Connects request packets specifying source and destination, as those same request packets lock up the target.

Fix: `http://support.microsoft.com/`

The LAND attack sent tremors through the Internet community, primarily because of the sheer number of systems affected. In particular, it was learned that certain network hardware was also vulnerable to the attack, including routers.

NOTE

Only certain hardware was vulnerable to LAND. It is known that NCD X Terminals, Catalyst LAN switches (Series 5000 and Series 2900), and Cisco IOS/700 were all vulnerable. If you fear that your router is vulnerable, I suggest compiling and using `land.c` as a test.

You should contact your vendor regarding fixes. It can take time to route out all LAND variations because so many mutations have cropped up. One version crashes Windows 95 and NT, even with Service Pack 3 installed. Windows NT is currently up to Service Pack 6a. If your systems are current, this attack does not pose a threat. Workarounds for Cisco hardware can be found at `http://www.securityfocus.com`. Otherwise, contact your respective vendor.

If your operating system is Windows 95, get the patch for the original LAND attack as well as several mutations. That patch can be found by searching for "land" under the Windows 95 knowledge base at `http://support.microsoft.com/`.

Winnuke

> Filename: `winnuke.c`
>
> Author: `_eci`
>
> Location: `http://www.packetstormsecurity.com` and search for "nuke"
>
> Background: See the below description
>
> Build Operating System: Linux, BSDI
>
> Target Operating System: Windows 95 and Windows NT. 98/2000 are not affected.
>
> Impact: Windows 95 and NT failed to react properly to packets with the out-of-band (OOB) flag set. Often caused a system panic requiring reboot.
>
> Fix: `http://support.microsoft.com/`

Winnuke will kill any unpatched Windows 95 or Windows NT box, forcing a reboot. This attack has gone through several mutations and is available for many build operating systems. The "nukenabber" tool helps to identify the presence of this tool on a network.

Nukenabber is a small, compact port sniffer written by `puppet@earthling.net`. The program listens on ports 139, 138, 137, 129, and 53. These are all ports on which DoS attacks have been implemented in the past. Nukenabber notifies you when your machine is under Winnuke attack. The program is available at `http://www.dynam-sol.com/puppet/nukenabber.html`.

DNSKiller

> Filename: `winnuke.c`
>
> Author: `_eci`
>
> Location: `http://www.packetstormsecurity.com` and search for "DNSKiller"
>
> Background: See the below description.
>
> Build Operating System: Linux, BSDI
>
> Target Operating System: Windows NT.
>
> Impact: Crashes DNS server, which can lead to other machines being unable to use Internet domain names correctly.
>
> Fix: `http://support.microsoft.com/`

DNSKiller will kill a Windows NT 4.0 box's DNS server. The source code was written for a Linux environment. However, it can also run well on BSD-ish platforms. For more information, see
`http://archives.neohapsis.com/archives/bugtraq/1997_1/0152.html`.

`arnudp100.c`

> Filename: `arnudp100.c`
>
> Author: `_eci`
>
> Location: `http://www.packetstormsecurity.com` and search for "arnudp100.c"
>
> Background: See the below description.
>
> Build Operating System: Linux, Solaris, FreeBSD, Novell
>
> Target Operating System: Old versions of Linux, Solaris, and FreeBSD. Does affect Netware 4 and 5, however.
>
> Impact: Worst case is that it can crash a system.
>
> Fix: `Upgrade OS`

`arnudp100.c` is a program that forges UDP packets, and can be used to implement a DoS attack on UDP ports 7, 13, 19, and 37. To understand the attack, I recommend examining "Defining Strategies to Protect Against UDP Diagnostic Port Denial-of-Service Attacks," by Cisco Systems. Another good source for this information is CERT Advisory CA-96.01.

NOTE

Cisco Systems' "Defining Strategies to Protect Against UDP Diagnostic Port Denial-of-Service Attacks" can be found online at http://cio.cisco.com/warp/public/707/3.html.

Distributed Denial-of-Service Attacks

In early 2000, the Internet community saw a new method of attack unleashed upon several popular Web sites, including CNN, E*Trade, Datek, Amazon.com, Yahoo!, and Buy.com that caused them to be unreachable for several hours. These attacks were unlike normal DoS attacks in that the flood of network traffic appeared to come from many different systems simultaneously. Network administrators and security personnel scrambled to identify the causes and sources of the attacks, as well as to find methods to stop them and bring their crawling Web sites back into service. Rumors spread about a coordinated underground cracking community conspiring to attack simultaneously. It appeared as though a new form of attack—the distributed denial-of-service (DDoS) attack—had arrived, and that it would become a nightmare for Web sites and businesses.

The good news is that over the past two years these attacks have not become as common as once feared. They do still occur every now and then. However, there have been relatively few new techniques, and many security products are now designed to deal with them. Administrators are also more aware of the attack methods, and are better prepared to defend against them.

Distributed denial-of-service attacks, as the name implies, occur when several systems, from a handful to thousands, simultaneously attack a specified target. Some of the well-known and analyzed attack forms are Trinoo (or Trin00), Tribe Flood Network (TFN), TFN2k (an updated version of TFN), and Stacheldraht (German for "barbed wire").

These attacks function via a master and slave mechanism. The master is the controlling station where the attacker defines the target and method of attack. The slave stations are remote systems that have been compromised and have had the attack tool installed. The master signals the slave stations to launch the attack. The attack is also stopped by another signal from the master system.

A good general overview of DDoS attacks can be found in "Distributed Denial-of-Service Attacks" by Bennett Todd at `http://www.linuxsecurity.com/resource_files/intrusion_detection/ddos-faq.html`.

This section provides an index of DDoS attack tools. The background information includes full analyses of the attack methods and source code.

Trinoo (Trin00)

Filename: `trinoo.tgz`

Author: Project DoS

Location: `http://packetstormsecurity.com/distributed/`

Background: `http://staff.washington.edu/dittrich/misc/trinoo.analysis`

Build Operating System: Unix

Target Operating System: Unix

Impact: Denial of service until the attack is stopped.

Fix: Patch systems to prevent compromise, monitor UDP traffic for Trinoo fingerprints, and run DDoS scanner tools such as RID (available at `http://packetstormsecurity.com/distributed/`) to detect the presence of the program on your network. Blocking UDP traffic on high-numbered ports might stop the problem, but might also cause other network applications not to work.

Tribe Flood Network (TFN)

Filename: `tfn.tgz`

Author: Mixter

Location: `http://packetstormsecurity.com/distributed/`

Background: http://staff.washington.edu/dittrich/misc/tfn.analysis

Build Operating System: Unix

Target Operating System: Unix

Impact: Denial of service until the attack is stopped.

Fix: Use RID (see Trinoo entry) to scan for the presence of the software on your network, and block all ICMP echo traffic. (This might not be possible depending on network needs of the organization.)

TFN2k

Filename: tfn2k.tgz

Author: Mixter

Location: http://packetstormsecurity.com/distributed/

Background: http://packetstormsecurity.com/distributed/TFN2k_Analysis.htm

Build Operating System: Unix

Target Operating System: Unix, Windows NT/2000

Impact: Denial of service until the attack is stopped.

Fix: Disallow unnecessary TCP, UDP, and ICMP network traffic. Protect systems against compromise by frequent monitoring and updating. Use application proxies to prevent the attack.

Stacheldraht

Filename: satchel.tgz

Author: Unknown

Location: http://packetstormsecurity.com/distributed/

Background: http://staff.washington.edu/dittrich/misc/stacheldraht.analysis

Build Operating System: Linux, Solaris

Target Operating System: Linux, Solaris

Impact: Denial of service until the attack is stopped.

Fix: Use RID (see link in trinoo entry) to scan for the presence of the software on your network, and block all ICMP echo traffic. (This might not be possible depending on the network needs of the organization.)

Summary

Denial-of-service attacks represent a growing trend in hostile Internet activity. After a few years of new techniques appearing for making DoS attacks, the past two years have been relatively mild in comparison. The care and diligence used to design and implement networks, software, and operating systems has a great effect on the ability of the attacker to cause denial of service. Prevention and awareness are two factors that have an immediate impact on the success of these attacks. Filtering unnecessary services and network data, stronger authentication and access control of remote systems and users, and the proactive monitoring and updating of systems and software can help protect your network against these attacks.

Other DoS Resources

Finally, here are several useful links for further information on DoS attacks.

Strategies to Protect Against Distributed Denial-of-Service (DDoS) Attacks: http://www.cisco.com/warp/public/707/newsflash.html

CERT Advisory CA-2000-01 Denial-of-Service Developments: http://www.cert.org/advisories/CA-2000-01.html

CERT Denial-of-Service Attacks: http://www.cert.org/tech_tips/denial_of_service.html

CERT Email Bombing and Spamming: http://www.cert.org/tech_tips/email_bombing_spamming.html

Denial-of-Service (DoS) Attack Resources: http://www.denialinfo.com/

Denial-of-Service Attacks—DDOS, SMURF, FRAGGLE, TRINOO: http://www.infosyssec.com/infosyssec/secdos1.htm

Denial-of-Service Database: http://www.attrition.org/security/denial/

Denial-of-Service Intrusion and Attack Reporting Center: http://www.doshelp.com/

Distributed Denial-of-Service (DDoS) Attacks/Tools: http://staff.washington.edu/dittrich/misc/ddos/

Distributed Intrusion Detection System: http://www.dshield.org/

Network Ingress Filtering: Defeating Denial-of-Service Attacks Which Employ IP Source Address Spoofing: ftp://ftp.isi.edu/in-notes/rfc2267.txt

Results of the Distributed-Systems Intruder Workshop: http://www.cert.org/reports/dsit_workshop.pdf

Consensus Roadmap for Defeating Distributed Denial-of-Service Attacks: http://www.sans.org/ddos_roadmap.htm

17

Viruses and Worms

IN THIS CHAPTER

- Understanding Viruses and Worms

- Objects at Risk of Virus Infection

- Who Writes Viruses, and Why?

- Antivirus Utilities

- Future Trends in Viral Malware

- Publications and Sites

Do you have a virus? No instruments, no senses can tell you if you are in the presence of the predator.

—Richard Preston, *The Hot Zone*

If doctors and pharmacists worked like antivirus vendors, we'd all be immunized against all illnesses. Would this improve our viability as a species?

—David Harley, *Icarus*

This chapter addresses one of the best known, most feared, and least understood problems in information security. It explains what viruses and worms really are (and aren't), summarizes the means of limiting their consequences, and most importantly, includes some pointers to further information.

Understanding Viruses and Worms

Computer viruses are perhaps the most well known and feared security threats of all. Certainly, they're among the most misunderstood. All viruses entail a certain degree of damage, but their impact, with some very prominent exceptions, is mostly social. That is, they cause more damage in terms of damage to morale and reputation than in terms of file or file system damage.

Every virus does cause some (usually) limited denial of service because they all steal disk space, memory, and/or clock cycles (processor time). Some cause unintended damage on some systems. Some do intentional damage to files and file systems, and a few can make some hardware effectively unusable by trashing firmware (CIH, also known as Spacefiller, and, incorrectly, as Chernobyl, for example). At this time, no known virus directly damages hardware, although the possibility of such a virus can't be discounted. However, some of the most successful viruses (in terms of survival) achieve longevity by virtue of the fact that they do nothing but replicate, and therefore aren't conspicuous. Direct damage tends to be noticeable. However, some viruses cause serious damage to data by slow and insidious corruption, and others continue to survive despite their high damage profile.

Email viruses and network worms can cause serious denial of service because of the load on networks and network traffic, servers and other infrastructural resources, as well as the load on first-line, second-line, and third-line support. Critical transactions may be hampered when servers have to be taken down to effect repairs. Other network services such as HTTP may be blocked during cleanup to stop the broadcasting of Nimda- or Code Red-like probes from infected machines, and by testing for other infectable systems.

Increasingly, legitimate services are being blocked completely by security-conscious administrators because they are potentially vulnerable to abuse by malicious software. The most obvious example is in restrictions applied to attachment file types that might contain malicious code: not only screensavers and other program files, but sometimes vulnerable data files such as spreadsheets and other macro-friendly documents, Microsoft Access databases, other scriptable data files, self-extracting zip files, and even encrypted zip files.

SELF-INFLICTED DENIAL OF SERVICE

Less obvious but common examples of blocked services include access to Web-hosted email, workstation-hosted Web servers, and scripting services such as the Windows Scripting Host (WSH). It would be naïve this late in the game to advocate a return to a laissez-faire "allow everything" approach to systems administration. The fact remains, however, that every legitimate file blocked because it has a .EXE filename extension is another victory for the bad guys.

It has to be said that even an innocuous virus can cause problems just by being there, or even by being misdiagnosed as being there. This can result in secondary damage because of inappropriate action taken by poorly informed virus victims. It can also result in social damage. Such damage can include loss of reputation, scapegoating of the victims of a virus attack, or even legal action. A victim might be accused of failing to apply "due diligence," of being in breach of contract, or of being in contravention of data protection legislation. He might even be accused of implication in the dissemination of a virus, which is illegal in many countries (even those in which the actual creation of viruses is not in itself a crime).

Viruses that do no intentional damage are sometimes described as *benign*, in much the same way that a tumor might be defined as malignant or benign. However, this usage is potentially misleading because the use of *benign* in this context does not mean harmless, let alone benevolent, as it might be understood to mean.

The meteoric expansion of Internet usage (especially email) since the early 1990s has raised the status of the virus from an occasional nuisance to everyone's problem. The vastly increased use of local networks and other means of sharing data and applications has also increased the risks by orders of magnitude. In brief, viruses can travel further and faster than was the case a few years ago. The big comeback story in the virus field is that of the computer worm. In the early 1990s, Internet usage became less specific to "big iron" mainframes and minicomputers reached via dumb terminals and terminal emulators. The first generation of worms declined in impact accordingly. Virus and *antivirus* technology became focused on the individual desktop PC. In the latter part of the decade, however, virus writers began to rediscover worm mechanisms as a means of accelerating dissemination, and now worms and worm/virus hybrids have become one of the most aggravating problems faced by system administrators.

The impact of fast-spreading email viruses has decreased dramatically in the last year, as industry has turned to increasingly strict regulation of allowable file attachment types, but at the cost of reduced convenience and functionality. Even worse, these inconveniences may actually have an adverse effect on security, in that end users may show surprising aptitude and cunning in their attempts to evade such restrictions. Nevertheless, we have recently seen a shift away from the explosive dissemination of infective emails from insufficiently protected corporate institutions, toward *malware* (MALicious softWARE), spread primarily by home users who rarely enjoy the benefits of obsessive regular updates of antivirus software and draconian blocking of infectable file types at the mail gateway.

This chapter, although it addresses worm mechanisms in detail, isn't particularly focused on differentiating between viruses and worms. Even within the industry, the terms are often used interchangeably in the context of the hybrid viruses/worms that dominate the current virus scene.

What Is a Computer Virus?

Most antivirus professionals will accept a working definition of the term *computer virus* like this: "a program that replicates by 'infecting' other programs, so that they contain a (possibly evolved) copy of the virus." (F. Cohen: *A Short Course on Computer Viruses*.)

Note that the emphasis here is on reproduction by infection. A virus is not destructive *per se*, whereas a destructive program is not a virus *per se*. Furthermore, although most viruses do attempt to operate without the knowledge of the system user, this isn't a requirement, either. The only defining characteristic is *replication*—the primary "intent" of the infective program is to reproduce.

NOTE

The term *program* does not necessarily imply a program file, although most viruses do in some way infect files. Nevertheless, we refer to infected and infective objects in this chapter unless we are specifically considering file infection, so as to include boot sector infectors and macro programs embedded in data files.

Infection is sometimes described in terms of attachment of the viral program to one or more programs on the target system. However, *attachment* is perhaps a misleading term, although it is conventionally used in this context because the word *attachment* has a rather different connotation in the context of email. It might be more useful to look at the process in terms of a chain of command. The viral code is inserted into the chain of command, so that when the legitimate but infected program is run, the viral code is also executed (in some instances, the infected program runs instead of the legitimate code—some viruses and worms replace legitimate files, rather than attaching themselves to them).

We often describe infection in terms of the viral code becoming physically attached to the host program, but this isn't always the case. Sometimes, the environment is manipulated, so that calling a given program calls the viral program. Sometimes, the viral program is activated before *any* program is run. This can effectively "infect" every executable file on the system, even though none of those files are actually physically modified. Viruses that take this approach include cluster or File Allocation Table (FAT) viruses, which redirect system pointers to infected files, companion viruses, and viruses that modify the Windows Registry, so that their own code is called before legitimate executables.

Except for a few extraordinarily primitive and destructive examples that actually trash the host program on infection, all viruses work along the following lines:

1. A computer user calls a legitimate program.

2. The virus code, having inserted itself into the chain of command, executes instead of the legitimate program.

3. The virus code terminates and hands over control to the legitimate program.

Companion or spawning viruses follow the same sequence, but the virus code is contained in a separate file, which is characteristically renamed, so that it will be executed instead of the program the victim thought he was launching. It then normally hands over control to the legitimate program.

Viruses that infect by overwriting the host file so that its normal functionality is impaired (or simply replace it) have not been particularly successful at spreading "in the wild," historically. However, some email viruses have gone against this trend by replacing legitimate program or data files with copies of the malicious program. The

"Loveletter" family of viruses used this technique with notable success (in terms of dissemination), often overwriting genuine graphics files such as JPEGs with a malicious Visual Basic script, in combination with the "double extension" trick of appending an extension signifying an executable filetype (in this case .VBS) to the filename, so that Windows recognized it as an executable file rather than as a non-executable data file.

The virus process is a little like the process of biological viral infection, although the analogy is overworked and can be misleading. Think of a person infected with an airborne disease. Whenever he exhales in a public place, he risks infecting others. Similarly, whenever an infected program is executed, the virus' infective routine also runs, and can infect one or more other objects "in range." Just as biological viruses infect hosts that are predisposed to infection, computer viruses target certain type of files and system areas, according to the virus type.

What Is a Computer Worm?

Replication is also the defining characteristic of a worm, and some authorities (including Fred Cohen, the "father" of computer virology) regard worms as a subset of the genus virus. However, worms present particular problems of definition. One viable definition distinguishes between worms and viruses in terms of *attachment*. Whereas a virus in some sense "attaches" to a legitimate program, a worm copies itself across networks and/or systems without attachment. It can be said that the worm infects the environment (an operating system or mail system, for instance), rather than specific infectable objects, such as files.

Some observers have used the term *worm* to refer to self-replicating malware that spreads across networks. This doesn't really amount to a meaningful distinction, because many viruses can travel between machines on a Local Area Network, for instance, without being "aware" that a target volume is not on the same machine. This isn't to say, of course, that viruses are never network-aware.

Objects at Risk of Virus Infection

Thousands of new viruses have been reported in recent years. Viral mechanisms differ widely, and any type of file can be affected. However, viruses can only spread when code is executed, which means that only files or other objects (such as the boot sector) containing executable code can be carriers for further infections. This doesn't mean, however, that only binary executable files such as DOS/Windows .EXE and .COM files can be infected.

Some data files can also contain executable code in the form of embedded macros. At present, Microsoft Office includes two of the applications (Word and Excel) that are most vulnerable to virus attacks that take advantage of interpreted macro/

scripting languages, such as Visual Basic for Applications and its siblings. Although macro viruses can and do exist for non-Microsoft applications, word processors that store macro code in separate files rather than within document files are arguably less vulnerable. People are far less likely to swap macros than documents.

Script viruses that take advantage of the Windows Scripting Host (WSH) to run Visual Basic Script (VBS) have declined somewhat in impact, as people have learned to recognize VBS as a "dangerous" extension, and turn off the WSH. Nonetheless, simple-minded VBS viruses continue to appear and enjoy some success.

Other types of macros, shell scripts, batch files, interpretable source code, even Postscript files also contain executable code, and are, in theory, vulnerable to virus attack. The likelihood of such an attack depends on a number of factors, however, such as the popularity of the platform and the access controls native to the operating environment. The restricted write access allowed to unprivileged accounts in a multiuser environment such as Unix or NT and its successors (Windows 2000, Windows XP) does tend to impede the spread of viruses and Trojans in such environments. However, it would be unwise to rely exclusively on this fact for protection of such systems. Some of the earliest experiments with viruses were in fact made on Unix systems, and some current worms are specific to NT-based operating systems.

As this chapter was being written, W32/Perrun, a proof-of-concept virus that infects JPEG files, was causing the kind of confusion that virus writers love to generate. Perrun works by attaching executable code to a pure data file. Windows does not normally attempt to execute a JPEG; it executes a JPEG viewer of some sort that displays the image. Perrun gets around this restriction by modifying the Windows Registry so that the infective file is executed as a program rather than displayed as a graphic. However, this means, effectively, that the infective file can only be executed on a system that has already been infected. Actually, an exploit such as this can be created for any type of data file, in principle. However, the writer of such a virus still has to find a way to execute code to modify the environment in the first place, nullifying the advantage of converting a non-executable data file to a program in the first place. Such exploits reinforce the need to avoid taking the innocence of data files for granted, but do not in themselves constitute a very likely major threat at present.

Who Writes Viruses, and Why?

There are certain stereotypes associated with virus writing. On the whole, they're rarely useful. Most virus writers try, for obvious reasons, to preserve their anonymity, so testing the truth of these images is somewhat problematic. Some virus writers do discuss and display their craft and angst in more or less public forums, such as the newsgroup alt.comp.virus. These groups are generally thought to be young males, and some research indicates that mostly they "age out" and leave the field as they acquire girlfriends and a life.

However, it's unsafe to assume that the "virus writers" who dominate such newsgroups are always who they say they are, let alone that they are as talented as they claim to be, or necessarily serious representatives of all virus writers. Indeed, it's possible that this group represents a constituency of wannabes rather than a group of real, competent virus writers. Certainly many (but by no means all) successful viruses seem to have been written by focused loners with no particular affiliations, rather than by groups.

It's also noticeable that many of the most vociferous individuals quoted and feted by the media, law enforcement agencies, politicians, and others are not widely respected among their peers. Of course, the same is true of other types of computer vandals, not to mention many self-styled security and/or virus experts.

Some virus writers have responded to the very few serious attempts at research in this area. However, quantitative research is not realistically possible, and the research that has been done leans to the ethnographic. That is, rather than try to establish numerical data with large samples, researchers in this field have tended to rely on qualitative data, using interviews with very small samples (just a handful of virus authors).

The acknowledged authority in this area is Sarah Gordon, who has written extensively in this area and in related ethical areas. Her papers for the Fourth and Sixth Virus Bulletin Conferences on *The Generic Virus Writer* are particularly relevant. A number of her papers, including both *Generic Virus Writer* papers, can be found at http://www.badguys.org/papers.htm.

A second widespread stereotypical notion is that people who write antivirus software also write viruses in an attempt to drum up business for their products. I can't say with absolute certainty that no vendor or researcher has ever written a virus, released a virus, or even paid a bounty for samples of original viruses. However, it's hard to comprehend why any antivirus professional would see a need to stray toward "the Dark Side" at this stage of the game. There are more than enough amateurs producing viruses. In *Generic Virus Writer II*, Gordon notes that older security professionals, especially systems administrators and such, make their own contribution to the virus glut through (probably well-meant) experimentation.

However, despite the eagerness of virus writers to implicate "the enemy" in the problem, there is no conspiracy between systems administrators and vendors to keep vendor profits high. Or if there is, no one has offered me a percentage. Indeed, systems administrators are increasingly aware that dependence on antivirus vendors as the source of all wisdom is sometimes counterproductive, and may lead to addiction to outdated technological approaches and partial solutions that fail to take into account the relationship between virus management and other areas of security. There might always be a place for malware management based on scanning for known viruses and other threats, but virus-savvy system managers would also benefit from sharing information with their peers outside the antivirus industry through lists such as AVIEN and AVI-EWS (http://www.avien.org).

There are probably as many reasons for writing viruses as there are virus writers, although the reasons cited by virus writers (actual or wannabe) don't always stand up to closer analysis. Some appear fascinated by the concept of a self-replicating and/or self-modifying program, and are curious to see how far their creations spread. Indeed, some apologists suggest that virus writing is a legitimate means of research into artificial life forms, or even artificial intelligence. (However, the adaptive behavior displayed by even the most sophisticated viruses is usually rather restricted.)

Many virus authors seem to enjoy matching wits with the antivirus establishment. Indeed, some viruses go straight from the creator to his favorite antivirus company without any attempt to spread it through the general population. Others, however, are more concerned with inspiring the admiration of their peers, rather than gaining the attention of the antivirus professionals. Others don't make a hard and fast distinction between writing viral and antiviral software, and might write both. This isn't normally the case in the antivirus industry, and those who have used their experience on both sides of the barbed wire to support their search for a job in the industry have usually been sadly disappointed. In fact, development teams in the industry have practical as well as ethical reasons for preferring to employ programmers whose experience is in other areas. It saves them having to clean ill-founded technical preconceptions out of the newcomer's head.

There are, of course, many viruses that are intended to cause widespread damage, although deliberate destruction is the goal far less often than most people seem to believe. (Often, virus damage comes from thoughtlessness or sheer incompetence on the virus writer's part.) Some virus writers argue that computer users who don't have the technical savvy to protect themselves deserve everything they get. On the other hand, some virus writers also claim that they have no personal involvement in virus dissemination, and are not responsible for the use made of their code by others. In other words, the distributors are the problem, not the authors. This would be more convincing if such authors never made their creations available as source code and/or binaries on Web sites, in e-zines, and other locations. Then viruses wouldn't be easily available to anyone who asks, or who trawls virus exchange Web sites.

How Are Viruses Created?

Some people seem to believe that computer viruses appear spontaneously in the same way that biological viruses seem to do. This isn't quite as silly as it sounds. Completely new viruses don't just pop out of the primeval soup without warning. However, it's not uncommon for a new variant (not necessarily a viable virus in terms of replication and the capability to infect) to be born without direct human intervention. For instance, a macro virus consisting of a fixed number of modules might mutate by losing some of its constituent macros, or gaining unconnected (not necessarily viral) macros. Some Word macro viruses have mutated without human intervention into many hundreds of variants. However, someone had to write the original virus.

It's not inconceivable that an operating environment might come into general use, in that a viral program *can* be created from scratch without direct human intervention, but it doesn't seem to have happened yet.

Most virus writers (and a high percentage of the rest of the world) have an exaggerated view of the ability necessary to produce a working virus. Undoubtedly, some virus writers produce technically competent code—but many more don't. Furthermore, as we've seen, many viruses are one-trick ponies. They might do the replication trick well or not so well, but replication, even when done efficiently, represents a somewhat limited functionality, compared to that of a compiler or business application.

Older viruses were often written in assembly language. In fact, it's difficult to write some types of viruses in a high-level language, even with the help of an inline assembler. This is an advantage, from the viewpoint of virus victims, in that it takes a certain level of programming expertise to create even a weak virus (or even to modify an existing virus so as to create a variant). Many variants are, in fact, simply existing viruses with a slight change that doesn't affect functionality (such as modification to unimportant embedded text). Such a change might require no programming at all.

Some virus writers and their admirers still regard proficiency in assembly language as the hallmark of programming excellence. This is actually in sharp contrast to the professional programmer, whose choice of tool, given a choice, is liable to be somewhat more pragmatic, based on the best tool for a given job, rather than a preference for the esoteric. However, the current is, by and large, flowing the other way in malware coding. The most recent and widespread viruses and worms are very often written in high-level languages.

As virus technology developed, some virus programmers turned their attention to creating kits to enable a wannabe virus author to "develop" other viruses without programming—that is, using *virus generators* to produce virus code. This has not, however, necessarily resulted in an increase in the total number of viruses "in the wild."

Kit viruses are often not actually viable (that is, they don't replicate), and are frequently detectable generically. A new kit virus might be identifiable as having been generated by a particular generator, simply by family resemblance. Thus, kit viruses have tended to contribute to the "glut" problem (the sheer weight in numbers), rather than to the "in-the-wild" problem (see the next section).

Certainly, assembly language is not necessarily the language of choice among the current generation of virus writers. Interpreted macro languages (especially Visual Basic for Applications) are generally harder to use than kits, but much easier than assemblers. Furthermore, disk space and main memory are no longer expensive, and grossly bloated files are less conspicuous in a Windows environment. Thus, its become more practical (as well as easier) to write viruses and worms in C++ or Delphi.

What Does "In the Wild" Really Mean?

A virus is deemed to be "in the wild" when it has escaped or been released into the general population. The *general population* refers to computing environments outside the development environment where the virus was created and tested, or the collections of antivirus vendors, researchers, and collectors. Viruses in these environments are typically (hopefully) processed under controlled circumstances, where no danger is posed to the surrounding communities. However, when a virus escapes a controlled environment, it might be said to be "in the wild" (often expressed adjectivally in the antivirus community as "In-the-Wild" or "ItW"). Note, however, that in the antivirus community, the fact that a virus is available on a virus exchange bulletin board or Web site does not make it In-the-Wild. Because access to such resources and exchange of viruses is voluntary, this counts as a controlled environment. However, it is perfectly possible for one of these "zoo" viruses to find its way into the wild long ater its author has forgotten about it, simply because someone picked it up off a virus exchange site and catapulted it into the real world.

In his conference paper "Counting Viruses" (Virus Bulletin, 1999), Paul Ducklin makes the distinction very clearly:

> For a virus to be considered In the Wild, it must be spreading as a result of normal day-to-day operations on and between the computers of unsuspecting users. This means viruses that merely exist but are not spreading are not considered 'In the Wild'.

In fact, the definition used by the WildList Organization is, historically, far stricter. For a virus to be on the WildList, the nearest thing to an industry standard metric for "In-the-Wildness," it must be reported by two or more of the virus professionals who report to the WildList Organization. Furthermore, these reports must be accompanied by replicated samples. (Viruses that are reported by only one reporter are put into the supplementary list.) Clearly, this strictness means that the WildList can't represent all the ItW viruses at a given time, but does represent viruses that are genuinely "out there." Such data are often more useful than absolute numbers to the organizations and individuals using the WildList as a basis for testing and research. (Note that the WildList indicates a virus's presence "out there," but not the total number of virus incidents in which a single virus is implicated. Thus the list only provides a very rough guide to prevalence.)

In fact, the WildList Organization, which has had some financial and resource difficulties recently, seems to have relaxed this rule somewhat as more corporate administrators have joined the ranks of reporters. System administrators who report to WLO are not always able to capture samples, usually because malicious code is discarded before it passes inside their organization's perimeter. This necessarily entails a change in the quality of information available from WLO. A reporter who cannot capture a sample has to accept that the discarded sample was the virus/variant the antivirus scanner reported it as being. A discarded sample cannot be verified against a central pool of samples, so its exact identity is unproven. However, reporters with large customer bases do increase the size and volume of virus reports. The organization seems somewhat confused currently in its balancing industry reporters against corporate reporters.

What matters most for our purposes, however, is the disparity between the number of In-the-Wild viruses at one time (a few hundred, according to the prevailing WildList), and the total number of viruses in existence. At the time of this writing, that total is usually taken as being in excess of 70,000, although precise figures are dependent on exactly what is measured. There is no universal standard for distinguishing between viruses, virus variants, worms and other malicious code detected by anti-virus software, and, for technical and administrative reasons, it would be a huge job to enforce such a standard retrospectively by crossmatching samples.

How Do Viruses Work?

A virus is, conceptually, a simple program. In its simplest form, a *direct action virus* can be modeled in terms of an algorithm such as the following:

```
begin
  Look for (one or more infectable objects)
    If (none found)
    then
      exit
    else (infect object or objects).
    endif
end
```

They don't remain in memory, but execute all their code at once, and then hand over control to the host program.

Many viruses go *memory resident* (install themselves into memory) after the host program is executed, so that they can infect objects accessed after the infected application has been closed.

The term *hybrid* is sometimes used for viruses that stay active as long as the host program is running. It is also (perhaps with more justification) applied to viruses that are both direct action and memory resident.

In fact, all viable boot sector infectors are memory resident—they have to be. Otherwise, their code can only be executed during the boot process, which rather limits their opportunities to infect other boot sectors. We'll consider boot sector viruses in detail later on in this chapter.

Of course, all but the most incompetent viruses are a little better error-trapped than this, and at least check that the infectable object hasn't already been infected. You'll notice that I've also skated over the infect object subroutine. We'll come to infection mechanisms when we discuss the main virus types later in this section.

Some viruses, of course, do more than just replicate. We sometimes describe viruses as having up to three components: an infective routine, a payload, and a trigger. The previous models demonstrate an infective routine, although it can be said that finding an infectable object is the trigger for the infective routine. However, we more often think of the trigger as being the condition that has to exist before the payload (or *warhead*) can be executed.

The payload can, in principle, be any operation that any other program can perform. In real life, however, it tends to be something flippant and irritating, such as visual or audio effects, or else downright destructive. So now our model looks like the following:

```
begin
  (Go resident)
  if (infectable object exists)
  then
    if (object is not already infected)
    then
    (infect object)
    endif
  endif
  if (trigger condition exists)
  then
    (deliver payload)
  endif
end
```

The trigger condition might, for instance, be the execution of a file, or a particular date or time. The combination of a trigger and a malicious payload is sometimes called a *logic bomb*, especially in the context of a malicious program with no capability to self-replicate, such as a Trojan horse (covered in Chapter 18, "Trojans").

Viruses can be classified conveniently (but by no means definitively) into five main classes:

- Boot sector infectors (BSIs)

- File infectors

- Multipartite viruses

- Macro viruses

- Scripting viruses

To these classifications we might usefully add memetic viruses, especially virus hoaxes and other types of chain letters, and worms, though the distinction between worms and some of the other types of malware listed above is not absolute. One of the best-known macro viruses, Melissa, is usually described as a worm, as are most VBScript viruses.

NOTE

Memetic viruses (virus hoaxes and other chain letters) are not viruses in the same sense as the preceding classes because they infect people, not programs. They are considered here because hoax management is usually the responsibility of the person responsible for virus management.

Boot Sector Infectors

BSIs are PC-specific viruses that infect the Master Boot Record and/or DOS Boot Record. At one time, these viruses accounted for the majority of reported incidents, but now they constitute a dwindling proportion of the total number of threats found in the wild, and new BSIs are something of a rarity. This might reflect that people now increasingly use email and networks rather than floppy disks to exchange files. The fact that these are harder to write than macro viruses and scripting viruses (or even file viruses) is also relevant.

When a modern PC boots up, it goes through a process called the Power On Self Test (POST). This stage of the boot process includes checking hardware components. Some of its information comes from information stored in CMOS, especially information relating to disk and memory type and configuration. If the CMOS settings don't match the actual drive geometry, the machine will not be able to find system areas and files where they should be, and will fail to finish the boot process.

The Master Boot Record (MBR), sometimes known as the partition sector, is found only on hard disks, where it is always the first physical sector. It contains essential information about the disk, giving the starting address of the partition(s) into which it is divided. On floppy disks, which can't be partitioned and don't contain a MBR, the first physical sector is the boot record, or DBR (DOS Boot Record). On hard drives, the boot record is the first sector on a partition. The boot record contains a program whose job is to check that the disk is bootable and, if so, to hand over control to the operating system.

By default, if there is a bootable floppy present, most PCs will boot from drive A, the first floppy drive, rather than from drive C, the first hard drive. This is actually an unfortunate default because this is the normal entry point for a boot sector virus. If the PC attempts to boot from a floppy with an infected boot sector (even if the floppy doesn't contain the necessary files to load an operating system and therefore can't complete the boot process), the infected floppy will infect the hard drive. Characteristically (although not invariably), once the hard drive is infected, the virus will infect all write-enabled floppies introduced subsequently.

CAUTION

You might have heard that boot sector viruses can be disinfected without antivirus software using FDISK with a (largely) undocumented switch (/MBR), known in some quarters as FDISK/MUMBLE. The good news is that this works a lot of the time. The bad news is that, if you try it with the wrong virus, you can actually lose access to your data. Antivirus software is a very imperfect technology, but it's almost invariably better and safer for removing viruses than general-purpose utilities that were never designed for that purpose. FDISK is *not* recommended as an antivirus measure unless you know exactly what you're doing.

The majority of boot sector viruses also contain some provision for storing the original boot sector code elsewhere on the drive. There is a good reason for this. It isn't because the virus programmer kindly intends to eventually return the MBR to its original state, although retaining a copy of the original boot sector can make disinfecting the virus easier. Rather, it is because she has to. Typically, a virus will keep a copy of the original boot record and offer it whenever other processes request it. This not only enables the system to boot in the first place, but also makes it harder to detect the virus without antivirus software that specifically recognizes it. However, some viruses simply replace the normal boot sector code with code of their own.

Some BSIs (Form is a particularly well-known and widespread example) only infect the boot record, even on hard disks. This creates particular problems with Windows NT and Windows 2000, and will usually prevent the system from booting at all. Thus a largely innocuous virus has suddenly become a major nuisance in some environments.

TIP

New boot sector viruses are comparatively rare. Nevertheless, even old favorites like Form still circulate among people who still exchange disks. Although reputable and up-to-date antivirus software is still a must for detecting them, a simple precaution eliminates most of the risk of infection on most PCs, even from unknown BSIs. Most PCs, by default, will attempt to boot from drive A if there is a floppy disk there. If there isn't, it tries to boot from drive C. However, nearly all PCs can be reconfigured in CMOS to change this default. On most systems, this is done by modifying the boot order, so that the system always tries to boot from drive C first (or in the order of CD-ROM drive, drive C, then drive A).

Other systems (notably some Compaq models) enable the setting of an option to disable booting from the floppy drive altogether. If the system user actually needs to boot from floppy, this simply involves resetting the option to default. Motherboard and PC system vendors use proprietary ways of setting CMOS options—consult the documentation that came with your system. Note that "file and boot" (multipartite) viruses are less likely to be contained by this precaution.

File Viruses (Parasitic Viruses)

File viruses infect executable files. Historically, most file viruses have not been particularly successful at spreading. Many thousands have been written, but the number actually seen in the wild has been comparatively small compared to BSIs, and more recently, macro viruses. Nonetheless, those that have survived in the wild have often spread surprisingly well—CIH, for example. Some of the most prevalent contemporary file viruses, however, are more commonly described as worms, as considered later in this chapter.

After a virus infects an executable file by direct attachment, that file, when executed, will infect other files. *Fast infectors* go for instant gratification. Each time the infection routine is executed, it infects a whole directory, all folders on the current path, a whole volume/disk, even all currently mounted volumes. Even file infectors that infect only one or two files at a time can spread quickly across systems and networks in a modern environment, where multiple binary executables are opened and closed many times over a single session. Every time you open an application, at least one executable file is loaded. Some applications will open several files at startup, whereas others periodically open multiple files when performing a particular operation.

Sparse infectors forgo the temptation to infect as many files as possible, usually in an attempt to make themselves less conspicuous. They may not infect every time the virus is executed, but infect only under very specific conditions, even when an infectable object is present.

NOTE

Binary executables are by no means restricted to `.COM` and `.EXE` files, but include DLLs (Dynamic Link Libraries), overlay files, VxDs and other classes of driver, overlay files, and even certain screensaver (`.SCR`) and font files. More recently, virus/worm authors have made increasing use of other file types such as `.PIF`, `.BAT`, and `.LNK`. Whereas `.EXE` and `.SCR` files, for instance, have the same essential structure, file types such as `.PIF`s denote quite a different type of executable file. However, Windows environments are not generally strict about checking that a file is the type its filename extension suggests. Renaming a program from `myprog.exe` to `myprog.pif`, for example, does not usually prevent its being executed "correctly"—that is, in the same way as the correctly named program file. The number of filename extensions that denote an executable file of some sort runs well into three figures, especially taking into account macro-bearing data file formats. This number holds even if we ignore executables associated with operating systems other than DOS/Windows, in which, like Linux or Mac OS, filename extensions do not have a particular significance to the operating system's command interpreter. It's unsurprising that most computer users can be tricked into running an obscure executable filetype, or an executable filetype masquerading as something else.

Multipartite Viruses

File and boot viruses are the most common example of multipartite viruses, viruses that use more than one infection mechanism. In this case, both boot sectors and binary executable files might be infected and used as the means of disseminating the virus. However, it's likely that there will be an increase in multipartite viruses consisting of other combinations of virus types.

In recent years, the term *multipolar* has also passed into vogue. This is usually applied to malware that comprises more than one type of threat (a worm, a parasitic virus, and a Trojan, for instance). Such malware is also sometimes referred to as *convergent*, or *blended*.

Macro Viruses

Macro viruses infect macro programming environments rather than specific operating systems and hardware. Microsoft Office applications are by far the most exploited environment. Macro viruses can be regarded as a special case of file virus, in that they appear to infect data files rather than binary executables. However, this way of looking at the process might actually confuse the issue. Macros are essentially a means of modifying the application environment, rather than (or as well as) the data file. Indeed, in the case of Microsoft Office applications that support macro programming languages (Visual Basic for Applications and, in earlier versions, WordBasic and AccessBasic), the macro language cannot be unbound from the application's own command infrastructure. Macro viruses usually infect the global template, and often modify commands within the application's menu system. Macro viruses are particularly successful against Microsoft applications because they enable executable code (macros) to exist in the same file as data. Applications that segregate macros and data into different files are less susceptible to this kind of attack.

Macro viruses have lost market share in recent years, in parallel with the recent growth in email viruses and worms. Indeed, it might be argued that Melissa, though itself a macro virus, and very successful in terms of spread, marked a watershed for this particular class of threat. It did so, perhaps, by demonstrating how successfully a virus of any type can spread by exploiting social engineering techniques to trick the victim into running compromised code.

Script Viruses

Script is a rather imprecise term, and actually suggests a slightly artificial distinction between macro viruses and script viruses (especially VBScript malware; VBScript being a script/macro language very closely related to Visual Basic for Applications). In this context, the term normally refers to VBScript and other malware that can be embedded in HTML scripts and executed by HTML-aware email clients through the Windows Scripting Host. Many of the viruses that use this entry point are often better characterized as worms, and are therefore treated under that heading later in the chapter. VBscript and Jscript are more virus-friendly than JavaScript (for instance), primarily because they have many of the file I/O capabilities of other variations on the Visual Basic theme. Extant JavaScript malware sometimes takes advantage of vulnerabilities in Internet Explorer for which patches exist.

This view of script viruses is rather restrictive. A broader definition might include HyperCard infectors, batch file infectors, Unix shell script infectors, and many more. However, these are currently of less practical importance.

Memetic Viruses

There is a further class of virus that is unique, in that it comprises viruses that don't exist as computer code. The term *meme* seems to have been coined originally by Richard Dawkins, whose paper "Viruses of the Mind" draws on computer virology as well as on the natural sciences. A *meme* is a unit of cultural transmission, of replication by imitation, much as a gene is a unit of inheritance (a rather imprecise unit, perhaps). The memes we are most concerned with in this chapter are those sometimes known as *metaviruses*. A metavirus is itself a virus (what Dawkins calls a "virus of the mind, not a computer virus"), but one that purports to deal with other computer viruses. These viruses don't exist. In other words, they are virus hoaxes. Virus hoaxes are not only a subclass of memes in general, but a subset of a particular type of meme: the chain letter. However, the virus hoax is particularly relevant to this chapter, because the administrator who manages virus incidents will usually also be the person who has to respond to plagues of virus hoaxes. The same might not be true of other hoaxes and chain letters.

The most commonly encountered hoaxes are derived from the infamous Good Times hoax of the mid-90s. They conform to a pattern much like this:

> [THIS WARNING WAS CONFIRMED BY SYMANTEC AND MCAFEE THIS MORNING.] IF YOU RECEIVE EMAIL WITH THE SUBJECT <GREEN EGGS AND HAM> DO NOT OPEN IT, BUT DELETE IT IMMEDIATELY!!! IT CONTAINS A VIRUS THAT JUST BY OPENING THE MESSAGE

TRASHES HARD DRIVES AND CAUSES MOUSE-MATS TO SPONTANEOUSLY COMBUST. MICROSOFT, AOL, IBM, FCC, NASA, CND, AND KKK HAVE ALL SAID THAT THIS IS A VERY DANGEROUS VIRUS !!! AND THERE IS NO REMEDY FOR IT AS YET. PLEASE FORWARD THIS TO ALL YOUR FRIENDS, RELATIVES, COLLEAGUES, AND ANYONE ELSE WHOSE EMAIL ADDRESS YOU HAVE HANDY SO THAT THIS DISASTER CAN BE AVERTED.

By the way, as far as I know there is no Green Eggs and Ham virus or hoax. I've just done what many real hoaxers have done and pulled a silly title out of thin air (or in this case, my daughter's bookshelf). In fact, the infuriating aspect of this problem is that most hoaxers are abominably lazy and unoriginal, and the subject of the email that carries the supposed virus is often the only bit of the hoax that varies between two variants.

This sort of hoax only continues to work because masses of people with little technical knowledge of computers (let alone computer viruses) join the Internet community for the first time every day. Each one is at high risk of passing on such a hoax because they don't know any better. Of course, a hoax can be much subtler than this, but I'm not here to tell you how to write a hoax that might fool even an expert.

Here are a few of the features that will alert the experienced hoax watcher to the unreliability of the Green Eggs and Ham alert:

- Uppercase is used throughout and the message carries clusters of exclamation marks for emphasis. Of course, this doesn't prove anything about the accuracy of the alert. Nevertheless, it's been observed many times that the use of uppercase, liberal exclamation marks, and poor spelling, grammar, and style characterize most common hoaxes. On no account, however, should you assume that an alert is accurate simply because it doesn't have these characteristics.

- The reference to McAfee and Symantec doesn't give contact or reference information. It's just there to add credibility to the hoax. There's no real indication of when it was written, either. There are hoaxes circulating the Internet right now claiming that IBM announced something "yesterday" that have been around for years. The "yesterday" is just there to give a false impression of urgency.

- It's true that some email viruses/worms arrive with a characteristic subject header. However, there are many others that don't, and it makes more sense to avoid executing *any* attachment than to try to remember what silly header goes with which virus. In fact, administrators trying to block particular viruses by filtering mail on subject alone using inappropriate criteria are responsible for a whole subclass of indirect denial-of-service attacks.

- It makes sense to be cautious about email, but just opening a message can only infect your system if you have certain mail programs (Outlook, primarily) set with overly permissive defaults. Most mailers don't execute code just by viewing the message. An alert that says this will happen but doesn't specify any particular mailer should be regarded with suspicion.

- It's implied that the malicious code works on any hardware. This is pretty suspicious. What's more, a payload that triggers as soon as you open the message/attachment will be pretty ineffective at spreading. You might think the mouse-mat payload is a bit over the top. Actually, real hoaxes are often as ridiculous as this (although they often conceal their improbability behind technobabble).

- Of all the organizations listed, only IBM has any real expertise in viruses (though the company is not actually in the antivirus research field any longer). The others are only listed to impress you.

- It's claimed that there is no "remedy" for the virus. Antivirus vendors can usually supply fixes for new viruses in hours, even minutes. Of course, the effects of some viruses might be impossible to reverse, but data recovery firms can perform near-miracles sometimes.

- A virus that trashes your system as soon as you execute it is unlikely to travel very far. What is being described here sounds more like a destructive Trojan, and they don't generally spread well through email.

- The warning urges you to forward the mail to everyone you know—that makes it a chain letter. Reputable and knowledgeable organizations don't send alerts that way, although clueless ones sometimes do.

How Do Worms Work?

The 1988 Morris Worm (the Internet Worm) and its siblings, such as WANK and CHRISTMA EXEC, usually targeted heavy-duty mainframe and minicomputer hardware, mail, and operating systems. More recent threats have been aimed primarily at PCs, and in one highly publicized incident (the AutoStart worm), Apple Macs. However, worms might also have the incidental effect of bringing down mail servers through the sheer weight of the traffic they generate. Some of these have been variously classified by different researchers and vendors as viruses, as worms, as virus/worm hybrids, and occasionally as Trojan horses.

Universally accepted classifications of worms don't yet exist, but Carey Nachenberg, in a paper for the 1999 Virus Bulletin Conference, proposed a classification scheme along the following lines:

- Email worms, unsurprisingly, spread via email.

- Arbitrary Protocol Worms spread via protocols not based on email (IRC/DCC, FTP, TCP/IP sockets).

As well as proposing classification by transport mechanism, Nachenberg also proposed classification by launching mechanism:

- Self-launching Worms such as the 1988 Internet Worm require no interaction with the computer user to spread. They exploit some vulnerability of the host environment, rather than in some way tricking the user into executing the infective code. However, KAK and the rather rare BubbleBoy are examples of self-launching worms. By exploiting a bug in the Windows environment, they can execute without user intervention. More recent examples include worms such as Code Red, which exploits vulnerabilities in Internet Information Services (IIS), and other malware that exploit buffer overflows and other weaknesses in Windows and Unix programs.

> **NOTE**
>
> For information on dealing with this problem by applying a patch, see `http://support.microsoft.com/support/kb/articles/Q262/1/65.ASP`.

- User-launched Worms interact with the user. They need to use social engineering techniques to persuade the victim to open/execute an attachment before the worm can subvert the environment, so as to launch itself onto the next group of hosts. Many of today's VBScript worms fall into this or the Hybrid-launch category.

In fact, some of the worms we've seen to date are probably better classified as Hybrid-launch Worms (by Nachenberg's classification scheme) or multipartite (in terms of conventional virus terminology) because they use both self-launching and user-launched mechanisms. Nimda and later members of the Code Red family are hybrid worms, using a variety of techniques to infect and spread.

Virus Characteristics

The following characteristics are not necessarily restricted to particular virus/worm classifications, but are of some importance if only because of the way the terms *stealth* and *polymorphism* are so often misused:

- Stealth—Almost all viruses include a degree of stealth; that is, they attempt to conceal their presence to maximize their chances of spreading. There have been viruses that asked permission before infecting, but this courtesy has not been rewarded by wide dissemination. Conspicuous payloads tend to be avoided, or are delivered fairly irregularly, or after a delay (on the nth iteration of the virus code execution, or on a trigger date, for instance). This gives them time to infect other systems before they're noticed. Stealth viruses use any of a number of techniques to conceal the fact that an object has been infected. For example, when the operating system calls for certain information, a stealth virus might respond with an image of the environment as it was before the virus infected it. In other words, when the infection first takes place, the virus records information necessary to later fool the operating system.

This also has implications for antivirus tools that work by detecting that something has changed, rather than by detecting and identifying known viruses. To be effective, such tools must use generic anti-stealth techniques. Of course, it isn't possible to guarantee that such techniques will work against a virus that has not yet been discovered. However, virus scanners that detect known viruses are at an advantage in this respect, because vendors will normally compensate for a new spoofing technique when they add detection for the virus that employs it. The trick employed by some BSIs of displaying an image of the original boot sector as if it was still where it belonged is a classic stealth technique. File viruses characteristically (but not invariably) increase the length of an infected file, and can spoof the operating system or a antivirus scanner by subverting system calls, so that the file's attributes before infection, are reported, including file length, time and datestamp, and CRC checksum.

- Polymorphism—Polymorphic viruses are adored by virus authors and feared by nearly everyone else. This is partly because of an overestimation of the impact of the polymorphic threat. Nonpolymorphic viruses usually infect by attaching a more or less identical copy of themselves to a new host object. Polymorphic viruses attach an evolved copy of themselves, so that the shape of the virus changes from one infection to another. Some polymorphic viruses use techniques such as changing the order of instructions, introducing noise bytes and dummy instructions, and varying the instructions used to perform a specific function. A more sophisticated approach is to use variable encryption, drastically reducing the amount of static (unchanging) code available to the antivirus programmer to use to extract a pattern by which the virus can be identified. You might imagine (as many people do) that this makes polymorphism a formidable technology to counter. Indeed, the emergence of polymorphic viruses and plug-in mutation engines (enabling almost any virus author to include variable encryption in his own work without reinventing the wheel) contributed to the disappearance of some of earlier antivirus packages.

However, although polymorphic viruses are popular with virus authors demonstrating their skills, they have been less well-represented in the field than in the collections of antivirus researchers, certification laboratories, comparative testers, and others who need as complete a collection as possible. Antivirus scanning technology has also moved on, and simple signature scanning for a fixed character string doesn't play a large part in the operation of a modern scanner.

The classifications of viral malware described earlier do not cover the entire range of objects detected by antivirus software. Some vendors are quick to point out that what they sell is antivirus software, not anti-malware software. Nonetheless, nowadays most commercial products detect some Trojan horses (see Chapter 18) and other objects that barely qualify as malware, let alone viruses. Such objects include intended (nonfunctioning) viruses, joke programs, DDoS programs, even garbage files that are known to be present in poorly maintained virus collections likely to be used by product reviewers. There are obvious commercial disadvantages to refusing to detect objects that are not viral or even malicious, when products may be marked down in poorly implemented comparative reviews for failing to detect them.

It might be noticeable that this chapter has been largely PC-centric. Certainly, there are more viruses that infect PC platforms (DOS and all flavors of Windows) than any other operating system. Native Macintosh viruses are far fewer. In fact, there are probably more native viruses on systems such as Atari and Amiga that have never had the same popularity (in corporate environments, at least). However, the fact that Macintoshes share with Windows a degree of vulnerability to Microsoft Office macro viruses makes them the other main virus-friendly environment today.

It should not be assumed, however, that other platforms don't have virus problems. Access controls can be imposed on unprivileged accounts in Unix (including Linux), NT, NetWare, and other platforms to restrict infection flow. However, they can't prevent unprivileged users from sharing files, if only by email. Nor can they prevent a privileged user from inadvertently spreading infection. Even systems that don't support any known native viruses (servers or workstations) can carry infected objects between infectable hosts, a process sometimes known as *heterogeneous virus transmission*. It's just as important to scan network file servers, intranet, and other Web servers, regardless of their native operating system. In fact, an increasing number of products detect viruses associated with other operating environments. Thus, some Mac products detect PC viruses, and vice versa.

A similar situation has arisen in Linux circles recently, as Linux worms have become more common, and possibly as more PC enthusiasts have taken to running multiple operating systems on a single PC. Indeed, the common hardware architecture hosting both Windows and some Linux versions results in some (limited) potential for cross-platform viral functionality.

Clearly, viruses do represent a risk on the Internet. That risk is higher for those running DOS, any variant of Windows, or certain macro-capable applications, especially the Microsoft Office applications suite. Mostly this is a matter of market share. Most virus writers target PCs and Windows because that's what they have access to. However, there are other factors that increase the risk: PC hardware architecture, Microsoft's dismissive stance regarding the need for security on single-user systems, and the dangers of having macro code and data in the same file.

There are some tools to help keep systems safe from virus attacks listed later in this chapter. Be aware though; the only way to guarantee safety is by obeying Richards' Law of Data Security—don't buy a computer, and, if you do buy one, don't turn it on. (A tip of the hat to Robert Slade, my fellow author and collaborator on "Viruses Revealed" for bringing that one to my attention.) Antivirus software is mostly reactive: It responds to a perceived threat, and works most effectively against threats it can identify with precision (known viruses). The best defense against unknown viruses is often to work in an environment that doesn't provide a host to particular classes of threat. Sadly, however, this is often not an option, particularly in some corporate environments where Microsoft products are considered obligatory.

Antivirus Utilities

Antivirus software can generally be defined as generic, malware-specific, or hybrid. Generic software commonly includes change detection software (integrity checkers), behavior monitors, and behavior blockers. It deduces the existence of a virus from a change in the environment or an infectable object (a file, for example), or from a process displaying behavior characteristic of malware. (Note that the term *malware* is increasingly used with particular reference to Trojan horses rather than viruses, though many researchers continue to use the term to cover all forms of malicious software. Trojans are considered at length in Chapter 18, as is change-detection software.)

Gateway machines in corporate environments are increasingly protected by another form of generic blocking. Filtering by file type is normally implemented by checking for "dangerous" filename extensions, though vendors are becoming increasingly aware of a need for mechanisms to check whether a program file's real structure conforms to the structure suggested by its filename extension. For instance, a batch file is simple text. If a file with the filename extension .BAT turns out to have an .EXE file structure, this in itself is a danger signal. However, filtering by filename extension is conceptually simple and catches most potential threats. Objects that might be blocked in this way include the following:

- Filenames that suggest an executable filetype that wouldn't normally be found as a legitimate file attachment—A .LNK file, for instance, is a shortcut, a pointer to a local file or one mounted from the local network. It's unusual to find one pointing to a remote system not accessible as a network share.

- Filenames that suggest an executable file type and blocked for policy reasons— It is very common for a policy decision to be made to block all executable files with extensions such as .EXE, .COM, and .SCR. It is considered acceptable in such cases to be worth the inconvenience in those instances in which such a file needs to be transmitted for entirely legitimate reasons. In some environments, files blocked for policy reasons might include filenames associated with macro-friendly Microsoft Office applications such as *.DOC, *.XLS, and *.MDB.

- Filenames matching a suspicious filename template such as *.jpg.pif (suggesting an executable masquerading as a graphic), *.txt.exe (an executable masquerading as a text file), or *.   .com (filename containing multiple spaces before the final 'real' extension in the hope that the final extension will be pushed off the screen and thus not noticed). This type of pattern matching is less necessary when the real file extension (the only part of the filename with any special significance for Windows, in general), is proscribed under one of the previous rules.

Malware-specific software checks infectable objects against a database of virus definitions. If a match is found, it alerts the computer user and might be able to remove the virus from the infected object. This is usually possible with boot sector and macro infectors. File viruses are sometimes harder (and sometimes impossible) to disinfect, and some vendors don't even try, taking the view that it's always better to replace a binary executable than to risk disinfecting it unsuccessfully. Many modern viruses/worms are comparatively easy to remove in that the whole file can be deleted, so that restoring an original file to its pre-infected state isn't an issue. However, collateral modifications to the environment, such as Registry changes, are still an issue in such cases, and can be very difficult to deal with. The increasing sophistication of detection algorithms also means that a virus-specific definition will also flag a close variant as infected, even where there is no specific detection for that variant. Some vendors are justifiably proud of the effectiveness of their technology in this area, and have developed generic drivers that can deal with whole families of viruses rather than a single variant. This is very useful in terms of detection, but can lead to difficulties with the disinfection and repair of collateral modifications to the environment.

Scanners can be *on-access* (real-time or memory resident) or *on-demand*. On-access scanners check files and other infectable objects as they are accessed (especially as they're opened for reading or writing), and can be implemented as a DOS TSR, Windows VxD, NT service, Macintosh System Extension, and so on. Most antivirus packages include an on-access malware-specific component, but on-access change detectors do exist. On-demand scanners are executed only when called by the user or by scheduling software. They do their job, then terminate.

Modern malware-specific scanners are better described as hybrid. Although they use more or less exact identification, most are also capable of a generic technique known as *heuristic analysis*, which is related to behavior blocking. Code is checked for characteristics that suggest a virus, either by passive analysis of the code, or by executing it under emulation, so that its behavior can be safely monitored.

Inclusion in the following list of antivirus products doesn't necessarily constitute a recommendation. Products change, and what works for one PC, environment, or organization won't necessarily work well in another. However, these are all competent products. In general, URLs in this chapter have been modified since the previous edition of this book, so that only the relevant domain name is given. Experience indicates that actual pages move around a lot. For a comprehensive list of vendors, the specialist antivirus magazine *Virus Bulletin* includes a comprehensive list of vendors on its Web site at `http://www.virusbtn.com/vb100/archives/products.xml?/`.

Network Associates

The NAI range includes the current incarnations of McAfee and Dr. Solomon's for a wide range of workstation and server platforms, including PCs/Windows, Macintosh, and Unix (including Linux). Visit NAI's Web site at `http://www.nai.com/`.

Norton Anti-Virus

Norton Anti-Virus is available for a wide range of workstation, server, and gateway platforms, including DOS, Macintosh, Windows 9*x*, and Windows NT/2000/XP. Find out more at `http://www.symantec.com`.

AVG AntiVirus

One of the few remaining desktop products free to some computer users. Visit `http://www.grisoft.com` for more information.

eSafe

Eliashim, producer of eSafe and now part of the Aladdin empire, focuses primarily on gateway protection from viruses and other malicious software. Contact them at `http://www.eliashim.com/`.

Antigen

Sybari's groupware security product supports a number of mail server products and configurations. More information is available at `http://www.sybari.com`.

PC-Cillin

PC-Cillin by Trend Micro can be found along with their InterScan gateway products at both `http://www.antivirus.com/` and `http://www.trendmicro.com`.

Sophos Anti-Virus

Sophos is focused on the corporate market. Products are available for a wide range of workstation, server, and gateway platforms, including PCs/Windows, Macintosh, and Unix (including Linux). Learn more at http://www.sophos.com/.

F-PROT Anti-Virus

A number of products have been based on the F-Prot detection engine. The original product (which is free for personal use, and also available as a commercial product) can be found at http://www.complex.is.

The product formerly sold by DataFellows as F-Prot Professional is now known as F-Secure, and is available at http://www.f-secure.com.

The Command Software version of F-Prot Professional is at http://www.commandcom. com/.

Integrity Master

Integrity Master by Stiller Research combines an advanced change detector with conventional known-virus scanning. The Stiller Web site is a good source of general information (hoax information, for example), and is located at http://www.stiller. com/stiller.htm.

There are hundreds of virus scanners and utilities. Those listed here have a good reputation, are easily available on the Internet, and are updated frequently. Viruses are found each day, all over the world. Most of them are unlikely ever to be seen In-the-Wild, but sometimes a formerly quiet virus will suddenly "get lucky" and go feral. New worms and other email-borne viruses such as Melissa or LoveLetter can go from unknown to global within hours. Strange to think that only a few years ago, it was still normal for antivirus software to be updated on a quarterly basis.

Future Trends in Viral Malware

Virus and antivirus technologies continue to increase in complexity and sophistication. The likelihood of contracting a virus on the Internet increases as "fast burner" virus dissemination techniques evolve, and the number of potential hosts increases with the expansion of the Internet itself. It depends on where you go: If you frequent the back alleys of the Internet, you should exercise caution in downloading any file (digitally signed or otherwise). Usenet newsgroups are places where viruses might be found, especially in those newsgroups where hot or restricted material is trafficked. Examples of such material include *warez* (pirated software) or pornography. Similarly, newsgroups that traffic in cracking utilities are suspect. However, the nature of the virus threat means that you are far more likely to receive an infection from someone you know, someone with no malicious intention, than from a known or anonymous virus author/distributor. We therefore recommend that you look through the guidelines to practicing "safe hex" for computer users and administrators summarized in the final section of this chapter.

Virus technology has been through a number of phases. The first big wave was the PC boot sector infector, mostly overshadowing even the parasitic fast-infector and "big-iron" infecting worms. The second wave was largely the rise of the macro virus. Among these, the first email-aware macro viruses foreshadowed the coming of the next wave: Melissa, LoveLetter, and the macro and VBScript worms that dominate the scene at the time of this writing. Many examples of the current wave of email viruses/worms are less sophisticated than the more complex, "traditional" viruses, relying to some extent on social engineering (psychological manipulation) as much as technical complexity. However, some recent examples (such as Hybris, MTX, and Yaha) combine technical complexity with social engineering. For example, some recent worms carry their own SMTP engines. An accelerating and related trend is for viruses such as Klez to spoof mail header information so that it becomes more difficult to identify the sender of infected mail. In such a case, not only is it more difficult to identify and warn the owner of an infected system, but individuals whose systems are not infected may be bombarded with misdirected warnings and complaints.

It's been suggested that upcoming operating systems will be so secure that viruses will cease to be a problem. However, experience indicates that as particular loopholes are patched, others are found and exploited. Expect the unexpected.

Publications and Sites

The following is a list of articles, books, and Web pages related to the subject of computer viruses. Some are only included or alluded to because they were in the previous edition. Some outdated links and unobtainable references have been removed, and several have been added. (We don't guarantee that those listed are still available—in fact, you might have trouble getting hold of any but the most recent.) Inclusion of a resource in this section doesn't necessarily constitute recommendation (as the comments make clear). However, it's important to know and recognize the more prominent but poor resources, as well as the good ones.

Bigelow's Virus Troubleshooting Pocket Reference by Ken Dunham. (McGraw-Hill) Well-meaning but not always accurate, and sometimes misleading.

CIAC/US Department of Energy(DOE)—This Web site (`http://ciac.llnl.gov/ciac/CIACVirusDatabase.html`) has a database of virus information that was recommended in an earlier edition of this book. The database is no longer being updated, but is worth checking for information on older viruses. CIAC/DOE have done sterling work in recent years on publicizing the problems associated with virus hoaxes and other chain letters. The relevant pages continue to be maintained and expanded at `http://HoaxBusters.ciac.org/`.

Computers Under Attack: Intruders, Worms and Viruses. Edited by Peter J. Denning. (ACM Press) Despite its age, this book is worth looking for. It contains some seminal papers on security, although its virus content is actually pretty outdated.

Computer Virus Prevalence Survey—TrueSecure (formerly the National Computer Association, then ICSA) publishes a yearly survey of virus prevalence, and has certification schemes for antivirus and other security software, papers, discussion groups, and so on. (`http://www.truesecure.com/`)

A Short Course on Computer Viruses, Second Edition, Frederick B. Cohen. (John Wiley & Sons) Solid material from the man whose early research contributed massively to defining the virus/antivirus field.

The Virus Creation Labs: A Journey into the Underground by George Smith. (American Eagle Publications) Smith's writings have long served as a very effective antidote to some of the self-righteous pomposity found in some corners of the security establishment. His book is an interesting, journalistic, alternative view across the virus/antivirus divide.

European Institute for Computer Anti-Virus Research—Despite its name, EICAR is not exclusively focused on viruses, and its members include representatives of academia and business: not all of them are European, either. Best known for its conference and for the publication of the EICAR test file, an industry standard for testing whether antivirus software is installed. (`http://www.eicar.org/`)

SherpaSoft Web page—FAQs including the VIRUS-L FAQ, the alt.comp.virus FAQ, the *Viruses and the Macintosh* FAQ, an email abuse FAQ, along with other papers, resources, and links. (`http://www.sherpasoft.org.uk`)

Mac Virus—Susan Lesch's antivirus resource for Macintosh users, now maintained by David Harley and containing his *Viruses and the Macintosh* FAQ, plus the definitive paper "Macs and Macros: the State of the Macintosh Nation." (`http://www.macvirus.com/`, `http://www.macvirus.org.uk`)

"Managing Malware: Mapping Technology to Function," by David Harley. Conference Proceedings, EICAR 1999. A comprehensive primer on malware management in corporate environments. (`http://www.sherpasoft.org.uk/papers/eicar99.PDF`)

Virus Proof: The Ultimate Guide to Protecting Your PC by Phil Schmauder. (Prima Tech) Lazily written, incompetent, misleading, and virtually useless. Avoid.

Virus Bulletin—The only monthly magazine entirely devoted to virus management (`http://www.virusbtn.com/`).

Viruses Revealed: Understanding and Countering Malicious Software by David Harley, Robert Slade, and Urs Gattiker. (Osborne) Covers a wide range of issues (technology, history, corporate protection, social issues, and ethics). Check the Web site at `http://www.viruses-revealed.org.uk`.

Mobile Malicious Code by Roger Grimes. (O'Reilly) Generally technically sound. Rather thin on references to other resources and authorities.

The Enterprise Anti-Virus Book by Robert Vibert. (Segura Solutions Inc.) Not the book with all the answers, but something arguably more important: the book with just about all the questions. (`http://www.segurasolutions.com/book.htm`)

Vmyths.com (formerly the Computer Virus Myths page at `www.kumite.com`)—Robert Rosenberger's essential resource for hoax hunters and other professional skeptics; highly recommended. (`http://www.vmyths.com/`)

WildList Organization International—The authoritative source of information on what viruses are known to be in the wild. An essential resource for antivirus software certification authorities, researchers, and so on. (`http://www.wildlist.org/` and `http://www.thewildlist.com/`)

`Association of Anti Virus Asia Researchers` (AVAR)—Also includes European and U.S. members. (`http://www.aavar.org/`)

Anti-Virus Information Exchange Network (AVIEN)—Network of anti-malware specialists in nonvendor organizations. Includes membership of AVI-EWS (Early Warning System) and the Anti-Malware Product Certification project (AMPC). (`http://www.avien.org`)

Most antivirus vendors have virus information databases and other resources, as well as information specific to their products. The following sites are generally dependable, but none are infallible. Precise URLs aren't given, as such pages move about a lot. Several of these sites have good hoax information, too.

`http://www.sophos.com/`

`http://www.nai.com/`

`http://www.symantec.com/`

`http://www.f-secure.com/`

`http://www.viruslist.com/`

Summary

This chapter can only give you an overview of the virus problem. If you have the misfortune to be a systems or network administrator responsible for protecting your customers from malicious software, you will need to do some serious research into virus and antivirus technology, and I recommend that you take advantage of the information resources listed in this chapter. If you're an administrator or manager, you certainly can't afford to rely on vendor sales executives or consultants to make all the decisions for you. More often than not, these people are better acquainted with the interface of their product range than with its real-world application to real-world virus management problems.

For your delectation, we offer some guidelines that should make your computing life safer:

- Check all warnings and alerts with your IT department. Whether you are a manager or administrator, make sure that there is a known policy by which only authorized personnel can pass on alerts. This cuts down on panic, curbs dissemination of hoaxes and other misinformation, and reduces the risk of inappropriate action that might be worse than no action.

- Don't trust attachments, even from people you know and consider trustworthy. The sender might have no malicious intent, but she might not be keeping her antivirus software up-to-date, either. Furthermore, email viruses and worms generally send themselves out without the knowledge of the person in whose account they are received. Even a legitimate, expected attachment can be infected with a virus. Anything that meets the following criteria should be considered particularly suspicious:

  - From someone you don't know, who has no legitimate reason to send them to you.

  - Attachment arrives with an empty message.

  - Message text doesn't mention the attachment.

  - Message text doesn't seem to make sense.

  - Message uncharacteristic of the sender.

  - Message concerns pornographic Web sites, erotic graphics, or other oddities.

  - Message includes no personal references at all.

  - Message attachments with filenames suggesting an attempt to disguise the fact that the file is an executable are, to the virus-literate, a dead give-away. The following is a list of filename extensions that indicate an executable program, or a data file that can contain executable programs in the form of macros. This list is not by any means all-inclusive. There are filenames such as .RTF that shouldn't include program content, but under some circumstances can (when it contains an embedded file, for example). Bear in mind that Word documents (for instance) can in principle have any filename extension, or none. Also, zipped (compressed) files with the filename extension .ZIP can contain one or more of any kind of file.

BAT	.CHM	.CMD	.COM	.DLL	.DOC	.DOT
EXE	.FON	.HTA	.JS	.OVL	.PIF	.SCR
SHB	.SHS	.VBS	.VBA	.WIZ	.XLA	.XLS

- Remember that worm victims don't usually know that they've sent you an infected attachment. There is no such thing as a trusted account. If someone sends you an attachment, especially if there's no obvious reason they should, or if it meets any of the previous criteria, confirm with them that they did so knowingly.

- Use antivirus software and keep it updated. However, don't assume that using the latest updates makes you invulnerable. Antivirus software cannot catch and disinfect every type of threat, especially new malware or variants, and might not completely reverse their ill-effects. Use on-access scanning and auto-updating of definitions wherever possible.

- If your environment allows it, disable the Windows Scripting Host.

- Don't install (or let others install) unauthorized Software. Programs such as games, joke programs, screensavers, and unauthorized utilities can cause difficulties even if they're not intentionally malicious. Be particularly cautious about programs found in unsafe environments such as Internet chatrooms, newsgroups, unsolicited email, and so on.

- If you use macro virus-friendly applications such as Word, ensure that macros are not enabled by default. Recent versions of Office enable macros in a document to be disabled as a default option. If you receive a document with macros from a trusted source, ask for verification. But don't trust this option absolutely. If it's possible to work with macro-hostile formats such as .RTF (Rich Text Format), do so.

- Disable default booting from floppy disk in CMOS. (This blocks infection from pure boot sector viruses.)

- Encrypted (passworded) attachments are normally legitimate mail, sent intentionally. However, if it started out infected, encryption won't fix it. Furthermore, encrypted attachments can't usually be scanned for viruses in transit.

- If you use macro-friendly applications and programs with known vulnerabilities such as IIS, Internet Explorer, Outlook, and Outlook Express, make sure they have the latest patches.

- Back up, back up, back up. And test your backups!

18
Trojans

"For they still prefer sheep to thinking men

Ah, but men who think like sheep are even better"

—*Brian McNeill, "No Gods and Precious Few Heroes"*

"Beware of geeks bearing gifts"

—*Anonymous*

This chapter examines a type of threat to system and Internet security that has been with us almost as long as the computer: Trojan horses, often simply referred to as Trojans.

What Is a Trojan?

Trojan horses present more difficulties in definition than at first appears. Whereas viruses are defined primarily by their capability to replicate, Trojans are primarily defined by their payload, or, to use a less emotive term, their function. Replication is an absolute value. Either a program replicates or it doesn't. Damage and intent, however, are not absolutes, at least in terms of program function. The first clue to their nature lies in ancient history and classical mythology.

Origin of the Species

Around the 12th century B.C., Greece declared war on the city of Troy. The dispute arose when Paris, variously described as a shepherd boy and as prince of Troy, abducted Helen, the wife of Menelaus, king of Sparta, and reputed to be the most beautiful woman in the world. The Greeks gave chase and engaged Troy in a 10-year war, but failed to take the city. This, of course, is the central plot of Homer's *Iliad*.

Finally, the Greek army withdrew, leaving behind a huge wooden horse. Greece's finest soldiers hid silently inside. The people of Troy saw the horse and, thinking with stunning naivete that it was a gift, brought it inside their city. That night, Greek soldiers under the leadership of Odysseus emerged from the horse, and opened the gates for the rest of the Greek army, who destroyed the city. It has been suggested that the Trojan horse story is the origin of the saying "Beware of Greeks bearing gifts."

In computing terms, the term *Trojan horse* is most often applied to an apparently attractive program concealing in some way an unpleasant surprise.

Definitions

One well-known definition is included in the now obsolete RFC 1244, the first draft of the *Site Security Handbook* (RFC 2196, a more recent draft, doesn't include a definition):

> A Trojan horse program can be a program that does something useful, or merely something interesting. It always does something unexpected, such as steal passwords or copy files without your knowledge.

This definition contains three useful ideas—not that they necessarily give us the best possible summary, but they serve as a good starting point for the discussion of some implicit ambiguities. First, the definition doesn't say that the Trojan *always* does something useful or interesting, but that it *might*. This generality opens a wide range of possibilities, from programs whose only function is to do something malicious, through programs that do something desirable *and* something malicious but covert, to *accidental Trojans*, which are intended to do desirable things, but somehow do something inadvertent and essentially undesirable as well (or instead).

Second, this definition includes the idea that a Trojan does something "unexpected" (unexpected to the recipient, or "victim," but not usually to the programmer). This assumption is common to nearly all definitions of Trojans.

Third, it contains the implication that the "payload" is something malicious. In fact, it's quite specific (intentionally or otherwise) about the fact that the cited example payloads (stealing passwords or copying files) involve unauthorized access rather than a breach of data integrity. For our purposes, this is less useful. It is overly specific about the type of security breach it appears to address (breach of privacy), and carries an assumption of malicious intent that is not universally accepted.

Most security professionals would accept a general definition along the lines of

> A Trojan is a program that claims to perform some desirable or necessary function, and might even do so, but also performs some function or functions that the individual who runs the program would not expect and would not want.

This is the baseline definition used in this chapter. We will consider variations in payload type in terms of subclassifications, rather than by defining the general malware class "Trojan" by a particular function, or by the type of security breach it attempts.

I Didn't Mean It

Like many definitions, the one in the previous paragraph misses out on the idea of malicious intent. It therefore raises a number of questions. Should we include Easter eggs (harmless code concealed more or less legitimately in production software by the original production team), for instance? Joke programs, installation routines that pass back information to the manufacturer and overwrite previous versions of system files, and accidental Trojans also present difficulties. However, as far as this chapter is concerned, these ambiguities are not bad things. This chapter will refer (not necessarily in depth) to a whole range of relevant issues, rather than ignore everything that doesn't conform to a strict single definition.

One common modern usage distinguishes Trojans (and related *malware*, or MALicious softWARE) from viruses and worms, based on the Trojans' inability to self-replicate. In fact, Ian Whalley, in a July 1998 article for *Virus Bulletin* ("Talking Trojan,") suggests using the term *nonreplicative malware* rather than Trojan horse, thus avoiding the popular confusion between replicating programs (viruses, worms) and static, *nonreplicative* code (Trojans, for instance). This certainly has advantages, but re-introduces the assumption of malicious intent (by using the word *malware*). Clearly, although we may prefer not to admit to malicious intent as a defining characteristic, we can't avoid considering it as a possible or even likely characteristic.

Apart from the intent to deceive implicit in many Trojan definitions, malicious intent can cover a wide range of intentions and mechanisms.

Using the classic tripod model of data security, Trojans can be divided into three broad classes of intent:

- Intent to gain unauthorized access

- Intent to obstruct availability (deny service)

- Intent to modify or destroy data and systems without authorization

By extension of this idea, we can also postulate three further classes of accidental Trojan that enable unauthorized access, obstruct availability, or compromise integrity, but are not *intended* to do so.

A problem here is that, whereas automated examination and analysis of the binary content of a program can sometimes tell us a great deal about function, it can tell us little about the intent of the author.

Dr. Alan Solomon gives a definition in *All About Viruses* that neatly illustrates the problem from the other end:

> Suppose I wrote a program that could infallibly detect whether another program formatted the hard disk. Then, can it say that this program is a Trojan? Obviously not if the other program was supposed to format the hard disk (like FORMAT does, for example), then it is not a Trojan. But if the user was not expecting the format, then it is a Trojan. The problem is to compare what the program does with the user's expectations. You cannot determine the user's expectations for a program.

Solomon's scenario is useful because it shifts the focus away from the programmer's or distributor's intent and onto the recipient/user's expectations. Implicitly, it also indicates that social engineering is a major component of a Trojan horse because it manipulates the victim's expectations. It's not unreasonable to expect that a computer user who consciously runs a program called FORMAT to know what to expect from a program of that name. However, if a legitimate disk formatting program is renamed to something that disguises its real function, or includes documentation that indicates that it is intended to display graphics, or optimize video performance, there is a clear intent to deceive and harm.

The passage also restates a problem that we will need to consider in more detail. It is (sometimes) possible to analyze a virus automatically, because the defining characteristic of viral code is replication. It is at least theoretically possible to deduce the capability to replicate by automatic or semi-automatic code analysis. (This is one of the ways in which heuristic virus scanners are meant to operate.) It is much more difficult, however, for an automatic analytical tool to deduce either the intentions of the programmer or the expectations of the program user by tracing what the code does, if the program is named inappropriately and deceptively, or whether its true functionality jibes with the description in the accompanying documentation.

Viruses and worms are sometimes referred to as a special case of Trojan horse. The argument is that, because the legitimate program now contains embedded malicious code, it has been *Trojanized* (or, less commonly, *Trojaned*). This is a defensible position, although it doesn't distinguish between a program written to be malicious and an "innocent" program hijacked by a malicious code. However, the main reason for disregarding this argument is that it compounds the popular confusion between Trojans and viruses. Nevertheless, email worms do conform to the working definition with which we closed the preceding section, differing from classic Trojans of other types only in that they include replicative functionality. Indeed, it has recently become more common in security circles (less so in the antivirus community) to refer to worms that use social engineering techniques to trick the victim into running them as Trojans, irrespective of their capability to replicate.

By extension, if we accept this view, we can also accept self-launching worms as Trojans, because they still use an element of deceit to persuade a potential victim that they are legitimate messages from trusted sources. This usage reflects a basic distinction between older parasitic virus types and the recent generation of email viruses and worms.

Despite the distinctions maintained by the antivirus community, it is still the case that all malicious programs are popularly described as viruses, irrespective of their replicative properties or the lack thereof. In fact, some programs and coding problems that aren't even malicious are also described as viruses (the so-called Millennium virus, for instance). The situation isn't helped by the fact that hoaxes almost invariably describe mythical "viruses" that are more properly described as Trojans, or sometimes as worms, if they're capable of existing at all. We should however note a degree of convergence between the descriptions of mythical viruses found in hoax alerts and the functionality of real email viruses and worms. I refer here particularly to the use of virus names in hoax alerts that correspond to real viruses, but ornamented by ascribing to real viruses a set of imaginary supernatural characteristics.

Even worse, some antivirus vendors, although fully aware of the distinction between replicative and nonreplicative malware, continue to display nonsensical alert messages such as `Virus Trojan/W32/xxx detected in file xyz.exe`. For a scanner to alert not only on Trojans but also on other non-viruses such as joke programs, garbage files, and intended viruses (attempted viruses that can't replicate) as if they were viruses, is misleading and might inspire panic quite inappropriately.

However, there is a point in alerting on intended viruses. Because such objects are often encountered in poorly maintained collections used for badly designed product tests, a product that only detects "real" malware, however technically and ethically correct, is in danger of being put at a competitive disadvantage, because a less "correct" product will fare better in such tests, by scoring a higher percentage of detected objects. The problem here is that to alert on such objects using messages that suggest that they *are* real viruses is poor practice, inaccurate, and confusing.

Trojan Classifications

Trojan horses are usually regarded as representing either an attack on privacy (password stealing, for instance, leading to unauthorized access and possibly modification), or on integrity (destructive Trojans). This is a little over-simplified. After all, unauthorized modification may be an attack on privacy (unauthorized access) as well as integrity. A privacy-invasive program often destroys files so as to cover its tracks, and an attacker might want to gain access for specifically destructive purposes. Furthermore, this approach presupposes malicious intent, which, as we've seen, isn't universally accepted as a defining characteristic. Consequently, some types are included here that are often not considered in this context.

The sort of payload you expect a Trojan horse (technically, I suppose it was a Greek horse) to carry might reflect your computing orientation. For many years, mainframe and minicomputer users tended to think in terms of programs that stole passwords or otherwise breached privacy, whereas microcomputer users tended to think in terms of destructive Trojans that formatted disks or trashed file systems. In real life, both destructive and privacy-invasive Trojans have been known at both ends of the Big Iron/PC spectrum for many years. However, recent years have seen more cross-fertilization as well as an expansion of the terminology to include some nonreplicative objects. Arguably, this has come about as the borders between server-class and desktop-class functionality has blurred, with the result that rootkits and *denial-of-service* attacks have become a threat to desktop users, while server administrators have had to take into account programs that endanger server and clients alike.

Destructive Trojans

Trojans whose main purpose is destructive have long plagued microcomputer owners. The Dirty Dozen list, first published via FidoNet in the mid-1980s, originally focused on such programs, and at one time the list defined a Trojan in terms of purposeful damage. Of course, the list quickly outgrew the original dozen Trojans and went through a number of changes through the 1980s and 1990s. It might still be possible to find it on some Simtel mirror servers in the DOS/virus directory hierarchy, but it is really only of historical interest. Old Trojans of the type generally listed in DIRTYD*.ZIP are almost invariably short-lived. Curiously, one vendor has revived the "Dirty Dozen" idea, but applied it to a list of the most reported current threats of all types for the current month. These will generally be viruses or worms, in the current climate, though it must be noted that Trojans (not necessarily destructive) have become much more of a concern to the antivirus community in recent years.

Malicious, nonreplicating programs have also been widely reported on Macintosh computers, including destructive Trojans. Virus Info purported to contain virus information but actually trashed disks. (It should not be confused with the informational but obsolescent HyperCard stack Virus Reference.) A PostScript hack that can effectively render certain Apple printers unusable by attacking firmware also excited much interest at one time. NVP modified the System file so that no vowels can be typed, and was originally found masquerading as New Look, which redesigned the display. More recently, destructive and privacy-invasive compiled AppleScript Trojans have been noted, as well as at least one worm. For more information on Macintosh malware, see http://www.sherpasoft.org.uk/MacSupporters/macvir.html.

With the increasing popularity of Linux as a PC computing platform, an increasing number of Trojans has been reported, although worms are more common at present. Some PDA platforms have also been associated with destructive and/or data-stealing Trojans, prompting some speculation about cellphone-targeted malware.

Regardless of platform, the social effect of such Trojans is often disproportional to their effect in terms of actual incidents. Because they don't self-replicate, unlike viruses and worms, they are less likely to be spread by innocent third parties. They tend to be crudely programmed. Simple batch files using DEL, DELTREE, or FORMAT are still common, sometimes compiled into an .EXE or .COM file using a batch-file compiler such as BAT2COM. This makes them harder to identify. Trojans are traditionally usually *direct action*; that is, as soon as a Trojan is executed, it does all its damage at once. This works against their being spread by previous victims. However, tradition has never been a good basis for complacency. This particular tradition has as much to do with the laziness and coding incompetence of the average script kiddie. There is no absolute reason a destructive Trojan should not be well-coded, persuasively presented, and include a multiple or deferred payload designed to give the victim more time to pass it on to other victims. Furthermore, resident Trojans exist that install themselves, so they're run during every computing session. Often, these are associated with activities such as password stealing or other unwanted effects, such as opening multiple windows or pornographic Web pages. However, any Trojan whose payload is not immediately and overtly malicious maximizes its own chances of being passed on.

The PKZip "Trojan virus" is described in the somewhat out-dated alt.comp.virus FAQ. Much of the FAQ text referring to this incident is included, because it makes an interesting case history:

> The threat described in warnings widely seen in the mid-90s was definitely not a virus, because it did not replicate by infection.
>
> A number of attempts were made at various times to pass off Trojans as an upgrade to PKZip, the widely used file compression utility. A recent example was the files PKZ300.EXE and PKZ300B.ZIP made available for downloading on certain Internet sites.
>
> An earlier Trojan passed itself off as version 2.0. For this reason, PKWare never released a version 2.0 of PKZip. In fact, there were hardly any known cases of someone downloading and being hit by this Trojan, which few people ever saw (though most reputable virus scanners will detect it). As far as I know, this Trojan was only ever seen on warez servers (specializing in pirated software).
>
> There are recorded instances of a fake PKZIP vs. 3 found infected with a real live in-the-wild file virus, but this too is very rare. The subsequent rash of resuscitated warnings about this was, at least in part, a hoax, and was certainly misinformative if not misinformed. It was not a virus, but a Trojan. It did not (and cannot) damage modems, V32 or otherwise, though a virus or Trojan might alter the settings of a modem—if it happened to be on and connected, or exploit other network- or broadband-specific vulnerabilities…
>
> It deleted files, it did not destroy disks irrevocably. This is not altogether impossible in all circumstances, but such exploits are virtually unknown.
>
> It's certainly a good idea to avoid files claiming to be unverified updates, system patches and such like PKZip vs. 3, but the real risk hardly justified the bandwidth this alert occupied.

Why is it an interesting case history? For one thing, the subject of the attack is a typical target for a destructive Trojan that passes itself off as something it isn't. PKZip was a popular and very useful shareware utility. Recently, it has been rather overshadowed by other utilities using the same compression format, which might explain why PKZip is a less attractive target for Trojanization nowadays. In the following pages, we allude to a similar utility for the Mac whose identity was also purloined to lure careless victims into running an imposter program.

Second, it was a counterfeit program that made no effort to assume the appearance or functionality of the program whose identity it claimed. This is characteristic of direct action, destructive Trojans, though not a defining characteristic. Disguising a Trojan as the program it claims to be is more characteristic of privacy-invasive programs, such as some password-stealers that are passed off as login programs. However, programs that look as if they are acting in accordance with their assumed function while carrying out some covert and destructive act have been reported.

Third and most interestingly, a program that very few people ever saw became a major nuisance because of the number of people who received and passed on a "semi-hoaxified" warning about the Trojan. In fact, the effect of the chain letter was more serious than the Trojan itself was ever likely to be. (This is a common side effect of direct action Trojans, but it rarely displays such spectacular effect.)

By *semi-hoax*, we refer to a misleading alert based on a real virus or Trojan, but into which enough misinformation has been introduced to render it too inaccurate to be useful. We should probably distinguish here between a number of possibilities:

- An alert based on real malicious software, but too imprecise to be useful. (Many virus alerts passed on by non-experts fall into this category.)

- An alert based on real malicious software, but rendered less useful by misinformation based on an imperfect understanding of the relevant technology. Even knowledgeable individuals can inadvertently introduce such an inaccuracy into an alert. Using the line of thought previously explored in relation to "accidental Trojans," we might refer to this as an accidental hoax, although the terminology is not in wide use.

- An alert based on real, malicious software, but invalidated by the introduction of deliberately misleading material, exaggeration, or complete fabrication of attributes and potential for damage.

Isn't a warning either a hoax or not a hoax? I think not. The intent to hoax (or the lack of it) might be absolute, but the mixture of fact and fiction is commonplace in hoaxes, where fact lends circumstantial support to an essentially fictional assertion. A particularly gross recent manifestation concerns hoaxes that describe legitimate Windows files such as SULFNBK.EXE and JDBGMGR.EXE as being malicious programs.

When a victim finds that she does indeed have a file of that name on her system, she is set to follow the advice and instructions on removal that accompanies some versions of these hoaxes. In such a case, we see what might be described as a memetic Trojan (see the section on memetic viruses in the preceding chapter): Whereas a real Trojan uses social engineering to persuade the victim to run malicious code, a hoax like this uses social engineering to persuade the victim to perform the destructive or otherwise undesirable act themselves.

As another example, in late 1997, a bogus version of StuffIt Deluxe was distributed. (StuffIt is a another popular archiving tool used primarily on Macs.) During installation, the program would delete key system files. Aladdin systems, makers of StuffIt, issued widespread advisories about the Trojan at the time.

Malicious Trojans have also been known to masquerade as antivirus software, in a manner analogous to the distribution of viruses by attaching them to legitimate antivirus or other software. A further refinement is to use the alleged antivirus program as a *dropper*—that is, a program that installs a virus, but is not a virus itself. Virus droppers are not always Trojans (they are not always intended to operate covertly), but a dropper that masquerades as a beneficial program yet actually installs a virus can certainly be described as a Trojan. Droppers are described in more detail later in this chapter.

A very well-known Trojan that combined sabotage and extortion was the PC CYBORG Trojan horse, or AIDS Trojan. In 1989, some 10,000 copies of an AIDS information floppy disk were distributed in Europe, Africa, Scandinavia, and Australia, many to medical establishments. After the program was installed and run, a hidden program encrypted the hard disk after a set number of reboots. The idea was that the victim would have to send a "license fee" to PC CYBORG's Panamanian address to get the decryption key. Fortunately, a virus researcher in the UK cracked the encryption very quickly.

TIP

You can find the CIAC bulletin "Information About the PC CYBORG (AIDS) Trojan Horse" at `http://www.ciac.org/ciac/bulletins/a-10.shtml`. This incident is also described in some detail in *Viruses Revealed*, by Harley, Slade, and Gattiker (Osborne McGraw-Hill).

Because it has become so common to distribute BIOS updates as software for flash BIOS systems, there have been attempts to take advantage of the potential for damage inherent in some such systems. Viruses and Trojans that attempt to trash a system by writing garbage to the flash BIOS have caused substantial damage from time to time (`CIH/Spacefiller/Chernobyl` is a well-known viral example, but Trojans such as Flashkiller have also used this vulnerability—indeed, Flashkiller seems to be just the destructive subroutines from CIH recompiled without the replicative code).

Interestingly, such payloads have come close to fulfilling the hoax writer's dream of a malicious program that causes irrevocable damage to hardware. Some flash BIOS systems cannot be recovered when the BIOS has been trashed except by chip replacement. Fortunately, some systems include stub programming to proceed far enough into the boot process to enable a reflash.

Privacy-Invasive Trojans

Privacy-invasive Trojans generally perform some function that reveals to the programmer vital and privileged information about a system, or otherwise compromises that system. Passwords are, for obvious reasons, a very common target.

They can also (or instead) conceal some function that either reveals to the programmer vital and privileged information about a system or compromises that system.

Some antivirus companies have differentiated between PC-specific privacy-invasive Trojans and destructive Trojans by restricting the use of the term *Trojan* to destructive programs. They use the term *password stealers* for the most common privacy-invasive programs. In the latter half of the 1990s, password-stealing programs aimed specifically at AOL users seemed to become very common (some estimates at the number of such programs rose to many hundreds). Some antivirus software uses an *APS* identifier for such programs, probably standing for AOL Password Stealer. However, AOL is not and never was the only vulnerable service. In their paper "Where There's Smoke, There's Mirrors," Sarah Gordon and David Chess describe running user simulations on AOL over a seven-month period. Although attempts were made to gain their dummy users' screen passwords, these attempts generally used direct social engineering techniques by correspondents masquerading as AOL staff, rather than indirectly with password stealing programs.

In recent years, viruses and Trojans have frequently appeared that attempt to steal other privileged information relating to a wide variety of applications and data formats. They have also been associated with the more-or-less random dissemination of possibly sensitive data to persons other than the author of the malicious software, including other intended victims.

Another recent development is the rise of convergent or blended threats, such as multipolar worms and viruses using a number of attack vectors, Trojan/social engineering techniques as a means of deceiving the victim into running malicious code, and installing back-door or privacy-invasive Trojans as part of the infective process.

Network Trojans

This diffuse class of malware includes a variety of subtypes and specific programs, but is often associated with programs like BackOrifice and NetBus that use particular network ports and a variety of subversive network-related activities, such as remote access and file modification, Registry and SAM modification, keylogging (password capture), display of local cached data, creation of network shares to allow unauthorized access, exploitation of victim systems to launch attacks on systems at one stage removed (WinTrinoo), ICQ and IRC exploits, (SubSeven) and so on. Some of these types of Trojan are examined in more detail below.

Back Door Trojans

Trojans have, from time to time, been planted in legitimate applications. Ken Thompson describes in his paper "Reflections on Trusting Trust" a number of interesting (not entirely hypothetical) scenarios, the most famous being the Trojanized compiler scenario. In this case, production software offers the means of privileged access to anyone who knows of the back door or trapdoor described.

Back doors and trapdoors offering unauthorized access (and maybe modification) are not the only instances of unauthorized code introduced into legitimate programs, however. Many Mac owners who bought a certain brand of third-party keyboard with a Trojan hardcoded into a ROM chip found that the text Welcome Datacomp was inserted into their documents at apparently random intervals. PC motherboards with a Trojanized BIOS were characterized by "Happy Birthday" played through the system loudspeaker at boot-up, apparently on the programmer's birthday. The term *back door Trojan* is also used increasingly to refer to a class of Trojan we have preferred to refer to as Remote Access Tools, and to software associated with the installation of commercial software that reports back to the vendor, or uses the host machine as a platform for further advertising. This type of activity is more often referred to as *spyware* or *adware*.

Remote Access Tools

Though few antivirus vendors will claim to detect all known Trojans, most do detect at least some on the platforms for which they have products, especially those Trojans that do direct damage. *Remote Access Tools (RATs)* such as Netbus and BackOrifice, however, straddle a line between legitimate systems administration (similar to that carried out by programs such as PC Anywhere) and covert unauthorized access. When the system owner is persuaded to run the installation program, a server program is installed that can be accessed from a client program on a remote machine without the knowledge of the user. The server is used to manipulate the victim machine.

Functionally, there might be no difference between a RAT and a "legitimate" tool. The difference lies not in the functionality, but in the facilitation of the covert availability of that functionality to unauthorized individuals. As with sniffers and network scanners, it's not what the program does, so much as the reason it's being used. Yet if RAT software is willingly installed, opening the system to an attack the user does not expect, does that make it a Trojan? Using Microsoft Word also makes the user vulnerable to attacks she might not have anticipated. It was, for instance, literally years before some computer users realized that using versions of Word and other Microsoft Office applications supporting macro languages made them vulnerable to macro viruses and Trojans. Does that make Bill Gates a Trojan author? No, because the functionality in this case is too generalized to be described as a back door. Arguably, any software with a significant degree of functionality also carries the risk of subversion by malicious software. However, a RAT broadcasting its presence to a hacker, who probes a characteristic range of port numbers, can certainly be described as a back door Trojan. It promotes the intentions of the author and subverts the expectations of the victim. Trojans that use specific ports are, along with a number of other examples of malware, listed at `http://www.simovits.com/trojans`. A number of sites also list the legitimate assignment of port numbers to given protocols and products: For instance, `http://www.iana.org/assignments/port-numbers/` includes both the Well Known Ports (assigned by the IANA, usually to system processes) between 0 and 1023, and the Registered Ports between 1024 and 49151 inclusive. 49152 through 65535 are known as Dynamic or Private Ports, and are not registered for particular uses.

This is a serious issue—not least in that the "Bad Guys" frequently allude to the shortcomings of legitimate software (especially Microsoft's), as if unforeseen bugs in Office justified their own premeditated activities.

Nonetheless, some RAT authors have exploited this ambivalence by producing "Professional" versions of such software and charging for them. This enables the authors to complain of the anti-capitalist, anti-competitive behavior of security vendors who detect their program as a Trojan (or, all too often and inaccurately, a virus). It works, too. Some antivirus vendors for a time dropped detection of the Professional version of Netbus, despite the murkiness of its antecedents and its continuing potential for misuse. Others have gone out of their way to distinguish between standard Netbus Pro installations and Trojanized installations. Clearly, the dividing line between a RAT and a back door Trojan can be somewhat hazy, because they may use very similar technology and functionality.

Droppers

A dropper is a program that is not itself a virus, but is intended to install a virus. Technically, a program that installs other nonviral programs, might also be referred to as a dropper. Curiously, given the popular association of Trojans and viruses, droppers are a comparatively rare entry point for viruses in the wild (see the preceding chapter on viruses). In the PC world, dropper programs are most commonly associated with transporting boot sector viruses across networks, and can be used for that purpose by both pro- and antivirus researchers. They can be used as a covert means of introducing a virus onto a system, if the victim can be persuaded by social engineering techniques to run the dropper program. Somewhat ironically, we have seen a number of instances in recent years where an email virus has installed a password-stealing or backdoor Trojan as part of its payload: W95/Matrix, for instance.

Droppers have been used with surprising frequency in the Mac world, though. The MacMag virus was introduced via a HyperCard stack called New Apple Products. The Tetracycle game was implicated in the original spread of MBDF. ExtensionConflict is supposed to identify conflicts between extensions (now there's a surprise), but installs the SevenDust virus. Both SevenDust and MBDF are still being reported in the field. Back in the PC world, the Red Team alert muddied the waters by attaching a virus dropper alleged to be a fix for a virus that didn't and couldn't possibly exist.

Jokes

Joke programs are almost as old as computing. One venerable example is the PDP Cookie program, which popped up and asked the victim for a cookie. PC and Mac users have both long been delighted or irritated by such programs. Confusion has arisen because of the habit of antivirus software of alerting (using the word *virus*) not only on viruses and Trojans, but on joke programs such as CokeGift. This widely distributed program offered the victim their CD tray as a holder for their fizzy drink (or possibly white powder for nasal ingestion or carboniferous fossil fuel). Cute for some, irritating for others, but not exactly life-threatening.

However, the practice of alerting on joke programs might have arisen in response to supposed joke programs that threaten to format disks, or claim to have done so, but make no such actual attempt. Indeed, there have been instances when, what one vendor has reported as a Trojan, another vendor reported as a joke. One real-life example concerned a program that changed the victim's desktop wallpaper to a pornographic photograph. (So who wallpapers their desktop in real life?) Such a payload might well be considered humorous by the Trojan author, and no more harm intended than is associated with other practical jokes. However, run on a system in an environment with a draconian policy towards trafficking in porno-graphic data, this payload might result in the victim's dismissal, a result that might well be regarded as being as catastrophic to that individual as the loss of data through deliberate destruction (though the corporate view of this comparison might be a little different).

There might be an argument for regarding this scenario, though, as an example of an accidental Trojan, an undesirable result unintended by the program's author. However, too much focus on accidental Trojans might also open up the possibility of the accidental non-Trojan, a program that fails to achieve a malicious intention. In the same way, perhaps, an "intended" (a virus whose replicative function never works) is of some interest to researchers, but not necessarily to the intended victim.

In recent years, a number of Trojans have carried payloads best described as annoy-ing, rather than data-threatening: opening multiple windows, opening dialog boxes that move away from the mouse cursor when the victim attempts to close them, or redirecting Web browsers to undesirable Web pages. Some versions of HTML/script Trojans such as JS/NoClose have made much use of such irritating side effects. Again, more significant damage may be incurred when attempts to remove such programs go wrong, as may easily happen with software that hooks itself deep into the operating system using modifications to the Windows Registry, for example. Does this also qualify as an "accidental Trojan"? Probably not. After all, programs on this particular borderline between Trojan horses and jokes are still employing the deception characteristic of some definitions of Trojan. Furthermore, I'd argue that a program that is intended to irritate a victim or make him feel foolish is as malicious in intent as a destructive Trojan. Only the type and extent of damage varies. Furthermore, such a joke cannot be described as harmless if the victim is driven to take unnecessarily stringent and time-intensive measures because of uncertainty about what other changes might have been introduced to the system.

Bombs

Logic bombs are malicious programs that execute their payload when a preprogrammed condition is met. When the trigger condition is a time or date, the term *time bomb* may be used. A *time out* is a logic bomb sometimes used to enforce contract terms. Characteristically, the program stops running unless some action is taken to indicate (for instance) that the license fee has been paid, or the contractor who wrote the code has been paid. It's not unknown for a contractor to introduce some more drastic time bomb to be triggered if a dispute over payment arises.

The use of the word *bomb* does suggest a destructive payload, but this need not, in fact, be the case. *Mail bombs* and *subscription bombs*, which don't really belong in a chapter on Trojans, are denial-of-service (DoS) attacks intended to inconvenience the victim by battering her mailbox with a barrage of mail. Often this is done by subscribing the victim to large numbers of mailing lists. Email Trojans certainly exist, although email is more commonly an infection vector for viruses and worms. Security vendors such as MessageLabs, which monitor email for known and unknown malware, are increasingly reporting the use of email to disseminate Trojans.

The term *ANSI bomb* usually refers to a mail message or other text file that takes advantage of an enhancement to the MS-DOS ANSI.SYS driver. This enables keys to be redefined with an escape sequence; in this case, to echo some potentially destructive command to the console. Such programs were at one time quite frequently reported on FidoNet. However, nowadays few systems run programs that require ANSI terminal emulation, and ANSI.SYS is not normally installed in Windows 9*x* or later.

There are alternatives to ANSI.SYS that don't support keyboard redefinition, or enable it to be turned off.

Rootkits

A *rootkit* is an example of a set of trojanized system programs that an intruder who manages to root-compromise a system might be able to substitute for the commands' standard equivalents. Examples include modified versions of system utilities such as top and ps, enabling illegitimate processes to run unnoticed, daemons to be modified to compromise log entries or hide connections, and utilities to be gimmicked to allow escalation to root privileges or to hide rootkit component files or other backdoor functionality (secret passwords to enable privileged access, for instance). Associated programs include packet sniffers and utmp/wtmp editors (used to doctor log files).

Rootkits exist for a number of flavors of Unix and NT-based systems. However, one-off Trojanized versions of login (that is, versions not included in a suite of programs such as a rootkit) have been used, for instance, to harvest passwords since Pontius programmed in PILOT.

TIP

You can find information on rootkits in the FAQ at `http://staff.washington.edu/dittrich/misc/faqs/lrk4.faq`.

Sarah Gordon's paper "Publication of Vulnerabilities and Tool" (Proceedings of the Twelfth World Conference on Computer Security, Audit and Control, 1995) includes a technical analysis of some rootkit components.

DDoS Agents

Distributed denial-of-service (DDoS) tools such as Stacheldraht, TFN2K, and Trinoo are Trojans designed with a very specific purpose. They are intended to bring down Internet servers by remotely coordinating packet-flooding attacks from multiple machines. Typically, the intruder controls a number of master machines. These in turn control daemons on remote machines. Covertly installed, their presence is often concealed by the installation of rootkits. Daemons can be installed on many hundreds of remote machines, all directing flooding attacks at the victim system.

Detailed analysis of DDoS attacks and counter-attacks is beyond the scope of this chapter. However, the installation and presence of a DDoS attack tool can be detected by the same means as other malware—that is, recognition of a specific search string (Known Something Detection), heuristic scanning, and change detection. Virus scanners usually detect known DDoS tools. Network traffic can be monitored for characteristics such as IP packets with spoofed source addresses. Intrusion detection systems can be configured to scan for patterns characteristic of communications between master software and daemon software. A number of papers are available discussing these issues at greater length:

`http://staff.washington.edu/dittrich/misc/stacheldraht.analysis`

`http://staff.washington.edu/dittrich/misc/trinoo.analysis`

`http://staff.washington.edu/dittrich/misc/tfn.analysis`

`http://www.cert.org/incident_notes/IN-99-07.html`

Worms

In principle, this should probably be the longest subsection in this chapter; however, this area has already been covered in the preceding chapter. Many system administrators now apply the term Trojan to what are often described as worms. Although I regard this usage as misleading, it is defensible, common, and can't be ignored.

It's defensible because, as discussed in Chapter 17, most present-day worms are reliant on social engineering to persuade the recipient to execute the malicious code. In other words, they conform to one of the definitions we've previously examined, suggesting that Trojans are programs that purport to do one desirable thing while actually doing some other, less desirable thing.

The usage is misleading because it defies the definition of Trojans as nonreplicative malware. In the virus business, most people hold the view that viruses and worms replicate. Some believe that the worm class is a subset of the virus class, and many regard Trojans as nonreplicative. These distinctions are not just academic. To fight malicious code effectively, we need to understand how it works, and distinctions are particularly important when we come to examine multipartite/multipolar threats such as MTX or LoveLetter. Modern mailborne malware might include components that can be described as parasitic (a file virus), a worm (a network virus that doesn't infect other files by direct attachment), and/or a classic Trojan.

The theoretical basis of computer virology might be a little shaky as we consider the effect of such recent developments. However, there is plenty of information on such programs on Web sites maintained by antivirus companies, such as those listed in Chapter 17.

Where Do Trojans Come From?

Usenet is a common source of Trojans and viruses, especially newsgroups that carry binaries of any sort, and more particularly, groups that traffic in warez (illicit software) or pornographic material. Trojans are also distributed through email and instant messaging services, as well as from Internet file repositories, and their distribution is increasingly associated with email viruses and worms.

The AOLGOLD Trojan horse was distributed via Usenet and through email. The program was claimed to be an enhancement package for accessing America Online. The distribution consisted of an archived file that, when unzipped, revealed two files, INSTALL.EXE and README.TXT. Executing INSTALL.EXE resulted in expanding 18 files to the hard disk. One of the new files, called INSTALL.BAT, attempted to delete several directories on drive C, as well as running a program called DOOMDAY.EXE that failed to execute because of a bug in the batch file. Destructive Trojans of this type have not captured the same attention recently, or caused as much damage. However, it would be naïve to assume that they no longer pose a threat. Furthermore, while Trojans such as FlashKiller, KillCMOS, and Winnuke V probably inspire more panic than their actual incidence might suggest, backdoor Trojans such as the wu-ftpd Trojan can be the means of entry for individuals set on causing equal or more damage.

TIP

You can find the security advisory titled "Information on the AOLGOLD Trojan Program" at `http://www.emergency.com/aolgold.htm` or `http://ciac.llnl.gov/ciac/bulletins/g-03.shtml`.

Trojans frequently masquerade as games, joke programs, screensavers, and other programs frequently exchanged by email, especially when strict system policies or security policies are not enforced. If software contains a privacy-invasive Trojan or a destructive Trojan with a delayed payload (a time bomb or other form of logic bomb, for example), the Trojan might be distributed by a victim who is not yet aware that the program is malicious.

AOL users are frequently targeted by privacy-invasive Trojans, as we've already seen, but also by destructive Trojans.

In April 1997, someone developed a Trojan called AOL4FREE.COM (not be to be confused with the AOL4FREE virus hoax that surfaced that same year—of course such confusion was part of the point of the hoax). The Trojan claimed to be a tool to gain unauthorized access to AOL and destroyed hard disk drives on affected machines. To learn more about it, check out the CIAC advisory at `http://ciac.llnl.gov/ciac/bulletins/h-47a.shtml`, though this advisory is inaccurate in at least one respect—many antivirus programs routinely detect Trojan horses.

In fact, attacks on AOL users are symptomatic of a mindset regularly encountered among computer vandals of all types. Like Usenet newbies and unwary IRC users, they are seen as a group of "lamers" lacking low-level knowledge of the systems they use. This is seen in itself as some twisted justification, not only for jokes and hoaxes, but for intentionally destructive programs.

Direct intrusion enables installation of rootkit components and other Trojanized files, especially if the intruder is able to gain root/administrator privileges.

How Often Are Trojans Really Discovered?

Trojans, especially password-stealers, are frequently discovered in communities such as AOL. AOL presents an Internet service for computer users who don't want or need to be computer geeks. Many newcomers to the Internet have no interest in the finer points of networking protocols and the mysteries of Gopher, Telnet, and Archie, and AOL emphasizes user-friendliness rather than 1970s geek cliques. Trojans in AOL usually target the least computer-literate members (new users, children) of those communities, already seen by technosnobs to be among the least computer-literate groups. This is significant because there are Black Hats (bad guys), who regard the technical ignorance of everyday users as justification of vandalism. They reason that if lame AOLers can't learn to protect their systems, they deserve everything they get.

In the corporate arena, Trojans are a major security concern on multiuser systems, which can, of course, include many desktop machines. They can be insidious, too, because even after they're discovered, their footprints may remain in dark corners of the directory system or Windows Registry, and it is often recommended that compromised systems be rebuilt completely in case undocumented or unconsidered residual compromises remain undiscovered. Trojans are often hidden within compiled binaries. The Trojan code is therefore not in human-readable form or machine language. Without using a debugging utility, you can learn little about binary files. Using a text editor or a utility such as *strings* to view a binary file or extract readable text from it, for example, is often unhelpful. Often, the only recognizable text strings will be copyright messages, error messages, or other data that prints to STDOUT at various points in the program's execution—stub loader messages, for example. In a graphical environment, recognizable strings will be even less frequent or useful. However, reverse-assembling serious quantities of potentially damaging code is not a task for the fainthearted or under-resourced. As we've already noted, such code is not always susceptible to automated analysis.

NOTE

Compiled binaries are not the only places you'll find Trojans. Batch files and other shell scripts, Perl programs, and perhaps even code written in JavaScript, VBScript, or Tcl can carry a Trojan. Scripting languages have been described as unsuitable for the creation of Trojans if the code remains humanly readable. This increases the victim's chances of discovering the offending code. In real life, though, victims often seem quite happy to run unchecked code, even when it's humanly readable. The LoveLetter virus was executed by countless recipients, even though the cleartext code clearly included a subroutine whose very name indicated that it was intended to infect files.

Nesting a Trojan within such code is, however, more feasible if the file is part of a much larger package—for example, if the entire package extracts to many subdirectories. In such cases, the complexity of the package can reduce the likelihood that a human being, using normal methods of investigation, will uncover the Trojan, especially if it's an easily overlooked short sequence, such as DELTREE C:\ or rm -rf.

Trojans don't usually announce their intent. Worse still, many Trojans masquerade as legitimate, known utilities that you'd expect to find running on the system. Thus, you cannot rely on detecting a Trojan by listing current processes.

In detecting a Trojan by eye, much depends on the user's experience. Users who know little about their operating systems are less likely to venture deep into directory structures looking for suspicious files. More proficient users are unlikely to have time to examine the complex system structures of modern operating systems, especially on server-class machines. Even experienced programmers can have difficulty identifying a Trojan, even if the code is available for their examination. Identification of malicious code by reverse-engineering can be more difficult and time-consuming by several orders of magnitude.

What Level of Risk Do Trojans Represent?

Trojans can represent a moderate-to-serious level of risk, mainly for reasons already discussed:

- New Trojans are difficult to detect using heuristic detection. (Unless you use the somewhat sweeping heuristic that a change in a file detected automatically is likely to indicate a Trojan substituted for a legitimate file.) There is no absolute test for code to determine whether it is (or is not) a Trojan because author intent and user expectations are not generally susceptible to automated analysis.

- In most cases, Trojans are found in binaries, which remain largely in non-human–readable form. However, the fact that the code is largely static does make Trojans at least as susceptible to "known-something" detection as viruses. In other words, when a known malicious program is identified, it can be detected by software updated with an appropriate search string. Remember that, by most definitions, replication is not a characteristic of the Trojan breed. Trojans spread through the action of being copied by an attacker or a victim socially engineered into carrying out the attacker's wants, not by self-copying. Thus it is not usually feasible for an attacker to use techniques such as polymorphism to reduce the chance of detection. Because the copying of the program is not a function of the program itself, the program has no means of evolving into a non-identical copy (a morph) of itself.

Nevertheless, undetected privacy-invasive Trojans can lead to total system compromise. A Trojan can be in place for weeks or even months before it's discovered. In that time, a cracker with root privileges can alter the entire system to suit his needs. Even when the Trojan is discovered, many hidden loopholes might be left behind when it is removed. It is for this reason that the complete rebuilding of compromised desktop and server software is sometimes recommended after the discovery and removal of Trojans, rootkits, DDoS agents, and so forth. Antivirus vendors tend to be over-relaxed in this respect, probably because historically they are used to dealing with a fairly small subset of the Trojan class.

How Do I Detect a Trojan?

Detecting Trojans is easy, if you have a static search pattern to scan for. Antivirus software routinely detects some Trojans using much the same pattern-searching techniques used for detecting viruses. In fact, known Trojans are often easier to detect than viruses, because they aren't usually embedded into other programs, or even polymorphic, though variations may be introduced, deliberately or otherwise, over time. However, identification of a known Trojan isn't always the best defense. Detection of previously unknown Trojans is also conceptually simple, provided you have always maintained the best security practices (literally always, at least as far as the protected system is concerned).

Most detection methods on traditional multiuser systems derive from a principle sometimes called *object reconciliation*. Object reconciliation is a fancy way of asking, "Are things still just the way I left them?" Here's how it works: *Objects* are system areas, such as files or directories. *Reconciliation* is the process of comparing those objects against a snapshot record of the same objects taken at some previous date when the protected object was known to be in a trustworthy, "clean" state.

> **NOTE**
>
> Strictly speaking, there is no such "clean state" time. Even a "day zero" installation of system software onto a virgin system assumes a program suite with no substitutions and back doors. Can you place unlimited trust in a system you didn't build totally from scratch yourself? "No amount of source-level verification or scrutiny will protect you from using untrusted code," says Ken Thompson. Does this mean we should give up on this approach? Of course not, but we should bear in mind that, even if we build an application from scrutinized source code, we might not be able to trust the compiler, or every snippet of hardware microcode on the system motherboard.

More commonly, the process described as object reconciliation is known as change detection, integrity checking, or integrity management. However, these terms are not strictly synonymous.

Change detection simply describes any technique that alerts the user to the fact that an object has been changed in some respect. *Integrity checking* has the same core meaning, but is often taken to imply a more sophisticated approach, not only to detecting change in spite of attempts to conceal it, but to ensuring that the reporting software itself is not subverted.

Integrity management is a more general term. It can include not only the detection of unauthorized changes, but other methods of maintaining system integrity. Such methods can include some or all the following, in no particular order:

- Maintaining trusted backups

- Blocking unknown intrusions at or after entry (for instance, by running system files from read-only media or refreshing system files from trusted read-only media)

- Maintenance of strict access control

- Careful application of manufacturer patches to block newly discovered loopholes

- A finely engineered change-management system, using only signed (trusted) code

A simple method of testing file integrity is based on reports of changes in file state information. Different file integrity tests vary in sophistication. For example, you can crudely test a file's integrity using any of the following indexes:

- Date last modified

- File creation date

- File size

Unfortunately, none of these three methods constitute a really adequate defense against more than the crudest attack. Each time a file is altered, its values change. For example, each time the file is opened, altered, and saved, a new last-modified date emerges. However, this date can be easily manipulated. Consider manipulating this file timestamp. How difficult is it? Change the system time, apply the desired edits, archive the file, and reset the system time. Better still, get and save the date/time information using standard C library functions (for instance), modify or replace the object, and restore the file modification date. On a single-user system (such as MS-DOS) with minimal or no access controls, the coding involved is trivial. For this reason, checking time of modification is an unreliable way to detect change. Also, the last date of modification reveals nothing if the file was unaltered (for example, if it was only copied, viewed, or mailed). On the other hand, if there is a disparity between the modification date returned by the system and the date of modification recorded by a system monitoring utility, there is a distinct possibility of malicious action.

Another way to check the integrity of a file is by examining its size. However, this value can be very easily manipulated, either by trimming or padding the file itself, or by altering the value reported by the operating system.

There are other indexes: For example, basic checksums can be used. However, although checksums are more reliable than time and date stamping, they can be altered, too. If you rely on a basic checksum system (or use change detection software, which relies on simple checksumming), it is particularly important that you keep your checksum list in a trusted environment. This might mean on a separate server or even a separate medium, accessible only by root or other trusted users. Checksums work efficiently and appropriately for checking the integrity of a file transferred, for example, from point A to point B, but are not suitable for high security applications. They simply aren't designed to guard against a malicious attempt to subvert them to return false information.

NOTE

If you've ever performed file transfers using communication packages such as Qmodem, you might remember that these programs perform *cyclical redundancy checksum (CRC)* verification as the transfers occur. This reduces the likelihood that the file will be damaged in transit. When dealing with sophisticated attacks against file integrity, however, this technique is insufficient. Tutorials about defeating checksum systems are scattered across the Internet. Most are related to the development of viruses. (Some older virus-checking utilities used checksum analysis to detect possible infection by new viruses; that is, viruses not yet known to the compilers of virus-specific scanner databases.) You can get an overview of CRC32 (and other algorithms) from RFC 1510 at `ftp://ftp.isi.edu/in-notes/ rfc1510.txt`.

A less easily subverted technique involves calculating a more sophisticated *digital fingerprint* for each file using various algorithms. A family of algorithms called the *MD series* can be used for this purpose. One of the most popular implementations is a system called MD5.

MD5

MD5 belongs to a family of one-way hash functions called *message digest algorithms*. The MD5 system is defined in RFC 1321 as follows:

> The algorithm takes as input a message of arbitrary length and produces as output a 128-bit "fingerprint" or "message digest" of the input. It is conjectured that it is computationally infeasible to produce two messages having the same message digest, or to produce any message having a given prespecified target message digest. The MD5 algorithm is intended for digital signature applications, where a large file must be "compressed" in a secure manner before being encrypted with a private (secret) key under a public-key cryptosystem such as RSA.

TIP

RFC 1321 is located at `ftp://ftp.isi.edu/in-notes/rfc1321.txt`.

When you run a file through MD5, the fingerprint emerges as a 32-character value. It looks like this:

```
2d50b2bffb537cc4e637dd1f07a187f4
```

Many sites that distribute Unix software use MD5 to generate digital fingerprints for their distributions. As you browse their directories, you can examine the original digital fingerprint of each file. A typical directory listing might look like this:

```
MD5 (wn-1.17.8.tar.gz) = 2f52aadd1defeda5bad91da8efc0f9800
MD5 (wn-1.17.7.tar.gz) = b92916d83f377b143360f068df6d8116
MD5 (wn-1.17.6.tar.gz) = 18d02b9f24a49dee239a78ecfaf9c6fa
MD5 (wn-1.17.5.tar.gz) = 0cf8f8d0145bb7678abcc518f0cb39e9
MD5 (wn-1.17.4.tar.gz) = 4afe7c522ebe0377269da0c7f26ef6b8
MD5 (wn-1.17.3.tar.gz) = aaf3c2b1c4eaa3ebb37e8227e3327856
MD5 (wn-1.17.2.tar.gz) = 9b29eaa366d4f4dc6de6489e1e844fb9
MD5 (wn-1.17.1.tar.gz) = 91759da54792f1cab743a034542107d0
MD5 (wn-1.17.0.tar.gz) = 32f6eb7f69b4bdc64a163bf744923b41
```

If you download a file from such a server and find that the digital fingerprint of the downloaded file is different, there is a good chance that something is amiss.

With or without MD5, integrity management is a complex process. Various utilities have been designed to assist with integrity management on complex and distributed systems. The following utilities were originally Unix-based, but similar programs are available for Microsoft operating systems.

Tripwire

Tripwire (originally written in 1992) is a comprehensive file integrity tool. Tripwire is well-designed, easily understood, and easily implemented.

The original values (digital fingerprints) for files to be monitored are kept within a database file in simple ASCII format that is accessed whenever a signature needs to be calculated or verified.

Ideally, a tool such as Tripwire would be used immediately after a fresh (day zero) installation. This gives you 100% assurance of file system integrity as a starting point (or nearly 100%—remember the Ken Thompson article). After you generate the complete database for your file system, you can introduce other users (who will immediately fill your system with junk that, optionally, might also be fingerprinted and verified on subsequent checks). Here are some of its more useful features:

- Tripwire can perform its task over network connections. Therefore, it's possible to generate a database of digital fingerprints for some entire networks at installation time.

- Tripwire was written in C with a mind toward portability. It will compile for many platforms without alteration.

- Tripwire comes with a macro-processing language, so your tasks can be automated.

Tripwire is a popular (especially in its commercial incarnation) and effective tool, but there are some security issues common to most or all integrity management tools. One such issue relates to the database of values that is generated and maintained. From the beginning, Tripwire's authors were well aware of this:

> The database used by the integrity checker should be protected from unauthorized modifications; an intruder who can change the database can subvert the entire integrity checking scheme.

TIP

Tripwire is discussed at length by its original authors in "The Design and Implementation of Tripwire: A File System Integrity Checker" by Gene H. Kim and Eugene H. Spafford. It is located at `ftp://coast.cs.purdue.edu/pub/papers/gene-spafford/Tripwire.pdf`.

One method of protecting the database is to store it on read-only media. This eliminates any likelihood of tampering. Kim and Spafford suggested that the database be protected in this manner, although they pointed out that this can present some practical, procedural problems. Much depends upon how often the database will be updated, and its size. Certainly, if you are implementing Tripwire or a similar utility on a wide scale (and using its most stringent settings), the maintenance of a read-only database can be formidable. As usual, this breaks down to a trade-off between the level of risk and the inconvenience of setting and maintaining paranoid defaults.

You can find Tripwire and some documentation at `ftp://coast.cs.purdue.edu/pub/tools/unix/ids/tripwire/`. However, Tripwire is no longer a supported research project at Purdue University. In its commercial incarnation, more information (and a downloadable evaluation version of the product for Windows XP Pro, 2000, and NT 4.0) is available from `http://www.tripwiresecurity.com/`.

TAMU/TARA

The TAMU Tiger suite (from Texas A&M University) is a collection of tools that greatly enhance the security of a Unix box. These tools were created in-house, in response to an extensive attack from a coordinated group of Internet crackers. The package has since been upgraded and renamed TARA (Tiger Analytical Research Assistant). It incorporates a number of scripts used to scan Unix systems for problems. More information is available from `http://www.securityfocus.com/tools/481`. TARA-PRO is available at `http://www-arc.com/tara/index.shtml`.

On Other Platforms

File integrity checkers exist for Windows—in fact Tripwire has been developed for Windows NT-based operating systems as well as for Unix. Integrity checkers are not necessarily expressly designed to check multiple machines and file systems over networks. Some older DOS and Windows tools use simple CRC checksumming as an index and therefore might be easier to subvert than tools that employ MD5 and related or equivalent algorithms. The majority are intended for use as a supplement to virus scanners (because detectable changes to an infectable object might indicate virus infection). This doesn't invalidate the potential usefulness of integrity checkers as a means of detecting possible substitutions of compromised code for system files.

However, change detection is less convenient on Windows platforms in that system files accessed by multiple applications can be replaced by legitimate installations and upgrades. There is often a sharper delineation on other platforms between files belonging to the system and files that belong to an application.

Furthermore, change detection only works well with certain types of binary executables, even in the context of virus detection. Many viruses and Trojans infect files whose main purpose is to contain data (spreadsheets, word-processing files, and so on). However, such files are usually *intended* to be modified as necessary, as are the log files used on many multiuser systems to track possible malicious action. Clearly, change detection based on the presumption that files remain static isn't going to work in these instances. In some instances, it's possible to specify changes that might signify a breach (the addition of macro code to a Word file, for instance). This approach requires that the inspecting software "know" more about the internals of the file, rather than just its digital fingerprint. That would entail serious administrative difficulties, so the approach is not well-favored at present.

Certain kinds of modifications to the Windows registry are particularly associated with viruses, worms, or Trojans, particularly those that set up the system configuration so that a (in this case malicious) program is executed each time the system is run. Unfortunately, Registry keys that are associated with such problems can also be used for legitimate purposes, so unless it is intended to lock down the registry and other configuration files, so that no modification at all is possible, it's difficult to evaluate and deal with modifications to such areas of the Registry. Attempts to prevent *any* modification to the system using this approach might have an adverse impact on the system.

The safest defense, though, is to block unauthorized modification of system files proactively by code signing, read-only media, and other preemptive measures. Sadly, safe and convenient are not always the same thing.

Resources

"Reflections on Trusting Trust." Ken Thompson. Reprinted in *Computers Under Attack: Intruders, Worms and Viruses*. Ed. Peter J. Denning. ACM Press, 1990. ISBN: 0-13-185794-0.

"Where There's Smoke, There's Mirrors: The Truth About Trojan Horses on the Internet." Sarah Gordon and David M. Chess. Virus Bulletin Conference Proceedings, 1998.
`http://www.research.ibm.com/antivirus/SciPapers/Smoke/smoke.html`

"Testing Times for Trojans." Ian Whalley. Virus Bulletin Conference Proceedings, 1999.

Practical Unix and Internet Security. Simson Garfinkel and Gene Spafford. O'Reilly & Associates, 1996. ISBN 1-56592-148-8.

Security in Computing. Charles P. Pfleeger. Prentice-Hall International, Inc. 1997. ISBN 0-13-185794-0.

MDx-MAC and Building Fast MACs from Hash Functions. Bart Preneel and Paul C. van Oorschot. Crypto 95.
`ftp.esat.kuleuven.ac.be/pub/COSIC/preneel/mdxmac_crypto95.ps`

Message Authentication with One-Way Hash Functions. Gene Tsudik. 1992. IEEE Infocom 1992.
`http://www.zurich.ibm.com/ security/publications/1992/t92.ps.Z`

RFC 1446—1.5.1. Message Digest Algorithm.
`ftp://ftp.isi.edu/in-notes/rfc1446.txt`

RFC 1510—6. Encryption and Checksum Specifications. Connected:
An Internet Encyclopedia. `http://www.freesoft.org/CIE/RFC/1510/69.htm`

RFC 1510—6.4.5. RSA MD5 Cryptographic Checksum Using DES (rsa-md5des).
`ftp://ftp.isi.edu/in-notes/rfc1510.txt`

"A Digital Signature Based on a Conventional Encryption Function." Ralph C. Merkle. Crypto 87, LNCS, pp. 369–378, SV, August 1987.

"An Efficient Identification Scheme Based on Permuted Kernels." Adi Shamir. Crypto 89, LNCS, pp. 606–609, SV, August 1989.

Trusted Distribution of Software over the Internet. Aviel D. Rubin. (Bellcore's Trusted Software Integrity (Betsi) System). 1994.
`ftp://ftp.cert.dfn.de/pub/docs/betsi/`

International Conference on the Theory and Applications of Cryptology. 1994 Wollongong, N.S.W. *Advances in Cryptology*, ASIACRYPT November 28–December 1, 1994. (Proceedings) Berlin & New York. Springer, 1995.

Managing Data Protection, Second Edition. Dr. Chris Pounder and Freddy Kosten. Butterworth-Heineman Limited, 1992.

A comprehensive Trojan database can be found at `http://www.simovits.com/ trojans/`, with Trojan descriptions sorted by name, filename, file size, action, affected system, country of origin, programming language, or port. This resource is particularly useful in relation to network-related Trojans such as Netbus, SubSeven, and Blade Runner.

Summary

Trojans are a significant security risk to any network, server, or workstation. Although Windows and Unix-hosted antivirus software usually detects known Trojans, though not necessarily for all platforms, there are strong arguments for using integrity management tools, especially on server-class machines, to reduce the possibility of system compromise from Trojans masquerading as system utilities. This approach is viable on workstations, too, although it may be harder to implement effectively. A combination of targeted integrity management, efficiently backing up data but restoring systems from a standard day zero image rather than from backup tapes, and sound user management controlling the installation and execution of unauthorized software, is more effective than any single strategy in any server or workstation environment.

PART V

Architecture, Platforms, and Security

IN THIS PART

19

Network Architecture Considerations

This chapter discusses considerations for network architecture that enhance the security of the computing and network environment.

Network Architecture

The Internet is known as the network of networks. Each network plays an important part in the greater security of the Internet. By emphasizing security when designing and implementing your network, you can make your little corner of the Internet a safer place to be. The creation of a network environment for an organization should be thought out well in advance, rather than simply plugging equipment together. The goal of this chapter is to present you with important considerations for your network design that will enhance the security of your organization and those with which it interfaces.

The term "network architecture" collectively describes the requirements, organization, methods, and equipment used to create a network, including its physical components and security awareness. A secure network architecture is achieved by considering all these elements, their use, and their relationship to each other. Before you can make a network architecture secure, it is important to know the components used to create the network and the threats against them. Once the organization of the components and their threats is understood, a valid architecture can be designed.

Network Components

Without network components, there is no network, and without consideration for these components, there is no security! The first step toward a secure network topology is to examine the devices and systems used to implement it. The following considerations and types of equipment are common to an organization:

- Access devices

- Security devices

- Servers and systems

- Organization and layout

Access Devices

The *access device* is the piece of network equipment that provides Internet access and intercommunication between networks, and is the first element required for an Internet-accessible organization. Organizations might not need an access device, but if they want to communicate with other networks, or to provide access from the outside to employees or Internet users, an access device is needed. Access devices come in many forms; the most common are modems and routers.

There are generally two (or more) interfaces on an access device. The interfaces to which the network of the organization connects are considered the internal interface of the router (or other equipment). The interfaces that connect to the Internet service provider (ISP) are the external interfaces. The internal network comprises those systems and equipment on the internal side of the router. The network or networks accessible from the Internet form the external network.

The use of the access device has a direct effect on the security of a network topology because it helps define the Internet access model used in the organization, and is the first point where defense is needed. There are many access models that designers can use, including highly restrictive exception-based access, open access, and a combination in between. Exception-based access models apply a default restriction that disallows all access, followed by exceptions for needed services and connectivity. This is a commonly used method of protection where the firewall is configured to block traffic to all but a few specified protocols and services on specific systems. An example of exception-based access is to disallow all traffic to the Web server except for TCP traffic to port 80 (the IP protocol and service port [HTTP] that the Web server uses). Exception-based access models are useful in simple network environments, where there is little network diversity or need for complex filtering rules.

An open model allows access to everyone unless otherwise explicitly prohibited. This model focuses on only the services provided by a network and its systems. It uses firewall rules to allow or disallow access from specific networks and systems to explicit services such as a Web server or email, and provides granular access control. This model takes no action on the remainder of the ports and protocols that are not in use, however, which can present a security risk in some network environments.

The following examples demonstrate the usefulness and dangers of an open access model.

In a simple network environment, where the Web server is connected directly to the Internet, an open model might create unnecessary security risks. In this case, the firewall allows access to the Web server from specific friendly networks and systems, but does not affect any other traffic to or from the Web server, including hostile traffic from the Internet. This presents a danger if an attacker compromises the Web server. The attacker can then set up a new and unauthorized service on that system, which runs unaffected by the firewall. An exception-based model would protect against this.

Open models are useful to provide granular access control and protect against unauthorized traffic to specific services, as is often used with domain name servers and email servers. Domain name servers and email servers often have secondary relays that provide service to Internet systems and protect the primary system from exposure to the Internet. The primary systems can be configured with an open access model that allows network traffic to the domain name and email services only from the relay servers. This example also assumes that the network topology protects the primary servers from external attack.

There are several schools of thought when determining which model of access should be used. The exception-based model is more restrictive, and places the brunt of the security responsibilities on the firewall's strengths. The open model relies more on the systems in use to assure that they are configured securely and provide minimal possibility for compromise and modification. Most experts these days strongly recommend the exception-based model, while trying to maximize system security as well.

Programmers over the last few years have been finding ways to bypass the access model. Security administrators closed access to IP ports such as the RPC (Remote Procedure Call), so programmers developed new RPC-like technologies such as SOAP (Simple Object Access Protocol). The major difference between SOAP and RPC is that SOAP runs over HTTP so that it can bypass firewalls, because the HTTP port is usually left open. Be aware if your programmers are doing this, because you might be wide open without even realizing it.

Security Devices

Firewalls, Virtual Private Network (VPN) servers, and intrusion detection systems (IDS) are commonly used examples of security devices. Firewalls are used to protect the internal network from external threats by allowing or disallowing certain types of network traffic and data. Firewalls are not meant only for the edge of the network, but anywhere that traffic restrictions are required or recommended. VPN devices are used to provide secure remote access from the Internet to users by creating an encrypted tunnel through which the remote computer accesses the internal network of an organization. Intrusion detection systems provide active monitoring and notification of known attacks on systems and networks by watching network data. These devices provide the first and most obvious level of security, and are vital to any network topology.

Servers and Systems

Servers and systems are all of the computers used within the organization. These systems include Web, mail, login, file and print servers, desktop computers, and network management systems. The requirements for these systems influence the network architecture and include the network services offered, and they also dictate to whom access is provided. Each service provided affects the security of the network and the system on which it runs. Consideration given to these effects results in a network architecture that minimizes the risks and effects of a security breach.

As you have learned throughout this book, attackers will often scan for servers that provide services to both the Internet and internal networks; the compromise of these systems allows the attacker a doorway into the organization. Servers that run multiple services present even greater security risks, because each service provides a potential doorway into that particular system. It is particularly important to examine the history of an application or service for security vulnerabilities. Email, Web, DNS, and FTP servers have a long history of vulnerabilities, and their simultaneous use on a single system provides several access points for an attacker.

Organization and Layout

The organization and layout of the network takes into consideration the implementation of these components. This includes the physical placement and organization of the network equipment and wiring, as well as the method by which Internet access is provided. Identifying network service requirements and the relationship of users to these services is important to the security of a network architecture.

Many operating systems and servers arrive configured by default to provide every service it supports, despite the fact that an organization rarely needs or uses all of them. If an organization needs file sharing, printing, Web, and email capabilities, the servers that provide these services should have all their other services disabled. If these services are provided to different groups within the organization, or if a clear need for these services to share information is not established, they should be run on different systems and networks that reflect the users' access needs.

Threats

The threats to a network should be known in advance of the design. The threats outlined here are organized into three categories:

- External attacks

- Internal attacks

- Physical attacks

Understanding the threats posed to a network connected to the Internet has several key benefits. This knowledge allows the network designers to protect against the attack and compromise of systems, limit the effects of vulnerabilities, and isolate their interactions. The secure network architecture affects the capability of an organization to react quickly to an incident and to recover safely without loss, while also adding to reliability and performance. The threats to a network and its systems are partially mitigated with a secure network architecture. Other factors that help alleviate risk are good security maintenance and diligence with regard to analysis of new and better security technologies.

External Attacks

External attacks are those that originate either from the Internet or from systems beyond the access device, and that target internal or external systems. External attacks are the most publicized and the most well-known form of attack. Stories of Web page defacements, viruses, Trojan programs, and denial of service by malicious system crackers and cyber-terrorists are common. Although invasive, reconnaissance probes and scans are not attacks. They are often precursors to an attack, however, because they provide vulnerability information to the attacker. The network components and their organization can minimize the risk associated with these attacks. External attacks occur against accessible services, systems, and networks; protection against external attacks includes the use of firewalls, network monitoring devices, distribution of services across multiple networks, and the establishment of bandwidth restrictions by protocol and service.

To protect against external attacks, it is useful to run services such as domain name servers, Web servers, and mail servers on separate systems, and to restrict network access to them with a firewall. It is also beneficial to isolate these systems so they are unable to access any other system.

These methods protect the systems from compromise by establishing only one point of access to each system. Multiple services on a single system might present higher risk for denial of service and system compromise because there are several points to attack and the compromise of one service can provide access to the data for all other services on that system. The example of a single system that acts as a mail, Web, and domain name server establishes three targets for attack. Denial of service against any of these targets results in a loss of service to all of them, and compromise of any one service provides the attacker with access to the data of the remaining two.

Internal Attacks

As the name implies, internal attacks originate from inside the organization. Despite the media attention given to external attacks, historically internal attacks are more widespread and frequent than those committed by outsiders. Disgruntled employees, curious users, or accidental misuse all contribute to the frequency of internal attacks. Defense against these attacks is more complex because designers attempt to provide high security without restricting the needed functionality of the network. Users should only be given enough access and privileges to accomplish their work and to protect against internal threats. Examining network data paths and splitting services across multiple networks and systems help provide higher security and minimize the effects of attack.

Users should not, for example, be given full network access to all systems, servers, and network equipment. Most organizations do not want all users to have access to financial systems, or for all users to have access to sensitive project materials. The use of multiple networks and servers to differentiate between groups and departments allows enforcement of these restrictions.

A key to having good internal security is to have good policies and procedures in place. This is discussed in detail in Chapter 25, "Policies, Procedures, and Enforcement."

Physical Attacks

Physical access is the final threat category. The ability to walk up to a system or piece of network equipment is the most dangerous of the risks. Simple actions such as unplugging equipment, rearranging cables, or physically damaging components can render the network unusable for long periods of time and at a high expense for repair. The location and access to the equipment that provides network service should be organized and secured.

Aside from physical damage to network equipment, another aspect of physical attacks is the ability for a user to see and analyze network traffic that travels over the same network wires of the user's desktop computer. If the network is not physically laid out safely, the user can use a packet sniffer to intercept and read the passwords and private information of other users. This can be prevented by physically isolating network traffic, based on the needs of a particular system.

Approach to Network Architecture

The approach to network architecture and its design is the philosophy and model used to outline the network requirements and components for an organization.

Although there are several schools of thought on this subject, the approach used here reflects a compromise between the idealistic and the realistic implementations. The ideal implementation provides complete and guaranteed security. The realistic model recognizes the need for services that have a higher potential for vulnerabilities. These services provide important aspects of service to the organization and to its customers and partners. In an ideal networked world, there are no vulnerabilities, and no risky services are used, which provides complete security.

As you know, there is no such concept as guaranteed or total security. The reality of the environment presses the network designer toward a high degree of security across the infrastructure. The level of security required in an organization should also be determined based on its needs, rather than on following a generic recipe. Despite the creation of a secure network architecture, security is still a continuous process that requires constant vigilance. Unfortunately, few organizations have dedicated teams to security development, implementation, and maintenance, though a greater focus and presence of security-specific staff is now developing. Because of the lack of dedicated personnel, organizations tend to focus security efforts on those areas deemed most vulnerable—the "squeaky wheel" approach to security. This often precludes the maintenance and upkeep of security for the internal network and systems, because they are considered protected by firewalls and other security mechanisms. Although lax internal security is not ideal, it emphasizes the need for a strong network architecture and infrastructure at its earliest stages of design. The higher the initial level of security, the easier it will be to develop and follow standards and procedures to maintain that level.

You can measure the security of a network architecture by its capability to manage risk and mitigate the effects of attack. When the threats to a network are understood, network designers should carefully consider the requirements, components, and features that are used in the network and their relationships with each other. The requirements establish the purpose for the network such as supporting the ability of its users to share data, communicate among each other, and interact with external sources. The components of a network include the actual hardware used to create the network and the organization and layout of the topology. The features are those capabilities and requirements outside of the initial needs that conform to a set of best practices and ancillary functionality. Finally, it is important to understand the relationships of all these components because security is only as strong as the weakest link in the chain.

Security Zones

Several zones of security are common to networks, and the consideration designers give to them affects the network architecture used. These zones outline security in relation to network access, and provide the initial sections of the network architecture. The security zones are organized into the external, the internal, and the intermediary tier.

The Great Beyond

The external network is, generally and in practice, the most open of the tiers, and consists of everything from the access device outward to the Internet. The organization has little or no control over the information, systems, and equipment that exist in this domain. The security of the ISP and all the external organizations to which it connects should not be assumed. It is useful to investigate the security practices and features that an ISP provides, including the control and management of the access device and the filtering and network topology of the ISP. Many ISPs manage the access device and secure it to prevent access and tampering by anyone other than the ISP; others require the organization to manage it. Many ISPs perform some level of packet filtering and firewalling on their own to detect and block improper data and attacks before they have a chance to reach the ISP's customers.

The network topology of the ISP also plays a role in the security for an organization. The physical relation between the individual customers of an ISP and the data paths established should be identified. Ideally, the amount of data from different organizations that travels across the same network wires should be minimized. This limits the effects on multiple customer networks in the event that the ISP falls victim to attack. The use of a common gateway by the ISP leads to a potential performance bottleneck and security risk as a single point of failure. ISPs with diversified networks and multiple points of access can provide higher security and reliability against attacks.

These considerations are beneficial to the organization, but finding a provider that implements many security measures might be difficult and expensive. An important philosophy to keep in mind when creating a secure network architecture is to secure the elements controlled by the organization as strongly as possible. Many organizations rely on the security provided by the ISP or any intermediary networks, and fail to implement any internal security measures. Therefore, the consideration of ISP security is important, but the emphasis should be placed on the creation of a secure network architecture for the organization. Solutions that mitigate weak ISP security include the creation of a Public Key Infrastructure, and the use of encrypted network communications with applications such as Secure Shell (SSH), SSL-enabled Web servers, and Virtual Private Networks (VPNs).

Internal Networks

The second zone is the internal network, where the vital computing assets should be safely protected. This area often has the most restrictive security measures, and is where the majority of users operate on a daily basis. The internal network is generally the least open, and has multiple layers of protection for the servers, desktops, and other computer systems and equipment used in the organization. The use of firewalls, multiple networks, and constraints on network data paths provides a higher level of security. The discussion of internal networks continues in greater depth in the section "Protecting the Castle" later in this chapter.

Intermediate Networks

The third zone is a compromise between the previous two zones and consists of the networks that provide services to both the internal and external networks. In general, it is considered very dangerous to make a single server or device exist simultaneously on an internal and an external network. A system configured in this manner is called a *multihomed* system, and should be avoided. Secure network architectures begin to differentiate between those systems and services to which the Internet has access, and those to which it does not.

Two intermediate networks are common in organizations. The first is a place for publicly accessible services such as the mail server, Web server, and Domain Name servers to internal users and those on the Internet. The second is a semiprivate network used by the organization, its business partners, and customers; this network requires specialized access only to those parties. This first area is often referred to as the "service network," or the De-Militarized Zone (DMZ), and is seen as a less protected area of the entire network infrastructure because it provides network services to the Internet.

A service network generally exists between the router to the ISP and the internal network. It can be created by adding another interface to the firewall, or by placing systems on the same network as the firewall. It is useful and more secure to create and protect the service network through another firewall interface in order to provide more restrictions of network access to the service network. Using this method, the organization can then restrict access to those services to authorized networks and systems, and prevent known hostile sites and competitors from accessing the Web site. The service network also benefits from a redundant or extra network link. With a single network connection to the ISP, a denial-of-service attack that utilizes all of the network bandwidth by attacking a system in the service network also denies service to the corporate network.

Multiple network connections can give a network a higher degree of security and reliability. Should an attacker attempt a denial-of-service attack, the access point under attack can be temporarily shut down, while the network remains operational through the secondary access point.

People often consider the service network as less secure and internal networks as more secure, but this is inaccurate. The internal network has a more restrictive protection method that severely limits access from the Internet. The service network has different requirements in that it needs to allow access from the Internet to certain services. Systems in the service network often have a higher degree of individual system security with a less restrictive protection method.

More care is often given to systems on the service network because of their increased exposure. In order to prevent compromise, an organization should maintain and patch the server software and operating system, protect them with strong filtering and access control policies, and monitor network traffic. In the ideal world, the same security considerations are given to all machines, regardless of their locations, but in practice, most organizations become more lax with the security of internal systems because of the other, broader security protection methods defined by the network architecture. The firewall used to protect the internal network is seen as the fool-proof defense mechanism. Equal focus should be placed on firewall policies such as access control and service restrictions, as well as system configuration and maintenance that keep the systems at their highest possible security levels.

The service network is a protective buffer zone for the company and is not the only intermediary network that might be needed by an organization. Many organizations partner with various other companies, provide support to customers, and share information between them. This function creates the need for an extranet in order to restrict access to sensitive information and resources from external users.

The *extranet* is a semiprivate network that shares data between the organization and its partners and customers. The information accessible on this network is often a subset of the information available on the corporate intranet, and requires explicit security measures to secure it. An extranet can be created by dedicating a piece of the network to these semiprivate servers and protecting them with a firewall. The access granted by the firewall should reflect the organizations that need it. Restricting access only to the networks and systems of the partner organizations instead of the entire Internet increases the security of the extranet.

Protecting the Castle

In this section, the discussion focuses on the architecture of the internal network. The security considerations for network design are applicable to all areas of network architecture, however.

Isolation and Separation

The idea of isolation and separation might seem contradictory to the concept of a network, where all things are connected, but the secure network architecture considers the relationship of each component and function to determine whether it needs to interact with the others. Separation of networks is the use of multiple physical and virtual networks to establish boundaries between unrelated network functions where no intercommunication is needed. It can also come in the form of physically disconnected networks, or virtually separate, wherein the devices do not allow network data to pass between them.

There are two levels to consider when dealing with isolation and separation. The organization of the packet or the low-level network data that travels electronically across the wire is the first level, and the organization of the systems that comprise the network is the second.

The relationships between users, groups of users, departments, and multiple locations within an organization require the network designer to consider the use of distinct networks in their network architecture. Some users might require access to the Internet without any other internal access, whereas others might need access to vital corporate information. The security of the network infrastructure becomes weak if these requirements are not assessed and if no distinction is made.

An organization often has several different and unrelated functions. A security risk is presented if these different groups are provided access to the networks and systems of the other. Publicly accessible terminals, for example, should not be on the same network as file, authentication, and email servers for the organization because that allows unauthorized individuals to access these systems.

Network Data

Network architecture does not focus only on the orientation of computer systems and their locations relative to each other, but also on the organization of network data. Security and performance are enhanced if consideration is given to the paths taken by packets. The topics discussed here are

- Networking concepts
- Segments
- Switches and hubs
- Routers
- Network numbers
- Physical considerations

Each of these topics has an important role in the security of a network architecture and should be examined prior to its design.

Networking Concepts   Before delving too far into the technical aspects of network data, it is important to further clarify the levels of networking that are discussed here. The term *network* refers to several facets of intercommunication between systems. The highest level of networking concerns the orientation of systems in relation to each other. The external and internal networks, service networks, extranets, and firewalls refer to the relationship of networked systems to each other.

Wading deeper into the technical details of networking, the next level is that of the protocol. Networks communicate via a number of different protocols. These protocols are independent of each other but often exist simultaneously. The most prominent of the protocols is the Internet Protocol (IP). Every system that interacts with the Internet uses IP. Each IP network is defined by a set of numbers that establish a range of values that can be assigned to systems. Routers are used to transfer information from one IP network to another. Although this discussion focuses on IP networks, other commonly recognized protocols include IPX/SPX, Systems Network Architecture (SNA), and NetBIOS.

An organization often has several different IP networks in use to isolate functional areas. The differentiation of IP networks has already been introduced with discussion of the service network and internal network. The internal network of an organization often consists of several networks, including a corporate network for all the users, management networks for network management of systems and devices, test networks to isolate laboratory systems, server networks, and even individual department networks. The need for all of these different functions requires consideration when designing the network. The decision to establish multiple networks in an organization is made by examining the function and organization of systems as well as the relationships they have with other systems in the organization, and determining which data sharing is acceptable.

The next area of networking discussed here is at the physical and electrical level. The wires and equipment used to create the network, their layout, and the factors used to determine the layout present a third area for consideration. The design of a secure network architecture examines all these components and determines the requirements and appropriate methods for their implementation.

Segments   Think of a segment as a single piece of wire, to which several computers can attach for network access. Each computer that attaches to a single segment can see all the network traffic on that segment, and shares the total bandwidth available for that segment. In the case of a 100Mbps network with several computers attached via a hub, they all share the available bandwidth. In the event that one of the machines is performing a network-intensive task, the availability of bandwidth for the other systems is diminished. Should a malicious person attack one of the systems on this segment and utilize the entire network bandwidth, denial of service occurs for every system on that segment. If a single system is compromised, it is possible for that individual to watch all the network traffic that is on that segment, identify the other systems, and proceed to compromise them. This includes communication between individual machines on that segment and any communication between one of these machines and other segments, networks, or the Internet.

Network segmentation is an important consideration when determining the relation and proximity of various systems. When designing a network architecture, it is important to understand the types of network data that will be traveling on the network. Web, file, and printer data are the commonly known information types that are first recognized.

Information such as user credentials, including usernames, passwords, encryption keys, and other private or sensitive information, such as financial data and company private information, also passes along the network segment, and poses even greater security threats. An attacker can view and steal sensitive information when care is not taken to define secure network segments. In the highest security environment, careful concern is given to the segmentation of systems. In the best-case scenario, user credentials and other sensitive information is not observable from any other system, and the electrical path taken by the data forms a direct line to the destination system.

Switches and Hubs   Network segmentation is affected by the network equipment chosen to provide service. Ethernet switches and hubs are two of the most common pieces of network equipment used in an organization. Along with Ethernet, some organizations use Asynchronous Transfer Mode (ATM) or Token Ring for their network interface type. Switches and hubs enable multiple systems to be connected to the same network. The difference is in the electrical methods by which this sharing occurs. All of the systems connected to a hub share the same segment. When data arrives on one port, the hub multiplexes the data to all of the other ports on that hub.

Network switches provide a higher level of security. Every port on a switch forms a separate segment from all other ports on that switch. When data arrives on one port, the switching technology determines to which port it needs to go, and switches it to that port instead of multiplexing it to all its ports. The only time a switch will multiplex data occurs when it receives a broadcast packet.

Broadcasts are special transmissions that have no particular machine as a destination. All systems see broadcasts and respond depending on their relation to the message. Broadcast storms occur under circumstances where one system sends an incorrect packet that causes all other systems to respond simultaneously, causing every system to again respond to those incorrect packets. This creates an endless cycle of broadcasts that saturates the network and causes a loss of service to the broadcast domain. Broadcast domains describe a single LAN or network wherein broadcast traffic propagates, and the desire to keep network traffic from permeating certain areas of the network or reaching particular machines should be examined.

Collisions are related to broadcasts. Whereas broadcasts occur at the IP layer of networking, collisions occur at the Ethernet layer. Collisions occur when two systems transmit network data simultaneously. All network transmissions occur as a series of electrical signals over the network wire. When two systems transmit data simultaneously, these signals collide, and the resulting signal and packet are corrupt. Collision domains are those areas wherein collisions are propagated, similarly to IP broadcasts. Hubs propagate collisions, but switches do not. Collisions also affect the performance of a network, so the use of Ethernet switches provides higher reliability.

By connecting a single system to each port on a switch, no system on the switch can view network traffic from another, unless they are communicating directly with each other. Careful thought during network architecture design allows for the creation of a well-organized and secure network. Using a switched network, it is feasible to ensure that each system has a direct electrical path to servers and important systems, thereby protecting it from eavesdropping. The benefit of a switched Ethernet is also weakened when a hub is connected to a switch, because it causes network traffic to be available to multiple systems. When attaching hubs to a switch in order to provide network access to more systems, the types of network traffic and the sensitivity of the information should be considered.

Routers   The use of routers at the network access point has been mentioned earlier in the discussion, but routers are not only useful at the edge of the network; they are used to create the separate networks and broadcast domains within an organization to form several internal networks isolated by function, data, or department. The equipment and management cost associated with routers versus network switches is higher, but in some cases a routed network makes more sense for the preferred architecture. Broadcast messages are transmitted across switches, but not across routers.

The use of routers is important to an organization for network isolation, as well as to add reliability. Routers enable the simultaneous use of multiple paths to a given destination and are capable of changing between them automatically in the event of failure. Routers often incorporate security measures akin to firewalls that allow restriction of network data types to and from its networks. Diversification, redundancy, and security of internal networks can be achieved at a higher degree with routers, at some expense to simplicity and ease of management and higher cost.

The configuration of the router is pivotal to the security of the network because an attacker can modify the path of network traffic via changes to the router. Detailed information on secure router configuration for Cisco routers (the most commonly used router products) can be found at "Improving Security on Cisco Routers," `http://www.cisco.com/warp/public/707/21.html`. You can also refer to Chapter 23.

Network Numbers   IP network numbers can be organized in many different ways, with various sizes. Consideration for the security of a network architecture when creating an IP network is useful to protect against rogue systems. A network is defined by a set of four numbers and an associated network mask. The network mask defines a network by carving out a range of numbers that are considered one network. All of the systems on a single network are configured with the same network mask, thereby ensuring that they can all communicate with each other. Subnetting is the method of dividing networks into small, arbitrarily sized chunks. In the early days of the Internet, networks were divided into several classes—A, B, C, and the special D/E classes of networks. These classes can accommodate different numbers of hosts:

- Class A: ~16 million hosts

- Class B: ~65 thousand hosts

- Class C: ~254 hosts

Network Classes D and E were specialized ranges of network addresses, reserved for multicast and experimental use. As the use of the Internet grew rapidly, these network ranges became impractical for organizations. Few organizations could utilize a complete Class A network, but might have had slightly more than could be accommodated in a Class B network; a similar effect occurs between Class B and Class C networks. The use of Variable Length Subnet Masking (VLSM) and Classless Inter-Domain Routing (CIDR) resolves the problem by allowing for the creation of small-sized networks and allowing for the dynamic routing of data between them. This is now the standard method by which ranges of IP addresses are given to companies by their ISP, and how traffic is routed to and from those networks.

These concepts are useful to an organization when creating a security-conscious network architecture. The temptation to implement large network classes is present because of their ease of use, but this is often not the best solution for security. The relationship between the network numbering and the organization of equipment needed to sustain it has an effect on the security of the network architecture. Large, flat networks where all the machines in an organization are on one network create several security risks. The effects of denial-of-service attacks via network data storms are widespread, affecting all the systems on the network. The network equipment required to maintain a flat network of this nature often results in many shared segments that can leave systems vulnerable to compromise. An attacker can easily add another machine to a flat network of this kind, because the capability to monitor and maintain a large network becomes difficult and unwieldy. This system can then be used to attack other systems, or to steal information as it travels over the network. Establishing a smaller-sized network is useful when determining which systems should be members of a single broadcast domain. You should take care to ensure that the network is not defined so small as to limit its scalability. As noted, the definition of network ranges should consider the ability of users and intruders to incorporate foreign network equipment into the environment.

The introduction of foreign computers and network equipment into the environment can adversely affect the network. Common cases of this occur when users initialize new systems and mistakenly configure them with an IP address that is already in use, or incorrectly configure the network address for the system. Two systems attempting to use the same IP address will attempt to fight for that address; this causes network confusion in the network equipment, and the loss of service or unreliable service for those machines. This is especially dangerous if the system attempts to use the IP address of an important system, such as the gateway or server, because all systems on the network will then flood the badly configured system and lose connectivity to the intended server or network. Attackers can use this tactic to assume the identity of a specific system, such as an email server or authentication server. Spoofing these servers by assuming their addresses and identities causes other systems to unwittingly transmit information to the falsified computer. The attacker can then gather information that enables her to compromise other systems.

A badly configured network address also causes an inability to communicate with other systems on the network, and results in abnormal network performance. Tightly controlled network addresses and subnet definitions help defend against these negative effects. The security of a network architecture is enhanced by defining and organizing networks based on their relationship and function to each other. Desktop computers often exist on the same IP network, using different physical segments to communicate with servers and gateways. This minimizes the capability of an attacker to compromise the servers, and limits the zone of vulnerability to desktop computers with limited privilege. Servers can be placed on different networks with higher bandwidth capacities in order to serve multiple clients without performance degradation. This is also useful to serve multiple networks that do not need to/should not communicate with each other, such as customer and internal networks. The separation by function also limits the effects of misuse and malfunction. The previous example of a user system misconfigured as the gateway would not affect the entire organization in a diversified network environment.

Other technologies that have increased the flexibility and security of internal networks are Network Address Translation (NAT) and proxy servers. This functionality allows greater control and restriction of network traffic and the protection of internal systems. With NAT, the network addresses of the internal network remain hidden, while still providing access to external resources. The router or firewall that performs NAT translates all of the network traffic that passes outward, so it appears to originate from that firewall or router. This is a useful capability because it obscures the layout of the internal network, as the external systems see network data arriving from the firewall only.

Attacks directed toward internal servers are then made more difficult, because NAT also protects the internal network. Unless configured explicitly to redirect incoming network data to a system on the internal network, a NAT device will only allow the return traffic for an internal system to pass. NAT also has the added benefit of allowing for the creation of new networks without acquiring new IP address ranges from the ISP.

A common example of Network Address Translation use for security occurs when an internal network is configured with a "reserved" set of IP addresses. The so-called RFC Networks are specified as private and internal networks that can be used by any organization simultaneously because there are no routes to them from the Internet backbone.

NOTE

See RFC 1597, "Address Allocation for Private Internets," at `http://www.ietf.org/rfc/rfc1597.txt?number=1597` for more information.

In this case, the internal network is a private network, and NAT is used to make all traffic appear to come from the NAT device—the firewall or router. The attacker can only scan and probe the NAT device, and has little or no information about the topology of the internal network and its systems. Consequently, the attacker cannot target specific systems, making compromise more difficult. The potential for denial of service does exist, though, because an attacker can target the NAT device if it is the single ingress and egress point for the network.

Proxy servers provide a similar functionality to NAT, but without any packet data modification. They obscure the internal network and system topology, and allow restrictive filtering rules to be applied. A proxy establishes a single system, or set of systems, that acts as the point of contact for a particular service. For example, a Web proxy server is the contact point for all internal Web-surfing users. The users' Web browser software is configured to point at the proxy server. Instead of contacting the remote Web server for a particular site, the Web browser sends the request to the proxy server, which then retrieves the appropriate Web content and passes it back to the requesting browser. The use of proxy servers allows a more restricted and controlled set of filter rules to be established on the firewall because all Web traffic to and from the Internet focuses on a single machine, the proxy server, instead of many different user systems. It also affords internal systems some protection against malicious content, such as viruses, because it can be filtered and analyzed by the proxy server before transmission to the requesting system.

Physical Considerations   The physical wiring used to create the network also requires consideration for security. As with most technology, there are several ways of obtaining a single result. Networking is no different, and the selection of cable types and implementation affects the security, reliability, and performance of a network. Twisted-pair telephone-style cable is the most commonly used in the networks of today. The use of twisted-pair cable forces a star topology for the network. A star has a center point with several tines protruding from it. Each individual cable forms a separate network segment that can be combined into a larger segment only via a hub. When connected to an Ethernet switch, the connection between the computer and the switch forms a single, private segment. Only one computer at a time is connected to the switch via twisted-pair cables. Other, older cable types are still in use today, including coaxial cable, often called thin-net. Coaxial cable allows for a less expensive network, but also a network with less bandwidth. This network cable is shared by several or many systems at one time, and forms a single segment on which each computer can see the traffic of the others.

When evaluating the cable type used for an organization, most designers will standardize on twisted-pair cabling. It is important to understand the benefit to security that is gained from the physical wiring, and to know that its inherent security benefits can be nullified with a poor network architecture. The privacy provided by a single segment can be done away with by the use of hubs that multiplex network traffic. In turn, the use of Ethernet switches does not guarantee privacy of the data if their use is not consistent and well-organized throughout the organization.

Along with the cable type, the location and organization of equipment also plays an important role in the security of a network architecture. As outlined in the discussion of threats to a network, physical disruption produces more difficult, expensive, and widespread effects on network service. Organizations need to consider the placement of vital network equipment and systems, including routers, access devices, firewalls, and servers. These important components should be physically secured from access by unauthorized individuals. Networking closets are often used for cable termination points and are also securely locked. A malicious user or unauthorized intruder should be prevented from modifying the network topology and adding a system to the network for the purposes of eavesdropping. Organizations that have large networks and multiple locations also build distributed redundancy into their network architecture. The ability to secure the network and systems is the most basic need for a secure network architecture. The flexibility and resilience of a network in the face of incidents provides the high level of security that separates adequate functionality from the robustness of a strong network.

Network Separation

Separation of networks often comes in the form of specialized network functionality, such as network management, monitoring, and remote access. Access to these functions might merit separation from the remainder of the network infrastructure. Different broadcast domains and network numbers communicate among each other via routers and by adding extra network interfaces to servers and network equipment.

Network Management

Network management refers to the control, configuration, and maintenance of the network hardware used throughout an organization. Many of these devices provide network, terminal, and Web browser-based access to administer and configure them. It is advisable to disallow the capability to manage these devices from the Internet and other in-band networks. *In-band* network management occurs when the administrators connect to the device over one of the networks that the device services. In-band management of a router, for example, occurs when the administrator connects to it from the Internet over the external interface, or from the internal network over the internal interface. Remote management of a router that ties the Internet to a service network or internal network should not be allowed from the Internet. Although outsiders cannot access the router directly from the Internet, they can access it from an Internet-accessible system in the service network. Compromise of a service network-based system provides the attacker with access to the network equipment. If possible, it is best to establish a management network on a third network interface, and to restrict management access to the router from only that special network.

A management network is often a separate physical connection to the devices and on which there are only a handful of dedicated management stations. No other network should have connectivity to the management network, unless controlled through a single, high-security system; access otherwise occurs by physical presence at one of the management stations. The use of a management network severely limits the capability of an attacker to access important systems and equipment, which decreases the risk of compromise.

Monitoring

Network monitoring is a useful function that aids in the security of a network by debugging problems and maintaining performance. The separation of network data might hinder the capability to monitor sections of the network. Therefore, it is important to consider what monitoring should be used and where, and to incorporate the required changes or equipment into the network architecture.

Several methods of network monitoring should be considered, as well as their placement in the design of the network. Intrusion detection is a relatively new innovation that is proving useful in the network. These intrusion detection systems (IDSs) are placed throughout the network, and actively monitor for known signs of attack. The placement of an IDS is often useful at network access points, including the service network, near the inside and outside of firewalls, remote access devices including VPNs and dial-in servers, and near key systems.

Firewalls also act as a form of monitoring for a network. Their role is more active, in that they manipulate network traffic by allowing or disallowing information to pass through. The effects of many attacks can be limited by regular and frequent analysis of these monitoring methods, including log analysis and configuration of the equipment to notify administrators in the event of an attack condition. An IDS can also be used to validate that a firewall is working properly.

Other considerations for monitoring include the capability for administrators to monitor network traffic and analyze it for insecurities as part of the regular maintenance. The network and its implementation affect the capability to monitor traffic in this way. Network equipment often supports monitoring with SNMP and RMON, two standardized protocols used for this purpose. A final method of network monitoring is via complex network management software suites. These packages use a number of different protocols and methods to acquire and analyze information and provide fast alert and responses to anomalous conditions. These tools often use special agents that run in conjunction with the systems and equipment being monitored; these packages are not affected by the physical orientation of the network, however.

Remote Access

If remote access methods are needed in the organization, the methods to provide it should be considered during the creation of the network architecture. Two methods are commonly used: VPN solutions and dial-in modem access. VPN solutions come in two forms—the hardware device and software application. The hardware VPN device provides several benefits; it is a specialized device that often provides a high level of performance and incorporates its own security methods. The software VPN solution runs as an application or service on existing server systems and often relies on the security mechanisms of its respective operating system.

The effects on the network architecture required to support a VPN are similar for each solution. VPN devices can be more easily integrated in a secure manner into the network environment because the access to and control of the device are more easily dictated. The software service requires more attention. To achieve the highest security, the VPN software should run on a dedicated server and be treated as a device with no other services present. The operating system should be configured in a secure manner, and no other internally used services should be run on the system in order to prevent access to the internal network. Software VPN solutions are affected by the vulnerabilities of the operating system as well as any insecurities in the software.

Dial-in support via modems and access servers provides a direct connection to the internal network. The considerations for dial-in methods include the use of a management network to control the device to protect it from unauthorized configuration changes. The dial-in server often relies on other servers on the network to provide authentication of its users. The network path used for authentication should also be private. Finally, dial-in servers should disallow remote networks to route traffic across their dial-in lines. Attackers will often use "war dialing" software to scan phone numbers for dial-in servers. Although the scanning cannot be prevented, the proper organization and configuration of dial-in equipment will limit the risk of compromise.

There are several considerations given to the placement of VPN and dial-in systems in order to protect the internal network. When defining the network architecture, the designers should identify the functionality supported and provided by the remote access. VPNs can provide transparent access to all the resources of a network, enabling the remote system to appear and function as it would if it were physically located at the organization. Dial-in access, unless combined with a VPN solution, is often used to provide more limited services such as email and Web access. Despite the differences in methods, both supply the same basic functionality—access from remote, distrusted networks and locations. Therefore, it is advisable to place remote access servers on a separate network and to control access to the facilities that it uses. The previously mentioned management network should also be used to control and configure these systems.

The placement of remote access equipment follows the same logic used for other network equipment: the limitation of the effects should an attack occur. Attackers will attempt to find the targets that provide them with the most access to other systems and equipment. Remote access devices are easily identifiable targets and should be protected adequately.

Network Isolation

Network isolation is a slightly different concept than separation. Isolation of networks affects the flow of network data, which services run on particular systems, and where they are located. It does not affect any of the internal or external network data from traveling across those same paths. Isolation is often used to enhance the security and efficiency of the network by isolating certain network traffic to certain physical wires and networks. Network isolation is achieved with the use of multiple physical and virtual networks within a single organization to separate functionality. Network designers can enhance security by organizing the network into its functional areas and considering the impact that each of these functions has on security.

One example of network isolation is to design the network so that the credentials of remote access users do not travel across any network wires or circuits that are exposed to users or other systems. The simplest method to provide this security is to connect the remote access server directly to the authentication server with a single cable. Another method is to use a switched network topology, keeping the authentication server and remote access device on their own private segments. The data sent from one to the other will then travel between only the two systems and their segments, where no other system can view it.

Isolation is discussed in the following contexts:

- Service differentiation

- VLANS

- Firewalls

The first and most obvious concept is the isolation of external from internal network traffic. Service differentiation is the identification and categorization of network services. The network services provided by an organization can be categorized as external-only, internal-only, or bridge services. As the name implies, external- and internal-only services provide functionality to either the external or internal network, but not both. Bridge services provide functionality to both the internal network and the external network. External services should be isolated in a service network, or hosted by the ISP for the organization. Also, the management of these services should occur via the previously mentioned management network. Internal services should be protected from external Internet and service network access.

It is considered dangerous to attach systems and equipment directly to the Internet without some form of protection, so be sure to protect service networks with protection mechanisms, such as a firewall.

The simplest network topology takes a router and connects one interface to the ISP and the other to a multiplexing device, such as a hub. All of the internal systems are then connected to the hub. Without getting into the details of network numbering, this is effective to provide Internet access to all the internal systems in the organization, but it also enables all systems on the Internet to communicate directly with each system on the internal network. Each system is susceptible to attack, and the entire computing infrastructure could be compromised.

The requirement for Internet access should be categorized into outgoing and incoming access. Outgoing access refers to the most common concept of Internet access—the capability to communicate with Web servers, send email, and download files. Most systems require outbound Internet access, but typically need securing from arbitrary inbound Internet traffic. All network communication and protocol details aside, the capability to perform these actions does not require internal systems to provide access to those on the Internet. When defining a network architecture, it is important to identify the services and systems that do require access initiated by Internet-based systems. The security considerations for the network architecture now take a basic shape as three organizational classes of network—the external, the intermediary, and the internal network.

Services Differentiation

The computing services provided by an organization form the basis of the network. Aside from the configuration and security methods used to protect the individual servers and operating systems, isolation of the network services is an important security tactic, because it protects from attack and restricts the effects of an attack. The services are those features that the users require and are provided by computers and network equipment. Common services include the following:

- Domain Name System (DNS)
- Email
- Web serving
- File sharing
- Printing
- Network login
- Directory services

DNS   The Domain Name System servers in an organization often serve the internal users as well as the external Internet. The application that provides DNS services has a history of vulnerabilities (as you will see in Chapter 21, "Unix") that have allowed attackers to compromise the system on which it runs and to corrupt its records. Given this history, careful attention to security is required. If the organization maintains its own DNS server, it is often best suited for the service network in order to protect the internal network from adverse effects of attack.

As part of the network architecture, security is also bolstered by redundancy. The use of multiple DNS servers provides a level of reliability in the event of failure or attack on one, and the placement of these merits consideration in the network architecture. Multiple DNS servers should not be placed on the same network; the purpose of redundancy is to provide a high level of reliability in the event of the failure of one network. If both DNS servers are located on the same network or on a single service network, they can both be taken out of service by a single attack. The ideal solution is to locate redundant DNS servers on separate networks that have differing paths to them. This prevents attackers from disabling all domain name services without a complex attack method. DNS servers should be protected by a firewall, and primary servers should be configured with access control restrictions that disallow arbitrary queries and DNS zone transfers to unknown servers.

The separation of DNS usage also requires consideration. Many organizations use a single DNS server, with or without redundancy, to answer both internal and external queries. This means that the Internet-based systems have access to the name server, as well as the internal systems. This bridging of the internal and external networks might present a high security risk if the name server is compromised. Another security risk when using a common name server is the revelation of information. The common DNS server stores all the name and network information for both internally and externally accessible systems. An attacker can glean this information from the server, arrive at a reasonable idea of the internal network architecture, and identify potential target systems.

One solution to these problems is a split-DNS topology, which creates two distinct name servers—one for systems on the internal network, and one for those on the Internet to use. The records in each are then updated independently, and external systems have no access to information about internally networked systems. The attacker no longer has a potential bridge between the internal and external networks, and the effects of the attack are limited.

TIP

For further information about securing specific DNS servers, see "Securing Domain Name Service" at http://www.jasakom.com/Artikel.asp?ID=111.

Email   Email is one of the most important network services to an organization, and the establishment of email services in the network architecture requires careful planning. It is inadvisable to support email with a single mail server. Mail servers often store the contents of users' mailboxes, including private and confidential company information. A single point of failure is present when using only one server. It is equally dangerous to provide access to the primary mail server from the Internet, because an attacker might expose or have access to its private information. One solution is to establish mail relays at different locations on the network, and then allow access to the primary mail server only from those relay systems. The mail relays are often located on the service network and further away at the ISP to provide several levels of redundancy in the event of attack or connectivity issues with the organization.

If an attacker succeeds in compromising the primary mail server, he can then access many other sensitive resources of the organization. The use of a mail relay defends the primary mail server and limits the effects of the attack. The mail relay can and should be protected with strong filtering rules on the firewall, and the primary mail server should also be strictly access-controlled to allow inbound mail only from the relay servers. It is also possible to do virus filtering on the mail relay as well.

TIP

The best archive of email security articles on the Internet is available from the SANS (System Administration, Network, and Security) Institute at `http://rr.sans.org/email/email_list.php`.

Web Serving   Many companies have a corporate Web site that provides the virtual storefront to the Internet, as well as an *intranet*, or an internally located Web site that contains private company information. The corporate and internal Web sites should be hosted on separate machines, to isolate the information accessible by Internet users from information available to employees. The network location of corporate Web sites should be determined based on how much traffic the site sees. An extremely popular Web site located on the service network with other network services such as mail relays and DNS servers might put those servers at risk in the event of a denial-of-service attack. The entire bandwidth can be consumed, rendering the other services unusable. The careful placement of redundant and distributed Web servers helps minimize the risks associated with this service. Web sites can be located on remote servers hosted by the ISP, or Web traffic can be load-balanced among several servers placed in close proximity to each other, or even in remote areas.

TIP

Further useful information to secure your Web server can be found in "Securing Public Web Servers" at http://www.cert.org/security-improvement/modules/m11.html.

File and Printer Sharing   File sharing is a staple of network life that is utilized at a majority of organizations. It is also one of the more common insecurities found on a network. The network architecture that supports security and services that hold potential risks does so by carefully controlling the network access to the file servers. When sharing filesystems among multiple systems on the internal networks, access should not be available to the extranets, service network, or Internet. File and printer sharing should never be allowed from unknown or external systems.

TIP

A useful article on the topic of securing multiple network server types can be found in "Securing Network Servers" at http://www.cert.org/security-improvement/modules/m07.html.

Network Login   Network logins are the methods used by users to authenticate to a remote or local system. This includes interactive access to Unix accounts, Windows Domain authentication, authentication to Web sites, and any other service that requires user credentials for access. There are many methods for network login, many of which are very insecure. The insecurities of network logins come from the use of cleartext authentication methods, wherein the user credentials are transmitted over the network without any encryption or other data obfuscation.

Security considerations for a network design include the isolation of traffic that carries credentials to minimize the opportunity for eavesdropping, and the use of VPN systems to provide encrypted communication that protects the credentials during transit. Other protection mechanisms include firewall rules to disallow the protocols that are known to function insecurely from passing the boundary of the internal networks.

Telnet, remote shells, and FTP are commonly used services whose traffic should not be allowed outside of the internal network, if used at all. These services transmit user credentials without any form of encryption, allowing an attacker to eavesdrop and intercept the information. SSH (Secure Shell, http://www.openssh.org) allows an encrypted network login. It is not without its own risks, but is much more secure than the unencrypted alternatives.

Directory Services   Over the past few years, directory servers have become increasingly popular as a place to store information about people, such as their phone number or their password. The most popular directory server systems are all based on LDAP (Lightweight Directory Access Protocol). The most popular types of LDAP-based servers are Sun ONE Directory Server (`http://wwws.sun.com/software/products/directory_srvr/home_directory.html`), Microsoft's Active Directory (`http://www.microsoft.com/windows2000/technologies/directory/ad/default.asp`), and Novell eDirectory (`http://www.novell.com/products/nds/`).

> **NOTE**
>
> Sun ONE Directory Server was formerly known as the iPlanet Directory Server and the Netscape Directory Server. Novell eDirectory was formerly known as NDS (Novell Directory Services).

These directory servers typically enable both unencrypted or encrypted authentication. Unencrypted authentication allows crackers to sniff the authentication packets and steal account passwords. Therefore, whenever feasible, directory servers should use encrypted authentication, which is usually performed by SSL. If encryption is not possible, it is recommended to keep the authentication traffic on a physically separate network.

Virtual Local Area Networks

The use of Virtual Local Area Networks (VLANs) is a relatively new approach to network topology that arose with the development of new network equipment. VLANs provide an alternative to the normal routed and switched network topology by simplifying diverse networks through more intelligent hardware. The VLAN allows groups of systems on different physical networks and segments to communicate seamlessly without the need for a router. One of the drawbacks of routed and switched networks is that the physical location of systems often dictates their presence on a particular network. For example, putting two systems that are physically in the same room onto two different networks requires that the network cables terminate at two different places, one at each network access point. If the network equipment is not physically located in the same area, this becomes quite unmanageable. VLANs allow for this capability and do so transparently.

The use of VLAN technology also has security considerations that might encourage their use. The nature of virtual and dynamically specified networks allows for fine-grained tuning of network traffic. The ability to shape the flow of network traffic is the ability to control it, which provides very flexible security capabilities that make it more difficult for network eavesdropping, and provide for more easily thwarted denial-of-service attempts. It is important to note that part of the benefit of VLAN technology comes from its manageability. Administrators can more easily monitor network information, gather statistical information, and notice and resolve anomalous conditions.

Firewalls

The use of firewalls in a network architecture is generally seen as a requirement for any organization that has Internet access. As you learned in Chapter 10, firewalls are useful tools, and their use in the network architecture provides greater security. As mentioned earlier, firewalls are often used to protect internal networks from access by unauthorized Internet-based systems. They can also be used to protect service networks and extranets. The use of firewalls is not a guaranteed preventative method, however. When designing a network, it is important to determine the restrictions needed for the organization, and where the firewall is most beneficial. Multiple firewalls are often used to protect network access points, and specialized networks throughout the infrastructure.

Firewalls come in several different forms, including dedicated firewall appliances, software-based firewall suites, and as a built-in functionality of network equipment. When considering security for a network architecture, it is often useful to use more than one of these methods. Routers are useful for the application of generic filtering rules, such as disallowing access to particular port numbers or services. Hardware and software firewalls can then work in conjunction with the routers to perform more fine-grained filtering based on more granular details, such as protocol flags and options.

Summary

The keys to establishing a strong and secure network architecture are to identify the features and functionality needed by the organization, to understand the relative security risks, and to make decisions about their implementation based on this knowledge. When designing the network, identify the parties who use it, their purposes for using it, and their requirements for effective work and functionality. Create a balance between security and functionality in order to arrive at a network architecture that is both secure and usable. When these aspects of network design are considered, along with the technical details presented here, you'll have a network architecture that is secure, strong, and flexible.

20

Microsoft

In earlier years, Microsoft products earned a reputation for poor security. Windows NT introduced a breakthrough in security for the Microsoft platform. Microsoft made great strides toward securing its platform with the introduction of Windows 2000, which Microsoft released in 2000. Windows 2000 ushered in even greater security with services such as Active Directory, Public Key Infrastructure (PKI), and Kerberos. Microsoft continued to improve the platform security with the release of Windows XP in 2001. Windows XP includes additional security capabilities and fixes in addition to all the Windows 2000 security features. Because the Windows 2000 and Windows XP operating systems offer the benefits of greater security and control, it would be in the best interest of your company to select at minimum Windows 2000 as your standard operating system. Microsoft officials have made their message clear: They have no intention of rewriting the security controls on Microsoft Windows for Workgroups, 95, 98, or Me.

Knowing this, I briefly discuss Windows 9x and Windows Me. To that end, this chapter begins with the minimum information necessary to break a non-Windows NT box.

Windows 9x and Windows Me

Windows 9x and Windows Me were never meant to have robust security features, and to be honest, never offered much more security than the original DOS operating system. Both Windows 9x and Windows Me use the FAT file system, which does not offer any file level security. Also, both rely on the PWL password file scheme, which is not secured and easily accessed. PWL files are generated when you create your password. By default, PWL files are housed in the directory C:\WINDOWS. However, you might want to check the SYSTEM.INI file for other locations. (SYSTEM.INI is where the PWL path is specified.)

The Password List Password Scheme

The PWL password scheme is not secure and can be defeated simply by deleting the files.

NOTE

If the cracker wants to avoid leaving evidence of his intrusion, he probably won't delete the PWL files. Instead, he will reboot, interrupt the load to Windows (by pressing F5 or F8), and edit the SYSTEM.INI file. There, he will change the pointer from the default location (C:\WINDOWS) to a temporary directory. In that temporary directory, he will insert another PWL file to which he already knows the password. He will then reboot again and log in. After he has done his work, he will re-edit the SYSTEM.INI, putting things back to normal.

In more complex cracking schemes, the attacker might actually need the password (for example, when the cracker is using a local Windows 95 box to authenticate to and crack a remote Windows NT 4.0 server). In such environments, the cracker has two choices: He can either crack the 95 PWL password file or flush the password out of cached memory while the target is still logged in. Both techniques are briefly discussed here.

Cracking PWL Files

Cracking standard PWL files generated on the average Windows 95 box is easy. For this, you need a utility called Glide.

Glide   Glide cracks PWL files. It comes with source code for those interested in examining it. To use Glide, enter the filename (PWL) and the username associated with it. Glide is quite effective and can be found online at the following location:

http://morehouse.org/hin/blckcrwl/hack/glide.zip

NOTE

To make your PWL passwords secure, you should install third-party access control software. However, if you are forced to rely on PWL password protection, you can still better your chances. Glide will not crack PWL password files that were generated on any box with Windows 95 Service Pack 1 or later installed. You should install, at a minimum, the latest service packs.

Flushing the Password Out of Cached Memory

Two different functions are used in the PWL system: one to encrypt and store the password and another to retrieve it. Those routines are as follows:

- WNetCachePassword()

- WNetGetCachedPassword()

The password remains cached. You can write a routine in Visual C++ or Visual Basic (VB) that will get another user's password; the only restriction is that the targeted user must be logged in when the program is executed (so the password can be trapped). The password can then be cached out to another area of memory. Having accomplished this, you can bypass the password security scheme by using that cached version of the password. (This technique is called *cache flushing*. It relies on the same principle as using a debugger to expose authentication schemes in client software.)

You can also force the cached password into the swap file. However, this is a cumbersome and wasteful method; there are other, easier ways to do it.

TIP

One method is to hammer the password database with multiple entries at high speed. You can use a utility such as Claymore for this, which you can download at `http://www.system7.org/archive/Passwd-Cracking/windows.html`. You fill the available password space by using this technique. This causes an overflow, and the routine then discards older passwords. However, this technique leaves ample evidence behind.

Either way, the PWL system is inherently flawed and provides very little protection against intrusion. If you are using Windows 9x or Windows Me, you need to install third-party access control. This chapter provides a list of such products and their manufacturers in the "Access Control Software" section later in this chapter. Not all products have a version for Windows Me. Check with the manufacturers for availability.

Summary on Windows 9x and Windows Me

Windows 9x and Windows Me were both excellent operating systems for their time. However, none of them are secure, and with the release of Windows XP replacing them, it is foolish in today's security threat environment to continue using them. If your firm uses these operating systems at all, the boxes that run them should be hidden behind a firewall. This is especially so with Windows Me because it has received little scrutiny due to it being specifically marketed as only a home user operating system. It might contain many vulnerabilities that have yet to be revealed.

With that settled, let's examine the Windows NT security features, which were initially introduced with the Windows NT operating system and were further enhanced with the introduction of the Windows 2000 and Windows XP operating systems.

Windows NT

Microsoft might be traditionally known for poor security, but not when it comes to Windows NT 4.0. Out of the box, Windows NT 4.0 has security measures as good as most other server platforms. The catch is that you must keep up with recent developments. Most of the security attacks that have been reported against Windows NT systems could have been prevented if the system had been running the current service pack release. If you have a connection to the Internet, you should consider subscribing to Windows Update so that it will automatically notify you about new service packs/updates.

Before you read any further, ask yourself this: Have I installed Windows NT 4.0 using NT File System (NTFS) and installed the service packs in their proper order? If not, your Windows NT 4.0 system is not secure and the rest of this chapter cannot help you. If you have not installed your system in this manner, go back, reinstall the service packs, and install with NTFS enabled.

> **NOTE**
>
> One would think that the order in which service packs are installed doesn't matter. Unfortunately, that is simply not true. There have been documented instances of users installing service packs in disparate order only to encounter trouble later. I recommend keeping a running record of when the packs were installed and any problems you encounter during installation. An important thing to remember when applying service packs is to always back up your system prior to installation.

General Windows NT Security Vulnerabilities

Windows NT, like most operating systems, has vulnerabilities. Please note that the list of vulnerabilities discussed here is not exhaustive—other vulnerabilities of lesser severity exist.

The Netmon Protocol Parsing Vulnerability

Windows NT Version: All versions

Impact: An attacker can gain control of your server.

Class: Critical

Fixes for Windows NT 4.0 Server and NT 4.0 Server, Enterprise Edition can be found at http://www.microsoft.com/Downloads/Release.asp?ReleaseID=25487.

As of this writing, no fix exists for Windows NT 4.0 Server, Terminal Server Edition.

Additional Information: http://www.microsoft.com/technet/security/bulletin/MS00-083.asp. The fix for this vulnerability will be included in Service Pack 7.

Credit: COVERT Labs at PGP Security, Inc., and the ISS X-force

NOTE

According to `http://www.microsoft.com/ntserver/ProductInfo/terminal/default.asp`, Microsoft discontinued NT Terminal Server Edition in August 2000, so there is little hope that this problem will be resolved for this platform.

Several protocol parsers in Netmon have unchecked buffers. When an attacker sends a malformed frame to a server that is monitoring network traffic, and if the administrator is using a protocol parser with unchecked buffers, the malformed frame either causes Netmon to fail or causes code of the attacker's choice to run on the server. If you are running Netmon under a local administrator's account, the attacker can gain complete control over the server, but not over the domain. However, if you are running Netmon under a domain administrator's account, the attacker might be able to gain control over the domain as well.

The Predictable LPC Message Identifier Vulnerability

Windows NT Version: All versions

Impact: A local intruder can impersonate your privileges, eavesdrop on your session, or cause your server or workstation to fail.

Class: Critical—denial of service

Fix:
`http://www.microsoft.com/ntserver/nts/downloads/critical/q266433/default.asp`. The fix for this vulnerability will be included in Service Pack 7.

Additional Information: `http://www.microsoft.com/technet/security/bulletin/ms00-070.asp`

Credit: BindView's Razor Team

An intruder can only exploit this vulnerability locally. The intruder causes a denial-of-service attack on either a client or server box by sending large packets of random data to it. If the intruder identifies a system process that has an existing Link Control Protocol (LCP) connection with a privileged thread, she can then spoof the client and make requests that she wouldn't ordinarily be able to perform. The amount of damage she can perform depends on which processes are running in the thread and what they permit her to do. The intruder can also eavesdrop on your session and potentially gather privileged information.

The Registry Permissions Vulnerability

Windows NT Version: All versions

Impact: Default permissions on certain Registry values can allow an attacker to gain additional privileges on a box.

Class: Moderate to severe

Fix: `http://www.microsoft.com/Downloads/Release.asp?ReleaseID=24501`. The Terminal Server Edition doesn't have a fix at the time of this writing.

Additional Information: `http://www.microsoft.com/technet/security/bulletin/MS00-095.asp`

Credit: Chris Anley, Milan Dadok, and Glenn Larsson

The SNMP Parameters key, RAS Administration key, and MTS Package Administration key all have inappropriately loose default permissions. This vulnerability could enable an attacker to manage or configure devices on the network, such as misconfiguring routers and firewalls and starting or stopping services on a machine.

The Remote Registry Access Authentication Vulnerability

Windows NT Version: All versions

Impact: Remote users can cause a Windows NT 4.0 box to fail

Class: Critical—denial of service

Fix for Windows NT 4.0 Workstation, Server, and Enterprise Server Edition: `http://www.microsoft.com/Downloads/Release.asp?ReleaseID=23077`. At the time of this writing, there is no fix available for the Terminal Server Edition.

Additional Information: `http://www.microsoft.com/technet/security/bulletin/ms00-040.asp`

Credit: Renaud Deraison

When an attacker sends a malformed request for remote Registry access, the request can cause the Winlogon process to fail, which in turn can cause the entire system to fail.

The Winsock Mutex Vulnerability

Windows NT Version: All versions

Impact: A local user can cause a box to stop responding to network traffic.

Class: Moderate—denial of service

Fix for Windows NT 4.0:
`http://www.microsoft.com/Downloads/Release.asp?ReleaseID=27272`

Fix for Windows NT 4.0 Terminal Server:
`http://www.microsoft.com/Downloads/Release.asp?ReleaseID=27291`

Additional Information: `http://www.microsoft.com/technet/security/bulletin/MS01-003.asp`

Credit: Arne Vidstrom

Inappropriate permissions assigned to a networking mutex can permit an intruder to run code to gain control of the mutex and then deny access to it. Doing this prevents other processes from being able to perform network operations with the machine.

Other Important Vulnerabilities of Lesser Significance

Windows NT is also vulnerable to a wide range of other things, which might not be absolutely critical but are serious nonetheless. Table 20.1 lists these problems, along with URLs where you can learn more.

TABLE 20.1   Other Important Windows NT Vulnerabilities

Vulnerability	Facts and URL
Out of Band	Out-of-band (OOB) attacks are denial-of-service attacks with a vengeance. Many platforms are susceptible to OOB attacks, including Windows NT 3.51 and Windows NT 4.0. The fix for Microsoft is available at the following site: `ftp://ftp.microsoft.com/bussys/winnt/winnt-public/fixes/usa/NT351/hotfixes-postSP5/oob-fix/`.
Port 1031	If a cracker telnets to port 1031 of your server and issues garbage, this will blow your server off the Net. This exploits a vulnerability in the file `INETINFO.EXE`. Check with Microsoft for recent patches.
NTCrash	A powerful denial-of-service utility called NTCrash can bring a Windows NT server to its knees. Source code is available on the Net at `http://packetstorm.decepticons.org/Exploit_Code_Archive/ntcrash.server.dos.zip`. Test it and see what happens.

Internal Windows NT Security

The majority of this chapter focuses on *remote security*, in which the attackers are on foreign networks. Unfortunately, foreign networks are not always the source of the attack. Sometimes, your very own users attack your server. That is what the next section is all about.

Internal Security in General

In general, Windows NT has only fair-to-good local security. This is in contrast to its external security, which I believe is very good (providing you stay current with the latest patches). At a bare minimum, you must use NTFS. If you don't, there is no point in even hoping to secure your boxes. Here's why: There are just too many things that local users can do and too many files and services they can use.

Some system administrators argue that they don't need NTFS. Instead, they argue that between policy and careful administration and control of who accesses their machines, they can maintain a more or less tight ship. They are dreaming.

The RDISK Hole

A perfect example is the RDISK hole. RDISK is a Windows NT utility that allows you to create emergency repair disks. This is a valuable utility for a system administrator. However, when it's accessible to the wrong person, RDISK is an enormous security hole. Here's why: A user can instruct RDISK to dump all security information (including passwords and Registry information) into the directory `C:\WINNT\REPAIR`. From there, an attacker can load a password cracker, and within hours, the box is completely compromised. This is just one more reason you should not walk away from your computer and leave it logged on. Would you like to try it yourself? Issue this command at a prompt: `rdisk /s`. Then go to the directory `C:\WINNT\REPAIR`, where you will find the necessary information you need to crack the box.

Achieving Good Internal Security

Achieving good internal security is not an end. There is no list of tools you can install that will permanently secure your box. New holes always crop up. Also, although Microsoft has done wonders to improve the security of Windows NT, pervading user-friendliness in its products continues to hamper efforts at serious security.

An amusing example of this was described by Vacuum from Rhino9 (a prominent hacker group), who made the observation that restricting user access to the Control Panel was a fruitless effort:

> If you do not have access to the Control Panel from Start/Settings/Control Panel or from the My Computer Icon, click Start/Help/Index. All of the normally displayed icons appear as help topics. If you click on "Network," for example, a Windows NT Help Screen appears with a nice little shortcut to the Control Panel Network Settings.

The problem sounds simple and not very threatening. However, the rule holds true for most system resources and even administrative tools. (Microsoft probably won't change it, either. Its defense would probably be this: It enhances user-friendliness to provide a link to any program discussed in Help.)

At a bare minimum, you should install logging utilities and a sniffer. I also recommend making a comprehensive list of all applications or resources that have no logging. If these applications and resources have no native logging (and also cannot be logged using other applications), I recommend deleting them, placing access restrictions on them, or (at a minimum) removing them from their default locations.

A Tip on Setting Up a Secure Windows NT Server from Scratch

To effectively erect a secure Windows NT server, you must start at installation time. To ascertain whether you should reinstall, you should measure your original installation procedure against typical preparations for a C2 system. To do that, I recommend downloading the *Secure Windows NT Installation and Configuration Guide*, which was authored by the Department of the Navy Space and Naval Warfare Systems Command Naval Information Systems Security Office. That document contains the most comprehensive secure installation procedure currently available in print. It is located at `https://infosec.navy.mil/TEXT/COMPUSEC/ntsecure.html`.

NOTE

C2 is an evaluation level in the U.S. government's Trusted Computer Security Evaluation Criteria (TCSEC) program. TCSEC provides a standard set of criteria for judging the security that computer products provide. TCSEC has also come to be known as the "Orange Book" because the base set of criteria specified by TCSEC is provided in a book with an orange cover.

The Navy guide takes you through configuration of the file system, audit policy, the Registry, the User Manager, user account policy, user rights, trust relationships, system policy, and Control Panel. It also has a blow-by-blow guide that explains the rationale for each step taken. This is invaluable because you can learn Windows NT security on the fly. Even though it spans only 185 pages, the Navy guide is worth 10 or even 100 books like this one. By using that guide, you can guarantee yourself a head start on establishing a reasonably secure server.

Summary of Windows NT

Windows NT 4.0 was the first step Microsoft took toward securing your network. Although Windows NT 4.0 and third-party software vendors provide you with many features to secure your Windows NT 4.0 network, Windows 2000 possesses even greater security. If you haven't yet taken the plunge to upgrade to Windows 2000, you should seriously consider doing so.

Let's move on now to examine Windows 2000 security.

Windows 2000

Windows 2000 has built on the existing Windows security by improving existing capabilities and adding new features. The NTFS file system has been redesigned for better performance, and Active Directory now replaces the Windows NT Lan Manager-style domain architecture. New security capabilities include Kerberos (used in Active Directory for authentication) and IPSec/L2TP (used with the Routing and Remote Access Service for network connections).

As with Windows NT 4.0, it is very important to install Windows 2000 using NTFS. If you don't install NTFS on your Windows 2000 desktop or server, you will not have a secure installation. Also, NTFS is required to install Active Directory. The focus of this section on Windows 2000 is on improvements to security and on general Windows 2000 security vulnerabilities.

Improvements to Security

Microsoft paid more attention to security with Windows 2000 and fully integrated security with the Active Directory directory service structure. Microsoft also designed the Windows 2000 platform to be more reliable than previous versions of Windows.

Some of the security features new to Windows 2000 are briefly discussed in the following list:

- First and foremost, Windows 2000 introduced Active Directory. It is the core of the flexibility of the Windows 2000 security model and provides information about all objects on the network. It is the basis for Windows 2000 distributed networking and facilitates the use of centralized management techniques, such as Group Policy and remote operating system operations. Active Directory replaced the security accounts manager (SAM) database area of the Registry on domain controllers storing security information such as user accounts, passwords, and group. Consequently, Active Directory has become a trusted component of the Local Security Authority (LSA). Active Directory stores both access control information to support authorization to access system resources and user credentials to support authentication within the domain. Windows 2000 Professional and member servers still retain the local SAM database for locally defined users and groups.

  Active Directory provides a single point of management for Windows clients, servers, applications, and user accounts. With Active Directory, you can delegate specific administrative tasks and privileges to individual users and groups, thus enabling the distribution of system administration tasks to either localized or centralized administration. For example, you can assign a specific management task, such as resetting a user's password, to office administrators in specific departments of your organization so that you can free up your time for more complex tasks.

  Active Directory includes built-in support for secure Internet-standard protocols such as PKI, Kerberos, and Lightweight Directory Access Protocol (LDAP). Learn

more about Active Directory at http://www.microsoft.com/windows2000/guide/
server/features/directory.asp.

- PKI also lies at the core of many of the security features in Windows 2000.
  PKI makes use of Microsoft Certificate Services, allowing the deployment of
  enterprise certificate authorities (CAs) in your enterprise, and is integrated
  into Active Directory. Active Directory uses the directory service to publish
  information about certificate services, which includes the location of user
  certificates and certificate revocation lists. When your organization begins to
  manage digital certificates, a range of enhanced security features becomes available to you in order to secure such technologies as Digitally Signed Software,
  the Encrypted File System (EFS), email, IP Security, and Smart Card Security.

- The EFS presents your users with the option to encrypt sensitive data on their
  hard disks, thus ensuring confidentiality should an intruder compromise or
  steal the disk.

- Kerberos is the default authentication protocol on Windows 2000, replacing
  Windows NT Challenge Response (NTLM) authentication. Kerberos has been
  around for a number of years, having been developed at the Massachusetts
  Institute of Technology during the 1980s.

- Internet Protocol Security Protocol (IPSec) provides advanced network security
  for you and your enterprise users.

Windows 2000 Distributed Security Overview

The Windows 2000 distributed security services include the following key business
requirements:

- Strong user authorization and authentication

- Users log on once to access all enterprise resources

- Secure communications between external and internal resources

- Automated security auditing

- Interoperability with other operating systems

Microsoft bases Windows 2000 security on a simple model of authentication and
authorization. After Windows 2000 identifies the user through authentication with a
domain controller, the user is granted access to specific network resources based on
permissions. This security model enables authorized users to work on a secure,
extended network. The Windows 2000 distributed security model is based on delegation of trust between services, trusted domain controller authentication, and object-
based access control.

Learn more about Microsoft Windows 2000 distributed security at `http://www.`
`microsoft.com/windows2000/techinfo/howitworks/security/distsecservices.asp`. Now
that we've briefly examined some of the new security features in Windows 2000, let's
move on to some potentially harmful vulnerabilities.

General Windows 2000 Security Vulnerabilities

Windows 2000, like most operating systems, has vulnerabilities. Please note that the
list of vulnerabilities discussed here is not exhaustive. Other vulnerabilities of lesser
severity exist.

The Malformed Data Transfer Request Vulnerability

Microsoft Windows Version: Windows 2000 Professional, Server, and Advanced Server

Impact: An attacker can send a malformed data transfer request and stop or severely affect
the performance of the SMTP service.

Fix: `http://support.microsoft.com/default.aspx?scid=kb;en-us;Q313450`. The fix for this
vulnerability will be included in Windows 2000_Service Pack 3.

The Windows 2000 Directory Service Restore Mode Password Vulnerability

Microsoft Windows Version: Windows 2000 Server and Advanced Server

Impact: A malicious user can install malicious code onto a domain server.

Class: Moderate to severe

Fix: `http://www.microsoft.com/Downloads/Release.asp?ReleaseID=27500`. The fix for this
vulnerability will be included in Windows 2000_Service Pack 2.

Additional Information: `http://www.microsoft.com/technet/security/bulletin/MS01-`
`006.asp`

Credit: John Sherriff of the Wool Research Organization

A malicious user with physical access to and administrative logon privileges on your
domain server can install malicious code if the server was promoted to a domain
server using the Configure Your Server tool. The only domain server in the forest
that can be affected by this vulnerability is the one that was installed first.

The Netmon Protocol Parsing Vulnerability

Microsoft Windows Version: Windows 2000 Server and Advanced Server

Impact: An attacker can gain control of your server.

Class: Critical

Fix: `http://www.microsoft.com/Downloads/Release.asp?ReleaseID=25485`. The fix for this vulnerability will be included in Windows 2000 Service Pack 2.

Additional Information: `http://www.microsoft.com/technet/security/bulletin/MS00-083.asp`

Credit: COVERT Labs at PGP Security, Inc., and the ISS X-force

Refer to the section "General Windows NT Security Vulnerabilities," for an explanation of this vulnerability. This vulnerability affects both Windows 2000 and Windows NT.

The Network Dynamic Data Exchange (DDE) Agent Request Vulnerability

Microsoft Windows Version: All Windows 2000 versions

Impact: An attacker can gain complete control over your box.

Class: Severe

Fix: `http://www.microsoft.com/Downloads/Release.asp?ReleaseID=27526`. The fix for this vulnerability will be included in Windows 2000 Service Pack 3.

Additional Information: `http://www.microsoft.com/technet/security/bulletin/MS01-007.asp`

Credit: DilDog of @Stake, Inc.

This is privilege elevation vulnerability. An attacker could exploit this vulnerability to take any action he wanted to on your box, because it enables him to run commands and programs with the privileges of the operation system itself.

The Phone Book Service Buffer Overflow Vulnerability

Microsoft Windows Version: Windows 2000 Server and Advanced Server

Impact: An attacker can execute hostile code on a remote server that is running the Phone Book Service.

Class: Critical

Fix: `http://www.microsoft.com/Downloads/Release.asp?ReleaseID=25531`. The fix for this vulnerability will be included in Windows 2000 Service Pack 2.

Additional Information: `http://www.microsoft.com/technet/security/bulletin/MS00-094.asp`

Credit: CORE-SDI and @Stake, Inc.

The Phone Book Service is used with dial-up networking clients to provide a prepopulated list of dial-up networking servers to the client. This service has an unchecked buffer in a portion of the code that does the processing of requests for phone book updates. When an attacker sends a malformed request, it can result in overrunning the buffer. This enables the attacker to execute any code that a user logged in to the server can run. In other words, the attacker can install and run code of his choice; add, delete, or change Web pages; reformat the hard drive; or do any number of other tasks.

The Telnet Client NTLM Authentication Vulnerability

Microsoft Windows Version: All Windows 2000 versions

Impact: An attacker could obtain another user's NTLM authentication credentials without the user's knowledge.

Class: Moderate to critical

Fix: `http://www.microsoft.com/technet/treeview/default.asp?url=/technet/security/bulletin/MS00-067.asp`.

The fix for this vulnerability will be included in Windows 2000 Service Pack 2.

Additional Information: `http://www.microsoft.com/technet/security/bulletin/MS00-067.asp`

Credit: DilDog of @Stake, Inc.

If a malicious Webmaster were operating a Telnet server and you initiated a session with that server, the Webmaster could collect your NTLM responses and then use them to possibly authenticate to your box. This is possible because, as part of the session, your box might pass your cryptographically protected NTLM authentication credentials to his server. After he has obtained these credentials, he could then use an offline brute-force attack to gain your plaintext password.

The Telnet Server Flooding Vulnerability

Microsoft Windows Version: All Windows 2000 versions

Impact: A remote user can prevent your box from providing Telnet services.

Class: Moderate to severe—denial of service

Fix: `http://www.microsoft.com/Downloads/Release.asp?ReleaseID=22753`

Additional Information: `http://www.microsoft.com/technet/security/bulletin/MS00-050.asp`

Credit: Unknown

This is a remote denial-of-service vulnerability. A malicious remote user can send a malformed input string from her box that would then cause the Telnet server to fail, causing the loss of any work in progress.

Summary of Windows 2000

Even though security for Windows improved greatly with the introduction of Windows 2000, new security violations occur all the time. Hence, it is important that you keep up with new advisories related to security holes in Windows 2000.

Windows XP

The Windows XP operating system was released in the fall of 2001 both to replace the Windows 9x/Me operating systems and as an improvement over Windows 2000 Professional. The two main versions of Windows XP are Home and Professional. The XP Home version is meant for home users and does not include all the capabilities of Windows 2000/XP Professional, such as the capability to join a domain. Windows XP Professional is the replacement for Windows 9x/Me and Windows 2000 Professional in a corporate environment and has all the capabilities of Windows 2000 Professional, with the addition of a new user interface and improved system operation and functionality.

Windows XP Security Improvements

Both Windows XP Home and Windows XP Professional offer numerous security improvements over Windows 9x/Me and Windows 2000 Professional.

Windows XP includes the following new security features:

- Personalized login—This feature provides the capability for multiple users to have secure user profiles, which prevent other system users from accessing or modifying the user information. This is similar in operation to user accounts on Windows 2000 and does not require a domain. This feature is not available on a Windows XP Professional system after it is joined to a domain. This replaces the Windows 9x/Me user account feature, which was not secured in any way.

- User switching—Used in conjunction with the personalized login feature, user switching allows multiple users to be logged on to a computer and to "switch" between user sessions. This feature is not available on a system that is the member of a domain.

- Internet Connection Firewall (ICF)—This feature provides security for your Internet connection by using active packet filtering. Packet filtering blocks all TCP/IP ports by default and dynamically opens ports as necessary. ICF provides protection from outside users gaining access to your system's data and services.

The following features are available only with Windows XP Professional:

- Blank password restriction—Windows XP provides a remote control feature based on the Terminal Services capability provided in Windows 2000 Server called Remote Desktop. The blank password restriction blocks user accounts with blank passwords from accessing the system using the Remote Desktop feature.

- Encrypting File System (EFS)—The EFS feature uses public-key encryption to provide an additional layer of security over the basic NTFS file security. EFS can be very valuable for protecting sensitive data for mobile and remote users where physical system security cannot be guaranteed.

- Smart card support—Windows XP Professional provides the capability to use Personal Computer/Smart Cards (PC/SC) in conjunction with a smart card reader to control access to the system. This feature is available only for systems that are members of a Windows 2000 Active Directory domain, because the card uses an X.509 certificate to authenticate the card holder with the domain controller.

With the release of Windows XP Home and Professional, Microsoft has continued to add to the security features that were provided originally with Windows NT. Windows XP also provides the capability for home and standalone users to have the benefit of NTFS security and user profile functionality, which is missing from Windows 9x and Me.

Modern Vulnerabilities in Microsoft Applications

In this section, I enumerate security weaknesses in some commonly used Microsoft applications: Microsoft Internet Explorer (Microsoft's Web browser, also known as MSIE), Microsoft Exchange Server (a mail administration package), and Internet Information Server (IIS) v4.0 and 5.0 (Microsoft's Web server, previously an add-on with the Windows NT Option Pack and now integrated into Windows 2000).

Microsoft Internet Explorer

Microsoft Internet Explorer v4.x and 5.x have several serious vulnerabilities; some of them are covered briefly here. Those vulnerabilities that are classified as either critical or severe can result in system compromise and are therefore of great interest to system administrators. With the release of Internet Explorer v6.0, these vulnerabilities have been addressed, and unless the older versions are required, it is recommended that you consider upgrading to 6.0. Windows XP and the upcoming release of Windows .NET are shipped with Internet Explorer 6.0 already integrated into the operating system (at least at this time—future versions of the OS might ship without a default browser, depending on the current government antitrust action). Although IE 6.0 has corrected the numerous vulnerabilities associated with the earlier releases, it is still recommended that you check the Windows Update site frequently to watch for new vulnerabilities and patches, as IE 6.0 has already had a few vulnerabilities identified.

Incorrect VBScript Handling Vulnerability

Microsoft Internet Explorer Version: 5.*x* and 6

Impact: Can allow Web pages to read local files

Class: Severe

Fix for MSIE 5.*x* and 6:

`http://www.microsoft.com/windows/ie/downloads/critical/q318089/default.asp`

Additional Information:

`http://www.microsoft.com/technet/treeview/default.asp?url=/technet/security/`
`bulletin/MS02-009.asp`

The Active Setup Download Vulnerability

Microsoft Internet Explorer Version: 4.*x*, 5.*x*

Impact: Malicious Webmasters can download a .CAB file to any disk on your box.

Class: Severe

Fix for MSIE 4.*x* and 5.01:

`http://www.microsoft.com/windows/ie/downloads/critical/patch8/default.asp`

Fix for MSIE 5.5:

`http://www.microsoft.com/windows/ie/downloads/critical/patch11/default.asp`

Additional Information: `http://www.microsoft.com/technet/security/bulletin/ms00-`
`042.asp`

Credit: Unknown

A malicious Web site can download a .CAB file to any disk on your box and then use the .CAB file to overwrite files, including system files. This could render your machine inoperable and create a denial of service on your box.

The Cached Web Credentials Vulnerability

Microsoft Internet Explorer Version: 4.*x* and 5.*x* prior to version 5.5

Impact: Malicious intruders can obtain your user ID and password to a Web site.

Class: Moderate to severe

Fix: `http://www.microsoft.com/windows/ie/downloads/critical/q273868/default.asp`

Additional Information: `http://www.microsoft.com/technet/security/bulletin/ms00-076.asp`

Credit: ACROS Security

When you use Basic authentication to authenticate to a secured Web page, MSIE caches your user ID and password to minimize the number of times you must authenticate to the same site. Although MSIE should pass your cached credentials only to secured pages on the site, it will also send them to the site's nonsecured pages. If an attacker has control of your box's network communications when you log on to a secured site, the attacker can spoof a request for a nonsecured page and then collect your credentials.

The IE Script Vulnerability

Microsoft Internet Explorer Version: 4.01 SP2 and higher, when Microsoft Access 97 or Microsoft Access 2000 is present on the machine

Impact: Permits an attacker to run code of her choice on your box, potentially allowing her to take full control of it.

Class: Extremely severe

Fix: `http://www.microsoft.com/windows/ie/downloads/critical/patch11/default.asp` or set an Administrator password for Microsoft Access

Additional Information: `http://www.microsoft.com/technet/security/bulletin/ms00-049.asp`

Credit: Georgi Guninski

This vulnerability enables an attacker to embed malicious VB code into Microsoft Access via Internet Explorer. Simply visiting a malicious Web site or previewing an email that contains malicious code can compromise your box.

The SSL Certificate Validation Vulnerability

Microsoft Internet Explorer Version: 4.*x*, 5.0, and 5.01

Note: MSIE 5.01 Service Pack 1 and MSIE 5.5 are not affected.

Impact: Two flaws exist in MSIE that can allow a malicious Web site to pose as a legitimate Web site. The attacker can trick users into disclosing information (such as credit card numbers or personal data) intended for a legitimate Web site.

Class: Moderate

Fix: `http://www.microsoft.com/windows/ie/downloads/critical/patch11/default.asp` or upgrade to MSIE 5.5

Additional Information: `http://www.microsoft.com/technet/security/bulletin/ms00-039.asp`

Credit: ACROS Penetration Team, Slovenia

When a connection to a secure server is made through either a frame or an image on a Web site, MSIE verifies only that the server's Secure Sockets Layer (SSL) certificate was issued by a trusted root and does not verify either the server name or the expiration date of the certificate. When you make a secure connection via any other means, MSIE performs the expected validation. If a user establishes a new SSL session with the same server during the same MSIE session, MSIE does not revalidate the certificate.

The Unauthorized Cookie Access Vulnerability

Microsoft Internet Explorer Version: 4.x, 5.0, and 5.01

Note: MSIE 5.01 Service Pack 1 and MSIE 5.5 are not affected.

Impact: This vulnerability can allow a malicious Webmaster to obtain personal information from a user's box.

Class: Moderate

Fix: `http://www.microsoft.com/windows/ie/downloads/critical/patch11/default.asp`

Additional Information: `http://www.microsoft.com/technet/security/bulletin/FQ00-033.asp#B`

Credit: Unknown

A malicious Web site operator could entice a user to click a link on the operator's site that would allow the operator to read, change, or add a cookie to that user's box.

Microsoft Exchange Server

The following sections list important vulnerabilities in Microsoft Exchange Server 2000 and Exchange Server 5.x.

Microsoft Exchange Encapsulated SMTP Address Vulnerability

Microsoft Exchange Server Version: 5.5

Impact: Intruder can perform mail relaying.

Class: Moderate—denial of service

Fix: `ftp://ftp.microsoft.com/bussys/exchange/exchange-public/fixes/Eng/Exchg5.5/PostSP2/imc-fix/`

Additional Information: `http://www.microsoft.com/technet/security/bulletin/fq99-027.asp`

Credit: Laurent Frinking of Quark Deutschland GmbH

This vulnerability could enable an intruder to get around the antirelaying features of an Internet-connected Exchange server. Because encapsulated Simple Mail Transfer Protocol (SMTP) addresses are not subject to the same antirelaying protections as nonencapsulated SMTP addresses, an intruder can cause a server to forward an encapsulated SMTP address from the attacker to any email address she wants—as though the server were the sender of the email.

Microsoft Exchange Malformed MIME Header Vulnerability

Microsoft Exchange Server Version: 5.5

Impact: A malicious user can cause an Exchange Server to fail.

Class: Severe—denial of service

Fix: `http://www.microsoft.com/Downloads/Release.asp?ReleaseID=25443` or Exchange 5.5 SP4

Additional Information: `http://www.microsoft.com/technet/security/bulletin/MS00-082.asp`

Credit: Art Savelev

The Exchange Server normally checks for invalid values in the MIME header fields. However, the Exchange service will fail if a particular type of invalid value is present in certain MIME header fields. You can restore normal operations by restarting the Exchange Server and then deleting the offending mail. The offending mail will be at the front end of the queue after you restart the Exchange service.

Microsoft Exchange NNTP Denial-of-Service Vulnerability

Microsoft Exchange Server Versions: 5.0 and 5.5

Impact: An attacker can cause the Server Information Store to choke.

Class: Medium—denial of service

Fix: `ftp://ftp.microsoft.com/bussys/exchange/exchange-public/fixes/Eng/Exchg5.0/Post-SP2-STORE/` or install SP1 or later

Additional Information: `http://www.microsoft.com/technet/security/bulletin/ms98-007.asp`

Credit: Internet Security Systems, Inc.'s X-Force team

When an attacker issues a series of incorrect data, an application error can result in the Server Information Store failing. It also causes users to fail in their attempts to connect to their folders on the Exchange Server.

Microsoft Exchange SMTP Denial of Service Vulnerability

Microsoft Exchange Server Versions: 5.0 and 5.5

Impact: An attacker can cause the Internet Mail Service to choke.

Class: Medium—denial of service

Fix: `ftp://ftp.microsoft.com/bussys/exchange/exchange-public/fixes/Eng/Exchg5.0/post-sp2-ims/` or install SP1 or later

Additional Information: `http://www.microsoft.com/technet/security/bulletin/ms98-007.asp`

Credit: Internet Security Systems, Inc.'s X-Force team

When an attacker issues a series of incorrect data, an application error can result in the Internet Mail Service failing.

Microsoft Exchange Error Message Vulnerability

Microsoft Exchange Server Versions: 5.0 and 5.5

Impact: An intruder might be able to recover encrypted data from your network.

Class: Moderate to severe

Fix: Download the latest version of `Schannel.dll`. Check out this URL for information on where to obtain the latest version:
`http://support.microsoft.com/support/kb/articles/q148/4/27.asp`.

Additional Information: `http://www.microsoft.com/technet/security/bulletin/ms98-002.asp`

Credit: Daniel Bleichenbacher

An intruder, running a sniffer on your network, might be able to observe an SSL-encrypted session, interrogate the server involved in that session, recover the session key used in that session, and then recover the encrypted data from that session.

Microsoft Exchange User Account Vulnerability

Microsoft Exchange Server Version: 2000

Impact: An intruder can remotely log on to an Exchange 2000 Server and possibly on to other servers in the affected Exchange Server's network.

Class: Moderate to severe

Fix: `http://www.microsoft.com/Downloads/Release.asp?ReleaseID=25866`

Additional Information: `http://www.microsoft.com/technet/security/bulletin/MS00-088.asp`

Credit: Unknown

A malicious user can log on to Exchange by using an account with a known username (`EUSR_EXSTOREEVENT`) and a password that Exchange creates during the setup process. Normally, this account has only local user rights, meaning that the account is neither a privileged account nor can it gain access to Exchange 2000 data. However, when you install Exchange 2000 on a domain controller, the system automatically gives Domain User privileges to the account, so it can gain access to other resources on the affected domain. Microsoft recommends that you disable or delete this account after the setup process has completed.

Internet Information Server

IIS is a popular Internet server package, and like most server packages, it has vulnerabilities. IIS 4.0 was released for the Windows NT operating system as part of the Windows NT Option Pack, and IIS 5.0 is included in the Windows 2000 Server operating system. Some of the most well-known IIS vulnerabilities are covered here in detail. However, please note that the list of vulnerabilities discussed is not exhaustive. Other vulnerabilities of lesser severity exist, and I am sure new ones are being found even as this is being written.

Buffer Overrun in HTR ISAPI Extension Vulnerability

IIS Version: 4.0 and 5.0

Impact: An attacker can cause the server to temporarily stop providing Web services, or in very unusual cases, the attacker can gain control of the server by sending a specially chosen request to an affected Web server.

Class: Severe

Fix for IIS 4.0 and 5.0: `http://support.microsoft.com/default.aspx?scid=kb;en-us;Q319733`

Cross-Site Scripting in IIS Help File Search Facility Vulnerability

IIS Version: 5.0 and 5.1

Impact: An attacker can send a request to an affected server that causes a Web page containing script to be sent to another user. The script executes in the user's browser as though it comes from the third-party site, which lets the script run by using the security settings that are appropriate to the third-party Web site, and also permits the attacker to access any data that belongs to the site.

Class: Severe

Fix for IIS 5.1: `http://www.microsoft.com/Downloads/Release.asp?ReleaseID=37857`

Fix for IIS 5.0:
`http://www.microsoft.com/windows2000/downloads/security/q319733/default.asp?FinishURL=%2Fdownloads%2Frelease%2Easp%3FReleaseID%3D37824%26redirect%3Dno`

The IIS Cross-Site Scripting Vulnerabilities

IIS Version: 4.0 and 5.0

Impact: An attacker can run code on your machine masquerading as a third-party Web site.

Class: Severe

Fix for IIS 4.0: `http://www.microsoft.com/Downloads/Release.asp?ReleaseID=25534`

Fix for IIS 5.0: `http://www.microsoft.com/Downloads/Release.asp?ReleaseID=25533`

Additional Information: `http://www.microsoft.com/technet/security/bulletin/MS00-060.asp`

Credit: Peter Grundl of Defcom

When a malicious user runs code masquerading as a third-party Web site, that code can take any action on your box that the third-party Web site is permitted to take. If you designate that Web site as a trusted site, the attacker's code could take advantage of the increased privileges. The attacker can make the code persistent, so that if you return to that Web site in the future, the code will begin to run again.

The IIS Malformed Web Form Submission Vulnerability

IIS Version: 4.0 and 5.0

Impact: An attacker can prevent a Web server from providing service.

Class: Severe—denial of service

Fix for IIS 4.0: `http://www.microsoft.com/Downloads/Release.asp?ReleaseID=26704`

Fix for IIS 5.0: `http://www.microsoft.com/Downloads/Release.asp?ReleaseID=26277`

Additional Information: `http://www.microsoft.com/technet/security/bulletin/MS00-100.asp`

Credit: eEye Digital Security

FrontPage Server Extensions ship with IIS 4.0 and IIS 5.0 and provide browse-time support functions. A vulnerability exists in some of these functions that allows an attacker to levy a malformed form submission to an IIS server that would cause the IIS service to fail. In IIS 4.0, you have to restart the service manually. In IIS 5.0, the IIS service will restart by itself.

The IIS New Variant of File Fragment Reading via .HTR Vulnerability

IIS Version: 4.0 and 5.0

Impact: An attacker can read fragments of files from a Web server.

Class: Moderate

Fix for IIS 4.0: `http://www.microsoft.com/Downloads/Release.asp?ReleaseID=27492`

Fix for IIS 5.0: `http://www.microsoft.com/Downloads/Release.asp?ReleaseID=27491`

Additional Information: `http://www.microsoft.com/technet/security/bulletin/MS01-004.asp`

Credit: Unknown

An attacker can cause a requested file to be processed by the .HTR ISAPI extension in such a way as to cause fragments of server-side files, such as .ASP files, to be sent to the attacker.

The IIS Session ID Cookie Marking Vulnerability

IIS Version: 4.0 and 5.0

Impact: A malicious user can hijack another user's secure Web session.

Class: Critical

Fix for IIS 4.0 *x86* platforms: `http://www.microsoft.com/ntserver/nts/downloads/critical/q274149`

Fix for IIS 4.0 Alpha platforms: Available from Microsoft Product Support Services

Fix for IIS 5.0: `http://www.microsoft.com/Windows2000/downloads/critical/q274149`

Additional Information: `http://www.microsoft.com/technet/security/bulletin/MS00-080.asp`

Credit: ACROS Security and Ron Sires and C. Conrad Cady of Healinx

IIS uses the same session ID for both secure and nonsecure pages on the same Web site. What this means to you is that when you initiate a session with a secure Web page, the session ID cookie is protected by SSL. If you subsequently visit a nonsecure page on the same site, that same session ID cookie is exchanged, only this time in plaintext. If a malicious user has control over the communications channel of your box, she could then read the plaintext session ID cookie and use it to take any action on the secure page that you can.

The IIS Web Server File Request Parsing Vulnerability

IIS Version: 4.0 and 5.0

Impact: Remote users can run operating system commands on a Web server.

Class: Critical

Fix for IIS 4.0: `http://www.microsoft.com/ntserver/nts/downloads/critical/q277873`

Fix for IIS 5.0: `http://www.microsoft.com/Downloads/Release.asp?ReleaseID=25547`

Additional Information: `http://www.microsoft.com/technet/security/bulletin/MS00-086.asp`

Credit: NSFocus

An attacker can execute operating system commands that would enable her to take any action that any interactively logged-on user could take. This would enable her to add, delete, or change files on the server; modify Web pages; reformat the hard drive; run existing code on the server; or upload code onto the server and then run it.

The Invalid URL Vulnerability

IIS Version: 4.0

Impact: Attacker can cause IIS service to fail.

Class: Severe—denial of service

Fix for NT 4.0 Workstation, Server and Server Enterprise Editions:
`http://www.microsoft.com/Downloads/Release.asp?ReleaseID=24403`

Credit: Peter Grundl of VIGILANTe

An attacker can send an invalid URL to the server which, through a sequence of events, could result in an invalid memory request that would cause the IIS service to fail. Microsoft engineers believe that the underlying problem actually exists within Windows NT 4.0 itself.

The Myriad Escaped Characters Vulnerability

IIS Version: 4.0 and 5.0

Impact: An attacker can slow an IIS server's response or prevent it from providing service.

Class: Medium to Severe—denial of service

Fix for IIS 4.0: `http://www.microsoft.com/Downloads/Release.asp?ReleaseID=20292`

Fix for IIS 5.0: `http://www.microsoft.com/Downloads/Release.asp?ReleaseID=20286`

Credit: Vanja Hrustic of the Relay Group

By sending a malformed URL with an extremely large number of escape characters, an attacker can consume large quantities of CPU time and thus slow down or prevent the IIS server from providing service for a period of time.

The Web Server Folder Traversal Vulnerability

IIS Version: 4.0 and 5.0

Impact: An attacker can take destructive actions against a Web server.

Class: Critical

Fix: `http://www.microsoft.com/windows2000/downloads/critical/q269862/default.asp`

Additional Information: `http://www.microsoft.com/technet/security/bulletin/MS00-078.asp`

Credit: Rain Forest Puppy

An attacker can change or delete files or Web pages, run existing code on the Web server, upload new code and run it, format the hard disk, or take any number of other destructive actions.

Tools

After you establish your Windows NT 4.0 or Windows 2000 server, you can obtain several indispensable tools that will help you keep it secure. No Windows NT 4.0 or Windows 2000 administrator should be caught without these tools.

Administrator Assistant Tool Kit

Administrator Assistant Tool Kit is an application suite that contains utilities to streamline system administration on Windows NT boxes.

Aelita Software

Windows Version: Windows NT 4.0 or Windows NT 3.51

Email: `Services@aelita.com`

URL: `http://www.aelita.net/products/AdminAssist.htm`

FileAdmin

FileAdmin is an advanced tool for manipulating file permissions on large Windows NT-based networks. This utility can save you many hours of work.

Aelita Software

Windows Version: Windows NT 4.0 or Windows NT 3.51

Email: Services@aelita.com

URL: http://www.aelita.net/products/FileAdmin.htm

Security Analyst

Kane Security Analyst provides real-time intrusion detection for Windows NT 4.0 and Windows 2000. This utility monitors and reports security violations and is very configurable. It assesses six critical security areas: access control, data confidentiality, data integrity, password strength, system monitoring, and user account restrictions.

Intrusion.com, Inc.

Windows Version: Windows 2000 and Windows NT

Email: info@intrusion.com

URL: http://www.intrusion.com/products/product.asp?lngProdNmId=4&lngCatId=23

LANguard Network Security Scanner

The LANguard Network Security Scanner not only enables you to monitor and control Internet usage on your network, but also monitors network traffic to detect break-ins from outside your network. With Network Security Scanner, you use keywords to block access to unwanted sites (such as IRC). You can also use keywords to block searches for objectionable material at search engine sites without blocking the entire search engine. With the network monitor, you can watch for suspicious incoming traffic to a specific server that shouldn't be accessible to outside traffic.

GFI Fax & Voice USA

Windows Version: Windows 2000 or Windows NT 4.0

Email: sales@gfi.com

URL: http://www.gfi.com/lannetscan/index.htm

LANguard Security Reporter

Security Reporter collects data about your Windows NT 4.0 or Windows 2000 network, such as user rights, users having administrative rights, and resource permissions, among others. This information is stored in a central database, and you use this information to generate reports that help you to identify and fix potential security problems.

> GFI Fax & Voice USA
>
> Windows Version: Windows XP, Windows 2000, and Windows NT 4.0
>
> Email: sales@gfi.com
>
> URL: http://www.gfi.com/lanselm/index.html

NT Crack

NT Crack is a tool that audits Windows NT passwords. This is the functional equivalent of Crack for Unix.

> Secure Networks, Inc.
>
> Windows Version: Windows NT (all versions)
>
> URL: http://www.system7.org/archive/Nt-Hacking/windows.html

Administrator's Pak

The Administrator's Pak includes a variety of tools for recovering crashed Windows 2000 and Windows NT 4.0 systems. This bundle includes the NT Locksmith, NTRecover, Remote Recover, and NTFSDOS Pro tools, just to name a few. The Administrator's Pak bundle is a great value for tools that will help with recovering your Windows 2000 and Windows NT boxes.

> Winternals Software LP
>
> Windows Version: Windows 2000 or Windows NT 4.0
>
> Email: info@winternals.com
>
> URL: http://www.winternals.com/

NTFSDOS Pro

NTFSDOS Pro allows you to copy and rename permissions on Windows 2000 and Windows NT 4.0 from a DOS disk. This is a great tool to keep around for emergencies (for example, when you lose that Administrator password).

> Winternals Software LP
>
> Windows Version: Windows 2000 or Windows NT 4.0

Email: info@winternals.com

URL: http://www.winternals.com/

RemoteRecover

RemoteRecover is a salvage program. It allows you to access dead Windows NT/2000/XP volumes via a network—now is that cool or what? NTRecover uses TCP/IP to access files and volumes on a dead NT box. You use the TCP/IP network connection to make the disks on the dead box seem as though they are mounted on your own system.

Winternals Software LP

Windows Version: Windows XP, Windows 2000, or Windows NT 4.0

Email: info@winternals.com

URL: http://www.winternals.com/

PC Firewall ASaP

PC Firewall ASaP is a bi-directional packet filter suite for Windows 9x/Me and Windows NT 4.0 clients.

McAfee Security

Windows Version: Windows 9x/Me or Windows NT 4.0

Email: support@mycio.com

URL: http://www.mcafeeasap.com/default.asp

RegAdmin

RegAdmin is an advanced tool for manipulating Registry entries on large networks, which is a big timesaver.

Aelita Software

Windows Version: Windows NT 4.0 or Windows NT 3.51

Email: Services@box.omna.com

URL: http://www.aelita.net/products/RegAdmin.htm

Sniffer Basic

Sniffer Basic (formerly named NetXRay Analyzer) is a powerful protocol analyzer (sniffer) and network monitoring tool for Windows NT. It is probably the most comprehensive NT sniffer available.

Sniffer Technologies

Windows Version: Windows 2000, Windows NT (all versions), or Windows 9*x*/Me

Note: Sniffer Technologies released Sniffer Pro 4.5 for laptop platforms in January 2001. This version includes support for Windows 2000.

Email: bcahillane@nai.com

URL: http://www.sniffer.com/products/sniffer-basic/default.asp?A=2

Somarsoft DumpSec

Somarsoft DumpSec dumps permissions for the NTFS file system in the Registry, including shares and printers. It offers a bird's-eye view of permissions, which are normally hard to gather on large networks.

SystemTools LLP

Windows Version: Windows XP, Windows 2000, Windows NT (all versions)

Email: sales@systemtools.com

URL: http://www.somarsoft.com/

Somarsoft DumpEvt

Somarsoft DumpEvt dumps Event Log information for importation into a database for analysis.

SystemTools LLP

Windows Version: Windows XP, Windows 2000 or Windows NT (all versions)

Email: sales@systemtools.com

URL: http://www.somarsoft.com/

Somarsoft DumpReg

Somarsoft DumpReg dumps Registry information for analysis. It also allows incisive searching and matching of keys.

SystemTools LLP

Windows Version: Windows XP, Windows 2000, Windows NT (all versions), or Windows 98

Email: info@somarsoft.com

URL: http://www.somarsoft.com/

Virtuosity

Virtuosity is a wide-scale management and Windows NT rollouts tool. (Good for heavy-duty rollouts.)

Raxco, Ltd.

Windows Version: Windows NT 4.0 or Windows NT 3.51

URL: http://www.domainmigration.com/fp_virtuosity.html

Access Control Software

The following section introduces several good packages for adding access control to Windows 2000, Windows NT, and Windows 9x/Me.

Cetus StormWindow

Cetus Software, Inc.

Windows Version: Windows 2000, Windows NT 4.0, or Windows 9x/Me

Email: cetussoft@aol.com

URL: http://www.cetussoft.com/stormwin.htm

Cetus StormWindow allows you to incisively hide and protect almost anything within the system environment, including the following:

- Links and folders

- Drives and directories

- Networked devices and printers

In all, Cetus StormWindow offers very comprehensive access control. (This product also intercepts most alternate boot requests, such as warm boots, Ctrl+Alt+Delete, and function keys.)

ConfigSafe Complete Recovery v4 by imagine LAN, Inc.

imagine LAN, Inc.

Windows Version: Windows 2000, Windows 4.0, or Windows 9x/Me

Email: feedback@imagelan.com

URL: http://www.configsafe.com

ConfigSafe Complete Recovery v4 records changes and updates made to the Registry, system files, drivers, directory structures, DLL files, and system hardware. You can instantly restore a system to a previously working configuration with ConfigSafe.

DECROS Security Card by DECROS, Ltd.

DECROS, Ltd.

Windows Version: Windows 2000, Windows NT 4.0, or Windows 9x/Me

Email: info@decros.cz

URL: http://www.decros.com/security_division/p_list_hw.htm

DECROS Security Card provides C2-level access control using physical security in the form of a card key. Without that card, no one will gain access to the system.

Desktop Surveillance Enterprise and Personal Editions

Omniquad, Ltd.

Windows Version: Windows NT 4.0 or Windows 9x

Email: support@omniquad.com

URL: http://www.omniquad.com/

Desktop Surveillance is a full-fledged investigation and access control utility. (This product has strong logging and audit capabilities.)

Omniquad Detective

Hanovia House

Windows Version: Windows XP, Windows 2000, Windows NT 4.0, or Windows 9x

Email: support@omniquad.com

URL: http://www.omniquad.com/

The Detective is a simple but powerful tool for monitoring system processes. Omniquad Detective enables you to monitor computer usage, reconstruct activities that have occurred on a workstation or server, identify intruders who try to cover their tracks, perform content analysis, and define user search patterns. In all, this very comprehensive tool is tailor-made to catch someone in the act and is probably suitable for investigating computer-assisted crime in the workplace.

Windows Task-Lock by Posum LLC

Posum LLC

Windows Version: .Windows 2000, Windows 4.0, or Windows 9x/Me

Email: support@posum.com

URL: http://posum.com/

Windows Task-Lock 6.2 provides a simple, inexpensive, and effective way to password-protect specified applications no matter how you (or someone else) execute them. It is easy to configure and requires little to no modifications to your current system configuration. Optional Sound events, stealth mode, and password timeout are also included.

WP WinSafe

PBNSoft

Windows Version: Windows NT or Windows 9x

Email: info@pnbsoft.com

URL: http://www.pbnsoft.com/

WinSafe allows you to encrypt your files using strong cryptography algorithms such as Blowfish and CAST. With WinSafe you can choose from among 28 different algorithms. Other tools included with this package are File Wiping and Merge Files. File Wiping rewrites deleted files with random trash for the number of times that you specify, whereas Merge Files enables you to merge two files so that you can hide one file in another.

CAUTION

The documentation suggests that using the Windows Policy editor to set the real-mode DOS settings could potentially conflict with WinSafe.

Secure Shell

F-Secure, Inc.

Windows Version: Windows 2000, Windows NT 4.0, Windows 9x, or Windows 3x

Email: Chicago@F-secure.com

URL: http://www.f-secure.com/products/network_security/

Secure Shell (SSH), .as you have seen throughout the book, provides safe, encrypted communication over the Internet or other untrusted networks. SSH is an excellent replacement for Telnet or rlogin. SSH uses IDEA and Rivest-Shamir-Adelman (RSA) encryption and is therefore extremely secure. It is reported that the keys are discarded and new keys are made once an hour. SSH completely eliminates the possibility of third parties capturing your communication (for example, passwords that might otherwise be passed in clear text). SSH sessions cannot be overtaken or hijacked, nor can they be sniffed. The only real drawback is that for you to use SSH, the other end must also be using it. Although you might think such encrypted communication would be dreadfully slow, it isn't.

Good Online Sources of Information

This section contains many good Windows resource links. Most are dynamic and house material that is routinely updated.

The Windows NT Security FAQ

If you are new to Windows NT security, the Windows NT Security Frequently Asked Questions document is an absolute must. I would wager that better than half of the questions you have about NT security are answered in this document.

```
http://www.it.kth.se/~rom/ntsec.html
```

NTBugTraq

NTBugTraq is an excellent resource provided by Russ Cooper of RC Consulting. The site includes a database of Windows NT vulnerabilities, plus the archived and searchable versions of the NTBugTraq mailing list.

```
http://www.ntbugtraq.com
```

NTSECURITY.com for Windows 2000 and Windows NT

This site is hosted by Aelita Software Group division of Midwestern Commerce, Inc., a well-known development firm that designs security applications for Windows 2000 and Windows NT, among other things.

```
http://www.ntsecurity.com/
```

Expert Answers for Windows XP, Windows 2000, Windows NT, and Windows 9x/Me

This is a forum in which advanced Windows XP, Windows 2000, Windows NT, and Windows 9x/Me issues are discussed. It is a good place to find possible solutions to very obscure and configuration-specific problems. Regulars post clear, concise questions and answers along the lines of "I have a PPRO II w/ NT 4.0 and IIS 3 running MS Exchange 5.0, with SP3 for NT and SP1 for Exchange. So, why is my mail server dying?"

```
http://www.zdnet.com/community/?ROOT=331&MSG=331&T=index
```

Windows IT Security (Formerly NTSecurity.net)

The Windows IT Security site, hosted by *Windows 2000 Magazine*, is full of information about the latest in security. You can subscribe to discussion lists about advanced vulnerabilities in the Windows 2000 and Windows NT operating systems. You can find it at the following URL:

```
http://www.ntsecurity.net/
```

"An Introduction to the Windows 2000 Public Key Infrastructure"

"An Introduction to the Windows 2000 Public Key Infrastructure" is an article written by Microsoft Press. It presents an introduction to one of Windows 2000's new security features, PKI.

```
http://www.microsoft.com/windows2000/techinfo/howitworks/security/pkiintro.asp
```

Windows and .NET Magazine Online

I know what you're thinking—commercial magazines are probably not very good sources for security information. *Windows and .NET Magazine* is the former Windows 2000 magazine, and the site offers numerous articles and FAQs on security for Windows .NET, XP, 2000 and NT. You can reach the site at `http://www.winntmag.com/`.

Securing Windows NT Installation

Securing Windows NT Installation is an incredibly detailed document from Microsoft on establishing a secure Windows NT server. You can find it at this site:

```
http://www.microsoft.com/ntserver/techresources/security/Secure_NTInstall.asp
```

Checklist for Upgrading to Windows 2000 Server

Microsoft lists the steps necessary to upgrade to Windows 2000. Included is how to check whether your hardware and software are compatible with Windows 2000 and how to choose a filesystem. You can find it here:

```
http://www.microsoft.com/TechNet/win2000/srvchk.asp
```

The University of Texas at Austin Computation Center NT Archive

This site contains a wide (and sometimes eclectic) range of tools and fixes for Windows NT. (A good example is a fully functional Curses library for use on NT.)

```
ftp://microlib.cc.utexas.edu/microlib/nt/
```

Books on Windows 2000 and Windows NT Security

The following titles are assorted treatments on Windows 2000 and NT security.

Securing Windows NT/2000 Servers for the Internet. Stefan Norberg, Deborah Russell. O'Reilly & Associates. ISBN: 1-56592-768-0. 2000.

Windows 2000 Security. Roberta Bragg. New Riders Publishing. ISBN: 0-73570-991-2. 2000.

Windows 2000 Security: Little Black Book. Ian McLean. The Coriolis Group. ISBN: 1-57610-387-0. 2000.

Configuring Windows 2000 Server Security. Thomas W. Shinder and D. Lynn White. Syngress Media, Inc. ISBN: 1-92899-402-4. 1999.

Microsoft Windows 2000 Security Technical Reference. Internet Security Systems, Inc. Microsoft Press. ISBN: 0-73560-858-X. 2000.

Microsoft Windows 2000 Security Handbook. Jeff Schmidt. Que Publishing. ISBN: 0-78971-999-1. 2000.

Microsoft Windows NT 4.0 Security, Audit, and Control (Microsoft Technical Reference). James G. Jumes. Microsoft Press. ISBN: 1-57231-818-X. 1998.

NT 4 Network Security. Matthew Strebe. Sybex. ISBN: 0-78212-425-9. 1999.

Windows NT/2000 Network Security (Circle Series). E. Eugene Schultz. New Riders Publishing. ISBN: 1-57870-253-4. 2000.

Windows 2000 Security Handbook. Phillip Cox. McGraw-Hill Professional Publishing. ISBN: 0-07212-433-4. 2000.

Windows NT Server Security Guide (Prentice Hall Series on Microsoft Technologies). Marcus Goncalves. Prentice Hall Computer Books. ISBN: 0-13679-903-5. 1998.

Windows NT Security Handbook. Thomas Sheldon. Osborne McGraw-Hill. ISBN: 0-07882-240-8. 1996.

Summary

Microsoft offers a number of excellent applications, and Windows XP, Windows 2000, and Windows NT 4.0 are excellent platforms. However, like their counterparts, they are not secure out of the box. To run secure Microsoft applications and servers, you must do three things:

- Patch the vulnerabilities discussed in this chapter.

- Apply the general security techniques discussed in other chapters.

- Constantly keep up with advisories.

If you cover these bases, you should be fine.

21

Unix

This chapter examines the Unix operating system from a security perspective. We'll start with a whistle-stop tour of Unix history, followed by an in-depth look at the issues faced when selecting a Unix distribution. We'll then consider the security risks and countermeasures—along with some thoughts about the decisions you'll face.

We'll cover the hardcore Unix security territory and some useful follow-up material written by respected security practitioners—that way, you can dip in and out as your interest takes you.

This chapter isn't a Unix security manual, nor is it a step-by-step set of instructions for securing a particular Unix distribution (see the "Host-Hardening Resources" section for pointers to checklists). You also won't find a list of the most "leet" Unix exploits here. There are a thousand hacker sites out there waiting for you, if that is all you seek.

My primary goal is to get you thinking about Unix security in the context of *your* environment. The way in which your organization deploys Unix has a fundamental bearing on what you can and should be doing to secure it. Sure, there are some common issues that face the majority of us, such as OS security bugs—but computer systems don't exist in a vacuum. They are used by people to get a job done—whether it is to serve your home page to an unsuspecting world, or to process credit card transactions through a major bank. Failure to grasp the local issues can lead to terminally flawed security "solutions" that simply don't fit your context. These are the "soft issues."

Also, understand that we're talking about an ongoing security process—not just an initial effort.

On a number of occasions, I'll reference specific programs or filenames. The names and locations of these programs might differ on your system—if you don't already know the differences, check your online man pages (`man -k search-clue`).

A Whistle-Stop Tour of Unix History

The seeds of Unix were sown in 1965 when Bell Labs, General Electric Company, and the Massachusetts Institute of Technology designed an operating system called Multics. From the outset, this was designed to be a multiuser system supporting multiple concurrent users, data storage, and data sharing.

By 1969, with the project failing, Bell Labs quit the project. Ken Thompson, a Bell Labs engineer began "rolling his own"—soon to be called Unix (a pun on Multics). The next year, Dennis Ritchie wrote the first C compiler (inventing the C language in the process), and in 1973, Thompson rewrote the kernel in C.

Unix was getting to be portable, and by 1975 it was distributed to universities. The attraction of Unix was its portability and low-end hardware requirements. For the time, it could run on relatively inexpensive workstations. Consequently, Unix developed a strong following within academic circles.

This popularity, coupled with the availability of a C compiler, lead to the development of core utilities and programs still included in our distributions today. Many utilities have quite a rich or comical history—I recommend you check the history books. With businesses recognizing that they could save on expensive hardware and training costs, it was only a matter of time before a number of vendors packaged their own distributions. From there, the Unix family tree explodes—splintering off into very different directions based on the motivation and financing of the maintainers.

TIP

For a comprehensive history lesson, visit `http://www.levenez.com/Unix/ /`. There is also a graphical family tree of Unix where you can trace the origins of your favorite distribution.

TIP

Matt Bishop maintains a fascinating archive of papers that record the findings of early Unix security reviews at `http://seclab.cs.ucdavis.edu/projects/history/index.html`.

Matt is probably best known for his research into secure programming techniques. Check out his research papers and presentations.

Vendors ported Unix to new hardware platforms and incorporated "value-added" items such as printed documentation, additional device drivers, enhanced file systems, window managers, and HA (High Availability) technologies. Source code was no longer shipped in favor of "binary-only distributions," as vendors sought to protect their intellectual property rights.

To stand a chance of securing government contracts, vendors implemented security extensions as specified in the Rainbow Books by the U.S. Department of Defense. Each book defined a set of design, implementation, and documentation criteria that an operating system needed to fulfill to be certified at a particular security level. Probably the best known level is C2, which we'll look at later.

Getting "accredited" was no mean feat. It required a significant amount of time and money. This tended to favor the big players who could afford to play the long game.

As it turns out, the security interfaces across different distributions are pretty incompatible. On top of this, the code running the C2 subsystems tended to be immature, buggy, and slow. The administrative tools were awful (and often still are), as was the support. Over time, the security of systems improved, as did the C2 subsystems.

Consequently, not enough administrators followed the advice they were given by security experts in securing particular Unix versions. Crackers were well aware of the shortcomings in popular distributions, and were running rings around the less capable administrators.

However, at the other end of the spectrum was a loose community of "security pioneers"—programmers cum administrators, who developed some of the most pervasive security tools ever written. We'll cover the best ones in due course. The authors openly shared their source code with the wider community via Usenet— way before the WWW (World Wide Web) had been invented.

Recent years have seen a significant rise in the popularity and business acceptance of open source Unix (`http://www.opensource.org/osd.html`). Traditionally, commercial support for open source distributions was limited to small specialist outfits that tended to have limited geographical presence. The recent explosion of business interest in GNU/Linux has vendors lining up to earn support dollars. Times have really changed in the Unix world. In the world of commerce, proprietary Unix systems still rule the roost. Now, everyone is talking open source. What does open source bring to the party? We'll cover that shortly.

Classifying Unix Distributions

Unix distributions offer very different levels of security out of the box. Today, there are hundreds of distributions, although only about a dozen are in very widespread use. From a security perspective, we can group these into the following categories.

Immature

Immature Unix distributions include experimental, unsupported, and poorly supported distributions. These distributions ship with programs that have security vulnerabilities that are either well known or easy to identify and exploit. You'll generally want to leave these well alone, except for maybe shooting practice in the lab.

Mainstream

Mainstream Unix distributions are characterized by a large installed user base, commercial support services, and up until recently, binary-only distribution.

The best-selling closed-source, commercial off-the-shelf (COTS) distributions as of this writing are

- Sun Solaris

- Hewlett-Packard HP-UX

- IBM AIX

The vendors started with the same common code. Serious security holes are found from time to time, but their occurrence is infrequent enough to consider the code reasonably mature from a security perspective.

The weak area tends to be the vendor enhancements. Writing secure software places certain demands on the programmer. There is little evidence to show that operating system vendors can produce secure code in a sustainable manner. It's not that the entire programming industry is stupid—that would be an injustice to some very talented code cutters. It's evidence that writing secure software, under commercial time pressures, is a "hard problem." This should not come as a startling revelation to the software industry.

TIP

In case you have a hard time believing that the commercial operating system you run has a security history comparable to Swiss cheese, you can look up your OS in the SecurityFocus vulnerability database (`http://www.securityfocus.com/corporate/products/vdb /`). This service used to be free, but is now a commercial product, so you will have to pay to search. You might be surprised by the results.

Mainstream vendors generally agree that security is important. However, the focus is on tangible security features like encryption, rather than security of design and implementation. It's a lot easier to sell features than it is to sell assurance. Insecure software is invisible—that is, until someone decides to break in.

Many IT decision-makers implicitly trust mainstream vendors to produce a secure operating system. However, comprehensive security testing is nontrivial. It requires significant expertise to do comprehensively and takes time—both of which come at a cost. However, some vendors aren't even trying. This is evidenced by the frequency of posts to BugTraq from independent security researchers reporting basic security flaws in COTS software.

This situation is exacerbated by a commonly held belief that exploiting security vulnerabilities is rocket science. That's a myth perpetuated by the news media and a section of the security industry—the truth is that anyone with even a modicum of IT skills can break into a computer system installed straight off the CD-ROM. Exploit scripts are widely available and simple to use.

This might lead you to think about legal liability issues. Surely, the law must protect the consumer? The truth is on the shrink-wrap clinging to your OS media. Read the big, fat disclaimer (known as the license agreement). Before you accuse me of being flippant, go on—read that agreement—every last word of it. Here is a snippet from a product disclaimer most likely installed on your workstation:

> DISCLAIMER OF WARRANTIES: YOU AGREE THAT XYZ HAS MADE NO EXPRESS WARRANTIES TO YOU REGARDING THE SOFTWARE AND THAT THE SOFTWARE IS BEING PROVIDED TO YOU "AS IS" WITHOUT WARRANTY OF ANY KIND. XYZ DISCLAIMS ALL WARRANTIES WITH REGARD TO THE SOFTWARE, EXPRESS OR IMPLIED, INCLUDING, WITHOUT LIMITATION, ANY IMPLIED WARRANTIES OF FITNESS FOR A PARTICULAR PURPOSE, MERCHANTABILITY, MERCHANTABLE QUALITY OR NONINFRINGEMENT OF THIRD PARTY RIGHTS. SOME STATES OR JURISDICTIONS DO NOT ALLOW THE EXCLUSION OF IMPLIED WARRANTIES SO THE ABOVE LIMITATIONS MAY NOT APPLY TO YOU.

> LIMIT OF LIABILITY: IN NO EVENT WILL XYZ BE LIABLE TO YOU FOR ANY LOSS OF USE, INTERRUPTION OF BUSINESS, OR ANY DIRECT, INDIRECT, SPECIAL, INCIDENTAL, OR CONSE-QUENTIAL DAMAGES OF ANY KIND (INCLUDING LOST PROFITS) REGARDLESS OF THE FORM OF ACTION WHETHER IN CONTRACT, TORT (INCLUDING NEGLIGENCE), STRICT PRODUCT LIABILITY OR OTHERWISE, EVEN IF XYZ HAS BEEN ADVISED OF THE POSSIBILITY OF SUCH DAMAGES.

Now ask yourself—what recourse do you have if someone drives a juggernaut through your systems security via a security hole in this software? The truth is, none—zero. What other product would you buy that basically says "We do not stand by this product at all, you use it at your own risk, and by using it, you free the manufacturer of any liability"?

Until the customer wakes up and demands security, vendors will spend more time trying to out-feature their competitors rather than auditing and fixing their existing codebase. Sexy features sell boxes.

How Secure Is Open Source?

Open source proponents argue that a transparent development process, with the benefit of "many eyes" debugging and reviewing code, adds security in itself. They cite the development process of new cryptographic algorithms/protocols as an example of the need for an open code development model.

> **NOTE**
>
> The open source development model contrasts sharply with that of the traditional closed source model. To find out more, see Eric Raymond's classic paper at `http://www.tuxedo.org/`
> `~esr/writings/cathedral-bazaar`.

Developing secure cryptography is a "hard problem"—as is developing secure and reliable program code. At their own cost, less experienced cryptographers have often learned that a closed development model results in seemingly hard-to-break algorithms. Under the glare of an experienced cryptanalyst, however, they are soon broken.

Others feel that developing secure program code doesn't work out that way in practice. They point to the lack of experienced code auditors, the sheer volume of code to audit, and the general lack of interest. This point is worth considering. How many people do you know actually review the source code they download? How many people do you know have sufficient experience to actually find most, if not all, of the security holes? We all assume that "someone else is doing it."

Open source code is at times reviewed—just don't expect every line of every program you download to have been reviewed by elite security researchers. In reality, high-profile or security-related software tends to grab the lion's share of attention. Even then, the sheer size of it and the codebase's complexity can make reviewing a formidable challenge—even for highly skilled reviewers (as evidenced by code errors that slipped by reviewers of ISC BIND V4 and SSH version 2). However, this means that code that is not high-profile might end up getting less review and testing than the closed source code.

It should also be noted that crackers get a chance to review open source code for security faults. Therefore, open source can be a double-edged sword. The good news is that most, but not all, of the crackers out there are script kiddies (see Chapter 9, "Dispelling Some of the Myths," for more information) without programming talent.

Customers reviewing closed source software relies on either *black box testing* (threat testing) or reverse-engineering. Both can be very time-consuming, and require a great deal of patience and sound methodology on the part of the reviewers. Reverse-engineering can be incredibly tedious and exhausting—it can also be illegal (refer to your license agreement again). The current trend in lawmaking might soon outlaw reverse-engineering altogether. Our lawmakers run the risk of outlawing one of the few methods available for finding security holes in closed source software. Open source eliminates that problem.

TIP

To learn more about software assurance testing (such as white box testing), check out the Cigital (formerly Reliable Software Technologies) Web site at `http://www.cigital.com/resources/`.

The view you take on open/closed source programs will strongly influence your selection of an operating system and the security tools available to you.

Some organizations can be particularly sensitive about using open source software—particularly those subject to regulatory or legal demands. The issues tend to revolve around trustworthiness (that is, no Trojan code), integrity concerns, and formal support.

The extent of the concerns will often relate to the role the software will play and who else is using it (the sheep theory). Back doors are pretty much unheard of in popular open source software. They are more likely to occur on the download site itself (after an attacker has compromised a site). This is exactly what happened to the primary TCPWrappers download site in January 1999. CERT released an advisory (`http://www.cert.org/advisories/CA-1999-01.html`) reporting that the site had been compromised and a Trojan had been inserted into the TCPWrappers source. The changes were spotted pretty quickly, as the modified archive files were not PGP-signed by the author. However, this kind of incident is extremely rare and easy to detect.

Rather than blindly trust download sites, I recommend that you follow a policy of downloading software from multiple, well-known, separately managed sites (for example, CERT, COAST, and SecurityFocus.com). Also, use cryptographic integrity software (such as MD5, PGP, or GnuPG) to verify the integrity of the archive against a known good signature (again, use unrelated sites for the comparison).

TIP

For tips on using MD5, see `http://www.cert.org/security-improvement/implementations/i002.01.html`.

For a Win32 version of MD5, visit `http://www.weihenstephan.de/~syring/win32/UnxUtils.html`.

Formal support is a separate (mostly commercial) issue that I don't plan to cover here.

But what about using an entire operating system that is open source, such as GNU/Linux? Some people perceive that open source systems suffer more security problems than other platforms. They point to the number of security patches released and the volume of vulnerabilities reported on lists such as BugTraq.

My view is that the kernel itself doesn't appear to suffer from any more security problems than any other Unix kernel. It's widely regarded as more widely analyzed from a security perspective than any mainstream closed source Unix.

However, a Linux distribution consists of more than just a kernel. In fact, SuSE has grown so large, the Professional Edition ships on seven CDs! Thousands of applications are available for Linux, many of which have not been written with security in mind. As a result, the distributors who package all this code are regularly sending out security advisories and patches. This can lead to the incorrect conclusion that all patches issued are relevant. The message: Don't install everything off the CD—be a little selective—install what you need. More on that later.

> **TIP**
>
> For more on the open versus closed source code debate, check out these links:
>
> "Musings on Open Source Security Models," by Michael H. Warfield:
>
> `http://www.linuxworld.com/linuxworld/lw-1998-11/lw-11-ramparts.html`
>
> "Rethinking Security Through Obscurity," by Simson Garfinkel:
>
> "The Myth of Open Source Security," by John Viega:
>
> `http://www.earthweb.com/article/0,,10454_621851,00.html`

The biggest win with open source software is that, if you know what you are doing (or know someone who does), you can change the system yourself by implementing additional defenses. However, if you are not a security programming expert, you are just as likely to create new holes in the process, so you have to be careful. We'll cover some of the more popular options later. There really is nothing to beat the sense of empowerment you get when you realize that you have complete control over the way your system operates.

Hardened Operating Systems

In this category I'm including distributions that meet one or more of the following criteria:

- The distribution shipped with "secure by default" configuration settings.

- It was programmed defensively. The programmer assumes any user could be an attacker.

- The distribution maintainers subject their existing source code to a security audit whenever a new class of security vulnerability is discovered.

- The distribution has been compiled in such a way as to limit a common class of security exploit, the buffer overflow.

OpenBSD

Probably the best known example of a free, open source, hardened Unix distribution is OpenBSD (http://www.openbsd.org/). In fact, OpenBSD is one of the only distributions in general circulation to meet the first three criteria (OpenBSD's developers would probably reasonably argue that they don't need to do point 4, because they do points 2 and 3!).

OpenBSD's publicly stated goal is to be "Number one in the industry for security." They achieve this by attracting security-conscious programmers and adopting a tireless approach to weeding out both possible and not-so-possible security exposures.

Security benefits of OpenBSD include the following:

- Has secure "out-of-the-box" system configuration; that is, no time-consuming hardening is required.

- Ships with strong cryptography ready for use. OpenBSD includes OpenSSH for secure network terminal access, IPsec, strong PRNG (Pseudo Random Number Generator), secure hashing, and wide support for cryptographic hardware. See http://www.openbsd.org/crypto.html for more details.

- Suffers fewer security vulnerabilities than any other Unix I am aware of. Equally important though is the turnaround of fixes—typically within a day or two.

- Provides source code for independent scrutiny.

- Includes simplified installation and management in recent releases.

OpenBSD has been ported to 10 hardware platforms.

At the time of this writing, OpenBSD has no SMP (Symmetric Multiprocessing) support—this is a major drawback confining OpenBSD to single CPU use. A project to rectify this has been under way for more than two years, but is dependent on hardware donations and developer time.

Immunix

The Immunix team has taken a very different, albeit limited, approach from that of OpenBSD. Instead of attempting to fix bad code through code auditing, they use a specially modified compiler, StackGuard, to generate object code that can detect a buffer overflow attack in progress and halt program execution. The most common type of buffer overflow is "smashing the stack":

> *"Smash the stack"* [C programming] n. On many C implementations it is possible to corrupt the execution stack by writing past the end of an array declared auto in a routine. Code that does this is said to smash the stack, and can cause return from the routine to jump to a random address. This can produce some of the most insidious data-dependent bugs known to mankind. Variants include trash the stack, scribble the stack, mangle the stack; the term mung the stack is not used, as this is never done intentionally.
>
> —Extract from Aleph One's all-time classic paper "Smashing The Stack For Fun And Profit,"
> available from `http://destroy.net/machines/security/P49-14-Aleph-One`

StackGuard technology does not protect against the many other classes of attack (or even every type of buffer overflow attack)—but it does limit the damage of a buffer overflow attack to a denial of service, rather than a system compromise.

TIP

For a full explanation of the StackGuard approach, check out Crispin Cowans' original research work at `http://www.immunix.org/StackGuard/usenixsc98.pdf`.

As a practical demonstration of StackGuard in action, the Immunix team created ImmunixOS—a complete distribution of Red Hat Linux compiled using their StackGuard technology (the kernel itself is not StackGuarded, however).

TIP

A free CD image of ImmunixOS and other goodies can be downloaded from `http://www.immunix.org`.

To gain maximum benefit from compiler-based stack protection technology, you will need to recompile all your applications. If you don't have access to source code, you will not be able to StackGuard them.

WRAPPERS

You can develop wrappers to sanity-check program arguments and environment variables whether you use StackGuard or not. This technique is useful for protecting a privileged (set-uid/set-gid) program that you suspect, or know, is vulnerable to a buffer overflow attack.

Sanity-checking involves creating a small C program that replaces the suspect program. The wrapper is programmed to inspect command-line arguments and environment variables for suspicious input *before* calling the real program. Attempted attacks are logged to the system log via syslog, and the vulnerable program never gets called. Arguments that satisfy your checks are passed to the real program for program execution per normal.

The wrapper will need to be installed with the same permissions as the real program. This will mean making it set-uid/set-gid. You'd better be sure your replacement code doesn't have any security weaknesses! The real program needs to be relocated to a directory only accessible by the owner of the wrapper—otherwise, users could bypass your wrapper and call the suspect program directly.

The ultimate wrapper approach is to wrap every privileged program on the system—if you have the time. Be on the alert for patches and upgrades that overwrite your wrappers with updated binaries. You'll also need to update your wrappers as new features are added to the protected programs. As you can see, there is some cost in doing this on a permanent basis.

Fortunately, someone else (AUSCERT) has done the hard work of creating a wrapper for us. Source code and instructions for use are available here:

`ftp://ftp.auscert.org.au/pub/auscert/tools/overflow_wrapper/overflow_wrapper.c`

The next time you learn of a suspected security problem in a set-uid/set-gid program, you can create a custom wrapper while you wait on the vendor fix.

While I'm on the subject of defending against buffer overflow attacks, I would be remiss if I didn't mention Solar Designer's Linux kernel patch. For those wishing to delve deeper into stack attack and protection, check out the links in the following sections. They only go to prove that security is often a game of cat and mouse.

Linux Kernel Patch

Author: Solar Designer

Platform: Linux (but principles apply to other distributions)

URLs: `http://www.openwall.com/linux/` and `http://www.insecure.org/sploits/` `non-executable.stack.problems.html` (In fact, explore the entire site.)

The patch provides the following features detailed in the README:

- Nonexecutable user stack area
- Restricted links in /tmp
- Restricted FIFOs in /tmp
- Restricted access to /proc
- Special handling of fd 0, 1, and 2
- Enforced RLIMIT_NPROC on execve(2)
- The destruction of shared memory segments when they are no longer in use
- Privileged IP aliases (Linux 2.0 only)

Multilevel Trusted Systems

The final category of Unix distributions is trusted systems.

TIP

Trusted operating systems (TOSs) provide the basic security mechanisms and services that enable a computer system to protect, distinguish, and separate classified data. Trusted operating systems have been developed since the early 1980s and began to receive National Security Agency (NSA) evaluation in 1984.

http://www.sei.cmu.edu/str/descriptions/trusted_body.html

Under the traditional Unix privilege model, the root user has full run of the system. Root can do anything—root is god-like.

Trusted systems, however, totally change the privilege paradigm. The root user becomes a mere mortal—subject to the laws of the trusted Unix universe.

Trusted systems provide a fine-grained mechanism for controlling what actions a user can take.

For example, as any regular reader of news:alt.security.Unix will tell you, a frequently asked question (FAQ) is "How do I prevent my Unix users from accessing other network systems via Telnet/rlogin from my server?"

On a standard Unix system, your options are limited and ineffectual. You could revoke access to the Telnet binary or delete it all together—but a user can simply upload another copy and set the permissions he desires (most likely with a innocent-looking filename to avoid detection). They could use a totally different program or even develop another one.

The solution is to stop trying to control user activity from userland—it's futile. Instead of trying to prevent the user from running a command through file permissions, take a different approach—identify which system resources the command needs to actually function.

So, to communicate with a remote system, the Telnet program must initiate a TCP network connection to the system specified by the user (for example, Telnet *yourhost*). To do this, it needs a communication endpoint on the local system called a *socket*. Only after it has been given a socket can it connect to the destination system. After initiating a connection, the receiving Telnet daemon can accept or deny the connection based on its access control policy.

Userland programs can't just create sockets out of thin air. They need to ask the kernel. Subsequently, the Telnet program must ask the kernel to create a socket for TCP communications. This is your control point. You could choose to wait until the call to connect, but why allow the program to allocate a finite system resource (that is, a socket) in the first place if you don't want it to connect? To implement this control, you need to modify the kernel. If you're running a closed source Unix, for most of you, the ride ends here. Modifying system call code without source is hairy. (It is possible—it's just totally unsupported.) However, admins of open source distributions win out in this situation.

TIP

Thomas H. Ptacek has documented the complete process for a BSD kernel—see `http://skoda.sockpuppet.org/tqbf/sysctlpriv.html`. Repeat that exercise for every other system call supported by your kernel, and you have one part of a basic trusted operating system.

NOTE

A user program (often referred to as a *userland program*) cannot modify the kernel in an arbitrary way. If it could, it would be a breeze to gain root access. You could simply overwrite the memory location storing the owner ID of your current process ID with the number 0—that is, root. The next time your process was subject to an access check, the kernel would look up your process owner ID in the process table and see the number 0—you would pass any access check!

However, userland programs need a way to ask the kernel to carry out actions on their behalf. This is because the kernel is solely in charge of access to system devices—for example, the display, hard drives, memory, network interfaces, and so on. Programs make requests of the kernel via system calls. A *system call* is a discrete action such as "Open this file." The system calls supported by your system are listed in `/usr/include/sys.h`. Inside the kernel is a syscall table listing the system call number and a pointer to the code that the kernel calls to do the work. The kernel returns control to the userland program when the code implementing the system call returns.

Trusted operating systems implement the following concepts/principles:

- The principle of least privilege—This says that each subject (user) is granted the most restrictive set of privileges needed for the performance of authorized tasks. The application of this principle limits the damage that can result from accident, error, or unauthorized use.

- Mandatory Access Controls (MAC), as defined by the TCSEC (Trusted Computer System Evaluation Criteria)—"A means of restricting access to objects based on the sensitivity (as represented by a label) of the information contained in the objects and the formal authorization (that is, clearance) of subject to access information of such sensitivity."

- Privilege bracketing—The principle of enabling and disabling privilege around the smallest section of code that requires it.

- A trusted computing base—The totality of protection mechanisms within a computer system, including hardware, software, and firmware, the combination of which is responsible for enforcing a security policy. *Note:* The capability of a trusted computing base to correctly enforce a unified security policy depends on the correctness of the mechanisms within the trusted computing base, the protection of those mechanisms to ensure their correctness, and the correct input of parameters related to the security policy.

Until recently, the predominant consumers of TOS technology were military and government agencies. With the explosion of e-business, this has changed. This attention to Internet-facing systems is a little ironic, given that survey after survey of IT security incidents conclude that 50%–80% of attacks originate from within the organization. Not only that, but internal attacks actually cost the most because insiders can cause the most damage.

At the time of this writing, there are five major commercial suppliers of Unix TOS products: Hewlett-Packard, Sun, Trusted BSD, NSA, and IBM.

Hewlett-Packard Praesidium VirtualVault

The HP TOS VirtualVault only runs on Hewlett-Packard hardware. The operating system is a hardened version of HP-UX. Focused on Web-based e-business applications, VirtualVault ships with Netscape Enterprise Server and a Trusted Gateway Agent.

VirtualVault replaces the all-powerful root user with 50 distinct privileges, granting each application only the minimum operating system privileges it requires to run properly. It incorporates many of the B-level Department of Defense Trusted Computer System (TCSEC) features. See `http://www.hp.com/security/products/virtualvault/papers/` for more information.

TIP

Even VirtualVault hasn't escaped the security bugfest unscathed. Check out `http://packetstormsecurity.nl/9905-exploits/hp.vvos.tgad.dos.txt`.

Trusted Solaris

Sun has taken Solaris and hardened it. The result is Trusted Solaris 8. Trusted Solaris 8 is similar to VirtualVault in that it removes the root account. It can also work with Sun's firewall product line. More information is available at `http://wwws.sun.com/software/solaris/trustedsolaris/`.

AIX TCSEC Evaluated C2 Security

IBM has a special version of AIX that has been evaluated at the C2 security level. It is a subset of AIX that eliminates some of the dangerous features. Check out `http://www-1.ibm.com/servers/aix/products/ibmsw/security/c2brief.html`.

Trusted BSD

TrustedBSD (`http://www.trustedbsd.org/`) lets you peek at the code.

Currently under development, TrustedBSD is a set of security extensions to the FreeBSD Unix operating system. The developers hope TrustedBSD will take FreeBSD into environments that have higher security requirements. The extensions are being integrated into core FreeBSD (`http://www.freebsd.org`).

NSA

The highly secretive U.S. National Security Agency (NSA), in conjunction with Network Associates, Mitre, and Secure Computing, has published an open source security extension for GNU/Linux. This includes a "strong, flexible mandatory access control architecture based on Type Enforcement." According to the online documentation, the NSA developed the Flask security architecture and prototyped it in the Mach and Fluke research operating systems. By integrating the Flask architecture into the Linux operating system, they hope to substantially broaden the audience of the technology. For more details, check out `http://www.nsa.gov/selinux/index.html`.

Realities of Running TOS

The substantial security improvement provided by a TOS does come at a cost, particularly:

- The need for specialized administration skills—The administrator(s) must be well-versed in both TOS concepts and real-world administration. Hiring experienced TOS administrators is not easy (they are few and far between). Also consider that internal support structures will need to change with the role-based administration inherent in TOS.

- The need to understand your application's security requirements in depth— Installing a TOS brings immediate benefits—your OS has suddenly become resilient against the majority of attackers. However, now you need to tell the TOS about your applications—that is, what OS resources your applications need to access. This can be tricky for two reasons. First, application documentation rarely includes anything like the kind of detailed information you'll need to do this. Second, applications are a moving target. Testing before upgrades becomes ultra-critical—a subtle, undocumented change in a rarely used application function could lead to access problems if the TOS application profile hasn't been updated. For commercial customers deploying popular corporate products (for example, ORACLE RDBMS), this will be less of a hurdle, because commercial providers of TOS technologies tend to have application security profiles for common enterprise applications. Unusual closed source applications will require significant testing and observation by administrators well-versed in troubleshooting TOS compatibility issues.

- Loss of flexibility—To fully realize the potential of using a TOS, you will want to lock down the privileges of applications and administrative accounts. By definition, this costs you flexibility—you will no longer be able to make major configuration changes to security-sensitive parts of the OS on the fly! If you value ultimate flexibility over hardcore security, then you probably don't want to run a TOS. It's a case of using the right tool for the right job. But don't forget: Flexibility benefits the attacker, too!

- TOS systems can still be hacked if they are not configured carefully or contain security bugs.

The decision to deploy a trusted Unix system will hinge on your analysis of risk: the value of the information you are trying to protect, the perceived threats, and the probability of attack. Security controls are an insurance policy of sorts. Your spending on security (both initial and ongoing costs) should reflect this.

Security Considerations in Choosing a Distribution

Consider the following key security factors when selecting a Unix distribution:

- Understand the intended use of the system. What threats must the system defend against? Consider physical, human, and technological threats.

- Gauge the technical security competence and awareness of the primary administrator(s). Distributions that are a significant departure from local technical security expertise should be considered a higher risk (unless technical security training will be provided). Vendor-provided security training classes tend to be weak. The SANS Institute offers good introductory courses.

- Learn about the vendor's approach to handling reported security vulnerabilities. Do they even acknowledge that vulnerabilities occur in their distribution? Do they have a clearly documented process for handling reports from outside? Do they watch BugTraq for reports of security problems in their software? Do they provide email addresses for reporting new security problems?

- Assess the vendor's response time when fixing security vulnerabilities. The SecurityFocus vulnerability database is useful for comparing the public announcement date and vendor fix dates.

- Consider the maturity and stability of built-in security tools and interface. Weak areas tend to be C2 audit log management and analysis, mixed coverage of daemon logging to syslog, and clunky security interfaces that can result in mistakes being made in security settings.

- Do a gap analysis, comparing the native security features against your Unix security policy. Consider the availability, cost, and installation overhead of third-party/open source tools required to plug the gap.

- Estimate the time it will take to lock down a virgin install of the distribution to comply with your policy. Calculate the cost of the administrator's time and possible delays on projects. This is the cost of buying distributions that are not secure by default. Ask the vendor to provide you with smart ways to lower this cost.

- Visit the vendor support site. How long does it take to find the security alerts/bulletins and security patches? Read a couple of security bulletins. Do they make sense? Do they tell you enough about the problem to figure out whether you would need the patch? Compare a security bulletin with the original announcement made on BugTraq (search the archives at http://archives. neohapsis.com/search/). Does the vendor's assessment of the problem tally with the original report?

- Assess the ease of security patching. Are stable tools available to identify missing patches easily? Are these kept up to date? Can patch installation be reliably automated for server farms? Are MD5 hashes available to validate patch integrity? Bear in mind the SANS finding that failing to update systems when security holes are found is the third most serious security mistake.

- Check the release versions of any bundled third-party software (for example, sendmail, bind, or wu-ftpd). Make sure they are current or that the vendor has backported fixes for security problems.

Unix Security Risks

You've chosen your Unix distribution (or someone else did it for you), and you need to know where the risks are. All operating systems have security problems—no matter what anyone might tell you to the contrary. Anything with some complexity, written by humans and managed by humans, inherits the wonderful flaws of the authors along the way.

The main risk areas on a typical, modern day Unix system tend to be the following:

- Misconfigured/buggy network daemons—These leave your system open to attack from anyone who can "see" your server across the network. The attacker doesn't need an account on your system to exploit these security holes. These are classified as *remote vulnerabilities*.

- Poorly chosen user passwords—Bottom line: Passwords are an inconvenience for most users. Systems configured to enforce fascist password rules only encourage users to write down their passwords. A middle ground is required—this is a people issue, rather than a technical one.

- Buggy privileged programs (set-uid/set-gid)—What happens when an attacker subverts a program that executes with special privileges? Well, it depends on the specific vulnerability. All too often, though, system security is breached, and the attacker can take control over the operating system. These problems are classified as *local vulnerabilities*, as the attacker requires a user account to exploit them (which might or might not be obtained legitimately).

- Filesystem nightmares—Badly set file permissions, sloppy handling of temporary files, race conditions, and insecure defaults are all culprits. Exploiting these can lead to leakage of sensitive information, introduction of Trojan code, and destruction of data. Bottom line: An insecure filesystem affects the integrity of the entire system.

- Insecure applications—Naive designs and sloppy programming practices combine to produce a giant sore on your system—exposed to anyone who tries to exploit the myriad of possible weaknesses. Bolting down your Unix server is not enough if someone can drive a tank through your application security.

The common trait these risk areas share is insecurely written code. We'll cover each category in more detail in the following sections.

BUZZT!

Actually, some people use these weaknesses to study attackers. Lance Spitzner used to get his kicks from blowing up things in his tanks. Today, he enjoys observing attacks launched against his honey pot system. A paper on his experiences is available at `http://www.enteract.com/~lspitz/honeypot.html` and `http://www.honeynet.org`.

A sacrificial host is built—with no security patches—and connected to the Internet (typically outside a firewall or within a DMZ). A series of logging mechanisms are activated to record probes and attacks. After a compromise, Lance is able to reconstruct all the attackers' activity via the captured packet trace.

This kind of exercise provides an insight into the way attackers compromise a victim machine, and more importantly, what they do when they have.

A number of organizations run honey pots to identify new attacks "in the wild." By coordinating their efforts, they are able to track new trends and issue alerts to the wider community.

Be warned though: Having drawn attackers to your site, you had better be sure they won't compromise your real network or discover you monitoring their activity. Sophisticated attackers can identify a honey pot very quickly.

User Accounts

If you haven't read Chapter 14, "Password Security," I recommend that you do so now.

Users, bless 'em, can give up your system's security no matter what lockdown procedures you have implemented. The age-old problem of poorly chosen passwords continues to plague any operating system or device that requires them.

One security practitioner I know describes passwords as "past their sell-by date." The problem doesn't seem to go away, and there is no reason to believe that it is going to. Therefore, a change of tack might be necessary, and you should give serious consideration to moving to other forms of authentication, such as one-time passwords (OTP), biometrics, or smartcards. No authentication system is perfect—many appear impressive until you start analyzing their issues. However, it doesn't take a giant leap to improve upon passwords.

Assuming you're stuck with Unix passwords, here's what can you can do to improve things:

- Limit access to the root account on a need-to-have basis. Root is all powerful, and you'll want to avoid giving this level of access to anyone who doesn't have a legitimate need for it.

- Don't give root access to anyone who can't demonstrate adequate technical expertise AND judgment. You get to define "adequate." Mistakes will happen from time to time, but allowing untrained newbies access to root is asking for trouble. At the same time, don't make a big thing about the root account to those you refuse—it might cause resentment that could lead to other security problems!

- Set a strong password on the root account. Stick to a minimum of eight characters and include special characters.

- Disable root logins across the network. Have admins make use of su, or better yet, deploy sudo.

NOTE

sudo is an incredibly useful utility. It allows the administrator to permit users to run commands for which they do not usually have the privilege. For example, you have a helpdesk that needs to be able to change passwords for everybody except the administrators. This is easy with sudo. You define a sudo rule to permit anyone in the helpdesk group (or using the helpdesk user ID, if you are not allergic to shared accounts) to run the passwd command as root—with a twist. You also define what arguments can or cannot be passed to the command. So, in this case, you would specify the administrator user IDs as invalid arguments (by using the exclamation mark to signify negation). sudo can be found at http://www.courtesan.com/sudo/.

- Store the root password offline in an envelope (signed across the join) in a secure place. In large environments, make sure that a log of access is kept.

- Don't use the same passwords across all machines. The compromise of a single password should not result in a complete giveaway. Categorize your systems in virtual groups, by either risk or data sensitivity. Assign a unique root password to each virtual group. In practice, these groups can be used for testing, development, and production. However, if you're storing the same data on all those systems, you either need to revisit your data security policy or think of another way to group your systems.

- Ban access to remote access servers that don't support encryption. Telnet and FTP send passwords in cleartext across the network. At a minimum, make sure your privileged users use ssh and scp.

- Implement password construction checks on the server. Set minimum values for password length, the number of alphanumerics, and where supported, special characters.

- Implement real-time password dictionary checks. Use software like npasswd (http://www.utexas.edu/cc/Unix/software/npasswd/)as a replacement for the stock password program. This type of software does require some configuration on the part of the administrator, but goes a long way toward solving the problem of easy-to-guess passwords.

- Instigate a password-cracking policy. Every month or quarter, attempt to crack all passwords (administrator accounts included). Track the percentage cracked and set targets. Use a decent-sized cracking dictionary (look for one at http://www.accessdata.com/dictionaries.htm) and add words that relate to your environment (for example, project names, team names, supplier names, nicknames, and so on).

- Create a password policy that states the required length and composition of passwords. Make sure all system users have seen it.

- Educate your users on strategies for choosing good passwords. For example, have them think of a line from a favorite song or quote and select the first letter of each word to make up a password—for example, "I Left My Heart in San Francisco" would be IlmhiSF. Then mutate the password by adding in special characters—for example, !lmhi$F_. That would take a while to crack. This can make hard passwords easy to remember.

- Don't think that by replacing letters with numbers in passwords you are going to outsmart a cracker. Password cracking programs do this automatically, too.

- Give serious consideration to enforcing account lockout after three or five failed logins. This can lead to a denial-of-service attack if you are in a hostile environment—a malicious user could lock out all the accounts on purpose simply by typing gibberish for users' passwords. (However, DoS is generally a low risk in an internal network.)

- Make sure that your helpdesk doesn't just re-enable locked accounts (or create new ones) for anyone who calls the desk with a friendly voice. It's a well-known fact that social engineering an over-obliging support staff is easier than bypassing a well-configured firewall.

- Don't let your support staff fall into the trap of using the same password when resetting locked accounts. Invest in some software that generates passwords that are phonetically easy to pronounce. (This won't work for multilingual support desks.)

- If a user calls to have her password reset, use a callback scheme on a prearranged number, or failing that, leave the new password on the user's voicemail. Don't tell the user the password there and then unless you know the person's voice well enough to spot an impersonator. This might sound a little too paranoid, but consider what someone might gain by doing this, and how stupid you'd look if you simply gave the password to them on a plate!

- Alternatively, to avoid these helpdesk issues about resetting accounts and passwords, implement a Password Reset product. These work by having users provide the answers to some identifying questions to which only they know the answer. A sample product is Password Station (http://www.passwordstation. net).

- Go on walkabout every now and then to check whether users are writing passwords down. For example, are passwords written on sticky notes on monitors? If they are, have a quiet word with the user. Persistent offenders might find remembering different passwords to different machines hard. Consider using software like Counterpane's Password Safe (http://www.counterpane.com/ passsafe.html). This installs on the client machine and can securely store passwords—unlocked via a single password. Just make sure this one is strong and not written down! This software is particularly useful for administrators.

- Make sure that your systems are using shadow passwords. Unix used to store passwords in the /etc/passwd file. However, as CPU technology forged ahead, it wasn't long before these passwords were being cracked. Check to make sure that your passwords are being stored in a location readable only by root.

- Avoid hard-coding passwords in scripts if at all possible. If you have to, make sure file permissions are set to user access only. stores Unix server passwords on the client in an easy-to-decrypt/decipher form. XOR'd in the NT registry does this, for example.

Filesystem Security

This section reviews fundamental filesystem and privilege concepts. When it comes to input and output, Unix treats everything as a file. In fact, the term *file* has multiple meanings in Unix—it can be a

- Regular file—A sequence of data bytes collectively regarded by the operating system as a file.

- Directory file—A list of filenames and pointers to file meta information (that's a fancy way of saying "information about a file"). If you have read access to a directory, it means you can read the contents of the directory—in other words, get a directory listing (ala ls(1)). However, only the Unix kernel has the capability to modify the contents of this file (for example, insert a new entry).

- Symbolic link—Contains the name of another file. When a symbolic link is accessed, the kernel recognizes the file as such by examining its file-type. It then reads the file contents. The kernel opens the file with the name stored in the symbolic link. System administrators frequently use symbolic links to relocate data to another filesystem while maintaining the path of the parent directory. Attackers, on the other hand, use symbolic links for more nefarious purposes, as we'll cover later.

- Character special—Represents a byte-oriented device. It is the Unix interface to devices that operate on a byte-by-byte basis, like a terminal device.

- Block special—Functions like a character special file, but for block-oriented devices such as disk drives.

- Socket—Allows one process to communicate with another process—whether on the local system (via Inter Process Communication) or a remote machine. Programs such as Telnet, rlogin, and FTP all use sockets.

- Named pipe—Supports local Inter Process Communication (IPC). Because of the type of queuing used, it is sometimes referred to as a FIFO (First In First Out).

Each of these objects is stored in the filesystem. Protecting the filesystem from abuse is critical to the ongoing integrity of your operating system, application programs, and data.

File Attributes

The Unix filesystem supports a standard set of file attributes or properties. These attributes are stored in a data structure called the *inode* (*index node*)—every file has an inode. On Solaris, the inode data structure for the traditional Unix FileSystem (UFS) is defined in /usr/include/sys/fs/ufs_inode.h.

From a security perspective, the most important attributes include the following:

- The owner ID—The numeric user ID that owns the file.

- The group ID—The numeric group ID that owns the file.

- Permissions—Combined with the owner ID and group ID, these determine the access controls on the file.

- Size—Measured in bytes.

- Time of last access—The time the file was last accessed, in seconds, since 1970.

- Time of last modification—The time the file was last modified, in seconds, since 1970.

- Time of last inode change—The time the file was created, in seconds, since 1970.

- Number of hard links—The number of files that "point" at this file.

The permissions attribute defines the access rights of the file owner, the group owner, and all other users on the system. The root user and file owner can control access to a file by setting permissions on the file and on the parent directories.

In the standard implementation of Unix, the root user is not subject to permission checking—root can read, write, or execute any file. Note that, in Unix, write access is equivalent to delete—by definition, if you can write to the file, you can erase the contents of the file.

Readers unfamiliar with filesystem permissions are encouraged to read the chmod man page. For further reading, I highly recommend W. Richard Stevens' *Advanced Programming in the Unix Environment*, Addison-Wesley, 1992, ISBN 0-201-56317-7.

Permissions in Practice
To access a file by name, a user must have execute privilege in every directory contained in the file path, as well as appropriate access to the file itself. In the case of files in the current directory, a user needs execute privilege for the current directory.

To be able to create a file in a directory, a user must have execute permission on every directory in the path, as well as write permission in the target directory.

When it comes to deleting a file, it isn't actually necessary to be the file owner or have write permission on the file. By having write and execute permissions on the parent directory, you can delete files. This can be a "gotcha" if you're not careful.

To understand how the various permissions are checked when a user attempts to open a file, you need to understand how process privileges work.

Put simply, when you execute a program, a process is created. Associated with a process are at least six IDs:

- Real User ID—The numeric user ID of your login account

- Real Group ID—The numeric group ID of your primary group (the group defined in your /etc/passwd entry)

- Effective User ID—The numeric user ID used during file access permission checks

- Effective Group ID—The numeric group ID used during file access permission checks

- Saved Set User ID—A copy of the numeric user ID saved by the exec function when you execute a program

- Saved Set Group ID—A copy of the numeric group ID saved by the exec function when you execute a program

In addition, if you are a member of more than one Unix group, a corresponding number of supplementary group IDs will be set.

At first glance, this might seem overcomplicated. To appreciate why so many IDs are required, we have to talk about a key security mechanism of Unix: the set-uid/set-gid privilege.

The set-uid/set-gid Privilege

Normally, when you execute a program, a process is created that runs with the privileges associated with your user ID. This makes sense; you shouldn't be able to interfere with files or processes belonging to another user. However, some programs need to carry out privileged operations. They can't do this if they execute under the user ID of an unprivileged caller. To make a program privileged, the program owner (or root) can assign the set-uid or set-gid bit to the program via the chmod command.

Unlike ordinary programs, a set-uid program executes with the privileges of the program owner—not the caller. By making a program set-uid, you allow it to take actions with the authority of the program owner on your behalf.

set-gid works the same way, but not surprisingly, for groups. A set-gid program runs with the privileges of the owning group rather than with the privileges associated with the group of the user ID that called the program.

set-gid can also be set on a directory. Files subsequently created within a set-gid directory will have their group ownership set the same as that of the set-gid directory. Usually the group owner would be set to the users' primary group. This way, a group of users can share data despite being in different primary groups.

An example of a set-uid program is the `passwd` program. When you change your password, the system needs a way to modify your password entry in `/etc/shadow`. This file is only accessible by root because it stores passwords; however, this prevents you from legitimately changing your password. By making the `passwd` program set-uid, you allow a nonprivileged user ID to update its password. Without the set-uid bit, users would have to ring up the administrator to have the passwords changed. Eventually, the administrator's temper is bound to fray—see the BOFH series at `http://members.iinet.net.au/~bofh/` for enlightenment.

In our example, the security of the shadow file is at the mercy of the passwd program. If the user running the password program can somehow influence the program in a way the programmer didn't consider, she might be able to directly modify the shadow file!

Therefore, set-uid programs must be programmed defensively to avoid being subverted by an attacker to gain extra privileges. In the case of a set-uid root program, the stakes are very high—one exploitable bug will mean game over, as the attacker is granted root privileges.

The umask

Our review of file permissions would be incomplete without studying the umask. The *umask* determines the set of permissions that will apply to a newly created file if no permissions are explicitly specified at creation time. In other words, it's the default file permission.

The umask is represented as the inverse of the file permissions. For example, if our default umask is 022, any files you create in which you don't explicitly set the file permissions will be created with 755 permissions; that is, user ID has read, write, and execute permissions, whereas group ID and Other have read and execute permissions. Just remember that the umask should be set to a value opposite of the permissions you want.

A common default umask value is 022. This is usually set in a system-wide login script such as `/etc/profile`. This can be overridden by a user who specifies a different (usually more restrictive) value in his local login script (for example, `~user/.profile`). The umask command is a built-in shell command; it can be run at the shell prompt—for example, as `umask 022`.

Every process on a Unix system has a umask setting—it doesn't just affect the users who log in interactively. When the system boots and executes the system start-up scripts, a number of network daemons (services) are started. They inherit the umask value of their parent process `init`—usually 022. Any files they subsequently create will be given permissions set by the umask unless the programmer has explicitly set permissions.

The umask setting is therefore incredibly important—if it is set too loosely, other users might be able to read, or in some cases, write over your files. Despite its importance, it is commonly overlooked by programmers.

Filesystem Risks

With the theory out of the way, let's examine the risks. The primary risks are

- Data disclosure—I don't want to belabor an obvious point, but this is so incredibly common that it deserves some attention. Users and programs create files in /tmp—it's a digital scrap yard. If the user doesn't specify file permissions, the umask value applies. Commonly, the default umask of 022 is set, and the file is given world-readable permissions—any user on the system can read the file.

  On a typical multiuser system, it is not unusual to find copies of scripts containing database passwords, confidential business data, sensitive log information, and core files containing encrypted passwords in /tmp. The same goes for user home directories and shared areas that have not been locked down to prevent access by Other. Why break in if you can read your way to root?

- Unauthorized data modification/deletion—This happens in two common ways. First, through lax user practices—someone sets world-writable permissions on a file. The second way is via world-writable directories. If I create a file in a directory that is world-writable, any local user can subsequently delete/modify it.

  This is also true for filesystems shared via NFS. The only exception to this is directories that have the sticky bit set (such as /tmp). If the file permissions are locked down, only the owner can write to the file. This is not always obvious, because the world-writable directory might be the parent of the parent of the current directory, or the parent of the parent's parent. In an extreme case, if the / directory is world-writable, an attacker can replace any file on the system—for example, by moving /usr/sbin out of the way and creating a replacement /usr/sbin, filled with Trojan programs of their choosing. This can easily lead to a total system compromise.

  The bottom line is that it's not just the parent directory that counts—but every directory along the way up to slash (/)! This problem is surprisingly common on system and application directories.

- Resource consumption—Each filesystem is built with a finite number of inodes. When all inodes are consumed, no more files can be written to the filesystem, regardless of available free space. On some versions of Unix, this can cause system daemons to crash or hang when /tmp is involved. Unless file giveaways (the capability for a non-root user to change the ownership of a file) have been disabled in the kernel, the culprit can cast the blame on another user simply by changing the ownership of the files she has created to the victim via the chown command. Consuming all free space is another approach.

- Temporary files with predictable filenames—Programs can be subverted to overwrite or remove arbitrary files if they create temporary files with predictable filenames in directories writable by Other (commonly /tmp). Other users can guess a filename in advance and create a symbolic link to a system file. When the program runs, it writes data to the system file resulting in data corruption. If that's the passwd file, you have a denial-of-service attack on your hands. This is incredibly common—especially in application code and administrators' shell scripts.

TIP

Privileged shell scripts that read filenames from the filesystem and blindly pass them to another program can be subverted. SNI (Secure Networks Inc.) posted an advisory way back in 1996 about this problem; it is archived at http://lists.insecure.org/bugtraq/1996/ Dec/0133.html. This weakness is still present in some commercial distributions today.

- World-readable/writable named pipes—One method for processes to communicate with one another is through the filesystem using a named pipe. If the pipe has been created with weak permissions, an attacker can read and write to the named pipe, subverting/crashing the process at the other end of the pipe or reading privileged data.

- Race conditions—Matt Bishop coined the acronym TOCTTOU (Time Of Check To Time Of Use) for a common race condition—namely, when a program checks for a particular characteristic of an object and takes some action based on the assumption that the characteristic still holds true. However, if a program is subject to race conditions, an attacker can swap the object between the time the check is made and the subsequent use of the object. This tricks the program, which will then operate on the wrong object. You can find more on race conditions in Chapter 26, "Application Development, Languages, and Extensions."

Filesystem Countermeasures

Here are some things you can do to minimize your filesystem exposures:

- Give clear direction in your security policy about the need to protect the organization's data. Classify information by sensitivity and define what access controls are required. Give examples.

- Set the TMPDIR environment variable to a private, per-user temporary directory. Well-behaved programs check TMPDIR before using /tmp.

- Audit your shell scripts and change all references to publicly-writable directories to your own tmp directory. For bonus points, create unique filenames without relying on the time, date, or process ID (or a weak pseudo-random number generator).

- Educate users about file permissions and the effect of the umask. In sensitive environments, have your users sign a usage policy that includes good stewardship of information.

- Ask users about their information-sharing needs. Create additional Unix groups as necessary and enroll users as appropriate to support data sharing at a more granular level. The group's mechanism can be used very creatively—think long-term and design a flexible group access model.

- Make sure that the system-wide umask is set to 027 in the system shell start-up files as a minimum.

- Modify system startup files to set the umask to 027.

- Create a cron job to check user start-up scripts for inappropriate umask settings.

- Audit /tmp and other shared directories now on your servers. Perform spot checks on /tmp. Persistent offenders should be warned that they are in breach of policy. If the warnings are not heeded and the information is sensitive, consider emailing a summary of interesting finds to management.

- Disable core file creation (not to be confused with kernel crash dumps) via the ulimit command. Modern Unix kernels will refuse to dump core when a set-uid program crashes because this might reveal sensitive information. However, privileged system daemons and application processes might dump core, resulting in chunks of sensitive system files being written to a world-readable core file. Validate your fix by sending a QUIT signal to an expendable network service, and check that it doesn't produce a core dump in its current working directory. (/proc or lsof can help find that out.)

- Monitor /tmp for predictable filenames using a tool such as L0pht's tmpwatch, available at http://www.atstake.com/research/tools/l0pht-watch.tar.gz.

- Make sure named pipes are included in your file permission checks! These are used for IPC, so lax permissions will allow an attacker to interact with processes in ways you don't want.

- Prevent file giveaways by setting CHOWN_RESTRICTED to true in the kernel configuration file. Note: Many versions of Unix do not allow file giveaways at all.

- Consider using extended ACLs (where supported) via the getfacl and setfacl commands (Solaris). These extend the access information stored in the inode. They can be used to give a user access to a file or directory even if that user is not in the owning group or is not the file owner, and the file permissions deny access by Other. However, ACLs can be a real pain to administrate. Personally, I recommend that you design a good group model and only use extended ACLs when you really need to.

The set-uid Problem

Programming mistakes in set-uid programs have been a real source of security headaches. A single security hole in just one set-uid root program can be all an attacker needs to gain root access.

The problem is widespread. We're not talking about one or two isolated instances—more like a graveyard of broken set-uid programs. Again, check the SecurityFocus.com vulnerability database for set-uid problems—there have been hundreds (thousands?)! The problem isn't going away, either—especially in third-party programs. New set-uid vulnerabilities are being reported to BugTraq on a regular basis.

TIP

Writing secure set-uid programs can be difficult. Just because you can program C doesn't make you a security god. Heck, even the security gods get it wrong sometimes. Take, for example, L0pht (`http://www.safermag.com/html/safer25/alerts/33.html`)—a group that knows its subject inside out.

The C language is pretty unforgiving to the developer of set-uid programs—C makes it too easy to screw up and open the barn door. Specifically, the lack of bounds-checking in C has allowed many developers to write programs with buffer overflows.

However, it would be pretty lame for us to blame a language for set-uid problems. After all, the security pitfalls of C are well documented—it's hardly a new language. Alas, the biggest source of security vulnerabilities is naive programmers slapping together code they think is secure.

A typical Unix distribution ships with a large number of set-uid root files—averaging between 70 and 100. Now, not every line of code necessarily runs with root privilege—the privilege has to be invoked by the program via a call to set-uid. But, even if the privileged lines of code are written super-securely, a wily attacker can exploit a hole in the nonprivileged section of code (that is, before the call to set-uid) with devastating consequences. If the attacker exploits a buffer overflow and can force the program to make a call to set-uid—boom, game over. Any code the attacker can supply for the program to execute will run with root privileges. Security-savvy programmers throw away the set-uid privilege as early as possible in the program.

So, given the number of privileged programs, the administrator is left to ponder: "Where will the next vulnerability be found?" The answer is, we simply don't know. Hence, the stock advice of any security textbook is to remove the set-uid bit from unnecessary privileged programs. This is much easier said than done. How do you know what is unnecessary? Sure, you know programs like passwd need to be set-uid, but what about all those others? Removing the set-uid bit has to be done with a great deal of care—unless you want to have a lot of free time on your hands.

Another more common example is the ping program. ping sends an ICMP ECHO REQUEST packet to a remote system and waits for a response (ICMP ECHO REPLY) to check whether the remote system is alive (although not necessarily functioning). The standard implementation of ping requires a raw socket to be capable of building the ICMP ECHO REQUEST packet. This is a privileged action, because having access to a raw socket means you can create custom packets—very dangerous in the wrong hands. So the ping command is set-uid root.

Unfortunately, allowing mischievous users access to seemingly innocuous programs like ping can result in a security nightmare. Remember the Ping of Death? The ping command has an option whereby the user can control the size of the ICMP packet sent. It turns out that some implementations of ping allow users to send out very large ping packets that have caused remote systems to crash. Was anyone expecting that? Of course not. Hence, the need to follow the least privilege principle. Only allow users to run what they need to run to do their job. Does every user on every system really need to be able to run network diagnostic tools?

Then there are those set-uid programs that don't even need to be set-uid—typically, system administration commands. The set-uid bit is redundant if only root is running it.

I am not aware of any vendors that provide any guidance or sufficient technical program documentation to help an administrator easily identify nonessential set-uid programs.

Fortunately for Solaris and Linux users, there is some good information out there on locking down your set-uid programs.

Solaris 8 set-uid lockdown information can be found at

`http://ist.uwaterloo.ca/security/howto/2000-08-17/` -

Solaris 7 information is here:

`http://ist.uwaterloo.ca/security/howto/1999-04-21`

and Solaris 2.6 information is here:

`http://ist.uwaterloo.ca/security/howto/2000-08-22`

So, how do you minimize your system's exposure to set-uid holes that are waiting in the wings?

1. Try to avoid installing the full distribution—install only what you need. This is a security best practice. If the code isn't on your hard drive, then no one can use it against you. But this can be hard to fulfill in a pressure-filled environment where the focus is on getting things live. Just remember the costs of post-live lockdown.

2. List all the set-uid/set-gid programs on the system. You can do this with the following commands:

```
find / -perm -u+s -print

find / -perm -g+s -print
```

3. Find out the stated purpose of each program. You're likely to find that some of them are totally unnecessary—neither you nor your users would ever need to run them. As long as these programs are not required for system operation, they can have the set-uid bit removed, or alternatively, all access by Other can be removed (that is, chmod o-rwx *file*).

4. Identify the set-uid root programs that only root needs to run and remove the set-uid bit—they don't need to be set-uid because you'll be running them as root. There's no point in leaving potential time bombs lying around for someone to play with. Remove the set-uid bit or access by Other (either is good). This can eliminate a large number of programs.

5. Identify set-uid programs that leak sensitive system information and thereby make an attacker's life easy—for example, ps, top, and netstat. ps and top display process information, including command-line arguments—these can contain application usernames and passwords. They also help an attacker identify usage patterns, which assists in the timing of attacks. Similarly, netstat reveals information about your network topology (via the -R switch) and current network connections (who is talking to your system).

   This kind of privacy disclosure can lead to client systems being attacked. Client systems are soft targets, the "low hanging fruit" of the network. They can be used as remote password sniffers (to compromise accounts on more systems), proxies to misdirect attack investigations, and conduits to other network segments that are unreachable directly (that is, they are behind a firewall or not directly attached). It's not hard to imagine the consequences if the client victim happens to belong to the system administrator level.

   Limit access to "leaky" set-uid programs on a strictly need-to-have basis. The side message is to secure your clients machines—they can be used against you!

6. Identify the set-uid root programs that only a trusted group of users need to run (for example, network operations). Create a dedicated Unix group and enroll the trusted users in this group. Next, change the group ownership of the set-uid programs to this group (don't change the owner, because that would make the set-uid call fail). Finally, and very importantly, remove all points of access by Other (that is, chmod o-rwx *file*). These include print queue management programs, network utilities, and application management interfaces.

7. Identify the set-uid root programs you think no one will ever need. Before you remove a set-uid bit, you need to be totally convinced you won't break something. In cases like these, you need to profile the programs' uses—that is, to log program invocation. One approach is to install an AUSCERT wrapper like the one discussed earlier. But we're not going to use the wrapper for its intended purpose here (although there is nothing stopping you from doing so). Instead, we're going to modify the wrapper to make a call to the `logger` command before the real program is called. This is unnecessary if you have C2 auditing configured and are logging calls to `exec()`. Review your logs after a month, and if no relevant activity has been logged, you probably have sufficient basis to remove the set-uid bit. You might want to leave your pager on for a while, though.

8. You should now be left with a handful of set-uid root programs that you consider essential. Modify the AUSCERT wrapper for those programs to make sure overly long arguments or environment variables cannot be specified. This won't protect you against all attacks, but will protect you against some of the common ones.

Pat yourself on the back—you've made it a lot harder for an attacker to succeed against your system.

Maintenance-wise, you will find that some vendor patches assume a vanilla install, and therefore patches and upgrades clobber your changes. Always run a file integrity checker after applying updates to identify changes—that way, you avoid your efforts being undermined by dumb scripts.

Make sure you keep an eye on BugTraq to keep up with new set-uid exposures, and subscribe to your vendor's security alert mailing list to ensure that you hear about patches quickly.

If you have only a few trusted users on the system, you might be tempted to skip the whole set-uid removal process. Before you do, consider this: You are unwittingly making life easier for a remote attacker. If an attacker gains shell access to your machine through some new exploit, she will use any vulnerability she can find to elevate her privileges to root. Set-uid root programs will be at the top of her list. If you fail to bolt down your this against you.

Understand, though, that gaining root is not always the attackers' endgame—it depends on what they are trying to achieve. For example, you can store all your sensitive company data in a relational database that is owned by a user called `datamart`. Clearly, the attacker only needs to target the data owner account (or privileged application accounts) to get full access to the database. This can be done through password-guessing, social engineering, or exploiting security bugs in set-uid application programs. Don't focus on root to the exclusion of your primary application accounts.

Application software often ships with set-uid/set-gid programs. In my experience, these tend to be rife with problems—ignore them at your peril. It is rare to find security-savvy application programmers.

Breaking set-uid Programs for Fun and Profit

NOTE

URLs and brief descriptions of tools mentioned in the following section can be found immediately after this list.

You're faced with a piece of software that smells of security problems. What can you do about it? Some homebrew security testing! You won't become an uber-hacker overnight, but the following techniques are a good place to start:

- Search the Web for information about previous product vulnerabilities. Include any other third-party code shipped as part of the product in your search (for example, library routines).

- Install a copy of the software on a test system and observe the installation routine closely. Check the contents of any logs or temporary files created during the install. They might contain passwords or other insightful information. Check the file permissions. Could an attacker read them? Also, study the default configuration. What are the weaknesses?

- Identify programs that are installed set-uid/set-gid and search available documentation for program information. (It might be sparse, though.)

- Run strings and grep on the binaries to identify weaknesses such as back doors, hard-coded calls to other programs without explicit paths, predictable temporary filenames, application-specific environment variables (which you might be able to overflow), and so on. Check for any hidden command-line arguments or back doors.

- If you can identify the actual developers of the code (through the RCS (Revision Control System) strings), search the Web for other code they have developed. If you can find any open source programs, check their coding style and observe any security errors. The odds are on your side that they've repeated the same mistakes in the code you're bashing away at.

- Observe how your target interacts with the kernel. As root, run the software via a program that can trace system calls (for example, strace or truss). If these tools aren't on your system, check your distribution media. Identify how the program works. Try to identify when it makes calls to the set-id family of system calls. Focus on the sections of code that execute with set-uid/set-gid privileges.

- Now watch the program's use of library files. Run the program under a call-tracing program such as ltrace or sotruss. Check for function calls that have known weaknesses (see http://www.whitefang.com/sup/secure-faq.html for a list). Keep rerunning it until you know which files it accesses. Examine those files, remove them, put spurious data in them, and so on.

- Play with the command-line arguments—feed the program data it doesn't expect. If the command takes a user-specified file as an argument, try and have the program read a file that you don't have access to (such as a database file or private configuration file). Some applications are so dumb they don't even check the original owner of the supplied file, and you could be staring at your own /etc/shadow file.

- Set crazy values for the standard and application-specific environment variables. Run the application to see whether it breaks. If it does, can you exploit it in some way? Does it dump core and leak sensitive information in the core file? (Use strings or gdb to check this.)

- Deprive the program of resources it expects and see how it reacts. For example, consume all available inodes on application-related (and /tmp) filesystems. Programs that haven't been coded with extreme situations in mind can behave unpredictably—use this to help you.

- If the application ships with a network server component, use Telnet (in the case of a TCP-based server), or better still, grab a copy of netcat (described in the following section) and connect to the network port(s) used by the application. Do you receive any output upon connecting? Try and stimulate a response by pressing Return or other various keys or by typing **help**. Try sending a large amount of nonsense data. Does it crash because of an overflow? If you can find specs for the protocol (or in the case of proprietary protocols, if you can reverse-engineer it), try overflowing specific protocol fields (for example, in the case of Web servers, the HTTP Referrer field). Granted, this is not rocket science, but just try things. You might be surprised how effective this crude approach can be at unearthing security bugs (or just general flakiness). Remember, you might be the first person scrutinizing it this way—you never know what you might find.

- Use a network sniffer like tcpdump or Ethereal and observe the communications between the client program and network server. Look for plaintext passwords flying across the network or other information leaks. Advanced testers will attempt to replay the network traffic to see whether they can re-authenticate using the captured packet data. Play "Man-in-the-Middle" (MITM) and intelligently modify the data in transit using a program like netsed.

- Check for inadequate settings on shared memory segments. Use the ipcs command to identify application-specific shared segments—check their permissions. Are they locked down enough? If not, read them as a non-root user. Try and decipher what you've read—check for information leaks such as weak passwords, encryption keys, fragments of database files, and so on. If you have write access, try and alter important values to affect what gets written to the user or application store.

Useful Tools for the Explorer

tcpdump

Author: Network Research Group (NRG) at Lawrence Berkeley National Laboratory (LBNL)

URL: `http://www.tcpdump.org/`

tcpdump is the de facto Unix network sniffer.

Ethereal

Author: Gerald Combs

URL: `http://www.ethereal.com/`

Ethereal is a GPL equivalent to commercial grade network sniffers. Featuring both a GUI display and a console-only version (tethereal), it can decode an incredible number of protocols. It also supports the capability to read capture files written by many other sniffers.

netcat

Author: Hobbit (ported to NT by Weld Pond)

URL: `http://www.atstake.com/research/tools/index.html`

Nicknamed the "Swiss Army Knife" of networking tools, netcat allows you to make outbound or inbound TCP connections to or from any port you choose. It can optionally hex dump traffic sent and received. Netcat can be used to bypass weakly configured packet filters, as well as to throw test data at a network service (useful when checking for basic overflows). Because it can run as a listening network service, you can play all kinds of interesting network tricks with it. See the README for some ideas. If you're bound to a MS desktop, you'll be glad to hear about the NT/95 port.

Ltrace

Author: Juan Cespedes

URL: `http://packages.debian.org/unstable/utils/ltrace.html`

Ltrace is a Linux-only program to show runtime library call information for dynamically linked libraries. This enables you to trace function calls whether they end up calling systems calls or not. If the program you are interested in is statically linked, this program won't help. Non-Debian GNU/Linux users should be able to find packages available from their favorite package mirror.

netsed

Author: Michal Zalewski

URL: `http://freshmeat.net/projects/netsed/?topic_id=43`

Michal is a very talented programmer active in security research. While he was black-boxing a Lotus product, he wrote netsed—a small GNU/Linux-based network utility that brings the functionality of sed (stream editor) to the network. netsed lets you change network packets on the fly as they pass your machine by specifying one or more search strings and a corresponding replacement. This automates an otherwise very tedious and repetitive process: Capture a data stream to a file, modify the capture file, and send downstream, for every client/server communication.

Subterfugue

Author: Mike Coleman

URL: `http://www.subterfugue.org/`

The author describes Subterfugue as a "framework for observing and playing with the reality of software." In a nutshell, you can mess with the program big time! The user creates "tricks" that affect the way the program operates (either directly or through throttling I/O). By manipulating the world that the application executes within, you can profoundly influence and analyze its actions.

Test Limitations

The previously described attacks can turn up surprising results for very little effort. It can be quite depressing though—you've locked down your Unix server only to find that the application gives up the goods to anyone who knows the magic incantation. DIY (Do It Yourself) testing is certainly valuable, and is the only option for most people. However, it is not a proper substitute for a thorough security audit by a seasoned security bug finder.

Perhaps the biggest problem with this approach is that there is really no way to know when you're done. All you can do is keep testing until you have exhausted all the tests you can throw at a program, or until frustration gets the better of you. It's often a case of diminishing returns—you find some interesting weaknesses, try to exploit them, and see what happens. Eventually, boredom sets in, and you find something more interesting to do.

If you do discover weaknesses, you can report them to the vendor. Depending on your point of view, you might have mixed feelings about doing so. Vendors have a spotted history when it comes to handling security problems. Some fix promptly and notify their users; others try to sweep problems under the carpet (worse still, some threaten the messenger).

If you are concerned about revealing your identity to a vendor, you can either use an anonymous remailer or ask the folks at SecurityFocus (`http://www.securityfocus.com`) to help you. They offer a free community service to help bug finders draft an advisory. With their experience in moderating BugTraq, they are also a good sounding board if you have concerns.

TIP

People have different views on the subject of full disclosure—it is a classic "religious" debate. Rain.Forest.Puppy (rfp), an active security researcher, developed a disclosure policy in light of his experience reporting vulnerabilities to software maintainers. You can read it at `http://www.wiretrip.net/rfp/policy.html`.

Rootkits and Defenses

Our contemplation of filesystem security isn't complete without a mention of rootkits.

After a successful root compromise, attackers might upload and install a *rootkit*, which is a collection of replacement system programs that enable attackers to hide their tracks and easily reconnect to the system at a later time. It is not unusual for an attacker to patch the hole that enabled him to gain access, to avoid losing the system to another attacker.

Rootkits typically include replacements for the following commands:

- `ps`—Shows process information. The rootkit version hides processes run by the attacker—they simply don't show up in the output.

- `netstat`—Shows network connections, routing information, and statistics. Attackers certainly don't want you discovering their connection to your systems. So they install a modified `netstat` binary that effectively cloaks connections on specific ports or specific client addresses.

- `ifconfig`—The attacker might want to sniff the network to pick off authentication credentials (among other things). To do this, the network interface card must be put into promiscuous mode. A very observant administrator might notice the "P" flag in the output of the `ifconfig` command. The modified `netstat` doesn't print the "P".

- df—Shows filesystem free space and inode usage. The attackers' toolkit and sniffer logs consume disk space that might be noticed on a quiet system. The rootkit df ignores files stored in a particular directory or owned by a particular user ID.

- ls—Lists files. Similar to the modified df, the rootkit ls behaves just like the standard ls, but it does not report files contained in a hidden directory or owned by a particular user ID.

- sum—Calculates checksum and block counts. Should the administrator become suspicious and attempt to checksum the files against known good files (on a "clean" system), the rootkit sum program will produce faked checksum values that match the original binaries. Never rely on sum for security. It is possible for an astute attacker to create modified programs that still output the same sum value as the originals. (Instead, use cryptographic routines like MD5.)

Rootkits are readily available across a range of operating systems and architectures, regardless of the public availability of source code. Patching binaries to include rogue code is not rocket science. It involves an understanding of binary file formats (for example, ELF) and some file manipulation—so don't assume you're invincible just because you are running a closed source OS.

Rootkit Countermeasures

The primary method to detect the presence of a rootkit is to use integrity assessment software. These programs take a digital snapshot of the system and alert you to changes to important system files.

When you first install integrity assessment software, a baseline database is created. This contains a unique signature for every file that is to be watched. Then, on a basis set by the administrator, new signatures are generated and compared with those stored in the integrity database. A mismatch means a file has been modified in some way—possibly indicating your system has been compromised. Alternatively, it could just mean you've applied an OS patch!

It used to be that system administrators would use a program like sum to generate file signatures of important system files. However, as they were to learn, these signatures can be faked. Attackers were able to cash in on the weaknesses of these checksum generators (or simply replace the program), thereby fooling the administrator.

In 1992, Gene Kim and Gene Spafford developed the Tripwire tool. Tripwire made use of digital hashing algorithms like MD5 to create file signatures that were impractical to forge. Even the slightest change to a file, or to the file's inode information, resulted in an unmistakably different hash. The software filled a real gap in the security toolkit and proved incredibly popular. It was ported to numerous platforms and became the de facto integrity assessment software, referenced in just about every security book you'll ever come across.

This software is today known as Tripwire 2.0.

For all its good points, this software has a major limitation—the database must be stored on read-only media like a write-protected floppy disk, a CD-R, or tape. Not surprisingly, this is an inconvenience and doesn't scale well. It might be the most common reason why sites give up using Tripwire. Storing the database on a read-only filesystem doesn't cut it either—an attacker can simply remount it read-write.

Realizing there was something of a market for this kind of tool, and that there was some mileage to be had in a major update, the authors set up a company, Tripwire Inc. This breathed life back into a popular tool. A number of new features were added, and the product was fully commercialized.

Possibly the most useful feature added is that you are no longer forced to store the integrity database on write-protected media—the database itself is signed using a 1,024-bit El Gamal encryption algorithm—you can store the integrity database on the system itself. That's not to say storing it on write-protected hardware is not a sensible idea. But, if that is not sustainable in your environment, then this might be for you.

Tripwire uses a policy language to define what to monitor. Check out the included documentation for a useful tutorial. The commercial version is somewhat easier to configure (no compiler required and the policy language seems friendlier) and ships with some reasonable defaults. Whatever version you use, though, don't forget to add in your application files and create the baseline database as soon after OS installation as possible.

For a stealthy way of running Tripwire, consider this. Create a cron job on a separate (hardened) system to remotely copy across the binary and database files and invoke the comparison. Don't forget to erase the files after the check. (The output can be stored on the invoking system ready for checking/filtering.)

Although the commercial version does offer some worthwhile benefits, don't feel you have to pay out to get the core benefit—many sites still run the ASR version without a hitch.

The commercial version is now available for Windows NT. Those running larger sites might be interested in the Tripwire HQ Manager product to centralize management of all V2+ Unix/NT Tripwire agents.

Good news if you're a Linux user, though—the Linux port of the commercial version was made open source, and can be downloaded free.

Binary and source copies are available from http://www.tripwire.org.

The commercially supported product is available at `http://www.tripwire.com`.

The original ASR release is available at `http://www.tripwire.com/downloads/` `index.cfml?dl=asr&cfid=265337&cftoken=18379700`.

Tutorials for installing Tripwire ASR can be found at `http://netweb.usc.edu/danzig/` `cs558/Manual/lab25.html`.

Solaris users should take a look at the CERT security improvement module at `http://www.cert.org/security-improvement/implementations/i002.02.html`.

Kernel Rootkits

We've covered userland rootkits, with which an attacker compromises the system and replaces important system files. Now we'll examine the ultimate form of deception—the *kernel rootkit*.

To appreciate the stealth provided by a kernel rootkit, it is vital to understand the role played by the kernel. The kernel is the huge C program that runs the show—it operates at a low level, interfacing directly with system hardware. An attacker who reprograms the kernel can change the behavior of the system in any way she chooses. Consequently, if an attacker modifies the kernel, she can literally change your world. Unless the attacker leaves the digital equivalent of muddy feet on the carpet, you'll probably never even know about the attack.

The means to introduce a kernel rootkit is a root-level compromise (just as for a standard rootkit). The usual purpose is to hide cracker activity and provide a convenient way for crackers to reconnect later on.

A kernel rootkit really is the most devious form of back door—it is the ultimate cloaking device. All bets are off when the kernel has been subverted.

Kernel rootkits typically modify the kernel call table to redirect system calls to rogue code introduced by the attacker. The rogue code performs whatever actions the cracker intends, and then calls the original OS code to let the call complete. The user is kept blissfully unaware of this.

A typical kernel rootkit

- Hides processes. No matter what tool the administrator uses, the attackers' processes are hidden—the kernel lies. This overcomes the limitations of back door-ing.

- Modifies system logging routines (process accounting, C2 kernel audit, utmp, and so on).

- Hides network connections.

- Modifies NIC (Network Interface Card) status to hide sniffer activity.

- Reports false file modification times.

- Hides the presence of the module (in the case of an LKM).

- Does anything else the attacker can think of.

TIP

The technical reference bible for Linux Kernel hacking can be found at `http://www.kernelhacking.org/`.

Three main methods exist to introduce rogue code into the kernel:

- Modifying kernel memory on a live system via `/dev/[kmem|mem]`

- Patching the kernel binary on disk

- Loading a kernel module

Traditionally, kernels were monolithic—a big slab of code did everything. Modern Unix systems support Loadable Kernel Modules (LKM), which enable the administrator to introduce new kernel code into the operating system while the system is running. This can be done to provide support for additional filesystem types, network drivers, or custom security routines. Check out your man pages for the following insertion commands: `insmod`, `lsmod`, and `rmmod`.

Whatever insertion method is used, kernel integrity is paramount—if the new code doesn't behave and tramples over key kernel structures, then the system is likely to crash. This isn't too subtle. Developers of kernel code know this all too well.

The act of patching a live kernel is actually less scary than it sounds (as long as you do it correctly). This technique is sometimes used to tweak kernel parameters where no userland utility exists. (It is generally unsupported, however.) Inserting new kernel code involves locating and overwriting unused areas of kernel space with your code and repatching the system call table to divert callers to your code.

Kernel patching on disk involves writing your changes directly to the kernel image using a binary patcher. You seek through the binary to specific locations and overwrite with your own code. File headers are likely to need modifying, so a basic understanding of object file formats is required.

All other previously mentioned methods are possible if root access has been gained. LKMs, however, provide the most convenient method for back door-ing the kernel. Consequently, LKMs appear to be the most common delivery mechanism for rogue kernel code in the wild. Inversely, LKMs provide the good guys with a way to enhance existing security, too.

At this point, you might be thinking that closed source operating systems should be safe from this kind of thing. Again, as with standard rootkits, access to source code is not a major factor. (Besides, source code for some closed source operating systems circulates within the underground community.) Kernel hacking requires a familiarity with kernel structures (documented in /usr/include), some skills with a kernel debugger, and an appreciation of kernel issues (for example, how to allocate memory correctly).

For example, in December 1999, mail was sent to BugTraq announcing the availability of a Solaris Loadable Kernel Module back door. The note was from Plasmoid, a member of The Hackers Choice (THC)—a Germany-based group with some very talented individuals. The paper is available at http://www.thehackerschoice.com/papers/slkm-1.0.html. Check out their other projects, too.

As with any program, it only takes one person to codify a kernel rootkit with a friendly userland interface. Then anyone can install and use it on a compromised system.

TIP

Rootkits come and go in popularity. A collection of current rootkits (both kernel and userland) can be found at the Packetstorm archive: http://packetstormsecurity.nl/Unix/penetration/rootkits/.

Even if you can't find a rootkit for your system, it is probably prudent to assume a kernel rootkit exists, and therefore, you should implement countermeasures. This might sound like unnecessary paranoia—perhaps it is. On the other hand, bear in mind that the cracker community is very effective at sharing tools. Crackers don't tend to advertise their tools with big neon signs, though.

Protecting Against Kernel Attacks

Safeguarding against kernel attacks can be summed up in one word: prevention. You need to prevent attackers from writing to kernel memory (directly or indirectly through LKMs) or the on-disk kernel. This is easier said than done because, if they have root, they can modify the kernel. To prevent this, you need to get in there first and change the rules. But, to do this, you need to modify the kernel itself—and, if your OS doesn't have LKM support, you're on your own.

TIP

The standard advice until recently has been "disable LKM support." This is now a waste of time—Silvio Cesare has created a program to re-enable LKM support. You can download Kinsmod.c from this site: http://ly-www.sd.cninfo.net/Anetroom/Aos/3-5-0328.htm.

If you're wondering why Tripwire isn't mentioned as a countermeasure here, you should probably re-read the introduction to this section. Tripwire is a userland tool. It doesn't run in the kernel—it makes calls to the kernel and bases its decisions on values returned by the kernel. Knowing this, an attacker can reroute calls made by Tripwire to custom code that generates false checksums that match Tripwire's expectations. This is usually implemented by a rootkit in order to hide the presence of the rootkit on disk.

Rootkit Detection

If you can't prevent, then detect. This is a sound security principle that can be applied to many security-related situations.

Currently, there is no generalized method to identify whether a given kernel on an arbitrary system has been subject to a rootkit attack. However, there are specific detect points for a number of published back doors.

Authors of kernel rootkits might include a routine to identify that the kernel rootkit is actually inserted. For example, the Adore LKM back door written by Stealth (http://www.team-teso.net/releases/adore-0.42.tgz) can be detected by making a call to setuid with a magic number. If you supply the right number, the kernel module announces its presence. Of course, you are relying on defaults here. If your attackers used any sense at all, they would have modified the magic number or even the particular call used, and this crude detection scheme would fail.

A program that implements a number of checks for common back door modules on Linux is rkscan. Using the technique outlined previously, rkscan can identify multiple versions of popular rootkits, Adore and Knark (written by Creed). rkscan is available from http://www.hsc.fr/ressources/outils/rkscan/index.html.en.

Host Network Security

This section focuses on network security at the host. This section does not discuss firewalls, network intrusion detection, and router network security issues. It deals solely with the services provided by a Unix server to its network clients.

Network Services: General Purpose Versus "Fit for Purpose"

Is your system having an identity crisis? It probably is if you've decided it's a Web server, but it's actually running all kinds of other network services, ranging from file-sharing services (NFS, Samba, and so on) to remote printing services.

What Are Network Services?

If you are familiar with the concept and implementation of network services, skip to the next section—otherwise, read on.

A *network service* is a process (daemon) that provides a service to clients. Apart from some internal housekeeping functions, its job is to process client's requests. It's called a *daemon process* because it is detached from its controlling terminal and runs in its own session group (of which it is the session leader). By doing this, the process can survive when the user who executed the program logs out of the system.

To respond to clients, network daemons bind to and listen on a TCP (Transport Control Protocol) or UDP (User Datagram Protocol) port. The program uses a network socket to send and receive data. A bound socket can be associated with a single IP address or all IP addresses on the system. This is determined by the parameters given to the bind() call. The port number selected by the programmer is based on a (voluntary) convention. For example, a Web server will listen on TCP port 80. A list of ports and their corresponding service names for your system is normally found in the /etc/services file. However, vendor-supplied services files are often incomplete.

For the official IANA (Internet Assigned Numbers Authority) port listing, visit http://www.isi.edu/in-notes/iana/assignments/port-numbers.

The IANA listing does not include a large number of ports in use today. Unless a software developer registers the port with IANA, it will not make it into the list. But that doesn't mean it can't be used—just that it might clash with an existing or future entry in their list. For an unofficial, but more comprehensive list, check out http://dhp.com/~whisper/mason/nmap-services.

The decision to use the TCP or UDP transport protocol will depend on the communication requirements of the application.

TCP is a connection-based protocol: One system (the TCP client) makes a *connect* call to establish a connection with another system (the TCP server). The kernels of both machines maintain state data about the connection. This includes the IP address of the remote system, the remote port number, sequencing data (to support reliability and the re-ordering of out-of-order packets), and a number of other parameters. The kernel examines the header of incoming TCP/IP packets to determine which socket should receive the payload of the packet. A connection is identified by the unique tuple of source IP, source port, destination IP, and destination port.

UDP is connectionless. Put simply, one system can send one or more packets to another system (or systems, in the case of multicasting/broadcasting). The remote system will not respond (that is, it's connectionless), and reliability therefore is not guaranteed. The application program is responsible for reliability. For further details about TCP/IP, refer to Chapter 6, "A Brief TCP/IP Primer."

The Risks of Running Network Services

Standard Unix distributions ship with a raft of network services. That should come as no surprise—after all, they are sold as general purpose operating systems. Unfortunately, all distributions—barring OpenBSD—ship with nonessential network services enabled—they are "on" by default.

Network services provide useful functionality to clients. Remote users can download mail, log in to the system, share data remotely, use printers attached to the server—in fact, all this and much more. Most significantly, they also enable remote attackers to break into the system, grab sensitive data, snoop the network, install Trojan programs, spy on end users, crash the system, or wipe the disks.

If you're new to IT security, you might find that last statement bewildering. Wouldn't they need to log in first? Why on earth would vendors ship software like that? Well, obviously the problems that allow attacks to happen are not part of their intended functionality. As history demonstrates, however, security bugs in network daemons are very common—so common, in fact, that when you're done installing your operating system, the chances are extremely high that your machine is vulnerable to remote attack.

Some administrators realize this and head straight for the vendor's support site to download and install the latest security patches. With that out of the way, they make the system available on the network, knowing that the system is "secure"—at least from a remote attacker. Right? Depends on the network. In general, this isn't enough. Even after applying every security patch available from the vendor, the system is still vulnerable to network attacks for four reasons:

- Insecure network daemon settings
- Insecure network kernel settings
- Insecure network protocols
- Unpublished security bugs in network daemons

Need convincing? Well, limiting ourselves to a subset of network daemons and a subset of their default insecure settings only (and that's quite a limitation), your system is probably vulnerable to some of the following post-installation problems.

Your system is most likely configured to run the X Window System (whether you know it or not). On some default installations, a remote attacker can grab screenshots and kill users' X programs—and that's just for starters. What about capturing every key the administrator types (think passwords) or remapping the administrators' keys to carry out additional commands when they hit a particular key?

Your system is most likely running an SNMP agent. SNMP agents enable remote Network Monitoring Stations (NMS) to collect system information. In its default configuration, remote attackers can also collect, and in some cases modify, your system settings. More on that later.

Your system gives away the names of user IDs on the system. Traditionally, the finger service was the culprit—vendors shipped with the finger server enabled by default, and remote users could query finger and gain a list of usernames ready for attempting brute-force logins. After pressure from customers, the majority of vendors now ship with this service disabled. But this isn't a comprehensive solution. In its default state, sendmail enables remote users to query user IDs, and will report whether they exist or not. Automating this check and building a dictionary of common usernames to check for is hardly rocket science.

In addition to the categories of problems previously mentioned, your system is also vulnerable to published security bugs in network services that the vendor hasn't even fixed yet. That's right—your system could be vulnerable to problems reported in public forums, and yet your vendor doesn't have a fix ready (yet). Again, this might sound crazy. Even worse—it might take six months for a vendor to fix a nasty security hole.

Your system is also vulnerable to so-called *0-day exploits*. These are exploits for unpublished vulnerabilities typically sent between friends with the accompanying message "Do not distribute." Ironically, they often spread like wildfire. In fact, this has lead to a number of security groups having to (somewhat embarrassingly) formally announce security problems they discovered simply because the information "leaked" from the group. The whole 0-day thing seems to generate a lot of excitement within certain sections of the security community (if script kiddies are actually considered to be part of the security community).

As someone with responsibility for securing a computer system, it's important for you to realize that thousands of people are trying to *break* (compromise) systems every day. Whether they are working for a security organization, a government agency, or an operating system vendor, or as a private individual, all around the globe people are in labs attempting to find security holes.

When security flaws are discovered, the finder has a number of options. Some people inform the vendor; some publish their findings to full disclosure mailing lists. Some tell their friends, and some tell nobody. (In fact, they might do some or all of these things at different times.)

Securing Network Services

Are you depressed yet? You might be feeling that all the "evil forces" of the world are against you. Fortunately, there are steps you can take to either eliminate or reduce your system's exposure to many of these network-borne threats:

- Disable network services you don't need.

- Use available security features of the services you do need.

- If an existing network server can't be secured as-is, find a replacement that has a proven track record.

- Assume that holes exist. Log relevant activity, analyze intelligently, and notify vendors and others.

- Keep on top of those patches or develop workarounds.

- Use a Network Services Wrapper such as TCP Wrapper to add IP-based restrictions and logging.

Disabling Network Services

Do you know what network services are enabled on your systems? Many administrators simply don't know. They've never bothered to question it—they never thought it was a problem. Hopefully by now you realize that not every program your system runs is necessarily healthy for it (or you) from a security point of view.

By turning off the services you don't need, you simply eliminate the risk inherent in running them.

CAUTION

Turning off the wrong network service might prevent users from doing work that they should legitimately be able to do. On a home system, that might cause you a minor inconvenience. On a production system, this can land you in hot water—and in some cases, cost thousands, even millions, of dollars. Learn before you burn! Follow sound change-management procedures to establish whether your user community requires a service. Overzealous hardening of systems can backfire in the long run, as managers will be hesitant to support your efforts. This is in nobody's interests.

Before turning off unused services, you need to audit what is enabled. Specifically, you need to figure out what services are currently active or will become active if requested by a client.

Network daemons are either standalone or started by a master (or super) daemon when the system enters multiuser mode. By examining each startup script, you can identify each daemon that is started and the command-line options it is invoked with.

Possibly the most famous master daemon is inetd. inetd reads a configuration file (often /etc/inetd.conf) to find out which services to listen for. Upon receiving a packet, inetd *forks* (creates a copy of itself) and executes (exec) the program specified in `inetd.conf`, handing over the new client connection in the process. inetd continues listening in the background.

Make yourself familiar with the inetd configuration file. Use the man pages to learn about services you don't recognize.

The startup (and shutdown) scripts are normally located in the `/etc/rc*` directories (rc means run command). Each `rc` directory represents a different system run-level. The startup scripts are easy to identify—they start with a capital "S" (the shutdown scripts start with a "K" for "kill") and are executed in numerical order (for example, `S01`, `S02`, `S03`, and so on). In fact, they are executed in the order generated by the filename shell wildcard character (just like `ls *`). The convention to use two-digit numbers avoids `S3` executing after `S24`, for example.

For our purposes, we're interested in run-level 3—multiuser mode.

Read the startup scripts on your system and make a list of services that are started. If you're not sure which program name represents a network daemon and which doesn't, there are several things to check:

- Check the man pages. If you are looking for a program called "nuked" and typing **man nuked** doesn't get you anywhere, try searching the man pages using the `man -k nuked` command. Man pages that describe the program as serving network clients or listening for connections are clearly good indicators of a network server.

- Run the `ps` command (`ps aux` or `ps -ef`). If the program is listed, run `lsof -I` and `grep` for the program name. If it appears, you can be sure it's a network daemon. The `-I` switch to `lsof` says, "List processes using a TCP/IP socket."

- Check whether the name of the program (minus the `d` if there is one) is listed in `/etc/services`. `grep` is your friend here.

- Last of all, if the program name ends in "d" (daemon)—it's probably a daemon. Okay, now we're starting to clutch at straws.

After you have identified the services, eliminate the ones you do not need. If they are started by inetd, comment them out of the inetd configuration file. If they are started by an `rc` script, either remove that script or comment the parts that start the unneeded service.

A Word About Privileged Ports

Programs written to listen on a port number lower than 1024 must be executed with root privilege (that is, UID 0). This rule protects sensitive system services because these run on ports lower in number than 1024 (that is, the reserved ports). The Unix kernel enforces this restriction to prevent nonprivileged users from launching fake network server processes on idle ports. Without this rule, a local user (that is, a user with an account on the system) could

- Start a fake Telnet server to capture user IDs and passwords of unsuspecting Telnet clients logging in to the system. If implemented properly, the victims would never realize their accounts had been compromised.

- Start a fake domain name server (DNS) and supply false IP addressing information to DNS clients. For example, a client system attempting to visit `http://www.pottedmeatfoodproducts.com/` could be redirected to an exact clone of the site created by the attacker. Sensitive information could then fall into the wrong hands.

- Start a malicious FTP server. Every time a user connects to the FTP service, the rogue FTP program spits back specially crafted data that exploits a bug in a client FTP program. By exploiting a security weakness in the client side program, the attacker is now able to run code on the user's workstation with the privileges of the remote user!

- ...and many, many more malicious acts.

On the other hand, nonprivileged processes are allowed to bind and listen on port numbers higher than 1024. Network-aware application programs make use of these nonprivileged ports. The advantage of using ports higher than 1024 is that programs do not need to be executed with root privilege just to bind and listen for client requests.

Unfortunately, this doesn't stop impersonation attacks. We noted earlier that when a program makes a call to bind(), it has the option of specifying a single IP address or a wildcard. The wildcard tells the kernel, "Bind to all available interfaces,"—or in other words, "Listen on every IP address on the system." You can tell which network daemons do this by using the netstat command. A very useful command to learn, netstat shows networking statistics. On most Unix systems, netstat -a shows all ports that are active or in the LISTEN state. The entries marked LISTEN either have a wildcard (*) source address or a specific IP address.

If a caller to bind() specifies a wildcard address, a subsequent caller (that is, another program) can still impersonate the server by binding "in front" of the original server. This wouldn't be possible if the original call had been made with a specific IP address. For example, a database listener binds to port 1999 and specifies the wildcard IP address. The kernel services the request. A local attacker notices the weak binding (via the netstat command) and runs a rogue database listener (that is, one she made earlier). This bind()s to the primary IP address of the machine, allowing the attacker to perform Man In the Middle (MITM) attacks or just to snoop on application usernames and passwords.

Some kernels prevent this kind of attack, but unfortunately, it is still possible on many popular distributions.

A further point to be aware of is the Strong versus Weak End System model, as defined in RFC 1122, "Requirements for Internet Hosts—Communication Layers." If your distribution follows the Weak model, remote attackers might be able to communicate with network services in ways you don't expect. Specifically, a multi-homed system can allow packets coming in on one interface to communicate with network services running on another (including a loopback) interface. So, binding network services to specific IP addresses might not gain you anything at all. See the following BugTraq thread for full details: http://archives.neohapsis.com/archives/bugtraq/2001-03/0009.html.

Protecting Against Service Hijacking Attacks

Either fix the kernel to prevent the bind()-related problems, or have network applications bind to specific ports. If you have source code for the kernel, you could, of course, modify the bind() call to check a list of unauthorized ports before binding. But, there is a wider question: Should end users have the capability to start up network services? Consider the other possible risks and the likelihood of these things happening in your scenario:

- A user runs a program such as netcat (renamed, of course) to listen on a high numbered port and execute a shell when a client connects. The next time the user wants to log in to the system, he just Telnets to the port running netcat, and, voilà, he has a shell waiting—no authentication, no logging in, no security! It won't take long for a curious person with a port scanner to find the port. (It takes about 10 minutes on a typical LAN to port scan all 65,535 TCP ports.) Hiding network services on unusual ports does not buy you real security.

- A programmer writes a network application program but fails to write it securely. A malicious client probes the service and attempts to blackbox her way to root.

Additionally, your usage policy should state that end users should not run unauthorized programs that listen for incoming network connections.

Detecting Fake Servers

As applies to preventing rootkit attacks, if you can't prevent attacks through fake servers, try to detect these fakes. Fortunately, in this case, detection is trivial. The key is noticing when an unauthorized program listens on a given port. You could write a custom program to do this, or use the following countermeasures:

- Run `lsof` on a regular basis and compare the results to an authorized baseline. `lsof` fills the gap that `netstat` leaves. `netstat` won't show you which process is listening on which ports—duh! Thankfully, `lsof` does. Create a list of authorized program names and their mapping to ports/IP addresses. Write a script to filter the output of `lsof` and compare the results to your baseline. Run via `cron` and have differences reported to the administrator for investigation.

- Run a port scanner and compare the results to an authorized baseline. This will tell you when an additional service is running (that is, a port is listening), but not what it is. This approach can be performed remotely without shell access to the system. The only requirement is that you be authorized by the system owner to perform port scanning, and that you have network visibility of the system (that is, you can send TCP and UDP packets to the server and receive replies).

- If you have kernel source code but are wary about modifying the `bind` call to limit listening services, try logging instead. Implement a simple logging routine each time `bind` is successfully called. Check the results against a baseline via a userland program, and report differences to the administrator for investigation.

At this point it's time to look at specific Unix services. What follows is not a comprehensive list—these are the mainstays of Unix network services.

Telnet

NOTE

As with many network services, the name Telnet might refer to the client program, to the protocol, and if you add the word *daemon*, to the server-side program. In our discussion of Telnet, we will be referring to the server program. To limit confusion, references to the TELNET protocol will use uppercase letters.

The Telnet server provides a network virtual terminal emulation service to clients. The server portion normally listens on TCP port 23. Check out RFC 854 for the technical specification.

Essentially, this means users can log in (authenticate) to the machine, perform some work on a text-based virtual terminal, and then disconnect. The TELNET protocol is defined in RFC 854. The Telnet daemon runs with root privileges.

TELNET is slowly being phased out. I say "slowly" because, although secure alternatives have been available for some time, a number of major vendors still insist on shipping distributions with TELNET enabled and no secure alternative installed.

TELNET Protocol Risks

The major security weakness of TELNET is that all communications between the Telnet client and server are passed in plaintext (unencrypted) across the network. That means usernames, passwords, sensitive system data, and other possibly confidential information is visible to anyone running a network sniffer located between the client and server. Worst of all, because of the way a routed IP network functions, machines on other parts of the network might also gain visibility of the data.

This makes TELNET unsuitable for use in environments where the security of the underlying network or every host en route cannot be completely trusted. To put it another way, as a Unix administrator, you probably have no control over security outside of your system—your options are confined to host-based network controls only.

Other attacks include insertion or replay attacks, in which a MITM changes the data on the fly or plays back an earlier data capture. Imagine finding yourself adding a user to the system with no hands!

Vendors can ship systems with default user IDs and passwords. Unless you change default passwords or lock the accounts, a remote attacker can gain access by using Telnet.

Information Leakage

By default, vendors tend to ship the Telnet daemon with a default login prompt that greets users with the name of the operating system, the version, and sometimes the system architecture. This kind of information helps attackers. With it, they can whip out their nastiest exploits geared specifically to your platform. Why give this information away so easily to an attacker? The reality is that removing this information won't stop your operating system from being identified remotely. (To find out why, read on.) However, I would argue that announcing your system details to anyone who makes a connection to your machine is making things a little too easy! Remove product/version info from your login banner, or insert the wrong information (see `http://www.all.net/dtk/` for a toolkit that does this). Some sites replace the vendor greeting with a legal "No unauthorized access" message. Check with your legal department for specific wording.

The TELNET daemon leaks information about your operating system in a less obvious way, too. The TELNET protocol defines a number of Telnet options. When a Telnet client connects to a Telnet server, either end can transmit Telnet options. These enable one side to express its capabilities and requested functionality to the other—for example, its terminal type. A remote attacker, able to connect to the TELNET daemon, can use this to her advantage.

There is no standard TELNET daemon implementation. Different vendors implemented different Telnet options. By examining the Telnet options and the sequence in which they are received, an attacker can fingerprint your operating system.

TIP

The TESO group has developed a tool that can identify a wide range of Unix flavors by using Telnet options. You can download it at `http://teso.scene.at/releases/` `telnetfp_0.1.1.tar.gz`.

I Spy with My Little Eye

Before launching an attack on a site, an attacker will perform remote reconnaissance. He will want to find out the type and version of operating system and the services you are running. Network daemons commonly announce their software version upon a client connection. This can help when you are remote troubleshooting, because network administrators can easily identify software version incompatibilities. This assists the attacker in the same way, however. Armed with this information, she can search vulnerability databases for known weaknesses, or in preparation for an attack, re-create an identical system in her lab for penetration testing.

A common reaction to this problem is to remove product/version information from system banners. This might mean

- Recompiling open source network daemons with this information stripped.

- Overwriting the banner strings in closed source binaries.

- Modifying configuration files (for example, `/etc/issue` on Solaris).

This will thwart banner grabbing.

However, even if you did this to all your network daemons, the version of your operating system and all its network software can still be identified remotely through the process of behavioral analysis.

Remote Determination of Network Service Versions

Software versions change because of bug fixes, additional software features, performance hacks, and so on. The attacker can probe for feature or bug differences between versions, thereby determining the specific version in use. This is not the long and complicated task it might sound like. The attacker can make the reasonable assumption that a site is running a relatively recent version and work backward. In fact, this kind of functionality is built into some commercial vulnerability scanners.

Remote Operating System Identification

Vendors' TCP/IP stacks respond differently to a given set of packets. By remotely fingerprinting the TCP/IP stack, it is often possible to identify the operating system in use and its version. You've already learned a bit about this in Chapter 3, "Hackers and Crackers." The attacker sends a sequence of packets with specific attributes. The response packets sent by the victim server contain unique elements that, when considered together, uniquely identify a vendor's TCP/IP implementation. The queso tool originally used this approach. This strategy was then adopted and expanded by Fyodor in his Nmap tool available from `http://www.insecure.org/nmap`.

Vendors TCP/IP stacks also exhibit distinguishing timing characteristics in their handling of packets. When a system receives a packet, the network interface hardware generates an interrupt. The kernel processes the packet based on information contained in the packet header. The time taken for a given platform to process the packet will vary depending on the code path taken (that is, if it's x, then do y; if it's x and z, do j). By sending multiple packets of varying complexity, it is theoretically possible to measure response times and compare them to known baselines to identify systems. This has been discussed in public forums, although no tool has been published as of yet.

Modifying network kernel parameters can defeat TCP/IP stack fingerprinting. These change the way that the TCP/IP stack behaves and will thwart known fingerprinting techniques.

This might leave you wondering whether it is worth removing system details from banners at all. There's certainly room for debate, but my personal view is that, for Internet-exposed hosts, it *is* worth the effort, as long as you understand it doesn't buy you any real security. What you're actually getting is security by obscurity—it might just be a reprieve from the less advanced attacker who relies on banner-grabbing-style scanning to identify potential victims. When the next remotely exploitable vulnerability is announced, your bannerless system is unlikely to appear on the script kiddies' radar. Sure, you'll need to apply patches—but at least you might avoid the embarrassment of being nailed by an amateur!

Securing Telnet

One option is to use router- or VPN-based encryption. This is a partial solution; it does not result in end-to-end encryption. This can still leave the TELNET data stream open to MITM attacks near either end of the connection.

The superior solution and stock replacement for TELNET is Secure Shell (SSH). SSH is deployed at thousands of sites worldwide, and has become the standard way of remotely accessing a Unix server across potentially hostile networks. SSH is a TCP-based service that listens on port 22 by default.

An Essential Tool: Secure Shell

According to the "What is Secure Shell" FAQ at `http://www.employees.org/~satch/` `ssh/faq/`:

> Secure Shell (SSH) is a program to log into another computer over a network, to execute commands in a remote machine, and to move files from one machine to another. It provides strong authentication and secure communications over insecure channels. It is intended as a replacement for Telnet, rlogin, rsh, and rcp. For SSH2, there is a replacement for FTP: sftp.
>
> Additionally, SSH provides secure X Window System connections and secure forwarding of arbitrary TCP connections. You can also use SSH as a tool for things like rsync (`http://rsync.samba.org`) and secure network backups.
>
> The traditional BSD r commands (`rsh`, `rlogin`, `rcp`) are vulnerable to different kinds of attacks. Someone with root access to machines on the network or physical access to the wire can gain unauthorized access to systems in a variety of ways. It is also possible for such a person to log all the traffic to and from your system, including passwords (which SSH never sends in the clear).
>
> The X Window System also has a number of severe vulnerabilities. With SSH, you can create secure remote X Window System sessions that are transparent to the user. As a side effect, using remote X Window System clients with SSH is more convenient for users.

NOTE

Historically, U.S. vendors have not shipped SSH in their Unix distributions. However, with the expiration of the RSA patent, recent (long overdue) changes in U.S. export legislation, and the release of public domain SSH implementations, this situation is starting to change.

As with many things in the Unix world, SSH is the name of the protocol and an implementation.

The SSH Protocols

Two major versions of the SSH protocol exist. They are quite different, and as a result, incompatible. The first version (SSH1) of the protocol had many security problems and has now been generally replaced by the second version (SSH2).

SSH Servers

Commercial SSH server software is available from SSH Communications (`http://www.ssh.com/`) and F-Secure (`http://www.f-secure.com`). Frustrated at the lack of a truly free, up-to-date SSH, the OpenBSD team started the OpenSSH project. The

stated goal of the project is to have Secure Shell technology shipped with every operating system.

The OpenSSH Project is great news for all Unix users—especially when you consider
it has been written and reviewed to the same security principles as the OpenBSD
project was. The source code has been significantly simplified to ease code review,
and all code has been subjected to an extensive security review. However, major
holes have been found in it nonetheless.

Unsurprisingly, a number of groups have integrated OpenSSH into their base operating systems. These include Solaris 9, most major Linux distributions, OpenBSD,
FreeBSD, BSDi BSD/OS, NetBSD, Apple Mac OS X, and AIX.

Don't worry if your favorite Unix isn't on that list. OpenSSH can be downloaded
from `http://www.openssh.org/` and installed as a separate utility. Official ports exist for
Sun Solaris, IBM AIX, Hewlett-Packard HP-UX, Digital Unix/Tru64/OSF, Irix, NeXT,
SCO, and SNI/Reliant Unix. A port to Windows is available as well. See `http://www.`
`openssh.com/portable.html` for an up-to-date list.

Compiler-shy Solaris users with a release before Solaris 9 can grab a compiled version
in Solaris package format from `http://www.sunfreeware.com`. For Solaris users who
want to install from scratch, check out this useful installation guide written by CERT:
`http://www.cert.org/security-improvement/implementations/i062_01.html`. (Although
the guide is described as Solaris-specific, it does include useful generic information.)

OpenSSH relies on two underlying packages:

- zlib, available from `ftp://ftp.freesoftware.com/pub/infozip/zlib/`

- OpenSSL, available from `http://www.openssl.org/`

In my opinion, OpenSSH is the way forward.

SSH Clients

Just like TELNET, SSH is a client/server protocol. To access a SSH server, the client
must be running SSH clients.

Unix users can use the OpenSSH client that ships the OpenSSH server.

My favorite Win32 client is called Putty. It's written by Simon Tatham, is free for
both commercial and noncommercial use, and is open source.

Putty supports both SSH protocols and runs on Windows 95, 98, Me, NT, and 2000.
It's a slick piece of code, weighing in at less than 300kb—so you can take it on a
floppy to your favorite Internet café. (Check out the Putty FAQ at `http://www.chiark.`
`greenend.org.uk/~sgtatham/putty/faq.html` to understand the risks involved should

actually you want to do this.) Putty can be downloaded from `http://www.chiark.greenend.org.uk/~sgtatham/putty/download.html`.

Simon has also created pscp, a Win32 port of the Secure Copy program (scp on Unix systems). Unsurprisingly, this can be used to transfer files across an SSH connection. Use this instead of FTP. A nifty GUI front-end for scp, written by Lars Gunnarsson, is available from `http://www.i-tree.org/`.

Commercial clients supporting features over and above Putty are available from F-Secure, SSH Communications, and Van Dyke. A full list of SSH clients can be found at `http://www.ece.nwu.edu/~mack23/ssh-clients.html` and `http://www.freessh.org/`.

SSH Resources

An excellent resource to learn more about SSH, written by Seàn Boran, can be found at `http://www.boran.com/security/sp/ssh-part1.html`. I consider this a must-read for anyone looking at using SSH in a serious way. Seàn has integrated a substantial amount of previously fragmented information with his own experiences (four-plus years) in implementing SSH. He covers the configuration options and describes some of the more advanced uses of SSH, such as

- SSH VPNs

- rdist over SSH for secure remote filesystem synchronization

- Using SecurID with SSH

- Tunneling VNC (Virtual Network Computing), a remote control program, over SSH (for NT administrators, he covers PC Anywhere as well). See `http://www.uk.research.att.com/vnc/sshvnc.html` for more details.

As with any complex piece of software, SSH has had security problems. For a comprehensive rundown of known security holes, check out the OpenSSH security page at `http://www.openssh.com/security.html`. If you are using a commercial version, I recommend that you check with are not vulnerable.

FTP

FTP is the File Transfer Protocol. An FTP client makes a TCP/IP connection to an FTP server (TCP port 21) and authenticates (or in the case of an anonymous server, supplies an email address). The client can list, put, or retrieve files.

Most client/server protocols use just one server port, whereas FTP uses two—one is a control connection for handling commands (port 21), and the other is a data connection (port 20) for transferring data. The data connection can be active or passive. The server initiates an active connection based on a port number specified by the client, whereas the client initiates a passive connection based on a port number specified by the FTP server. This has implications for your ability to successfully firewall FTP, as the firewall must dynamically allow data connections based on information transferred via the command connection. This requires the firewall to be capable of decoding FTP command connections properly and tracking FTP protocol state transitions. The data connection takes place over an ephemeral port (that is, a port greater than 1024). Some routers don't offer this level of sophistication, which means that network administrators have to implement very relaxed ACLs. A better option is to buy a router that can handle this.

FTP Risks

The FTP protocol design is tricky to secure. The base FTP specification can be found in RFC 959—however, there are many extensions (see `http://war.jgaa.com/ftp/?cmd=rfc` for a comprehensive list). Firewall vendors hate it, warez peddlers love it, and security practitioners try to avoid it.

Some of the risks of running FTP are as follows:

- As with TELNET, there is no encryption, so MITM attacks apply.

- As with Telnet, many FTP daemons announce system/daemon version information when a client connects. This is an information leak.

- RFC-compliant FTP daemons permit port-bouncing attacks. *Port bouncing* is a technique whereby an attacker instructs a remote FTP server to port scan an unrelated system through judicious use of the `FTP PORT` command. The victim machine sees connections from the FTP server, hence the attacker doesn't get the blame. Bounce attacks can also be used to bypass basic packet-filtering devices and export restrictions on software downloads.

  This is an old problem, and some vendors eventually broke with RFC compliance to prevent this. Other vendors still ship FTP daemons susceptible to this "feature." Hobbit is credited with discovering this weakness. His paper can be viewed online at `http://www.insecure.org/nmap/hobbit.ftpbounce.txt`.

- The FTP protocol is hard to firewall properly. To set up the data connection, TCP/IP addressing information is passed down the control connection. To figure out the correct address/port pair to allow through, the firewall must carefully monitor the control connection. Basic packet-filtering devices don't have the application layer protocol intelligence to do this, and therefore large holes have to be punched in network ACLs just to support FTP. A second, more serious problem is the difficulty firewalls seem to have correctly understanding the application dialogue between client and server. This can be exploited to attack other network services running on the same system with the FTP server.

NOTE

Originally reported by Mikael Olsson, the same problem was independently discovered by John McDonald (also known as Horizon) and Thomas Lopatic. This was against Checkpoint FW1 and a Solaris FTP server, but the principle applies to any other combination where the firewall incorrectly parses the FTP control stream. A technical paper demonstrating the successful exploitation of a buggy Solaris ToolTalk daemon via an FTP data channel can be found at http://packetstormsecurity.nl/0002-exploits/fw1-ftp.txt.

- FTP servers that ship with proprietary distributions typically provide very little access control capability.

- Access control can be confusing and prone to procedural failure. Some FTP daemons consult a file called ftpusers, which contains a list of users who may *not* use FTP. This tends to confuse novice administrators, and even in experienced hands, leads to new users not being included; that is, when a new user is added to the system, he gets FTP access by default. If your site policy is based on the least-privilege principle, this is not helpful.

- Writable, anonymous FTP servers are incredibly hard to secure. Allowing anyone to write to your filesystem is hard to do securely.

- The default umask setting on many FTP daemons results in newly created files that are accessible to everyone. This is commonly a result of inheriting a weak umask from inetd (the daemon that spawns the FTP daemon).

- By default, many proprietary FTP daemons do not log client connections.

Securing FTP

If you want to offer anonymous FTP services to untrusted clients, give serious consideration to using a dedicated, standalone system (on its own DMZ off the firewall). This isolates any break-in to the FTP service only. And, as the old saying goes, "A chain is only as strong as its weakest link."

TIP

For an illuminating read on the pitfalls of running a misconfigured FTP and Web server on the same system, check out the following article: http://www.dataloss.nl/papers/how.defaced.apache.org.txt.

The server should be stripped down. Only the FTP service should be accessible to the untrusted clients (for example, the Internet).

A popular alternative to running a proprietary FTP daemon is the Washington University FTP daemon available from `http://www.wu-ftpd.org/`. This enhanced FTP server provides additional functionality useful for minimizing abuse. However, it has a spotted security history. If you choose to run it, be prepared to upgrade in a hurry when the next major hole is discovered, and every script kiddie is trawling the Internet looking for vulnerable wu-ftpd installations.

Alternatively, evaluate the benefits of running a cut-down FTP daemon. Dan Bernstein has written a drop-in FTP replacement called Publicfile, designed and written with security as its primary goal. It is ideal for anonymous FTP. The download page is `http://cr.yp.to/publicfile.html`. Publicfile can also serve as a very basic Web server—serving static content only.

If at all possible, avoid running an anonymous writable FTP server altogether. You're likely to end up acting as a mirror for pirated software hidden in surreptitiously named directories. Not only that, but write access to the filesystem aids an attacker who can leverage even a minor misconfiguration on your part. For a pretty comprehensive list of anonymous FTP abuses, check out `http://www.uga.edu/ucns/wsg/security/FTP/anonymous_ftp_abuses.html`.

Various schemes have been proposed to date, but none seem to be bulletproof. However, that said, you could do worse than follow CERT's advice at `http://www.bris.ac.uk/is/services/networks/anonftp/anonftp.html`.

Finally, activate FTP daemon logging and make sure that syslog is configured to log LOG_DAEMON messages. (Check your ftpd man page for the specific logging facility used.)

The r Services

rlogind and rshd are the remote login and remote shell daemon. These so-called *r services* use TCP ports 513 and 514, respectively. The RLOGIN protocol is described in RFC 1282.

The r services were developed at Berkeley to provide seamless "Look, Ma—no password" authentication between trusted hosts and/or users.

Authentication between client and server is based on the client IP address, TCP port, and client username. The client IP address and username must match an entry in either the system-wide trusted hosts file (`/etc/hosts.equiv`), or a user trust file (`~/.rhosts`). An additional so-called safeguard is that the client connection must originate on a reserved TCP port—as only programs running with root privilege can do.

The r services are very popular with end users and administrators, as manual entry of the password is not required (unlike with TELNET). Unfortunately, they are terminally insecure.

r Services Risks

Security of the r services is based on an extremely weak authentication model, known as a trust model.

Authentication is based on weak credentials: the source IP and TCP port. The source IP and TCP port can be forged. The original designers assumed a trusted network. Even the Unix man page for these commands recognizes this fact.

Combined with predictable sequence numbers, crackers had a field day with these services. Steve Bellovin described address-based authentication as "a disaster waiting to happen."

The following post gives a line-by-line account of a real hack where the weakness of rsh was exploited: http://www.cs.berkeley.edu/~daw/security/shimo-post.txt.

Countermeasures

Avoid the r services totally—switch to SSH. This protocol is just plain broken from a security perspective. Expend your security efforts on bigger rocks (for example, host hardening and security patching).

REXEC

REXEC is often confused with the other r services. However, it bears no relationship to them. REXEC runs on TCP port 512.

Unix distributions often ship without an REXEC client program—for some, this makes the service all the more mysterious.

The REXEC protocol is predominately used by application programmers to connect to a Unix system remotely, run a command, and exit. They do this via the REXEC REXEC library call. REXEC uses standard username and password authentication. All communications are sent in clear text between client and server.

REXECREXEC Risks

- Brute-force login attempts might go unnoticed as the REXEC daemon performs pitiful logging.

- Communications are unencrypted so that all the Man In The Middle attacks apply, as well as passive attacks.

- There is no access-control built into REXEC. Beyond disabling the service or using third-party software, you cannot define which users can use the service. Therefore, a user who normally logs in via a secure protocol could end up inadvertently sending his password (and more) across the network in plaintext, simply by using a client application that relies on REXEC.

- Some REXEC daemons produce a different error message to a client, depending on whether the username or password was incorrect. This behavioral difference permits attackers to ascertain valid usernames. Again, your system is disclosing information.

Securing REXEC

- Disable REXEC. If client applications rely upon it, figure out a migration path away and then disable it.

- If disabling is not an option, consider using SSH to tunnel the protocol. SSH provides remote terminal access.

SMTP

SMTP is the Simple Mail Transfer Protocol (defined in RFC 821). Among other tasks, its job is to receive mail by accepting connections on TCP port 25 from remote mail servers. By default, Unix comes with the sendmail program, an age-old program that implements the SMTP protocol (and more).

SMTP Risks

sendmail is one of those programs every administrator seems to have heard of. Its history of security problems is well known. It could be the most maligned Unix software ever written. With that reputation, it should be clear that something is fundamentally wrong with sendmail—and that something is its monolithic design.

However, the security of sendmail has improved significantly in recent years because of the efforts of its author, Eric Allman, in response to the many security problems it has suffered. It's debatable whether sendmail is totally "out of the woods," or ever will be, because of its design. It was designed for the old world in which the Internet was one of many networks, and email addressing/routing was much more complex than it is today. Therefore, it is full of features that still exist, but are obsolete.

Rather than repeat a history of security flaws here (I don't think there's space), these are some generic problems that a default installation of sendmail presents:

- sendmail is "Yet Another Daemon" that runs as root. Therefore, an exploitable vulnerability in sendmail can mean giving away root access to an attacker. Even though a root-run program might temporarily drop privileges, an attacker who is able to run shellcode (through a buffer overflow or string format exploit) can simply make a call to seteuid() to re-establish those privileges and have her shell code running as root.

- sendmail is incredibly complex. Its configuration file uses m4, the GNU implementation of the Unix macro processor. Few people truly understand m4, and fewer still understand sendmail configuration. As a result, it's easy to make blunders, and hard to lock it down without outside help.

- sendmail can be used to elicit usernames. By connecting to port 25 and issuing VRFY and EXPN commands, sendmail will confirm valid usernames. This is the first step in taking over an account. Attackers can then use remote login services and attempt to guess passwords. This guessing attack can be automated, using a large dictionary of common usernames to increase the chances of finding a valid username.

- Older versions of sendmail allow spammers to relay mail through your system. Apart from using your resources, this can make you very unpopular and result in your site being listed on RBL (Realtime Blackhole List at http://mail-abuse.org/rbl/). This is bad news for you, as any mail servers your site attempts to connect to will drop the connection if they follow the RBL list.

- If incorrectly configured, sendmail leaks internal address information to the outside. Attackers can send probe emails to a company mail server. By sending a malformed message, they can elicit a bounce message possibly including internal IP addresses. This assists an attacker in mapping the internal network.

- The sendmail daemon outputs its version number upon client connection. This information helps the attacker select a relevant exploit.

Securing SMTP

In my experience, few machines on an organization's network actually need to be listening for mail—they just happen to be because sendmail is active by default. Put simply, don't run mail transfer unless you need it. Turning off your mail transfer agent does not affect your systems ability to actually send mail (such as for the output of cron jobs).

- Consider using Qmail instead of sendmail. It has been designed and coded following sound security principles and has an impressive security track record—zero security holes. Visit http://www.qmail.org/ for more details. Recent versions of Qmail go further in easing the migration from sendmail. Qmail is available on a wide range of platforms.

- Postfix (formally Vmailer), written by Wietse Venema, is a popular sendmail-compatible alternative written to be fast, easy to install, and secure. Full details are at http://www.postfix.org/. If you can't face Qmail, check out Postfix.

- If you must run sendmail, don't run it as root—build a `chroot` environment and run it as a nonprivileged user. Russell Coker has detailed how he does this at `http://www.coker.com.au/~russell/sendmail.html`.

- A common misconception among administrators is that sendmail needs to be listening to the network to send mail from the local machine. Although this is the default on many systems, it's not required. sendmail can be invoked via `cron` with the `"-q"` flag to service the queue of outgoing messages on a regular basis. If all you want is the capability to send mail, then disable the sendmail startup script—you don't need sendmail listening on port 25.

NOTE

The authors of Qmail and Postfix have publicly locked horns a number of times on security-related mailing lists. There is clearly no love lost between them as they try to find security bugs in each other's software. Although this might not be a pleasant sight to the uninitiated, it does give a valuable insight into the security issues facing designers of Mail Transfer Agents (MTA), such as where the weaknesses are and how to avoid them. The bottom line is, if you want secure mail servers, use dedicated, hardened systems with shell access given to trusted users only.

DNS

DNS is the Domain Name System. It's a UDP- and TCP-based protocol that listens on port 53. TCP connections are commonly used for zone transfers.

The DNS matches IP addresses to hostnames (and hostnames to IP addresses). A DNS server is responsible, or *authoritative*, for a given part of the domain name system (for example, `mybitofthenet.com`).

Clients make requests of the DNS servers when they want to communicate with systems for which they have only the fully qualified hostname (for example, `myserver.mybitofthenet.com`).

The DNS is a critical part of the network infrastructure. Its failure—whether through administrative incompetence or denial of service—can have major consequences.

DNS Risks

The DNS protocol has security problems. A detailed description of DNS and its protocol weaknesses can be found at `http://www.geocities.com/compsec101/papers/dnssec/dnssec.html`. DNS is defined in a number of RFCs—see `http://www.dns.net/dnsrd/rfc/` for full details.

As far as Unix host security goes, the most widely used DNS server software is BIND (Berkeley Internet Name Daemon), developed by the Internet Software Consortium (ISC).

Let's look at the track record of BIND. The first problem is that three major versions of BIND are in common deployment around the world: 4, 8, and 9. BIND 4 has long been considered obsolete and should not be used as it is no longer maintained, but many sites have it installed. If an upgrade to BIND 8 or 9 is not possible, BIND 4.9.9 should be used, as it is the most secure of any of the 4.x line.

BIND 8 has been out for a long time, but it is still being maintained, unlike BIND 4. The main developer on BIND 4 and 8 was Paul Vixie. In an interview (http://www.linuxsecurity.com/feature_stories/conrad_vixie01.html), he trashed the code:

> "...every bit of effort I ever put into BIND, from version 4 to version 8, was patchwork. The basic sleazeware produced in a drunken fury by a bunch of U.C. Berkeley grad students was still at the core of BIND."

On the whole, the security record of BIND 8 hasn"t been that bad compared to something like Windows, but for a system that runs part of the Internet's core, any security hole is bad. History shows that BIND 8 has averaged about one major security hole per year, the most recent of which was discovered in June 2002. BIND 8.3.3 fixes this problem.

BIND 9 is an almost complete rewrite of BIND from the ground up. The primary reason is that the BIND 8 code had reached a point where no new features could be added to the code. The Internet Software Consortium (ISC), which is in charge of BIND development, is recommending everyone upgrade to BIND 9, but that could be because they don't want to maintain the old versions.

However, is BIND 9 any more secure? Security was one of the primary goals of BIND 9, whereas it was an indirect goal with the older code. BIND 9 has only been out since 2000, and the old BIND code dates from the early 80s. Security holes have been found in BIND 9, which is not surprising for relatively new software. The choice between correctly designed code versus battle-tested code is a tough one to make.

It turns out attackers like breaking into BIND servers. DNS servers are tasty targets because so much of the Internet relies upon then. With control of a BIND server, you can do truly nasty things, for example:

- Deprive a site of traffic by changing the IP/name mappings to a nonexistent address. Worse still, you can redirect traffic to a pornographic or competing site. Lost revenue and bad press don't help a company's stock price.

- Clone an e-business site, modify the site's DNS server to map your imposter site, and collect credit card details, user account information, and password details.

- Exploit trust relationships between systems by mapping an IP from one side of the trust relationship to your machine.

- Compromise one of the root nameservers.

That last one is particularly worrying. The root nameservers are the starting point for addressing on the Internet. There are only 13 root nameservers in total (because of protocol limitations).

Aside from security flaws, misconfiguration is common. When sizing up your site, attackers will request zone transfers from your DNS server. This is basically a dump of all the information pertaining to a particular DNS zone. This is as good as a network map! You don't want this.

Another configuration hole is version numbers (again). To discover the version of BIND you are running, a client can query your DNS server, and your server will tell them. This isn't so good.

The other major). risk facing the DNS protocol and the BIND implementation are denial-of-service attacks. Numerous DoS vulnerabilities have been found in BIND. Disabling DNS servers prevents DNS queries from being resolved, thereby stopping clients relying on the DNS resolution services (that is, almost everyone) in their tracks.

Securing DNS

The obvious countermeasure is to find an alternative to running BIND. Here your choices are limited—we live in a BIND monoculture. You could switch to Microsoft's DNS implementation (that's not a recommendation), or look for a DNS server where security of implementation is a primary goal. The only viable alternative I am aware of is the djbdns package by Daniel Bernstein. This package has had sufficient production usage to be a serious contender to BIND. It was designed and written with security in mind by a programmer experienced in writing secure code. You can find out more at http://cr.yp.to/djbdns.html.

If you stick with BIND, there are some things you can do. A useful summary of the issues and countermeasures is available at http://www.acmebw.com/papers/securing.pdf. You should at least give serious thought to the following points:

- Don't run BIND as root. Instead, create a new user and group. Specify these as command-line options when you execute BIND.

- Use the chroot command to run BIND so that it has restricted access to the filesystem. The chroot program enables you to specify the directory that a process will treat as its root directory (enforced by the kernel). To do this, you need to create a mini-duplicate of your operating system, because BIND will no longer be able to see important system libraries and configuration files. Full instructions can be found at `http://www.etherboy.com/dns/chrootdns.html`. See the section on `chroot` later in the chapter for some important caveats.

- The version number is hard-coded in the BIND code, so if you have source code, you can simply remove it or replace it with a fake version or silly message (have fun). Otherwise, you'll have to binary patch the executable—good luck! Recent versions of BIND can be configured to enable version requests from specific addresses only.

- Configure BIND to disallow zone transfer except to authorized servers (such as DNS slaves).

finger

finger has been around for years. Its problems have been discussed numerous times and are well documented—even vendors today ship it disabled. You can refer back to Chapter 8, "Personal Privacy," for more about finger as well.

Don't enable finger unless you don't mind your systems leaking sensitive system information like usernames, home directories, and login patterns.

finger can be used as an early warning system that someone is checking out your site. Use TCPWrappers to wrap the finger service and enable logging. Some administrators configure TCPWrappers to return bogus finger information, feeding less savvy attackers false usernames that they subsequently fail to log in with.

SNMP

SNMP is a protocol to support network monitoring and management. Its use is widespread, and most network monitoring products rely upon it. It runs on UDP ports 161 and 162 (for SNMP traps).

For the technical details behind SNMP v1, consult RFC 1157. RFC 1441 introduces the various RFCs that make up SNMP v2.

SNMP Risks

An SNMP client authenticates to an SNMP agent via a string known as a *community name*. This community name works very much like a password. Unix hosts often ship with an SNMP agent enabled by default—so your system could be exposed to SNMP flaws already. Problems with default SNMP installations include the following:

- The default read-only community name is `"public"`, and the default read/write community is often `"private"`. Hard-coded "passwords" like these have blighted

IT security for as long as I can remember. A full list of common passwords including SNMP community names is at `http://www.phenoelit.de/dpl/dpl.html`.

- If the read-only community can be guessed, serious information disclosure issues can crop up. The extent of the data disclosure is dependent on the MIB (Management Information Base). MIBs vary between vendors, but they usually contain the following types of information: network interface settings, network services, current network connections, administrative contacts, and server location. This assists attackers in mapping your network topology (think multihomed hosts), in performing traffic analysis (who is talking to whom), and maybe even in getting some social engineering info.

- If the read/write community name can be guessed, you have the problems previously mentioned, but also the attacker can now modify the status of network interfaces and even reboot systems. Vendor-enhanced MIBs can allow even more devastating operations.

- Access to SNMP agents is not logged by default. You won't notice authentication failures.

- Some SNMP implementations, notably Solaris, actually run other SNMP daemons on high-numbered ports. Blocking access on a firewall to UDP port 161 might not be sufficient. Solaris users should check out `http://ist.uwaterloo.ca/security/howto/2000-10-04/`.

Securing SNMP

- Decide whether you need SNMP. If your network operations team isn't monitoring servers via SNMP and you're not running any special software that relies on SNMP (some clustering implementations do), then disable it.

- Modify the default community strings to be hard-to-guess, random-looking strings. Make them long (at least 10 characters), and whatever you do, don't use the name of your network supplier! (I've seen this too many times.)

- Configure SNMP authentication traps. If someone is trying to guess your SNMP community string, you want to know earlier rather than later. By configuring authentication traps, you can have the agent inform the SNMP master (normally the network management console) when an authentication failure happens. You might think it improbable that someone could guess a long SNMP community string. The savvy attacker will use a tool like ADMsnmp, written by the highly respected outfit ADM. Check out this post to BugTraq for more info: `http://archives.neohapsis.com/archives/bugtraq/1999_1/0759.html`.

Network File System

The Network File System (NFS) protocol defines a way for cooperating systems to share filesystems. Today, everyone seems to refer to NFS mounts as *shares*.

NFS is based on the RPC (Remote Procedure Call), a protocol that defines how machines can make calls to procedures on remote machines as if they were local.

NFS implementations consist of more than just a single NFS server process. In fact, they require mountd, statd, and lockd. These daemons have had a plethora of problems—especially statd.

NFS is a very useful protocol, but is rather weak from a security point of view at the same time. Its use needs to be carefully thought out. Full details of NFS v2 can be found in RFC 1094. NFS v3 is defined in RFC 1813.

NFS Risks

- If you're running an unsupported or unpatched version of NFS, you're dead in the water if someone takes a shot.

- Misconfigurations are common with NFS. Sharing system-related filesystems is asking for trouble.

- Weak authentication is used. The requests can be spoofed or sometimes proxied through the local portmapper.

- No encryption is used, so your darkest secrets go across the network in plaintext.

- NFS-related daemons commonly run as root. An exploitable security hole can leave you with a root compromise on your hands.

- Watch your defaults! The file /etc/exports (or /etc/dfs/dfstab) controls which filesystems you share and with whom. Unless you specify otherwise, your implementation might default to using insecure options or giving write access by default.

Securing NFS

Don't run it! Solve security headaches in one fell swoop—turn if off! OK, so you want this functionality? Read on...

- Is NFS the right file sharing mechanism for what you want? Given its security problems, examine your file sharing requirements. For example, if you want a mirror of some files, you could just buy another disk (they are cheap these days) and use rdist over SSH to make replicas to other systems. If you can find a way around using NFS, then do so.

- Avoid using NFS for sensitive information, and never run Internet-facing NFS servers.

- Firewall NFS to limit your exposure on the wider network.

- Stay up to date with vendor security patches! NFS-related patches seem to come out thick and fast. If your vendor isn't supplying patches, this could be a "Bad Thing." They might not be patching known holes.

- Share filesystems on a need-to-have basis. Restrict this to read-only sharing wherever possible. Always specify nosuid as an option, to ensure that the set-id bit is not honored on files created on exported filesystems.

- Remove any references to localhost in your exports file.

- Do not self-reference an NFS server in its own export file.

- Limit export lists to 256 characters (including expanded aliases if aliases are in use).

- Consider using a replacement portmapper that won't forward or proxy mount requests. Check Wietse Venema's modified portmapper at `http://www.ja.net/CERT/Software/portmapper/`.

- Where read-only sharing is possible, consider mounting a locally exported filesystem as read-only (that is, in `/etc/vfstab` or similar).

Samuel Sheinin has written an excellent article on the risks of NFS and how to reconcile them; find it at `http://www.giac.org/practical/Samuel_Sheinin_GSEC.doc`. If you are running NFS, consider installing the tool nfswatch.

NFS version 4 is the next generation of NFS. Production-ready implementations are not readily available as yet. See `http://www.nfsv4.org` for more information.

Alternatives to NFS include AFS (`http://www.contrib.andrew.cmu.edu/~shadow/afs.html`) and CODA (`http://www.coda.cs.cmu.edu/`).

The Caveats of chroot

A common countermeasure aimed at security network services is to run them in a chroot environment. chroot changes the process's idea of its root directory. The idea is to prevent the process from having access to any files outside of the chroot directory. Therefore, if the network service is compromised, the rest of the system is protected. However, it's not as simple as that.

The most common mistake is to think that chroot is like a virtual computer—a totally distinct environment. It isn't. It's a filesystem abstraction; there are escape routes from chroot environments. Here are some details:

- If the process can run as root, your security is hosed. After compromising a chroot'ed network service running as root, the attacker can create device files to access RAM directly via the mknod command. The attacker can then modify the process's idea of the root directory and have unrestricted access to the system.

- Some distributions suffer from a bug in their chroot call. An attacker who has compromised the chroot environment can force a second chroot and then cd out of the restricted area. For more details, see http://www.bpfh.net/simes/computing/chroot-break.html. Preventing this requires a kernel change—see http://archives.neohapsis.com/archives/nfr-wizards/1997/11/0091.html for more details.

Better the Daemon You Know...

Take a multilayered approach to securing network services—that way, if one layer of defense fails, you haven't given up the farm.

- Disable the services you don't need.

- Add firewall services you do need. (This could be an expensive market-leading product or a hardening Unix system with packet forwarding enabled and kernel-based IP filtering in effect.)

- In addition to a network firewall, consider the use of kernel-based access controls to protect your network services from internal systems (which themselves might have been breached, or are simply in the hands of a malicious employee). Today, many Unix systems ship with kernel-based IP filtering. Learn how to use this feature.

- Use switches instead of hubs in your network as much as possible to avoid packet sniffers.

- Consider the use of TCPWrappers. This software protects TCP-based network services that are launched by inetd. Normally, when inetd receives a connection from a client, it consults inetd.conf and launches the program that corresponds to the port on which the connection was received. With TCPWrappers installed, inetd calls tcpd, which consults the hosts.allow and hosts.deny files. These files control client access to services based on IP address. For example, you might want to limit SSH access to a range of addresses where you know your shell users are located. Or, you might allow only cluster members to access cluster-based daemons. For extra bonus points, you can set up fake daemons to pick up on suspicious activity. For example, create a fake finger daemon that outputs nonsense data, or an HTTP daemon that sends out redirects to the attacker's machine. Parse the logs using a tool like swatch (covered in Chapter 13, "Logging Tools").

- Read the man page for the network service you want to protect and identify command-line options that can be used to control access, improve logging, or limit dubious functionality. For example, on many systems, syslogd listens to the network for syslog messages. Therefore, an attacker can send spurious messages to either mislead you or fill up the disk. By specifying a command-line switch, you can disable this function.

- If you have a source to the service, consider compiling with StackGuard. This will eliminate common types of buffer overflow.

- Make sure the service is launched with a sane umask value. Umask is inherited from the parent process, so this could be inetd or init. Limit this value to no access by Other as a minimum. Check it out on your system.

- Verify that network server programs and configuration files cannot be overwritten by a nonprivileged user. Check for weak permissions on the files themselves and their parent directories.

- A common sign of intrusion is a second inetd appearing in the process list. Intruders start another copy of inetd with their own configuration file to install a back door—such as a password-protected shell—when they connect on a specific port. Consider moving the real inetd to an alternative location and replacing it with a fake inetd that notifies you when it is executed. (You'll need to update your startup files to reflect the path change.) Of course, this is an attack-based countermeasure specific to only one kind of attack, albeit a popular one.

- Install a lightweight intrusion detection system such as snort (`http://www. snort.org`), with a signature set that reflects the services you are offering. Integrate this into a centralized monitoring scheme, such as a central syslog server and swatch (see Chapter 12, "Intrusion Detection Systems," and Chapter 13).

Sun has several good patch analysis tools that help you figure out what patches you need to install on your system. More information and the tools themselves are available at `http://sunsolve.sun.com/pub-cgi/show.pl?target=patchpage`.

Also very good is the Red Hat Update Agent (`http://www.redhat.com/docs/ manuals/RHNetwork/ref-guide/up2date.html`), which automatically identifies missing patches. You can either manually select which patches to download and install, or let the Agent do it all for you. Unregistered users can use the (much slower) public download site.

Unless you run a trusted Unix distribution, vendor security extensions or third-party software will be required. A popular option is sudo—we'll cover this and alternatives later. Mainstream vendors have started picking up the ball—Sun introduced the Role Based Access Control (RBAC) System in Solaris 8.

Assessing Your Unix Systems for Vulnerabilities

A common strategy to assess your system for vulnerabilities is to do it in a number of phases:

1. Use a network-based vulnerability scanner to identify remotely exploitable security holes. Attackers can exploit these vulnerabilities from across the network—they don't need a Unix account on the victim machine. Fixing these tends to be priority #1 in most shops.

2. Eliminate false positives by manually double-checking the results. For a number of reasons, scanners sometimes report false positives. Log on and check for them. There is probably nothing worse than a security newbie running a vulnerability scanner, taking the results as gospel, and dumping the output on the system administrator's desk. (A number of large, respected accounting firms gained a reputation for doing this.) Know the weaknesses as well as the strengths of your tools, or look a fool in front of a knowledgeable system administrator.

3. Prioritize the findings based on your understanding of the vulnerabilities and the risk they pose in the context of your site. The scan reports generally include background information on specific vulnerabilities to help you do this. Hopefully this book will serve to sharpen your understanding of the issues.

4. Draw up a plan for fixing the problems. Identify what needs to be done and who is going to "own" the change. Test the changes on a nonproduction system and ensure applications are fully tested. Start fixing, one major change at a time.

5. Use a host-based vulnerability scanner to identify locally exploitable security holes. Host-based scanners should produce few false positives because they run on the machine itself. Manual checking should be minimal if the product is even remotely decent. At a minimum, your host-based scanner should be able to identify missing security patches, insecure network services, user account problems, and common filesystem insecurities. Don't just take the tool vendor's word for it either—always evaluate before you buy against a system build that you are familiar with.

6. Identify the biggest risks. Given your knowledge of the local user base, state these risks in the fix plan and start fixing.

TIP

Commercial and freeware network vulnerability scanners have been around for some time. Personally, I like the Nessus network vulnerability scanner. It's reliable and extensible—new checks are relatively easy to add via the NASL scripting language. The wide and enthusiastic user base and scripting language result in a fast turnaround for new tests. Often, NASL scripts are available within a day of vulnerability being announced. This is significantly faster than other scanners I've used—even expensive commercial products. Another useful feature is automated updates of new checks, ensuring that you keep current.

TIP

If you're assessing vulnerability scanners, take a look at `http://www.networkcomputing.com/1201/1201f1b1.html` for some interesting insights into the effectiveness of popular scanners.

As with any vulnerability scanner, you can get false positives. The comprehensiveness of the NASL scripts varies, so I recommend that you manually check the results to save embarrassment. However, unlike with the commercial scanners, you can at least review the source and improve it if you have better ideas.

The freeware site is at `http://www.nessus.org/`.

For those who want formal support, the creators of Nessus will happily sell you a support contract.

TIP

Host-based scanners are specific to a particular Unix flavor, so your options will be tied to the popularity of your platform. A comprehensive list of commercial scanners is available at `http://www.networkintrusion.co.uk/h_scan.htm`.

Just remember that the market leader is not necessarily the best—it might just have the nicest GUI. If the guts aren't up to the task, no GUI will make up for it. The host-based scanner market is relatively immature compared with network vulnerability scanners—be sure to validate vendor claims before you buy (and watch out for ancient checks being touted as "state of the art").

One thing I can promise you though—as you go through the dragged-out process of locking down a fully operational production system, you'll soon realize that applying your security standard to a virgin system is a walk in the park.

THE COST OF BELATED SECURITY HARDENING

The next time someone (your manager, the project manager, the marketing manager) asks you to release a system to your user community before you've had a chance to harden it (for example, because of late hardware delivery), ask him to sign a purchase order. Tell him that this is to cover the costs of making the system compliant post-go-live. When they laugh, point out that making security changes to operational systems increases risk—however well researched, things might just break. To reduce the risk of a bad change hitting during peak activity, many organizations have change policies that only allow changes to be made off-peak. Personally, I don't know any CIOs that allow changes to be made to systems without application people running some tests—the costs start to skyrocket. It's also a bad practice to make a whole slew of changes in one shot, because backing out the change becomes nontrivial. This results in a string of late nights that further amplifies the cost of post-live hardening. Factor in "just-in-case" data backups, and you're talking serious money.

The rush to save a day before the hardening activity can easily cost an organization thousands of dollars in overtime to put things right later, as well as leave a drawn-out window of exposure. The decision-makers in your organization should be made aware of this problem before you hit it. With their buy-in, this kind of situation can be avoided. As well as the overtime savings, the other selling point is avoiding low staff morale. Unless someone is shooting for overtime cash, I don't know of anyone who wants to arrive back in the office at midnight to make a change. If the change goes wrong, they could be left with a night's restoration activity. Losing key personnel the following day is also not a good thing.

Host Lockdown

Host lockdown is the process of making a system compliant with your Unix security policy. In other words, it is configuring the system to be significantly more resistant to attack.

There are three common approaches:

- Manually make the changes required by your policy—This is certainly useful the first couple of times you do it, because you get to see what you are changing. After that, making changes manually is a boring waste of time, which can easily lead to things being missed or mistakes being made.

- Write some scripts to automate the changes—This requires some scripting capability, a test machine, and some time (in fact, quite a lot of testing time if you want to cover everything). This time is probably best spent on site-specifics (like in-house application hardening), because writing operating system-hardening scripts is a bit like reinventing the wheel (see the following section).

- Identify a hardening tool that can best match your security standard—Recent years have seen the development of some excellent hardening scripts for the most popular platforms. In the following section, we cover the primary ones. The key here is to understand what the tool does and doesn't do, and how to configure it for your site policy. You can fill in the gaps through homegrown scripts.

Host-Hardening Resources

These tools are distribution-specific because of the differing Unix security interfaces and platform-specific risks. This shouldn't be treated as a definitive list, though—for example, Linux has many, many hardening projects. I've been a little selective and picked out the ones that are sufficiently well developed enough to be usable in a production environment. As per usual, test any such tools on a nonproduction system first.

For some distributions, I don't know of a specific tool—so I've listed well-regarded hardening documents. So with that disclaimer in place, let's look at the options.

Sun Solaris

Solaris users are spoiled for choice these days. The obvious question is, "Which hardening tool should I go for?" To help you decide, check out this SANS-sponsored report that compares the most popular Solaris hardening tools: http://www.sans.org/sol11c.pdf.

YAASP (Yet Another Solaris Security Package)

Primary Author: Jean Chouanard

URL: http://www.yassp.org/

YASSP supports Solaris versions 2.6, 2.7, and 8 on both Sparc and Intel. YASSP looks set to become the de facto tool for hardening Solaris. The SANS Institute has stated that it will promote YASSP's use globally.

YASSP ships as a tar ball containing packages in Solaris package format, some shell scripts, and a set of security tools to replace or supplement stock Solaris programs.

The following packages will be installed by default:

- SECclean—The core package, securing your Solaris installation
- GNUgzip—gzip 1.2.4a [GNU]
- PARCdaily—Some daily scripts, logs rotation, backup, and RCS for systems files
- WVtcpd—tcp_wrappers 7.6 and rpcbind 2.1 [Wietse Venema]
- PRFtripw—Tripwire 1.2 [Purdue Research Foundation of Purdue University
- OPENssh—OpenSSH 2.3.0p1 [OpenSSH.com]

From a general Solaris-hardening perspective, YASSP does the following by default:

- Turns off ALL network services in /etc/inetd.conf (configurable) and disables nonessential services started from /etc/init.d.
- Turns off rhosts authentication, disables unused system accounts, disables FTP access to system users, and sets minimum password length to eight.
- Disables stack-smashing attempts (commonly caused by buffer overflows) and activates logging at the kernel level by a parameter change in /etc/system.

(Note that this doesn't prevent data segment buffer overflows.) This can actually break your applications, so testing, as ever, is essential.

- Runs Casper Dik's "fix-modes" script to lock down filesystem permissions. It also disables honoring of set-uid bit on newly mounted filesystems.

- Modifies behavior of the TCP/IP stack to both improve security and increase resilience to DoS attacks. (This is helpful, but it will not defeat the problem.)

Don't be alarmed by that thorough approach—the default packages and installation settings are certainly appropriate for an Internet-exposed or highly sensitive internal server. However, for internal multiuser systems, you'll definitely want to investigate the configuration options available in yassp.conf. You could easily end up breaking application functionality if you don't modify the defaults.

For those installing Solaris from scratch, primary YASSP author Jean Chouanard has helpfully documented that process (starting with the Solaris CD in hand) at http://www.yassp.org/os.html.

YASSP is) a no-brainer to install. After you've downloaded the YASSP tar ball, you install as follows:

```
# uncompress yassp.tar.Z
# tar xvf yassp.tar
# cd yassp
# ./install.sh
... check and modify all the configuration files ...
# reboot
```

The post-install steps require you to edit a small number of configuration files and create the Tripwire integrity database, as follows:

- Edit and configure /etc/yassp.conf.

- Edit and configure /etc/hosts.deny /etc/hosts.allow.

- Edit and configure /etc/sshd_config /etc/ssh_config.

- Read http://www.yassp.org/after.html and the papers linked under http://www.yassp.org/ref.html.

- Make any additional changes and install any additional software.

- Create the Tripwire database and save it to read-only media.

Personally, I think YASSP is the future of Solaris hardening (at least for virgin systems). It's been well tested, can be uninstalled as easily as it is installed, and seems to have attracted some talented individuals to keep it updated.

TITAN (Toolkit for Interactively Toughening Advanced Networks and Systems)

Primary Author: Brad Powell

URL: `http://www.fish.com/titan/`

TITAN predates YASSP and takes a different approach. It is based on the KISS approach (Keep It Simple, Stupid).

Rather than create a mammoth script that attempts to do everything, TITAN's authors wrote a set of Bourne shell scripts (referred to as *modules*) invoked by the TITAN program itself. Each module targets a specific aspect of operating system security. Modules can be included (or excluded) via the use of a configuration file specified at runtime. This enables you to create different configuration files to reflect the different security postures required by individual systems (for example, firewall, mail server, workstation, and so on).

A TITAN module consists of two primary functions: fix and check. As you'd expect, the fix function does the actual work—it makes the changes—whereas the check function looks to see if the fix has already been applied. You tell TITAN in which mode to run a particular script through the configuration file.

This makes it easy to check that a system has been configured to your security policy. For me, this is the real strength of TITAN.

To install TITAN, copy the TITAN archive to a target server, run the install program, and customize the configuration file. You're all set to invoke the main TITAN shell script (supplying the name of your configuration as an argument). If you're having problems with a module, you can run TITAN in debug mode.

Run TITAN periodically via `cron` in check mode, and you have an extensible, host-based scanner.

TITAN version 3.7 supports Solaris only. Version 4.0, which is in beta as of late summer 2002, also supports Linux and FreeBSD. The tool itself is structured to accommodate any operating system, but until now few modules actually existed for any other distribution.

Another great thing about TITAN is that you don't need to be a programming genius to add extra modules—nor do you have to jump through hoops. (Remember KISS?) Assuming you are competent at Bourne shell scripting, there is no new programming language to learn—just some conventions to follow (just copy and customize the supplied template file).

Note that, unlike YASSP, TITAN doesn't install any security tools. (It does include Casper Dik's fix-modes script, but that's a one-shot tool, so I'm not counting that.)

I recommend that you run YASSP first to harden and install the tools, and then monitor with TITAN on an ongoing basis. For huge server farms, TITAN output can get overwhelming—consolidate the output using Perl.

When I first started using TITAN, it had an annoying habit of changing things even when you asked it to only check them. The principle of a passive check mode hadn't been implemented consistently throughout all the modules. A quick check through the most recent set of scripts suggests the authors have rectified this problem (although I couldn't find a reference to it in the change log).

This is a handy reminder: Always understand what actions a hardening script will take *before* you run it.

NOTE

The authors comment that TITAN doesn't actually stand for anything. They just came up with the name, and it stuck.

GNU/Linux

There are a host of projects seeking to protect the world's favorite penguin (The Linux mascot, in case you've been living under a rock). Here's a select few:

Bastille Linux

> Bastille Linux (v2.0)
>
> Primary Author: Jay Beale
>
> URL: http://www.bastille-linux.org/

The Bastille Hardening System is an open source, community-run project suitable for Red Hat and Mandrake systems. (The authors have declared it should be portable to any Linux distribution.)

The stated mission of the project is to provide the most secure, yet usable, system possible. The authors have drawn on a wide range of security sources, including the SANS Linux hardening guide, Kurt Seifried's Linux administrators security guide, and more. The creators, Jon Lasser and Jay Beale, list administrator education as a key goal.

Bastille focuses on four key lockdown areas:

- It implements network packet filtering in the kernel (using ipchains). This limits your visibility on the network. (This doesn't "hide" your system—rather, it sets up access controls to your systems' network services.)

- It downloads and installs the latest security patches (not many tools do that). The caveat here is that it doesn't check the digital signatures on the downloaded files. (You can do this manually using PGP or the open source GnuPG software from `http://www.gnupg.org/`.)

- It increases the system's resistance to many types of local attacks by removing the privilege bit from a number of set-uid programs.

- It disables nonessential network services.

As a tool, Bastille's notable features include the following:

- Bastille can be run on living systems (that is, not just new installs).

- Bastille is self-aware. This has more to do with multiple runs on the same machine. Bastille knows what it did the last time it was run, so it won't repeat itself. Note that Bastille does *not* detect your initial security settings during its first run. (It will prompt you to turn off things that you might already have disabled.)

- Bastille has a primitive but handy Undo feature. Essentially, it makes a backup of files before modifying them. It replicates the directory structure and permissions under the Undo directory. There is no automagic back out—if you need to undo an action, you do it by hand.

- Bastille has a so-called *impotent mode* (also known as *shooting blanks mode*). This is definitely recommended for first-time users. Bastille will tell you what it would have done, given your answers, without actually doing it. This might save you having to undo things later.

The `Interactive-Bastille.pl` Perl script is written with the novice in mind. The user is prompted to answer yes or no for each hardening question. Each question is supplemented by explanatory text to help someone unfamiliar with Linux security. At the end of the Q&A session, the user runs `BackEnd.pl`, and the changes are made.

To make those exact same changes across a number of machines, just copy the Bastille input log—generated during the first run—and feed the log results as input to the `BackEnd` Bastille script on the target servers. This technique is fully explained in the Bastille documentation (`docs/readme.automate`). A slicker automation procedure is apparently in the works, but the current approach, although basic, does work.

Linux novices will have a steep learning curve with whatever tool they end up using. Bastille makes a lot of effort to ease this burden, and to some extent, achieves this. (I know of nothing better.)

Hewlett-Packard HP-UX

HP has ported Bastille to HP. It is available from `http://www.hp.com/products1/Unix/operating/security/`.

Additionally, Kevin Steves from HP has created a very useful hardening guide.

The papers for HP-UX 10 and 11 can be found at `http://people.hp.se/stevesk/bastion.html`.

Kevin has written a very readable guide, starting from the installation of HP-UX through securing the host and creating a recovery tape.

IBM AIX

Scripts for hardening AIX 4.3 are available at `http://ist.uwaterloo.ca/security/howto/2001-01-15/kit.html`. Unfortunately, I am unaware of any publicly available hardening scripts for AIX 5.X. A basic guide for securing AIX has been developed by IBM. It is available at `http://www.redbooks.ibm.com/redbooks/SG245971.html`.

FreeBSD

FreeBSD users should check out the Security HOWTO available at `http://people.freebsd.org/~jkb/howto.html`.

The FreeBSD ports collection (security tools ported to FreeBSD) is available at `http://www.freebsd.org/ports/security.html`.

What do you do if you're unable to find a hardening tool for your operating system's specific distribution or version? Unfortunately, vendors have a poor track record of creating credible hardening tools. Check with your user group (if it exists) and the Usenet newsgroup for your distribution. You might wind up having to rewrite the scripts from one of the tools previously mentioned. If you're an HP-UX or AIX admin interested in security, here is the perfect opportunity to make a name for yourself!

Summary

A single chapter on Unix security never can do the subject justice. Rather than attempt to cover all aspects of Unix security, I've hopefully got you thinking about the issues. Specific technology problems come and go (well, they don't always go), but the thought processes and security principles tend to remain static. If I've got you thinking about your environment in a new way, then I've met my goal. The great thing about Unix is the open community that supports her. Although there are many problems, there are many more solutions. Good luck keeping her safe!

22

Novell NetWare

IN THIS CHAPTER

- The OS Facts of Life
- Watching the Big Three
- Further Reading

A little neglect may breed mischief...for want of a nail, the shoe was lost; for want of a shoe, the horse was lost; and for want of a horse, the rider was lost.

—*Benjamin Franklin,* Poor Richard's Almanack, *1758*

A venerable operating system still in use in many shops, NetWare isn't as dead as pundits would have you believe. Here we discuss pointers, practices, tools, and tips for locking down this operating system—which is still frequently found at the heart of an enterprise's authentication infrastructure.

The OS Facts of Life

Let's cut to the chase here: What I *don't* find interesting are exploits or practices that cover older, unpatched versions of the operating system. These are cases of simple neglect—about as interesting as listening to your father's apocryphal college stories or last year's stock reports.

We've said it in earlier chapters and will say it again: Running an unpatched OS is begging for trouble. Your first rule of thumb with *any* OS has got to be "stay current."

With this in mind, here I'll rudely ignore anything before NetWare 4, and talk about NetWare 4.11, Netware 5.1, and NetWare 6.0. Novell hasn't supported NetWare 3.11 since January 1999, and it recently announced that it would stop supporting NetWare 3.2 as well. Your initial reaction might be, "So what? Why should I care whether it's supported, as long as the current config is working?"

However, because the frequent discovery of operating system security problems is a fact of life, to stay secure you need some way to fix these problems. Specifically, you either need source code to the operating system (plus the requisite know-how) to fix a given problem, or you need vendor support.

Source code isn't available for NetWare—so you *must* have Novell's support to address newly discovered OS problems.

Conclusion: Using a version of NetWare with no support is not exactly a smart or secure thing to do. If you use NetWare 3, or (egads!) NetWare 2.86, you're *on your own*. Not much fun. Stop reading here, and go do something about it. After you've upgraded, come back; we'll talk more.

Still here? Okay, so you're using NetWare 4 or NetWare 5—go out and get the latest patches. There is a *huge* number of security patches available. For reference, in this chapter, I discuss NetWare 4.11 SP 9, Netware 5.1 SP 5, and NetWare 6.0 SP 2. These *minimum patch levels* are surely different now, so go download the latest ones.

> **NOTE**
>
> Novell's Minimum Patch List for all its products can be found at `http://support.novell.com/produpdate/patchlist.htm`.

Finally, if you are a true-red Novell shop, it's likely that you are using Novell's BorderManager as a software firewall and that you're using GroupWise as your email system. Although the following does apply to the host operating system that these products live on, it's not a guide to securing these specific products. See Chapter 10, "Firewalls," for firewall information; see Part V, "Architecture, Platforms, and Security," for more guidelines on securing network applications.

Watching the Big Three

After you patch, life with NetWare consists of being careful about three environments that substantially affect your security:

- Server environment—Server console and configuration
- Client environment—Workstations, client software and configuration
- NDS (Novell Directory Services) environment

In what can be a hugely complex system, it's useful to distill all your NetWare security concerns into these three groups. Not every individual is responsible for each group, but every individual suffers the consequences if these categories are not tended to. (If you're "lucky" enough to be the only person in your shop who tends to all three of these, pat yourself on the back and demand a raise.)

Accordingly, you'll want to figure out who's responsible for what in your organiza-tion—it doesn't do any good for only one of these subsystems to be locked down.

Server Environment

It's an understatement to say that, when an intruder is able to access your server console, the battle is lost. If you're new to NetWare, here's a basic, horrible fact about the OS:

> There *is* no explicit login to the console. The default access when you boot up amounts to "The dude who's driving is large and in charge."

Huh? This sounds awfully weird, if you're used to Unix or (properly configured) NT. Why would the console offer supervisor privileges to just anybody?

The answer is, it doesn't *explicitly* offer these privileges. Many of NetWare's NLM (NetWare Loadable Module) tools require authentication before they permit you to perform privileged operations.

But because NetWare in its default configuration permits anybody driving the keyboard to load an NLM, it implicitly allows them to perform *any* privileged opera-tion coded into that NLM.

For example, simply by loading an NLM (and without causing undue suspicion—you don't have to reboot to do these things), you can

- Set the administrative password (which would alert the real administrator that something's awry).

- Add an additional administrative user to the system with a password of your choice (which would not alert the administrator).

- Snag the entire NDS database (if you're driving a server with a replica on it) for offline decryption with publicly available tools.

- Commit other mayhem at will.

Sound bad? It is. Again, merely by inserting the right floppy diskette in the drive—or by loading an NLM from a user's directory on the server—you can, as an untrusted user, be treated as a trusted user at the console.

Novell offers a partial solution: the SECURE CONSOLE command.

It's a hard call: On the one hand, SECURE CONSOLE protects your servers from a keyboard interloper who wants to

- Load NLMs from anywhere but `SYS:\SYSTEM` or `C:\NWSERVER`

- Gain access to the NetWare debugger (Right-shift + Alt + Left shift + ESC), and possibly hand-enter malicious code

- Change the time to try to break security

On the other hand, `SECURE CONSOLE` can be a real pain when you have to do maintenance. Even a legitimate user (you) can't change the time to correct for clock drift; you can't add a search path; and you cannot load NLMs from anywhere but the two system locations. It would be a wonderful thing if you didn't have to reboot the system to disable it.

Unfortunately, using `SECURE CONSOLE` is a must if your physical security is at all in question—if there's even a possibility of an unauthorized person sitting down at your server keyboard for even a moment.

Physical Security

Here's the obvious: Keep your consoles (*and backup tapes!*) behind locked doors. But as with other operating systems/routers/pieces of key infrastructure, there is usually some point when your space is shared, be it with the cleaning people, outside consultants, or your own folks.

NOTE

I was once in an IT shop where an application consultant was invited to set up his office in the computer room—there wasn't any extra office space. That's Huge Problem #1. Then, the consultant started doing ad hoc training for users of his application—right in the data center.

Huge Problem #2? He gave out the passcode to the data center door, and the user was sitting at an NT console merrily playing Solitaire when the consultant arrived. ("Oh, was that a server?") Notwithstanding how trusted the consultant was, the user could have been anybody. All of the data center's physical security was compromised the instant the consultant was trusted in the data center.

A corollary: Any server that is *not* physically secure *must not* be part of your production NDS tree. Any machine that isn't physically secure can't be considered trusted, and any untrusted console can wreak havoc on your tree. This means new servers that are being set up on an unsecured workbench, lab machines, test machines, and so on.

Naturally, any switches or hubs that your servers—or administrative workstations—are connected to also need to be behind locked doors, particularly in light of how easily NetWare's default remote control encryption is defeated. (See the section "RCONSOLE," later in the chapter.)

Physical security can be a pretty large and ongoing task (for more on physical security, you can refer to Chapter 25, "Policies, Procedures, and Enforcement"). After you've set up physical security for your production servers, you need policies, procedures, and regular checkups to make sure that your secured areas *stay* secure.

Securing an Insecure Console

The best thing to do with an idle console is to use a utility to lock down the keyboard, and only unlock it if someone authenticates. NetWare 5.1 and NetWare 6.0 have just such a utility, scrsaver.nlm. It's pretty easy to use—just type

scrsaver help

at the console prompt for on-the-fly directions.

I like to set up the screensaver to kick in and lock down after four minutes of idle time. (You can see what this looks like on NetWare 5.1 in Figure 22.1) The screensaver is not a default action; you must load and configure the screensaver each time. You can do this by putting the following line in your AUTOEXEC.NCF:

```
scrsaver enable; delay=240
```

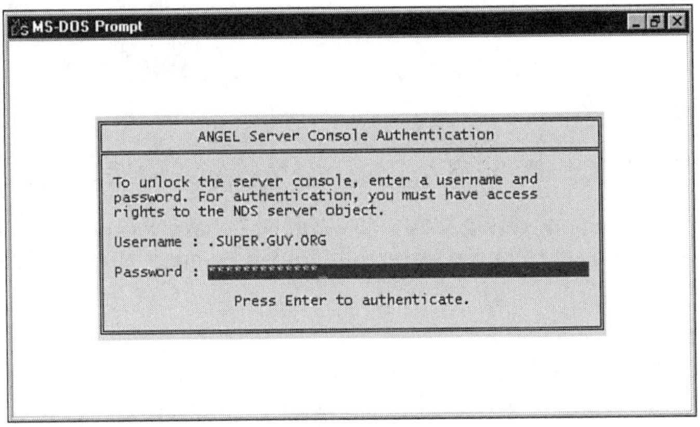

FIGURE 22.1   It's a good idea to load scrsaver.nlm upon server startup so it locks down the keyboard when the console has been idle.

Some folks also like to start the screensaver up as the last action of the AUTOEXEC.NCF. This way, even if someone does get access to one of the servers right after boot-time, they need to authenticate.

In this case, the last line of your AUTOEXEC.NCF should look like this:

```
scrsaver enable; delay=360; activate
```

NOTE

Activating the screensaver at boot-time is not a sure-fire way of keeping someone out of your console; an intruder could, at first-stage boot-time, avoid execution of the AUTOEXEC.NCF by typing **server -na** from the DOS prompt.

NetWare 4.11 Console Lock   NetWare 4 doesn't have a cool password-protected screensaver like NetWare 5 now offers.

However, you can always use the MONITOR.NLM to manually lock your console down when you're not using it (see Figure 22.2), or get a third-party tool (check the end of this chapter for product listings).

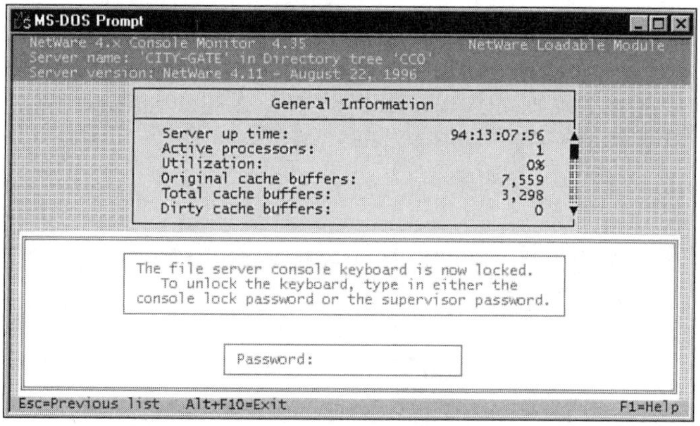

FIGURE 22.2   Although NetWare 4's MONITOR.NLM has a lock function, it requires an administrator to explicitly lock the server, rather than doing so after a timeout.

RCONSOLE

RCONSOLE, the remote-control tool for NetWare servers, can be a NetWare administrator's best friend. Unfortunately, it's not exactly a very secure friend.

The first problem with RCONSOLE is that, by default, its password is stored in plain text. If you're an old-style CNE (Certified NetWare Engineer), your AUTOEXEC.NCF might have a line like

```
LOAD REMOTE MYPASSWORD
```

in it. (If you use INETCFG.NLM to configure remote access, the password is stored in plain text in SYS:ETC.)

Obviously, this is a bad thing. You don't want someone printing out your AUTOEXEC.NCF for troubleshooting purposes and then accidentally leaving it around for the entire world to see. Furthermore, because RCONSOLE sends screens over the network "in the clear," someone with a sniffer could watch you scroll through or edit your configuration file and read your password.

What to do? NetWare has a method of "encrypting" the REMOTE password (REMOTE ENCRYPT at the server console), but it is worthless in terms of secure encryption. In less than a second, you can use a DOS-based, publicly available tool, REMOTE.EXE, to break even the largest passwords encrypted this way. Don't use REMOTE ENCRYPT; it will do nothing but give you a false sense of security.

In short, using RCONSOLE over potentially untrusted networks is a really bad idea. If you really must use it, make sure that

- Your data link and network infrastructure is secured from eavesdropping.

- The two server-possible directories in which the password might be stored are unreadable by anybody but Admin-equivalents (directories such as SYS:SYSTEM and SYS:ETC).

RCONJ, the "pure Java" version of RCONSOLE, has similar problems, and should be treated with similar care. If you are serious about secure remote control of the console—and you should be, if you are responsible for an enterprise's security—see the end of this chapter for third-party tools that are much more secure.

Network Computing's October 16, 2000 issue has a detailed workshop by Kevin Novak that discusses RCONSOLE and RCONJ, available at http://www.networkcomputing.com/1120/1120ws1.html.

Unix Compatibility Utilities

Speaking of plain text remote control utilities, XCONSOLE, the Telnet server for NetWare, is no safer than RCONSOLE. It uses plain text Telnet for the authentication and either Telnet or the X protocol—both nonencrypted protocols—for the session data. You should avoid XCONSOLE as well, unless you're absolutely sure that your infrastructure is untappable.

The same goes for FTP. Although FTP is arguably less of a risk than RCONSOLE if nonadministrative users are ftping, FTP is just as grave a risk as RCONSOLE if administrative users ftp in to the server. All passwords for FTP are sent in the clear. Avoid, avoid, avoid.

As with any service, if you have no pressing business reason for using the service, you should probably use UNICON.NLM to deconfigure both of these tools (see Figure 22.3).

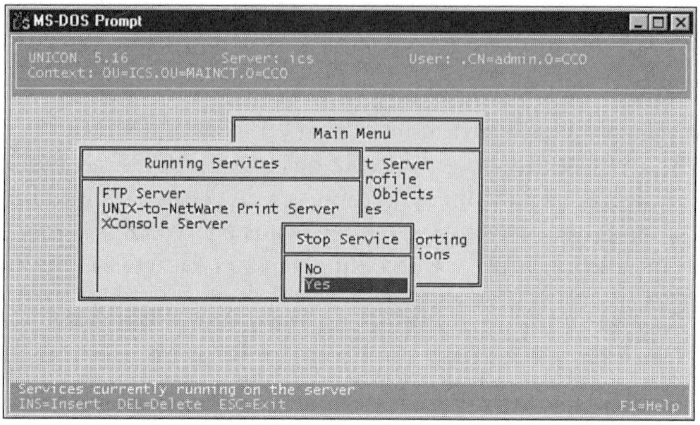

FIGURE 22.3 Use UNICON, NetWare's Unix Services Configuration tool, to stop unwanted Unix compatibility services from running.

WWW Services In the past, NetWare 4.11 and IntranetWare shipped with the NetWare Web Server—not the Netscape Enterprise Server. The Web server included a PERL.NLM that allowed arbitrary execution of code on the server—a very bad thing indeed.

Although this hole has long been plugged in newer versions of the Web server, we mention this because the Web server is *not* part of the NetWare 4 core OS, and thus, not part of the OS's service pack. You need to go out and separately update it (or upgrade to NetWare 5.1 or 6.0).

Finally, as with any Web server, you'll want to search-and-destroy any sample scripts. Leaving them there is simply asking for trouble.

NETBASIC.NLM Get rid of NETBASIC.NLM unless you have a pressing need for it. There are several attacks involving NETBASIC. This is particularly true of NetWare 4, which doesn't have the later NetWare version's SCRSAVER.NLM. Even if you've used the SECURE CONSOLE command, NETBASIC.NLM allows someone who accesses the console to

- Drop to a NETBASIC shell.

- Copy untrusted NLMs into the SYS:SYSTEM directory.

- Copy the NDS files from the hidden SYS:SYSTEM_NETWARE directory to arbitrary locations on the file server.

- Perform trusted file operations that could potentially make your life miserable.

Again, if you've got NetWare 5.1 or 6.0 and SCRSAVER.NLM (or NetWare 4.11 and a third-party utility), this isn't as hot an issue, but it is still due diligence to remove this tool from the server unless you need it.

TOOLBOX.NLM   Toolbox is one of the most useful administrator tools available for NetWare. It even attempts to keep its operations secure—you must authenticate to the tree before it will obey your commands. However, Toolbox is frequently used in batch files, and administrators tend to save authentication information to the Toolbox database. (For example, many administrators use Toolbox to reboot the server, purge limbo blocks from volumes, and so on.)

In a nutshell, an intruder who's familiar with Toolbox will likely type

```
AUTH LOAD
```

at the console. If an administrator has previously done an AUTH SAVE, then the intruder can use Toolbox's functions without logging in.

Basically, if you're doing AUTH SAVEs, the same rules apply to Toolbox as were previously described for NETBASIC. If a screensaver is unavailable, the potential amount of damage is huge. If a screensaver is in use, AUTH SAVE has a more acceptable level of risk.

Server Environment Parameters

There are publicly available tools that can spoof NCP (NetWare Core Protocol) packets—thus making hijacking a session a real possibility. To prevent this from happening to your users, you'll want to set your server's NCP parameters to include packet signature, packet length, and packet component checks.

For example, to get the highest level of NCP security, you'd type

```
SET NCP Packet Signature Option = 3
SET Reject NCP Packets with bad components = ON
SET Reject NCP Packets with bad lengths = ON
```

at the server console. (NetWare 4 users have to put these in the AUTOEXEC.NCF as well.)

NOTE

You will definitely want to do tests in your environment before you enable a packet signature level of 3. Level 3 means, "Don't communicate with ANYBODY if they don't sign their packets." This might be a bad thing if you haven't enabled your clients' packet signature options. (Although, Novell's latest client defaults to "will-do," as discussed later in the chapter.)

Furthermore, you will want to test your servers to see how they'll hold up under the load with a signature level of 3. The amount of processing dedicated to cryptographically signing packets is nontrivial.

Bindery Context   A bindery context is *only* necessary on a server if its third-party software doesn't understand how to communicate via NDS. Unfortunately, there are still NetWare utilities that don't. Upgrade them, if you can, to utilities that are NDS-savvy, because there are publicly available tools that attack based on bindery contexts. (See the "Guest and Other No-Password Users" section for an example of this.)

NetWare servers default to having a bindery context; get rid of it by typing

`set bindery context=`

(That's right, there's nothing to the right of the equal sign.) The system will warn you that bindery services have been disabled. If you don't need 'em, this is a good thing.

Client Environment

You'll want to stay native with your NetWare client—that is, use Novell's client, *not* Microsoft's. Microsoft's client doesn't support packet signing—neither advisory (Level 2) nor mandatory (Level 3).

The NetWare client defaults to the same thing that the server does—Level 1: "Perform packet signatures only if the other side requires it." So, if you're using the latest version of the NetWare client, you won't have a problem setting the server to a mandatory packet-signature level. Still, if you're serious about requiring packet signing, you'll want to set your clients to Level 3.

Again, *make sure to test* any parameter changes in your environment before rolling them out. As advisories come out, you might find yourself changing a large number of client workstations at a time. ZenWorks or other desktop management can make this easier and quicker. You can find out more about ZenWorks at `http://www.novell.com/products/zenworks/`.

Windows: The Weakest Link

Without getting into operating system holy wars here, let's just say that you need to pay special attention to Windows workstations where administrative users log in. The PWL files (in Windows 9*x*) and the SAM (of Windows NT/2K workstations) are very easily cracked.

This is fine if you only log in at workstations that have tight physical security. But what about when administrators need to log in from the field? If you must do this, consider using some sort of encrypted remote control rather than using the desktop of the workstation that you are working on (for example, Citrix, PCAnywhere, and so on). The last thing you want to do is leave your administrative NDS password—and username—as a dropping on the user's highly insecure workstation.

Also, check out Chapter 18, "Trojans," for information on protecting your workstations from programs that can hijack login information. Because it's likely that if you're in a NetWare environment, you might want to use ZENWorks to assign policies that lock down your client workstations.

Finally, if you have public terminals, or a Citrix remote login system, you will definitely want to disable the "Advanced" function of the client. The browse functions of the Advanced tab provide more information to an intruder than you want to disseminate. (If you do this, you'll want to enable "context-less" login, unless you want your users typing *.myname.mydepartment.mylocation.myorg* as their username.)

Novell Directory Services (NDS) Environment

Any directory service (DS) needs to be maintained from birth and throughout its life. Neglect and oversight are the main reasons a DS fails—whether in the security space or simply from the functionality perspective.

A Good Start: Intruder Detection

Intruder detection is a way of making NDS count the number of failed login attempts within a certain time frame—and lock the account for a certain amount of time if the number of failed logins exceeds a certain limit.

Let's look at an example. An intruder writes a program to perform a dictionary or brute-force attack on a given user's login, say, user name JOE, using the authentication calls that are available via the NetWare API. If there is no intruder detection, the intruder can cycle through thousands of possible passwords in a relatively short time.

If the admin has enabled Detect Intruders, as shown in Figure 22.4, the following happens: Because the intruder is trying more than seven passwords in a 30 minute period, the account is locked for 15 minutes. All of a sudden, rather than being able to cycle through thousands of passwords, the intruder can only cycle through seven before the account is locked. This is an extremely good protection against systematic, online, real-time password cracking.

The bad news is intruder detection is not enabled by default. You'll need to go into NWAdmin and enable it per OU (organizational unit) as part of your "new tree SOP (Standard Operating Procedure)."

User Names: Admin

Admin is the first user created in a new NDS tree. The first thing a lot of folks do after installing a new NDS tree is rename the Admin user to something non-obvious and put Admin into a non-obvious container (like .GSmith.abc.myorg.) This container should be stored separately from that of regular users.

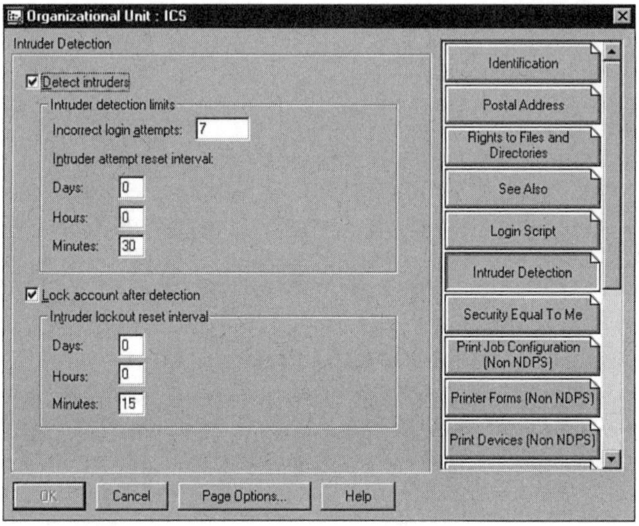

FIGURE 22.4   You'll want to use NWAdmin to enable intruder detection on each organizational unit in your tree.

This is a good measure, as far as attacks from outside your organization go, but it's not foolproof. As we've discussed elsewhere, lots of security problems come from the inside. A temp worker—intern, air conditioning repair person, or receptionist—might see an administrative user log in (like, um, YOU while you log in to solve a problem for this person)—and thus gain information about an administrative user's login name. Perhaps it's not THE Admin user, but it's *an* Admin user—which is all potential crackers are looking for. So, move the Admin user if you want, but know that this is not a cure-all.

Naturally, you'll want to make sure that *all* administrative users have *very good* passwords. Use NWAdmin to make sure that administrative users have policies in place to require a password of sufficient length.

Guest and Other No-Password Users
Unless you have a need for a Guest account—and most organizations do not—delete the Guest user. (NetWare 5, happily, does not supply a Guest user by default when you install a new NDS tree.)

If you're administrating an existing NDS tree, you will want to check for users with no passwords on a fairly regular basis (or use NDS auditing software, discussed later in the chapter). Even if these accounts have no special privileges, they will permit an attacker to browse the tree and gather an intruder's best friend—more information. If they belong to a container that's been given special authority (a bad idea—see the section "Unintended Consequences of Container Rights"), suddenly you've got a problem on your hands.

How do these no-password accounts "show up?" There are tools (for example, backup, antivirus, print servers) that generate accounts so that the program can log in to the tree without operator intervention. You'll want to make sure that these accounts do NOT allow an interactive login—at least, not without requiring a password. Try it; if the tool account allows you to log in, restrict the account to certain network addresses only—the network addresses of the station that runs the program, such as the anti-virus console, the print server, and so on. (Some of these types of tools don't permit you to specify a password, so changing the password won't fly.)

You—and an intruder—can find accounts with no passwords, if you have a bindery context set (see why a bindery context isn't a good thing?), with the freely-available CHKNULL program. A good NDS auditing tool will also find these.

NOTE

There is literature out there that implies that you can also use NLIST to find null password information. This is not the case. NLIST will show you what the policies are for users—that is, if a null password is allowed and the minimum password length. These are useful things to know (because you don't want a user to have too short of a password, or to be allowed to blank it), but be aware of the difference.

Enforcing User Authentication Policies   NetWare has a bunch of good password management built into NDS. Each site is different, but typically, enabling the password management can greatly increase your security. Using NWAdmin, you can set

- Whether a user can change his password.
- Whether a password is required.
- The minimum password length.
- Whether periodic password changes are required, and how many days are required between changes.
- The number of times the user can procrastinate a required periodic password change before getting locked out (called *grace logins*).
- Whether unique passwords are required.

These policies are delegated *per user*, not as part of a group. You'll want to use NWAdmin's Details on Multiple Users feature (see Figure 22.5) if you want to change the policies of many users at once.

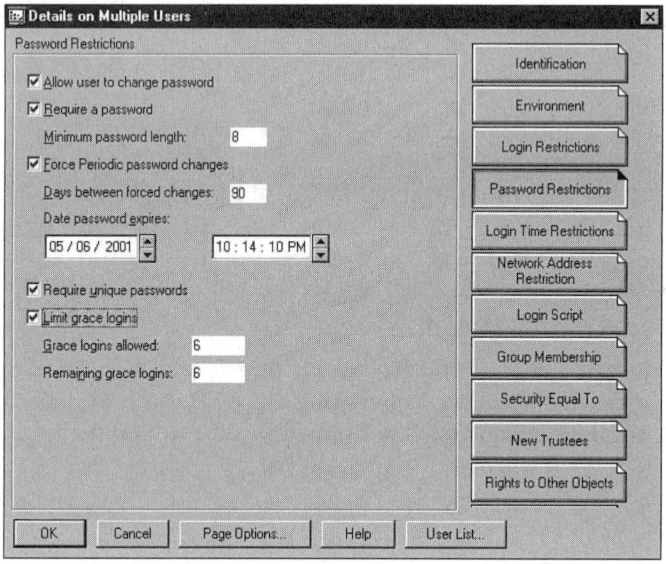

FIGURE 22.5   If you are changing the password policies of a bunch of users at one time, use NWAdmin's Details on Multiple Users options.

If your organization believes that passwords are too easily compromised (by users writing them down, sharing them, and so on), you can investigate alternative login methods, such as biometrics. The Novell Modular Authentication System (NMAS) supports third-party authentication such as fingerprinting, SecurID, and so on. You can read more about NMAS at `http://www.novell.com/products/nmas/details.html`.

Understanding and Applying NDS "Best Practices"

The Novell Directory Service is the heart of your NetWare network. Servers, accounts, file systems, certificates—everything—relies on NDS being configured correctly. If you or your system administrators don't fully grok NDS, or take short cuts, you are likely to make mistakes that will leave you vulnerable to attack.

> **NOTE**
>
> There is a huge body of work about NDS—most of it, naturally, written by Novell. If you are shaky on your NDS understanding, or want to make sure you fully understand it, a good place to start is the Novell Research AppNote, "Learning and Applying the Rules of NDS Security," found at `http://developer.novell.com/research/appnotes/1997/august/02/index.htm`.

Unintended Consequences of Container Rights   Container rights are one of the most convenient NDS features—you apply rights to an organizational unit (OU), and the rights flow down so that children containers and their objects inherit these rights. Convenient—yet dangerous.

With many objects and subcontainers in a tree, it can be difficult to visualize just what the consequences of inherited rights can be.

One common—and bad—practice that some IT shops have is to link administrative rights to an OU, for example, the SysAdmins OU. They figure, "Anybody in this OU is an administrator, so what's the harm?" The answer is it can do plenty of harm.

For example, a problem with the initial version of ZenWorks workstation manager allowed *any* workstation object to assume the rights of its container—without a user being logged on (this problem has since been corrected in later releases). This made it easy for an untrusted user to get sneaky and run programs with those rights. In the case of a container that was assigned Admin rights, the *workstation* assumed the Admin rights—because it was part of the container. All of a sudden, the intruder had admin rights, too.

If the container had *not* been given special rights, the damage of this exploit would have been minimized. Lesson: Don't assign sensitive rights to a container, ever.

What are *sensitive rights*? Some of them include the following:

- Security equivalencies to administrative users

- Any rights to the root of any volume

- Any rights to SYS:\etc

- Any rights to SYS:\system

Use groups instead of containers to assign these types of rights. This is a good administrative practice. Because a group is a central point of administration, the potential for admin error is decreased.

There's nothing inherently wrong with grouping; the problem only has to do with *inheritance*—and thus, containers. Although Novell (and other literature) will tell you that problems with inheritance can be handled with an IRF (Inherited Rights Filter), consider the previous problem. Would an IRF block rights to *workstation objects* in the *same* OU as the administrative users? No! An IRF "flows down" through the tree. Objects in the *same* container get the same rights as the user in the container.

In a nutshell, inheritance can be a tricky beast. Be careful.

NDS Auditing Tools

NDS can be a big and complex beast—the fact of the matter is that any good directory service is. Your best bet if you are serious about keeping an eye on NDS is to invest in third-party auditing software. NWAdmin enables you to do searches on various NDS attributes (for example, the `Security Equivalent to Me` search shown in Figure 22.6, which reveals all the users that other users are equivalent to). However, searching on every single property from NWAdmin can be cumbersome and/or impossible. I do not recommend Novell's AUDITCON for anything but a very small organization.

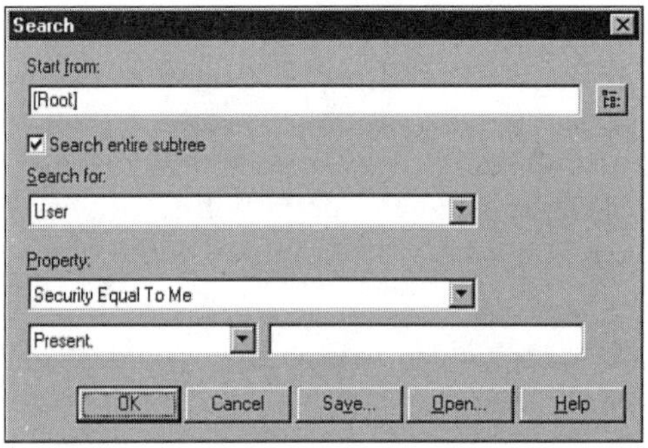

FIGURE 22.6   NWAdmin will enable you to do basic property searches, but isn't sufficient for hardcore auditing.

It's beyond the scope of this chapter to review every auditing tool available, but the following are a sampling of what's available.

AuditWare for NDS

Manufacturer: Computer Associates

URL: `http://www.computerassociates.com/products/auditware_nds.htm`

A Windows-based advanced NDS reporting and security analysis tool. Generates comparison, analysis, security, and documentation reports.

Can locate potentially hazardous stealth users that cannot be seen because the Browse privilege has been filtered out. Can also locate "dangerous" users—those who have supervisor privileges but do not meet minimum password requirements.

bv-Control for NDS

Manufacturer: BindView

URL: `http://www.bindview.com/solutions/Novell/`

A tool to automate the analysis and documentation of server and NDS configuration; it looks for improperly configured servers and out-of-date or conflicting executables (including EXEs, NLMs, services, and device drivers) that can cause your servers to perform poorly and crash.

JRButils

URL: http://www.jrbsoftware.com

Command-line-based utilities for the rugged individualist who lives for the CLI. Users can use these utilities to perform operations on objects selected via wild cards, container, membership of a group, or via a list in a file. When displaying information, filters can be applied. Can be used for automation of operations such as mass user creation, customization, deletion, and for performing security checks.

LT Auditor+ 8.0

Manufacturer: Blue Lance

URL: http://www.bluelance.com/products/lta_nw/

A Windows-based intrusion detection/audit trail security software solution. LT Auditor+ supports NT and/or Novell networks. Alerts can be configured to respond to specific events either system-wide or at particular workstations; it also provides off-site paging and email alerts via an SNMP console.

Commercial Secure Remote Control Products

SecureConsole for NetWare 3.4

Manufacturer: Protocom Development Systems

URL: http://www.serversystems.com/SecureConsole.htm

A native Win32 application, which provides single sign-on to a NetWare console. It does this by checking a user's current NDS credentials and looking them up in the SecureConsole database. Standard NDS security features such as secure password authentication, single sign-ons and intruder lock out are supported. Generates SNMP alerts to one or more network management consoles when it detects attempted unauthorized access or other abnormal server conditions.

AdRem sfConsole

Manufacturer: AdRem Software

URL: http://www.adremsoft.com/arcon3/sfcon/sfcon/index.php

Offers 128-bit encrypted remote console operations. Access control is available that allows users and groups of users to be permitted specific console commands and server screens.

Useful Freeware

Most of the following is available from `http://www.netwarefiles.com`, a repository of free or shareware utilities.

BURGLAR.NLM   A venerable tool, Bart Mellink's BURGLAR.NLM creates a supervisory user of your choice. You need access to the server console and about five free nanoseconds to do this—reason #9,285 to secure your server consoles from unauthorized personnel.

HOBJLOC.NLM   Novell Consulting's answer to crackers who create "hidden" users; that is, users invisible even to administrative users. Finds them so you can root them out. (Commercial auditing tools do this too, but this is free.)

REMOTE.EXE   Written by TheRuiner, REMOTE. EXE *instantly* cracks even the longest of "encrypted" remote console passwords. Want to see some fun? Type `remote encrypt` at the server console, and enter the longest password you can. Then take the remotely encrypted string, and feed it to REMOTE.EXE.

`985FF510136420112F1D366A207616903FBEEDEBCDCDDCCCDCCBDB4CCBCCDCD4BCDBB03`

is instantly decrypted to

`THEREISNOREMOTEPASSWORDSECURITY`

It's a small and useful demo tool that turns even the most doubting Thomas into a true believer in REMOTE's lack of real encryption.

SETPWD.NLM   Developed at the University of Salford in the U.K., P.R. Lees' SETPWD.NLM enables you to set anybody's password from the server console. Is this reason #9,286?

Further Reading

Novell's Guide to NetWare 6 Networks. Jeffery F. Hughes and Blair W. Thomas. John Wiley & Sons, March 2002. ISBN: 076454876X.

Novell's NetWare 6 Administrator's Handbook. Jeffrey Harris and Kelley J. P. Lindbergh. John Wiley & Sons, March 2002. ISBN: 0764548824

Mastering NetWare 6. James E. Gaskin. Sybex, February 2002. ISBN: 0782140238

Mastering Netware 5.1. James E. Gaskin. Sybex Publications, July 2000. ISBN: 078212772X.

The Complete Guide to Novell Directory Services. David Kearns and Brian Iverson. Sybex, March 1998. ISBN: 0782118232

Special Edition Using Netware 5.0. Peter Kuo, John Pence, and Sally Specker. Que, August 1999. ISBN: 0789720566

Novell's Guide to NetWare 5 Networks. Jeffrey F. Hughes and Blair W. Thomas. IDG, 1999. ISBN: 0764545442

Novell's Guide to Integrating NetWare 5 and NT. J. D. Marymee, Sandy Stevens, and Gary Hein. IDG, October 1999. ISBN: 0764545809

Novell's Guide to NetWare 5 and TCP/IP. Drew Heywood. IDG, March 1999. ISBN: 0764545647

Novell's Guide to LAN/WAN Analysis. Laura A. Chappell. IDG, March 1998. ISBN: 0764545086

Novell's Four Principles of NDS. Jeff Hughes. IDG Books Worldwide, 1996. ISBN: 0-76454-522-1.

NetWare Web Development. Peter Kuo. Sams. 1996. ISBN: 1575211866

Summary

As with other operating systems, keeping NetWare secure is a matter of being diligent about staying current with OS levels, patches, and best practices. Some NetWare tools and/or services are security liabilities; as with any other OS, your rule should be "If I don't need it, I won't run it." Some of NetWare's more insecure tools have third-party replacements that are more secure.

Understanding NDS rights is vital to making sure that you don't cause unintended security consequences. And NDS-specific auditing tools can help make sure that your secured network stays secure.

Routers, Switches, and Hubs

Administrators and security professionals alike often spend a significant amount of time configuring and securing the various firewalls, Web servers, and surrounding systems that make up their enterprise environments. Unfortunately, infrastructure devices such as routers and switches are frequently neglected in this effort. This neglect can often lead to sniffed sessions, route changes, and some overall Really Bad Things.

In this chapter, I will be focusing on the steps necessary to configure, deploy, and keep your infrastructure equipment safe from hostile attackers. I have chosen to focus on Cisco products simply because they are by far the most predominantly used. However, users of products from Extreme, Juniper, Nortel, or other routing and switching vendors might still find this chapter useful, as many of these techniques apply to non-Cisco equipment as well. Please note that this chapter assumes basic familiarity with Cisco routing equipment. Most of the examples in this chapter will be demonstrated on the "router" versions of IOS. Although the versions of IOS found on switches are similar, for simplicity's sake we will only be showing examples from the router version of IOS.

NOTE

The authors of the book *@Large* write about a cracker who had stolen thousands of passwords by compromising Internet backbone routers and setting up customized sniffers. Although it is true that sniffing was easier back then (because many of the routers in the earlier days of the Internet were based on Unix operating systems such as IBM's AIX), source code for Cisco's IOS has been seen circulating through some underground channels. Although I know of no documented cases of Trojaned IOS code, it is certainly possible. People taking comfort in IOS being more "specialized" and subsequently more obscure, do so foolishly.

The Problems with Infrastructure Equipment

Although it is safe to assume that most hacking targets are end-node systems—such as Web, application, or database servers—many people foolishly ignore the security issues surrounding their infrastructure equipment. This can, unfortunately, be a colossal blunder. The truth of the matter is that not only can routers and switches be compromised, they can be used as stepping stones for further attack, as well as become incredibly useful information gathering devices for attackers.

Routers, switches, and hubs have their own OS. Cisco calls theirs IOS (Internetwork Operating System). Although Cisco's track record with security is fairly good, it is by no means flawless. Cisco has had some security problems in the past, and as with any OS, if those problems are not patched or addressed, you leave yourself open to further troubles.

Of particular concern is the fact that routers and switches can be used to not only map target networks, but also to mask one's identity, help create sniffing stations, and create some overall widespread chaos. For example, most Cisco switches have the capability to create a *monitor port* that can mirror or *port span* any other port on the switch. This effectively allows an administrator—or an intruder—to duplicate any traffic that the switch sees, and dump it down a specified switch port. So, although administrators might take comfort in their switched environment's apparent immunity to the sniffer-based eavesdropping problems that HUBed environments face, all bets are off if the intruder has access to configuring the switch.

Other shenanigans can include static route entries and ICMP (Internet Control Message Protocol) redirect messages, conveniently disabled access control lists (ACLs), or even bizarre network address translation (NAT) rules. Rest assured that if an experienced intruder gets into your routing and switching architecture, you will have a *very* difficult time permanently locking him out of your systems and network.

Keeping Up with OS Revisions

Keeping "current" with OS changes is pivotal. Much as this point was driven home in the Microsoft, Novell, and Unix chapters of this book, the same holds true with Cisco IOS. However, Cisco actually does a better job with OS revisions, version control, and release strategies than most other software vendors. When Cisco says that a version of their software "is stable," it might actually, in fact, be stable.

The first thing you should do while analyzing the state of your infrastructure equipment is investigate the various versions of IOS running on your systems. This can be accomplished by using the Show Version command. Should you discover that you are running older versions of IOS, consider the phrase "If it isn't broken, don't fix it" before moving towards massive upgrade efforts. More important than the age of the IOS version is where that version is in its release life cycle. Cisco has designated three stages that a particular IOS version resides in during its release cycle:

- Early Deployment (ED)—This is usually a version of IOS with new features that might still have some bugs in it.

- Limited Deployment (LD)—These IOS builds are usually considered "interim" builds. They are usually released with fixes to specific problems found in ED builds.

- General Deployment (GD)—General deployment builds are focused on stability, and are usually fairly "bug free."

TIP

Cisco's full release strategy is actually a fair bit more complex then what we've outlined previously—we are simply going over the basics here. A great document that details numbering, life cycles, and other versioning tidbits can be found on Cisco's site at http://www.cisco.com/warp/public/cc/pd/iosw/iore/prodlit/537_pp.htm.

Although you might be tempted to use the "latest and greatest" version of IOS, I caution you to only use what you need, and to stick to GD builds whenever possible. GD builds tend to have the majority of the bugs worked out of them, and are usually quite solid. The only exception to this rule of thumb is in relation to security problems—if an IOS version contains a known security vulnerability, you really have no choice but to upgrade.

TIP

If you maintain Cisco equipment, it would be wise to subscribe to Cisco's mailing list that announces the security field notices. You can find subscription information for the list at http://www.cisco.com/warp/public/707/sec_incident_response.shtml.

Securing Hubs

Hubs are the simplest of the three types of devices in this chapter by far. All hubs do is repeat all the packets they receive out of all the other ports. Two kinds of hubs are available: managed and unmanaged.

Unmanaged hubs are very simple. You plug them into the network, and that's all you can do with them. The good news is that there is nothing a hacker can break into. The bad news is that it won't provide you with any data when you have a problem.

Managed hubs will usually give you some traffic statistics and the ability to disable individual ports. Traffic statistics are good for looking for abnormal conditions. These devices enable you to remotely disable a port, which can be handy, especially if it is the weekend and you don't have the keys to physically get to the hub.

The downside to a managed hub is that it will have either an SNMP, Telnet, and/or HTTP interface that enables you to perform remote management, which is another point of attack for crackers. If you are not using the remote management features, you should turn them off. How you do this depends on the vendor. If you are leaving them on, make sure to pick good passwords. We will discuss SNMP in more detail later in the chapter.

Securing Switches

The difference between hubs and switches is simple. Switches only send traffic to those ports to which it needs to go. This stops users on a port from seeing all the traffic. This helps with network performance and security at the same time. Telling the difference between a switch and a router gets fuzzy because many "switch" products have routing-like functionality such as VLANs (Virtual Local Area Networks). Because this advanced functionality overlaps with routers, if you are using it, please read the router material below as well.

Virtually all switches are managed. The issue is the same as with hubs—turn off the management features if you are not using them. If you are using it, make sure to secure it as much as possible.

Securing and Configuring Routers

Routers are easier to protect at a host level than many Unix or Windows systems are, simply because they have fewer services that can be accessed remotely. Sure, they perform some complex routing calculations and play pivotal roles on the Internet, but they don't have services running on them like BIND, IMAP, POP, or sendmail—services that have proven to be points of entry on Unix and Windows platforms again and again.

However, despite the fact that routers tend to be generally less accessible, a number of configuration tasks should be performed to limit a router's accessibility even further.

Securing Login Points

Unfortunately, the majority of routers today are still managed over Telnet, which does not employ any type of encryption. Telnet passes all traffic in the clear, so it is quite easy to pick up login passwords if you have sniffers in place. Cisco IOS version 12.1 brought SSH version 1 to most of its router platforms. Unfortunately, Cisco is using the less secure SSH version 1 instead of version 2. Fortunately, we can do a number of things to help restrict access to Cisco routers, and help limit the chances of unauthorized users accessing our routers. On the other hand, Extreme Networks has a SSH2 Download for their ExtremeWare.

TIP

SSH is a secure replacement for Telnet (among other things). You can find out more about SSH at `http://www.tigerlair.com/ssh/faq/ssh-faq.html`.

You can log in to a Cisco router four ways:

- Via the physical *console* port

- Via the physical *auxiliary* port

- Via other physical serial ports (only on models equipped with such ports, or *lines*)

- Via telnetting into one of the unit's IP addresses

Three of these methods require physical access, which makes our life a little easier. We will discuss the fourth method, logging in using Telnet, first.

Cisco routers have five *virtual terminals*, or *vtys*, that you can telnet to. There are two things you need to worry about with Telnet logins. First, you want to make sure that all the vtys have passwords enabled. You can do this by issuing the following commands from the configuration mode:

```
Router1(config)#line vty 0 4
```

```
Router1(config-line)#password fabi0!
```

This sets the vty password to `fabi0!`. Next, you will want to add a level of defense to help prevent attackers from telnetting into the router and remaining idle, which can tie up all five vtys. The following commands will not solve the problem entirely, but will definitely help:

```
Router1(config)#line vty 0 4
```

```
Router1(config-line)#exec-timeout 1
```

```
Router1(config-line)#exit

Router1(config)#service tcp-keepalives-in
```

These commands set the vty timeout value to one minute, and force the use of TCP keep-alives to help combat orphaned sessions. In addition to these commands, you can use a standard access list to limit the number of workstations that can telnet into the router itself. For example, assuming your management segment (where you will be telnetting from) is 10.1.1.0, the following will limit inbound Telnet sessions to this range:

```
Router1(config)#access-list 1 permit 10.1.1.0 0.0.0.255

Router1(config)#access-list 1 deny any

Router1(config)#line vty 0 4

Router1(config-line)#access-class 1 in
```

When it comes to physical access concerns, there are two things we want to watch out for: the console port and the auxiliary port. The auxiliary port is often used for "out of band" management via devices such as modems, so it is extremely important that this port be protected as well. You can protect both ports using passwords by issuing the following commands:

```
Router1(config)#line aux 0

Router1(config-line)#password fabi0!

Router1(config)#line console 0

Router1(config-line)#password fabi0!
```

NOTE

There is one other method of helping combat the problems surrounding Telnet—don't use it. Some administrators resort to recycling their terminal server and dial-up equipment, then attaching it to the Cisco router AUX or CONSOLE ports. They can then SSH or dial into the terminal server, and then hop onto the router from there. Also, directly connected dial-up access to routers is actually quite feasible because bandwidth is not an issue during text-based configurations. Just make sure that you require authentication.

Keeping Administrators Accountable

Finally, in the interest of good auditing/accounting practices, it's a good idea to remove the use of "shared" accounts. A shared account is one that is used by multiple people, with no method of clarifying true ownership. By default, Cisco devices have two levels of access: User mode and the privileged Enable mode. You can think of Enable mode as the equivalent of root in Unix, or Administrator in Windows NT.

By default, users are authenticated based solely on passwords—no usernames are required. This is true for both the regular Login mode, as well as Enable mode. Unfortunately, most organizations never move away from this model, and therefore have multiple people sharing the router passwords. By implementing AAA (Authentication, Authorization, and Accounting) services in conjunction with the RADIUS or TACACS authentication mechanisms, administrators can tie their Cisco infrastructure to a centralized username repository such as LDAP (Lightweight Directory Access Protocol), NDS (Novell Directory Services), AD (Active Directory), or any other centralized password store. By implementing such an authentication model, administrators will be forced to log in to routers using their username and password credentials, leading to the possibility of clean audit trails.

> **TIP**
>
> AAA configuration is beyond the scope of this chapter, but a good start to learning more on the subject (including sample configurations) can be found at `http://www.cisco.com/univercd/cc/td/doc/product/software/ios120/12cgcr/secur_c/scprt1/scathen.htm`.

Disabling Unnecessary Services

The next step in securing your Cisco equipment is to disable unnecessary services. Sound familiar? It should—this is the standard technique that should be employed across all OS platforms.

First, disable the small servers. These services are rarely used, and are not needed in most environments:

```
Router1(config)#no service udp-small-servers
```

```
Router1(config)#no service tcp-small-servers
```

Next, disable the `finger` service:

```
Router1(config)#no ip finger
```

Although the `finger` service doesn't pose any threat by itself, it can be used as a reconnaissance tool by hackers to scope out further information. After disabling finger, make sure that the HTTP (Web) server is not running. Although it is disabled by default, it's better to be safe than sorry by using this command:

```
Router1(config)#no ip http server
```

Cisco devices have a Cisco-proprietary protocol called Cisco Discovery Protocol (CDP). Like finger, CDP is not a threat in and of itself, but can be used to gain information that an intruder shouldn't have access to. You can disable CDP on a per-interface basis with these commands:

```
Router1(config)#int eth0/0
```

```
Router1(config-if)#no cdp enable
```

Or you can choose to disable it entirely by issuing the following:

```
Router1(config)#no cdp run
```

Finally, although I recommend using the Network Time Protocol (NTP) to synchronize time across your infrastructure (see the next section for NTP implementation issues), if you do not plan on deploying NTP, you should make sure it is disabled by issuing this:

```
Router1(config)#no ntp
```

> **TIP**
>
> It never hurts to double-check your work. Consider periodically running nmap against your routers to check for running services. It's a good habit to form, and it might save your butt some day.

Network Management Considerations

Locking down terminal access and disabling unnecessary services are important steps in securing your infrastructure. However, the task does not end with a few configuration settings. There are a number of procedural and management aspects of infrastructure security that should be taken into consideration as well:

- Do you keep backups of your router and switch configurations? If not, why not?

- If so, where are those configuration files stored? Are they secure?

- Are the passwords in those configuration files secure?

- Do you track when people log into your routers, change configurations, or bring WAN links down?

- Have you centralized your logging efforts for coordination purposes?

- Can you monitor and manage your infrastructure securely?

Fortunately, down it's not too hard to address most of these issues. With a little planning, a few service additions, and some configuration changes, even shaky situations can be drastically improved.

Centralizing Logging

Security gurus will down explain that syslog is not the most secure protocol out there because it passes its information in the clear over UDP. Unfortunately, right now there are few alternatives. Assuming you have a syslog server set up, you can use the following commands to pipe your output to that server:

```
Router1(config)#logging trap notifications

Router1(config)#logging facility local6

Router1(config)#logging 10.1.1.2
```

These commands will instruct the router to output all notifications (trap notification) to the logging host (10.1.1.2), using the facility local6.

NOTE

syslog uses *facilities* to help designate between log entry types: auth, auth-priv, cron, daemon, kern, lpr, mail, mark, syslog, user, uucp, and local0 through local7. You can think of these as simply categories of message types. Although you can configure your router or switch to report using any of these, most administrators pick one of the "local" settings for their infrastructure equipment. See the Unix man pages for syslogd and syslog.conf for more information.

Password Storage Considerations

Many people store their router configuration files and images on FTP or TFTP servers. Although keeping backup copies of both images and configuration files is a great practice, it is *crucial* that these files be protected. Make sure that the server they are hosted on is secure, and that the file permissions on those configuration files limit their accessibility. One good security measure is to only have the FTP or TFTP server up during the transfer and then shut them down immediately afterward.

NOTE

Frequently during penetration tests you will come across the systems that store the router configuration files. Although the routers themselves can be quite difficult to break into, after stumbling across unprotected configuration files you can usually decrypt the passwords and subsequently access the routers fairly easily. In these scenarios, the configuration files—not the routers themselves—become the weak link in the chain. You can read more about Cisco password storage at `http://www.cisco.com/warp/public/701/64.html`.

Next, consider implementing two precautionary measures on the password front. First, use Cisco's "secret" password convention, as opposed to the normal "enable" password. The storage of the "enable secret" password uses an MD5 hash that is not reversible, but the regular "enable" password can be trivially decrypted. You can make the switch to using "enable secret" by using the following commands:

```
Router1(config)#no enable password
Router1(config)#enable secret #fabi0!
```

This code removes the regular "enable" password, and replaces it with the "secret" password of `#fabi0!`. Another precautionary measure is to use the password encryption service available on most Cisco devices. This service applies to usernames and first-level login passwords only. Although the password encryption service still implements an incredibly weak encryption mechanism, it will at least allow you to avoid storing your user and login passwords in clear text. You can enable the password encryption service by using the following:

```
Router1(config)#service password-encryption
```

Time Synchronization

The network time protocol (NTP) was designed to synchronize the clocks of systems and network devices to some sort of time reference. NTP is an industry-standard Internet protocol, whose foundation was defined in RFC 1059. NTP is considered to be highly accurate, and quite transportable—there are implementations of it on Windows-based operating systems, Unix systems, and a myriad of routing and switching devices.

NOTE

Although something as seemingly trivial as time might not seem critical in the area of security, this couldn't be farther from the truth. Time plays a critical role in basic auditing, accounting, and event correlation. I personally learned this the hard way when I was once asked by a client to track an internal user's illegal activity on the Internet. The trail lead me to the proxy server logs, which were slightly out of sync with the log data I was given. I didn't think this was a big deal until I realized that the proxy servers were servicing requests at the rate of 60-per-second! That minute's worth of discrepancy sent me sifting through thousands of requests.

If you can successfully deploy NTP in your environment, you might be thanking yourself later. Assuming you have some NTP servers to poll from, the following commands will configure your router to synchronize with an NTP-enabled time source (in this case, an NTP server at 10.1.1.9):

```
Router1(config)#ntp server 10.1.1.9
```

TIP

The official NTP home page, which contains links to FAQs, RFCs, and code can be found at http://www.eecis.udel.edu/~ntp/.

You can also find a brief primer on NTP at http://www.nwc.com/1002/1002ws1.html.

SNMP Considerations

Some organizations use SNMP heavily. Others do not, but leave the protocol enabled in hopes that some day their horrendously expensive network management "framework" product will do something useful. Regardless of what role SNMP plays in your environment, here are two bits of advice:

- If you aren't going to be using SNMP, disable it.

- If you are going to use it, configure it properly.

Disabling snmp is pretty simple—simply find all your snmp statements and negate them with the no command, like this:

```
Router1(config)#no snmp-server community fabio RW
Router1(config)#no snmp-server packetsize 2048
Router1(config)#no snmp-server engineID local 00000009020000107BCDE841
```

However, if you are using SNMP and cannot disable it, you can do a number of things to further secure its use. First, SNMP has essentially two modes: a READ-ONLY (RO) mode, and a READ-WRITE (RW) mode. If at all possible, use the READ-ONLY mode. By restricting the use of SNMP to READ-ONLY, even in the event that the community string is discovered, attackers will be limited to using SNMP for reconnaissance purposes. They will be unable to use it to modify configurations. If you must use the READ-WRITE mode of SNMP, make sure that your READ-WRITE and READ-ONLY community strings are different. Finally, you can use ACLs to restrict SNMP usage to only the workstations or management machines that need it. For example, if your network management segment is 10.1.1.0, the following ACLs will block SNMP from everything but that segment:

```
Router1(config)#ip access-list standard 1
Router1(config-std-nacl)#permit 10.1.1.0 0.0.0.255
Router1(config-std-nacl)#deny all
Router1(config)#snmp-server community fabio RO 1
```

Remember, it is a good strategy to keep necessary services exposed to as few machines as possible.

NOTE

If you are not worried about the potential of SNMP being a security problem, please read the article at `http://www.informationweek.com/story/IWK20020212S0007`, which details SNMP vulnerabilities.

Preventing Spoofing and Other Packet Games

You might be tempted to skip this section. Don't. If there is one thing you do with your infrastructure, I beg of you to implement these recommendations. The following material is so important that, had the majority of network administrators implemented these suggestions, the massive distributed-denial-of-service (DDoS) attacks that occurred in February 2000, and repeated on a smaller scale since then, might not have been possible.

Although certain types of DDoS starvation attacks will continue to be virtually impossible to stop, some preventative measures can be taken. Many of the denial-of-service attacks that occur on the Internet originate with forged, or *spoofed*, source addresses. This makes it incredibly hard for a victim to trace an attack back to its origin, much less stop it. The following precautionary measures will not only protect your network from some types of potentially hostile traffic, they will also help protect the Internet community as a whole from your network. Should any of your machines fall prey to malicious intruders, you can use your border routers to help shield your fellow netizens from your misfortune. If your infrastructure is designed and protected properly, in the event that any attackers beat your system administrators to the implementation of a patch, your routers might still be able to help stop hostile activity.

In short, implementing the following recommendations is not only a good idea for your own safety, but for the safety of the Internet community as a whole.

Egress Filtering

Frequently, network administrators keep a sharp eye on what enters their network, but never watch for what exits it. Filtering the traffic that leaves a network, or *egress filtering*, will help lower the risk of your environment being used as a DDoS platform, as well as make it less attractive to intruders.

The primary method used to stop outbound spoofing is the implementation of ACLs on the perimeter routers. It is generally considered a good practice to configure and apply these lists to the interface through which the packets come into a network, rather than the interface through which they leave. This not only makes the lists easier to read, but it also protects the router itself from spoofing attacks.

For this example, assume that the local network uses the address block of 172.16.1.0 (mask 255.255.255.0—a Class C). Also assume that the local area network is attached to the first Ethernet port, Ethernet 0/0.

With this configuration, you would want to make sure that all IP packets leaving the network have a source address falling in the 172.16.1.0 range. Anything not having a source address in that range is obviously spoofed. There are two steps to enforcing this policy. The first is the creation of the ACL itself:

```
Router1(config)#access-list 100 permit ip 172.16.1.0 0.0.0.255 any
```

The second is the implementation of the ACL on the proper interface, in this case, Ethernet 0/0:

```
Router1(config)#int eth0/0
Router1(config-if)#ip access-group 100 in
```

TIP

Chris Brenton has written a brief but good paper on egress filtering for the SANS Institute. It's worth a quick read, and you can find it at http://www.sans.org/y2k/egress.htm.

Ingress Filtering

Ingress (or inbound) filtering is very useful in defeating denial-of-service attacks against your network. RFC 2267 (http://archives.neohapsis.com/archives/rfcs/rfc2267.txt) describes it in detail.

You can manually configure ingress filters. The process is similar to egress filtering, except the filters here are on the external connections instead of the ethernet port. However, we are going to look at an easier way to implement it.

Cisco released the Unicast RPF (Reverse Path Forwarding) feature in IOS 12.0 (it was also in an earlier 11.1(CC) release) to try to mitigate problems caused by bad source addresses in packets. If this feature is enabled on a router interface, the router will verify that the source address is in the routing table for that interface. If it is not, the packet is dropped.

What's nice about this feature is it's much easier to implement than specific egress filtering, though it serves the same purpose. One major downside is that it assumes symmetrical routing. If you have asymmetrical routing in your network, this feature will cause a lot of connections to fail.

> **NOTE**
>
> Symmetrical routing is when packets going out and packets coming back in follow the same path across the network. Asymmetrical routing is when the packets going out take one path across the network, but the packets coming back in take a different one.

This feature depends on the Cisco Express Forwarding (CEF) feature, which is an easy to setup switching system built into Cisco router. CEF must be enabled on the router first:

```
Router1(config)#ip cef
```

Then you enable it on each interface:

```
Router1(config)#int ethernet 0/0
Router1(config-if)#ip verify unicast reverse-path
```

Stopping Silly Packet Games

There are a number of tricks and miscellaneous packet nonsense that attackers might attempt when attacking your network. Although the likelihood of their success using only these techniques is rather limited, you still don't want this type of traffic bouncing around on your network.

First you'll want to disable IP source routing. IP source routing allows for the specification of a predefined path that a packet should take, and is often used in spoofing-based attacks. Packets being source routed rarely have a legitimate origin. It is therefore safe to disable this feature on at least your Internet-facing routers, with this command:

```
Router1(config)#no ip source-route
```

Another common attack uses directed broadcasts in an effort to flood a victim's network with ICMP echo replies. This attack, otherwise known as *smurfing*, can be used to channel a number of networks to mistakenly respond to ICMP echo requests that were forged en masse. Unless you know of a specific application in your environment that might rely on directed broadcasts, you should disable this feature on every active interface of every active router:

```
Router1(config)#int ethernet 0/0
Router1(config-if)#no ip directed-broadcast
```

It is a good idea to disable `proxy-arp` on interfaces that don't require it:

```
Router1(config)#int ethernet 0/0
Router1(config-if)#no ip proxy-arp
```

Finally, there are a number of ICMP services that you might want to disable. However, because a number of ICMP services are quite useful, and sometimes even required for proper functionality, our recommendation is to start by disabling ICMP redirects and move on from there, if necessary. The easiest way to disable ICMP redirects is with the following:

```
Router1(config)#int ethernet 0/0
Router1(config-if)#no ip redirects
```

However, if you want to gain more granular control over ICMP, you might want to look into using ACLs.

Summary

Securing infrastructure equipment is critical for two reasons:

1. If an attacker gains access to your infrastructure equipment, she can do an incredible amount of damage.

2. If security is executed properly, not only will you protect your own network, you will help protect the Internet as a whole.

The steps we've outlined are fairly simple to implement, but can still be very effective. You should try to test your configuration as much as possible. The NCAT (Network Config Audit Tool) and RAT (Router Audit Tool) can be found at `http://ncat.sourceforge.net/`. Finally, as in dealing with any vendor, make sure that someone in your organization is monitoring the security advisories of all the network equipment vendors you have in your shop. Timeliness counts with routers and switches, too.

Further Reading and Reference

The following are *highly* recommended for further reading on the subjects of Cisco security features, and infrastructure security in general.

Cisco IOS Password Encryption Facts

http://www.cisco.com/warp/public/701/64.html

Cisco Product Security Incident Response

http://www.cisco.com/warp/public/707/sec_incident_response.shtml

Essential IOS Features Every ISP Should Consider

http://www.cisco.com/warp/public/707/EssentialIOSfeatures_pdf.zip

Extreme Networks Countering Denial of Service

http://www.extremenetworks.com/technology/whitepapers/security.asp

Improving Security on Cisco Routers

http://www.cisco.com/warp/public/707/21.html

Juniper Networks Router Security

http://www.juniper.net/techcenter/app_note/350013.html

Mastering Cisco Routers, Chris Brenton. (Sybex)

Nortel Security Document Library

http://www.nortelnetworks.com/solutions/security/doclib.html

Phrack 55: Building Bastion Routers Using Cisco IOS.

http://www.phrack.com/

24

Macintosh

Security issues plague every operating system, and the Macintosh operating system is not excluded. Hundreds of hacking programs targeting the Macintosh (and for the Macintosh, targeting other systems) exist, so it isn't hard to see that it has its flaws. Yet many people still believe that security on the Macintosh platform isn't an issue! Until Mac OS X, Macintosh operating systems offered greater security than many alternative systems, but many of the issues and hacks seen now are the result of modifications to the system and third-party software exploits.

When security issues and hacks began increasing for the Macintosh, many of the Mac OS news sites never reported on any issue that arose for fear of losing readers by reporting such negative issues. Times have changed for these news sites; when one site posts on an issue, the others must follow suit, as security has become such a hot topic and is recognized as a high priority subject. If not for all the competing news sites and concerned readers, some security issues still wouldn't be reported.

Security issues and hacking topics for the Macintosh formerly could only be found at select sites, most of which specialized on the topic or were underground-related. Sites like mSec (http://www.msec.net), SecureMac.com, and Freaks Macintosh Archives (http://freaky.staticusers.net/, a Mac hacker site) have reported on hacking vulnerabilities since they opened. Macinstein.com was one of the first sites to cover Macintosh security issues openly, and now MacSurfer.com and MacFixIt.com have no fears of discussing or reporting the issues, either.

Apple has also adapted to security publicly by offering a mailing list specific to Macintosh security and has set up a Web site with information at (http://www.apple.com/support/security/). This mailing list will only discuss topics related to the operating system—third-party products won't be discussed on this list.

The security updates page (http://www.apple.com/support/security/security_updates. html) within Apple's security site currently only has information on Mac OS X and Mac OS X servers. The details include the affected piece of software the system uses, and any known references.

In the rest of this chapter, I will cover Macintosh security topics ranging from internal desktop security to Internet security, covering both the classic Mac OS (prior to X) and Mac OS X. First off, I would like to explain the differences between Mac OS X and Apple's previous version of its operating system.

Mac OS X—Apple's New Operating System

Unlike any of Apple's other operating systems, Mac OS X is a new breed, created by mixing the Macintosh interface with the advanced technology of Unix underlying the system. Mac OS X is Unix-based, running on what is known as Darwin (http://www.apple.com/darwin/), the core of Apple's system. The most notable difference is the integration of Mach 3.0's OS services based on BSD. Apple has brought back many users with the release of Mac OS X by catching the attention of technical users, allowing them to interact with the Unix interface through the Terminal application (see Figure 24.1), providing the best of both worlds.

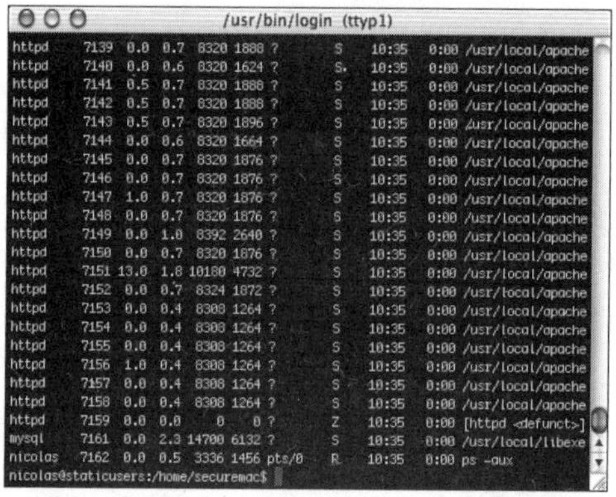

FIGURE 24.1   The Mac OS X Terminal console—the gateway into the core of the Unix portion of the system.

The Terminal application allows users access to the Unix built into Mac OS X. With the developers tools installed, many Unix programs can also be compiled and run from the command prompt. This includes many of the security tools available for

Unix, as well as hacker's exploits in C or Perl found on sites such as PacketStorm Security (`http://www.packetstormsecurity.org`).

In basing OS X on Unix, Apple has introduced the security concerns that exist for the Unix operating system, as well as those of the Macintosh. Mac OS systems prior to OS X were considered more secure because remote administration utilities were not built-in. Additional software was necessary to remotely control or administer the computer; without it, remote attackers had no way into the computer if no services were enabled or server software was installed. Unix offers an advanced multi-user environment—there are dozens of services and programs to be activated or launched to allow remote users access to the system (such as FTP, SSH, Telnet, Web, and back-doors accessible via Telnet).

Mac OS X offers many services that are disabled by default, so unknowing users would not be open to remote connections without activating the services first. Early versions of Mac OS X came with a Telnet service that allowed a user to connect with a Telnet application and navigate and control the system remotely. However, due to insecurities in the protocol, Telnet service was promptly replaced with SSH, a secure non-plain-text encrypted type of Telnet functionality.

Enabling the SSH service (daemon) on a Mac OS X system will allow a user to SSH to the computer, and with the correct authentication password, the remote user can access the computer via the command line (for more on SSH, see Chapter 6, "A Brief TCP/IP Primer"). If you do not intend to access your computer remotely, turn this service off, especially if you have not set up a firewall restricting access to the port SSH runs on (port 22). SSH has had its own security issues as well; running the software without following up on security issues can be hazardous to your system. In short, don't run it for fun—use it when needed and when the computer is protected properly.

Establishing the Macintosh as a Server

Today, it is common to have Macintosh computers in every environment, and it is becoming more common to see them used as servers. There are many server software packages available, including IRC, FTP, Hotline, Mail, and Web for the Macintosh.

Establishing a Macintosh Internet information server was once a pretty daunting task—not any more. Today, there are many server suites available that will have you up and running in minutes. I list a few in Table 24.1.

TABLE 24.1   Popular Macintosh Server Suites and Their Locations

Server	Location
AppleShare IP	`http://www.apple.com/appleshareip/`
CL-HTTP	`http://www.ai.mit.edu/projects/iiip/doc/cl-http/`

TABLE 24.1   Continued

Server	Location
FirstClass	http://www.softarc.com/
HomeDoor	http://www.opendoor.com/homedoor/
MacHTTP	http://www.machttp.org/
4D WebSTAR	http://www.webstar.com/
WebTen 3.0.4	http://www.tenon.com/products/webten/

Of the server suites listed, I will only go into detail with two of them, WebSTAR and Hotline.

Of the servers mentioned in Table 24.1, the one that has received the most publicity is WebSTAR, mostly for its security features. The first mainstream media attention the software package received occurred when a cash reward was offered for anyone who could penetrate the Web server. Most recently, the U.S. Army decided to switch its Web server platform to the Mac OS and run WebSTAR. Before discussing other vulnerabilities for the Macintosh platform, I want to briefly cover that story.

WebSTAR Server Suite Recruited by U.S. Army

On September 14, 1999, StarNine (now known as 4D Inc.) announced that the U.S. Army's main Web site, http://www.army.mil, was being served by WebSTAR Server Suite software on the Mac OS. A Windows NT–based server had previously been serving the Army site when it was hacked in late June 1999 by a 19-year-old Wisconsin man. Perhaps old news, but the Web server is still in place running on a Macintosh using WebSTAR.

NOTE

For more information, refer to http://www.webstar.com/press/press_releases/ pr091499.html.

This sudden switchover caught the attention of everyone. WebSTAR's press release was plastered all over the news, and Apple ran commercials showing Army tanks surrounding the G3 Macintosh.

WebSTAR for Mac OS X allows for the easy configuration of all the services offered in one package. Even though Mac OS X has the Apache Web server built in, the ease of WebSTAR and the added features/security make it a complete server suite. Last time I checked, the Army wasn't running WebSTAR on Mac OS X—more than likely it hasn't passed the tests, as the OS is rather new, or the Army prefers Macs without remote administration methods, so it would be ideal to stick to running WebSTAR on an OS prior to Mac OS X.

Hotline for Sharing Ideas and Files

Hotsprings, Inc., took over the development of Hotline from Hotline Communications, the recent event has put many questions into the picture as to where this program will go. Both the client and server software are available for download on such sites as VersionTracker.com and Download.com from mirrored locations. Grab your client, put in an alternative Hotline server, and connect.

Hotline is not a Web server or email server; you do not use a Web browser to access it. Hotline is its own server and its own client. Anyone can host a server, run the application, and become an administrator capable of sharing files with the world. You can find anything you want to download somewhere on Hotline. Hotline was first made for the Macintosh, and demand was sufficient for a Windows-compatible version, which is now also available. Let's go through some of the details.

Hotsprings, Inc., made two products: a server that enables users to connect, and a client application that enables users to chat, send messages to each other, download files, stream media, and post news.

The software is free, and with the tracker system, anyone can find a server to fit their needs. The tracker is a list of online servers. You can search the servers' descriptions or names to find a server that will fit your needs.

To list all the uncensored servers, open the server window and click the Add Tracker button. Enter **tracked.group.org** for the name and address. Refresh the list, and you now have access to anything you desire.

> **TIP**
>
> For a Macintosh hacking server where you can find all the Hackintosh files, get the Hotline client and connect to the Freaks Macintosh Archives server. The address is `fma.nedline.com:1234`, or search for FMA on the tracker or from the Web at `http://tracker.staticusers.net/`. From there you can talk to Macintosh hackers, programmers, and power users whose ideas exceed most Mac users. Plus you can talk to some of the original Macintosh hackers, like The Weasel, who started the e-zine *HackAddict*.

For Hotline resources such as news sites, articles, search engines, servers, and trackers, visit `http://www.hotspringsinc.com/`.

Mac OS X Server Ability

There are two different versions of Mac OS X: the standard package for the client side, and Mac OS X Server, which is intended for use as a server. The difference between the two is that the Server version has added tools and services pre-bundled with it to easily manage a server.

The standard edition of Mac OS X does have the capability to be run as a server. For starters, it comes with an FTP server, Web server and SSH server, and with the right knowledge, additional server functionality can be added. However, the nice, easy-to-use interfaces to configure, set up, and install the server software will be absent, unless third-party developers create them.

The Web server bundled with Mac OS X is the most used and popular Web server in the world—Apache (`http://www.apache.org`). Adapted to Mac OS X, users can now publish and serve their sites from their own computer with all the functionality of Apache for the Unix platforms. Mixed with PHP and MySQL, the Apache Web server is far from lacking functionality. Mac OS X Server Edition has GUI-based configuration utilities to help manage the Apache Web server. The standard version of Mac OS X doesn't come with any configuration utilities, so any changes to the server need to be done by command line. Reading the help manual and additional documentation on the Apache Web site will be useful.

Each user has a directory called Sites in his Home Directory where the files are accessible from a Web browser when the Web Service is active. Accessing `http://127.0.0.1/~username/` from your Web browser on the local machine will show the files in the users directory. Be aware that files stored within the Sites directory are accessible by anyone if the Web server is active. If you use this directory for only yourself without intending to allow access to anyone else on the Internet, be sure to configure the firewall settings to deny access to whichever post the Web server is running on (generally port 80).

There are Unix variants of Hotline, one of which is called HXD. Mac OS X is capable of running HXD in the background (a daemon) by having the system take care of it; setting up, starting, and stopping the service is done through the Terminal application. HXD is just one example of what is available to run on Mac OS X as server software; Apache is another, and there are still others, such as mail servers and various file sharing servers.

Vulnerabilities on the Macintosh Platform

I will now go over some different software vulnerability issues for the Macintosh. I don't believe that you can understand security fully without understanding what the hacker uses and knows. Some vulnerabilities only affect older versions of the software titles or systems, but you'd be surprised how many people are still using older versions, whether it's because they were unaware of the update, the security alert wasn't made public enough (such as just saying it's an update, instead of advising of a security hole), or the new version had too steep a price tag.

AtEase Access Bug

Application: AtEase 5.0

Impact: This opens documents with other programs.

Class: Not critical

Fix: Disable the programs that allow this access.

Credit: charlie chuckles

I spoke with charlie chuckles a while ago (in October 2000). He had noticed that no papers had been written on the unusual way of accessing files with AtEase, so he wrote the following:

> This is a [problem] for AtEase 5.X...When I say the phrase "AtEase," it usually implies some sort of inferiority to everything else. But AtEase isn't really the problem here. It's the applications and some of their roundabout ways of opening files and the system administrator's not noticing. So I guess it sort of IS an AtEase problem by not covering every single [strange] way that programs ask for files. That was pretty deep.

> The first thing I want to cover in here are the older tricks that have been on the market for a while. Everyone knows about the Web browser trick (type `"file:///drive name/"` and read all the files on the drive). That is commonly accessible because all users are given access to some browser in their user folder. There was another trick that I'd seen using Apple Works, but I could never get it to work. I think it's because the person who wrote it was a failure with a wooden leg and real feet.

> Now forward! to read/write! Let's pretend you are in a biosphere. Now let's pretend your user has access to MS Word. In version 8 (and the equivalent Excel release and probably the rest of Office) there is a find file function. Here's how to use it:

> Launch MS something. File>open. Click the Find button. On the Find Window select the drive you want to search and what you want to search for. If you want all the files list leave the search field empty. It will take a while if there are a lot of files on the drive to be searched (4 minutes for 30,000 on beige g3s). The files will list and you can select what to open with read/write privileges.

> I'm pretty sure this works because the method of opening the files was not covered in AtEase. There are other examples of this. In a graphic converter, you can go to file>browse folder and look at the drives with read/write access. Same with Netscape (read only). These are all very [strange] methods of opening and browsing the files. I'm sure there are many other applications that are like them. Keep your peepers on the screen, squire.

AtEase PowerBook 3400 Bug

Application: AtEase 4.0

Impact: Disk drives can be corrupted.

Class: Critical

Fix: Upgrade; the fix is out.

Credit: Unknown

If you have a PowerBook 3400 and are thinking about installing At Ease 4.0, do not enable the floppy disk boot security feature. If you do, your disk volume will become permanently corrupted, and you will be unable to access the disk by any conventional means (including boot floppy, SCSI drives, CD-ROMs, or other methods).

Denial of Service by Port Overflow

Mac OS Versions: 7.1, 7.8

Impact: Attackers can take down the machine by port scanning.

Class: Moderate

Fix: Get OpenTransport 1.2.

Credit: VallaH

Mac OS machines running TCP/IP and System 7.1 or System 7.8 are vulnerable to a denial-of-service (DoS) attack. When these machines are the target of heavy port scanning, they die (7.1 crashes, and 7.8 runs the CPU to 100% utilization). This was reportedly repaired in OpenTransport 1.2.

Besides the systems themselves being affected from the attack, it is common for third-party server software to also have flaws causing denial of service. In case of constant crashing, look over the log files carefully for something suspicious, then put a stop to the insanity! Report your findings to the developers of the application. Be sure to update your software if new versions are available from the vendor, as the issue may have been tackled previously.

DiskGuard Security

Application: DiskGuard

Impact: DiskGuard can deny even authorized users access to their disk drives.

Class: Serious

Fix: Available

Credit: Unknown

Even the security applications themselves can create security problems. DiskGuard, created by ASD Software and now owned by Intego, is a security application that restricts access to folders, files, and disk drives. In a prior version of the software (1.5.2), users who installed the software found that their drives were inaccessible. The company at the time (ASD Software) released a patch upgrading the software to 1.5.3, resolving the issue. Even with the current version, security software that restricts drive access can be very harmful when misconfigured or tampered with by a vicious attacker.

The current owner Intego (`http://www.intego.com`) has taken further steps to ensure that the software is understandable and well-documented. New versions of DiskGuard don't have the problem found in version 1.5.2, but there is still the possibility of administrator error causing lockouts to the computer unintentionally.

Be cautious of how the computer is set up—if it is in a high-risk environment, invoke more restrictions and policies. Make sure the administrator is the only one who knows the password used to administrate DiskGuard; in the wrong hands, it could be used to cause lockouts, making it a very time-consuming task for the administrator to regain access to the system.

For example, a user with enough permissions could load and run a program created by mSec called Disengage (`http://freaky.staticusers.net/security/fileguard/Disengage.sit`), allowing the person running it to see the results after the program decrypts the user information stored in DiskGuard. Once the user had the administrator password, she could log in as the administrator and have full access to the computer or change the permissions.

Users can contact the software developer to voice their concerns. In the end, it's a cat and mouse game—the developer will change the encryption method the user information is stored in, and crackers will figure out how it was done and create a new program to decrypt it. The best thing to do is watch user activity on the computer and restrict access as much as possible when in a high-risk environment.

FWB Hard Disk Toolkit 2.5 Vulnerability

Application: FWB Hard Disk Toolkit 2.5

Impact: Removes drivers for protection to access hard drive.

Class: Serious

Fix: Upgrade

Credit: Space Rogue

In an advisory, Space Rogue explains the problem, the exploit, and the fix: in short, replace the driver for the drive. The hard disks blocking functionality won't be fully operational, and the data can be accessed.

TIP

The full advisory written by Space Rogue back in 1998 is at http://www.atstake.com/research/advisories/1998/fwb.txt.

MacDNS Bug

Application: MacDNS

Impact: MacDNS is vulnerable to DoS attacks.

Class: Moderate

Credit: Matt Leo

MacDNS provides Domain Name Service lookup for networks and runs on Macintosh Internet servers. Unfortunately, MacDNS will die when bombarded with requests at high speed. (The problem was initially discovered when a firewall tried to resolve forwards on each and every URL requested. This flooded the MacDNS server with thousands of requests.) This has now been confirmed as a bona fide DoS attack that can be reproduced by remote attackers. Leo suggests packet filtering. Otherwise, contact Apple for further information.

NOTE

Apple has released more documentation on the configuration of MacDNS to allow more connections. Full documentation can be found at Apple's Technical Information site, linked from Apple.com's support section.

Network Assistant

Application: Network Assistant

Impact: Remote users can access your drives and network.

Class: Serious

Fix: Change the default password.

The default password for Network Assistant is "ZYZZY". Do us all a favor; change the password so it is not the default. For any type of program which has default passwords, documented or not, change the password right away to avoid unauthorized entry.

Password Security on Mac OS 8.0 Upgrades

System: Mac OS 8.0 with PowerBooks 2400 and 3400

Impact: Password protection will not work.

Class: Serious

Fix: Find patch at `http://til.info.apple.com/techinfo.nsf/artnum/n26056`.

Credit: Apple

If you install 8.0 over earlier versions, the Password Control Panel is disabled, and password protection will not work. To remedy this, either install the patch or install 8.0 clean and keep an earlier version with which to boot. Whenever you want to adjust the password settings, boot with the earlier version.

Sequence of Death and WebSTAR

Application: WebSTAR and NetCloak combined (not WebSTAR alone)

Impact: WebSTAR servers with NetCloak can crash after receiving the Sequence of Death.

Class: Serious

Fix: Upgrade

Credit: Jeff Gold

This is a garden-variety DoS vulnerability in early WebSTAR releases, and has nothing to do with Apple. (In fact, this hole can only be reproduced on a server that is also running NetCloak.) Gold found that if you append certain strings to an URL, the WebSTAR server will crash. *Macworld* ran a story on this hole, and the folks at that magazine did some testing themselves:

> ...for Mac Webmaster Jeff Gold, frustration turned to alarm when he realized that a mere typo caused his entire Mac-served site to crash. Gold's crash occurred while he was using StarNine's WebStar Web server software and the plug-in version of Maxum Development's NetCloak 2.1, a popular WebStar add-on. Adding certain characters to the end of an URL crashes NetCloak, bringing down the server. To protect the thousands of sites using NetCloak, neither Gold nor *Macworld* will publicly reveal the character sequence, but it's one that wouldn't be too difficult to enter. After further investigation, *Macworld* discovered that the problem surfaces only when a server runs the plug-in version of NetCloak. When we removed the plug-in and used the NetCloak CGI instead, the Sequence of Death yielded only a benign error message.

TIP

The previous paragraph is excerpted from an article by Jim Heid, titled "How to Crash a Web Server." (*MacWorld* 1997)

NetCloak is manufactured by Maxum Development. You can contact Maxum for upgrade information at `http://www.maxum.com`.

Mac OS X Software Vulnerabilities

Mac OS X has had more security issues discovered and fixed within the last three months than Mac OS 9 has had in the past two years. This is because Mac OS X runs many programs that are for Unix in general, and as much of it is open source, the developers, hackers, and coders can pick at the code inside and out to find insecurities.

If you were to look at a Unix security mailing list there would be 100 times more posts to it than there would be for a Mac OS 9 list. With past Mac OS releases, nothing has really been open source, so the flaws discovered were generally super-probed in order to find them.

Take a look at Mac OS X's software vulnerability page (`http://www.info.apple.com/usen/security/security_updates.html`) and subscribe to their mailing list (`http://www.info.apple.com/usen/security/`). Within each Security Update you install when you subscribe, you will see what is actually being updated. These titles are being updated for one reason or another because of the lack of security. Many of these programs being updated are Unix distributions, so when a version of the software is found to be vulnerable, Apple will have to evaluate the program and see if a security risk exists on their platform. If the risk exists, Apple will make the update available promptly.

Upon finding a vulnerable item in Mac OS X, you should contact Apple's security team so they can get right on it, and of course email `macsec@securemac.com` with the details so they can be verified.

For instance, I just received an email from a user named Olivier notifying me of a security risk that was just discovered for OpenSSL. This particular vulnerability would require Apple to update many other packages that utilize OpenSSL functionality. The issue was posted to bugtraq by the people who found it—Olivier is just one of the Mac OS X readers who follow up on security, therefore knowing his system is insecure before Apple even announces it. He told me he applied all the necessary changes detailed in the advisory, and his system is no longer vulnerable.

Localhost Security Concern

Mac OS X's first major security glitch affects all systems that have not upgraded to Mac OS X 10.1. The issue revolves around Setuid root applications allowing root access. This was demonstrated in four easy steps:

1. Open up the Terminal.app (located in Applications/Utilities/).

2. Quit Terminal.app (File Menu, Quit Terminal)

3. Open up NetInfo Manager (Applications/Utilities) and leave it in the foreground.

4. Launch the Terminal.app from the Recent Items list from the Apple Menu.

If the computer has not been patched, the command prompt will be #, representing root, or the owner of the computer, who can do anything. Apple took this issue very seriously and updated the software fixing the hole. New builds of Mac OS X are not affected in the manner described.

Added additional security measures, such as applying the Open Firmware protection described later in this chapter, will increase local user security—they will not be able to boot from any other drive or media without supplying proper passwords.

About File Sharing and Security

Yet another security concern for Macintosh users is permitting file sharing. Notice the word *concern* is used, because the problem depends on what disks and resources are actually shared, if any. The Macintosh file sharing system is no less extensive (nor much more secure) than that employed by Microsoft Windows versions.

Sharing files is the act of allowing others to have access to the files. Sharing can be complex, and the choices you make in configuring the file sharing are dependent on the trust relationship in your organization. For example, I will share with you a story of one of my clients—I can assure you this happens a lot, and with networks being used in every environment, security rules must be implemented.

It doesn't matter how large or small the network may be, when people are grouped together, each group has its own tasks. My client's office wasn't the largest setup; however, he had enough computers, and a few extra that weren't used on a daily basis. Everyone who was a part of the company was trusted—the owner fully believed that each employee loved his company and the business, as well as cherished their jobs.

I was called on to do some security assessment because many of the company's confidential files and client contact sheets had been distributed to a competing company. The network was composed of both Window and Mac machines sharing resources amongst each other. The computers in the billing department only showed the billing information, and the computers in the lab only showed the users' shared resources.

Instead of setting up file sharing with permissions for each group of computers, the prior administrator just made it so that a computer in a particular group (for instance, billing) only showed a directory on the desktop, which the user could double-click to access. No restriction whatsoever was implied. The users could hold down the option key and click on the title bar to navigate a directory and see all the other users' files, with the permissions to copy, delete, and so on.

I set up each user with their own login and password, and they were still able to share files with other users in the department, but now the other departments were restricted from navigating another's directory.

Log files on the server showed that the files were downloaded from someone on an IP address that was assigned to a unused computer in the billing department. The computer had the exact same setup, but there wasn't any sort of login authorization upon boot up. The other computers were protected with a screensaver password.

To prevent situations like this from occurring, you should carefully plot out sharing privileges at the time of installation. (And, naturally, if you don't need file sharing, turn it off. Later in this chapter, I examine programs that can block unauthorized access to folders and control panels, so you can ensure that sharing stays off.) However, perhaps the most important step you can take to keep a Macintosh network secure is this: Educate your users.

Macintosh users are not security fanatics, but that's no crime. Still, a lot of Unix and Windows NT users ridicule Macintosh users, claiming that they know little about their architecture or operating system. With Apple's release of Mac OS X in 2001, which is based on the BSD platform, security has changed. Apple is taking security issues very seriously, and reacting to security flaws in a timely manner.

However, most Macintosh users are not very security conscious, and that's a fact. So, anything you can do to change that is wonderful. At the very least, each user should establish a strong password for himself as the owner of the machine. (Macintosh passwords are subject to attack just the same as any other password on other platforms.) Finally, (and perhaps most importantly), guest access privileges should be set to inactive.

Mac OS 9 File Security

Mac OS 9 offers many more security features, such as voice authentication. One of the more notable features is the capability to encrypt and decrypt files using the built-in File Security program. It doesn't offer the highest level of encryption, but it is enough to keep people from opening them and still be quick enough to encrypt and decrypt on the fly.

To encrypt your files on the fly, open the Apple File Security program located in the security folder within the Application folder on the hard disk.

Mac OS X File Security

Mac OS X offers much more user security than their previous operating systems. The administrator can add, modify, and delete multiple users through the System Preferences Users control pane. Each user's account has its own home directory. This is a place where the user's files are stored and protected by default from other users making changes to them without the proper privileges. The permissions used for the files are the same setup as permissions used in Unix.

Using the Terminal application to access the command line, users can learn more about file permissions via the command man chmod. Users can also change the permissions through the graphical user interface (GUI) of Mac OS X by choosing Information on the particular file or folder and selecting Permissions.

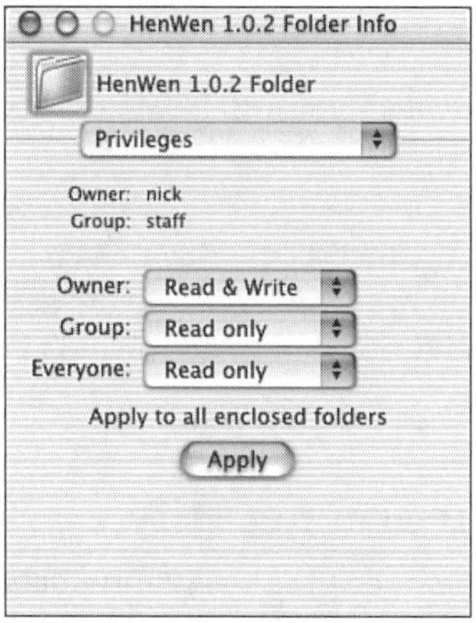

FIGURE 24.2   Permissions screen for a file or folder.

Owner is the person who owns the file/folder. If you're looking at one of your own, you should be the owner, and Group defines which group you are associated with. Because I logged in with the administrator account, I am part of the group Staff.

If you have a sufficient permission level, you can change the permissions of the files, allowing the owner Read & Write or Read Only access. The group setting allows you to select what the other accounts in your group can do to the file: Read & Write, Read Only, or None.

The Everyone permission is what everyone can do. These are the users who are not a part of the group, or who aren't the owner of the file. In Mac OS X, your home directory is set to Read Only for Everyone, meaning that everyone can peek through your files. If you want to restrict all the other users, simply get info on your user folder (by clicking the home button and then going up a directory) and select the Privileges option from the pull-down menu and toggle the settings. Once the changes are selected, they are made. There isn't a choice to save permissions or cancel, so pay attention to what is being done, in case you accidentally or incorrectly select incorrect permissions.

The root user has permission to change any file permission, or to open or delete any file—essentially, whatever she wants. This user should be protected—in Mac OS X, Apple decided it was wise to disable the root user. Those who really want to enable it can do so by following these instructions (this same method can be used to disable the root account, also):

1. Within the Applications folder on the hard drive is another folder called Utilities with a program called NetInfo Manager—double-click it.

2. Follow the Domain Menu, Security, then click Authenticate. A dialog will show up asking for the administrators password.

3. After you're authenticated, you will be able to click the Menu Domain, Security, Enable Root User.

The Administrator account, which is the first one created when installing Mac OS X, should not be used for everyday normal use. Avoid selecting new users as Administrators when there is no need to do so, and avoid doing everyday tasks as root.

Server Management and Security

For many, establishing a Web server is a very formidable task, but there is no comparison to actually maintaining one. This is especially true if that Web server is only a small portion of your network, or if numerous people need to be called upon to handle security privileges with different departments or clients.

Handling the management of a server is a very important task; even more important is ensuring that the server remains secure from intruders. Two approaches can be taken to assist with such tasks: You can contract out for custom programming, or you can rely on third-party applications for assistance.

Custom programming is expensive and time-consuming. If you want to throw up a few Web servers and manage them remotely, I recommend using prefabricated tools for the task. If your environment is predominantly Macintosh, the applications that follow are indispensable.

For Unix systems, there have been dozens of applications for security-related research. As Mac OS X is Unix based, we are already seeing ports of many of the popular security analysis tools for Unix to Mac OS X. Currently, many of the programs lack a GUI and must be set up and installed via the command line. If you're not quite grasping the Unix aspect, search Google.com for Unix tutorials or howto's—just reading over and trying the commands will familiarize you with it.

The benefit of many of the Unix applications is that they're open source. This means they're not compiled applications; instead, they include the source code, and have a cost that's priceless to end users—free. If you find a program that runs on Unix and the developers have created builds for various flavors of Unix, there is a chance they are developing a version to work flawlessly with Mac OS X, or would be able to if they had access to a Mac OS X computer to debug, compile, and run it on.

After understanding the benefits, take a look at some of the management utilities built into the system. Bring up Mac OS X's Sharing Preference window to make sure you know what is running and what isn't. Open the System Preferences window, then click the Sharing icon. Within the window you will see the status of the following options:

- File Sharing

- Web Sharing

- Allow FTP Status

Both File Sharing and Web Sharing have buttons to activate and deactivate the service. When the File Sharing status says File Sharing On, the service is active, and can be turned off by clicking the Stop button. At that point, the status will change. Allowing FTP access by checking that check box is generally not a good idea unless you are aware of the access it grants—any user on your system with an account can FTP in. FTP is also an insecure protocol; by this I mean that the authentication that's performed when it asks you for a login and password when FTPing into the server is sent in plain text format. Anyone sniffing the network to monitor traffic between you and the destination host can see all the traffic passing by, including the files being transmitted.

Under the Applications tab of the Sharing Preferences is a check box that should be unchecked by default labeled Allow Remote Login. When this option is checked, your computer is running the SSH daemon (SSHd), waiting for connections to be established. Upon correct authentication, users who have an account on the system can operate the computer via the command line as if they were in the Terminal application. By trusting users to connect remotely, you also run the risk that the SSHd running on your computer might be vulnerable to some sort of exploit.

That is why I suggest you follow SecureMac.com for any sort of issue that might occur concerning your Mac's security. If you aren't one to compile your own builds of software when new versions come out, keep checking back with Apple's Software Update, located in Systems Preferences. Check this periodically for new updates that might close any open holes until updates are available. Often, the only route is to disable the affected application containing the holes. If the application is a service that allows for remote users to create a connection remotely to your computer, it might also be wise to disallow access by denying connections to the port from the firewall.

EtherPeek

WildPackets, Inc.

Email: info@wildpackets.com

URL: http://www.wildpackets.com/

WildPackets, Inc., formerly known as AG Group, has the most outstanding network utility around. EtherPeek is a protocol analyzer for Macintosh that supports a wide range of protocols, including but not limited to the following:

- IP
- AppleTalk
- Netware
- IPX/SPX
- NetBEUI
- NetBIOS
- DECnet
- SMB
- OSI TARP

EtherPeek is not your run-of-the-mill protocol analyzer, but a well-designed commercial sniffer. It includes automatic IP-to-MAC translation, multicasts, real-time statistics, and real-time monitoring. EtherPeek also includes integrated support for handling the LAND denial-of-service attack that took down so many servers. If you are in a corporate environment, this would be a wise purchase. Security administrators will love this program for analyzing network activity.

InterMapper 3.6

Dartware, LLC

Email: info@dartware.com

URL: http://www.dartware.com/intermapper/

InterMapper is an excellent tool that can save Macintosh system administrators many hours of work. The application monitors your network for possible changes in topology or failures in service. Network management is achieved using the Simple Network Management Protocol (SNMP).

One especially interesting feature is InterMapper's capability to grab a network snapshot. This is a graphical representation of your network topology. (Network topology is more or less automatically detected, which saves a lot of time.) InterMapper even enables you to distribute snapshots across several monitors for a wider view.

The network snapshot is extremely detailed, enabling you to quickly identify routers that are down or having problems. You can actually specify how many errors are permissible at the router level—when a particular router exceeds that limit, it is flagged in a different color. Clicking any element (whether machine or router) will bring up information boxes that report the element's IP address, the traffic it's had, how many errors it's had, and so forth. If there has been trouble at a particular node, you will be paged immediately. In all, InterMapper is a very complete network analysis and management suite.

InterMapper provides simultaneous support for both AppleTalk and IP. The software has full Mac OS 9 and Mac OS X support and is ready to run on Apple's 1U rack-mountable XSERVE machines with a plethora of user-contributed plug-ins for added functionality.

MacAnalysis

Lagoon Software, Inc.

Email: support@macanalysis.com

URL: http://www.macanalysis.com/

OS: Mac OS 9, Mac OS X

MacAnalysis is one program that belongs in any administrator's toolbox for security auditing. MacAnalysis includes over 300 vulnerabilities, and retrieves passwords and information in over 200 different manners. It runs from a Mac, but has the information to scan many operating systems for known holes, reporting and analyzing the results, and giving the administrator insight into his network along with tips on fixing the problems.

Besides the security auditing features and the capability to test the results within the program to prevent false alarms, it also has schedulers and instant updates for the newest security holes available for download from their server through the software.

I said it belongs in any Mac administrator's toolbox, but it isn't just a security admin's tool because of the entire built-in network testing and analysis tools:

- Traceroute with graphical map locating
- Firewall (Mac OS X)
- ping
- TCP bounce
- finger
- Port scan
- Reverse IP
- Brute force pop3/SMTP
- DUP broadcast scan
- WHOIS
- OS fingerprinting
- Network info, ICMP logger, news grabber and more...

In only a few seconds, MacAnalysis finds dozens of ways to exploit a system in many protocols, analyzing your network for any open holes, bugs, or tricks you might not be aware of.

MacSniffer—Mac OS X

Brian Hill

Email: brianhill@mac.com

URL: http://personalpages.tds.net/~brian_hill/

MacSniffer is a graphical front-end for Mac OS X's built-in tcpdump. With MacSniffer and tcpdump (see Chapter 15, "Sniffers," for more on tcpdump), you can view Mac OS X's network traffic to look for network flaws or to analyze traffic.

From the command line, you can access the built-in text-only interface by typing **tcpdump**, or **man tcpdump** for instructions. If this screen confuses you, or you just enjoy having the graphic feel to control and change settings, MacSniffer is for you.

MacSniffer's options include filters to easily sort out traffic, and various view modes for diagnosing the packets being captured. You can choose to view just the headers, or the full ASCII dump of the packet data in real-time.

ettercap

Alberto Ornaghi and Marco Valleri

URL: `http://ettercap.sourceforge.net/`

In short, ettercap is a sniffer, interceptor, and logger for switched LANs used for multiple purposes. Developed on Unix and adapted to Mac OS X requirements, ettercap is simply one of the neatest network analysis tools on the block.

For a while, many people using Mac OS X had to modify the source before ettercap would compile, but currently ettercap compiles flawlessly on Mac OS X.

The ettercap developers keep adding new features to it on a regular basis. Here are some interesting functions that ettercap can show you while analyzing the network traffic. Many of the features of the program offer the capability of looking into and deciphering what the packets are for, so in the wrong hands this program could be dangerous (it can quickly pick out passwords from packets crossing the network). Many of these features will show you why you need to implement encryption in your everyday use. Even earlier standards on secure connections have been found insecure, such as SSH. Using SSH2 connections is recommended when possible.

- Password collection—BGP, FTP, *Half Life*, HTTP, ICQ, IMAP 4, IRC, LDAP, MSN, MySQL, Napster, NFS, NNTP, POP, *Quake 3*, RLOGIN, SMB, SNMP, SOCKS 5, SSH, Telnet, VNC, X11, and YMSG.

- Packet filtering—This feature sets up rules that will filter for a specific string, and there is also support for packet dropping. Packet dropping in ettercap allows for a filter to be enabled that will catch a particular string and replace it with something else.

ettercap also features OS fingerprinting, a connection killer, network scan, and plug-in support. You can find out more on ettercap as well as help forums at its Web site.

HenWen with Snort

Nick Zitzmann

Email: `nickzman@mac.com`

URL: `http://homepage.mac.com/nickzman/`

Nick Zitzmann's HenWen is a application developed to easily set up the popular Unix-based Network Intrusion Detection System (NIDS) Snort (http://www.snort.org) on Mac OS X. HenWen makes it possible for Mac users to interact with Snort without using the command line or having to compile the software. The hardcore geeks will always compile and run their software from the original source, but HenWen reaches out for free.

Snort alone is a network intrusion detection system for analyzing traffic in real-time, capable of handling protocol analysis and content matching to detect attacks and probes. Snort has very flexible rule sets; besides functioning as a straight IDS (intrusion detection system), it also can be used as a packet sniffer, and as a packet logging utility, making it very useful for security administrators. For more on Snort, see Chapter 12, "Intrusion Detection Systems."

StreamEdit

Weedo

URL: http://weedo.accesscard.org/streamedit/

StreamEdit is a utility that allows you to modify a stream of TCP or UDP datagrams. The process works by tunneling the data through itself, then allowing you to edit it or apply filters in real time. StreamEdit can be used for many different system administration purposes, but it's a great application for performing security analysis tests on the network.

The documentation with the application goes over the program step by step in setting up a tunnel for whichever type of stream you wish to analyze or manipulate. StreamEdit is currently on version 1.0b2, but any suggestions or comments should be brought to the attention of the developer, as the program is still in the beta stage.

MacRadius

MCF Software

URL: http://www.mcfsoftware.com

RADIUS technology is imperative if you run an ISP or any system that takes dial-in connections. Management of user dial-in services can be difficult, confusing, and time-consuming. That's where RADIUS comes in. Authors of the RADIUS specification describe the problem and solution as follows:

> Since modem pools are by definition a link to the outside world, they require careful attention to security, authorization and accounting. This can be best achieved by managing a single "database" of users, which allows for authentication (verifying user name and password) as

well as configuration information detailing the type of service to deliver to the user (for example, SLIP, PPP, telnet, rlogin). RADIUS servers are responsible for receiving user connection requests, authenticating the user, and then returning all configuration information necessary for the client to deliver service to the user.

TIP

To learn more about RADIUS you should obtain RFC 2138, which is located at `ftp://ftp.isi.edu/in-notes/rfc2138.txt`.

In short, RADIUS offers easy management of a centralized database from which all dial-in users are authenticated. RADIUS implementations also support several different file formats, including native Unix passed files. Lastly, RADIUS implementations offer baseline logging, enabling you to determine who logged in, when, and for how long.

If you've ever dreamed of having RADIUS functionality for Mac OS, MacRadius is for you. It is a very refined application, offering you the capability to build complex group structures. In this way, adding new users (and having those new users automatically inherit the attributes of other users) is a simple task. And, of course, all of this is packaged in an easy-to-use, graphical environment characteristic of Macintosh applications.

Currently, the only concern with running a MacRadius server is the physical security of the computer. Keep it out of the reach of others, because if anyone were to gain physical sit-down access to the computer or remote control of it as if they were sitting in front of it, they could use a program that decrypts the administrator's password. The intruder would then have access to change users' password, or to make other modifications or additions to the server.

Network Security Guard

MR Mac Software

Download: `http://freaky.staticusers.net/network/NetworkSecurityGuard.sit.hqx`

Have you ever dreamt about NESSUS for Mac OS? What about a program (HyperCard Stack) that would automatically scan your Mac OS hosts for security vulnerabilities? If so, you need to get Network Security Guard.

Network Security Guard operates over AppleTalk and checks for the following in versions of the Mac OS prior to Mac OS X:

- Default passwords

- Accounts without passwords

- File sharing

- File permissions

But wait—there's more. Network Security Guard has a brute force password cracking utility, so you can test the strength of network passwords, and your reports can be formatted in several ways and forwarded to you over the network. Lastly, you can schedule timed security assessments. All these features make Network Security Guard a great choice. It can save you many hours of work.

The software is unsupported now, as the developer's site went offline. A more advanced product that is supported and scans for more vulnerabilities is MacAnalysis, which is covered later in this chapter.

Oyabun Tools

Team2600

Email: sixtime@team2600.com

URL: http://www.team2600.com/

Oyabun Tools, released by Team2600, is an application you can use to send remote commands to control your Mac. For example, if you notice your Macintosh server is slowing down and you are not at the office to reboot it, you can use the Oyabun Send to restart the machine. This program does not require any installation—just double-click it! Oyabun Tools consists of two products:

- Oyabun Send lets you send shutdown/restart/sleep commands over the Internet to other Macs that already have Oyabun Tools Pro installed.

- Oyabun Tools Pro lets you send shutdown/restart/sleep commands to other Macs over the Internet. It also lets you set up Macs to receive these commands. This package has everything that comes in the Oyabun Send package.

The Oyabun Send tool was made open source, allowing developers to do whatever they choose with the code as long as it is referenced to Team2600. Currently the software does not run on Mac OS X except under classic mode. Users seeking remote control of a server should look into Mac OS X's built-in SSH daemon.

Silo 1.03

Logik

URL: `http://logik.accesscard.org/`

Download: `http://freaky.staticusers.net/update.shtml`

Silo, created by Logik, a Macintosh security guru, is a remote system analysis tool designed for security and administrative evaluation purposes. It features full documentation, remote concept password and file structure generation, network mapping, OS fingerprinting, and remote system, client, administrative, domain, protocol, and network analysis and monitoring.

Logik is said to be working on a new version of Silo that has Mac OS X support, so keep your eyes peeled and his site bookmarked.

Nmap

Nmap, short for Network Mapper, is an open source utility that allows for network examination, or security auditing, as you learned in Chapter 3, "Hackers and Crackers." Of all the classic network utilities that exist for Mac OS 9 and below, nothing can compare to the speed and reliability of Nmap. Luckily for Mac OS X users, Nmap can be installed and run from the command line!

Matthew Rothenberg has developed a GUI front-end application for Mac OS X designed to interface with Nmap called NmapFE. Written in Objective-C, the application is available at `http://faktory.org/m/software/nmap/`.

Nmap can scan a single host or large network very quickly. The program utilizes raw IP packets to determine the status of hosts on a network. Besides the hosts' status, it will also determine the hosts' operating systems, and what type of firewalls are in place, along with which services are running on the computer by using known characteristics.

The help screens and documentation included with Nmap are priceless in getting you started. Need help with the installation of Nmap? Install FINK (`http://fink. sourceforge.net/`). FINK is a project that ports Unix software and ensures its compatible with Mac OS X. Once FINK is installed, read over its documentation to see how to quickly install Nmap.

TIP

Nmap is available for download for free from `http://www.insecure.org/nmap/`.

Timbuktu Notes

Netopia, Inc.

Email: pfrankl@netopia.com

URL: http://www.netopia.com/

Timbuktu Pro 2000 for Mac OS is a powerful and versatile remote computing application. Although not specifically a security program, Timbuktu Pro is a valuable tool for any Web administrator. Timbuktu Pro currently supports TCP/IP, AppleTalk, IPX, and Open Transport. Through these protocols, you can remotely manage any box (or series of them).

With a simple port scan to an unprotected computer running Timbuktu on port 407, the outsiders have inside knowledge of what is running on your network. Because Timbuktu, along with the other remote control administrative utilities, offers so much control, this is a prime target for attempted intruders.

Also note that the Mac OS X Preview release of Timbuktu included a security risk. Users usually found it by simply clicking the About Timbuktu menu before even being logged in, which granted them access to the computer. Netopia quickly released a fix for the paid version of the preview software, accepting it as a security issue. By now this preview release of the software should NOT be running on your system, as newer versions have been released.

TIP

The Timbuktu Preview release security issue, documentation, and fix can be found at http://www.securemac.com/timubktuosxpreviewhole.php.

Firewall Protection

No matter which operating system you choose to run, if your computer is connected to the Internet or a network accessible by outsiders, you will want to add firewall protection. Here's a perfect illustration of why you need firewall protection: You are running Mac OS X, and have FTP or SSH service enabled so you can connect to the computer from home or work. You're the only one connecting to the computer, and there's no need for others to access those ports. With the firewall protecting those ports, allowing only your remote IP to connect, your computer is safe from any infiltration attempts.

When using your computer as a server for others to connect to, it's really easy to configure the firewall in Mac OS X (or any other OS) to restrict all access to any other port except the ones you wish others to connect to. You should become familiar with how the firewall's filter or rule editor works. Once you have the settings in place, the first thing to do is test that what you put in place actually works. Feeling secure with an improper setup can often be a greater risk than having nothing, because you incorrectly believe that a intruder can't gain entry.

In the Mac OS X Jaguar release and higher, there is a firewall control setting in the System Preferences with which you'll construct your firewall settings. Planning out what you want others to have access to on paper, then implementing it into the program works best. If you're unfamiliar with what ports each software runs on, the port numbers should be included in the documentation for the program. Alternatively, you can simply set the firewall up to deny all access to all ports, then figure out which ports require access and enable them so that either everyone or only specific IP addresses or ranges can access them.

The administrator can type `lsof -i` from the Terminal application in Mac OS X to see what applications are bound to which ports, and which ports are actively listening or connected. The command `netstat -a` will also show connection information. More variables like `-a` can be found by using the `man netstat` command from the console.

The next firewalls listed are some of the best firewall software for Mac OS 9 and earlier. Not every machine can run Apple's new latest and greatest system, but no matter how old or new your system is, you should be protected from outsiders.

IPNetSentry

Sustainable Softworks

Email: brad@sustworks.com

URL: http://www.sustworks.com/

IPNetSentry can be downloaded and used immediately, as it is shareware. The developers of this application strongly felt that Mac users should be able to use software first to see if it meets their needs before they dish out the money. Unlike any other firewall for the Macintosh, IPNetSentry does not barricade your computer behind a wall, making it inaccessible from the world. Instead, it works with you, building the rule sets. Of course, you can make your own filters and rules for it to follow. The program watches the type of connections; for instance, if someone port scans your computer, the program notifies you that the attempt has been blocked, and allows you to take the appropriate action.

The developers took this approach because not enough people could configure their firewall properly. Some people were so protected that they didn't know how to unprotect themselves for a particular port or program—they just took down the firewall completely and forget to put it back online.

IPNetSentry knows when you're doing something and permits it, as well as alerting you when others are connecting. Indeed, you can test your own firewall by having IPNetSentry's servers test it and informing you of the outcome. Everything is configurable, and you can be kept apprised of what's going on with the connections.

NetBarrier

Intego

Email: support@intego.com

URL: http://www.intego.com/

Intego's NetBarrier is a fully functional firewall for the Mac OS. The GUI of the program is very friendly to use and navigate. With all the gauges and valves going up and down as traffic comes and goes, users can get a real feel for what is happening and at what level.

NetBarrier also protects against ping flooding, SYN flooding, port scans, unknown packets, and features localhost hacking with password protection to protect NetBarrier. It also covers pings of death and many of the well-known webworms.

Norton Personal Firewall

A Symantec product, Norton Personal Firewall offers a great way to protect your Macintosh from intruders. This program has predefined applications and the ports they run on. For instance, if you know you are running ICQ, you simply select ICQ from the list and allow it. This works the same for many of the popular games or known services.

For those users familiar with OpenDoor Firewall by OpenDoor Network (http://www.opendoor.com/), Norton Personal Firewall is based off that code.

TIP

Norton Personal Firewall will run on both Mac OS and Mac OS X. More information about this product can be found by visiting http://www.symantec.com/sabu/nis/npf_mac/.

Internal Security

Internal security is one of the most important parts of security. Even if your computer is secure from others on the Internet, if someone sits down at your computer for 10 minutes while you are out, your computer is at risk. Or what if someone were to sit down and see your password on a sticky note, or one of your various other hiding places (under the desk, or perhaps under the keyboard)? All your data could be stolen, or your computer could be compromised. You need to take a look at as many utilities as you can to help protect you, and to see what is most commonly used when intruders want to bug your system.

For Macintosh computers running Mac OS X and below, you will find many indispensable programs throughout this section to assist you in running a tight ship. Mac OS X has added security pre-installed that takes just seconds to get running.

Mac OS X Screensaver Password Protection

I remember many screensavers for Mac OS that just didn't offer any sort of security, or the ones that did would crash, or could be force quitted in one way or another, disabling the security at hand. One thing to remember about screensaver passwords is that they are meant to protect your computer while you are away for a short period of time. If your computer is set to automatically log in when started, someone could just as easily restart your computer and wait for it to come back up, and the screen would no longer be protected.

I will assume you have multiple users in place, and auto-login disabled when you plan on working in a secure environment (if not, do so!). In the Screen Saver System Preferences window, there is a tab called Activation. You can set the time for the screen to lock automatically. Below that, you have these options:

- Do Not Ask for a Password

- Use My User Account Password

Upon selecting Use My User Account Password, you will have to enter the same password you use to log in to the system. Without this checked, the screensaver offers no sort of security whatsoever, and is just pretty pixels flying around your screen.

Mac OS X Login

Like Mac OS 9, Mac OS X supports multiple users. This makes it possible to restrict access to your computer by having it protected upon startup, giving the user the option to log out when she is finished without shutting down.

It's important to note here that there can be only one administrator! Well, there *can* be more than one administrator, but it's best to limit it to only one—and don't get click-happy when creating new users. Granting administrative options by clicking that box when creating a new user will give that user admin privileges to make modifications and changes to the system, including deleting your account, or installing software that could alter the system and allow a backdoor to be put into place. Hope I scared you—be cautious to whom you permit admin privileges. From the command-line view, being an administrator means you're in the Group Admin.

Create a login and password for each user that's going to access the system. Advise the users to keep it confidential and private so others do not use it. If the chosen password is weak, it can be cracked very easily. Examples of weak passwords are those that can be found in a dictionary, are short, are the same as the user's name, or are common knowledge for an insider (friends, family, co-workers). When choosing a password, keep it very private, and do not write it down—just remember it, and don't use the password to log in to the system as any other password. A good password would be kP@#!3KA, instead of the normal password of your last name or license plate number.

I'd like to recommend that you choose a password up to 18 characters in length, but Mac OS X only stores the first 8 characters for the login password—be sure to mix it with numbers and extended characters. However, in later versions of Mac OS X, this may be fixed. To find out whether this is the case in the version you're running, set your password for more than eight characters, then log out. When typing your password to log back in, type the first eight characters, then randomly type some other letters—if it works, it's hasn't been fixed.

BootLogger

BootLogger is one of the simpler security applications. It basically reads the boot sequence and records startups and shutdowns. It is not a resource-consuming utility. I suggest using this utility first. If evidence of tampering or unauthorized access appears, then I would switch to Super Save (detailed later in this chapter).

> **TIP**
>
> BootLogger is available at `http://freaky.staticusers.net/security/BootLogger.sit.hqx`.

DiskLocker

DiskLocker is a utility that write-protects your local hard disk drive. Disks are managed through a password-protected mechanism. (In other words, you can only unlock the instant disk if you have the password. Be careful not to lock a disk and later lose your password.) The program is shareware (written by Olivier Lebra in Nice, France), and has a licensing fee of $10.

> **TIP**
>
> DiskLocker is available for download from `ftp://ftp.amug.org/`.

Empower

Magna

Email: mailto:sales@magna1.com

URL: http://www.magna1.com/

Empower offers powerful access control for the Macintosh platform, including the ability to restrict access to both applications and folders.

Ferret

Ferret is a small application that quickly gathers all important information (logins/ passwords) from a system by descrambling all passwords into plain text. It is meant to be used with a startup disk, or when you only have a few seconds of access to the machine. You can also drag and drop preferences onto it to get the information you want from a particular file (for example, when you are only able to access a preference file, and cannot directly access the machine).

Ferret can gather important information from preference files on any mounted volume, including AppleShare-mounted hard drives. Ferret can discover logins and passwords stored in any of the following applications: FreePPP, MacSLIP, OT/PPP (ARA), Internet Control Panel (Internet Config), Netscape Communicator, Eudora, AIM, ICQ, Gerry's ICQ, Apple File Sharing Registry (Users & Groups), Carracho Bookmarks/Server Data Files, and Hotline Bookmarks/Server Data Files.

Currently, Ferret works with Mac OS 9 and earlier. Word is, the source code was lost, so future development of the program has been halted. As it currently stands, the application is still very useful.

TIP

Ferret can be downloaded from http://freaky.staticusers.net/hacking-misc/Ferretv0. 0.1b4.sit.

Filelock

Filelock is a little more incisive than DiskLocker. This utility will actually write-protect individual files or groups of files or folders. It supports complete drag-and-drop functionality, and will work on both 68KB and PPC architectures. It's a very handy utility, especially if you share your machine with others in your home or office. It was written by Rocco Moliterno of Italy.

TIP

Filelock is available from http://macinsearch.com/infomac2/disk/filelock-132.html.

FullBack

> Highwinds Trading Company, LLC
>
> Email: support@highwinds.com
>
> URL: http://www.highwinds.com/

Highwinds has been creating security/encryption products since 1999. FullBack is a secure, easy-to-use archiving and backup program for Mac OS 9 and earlier. The deluxe version provides 512-bit, randomly generated encryption keys. Product information is available at http://www.highwinds.com/BackupSystem.html.

Invisible Oasis

Invisible Oasis is a keystroke logger. This application records everything typed into a daily log. The installed extension is invisible, as is the folder where the logs are kept. To see whether you have this extension installed, use a program such as Apple ResEdit and go to Get Info Menu, and navigate to the Preference folder located within the System Folder on the Hard Disk (Hard Disk → System Folder → Preferences). Go into your preference folder, Get Info on the hidden folder and Unhide. You can open the logs with any text-editing program.

> **TIP**
>
> Invisible Oasis will work with systems prior to Mac OS 9. Download it at http://freaky. staticusers.net/security/keyloggers/InvisibleOasis_Installer.sit.
>
> ResEdit can be found by searching for it on http://www.versiontracker.com.

TypeRecorder

Valid uses have been found for keystroke recorders, such as recovering documents after a crash, even before it was saved, and for development/testing purposes to ensure activities happened in the same manner. TypeRecorder is a shareware-based keystroke recording application, currently only for systems prior to Mac OS X. If you don't pay the shareware fee, a dialog is displayed upon startup, so the program is not intended to be a sleek, hidden, you-can't-find-me type of spy software.

> **TIP**
>
> Find TypeRecorder at http://rampellsoft.com/products/typerecorder/.

KeysOff and KeysOff Enterprise

Blue Globe Software

Email: cliffmcc@blueglobe.com

URL: http://www.blueglobe.com/~cliffmcc/products.html

KeysOff enables you to lock out certain keys, preventing malicious users from accessing the menu bar, using mouse clicks, the power key, or command-key shortcuts. The program also prevents unauthorized users from loading disks. This is one of the most simple, cost-effective, and useful security programs available. Mac OS systems prior to OS 9 have it made when using KeysOff for desktop security—most definitely a favorite for security, and not a favorite of the hackers when all the security is in place, disabling many bypass features.

LockOut

Maui Software

Email: development@mauisoftware.com

URL: http://www.mauisoftware.com/#LockOut

LockOut, available for both Mac OS 9 and Mac OS X, is an easy-to-use application. It doesn't pretend to offer a vaulted, secure solution—the documentation states its faults, so users are not fooled by false claims. Another positive aspect to the program is the low price, as Mac computers need some sort of security. Lockout can offer it, and the development staff implement user suggestions with each new version.

Before accessing the Macintosh, a valid password must be entered. While you're away from the computer and it has been locked out, users may leave messages. If a password is entered incorrectly, LockOut enables the administrator to set up a voice warning to alert the user trying to gain access. When the maximum amount of idle time has been reached, LockOut will reactivate. When the program detects break-in attempts, it can automatically email a address with information about the attempt.

OnGuard Emergency Passwords

Several security programs use emergency passwords. These are passwords generated by the program in case the admin forgets his password. They usually give the user complete access to a computer.

In theory, you would need all sorts of software registration information for the software vendor to give away the emergency password. In reality, you only need to find the algorithm used to generate the emergency password.

nOGuard is a program that generates emergency passwords for PowerOn Software's OnGuard 3.1 and 3.3. It was created by mSec.

> **TIP**
>
> The most up-to-date version of nOGuard is available for download at `http://freaky.`
> `staticusers.net/security/onguard/nOGuard2.sit`.

Password Key

> CP3 Software
>
> Email: `carl@cp3.com`
>
> URL: `http://www.cp3.com/`

Password Key logs unauthorized access attempts, locks applications, and temporarily suspends all system operations until the correct password is supplied. Password Key is not Mac OS X-ready; it's only for use on systems up to Mac OS 9 currently—check their site for more current information.

Password Security Control Panel Emergency Password

PowerBook users use the Password Security Control Panel to protect their computers. Displaying a dialog box that requests a password every time the hard drive is mounted, Password Security provides a convenient security measure.

As pointed out by a previous advisory, Password Security generates an emergency password every time it displays the password dialog box. This emergency password gives the same access level to the laptop as the owner's password does.

This is, of course, a huge security breach, allowing anyone who can figure out the emergency password to access the computer, and even to change the owner's password. The program PassSecGen (created by a member of the Macintosh security group mSec) generates the emergency passwords for the PowerBook security control panel to gain entry without knowing the real administrator password. This does not to appear to be a risk when using Mac OS X as the operating system.

> **TIP**
>
> The most up-to-date version of the Password Security Generator is available for download at
> `http://freaky.staticusers.net/security/powerbook/PassSecGen1.0.sit`.

Aladdin Secure Delete

Aladdin Systems

Email: sales@aladdinsys.com

URL: http://www.aladdinsys.com

Secure Delete in the past has been a part of the Stuffit Deluxe package for file compression. Secure Delete does exactly what it says—it deletes the files in a secure manner in which they are not recoverable with software such as Norton Utilities. When deleting a file by dragging it to the trash can, the file remains on the hard disk until the data has been overwritten on the areas of the disk where the original data was. Secure Delete overwrites the erased data blocks on the disk numerous times to ensure a safe deletion.

Stuffit Expander has become a part of the Mac compression lifestyle, offering the capability to expand every type of file. Stuffit Expander comes pre-installed with Mac OS X, so Aladdin decided to offer Secure Delete as a stand-alone deal. It can also be obtained with the Stuffit Deluxe package.

SecurityWare Locks

SecurityWare, Inc.

Email: sales@securityware.com

URL: http://www.securityware.com/

SecurityWare offers physical security devices for all makes and models of Macs to prevent theft and tampering. From iMacs to desktops, there is hardware protection to physically protect your computer, including iBooks and PowerBooks.

Having some sort of physical security is always important no matter what environment you're in. Once that computer is out the door, it's gone—the only chance you have after that is Stealth Signal.

Stealth Signal

Stealth Signal, Inc.

Email: sales@stealthsignal.com

URL: http://www.stealthsignal.com/

You can track lost or stolen laptops with Stealth Signal for a secure recovery. Stealth Signal silently sends information to the tracking servers that are watching your laptop. If for any reason you lose it, simply log on to the Web site and report it stolen. With the help of Stealth Signal, you might be able to recover the computer—although chances are what is on it has more value than the computer itself.

Through their research, the developers at Stealth Signal came to the conclusion that when hardware is stolen, it is usually sold quickly, wiping minimal, if any, amounts of data from the hard disk. This may or may not be the case, depending on who has stolen it. If the computer is connected to the Internet or has a phone line connection, Stealth Signal will make contact with the tracking servers. The computer can be tracked by the IP address used to connect to the Internet. Stealth Signal also has additional security features that they didn't want me to talk about, but I can assure you that if your computer is stolen and someone is connecting to the Internet with it, they can help recover the hardware.

Stealth Signal is available for Mac OS, Mac OS X and the Windows platform. Connection statistics and other neat information can be viewed from the reporting Web interface.

Mac OS X Single User Root Mode

Single user mode is a startup method you might choose to boot into when in front of the computer. This mode offers root access to the computer without authentication—it exists for emergency cases to fix problems.

To boot into single user mode, during the startup progress hold down the Command + S key. Once you are in and the computer has started up, you will have a black screen (command line) with the # facing you. Before any changes can be made, you must mount the hard disk.

```
/sbin/fsck -y
```

```
/sbin/mount -wu /
```

In single user mode, it's just you and the machine—no services are started. So, if you need to start services to change information, such as NetInfo, you must load it up.

Full documentation on single user root mode can be found at
`http://www.securemac.com/macosxsingleuser.php`.

Super Save 2.02

For the ultimate paranoiac, Super Save will record every single keystroke forwarded to the console. However, in a thoughtful move, the author chose to include an option with which you can disable this feature whenever passwords are being typed in, thus preventing the possibility of someone else later accessing your logs (through whatever means) and getting that data. Although not expressly designed for security's sake (more for data crashes and recovery), this utility provides the ultimate in logging. Super Save does not work with Mac OS 9 or Mac OS X, and does not record mouse movement—only keyboard activity.

TIP

Super Save is available at `http://wuarchive.wustl.edu/systems/mac/amug/files/system/s/`.

SubRosa Utilities

SubRosaSoft.com Ltd.

Email: `contact@subrosasoft.com`

URL: `http://www.subrosasoft.com/`

SubRosa Utilities is a set of security applications, two of which are for encryption. The software-suite consists of three pieces of software, all of which are compatible with the Windows OS, Mac OS, and Mac OS X:

- SubRosa Encryptor—Featuring 128-bit encryption with rolling keys, this program will encrypt your files and folders utilizing keys instead of insecure passwords. The files are encrypted in a format that's Internet-ready; once it has been uploaded, it can be downloaded without being corrupted on both the PC and Mac.

- SubRosa Decryptor—The Decryptor will decrypt the encrypted archives created with the encryption application. Best of all, the entire Decryptor program is free of charge from SubRosa's Web site, so you can transmit files in a secure manner, and the recipient of the file does not need to purchase any software to decrypt it.

- SubRosa Shredder—If you want a file encrypted in the first place, a potential data thief already knows it has confidential value. After a file has been encrypted, it is suggested that it be securely deleted using the SubRosa Shredder. The settings can be manipulated to specify how many times the file should be overwritten for a secure delete—by default it is set to three; if you feel extra special, raise the number. The higher the number, the more times Shredder manipulates the data, and the harder it is to recover.

Open Firmware Password Protection

Apple Open Firmware (`http://bananajr6000.apple.com/`) is the firmware used in Macintosh hardware—all specifications and details can be found at the included URL. For our purposes, we will only cover the password feature of the firmware.

Similar to the PC's BIOS password, the Open Firmware password protects the system in many levels. Mac hackers know that they have many different ways to bypass internal security while sitting in front of the machine. They can try disabling extensions, booting from a media device or SCSI ID, and they'll be successful in one way or another. Open Firmware puts a stop to bypassing security by disabling the user from bypassing the operating system's instructions without supplying the proper password.

The newer Macintosh hardware models come with Open Firmware capable of setting up password support. Apple has also prepared software for Mac OS X to easily set up the password and enable or disable restrictions. For Mac OS X running Firmware 4.1.7+, use Apple's application Open Firmware Password available for download at `http://www.apple.com/downloads/macosx/apple/openfirmwarepassword.html`.

The password protection feature of Open Firmware goes beyond standard Firmware specifications; a notable feature is the anti-brute force password attack methods. This means a user cannot keep on entering the password over and over until he finds the correct one—the Open Firmware will stop the user from making further attempts.

NOTE

Full instructions for enabling Open Firmware Password protection on Mac OS 9 and Mac OS X through Open Firmware can be found at `http://www.securemac.com/openfirmwarepasswordprotection.php`.

There are two ways to bypass the Open Firmware Password, but the first one doesn't quite bypass it. Instead, it's a program that will grab the password if the computer is started up. If you're locked out already, this program will do you no good, but it's useful if you need to recover the password. The program name is FWSucker, short for Firmware Password Sucker. Keep in mind that if a user on your system is already at the desktop and has the capability to load/run software, she can obtain the Open Firmware Password and make alterations. You can find out more about FWSucker at `http://www.securemac.com/file-library/FWSucker.sit`. Keep this out of the reach of children—you wouldn't want someone to obtain the password and then protect the system and lock you out.

The second method for getting around the Open Firmware password is by resetting it. Without knowing the current password, the only way to gain entry is to reset the password. To do so, you will need to open up the computer and add or remove the necessary RAM so the total amount in the computer is different from its original amount, then ZAP the PRAM three times by holding down Command + Option + P + R during startup. After it has been reset, you can replace the hardware with the original components.

Apple did a good job requiring physical access to the insides of the machine to bypass the security. In a multiuser environment (work, lab, school), the computers would be locked anyhow, and someone wouldn't be able to open the machine up unnoticed.

Password Crackers and Related Utilities

The following utilities are popular password crackers or related utilities for use on Macintosh. Some are made specifically to attack Macintosh-oriented files. Others are designed to crack Unix password files. This is not an exhaustive list, but rather a sample of the more interesting tools freely available on the Internet.

> **NOTE**
>
> FileMaker Pro is a database solution from Claris (`http://www.claris.com`). Although more commonly associated with the Macintosh platform, FileMaker Pro now runs on a variety of systems. It is available for shared database access on Windows NT networks, for example.
>
> Many of the applications that crack FileMaker Pro files are version-specific. There has not been a crack for recent versions of FileMaker Pro in years. If you find an old FMP file on disk and it is protected, the FMP-cracking applications in this section would be useful.
>
> There are also FileMaker Pro Password crackers available for the Windows platform that might cover more than the other software titles mentioned.

FMP Password Viewer Gold 2.0

FMP Password Viewer Gold 2.0 is another utility for cracking FileMaker Pro files. It offers slightly more functionality (and is certainly newer) than FMProPeeker 1.1.

> **TIP**
>
> FMP Password Viewer Gold 2.0 is available at `http://freaky.staticusers.net/cracking/` `FMP3.0ViewerGold2.0.sit.hqx`.

FMProPeeker 1.1

This utility cracks FileMaker Pro files. In any event, FMProPeeker subverts the security of FileMaker Pro files.

> **TIP**
>
> FMProPeeker is available at `http://freaky.staticusers.net/cracking/FMProPeeker.` `sit.hqx`.

Macintosh Hacker's Workshop

Grungie

Email: grungie@code511.com

URL: http://grungie.code511.com/

Macintosh Hacker's Workshop (MHW) is a suite of hacking tools that will run under Mac OS 9 and Mac OS X. The program was developed to beat the performance of the existing graphical user interface password crackers for the Macintosh, and under Mac OS X it did indeed offer quicker speeds and better functionality.

MHW includes a wordlist generator used to test passwords. The cracking can be done using wordlists, or by brute force attacks. Many password crackers exist for Unix, but the advantage of using a Unix-based password cracker is purely in the performance.

John the Ripper

URL: http://www.openwall.com/john/

John the Ripper is a Unix-based password cracking utility, and as mentioned previously, the advantage of using a Unix-based password cracking utility like this is for the performance. Because of all the system resources the program uses to test and audit the password, there is no need to bog it down with graphical user interfaces. This program must be compiled from the command line via the Terminal application.

To start off, go to the Web site listed here and download the Development release (dev) of the program, which supports Mac OS X. Compilation might require you to become acquainted with the user manual or install instructions.

After compilation is complete, run John the Ripper on a Unix password file, or export the password file stored in Mac OS X by using the following command:

```
nidump passwd .
```

The program is well-documented and discussed at the Web site provided. Happy cracking—this has to be one of the quickest password crackers available to run on Mac OS X!

Killer Cracker

Killer Cracker is a Macintosh port of a password cracker formerly run only on DOS- and Unix-based machines (http://www.hackers.com/html/archive.2.html).

MacKrack

MacKrack is a port of Alec Muffet's famous Crack 4.1. It is designed to crack Unix passwords. It rarely comes with dictionary files, but still works quite well, and makes cracking Unix /etc/passwd files a cinch. (It has support for both 68KB and PPC.)

> **TIP**
>
> MacKrack is located at http://freaky.staticusers.net/cracking/MasterKrack1.0b14.sit.

MagicKey 3.2.3a

Made by System Cowboy of the hacker group Digital-Rebels.org, MagicKey is a password-auditing tool for AppleTalk. The application audits an AppleTalk user's file for weak passwords or no passwords with the brute force method.

> **TIP**
>
> MagicKey3.2.3a can be downloaded from http://freaky.staticusers.net/security/auditing/MK3.2.3a.sit.

MasterKeyII

MasterKeyII is yet another FileMaker Pro-cracking utility.

> **TIP**
>
> MasterKeyII is available at the following site http://freaky.staticusers.net/cracking/MasterKeyII1.0b2.sit.hqx.

McAuthority

McAuthority is a password-security application that uses brute force to attack a server to gain access to the password-protected areas. This application was made by nulle, one of the greatest Mac hack programmers.

> **TIP**
>
> McAuthority can be downloaded from http://freaky.staticusers.net/jp/McAuth1.0d6-FAT.sit.

Meltino

Meltino is a sleekly designed Unix password cracker by the Japanese programmer nulle. This is one of the most popular Macintosh Unix password crackers. This application supports MD5 encryption as well as DES encryption. Meltino also supports the UltraFastCrypt (UFC) algorithm.

> **TIP**
>
> Meltino 2.0.1 can be downloaded at `http://freaky.staticusers.net/cracking/Meltino/`
> `Meltino2.01_PPC.sit.bin`.

Password Killer

Password Killer is designed to circumvent the majority of PowerBook security programs. PowerBooks are the only Apple computers susceptible to the security bypass circumvention, because the security software affected is only installed on PowerBooks.

> **TIP**
>
> Password Killer (also referred to as PowerBook Password Killer) can be found online at
> `http://freaky.staticusers.net/cracking/Passwordkiller.sit.hqx`.

Anonymous Email and Mailbombing

Mailbombing is the act of sending a lot of email to a person to flood his mailbox. I do not suggest sending a mailbomb to anyone. Try sending it to yourself to see how it works. If you have ever received a mailbomb, you understand.

Sometimes you have to send anonymous email—things you don't want people seeing and knowing you sent.

Caem

Caem lets you send mail anonymously with attachment support by utilizing proxy servers and certain mail servers. Some of the advanced features included for sending mail are the capability to build custom message headers and to import/export contacts and data.

> **TIP**
>
> Logik, the programmer of Caem, takes his work seriously and updates the program often. You
> can find his program at his Web site: `http://logik.accesscard.org/`.

Bomba

Bomba is another mailbombing application. One of the techniques that the program has to send mail quicker is to connect to several mail servers simultaneously with proxy support for privacy.

Bomba is available for download at `http://www.team2600.con` or at `http://freaky. staticusers.net/attack/mailbombing/bomba.sit`.

NailMail X

Another Team2600 development, NailMail works on both Mac OS and Mac OS X, delivering what the group considers their fastest mailbombing application ever. You can be the judge of that by going to `http://www.team2600.com` and downloading the program free of charge.

Spic & Spam

Created by a Macintosh developer who goes by the alias of Mancow, this is a very slick, easy-to-use mass emailing program that supports HTML email. Spic & Spam has been built for Mac and Mac OS X. You can download it and see screenshots at `http://mancow.forked.net/products/spicnspam/`.

ATT Blitz

A different kind of bulk mailer, ATT Blitz is a application that takes advantage of mobile messenger Web site services for many popular cellular services. The program allows the user to send a certain amount of messages to the target's phone, hiding their IP address by specifying a proxy.

ATT Blitz has been tested to work with AT&T, Verizon, Nextel, Sprint PCS, VoiceStream, and PrimeCo. Many users do not have free messaging services, thus they are paying per message. Bombing someone's phone with this program is not recommended, but if it ever happens to you—you are aware the program exists. You can download it at `http://mancow.forked.net/products/spicnspam/`.

Macintosh Viruses, Worms, and Antivirus Solutions

Viruses exist for the Macintosh. However, unlike the widespread Melissa or I Love you Bug viruses, unless the user's whole network or a majority of its contacts were Macintosh users also, the virus or Trojan wouldn't make it far. The reason Windows-based viruses/Trojans go so far is that there are more Windows users than Mac users around the world. Each time the virus comes to a Macintosh computer, chances are it has no affect on the system, so it's a dead bug—you're not spreading it. Good for you for being a Mac user.

Viruses spread globally on the Macintosh don't work that well, because once they hit a Windows users computer, chances are it wouldn't know how to run the Mac program or script. Of course, in due time, one could be set up to work on both systems with the right mind and programming.

Picture an office work network: hundreds of Macintosh computers in one place, an environment in which a worm or virus could easily spread across the network. All it takes is one person and a network that shares resources.

I've seen it time and time again: developers who create the software distribute files that are infected. They could be doing so intentionally or unintentionally, but the fact remains that when the programs are put on Internet sites like Download.com, AOL Archives, and VersionTracker.com, millions of Mac users flock to the sites to download the software.

The most widespread event I can reference was an incident in which a CD packaged with an issue of *MacAddict* magazine was distributed to its subscribers and newsstands. The CD was accidentally infected with the AutoStart worm. The worm was activated when the PowerPC computer's QuickTime (2.0) control panel was set up to automatically play CDs when inserted.

Users had to download removal tools to get rid of the worm that caused the computer to read the hard disk in intervals of 3, 6, 10, and 30-minute intervals.

Detecting and preventing viruses and other malicious activity from taking place on your computer is the most important part. Even though you might feel that your computer is safe, you don't know what viruses other computers have, or what the disk a client has sent you could be infected with. It's even easier to become infected nowadays from the Internet being so handy. Imagine a hostile employee or enemy that knows you use a Macintosh. He sends you an email with a virus attached—of course, he faked the address, so you don't think twice about opening it. Your Mac could be gone at this point.

The following are a few popular Macintosh antivirus solutions and resources.

MacVirus.Info

No, its not a .com, . net, or .org—it's http://www.MacVirus.info/, a site devoted to Macintosh virus education and antivirus solutions. Get the latest antivirus definitions, news, and facts about viruses from this site.

Read comparisons between different antivirus products, vendor facts, and get your questions answered about Mac viruses.

.Mac

Once known as iTools, but now known as .Mac, this once-free service has moved to a yearly service fee. Along with the Email@Mac.com and Web hosting that iTools offered, .Mac offers antivirus solutions for subscribers. The bundled Apple .Mac service comes with hard disk space on Apple's server to backup onto, as well as the well-known antivirus software title Virex and updated virus definitions.

The Virex application is developed by McAfee, and is available for both Mac OS and Mac OS X. Virex scans emails for infected attachments, archived formats, and easy drag-and-drop checking. Combined with Mac OS X's pre-existing security features, .Mac's backup and Virex make for a great combination.

> **TIP**
>
> .Mac service can be obtained by visiting `http://www.mac.com/`; free trial accounts are available. Virex for the Macintosh may be obtained from `http://www.mcafeeb2b.com/products/virex/`.

Norton Anti-Virus

Symantec Corporation

URL: `http://www.symantec.com/`

Symantec has a long history and good reputation for their products. Norton's Anti-Virus for the Macintosh offers the same level of satisfaction as their other products offer. The features of NAV (Norton Anti-Virus) for the Macintosh compare to the other antivirus vendors in that it scans for viruses, and checks email attachments and archived files for viruses hiding within. A popular yet easily forgettable feature of NAV is that the virus definitions are automatically updated via Symantec's LiveUpdate technology, so having to remember to download new definitions to be protected is in the past.

The Mac OS X version of NAV is lacking a few features, as developers hurry to adapt to the new technology and standards that Mac OS X offers. As reported on VersionTracker.com and other news sites, the Mac OS X version still has a few memory leaks, and the AutoProtect feature isn't yet what the Mac OS version offered. It will be worked out in due time, and as of this writing there have not been any Mac OS X-specific viruses released into the wild.

> **TIP**
>
> Norton Anti-Virus product information is located at `http://www.symantec.com/nav/nav_mac/`. Downloadable demos, and more can also be found at Symantec's Web site.

Intego VirusBarrier

Intego

Email: support@intego.com

URL: http://www.intego.com/virusbarrier/

VirusBarrier is Intego's antivirus solution, available for Mac OS now, and with a planned release for Mac OS X in the third quarter of 2002. The developers have truly created a program that runs itself right out of the box. The features offered grow with every version:

- NetUpdate virus definitions (download new viruses instantly)
- Log file functions
- Drag-and-drop virus scan
- Protects against viruses and macro viruses
- Stuffit archive scanning
- Voice alert and email alert upon locating viruses
- Password-protected settings (intruders cannot simply disable the password, but must authenticate first)

This software title can be purchased online or at any authorized Macintosh dealer, or you can download a demo from http://www.intego.com.

Disinfectant

Disinfectant definitely has served its purpose, and has been used by thousands of Mac users seeking to detect and remove virus-infected files. The program isn't Mac OS X ready; in fact, the program has been discontinued completely but can still be found. The program file is small and very quick at doing its job. If you're running a system prior to Mac OS X, this program is free of charge to use; however, you will want to note that it doesn't protect against worms, and it doesn't protect against Microsoft Word macro viruses.

> **TIP**
>
> Because the program's development has been halted, there is not a centralized homepage to visit. Try the link http://hyperarchive.lcs.mit.edu/HyperArchive/Archive/vir/disin-fectant-371.hqx, and if it doesn't work, simply go to an archive site such as http://www.download.com and perform a search for Disinfectant.

AutoStart Worm Remover

The AutoStart worm affects older Macintosh systems when QuickTime's AutoPlay feature is enabled in the control panel. In version 2.0 of QuickTime, AutoPlay was enabled by default, so users commonly found themselves with computer problems and errors. After the computers were taken to the shop, it was found that many of them had the AutoStart worm. Users can check to see whether their computer is a victim to the worm and download free removal tools at the following sites:

- WormScanner—http://www.jwwalker.com/pages/worm.html

- WormFood—http://www.users.qwest.net/~baerd/wormfood.html

- Worm Gobbler—http://www.lineaux.com/html/body_autostart.html

The Little Dutch Moose

Webmasters who have ever viewed their Web logs have seen evidence when their site has been hit with such worms as CodeRed and Nimda, as their requests fill the logs. Hopefully, any request from those two worms show up under File Not Found and Not a Valid Request. Whether they actually affect your system or not, the worm is using bandwidth and filling up log files rapidly by requesting files that could be nonexistent.

The Little Dutch Moose is a program for blocking and stopping these worms and illicit requests from arriving at your Mac OS X Web server (Apache) before they are even processed. The program watches over the connections and notices when connections are made in worm- or virus-like methods, and puts a halt to the requests.

Mac OS X users who are taking advantage of the built-in Apache Web server now have a way to protect and prevent against these type of connections, which could lead to denial of service or other malicious activities.

> **TIP**
>
> Customers of LDM (Little Dutch Moose) receive free updates. The software is shareware-based, so you can try it out by downloading it from the developer's Web site at http://www.wundermoosen.com/.

Mac OS X Virus Overview

As it stands, Mac OS X does not have any viruses designed for it. Before long (or when someone reads this statement), a new virus might be discovered. Viruses have been sparse for the last few years on the Macintosh; for the most part, we only update our monthly virus definitions to protect against Word macro viruses.

Email, software archives, and Web sites are all great ways to catch a virus, simply by downloading software without being protected. Antivirus software does more than just look for known viruses—it watches the system and its resources, looking for tactics that viruses are known to use. Not being protected is just dumb. Getting an infected file is as easy as downloading a movie from the Internet, so be cautious. Use one of the antivirus solution titles listed above and join their mailing lists to stay advised of current viruses in the wild.

Because of Mac OS X's Unix core, many are concerned that remote users will gain access because of misconfigured or outdated services, and that access will be granted by software unintentionally. The main concern is a Trojan horse that can backdoor the computer, allowing remote access or sending system files without your knowledge. Set up your firewall to deny connections when you are not allowing others to connect to your computer. One of the easiest ways to ensure that you don't get hacked is to put up a barrier ensuring that intruders can't get close enough to try.

Spyware and Detection

Besides viruses, Macintosh users have to be aware of spyware. *Spyware* are programs that run in the background, allowing someone to monitor user activity. This can include Trojan horses, remote administration type utilities, and keystroke loggers.

Keystroke loggers monitor and log everything typed on the keyboard. Hackers use these types of programs to capture user passwords, and others use them to snag confidential information, such as credit card numbers or social security information. These programs are generally undetected, and without the right knowledge of every keystroke logger out there, you can be left in the dark.

Trojan horses for the Macintosh often offer some sort of way back into the system. Once the Trojan has been installed, it remains undetected, just waiting for the remote user to make the connection. Users without a Internet or network connection need not worry about Trojans if in a isolated situation, but those who are in constant movement on the Internet should take extra steps to make sure their computer isn't a playground for hackers.

Not all remote administration tools are considered Trojan horses. Programs such as Timbuktu and Apple Remote Desktop offer remote control over the computer, but in a commercial way. Usually when connections are established to one of these commercial products, the remote user can see that the user has connected to his computer, but there are some set to work in the background, so the present user need not be interrupted when another remote user is connected. Any of these programs, if installed without knowing what it does or knowing who installed it, can be a security risk—your computer could be waiting for people to connect to, administer, or control your Mac remotely.

MacScan

You need to detect, isolate, and remove spyware and any unwanted administrator programs that might be plaguing your system without your knowledge. The job of MacScan is simple: Find any sort of software on your computer that can be construed as spyware, and detect any programs that offer remote administration functions you might be unaware of.

MacScan checks the hard drive for all known keyloggers for the Macintosh. It will also isolate any log files created by the keystroke loggers and move them to a secured location. Those log files could have years of your emails, confidential documents, passwords, and other affairs you don't want recovered.

Ever keep changing your password and feel like someone keeps getting your new passwords every time? If a keystroke logger is installed, all the user has to do is view the log files and search for your old password and look at what follows: chances are, it's the new password. If someone is capturing every keystroke, you're no better off than if they knew your password in the first place. They could also be learning the passwords you commonly use for other systems or resources that require your authentication. Before typing in that secret information, make sure someone isn't snooping on your keystrokes.

Included in the definition of spyware are Trojans and admin utilities. Many Trojans are configured to contact the attacker by email, notifying them of your IP address and other information that lets them know your computer is online and accessible. A firewall can protect intruders from coming in, but you will have to protect your machine to deny access to all ports, because you just can't tell what port the Trojan may be set up for without analyzing it.

MacScan also detects these known Trojans, offering administrator functions remotely to the computer. Furthermore, when it finds any Trojan, it will notify the administrator of the configured settings, such as email address, passwords, and logins. For example, consider a Trojan horse—if it was set up to email nick@securemac.com, you know immediately that the intruder is linked to that email address. You also know what port the Trojan is set to communicate over and the password if any. With a little more research, you can try connecting to your own infected computer, or simply remove the spyware program all together.

Regarding valid system administrator tools such as Apple Remote Desktop and Timbuktu, MacScan does not divulge any passwords, and does not allow the user running the program to remove the admin tools. Instead, it will let the user know the software is running so she can take the appropriate action.

MacScan also has Mac OS X functionality, protecting the system so it is a security resource for everyone interested in keeping their privacy.

TIP

A trial version of MacScan can be downloaded at `http://macscan.securemac.com/` and purchased from the same site. Becoming part of the MacScan user base ensures that you will be included in special deals, price cuts, and many free updates as new features are added.

Resources

The following list of resources contains important links related to Macintosh security. You'll find a variety of resources, including books, articles, and Web sites.

Books and Reports

"Secure Installation of OS X."—This article written by `mpetey@securemac.com` is a good paper to have on hand when installing Mac OS X. Security will become more of an issue as the hackers get to play around with OS X. The article is available at `http://www.securemac.com/osxsecurity.php`.

"Macintosh Security Auditing"—This article explains different tools that can be used to audit your network for security problems. One of the main points of the article is that commercial auditing programs do not exist for the Macintosh, so you can use the efficient, free tools that were made by hackers. The article is at `http://www.securemac.com/secauditing.php`.

"Macintosh Security Internet Basics"—Sans.org published this excellent white paper. Written by Patrick Harris, this document covers the basics of Macintosh security. It can be viewed at `http://www.sans.org/infosecFAQ/mac_sec.htm`.

"Macs & Cable Modems"—Everyone has heard about the security issues of cable modems, and that cable modem networks are easy targets to be scanned. If you use a cable modem at home or at work, read up on this issue at `http://www.securemac.com/secauditing.php`.

"Macintosh OS X Security"—This is a three-part information guide to setting up, structuring and advancing Mac OS X security, written by Chevell. Find it at `http://www.securemac.com/macosxsecurity.php`.

"Connections and Protections—Cable and DSL Connections and Security Measures."—Peter N. Heins (`mpetey@securemac.com`) describes the difference between DSL and cable, and covers security aspects of what the snoopers can see and how. Read this article at `http://www.securemac.com/dslcable.cfm`.

Apple has set up a developer area devoted to implementation of security at `http://developer.apple.com/macos/security.html`.

Apple also has a Mac OS X security information page set up with contact information, updated information and mailing list subscription info at http://www.apple.com/support/security/.

Many firewall documents for the Mac OS can be found at the Firewall Guide Mac OS section at http://www.firewallguide.com/macintosh.htm.

How Macs Work by John Rizzo and K. Daniel Clark. Que. (2000) ISBN: 0-789-72428-6

Voodoo Mac by Kay Yarborough Nelson. Ventana Press. (1994) ISBN: 1-56604-028-0

Sad Macs, Bombs, and Other Disasters by Ted Landau. Addison-Wesley. (1993) ISBN: 0-201-62207-6

The Whole Mac: Solutions for the Creative Professional by Daniel Giordan, et al. Hayden Books. (1996) ISBN: 1-56830-298-3.

Building and Maintaining an Intranet with the Macintosh by Tobin Anthony. Hayden Books. (1996) ISBN: 1-56830-279-7

Sites with Tools and Munitions

Freaks Macintosh Archives—Warez, security, cracking, hacking. http://freaky.staticusers.net/

CIAC U.S. Department of Energy—http://ciac.llnl.gov/ciac/ToolsMacVirus.html

SecureMac.com—Security site. http://www.securemac.com/

Macman's Mac site—http://www.macman.net/

Macintosh Underground Forum—http://freaky.staticusers.net/ugboard/

AOL Specific Tools—Hacking and cracking utilities for use on America Online. http://freaky.staticusers.net/aol/

Cyber-Hacking—Security and hacking site in both German and English for the Macintosh. http://www.cyber-hacking.com/

E-Zines and Web Sites

Macinstein—The ultimate Macintosh resource site on the Net. Search engine, daily Mac news, Sherlock plug-in, press releases, top sites, message boards, polls, contests and more! *Macinstein* now has free Web pages for Mac enthusiasts. http://www.macinstein.com/

MacCentral—Extensive and very well-presented online periodical about Macintosh. http://www.maccentral.com/

MacHome Journal Online—Good, solid Internet magazine on Macintosh issues. A printed version is available on newsstands and via subscription. `http://www.machome.com/`

MacAssistant Tips and Tutorial Newsletter and User Group—A very cool, useful, and, perhaps most importantly, brief newsletter that gives tips and tricks for Mac users. Commercial, but I think it is well worth it. A lot of traditional hacking tips on hardware, software, and special, not-often-seen problems. These are collected from all over the world. Subscriptions are $12 per year. `http://www.macassistant.com/`

MacFixIt.com—Troubleshooting solutions for the Macintosh. If there's a issue with anything Macintosh-related, you'll find it here. This site has very active responsive message boards for good technical interaction. `http://www.macfixit.com/`

MacDirectory—This full-color magazine, with daily e-news featuring press releases, news, product info, and much more, is a must for all true Mac peepz. It frequently covers security issues dealing with firewalls and networking. `http://www.macdirectory.com/`

MacSlash—MacSlash is a well-organized, Macintosh-specific site. This site utilizes the Slashcode, which is the same code used by Slashdot.org. Well worth a daily visit! `http://www.macslash.com/`

MacTech—Well-presented and important industry and development news. You will likely catch the latest dope on new security releases here first. Also, some very cool technical information. `http://www.mactech.com/`

Happle—The Macintosh underground e-zine dedicated to Macintosh hacking, warez, and much more—11 issues of jam-packed Happle! This publication was started by a Macintosh hacker named hackmak, and then soon after taken over by Jambo. Jambo is the only machacker I know who wears a skirt. Seriously though, Jambo is from Scotland, and he plays a bagpipe. To this day, his e-zine Happle is the most downloaded Mac hack zine around. Jambo has reportedly been schooling in the United States—if you see him, give him a hug. Each issue is filled with articles ranging from coding, phreaking, and cellphones to hacking, cheats, and warez. If you're interested in Macintosh hacking, this would be a good site to read. `http://freaky.staticusers.net/textfiles/zines/Happle/` or `http://jambo.accesscard.org/`

25

Policies, Procedures, and Enforcement

This chapter discusses the creation and enforcement of security policies for an organization.

The Importance of Security Policies

The computing and network environment within an organization is often the component that draws the line between success and failure of the company. The reliance on computers and the Internet in our daily work requires security considerations in many areas. The security of the network, servers, and desktop computers is understood to be a complex and serious undertaking, but not the only factor that brings security to a company. The work done to bolster the security of the network and computer systems can be rendered useless if users do not work in a secure manner. It can also become a wasted effort if administrators do not maintain it. Security also decreases if it does not adapt to the changing work environment. Security is the responsibility of every person within an organization. All computer administrators, computer users, and even those employees who do not use computers in their daily practice share the responsibility for the overall security of a company.

The goal of this chapter is to provide a basis by which security policies can be created and enforced. The examples used are drawn from real security policies but organized as a sample security policy for Company Z, a hypothetical high-technology firm.

This chapter organizes the discussion of security policies around the following themes:

- Site and infrastructure security policies

- Administrative security policies

- User or employee security policies

The issues of physical access, acceptable use, authentication, and incident response are common to each of these subjects and important to the creation of a security policy. This chapter uses sample Company Z policies to demonstrate these important components.

Site and Infrastructure Security Policy

A site and infrastructure security policy outlines security in regards to the office, building, or buildings in which the company functions, and the computing and network infrastructure it uses. The business site provides the first physical perimeter for the organization, as well as the first focus for security. The computing infrastructure includes desktop systems, servers, network equipment such as routers and firewalls, and other computing resources used within the organization. The procedures and methods applied to these systems, the environment in which they exist, and their use constitute the site and infrastructure security policy.

Facilities and Physical Security Considerations

In this inter-networked age, many people often associate security with the more virtual aspects—network, operating system and application security, the underground, crackers, and all of the media-hyped fear, uncertainty, and doubt that surrounds these aspects. Prior to this time, the term *security* conjured images of armed guards or large, burly men posted by each door. Physical security is a large component of any security policy, and rightfully so. The front door is the most easily utilized point of attack.

The site and infrastructure security policy should outline the methods used to provide and control physical access to the building and the conditions under which access is granted. Important elements are

- Methods of physical access

- Procedures by which access is granted, modified, or denied

- Access restrictions based on employee status

- Hours of operation

- Points of contact for access

- Procedures for incident handling and escalation levels

Physical access methods describe the actual means of accessing the facility, offices, labs, or other areas. These are often a lock and key, proximity cards, or biometric methods. Consideration should also be given to guidelines for the appropriate use and handling of the keys. The procedures used to obtain keys/cards and by which access is granted or modified should be outlined clearly, as it is often a point of confusion for both new and long-time employees. Equally important is a list of the people and departments to whom an employee must go to gain access to the business site—filling out forms or asking approval becomes futile if the person to whom these request should be addressed is unknown.

Many organizations distinguish between full-time, part-time, and contract employees and limit facility access based on these categories. Along with the hours of operation, the site security policy should specify any restrictions for special employees during and outside of regular working hours. Related to the segmentation of employees, the segmentation of the facility is also common. Labs, offices, and storage areas often merit access restrictions in order to prevent unauthorized entry.

Should an incident occur, the procedures for incident handling are vital to the security of an organization, as well as the safety of the employees. Incidents vary in nature, from unauthorized visitors and broken access methods to the removal of employees. Many organizations have security personnel to assist in these matters, and suggested methods to react to specific situations. Defined escalation levels help an employee understand incident seriousness, and to determine the appropriate time to notify external support, such as local law enforcement and legal counsel.

Company Z has installed and uses proximity-based card readers at all external entrances, lab doors, storage closets, and key financial offices for access control.

The administration has defined the following security policy that regulates access into the facility:

- During weekday business hours—between 8 a.m. and 6 p.m.—card access is not required for full-time and part-time employees.

- Contract employees are required to sign in with the receptionist.

- All external doors are locked outside normal business hours, and card access is required for full-time and part-time employees.

- Contract employees are restricted from access outside normal business hours unless specialized access forms are filled out and approved by the hiring manager.

- Access to restricted labs, storage areas, and financial offices is gained via specialized access forms and management approval.

- Access cards are obtained at the security office after the hiring manager approves access forms.

- Misplaced or stolen access cards must be reported immediately to security.

- Access cards should be kept on the person at all times; cards should not be loaned to anyone or left unsecured.

The following security policy for incident response is also provided to employees:

In order to ensure safety and security within the Company Z facility, employees should read and understand the following guidelines for dealing with incidents:

- In the event of an unauthorized visitor, the employee should immediately notify the security department and request assistance for removal of the visitor.

- Should the visitor be witnessed committing an act of larceny, attack, or destruction of property, the employee should notify the security department, and they will then contact the appropriate authorities.

- All witnesses should provide the security department with an affidavit indicating their presence and the details of the incident, and should be available for further questioning by the security department and the appropriate authorities.

- All doors, locks, and access methods that are nonfunctional should be reported to the security department. Security will coordinate with maintenance to fix the broken equipment.

- Managers should be notified when an employee is involved with a breach of security.

- Employees should not handle these situations alone, but should instead notify security and allow the security staff to control the situation.

This example demonstrates important aspects of a site and infrastructure security policy. Constraints on physical access are defined, including the actual methods that employees use to enter the facility and the differentiation between employee types. The processes and procedures used to control access and to acquire the appropriate privileges are outlined, including the identification of the responsible individuals. The response guidelines for any incidents are clearly outlined with the safety of the employee in mind. Individuals trained to handle incidents of this nature are identified and involved in each response method.

Infrastructure and Computing Environment

The following aspects of security are commonly considered when creating a security policy for the infrastructure and computing environment:

- Physical access to computer systems and facilities

- Security considerations for laptop computers and PDAs

- Voice and data network security

- Remote network access to computer systems and resources

- Security monitoring and auditing

- Authentication and access control

Physical Access to Computer Systems and Facilities

The computer systems used throughout an organization can be categorized into the following classes:

- Public terminals

- Desktop systems

- Server systems

Each of these classes of systems can be addressed individually within the site and infrastructure security policy.

Public Terminals　As with the building and facilities, control of physical access to the computing environment is an important component to its security. Once someone is inside a building, finding an unoccupied terminal or computer system is often easily accomplished. Without a policy for protecting these systems, unauthorized users can gain access to important and private resources, information, and files. Computer terminals in publicly accessible areas should be controlled carefully by limiting access to network facilities and resources, and establishing usage policies for employees and guests.

Returning to the hypothetical case, Company Z has an open atrium area that contains several terminals accessible to employees and visitors. The following security policy, which provides regulations for the use of these public terminals, is posted in plain view:

Rules and Restrictions for Public Terminal Usage

- Visitors must see the receptionist to receive a guest account.
- Guest accounts are capable of accessing the Internet only.
- No internal systems or resources are available via guest logins.
- Guest accounts are automatically logged out after 15 minutes of idle time.
- Employees should log out before leaving the terminal.
- Please report all malfunctioning systems to the IT department.

Administrative Policies for Public Terminals

- Public terminals are secured to the desktops via anti-theft alarm devices and cable locks.
- All systems configured for public use are on a restricted-access network.
- Systems are configured with guest accounts that have no access to company resources or systems.
- Guest accounts are automatically logged out after a specified amount of idle time.
- Guest accounts should be set to expire when no longer needed, based on the requirements of the guest.
- Publicly accessible systems should allow no access to internal systems or resources.
- Publicly accessible Unix systems should be configured with a minimal set of utilities, have no network services running, and provide a restricted and inescapable shell to guests; the account should be removed when the visitor leaves the premises.
- Publicly accessible Windows systems should not be domain members, and guest accounts should have only the local user-group privileges.
- Operating systems and software should be updated when new vulnerabilities and subsequent patches are released. This includes updating virus signatures in anti-virus products.
- Menus and commands should also be configured to allow access only to the appropriate Web browser program on the system and no other applications.

Public terminals are often presented to accommodate the network needs of visiting employees, vendors, and business partners. These terminals require special considerations for security, along with posted regulations for their use to protect the computing infrastructure. The Company Z policy distinguishes between visitors and employees who use the terminals, and presents significantly more restrictions to the visitors. The administrators of these systems also have a security policy that outlines the measures used to configure the systems. This ensures that all publicly accessible systems are configured alike, and helps ensure a known level of security.

Desktop and Server Systems   Public terminals are not the only systems that require guidelines. Desktop systems often have the most lax security because individual employees often administer their own machines, or have special privileges and access to their respective system. It is often infeasible for the Information Technology staff to administer all desktop workstations; therefore, the development of a security policy that governs their creation and use is very important. The site and infrastructure security policy for desktop systems establishes the standards used to create them, including operating systems, applications, and utilities. The security constraints generally consist of configuration information by which administrators can replicate the desktop system at a known level of security. The policies also present the guidelines for the desktop system's interaction with servers and the network. The security policy for desktop users is discussed later in the chapter.

Given the understanding that desktop systems are likely to be uncontrolled by the IT staff, effective infrastructure policies attempt to minimize the amount of data, applications, and other information that remains on the desktop system. This enhances both the security and availability of information within the organization. Many companies centralize storage of user data and applications to a single server or set of servers. In the event of a failure of a desktop, the effort required to make it functional again is minimized—all the essential and important data is on the server, and isn't lost or require significant time and effort to restore.

Server systems become a focal point, as they have the responsibility to reliably store and provide access to shared data, private user information, applications, and services for the organization.

A server security policy should encompass the following components:

- Service configuration
- Shared data permissions and access control
- User private data permissions and access control
- Backup and restoration procedures
- Incident response

The service configuration is the initial method used to secure the server. Most operating systems provide a vast array of potential services and capabilities, not all of which are needed or desired by the organization. Each of these services has its own security ramifications that should be considered when enabling or disabling it.

The decision to allow a service is often an issue of cost versus risk analysis. If the service provides a required function that has inherent security risks, the administrators should determine whether there are suitable replacements for the service. If any substitutes are available, the cost and effort required to implement them should be weighed against the security risks and cost of the original. It is important to document within the security policy the foundation for decisions, and to identify the known security risks accepted by the organization.

Also related is the maintenance of the software and operating systems running on the servers—security measures should be updated frequently, as new vulnerabilities are discovered. Updates should be applied and monitored. The people writing the security policy probably will not always be employed at the organization; therefore, knowing the background of a decision is important to the future maintainers of the security policy.

Company Z's Server Security Policy is as follows:

- Servers should be configured to support only the required services, and to disable unnecessary software and services in order to minimize security risks.

- Server systems should be physically secured, allowing only administrative access.

- Server operating systems and software should be updated when new vulnerabilities and subsequent patches are released. This includes updating virus signatures in anti-virus products.

- In the event of incidents such as hardware failure, system compromise, or other attacks, the server should be removed from the network and left in its current state in order to allow effective forensics work.

- A contingency plan should be created and followed to recover from disasters. For in-depth information on their content and creation, see the Disaster Recovery Journal sample recovery plans at `http://www.drj.com/new2dr/ samples.htm`.

Focusing on security policies instead of system configuration, the Company Z Server Security Policy leaves out most of the technical details related to the secure lockdown of servers and operating systems. The standards of configuration, access, and maintenance are important components that should be incorporated into the policy. Incident response for servers is reasonably complex; to avoid damaging potential evidence after an attack is discovered, the system should be left intact for security analysis and forensics work.

Shared data is often the primary purpose of a server—allowing employees access to common files, applications, and other data. Server operating systems generally support multiple methods to provide multiuser access to data. When establishing the infrastructure security policy, the technical details surrounding shared data should be clearly outlined.

The Site and Infrastructure Security Policy for Company Z establishes the following criteria for shared data on servers:

- No data sharing should be initialized via the Everyone group on Windows servers, or World read/write access on Unix systems.

- Access by the Everyone group and World read/write permissions should be removed or disabled from the shared data.

- Global or common access to all employees should be controlled via membership in the specially created Employees group on the servers.

- When needed, smaller privilege groups should be created and shared data coordinated with those groups to meet the access control requirements for a user.

Company Z's policy emphasizes a strict level of security for shared data. It identifies and distinguishes between unconditionally shared data and the true need for shared data. Data is shared only between employees, and security control is exercised to ensure that only authorized individuals have access to it. In this model, access control is achieved via membership in various user groups, and permission is adjusted accordingly.

Private user data includes a user's respective "home" directories, or the areas in which his personal files are stored. Because these files are also often kept on the server, it is important to outline the level of security the user can expect, as well as the method by which it is provided.

Company Z details this security policy for user home directories and private storage areas:

- Server-based user home directories are provided for the storage of private and personal data.

- On Windows servers, the permissions should be set to allow the respective user full read and write permissions for a directory, and also to allow the system backup process to access the data when backing up the storage system.

- No other users should have access to any home directory aside from their own.

- Users are encouraged to use their server-based directories for data storage in order to provide security and to facilitate the simple recovery of data in the event of an incident.

Employees often store personal and sensitive information on their systems as work and personal life cannot be completely segregated. Ideally, employees should not do this, and a good policy might be to prohibit it. To provide data security and avoid data loss in the event of a desktop system failure, users at Company Z are encouraged to store their data on the servers, and are provided a high degree of protection from prying eyes.

Backup and restoration procedures serve many functions in an organization. These include protection of data in the event of a catastrophic incident, restoration of accidentally removed files, and provision of general infrastructure reliability. Backup data is often used in the forensics of security incidents to assess the reliability of data—data altered by an attacker can often be detected by a comparison between it and the version on the backup media. The physical storage of the media on which the backups are made is also important to security. Many organizations use special offsite storage organizations to assure that the backups are securely stored.

Company Z's security considerations for system backups include the following:

- All backups are to be stored in a locked storage area prior to offsite storage.

- Backups should be periodically tested to make sure they worked correctly and can be restored.

- Weekly backups are moved into offsite storage via a storage company representative at a scheduled pickup time.

- Backups consist of one full system backup, per system, per week, with nightly incremental backups of all modified data.

- Use of backup and restoration applications should be restricted to authorized administrators only.

- In the event of a disaster, hardware failure, or other event that results in the loss of data, the employee should notify the IT staff.

- Information will be restored from the last full archive with the incremental changes layered over, up to the time of the event.

Backups provide a level of reliability and security to the information stored and used within the organization. The security policy specifies the method for backups, recovery during incidents, and privileges required to access the information. The physical security of the backup data is also emphasized to create a comprehensive policy that effectively protects the organization.

Incident response takes on several meanings, but can be summarized as the best course of action in the event of anomalous circumstances. For the purposes of this discussion, the actual circumstances are not as important as the reaction to them. Security policies provide key benefits in the area of incident response by identifying and organizing information vital to a safe reaction. Security policies should include the suggested methods to react to incidents and pertinent contact information. The primary goal of incident-response guidelines is to avoid the knee-jerk, emotionally motivated responses that often happen quickly and without careful analysis. By having a step-by-step approach to handling incidents already in hand—including the proper steps to identify, control, and resolve issues—those involved can react safely.

Physical Security Considerations for Laptop Computers and PDAs

As technology advances, we see the creation of new, smaller, and more powerful computing devices. In light of the prevalence of telecommuters and remote offices, and the frequency of business travel, these small computing devices, such as laptops, cell phones, and PDAs, require special security considerations. The theft and misuse of these devices present a high risk to the infrastructure of an organization, as they often function with the same level of access as their larger and less portable cousins. Many of these portable computers have special security methods that enable the user to protect the device and the information stored on it. Chapter 29, "Wireless Security," will cover the wireless security aspects. The company policies that govern the use of laptops, phones, and PDAs should require putting these capabilities to use.

Company Z has established a set of Security Policy Considerations for laptops, phones, and PDAs. These physical and configuration considerations include the following:

- Laptops, phones, and PDAs should be configured to support power-on passwords if possible, in order to protect against unauthorized use if stolen.

- For laptops and PDAs, users should log out and power off the system when not in use, instead of putting the system into standby mode. This prevents unauthorized users from impersonating you, should they gain access to the system.

- Private and sensitive data should be protected via encryption and passwords, if possible.

- Users should use different passwords on all of their portable and nonportable systems to defend against the compromise of multiple systems via a stolen password.

- When temporarily leaving your workspace, care should be taken to either lock the system via a password-protected screensaver or log out completely.

- Laptops and PDAs should be physically secured by a locked cable, tether, or other security device at all times.

- If no security method is available, the system should be locked in a cabinet drawer or other secured storage area when not in use.

Voice and Data Network Security

The network is the lifeline for the computing infrastructure. The phone system that provides voice communications forms a network of interconnected phones. Desktops connect to servers and the greater Internet via the local area network. Customers, partners, and employees contact the company via the network. The majority of internal communication likely occurs via the voice and data networks. Security policies should attend to the security of network communication. By addressing the risks and defenses against them, the networks can function more securely.

The phone system within an organization often crosses the boundaries of voice and data communications. The desktop computer can interact with modern phone systems to retrieve voice mail, leave messages for others, and administer the system. As with the previous areas of concern, physical access should controlled. The operational constraints—such as Personal Identification Numbers (PINs) for users—and standard configurations should provide a more secure environment. An often forgotten security aspect of the phone system is the provision of remote dial-in capabilities that support both phone system administration and network access.

Several concerns for the phone system are outlined in this Company Z security policy:

- Physical access to the phone system hardware and system configuration terminals is restricted to phone administrators and phone company personnel.

- The phone system hardware should exist in a secured area that requires specialized access methods via keys or electronic cards.

- Default PINs for new users should be randomly chosen.

- When establishing a voice mail account, avoid using PINs that can be easily guessed, such as an extension number, the surname of the user, or other identifiable information.

- Dial-in modems used for administration of the phone system should be protected with passwords.

- Dial-in lines should have caller ID to make tracking security incidents easier.

- Network access via dial-in modems should be authenticated and logged via a centralized authentication and reporting system.

- Modems meant for dial-in should be programmed to prevent dial-out capabilities.

- Installation of new modems should be coordinated through the phone and IT group to provide the necessary security and network infrastructure to maintain security.

- Phone line audits should occur regularly to verify the functionality of existing modems and to identify unauthorized modems.

This security policy addresses the phone system rather extensively. A comprehensive security policy takes into consideration all aspects of an organization, and does not focus only on the computing environment. All aspects of security in an organization are related; a breakdown in the security of one area provides access despite the security measures of another. A weakness in the phone system security policy might permit an unauthorized intruder to access system and network resources even if other system and network security measures are in place.

The data network should be extended the same security features as the voice network. Network and telecommunications hardware such as routers, switches, and network lines (ISDN, DSL, T1, and so on) should be physically secured to avoid accidental or intentional disruption of network services. Beyond the physical aspects, the network requires a high degree of security and diligence to maintain that level. The first tier of protection is generally a firewall at the Internet access point (as you learned in Chapter 10, "Firewalls"). The specific firewall rules and filters should be defined based on the network access needs of the organization. A reasonably safe, but somewhat restrictive, guideline is the exception method. This dictates a global rule to deny access to everything first, and then makes exceptions for those network services deemed necessary.

After the firewall, network architecture and organization should also be considered to protect and isolate information as it travels on the network wire. The network hardware must be protected from network attacks and unauthorized configuration attempts.

Company Z has a diverse network that separates servers from the normal desktop computing network. The Internet access point is protected by a firewall. The data network portion of its security policy reads as follows:

- Firewalls are used to protect the internal networks in a restrictive fashion.

- Filtering and rules on the firewall support outgoing connections from employees so as not to restrict their ability to use the Internet.

- Filtering and rules on the firewall allow only incoming connections to the company Web server, mail servers, and name servers (DNS).

- The customer support network exists on a different network number and interface than the administrative and corporate network, and with fewer restrictions, in order to support the required services of that organization.

- All access to network equipment, where supported, shall be protected via non-default passwords.

- Managed network equipment, including firewalls, routers, switches, modems, and other communication devices, are configured to allow administrative access from only a small number of administrative systems, in order to protect them from unauthorized configuration changes.

- All configuration changes to network equipment must be logged for reference.

- In the event of network attacks, the network administrators should notify the corporate security department, in case legal intervention is required.

- Network equipment should be configured to enable only those protocols in use by the organization, disabling all other features.

- Response to incidents should occur in the following manner:

    1. Attempt to identify the cause.

    2. In the event of network disruption and loss of service from attack, network administrators should attempt to identify the source of the attack. Firewall rules should be modified to control the effects, if possible.

    3. Restore service to the company as quickly as possible while attempting to preserve evidence of the issue.

    4. Upon resolution of an incident, incident forms should be filled out and submitted to the manager of the network group.

    5. Analysis of the incident should be discussed in a group meeting to identify weaknesses in the organization and help prevent future issues.

- To protect against equipment failure, spare network hardware should be available.

- To facilitate ease of replacement and security of the configuration of network equipment, the configuration information should be maintained on the administrative servers.

- Where possible, network equipment should be configured to boot and download its configuration from the administrative servers, in order to preserve the integrity and reliability of the configuration.

- Network equipment that is not managed via SNMP should have that protocol disabled. The SNMP (Simple Network Management Protocol) allows administrators to see and modify the settings and configuration for a device with little or no authentication and access control.

- If using SNMP for management of the device, SNMP access should be restricted to administrative servers. The community strings should be changed from the defaults as well.

Network equipment presents a complex set of security requirements that should be outlined in the security policy. This allows for a safe installation and a maintained degree of security. The security policy incorporates physical orientation and configuration to defend against unauthorized access and management of the device.

Authentication and access restrictions are implemented, as well as reliability in the configuration methods. The services provided by the equipment are tailored to the needs of the organization, allowing a known set of security concerns to be identified and resolved.

Remote Network Access

Remote network access is a convenience that allows employees to do their daily work, regardless of their location. This functionality requires an extension of the network security policy discussed previously, focused on the methods and use of remote access. Remote access can be provided via Virtual Private Networks and the previously mentioned dial-in modems. The provision of these capabilities often conflicts with the security policy for the network, because the policy generally seeks to keep outsiders from accessing internal information and resources.

Here is Company Z's Remote Access Security Policy:

- The company provides remote access capabilities via a Virtual Private Network solution that supports remote dial-in Internet service providers and broadband cable-modem users.

- Configuration of the VPN hardware and software follows the security policy set forth for other network equipment.

- Users requiring remote access capabilities must receive approval from their manager and the IT department and fill out the required forms before remote access is provided.

- Remote access is authenticated via passwords, security tokens, or single-use passwords.

- Remote access passwords should follow the security policy guidelines for authentication.

- Remote access software, configuration, and account information is to be used only by the employee for whom it is intended.

- If access by multiple remote machines is required, this should be indicated on the Remote Access Form.

- Remote access should be used only when required and not left unattended by the employee.

- Acceptable use of this resource is outlined in the User Security Policy.

Remote access is a subfunction that inherits security policy guidelines from several areas. The administration and configuration of the VPN falls under the Company Z's

Network Devices Policy, whereas the authentication and use of the VPN by employees is governed by the Authentication and User policies, discussed later in the chapter.

As you can see, a comprehensive security policy is very easily scaled to meet new requirements and functionality within an organization. The effort expended in the early development stages of the security policy or policies simplifies its extension greatly.

Security Monitoring and Auditing

Central to a comprehensive security policy, and the components that unify procedures and response, is the discussion of monitoring and auditing. *Security monitoring* verifies the configuration guidelines and technical requirements outlined in the security policies. *Security auditing* entails a consistent set of practices that enforce the security policies set forth for the organization.

Monitoring is the policy action that becomes part of the ongoing standard security process in the company. The installation of a firewall is one element of the security monitoring system—it focuses on the network access points. Other aspects of monitoring are the use of security cameras, anti-virus software, server disk quotas, intrusion detection devices, and network management software. The monitoring component of a security policy enhances the security in an organization by validating the other elements in the policy, ensuring their existence and correctness.

Monitoring capabilities also affect the safety and effectiveness of incident responses. It provides evidence for legal issues and an informative basis for post-mortem analysis of incidents. This analysis is very useful to assist in prevention and understanding of problems.

Finally, security monitoring provides the capability for the organization to recover from incidents by providing in-depth information about it. Network attacks can be monitored and defended against, spurious hardware failures can be traced and rectified, and the actions of unauthorized intruders can be watched and recorded.

The monitoring methods for a server, network, or other computer equipment are often those that gather and analyze statistics. The statistics gathered provide the reference point for normal operation, and for that which is abnormal. This information is often gathered by hand, or eye, in the case of security cameras and monitoring. The level to which the monitoring is automated increases its effectiveness.

To allay the fears that this task is incredibly difficult, it is important to note that many operating systems and software have the capabilities to perform a large portion of the monitoring and auditing functionality—the features simply need to be enabled. Authentication policies including the identification of password criteria, the use of password aging, and keeping a password history to avoid repetition are enforced by common features in most operating systems. Access control methods and auditing capabilities are inherent parts of server operating systems. Network management protocols allow for special alerts and notices to be sent under special conditions. An example is SNMP, which can be configured to notify administrators when special events occur. SNMP has weak security and should be investigated prior to its implementation, and is mentioned here because of its wide use. An alarm company, monitors the alarm system, and the proper authorities are notified automatically when it is set off.

Company Z's Security Monitoring Policy reads as follows:

- Closed-circuit television cameras are installed throughout the organization and at entry/exit points.

- This video information is recorded and monitored by the security group.

- Network equipment management and monitoring occurs via automated management software that notifies administrators via pager in the event of anomalous issues.

- Anti-virus software monitors all programs, documents, and email messages for viruses and automatically cleans discovered viruses.

- Users and administrators are automatically notified via email when a virus is discovered.

- All servers are monitored via monitoring programs and built-in functionality that complies with the established security policy.

Auditing ensures that the security policy is in place and followed. The measures used to audit include the services of contract security firms to analyze an organization's networks, systems, and policies—often unbeknownst to the employees. Other forms of auditing include random and frequent verification of the policies by administrators or special internal teams designed for such tasks. The reference to auditing in the security policies of an organization also has a psychological effect that helps foster greater security awareness and action. Employees are less likely to adhere to security policies if they feel there is no enforcement. By outlining the presence of auditing methods, without necessarily clarifying the exact procedures, frequency, or schedule, an organization makes its employees more aware of security issues. A greater emphasis on secure thought and use is the natural result. Consider Company Z's Security Policy for Enforcement and Auditing:

- Periodic and random security audits will be performed on servers and network equipment to ensure proper configuration, diligent updates and application of patches, and compliance with other security policy regulations.

- These audits can be performed by internal staff or external agencies with or without the knowledge of the administrators and users of the systems. (For some useful information about audits and pitfalls to avoid, see the article "Audits from Hell" by Carole Fennelly at `http://www.theiia.org/itaudit/` `index.cfm?fuseaction=forum&fid=177.`)

- Desktop systems and users will be audited for compliance with the Site and Infrastructure Policy, with regard to configuration, up-to-date software, and network services.

- Audits of users for compliance with the Acceptable Use Policy will also be conducted to assure the safety and security of the computing environment.

Notification to employees of the audit policy enforces compliance of security policies and also forewarns them of repercussions for compliance failures. Administrators have the largest responsibility and expend the most effort to enforce adherence to security policies. Audits might seem forceful, but an environment with so many security components requires dedication and diligence to maintain security.

Authentication and Access Control

Authentication and access control are two aspects of security in which administrators and users must participate equally for any level of effectiveness to exist. Security policies need to present the regulations and requirements clearly, and should help employees understand the seriousness of compliance. Authentication policies establish the best practices and exact implementations used to provide access to desktop systems, servers, and local network resources, and from remote sites. There are well-known methods to provide authentication, and several guidelines that create a more highly secure environment. The authentication issues addressed by the security policy are important to most other areas covered within the policy. Access control is related to authentication, and is often used simultaneously because the authentication of a user instantiates group membership and provides access to resources.

Not surprisingly, authentication security involves the implementation and use of various forms of authentication. Commonly used means are passwords, Personal Identification Numbers (PINs), single-use passwords, public-key encryption, proximity cards, smart cards, other code-generation tokens, and biometric agents.

The most commonly used authentication method is the username/password combination. In comparison to other authentication methods, this is also the most easily compromised—theft of passwords comes in many different forms, often because of the individual's choice of password. People tend to gravitate toward easily remembered words or phrases when selecting passwords, such as names of family members, pets, hobbies, or other interests. Unfortunately, attackers often easily guess these passwords. In the quest to balance ease of use with high security, authentication security policies help users create stronger passwords that might not be so easily discerned. The policies also provide guidelines by which users can increase the security of their daily work. The enforcement of these guidelines often occurs as a feature of the operating system or programs doing the authentication.

Authentication security policy also differentiates between where and how authentication methods are used. Security requirements for access to different systems, networks, or facilities often mandate the need for each user to maintain several authentication methods. This is especially true for computer and network administrators. Users are not the only group governed by authentication policies. Administrators need to be even more concerned with authentication security because they control access to highly privileged accounts, systems, and resources. There are several guidelines for the handling and use of passwords, also. These guidelines help to keep users continually thinking of security in everything they do.

Company Z's Authentication Security Policy for users and administrators includes these guidelines:

- On systems where credentials are the username/password pair, passwords should meet the following criteria:

  - Passwords should be at least eight characters.

  - Passwords should be a combination of letters, numbers, and extended or special characters.

  - The company will maintain a history of a user's last five passwords to prevent repetition.

  - Passwords should be sufficiently different from any password in the history to prevent patterns of easily obtained passwords.

  - Common dictionary words are not allowed.

  - Passwords will expire every 12 weeks, requiring the user to create a new one.

  - Passwords should be chosen carefully by avoiding family or pet names, personal interests, or other information that can be linked and easily identified.

- Administrators must abide by the criteria set forth for users, with the addition that their passwords will expire more frequently, at six weeks.

- Passwords for privileged accounts will change every four weeks to provide higher safety, because these accounts are shared among several administrators.

- Remote access will be granted using single-use passwords and code-generating security tokens to prevent theft of user credentials.

- All user accounts will have a password. Any user account without a password will be disabled, or have a random password generated for it.

- Newly created accounts will have randomly generated passwords that expire upon first login, requiring the user to set a new password.

- Passwords should never be written down or stored on a recoverable medium such as paper, sticky notes, or white-boards.

- Users should never tell anyone their passwords.

- Administrators will never ask users for their passwords. In the event that someone does ask for the password, please report it immediately to IT and the security group.

- When automating tasks that require authentication, avoid storing passwords clearly in data files. If possible, encrypt or hash the password prior to storing it, in order to prevent the theft of the passwords.

- When using smart cards, proximity cards, or other hardware token-based authentication methods, keep the device on your person at all times, and do not let others borrow it.

- When using public-key encryption methods for authentication, private key information should be protected via file access restrictions, or storage on external devices such as smart cards.

- When using encryption, private and secret keys can be escrowed by the administration to protect the data from loss and to ensure that access is attainable when required.

- All authentications, whether successful or failures, are logged by the system being accessed.

- Systems should be configured to allow three failed login attempts before account lock-out occurs.

- In the event of login failure and account lock-out, internal accounts should be configured to allow logins again after 30 minutes. The use of permanent lock-outs is also supported by many operating systems. These require an administrator to intervene and reopen the account. A permanent lock-out can result in a denial-of-service condition if an attacker attacks multiple accounts.

- Remote access accounts should be disabled after three failed login attempts, requiring administrative intervention for the reuse of the account.

- Administrators should implement login notices that are displayed prior to login prompts. These notices should warn unauthorized users that their actions are monitored and attempts to enter the system are prohibited. Legal ramifications might result from continued use by unauthorized personnel.

- In the event of lost or stolen passwords and authentication devices, the IT department should be notified immediately to disable access for that account, and to begin the creation of new access credentials.

- Administrators should confirm the identity of users before issuing new passwords. This can be done in person with the presentation of a badge or photo ID, the use of a special recovery password, a personal identification number, Social Security number, or other method that is normally known only by the user and administrator.

As you can see, the use of authentication is serious business. Users and administrators need to be made aware of the negative effects of authentication misuse. To summarize, the important components of authentication are as follows:

- Teaching users and administrators to use authentication methods securely through strong password creation, as well as keeping passwords secure.

- Authentication logging and monitoring.

- Different authentication methods should be defined and used for different applications to provide the highest level of security, instead of standardizing on a single authentication method. For example, remote access often merits a stronger authentication mechanism than internal server access does.

- The importance of strict authentication security policies, such as password expiration and selection criteria, to make attack and compromise difficult.

Access control is the next related component to authentication. Access control exists at several levels—network access, data file access, and resource access. Network access is determined by protocols, port numbers, source and destination systems, and networks. Network access control is most likely maintained by the firewall, and these policies are discussed earlier in this chapter. Data file and system resource access control is accomplished via operating system functionality, such as file permissions linked to user and group memberships. An access control security policy presents the user with a set of best practices for utilizing this functionality. Consider Company Z's Access Control Policy:

- Network access control occurs via the firewall, which is configured to allow Internet access for employees. If a required service is blocked by the firewall, contact the IT or network administration group to discuss possible solutions.

- Employees are granted access to global company computing resources via their desktop login procedure.

- Common file shares are automatically initialized at login time. The user has rights to add to common areas, but not to remove files or folders unless the user created them.

- Unix user accounts should be created with membership in the Global users groups or equivalent (operating system dependent).

- Unix user accounts should have their own private group as the default group membership, which allows them to set permissions safely on their files and directories.

- Windows accounts should be members of the Domain Users group.

- Home directories should be created to allow access only by the owner of the directory.

- The Unix umask setting allows users to specify a default permission level for newly created files. This should be set to create files that disallow everyone else to modify or execute them. (The default umask is generally 022, which creates files with read and write permissions for the owner and read permissions for the group and world.)

- The Unix SetUID/GID settings should be avoided unless absolutely necessary.

- The permissions of user resource settings including .login, .profile, and .rhosts should be secured against unauthorized modification.

- Users should contact the IT department if any uncertainty exists when setting access control methods.

- If unauthorized access to files, folders, or other data is suspected, notify the IT department for an investigation.

- Automatic scans will execute on a regular basis to search for unsafe access control settings on systems, user files, folders, and applications.

- The Windows NT and 2000 operating systems provide access to everybody (via the special Everybody group) by default. This group access should be removed and replaced with the Domain Users group, if access to all employees is to be granted.

NOTE

The Windows NT and 2000 operating systems support a slightly different access control mechanism than Unix. The Windows mechanism has the standard read, write, and execute permissions like Unix, but it also has several special attributes, such as full-access and modify. The full-access permission allows the individual to modify all the permissions, including the permissions for others. This is often not the desired effect, so in cases where the user requires only read, write, and execute access, `full-access` should not be enabled. The `modify` attribute allows a user to make changes to a file already in existence, but not to create new files or folders.

Access control policies can present useful technical information to the users and promote security awareness. Noting the technical details of access control mechanisms for the operating systems in use is beneficial, because the casual user is often unaware of their existence or use. The identification of contacts and procedures for access control issues is used to help the user learn and implement secure settings.

Acceptable Use

Acceptable use is a general set of guidelines for administrators and users that emphasizes best practices and security awareness in daily work. Administrators and users share most responsibilities for security, but the privilege and access levels of administrators mandate several strict rules to prevent the misuse of their power.

Administrative Security Policies

The administrator's job is to adhere to the site and infrastructure policies, as well as to work in a secure manner outlined by his own acceptable use policies. Given the nature of administrator privileges and access, certain rules are required to govern their use and prevent the abuse of those privileges. Because of these higher privileges, the administrator also needs to be extremely diligent in his security awareness and action.

None of the policy issues presented here are exclusive or independent of the others. This is also the case for administrative and user security policies. The administrative security portion of the security policy outlines acceptable use and procedures for administrators to consider and abide by when following the entire security policy. Administrative policies define rules and accepted processes by which the computing infrastructure is established and maintained. They also outline a hierarchy of responsibility, escalation matrices, and procedures for everyday security awareness and implementation, as you can see in Company Z's Administrator Acceptable Use and Procedures Policy:

- Unauthorized access to user files and information is prohibited unless the administrator is actively resolving an issue with the user.

- Administrators monitoring user data and voice communications, including authentication, email, Web traffic, and phone conversations, is acceptable only when working to solve problems or during security audits. The practice of automated monitoring via intrusion detection systems and other equipment should be identified and outlined separately.

- When troubleshooting problems, administrators should ask permission and make the user aware that access to these forms of information will occur.

- Administrative adherence to this policy and the remaining security policies outlined in these documents will be randomly and periodically audited for compliance.

- Noncompliance with the security policies results in notification to management and a documented warning. Further noncompliance or abuse may affect the employment status of the administrator.

- Purposefully executed events that result in loss of service, compromise of a system, or altered functionality will be investigated, and the appropriate actions will be taken against the administrator.

Acceptable use policies should be clear and concise when presenting the rules and regulations. Serious security and confidentiality issues can arise when acceptable use is not well defined. The policy should discuss acceptable use with regards to administrative interaction with users, their data, and private information. Earlier in the general security policy, it is recommended that users store their personal files in protected home directories on centralized servers. Users are unlikely to do so if the administrator who maintains those servers does not have her own rules regarding access to these files. Computer and network administrators often have complete access to every action and keystroke of users. This is a very powerful position that can easily be abused if strict policies and enforcement are not in effect. It is not sufficient to simply state the rules; the results of failure to follow the rules should also be clarified.

Acceptable Use Policies for Users

This section outlines the rules for acceptable use that apply to the users in an organization. The previously outlined security policies should also be adhered to and practiced as a normal part of daily operation.

Company Z's User Acceptable Use Policy reads as follows:

- Use of computer, network, and company resources is granted under the proviso that users read, understand, and comply with the security policy in full, and indicate so by signing and returning the policy to the IT department.

- Users should adhere to the authentication policy and treat all passwords as private, personal property.

- Users agree not to abuse the computer, network, or other company resources to create loss of service, system compromise, or to weaken existing security measures. Failure to comply might result in punitive action by the company and affect the user's employment status.

- Users agree to participate in random periodic audits of their processes and procedures for compliance with the outlined security policy or policies.

- All incidents including hardware failures, computer attacks, and unauthorized entry or access should be reported to the appropriate security or IT departments.

- Employees should request identification from unknown visitors seeking entrance to the facilities and direct them to reception or security for access.

- Employees should not allow unknown individuals or non-employees to access computer and network resources.

- Laptops, PDAs, and other portable devices should not be left unattended. (Also refer to the security considerations for these devices outlined earlier in the policy.)

- Users should lock their terminals prior to leaving the work area.

- Users agree to follow the site and infrastructure security guidelines with respect to the security of desktop computer systems, their use, and the services provided by them.

Acceptable use encompasses more general guidelines that relate to the technical implementation details provided by the security policy. These regulations emphasize the importance of security to their daily work habits by summarizing some of the important components of the overall security policy. Authentication, physical security, and proper contact and response are important elements with which the user is frequently involved.

Enforcement of Policy

A set of regulations and guidelines is only useful when it is followed. This section summarizes the methods of enforcement presented throughout the chapter and discusses the need for enforcement measures. Without enforcement, security policy is likely to be followed for a short time after implementation, but generally falls into a state of disuse. The goals of the security policy at a global level are to instantiate a set of processes and methods that enhance the security of an organization, and to create a state of security awareness in the minds of all employees. The processes and procedures provide the means to implement security, and security awareness allows it to be sustained in the organization.

The first aspect of the security policy that enforces compliance is the binding nature of a written contract. The employee should read and agree to the security policy by signing it. The policy should then be securely stored. The legalities of a signed contract should be discussed with the legal counsel for the organization. The psychological effects are also beneficial to security policy enforcement. People have a heightened awareness when they feel bound, legally or otherwise, to a particular set of rules.

Auditing the environment and its users for compliance with the security policies is a common method of enforcement. There are generally two types of audits—notified or scheduled audits, and blind audits.

Scheduled audits are announced to the employees, and help establish compliance where it is otherwise lacking. As in a military inspection, users have an established period of time to ensure their practices are in line with the documented security policies. These audits are useful to bring the security of an organization up to an acceptable level, as the employees scramble to comply. Inspections of this nature often involve several stages. The first occurs at the technical level, wherein the systems, network, and facilities are analyzed for their security components, to assure they meet the requirements of the security policy. The practices of users are then assessed to determine whether there are improper habits or actions that negate security. A final stage is the analysis of the auditing methods to ensure that they gather the appropriate information and meet the goals of the audit.

Blind audits—audits that are random and periodically scheduled without any notification to those being audited—are useful to establish the constant security awareness needed to maintain security as the organization flourishes. Blind audits come in the form of simulated attacks or planned scenarios to exemplify a particular security practice. Blind network and computer system analysis often appears as a real attack, and the results are generally surprising, even in organizations with strict security policies. Social engineering is a particularly important aspect of these audits, because it demonstrates the level of security awareness present among the employees. This aspect of the audit might include attempts to enter the facility, acquisition of passwords or access keys, and attempts to gather private information about the organization. The response of the employee and the ability of the auditor to garner this information demonstrates the level of awareness and the level of compliance with current security policies. The knowledge that an audit could occur at any time, without notification, forces employees to incorporate security awareness and practices into their daily routines. This enhances the security of an organization over the long run.

Another way to ensure compliance is to automate the enforcement of the security policy. One example of this is a program such as Password Bouncer (http://www.passwordbouncer.com/), which helps enforce the Authentication Security Policy discussed a few pages back by not allowing users to specify passwords that do not meet the policy.

Summary

Security policies are dynamic and complex procedures, processes, and methods used to enhance the security within an organization. It is important to remember that the creation of security policy is not a one-time event. Policies must be flexible and scalable to meet the ever-growing and changing demands of the organization. Enforcement of the policies also helps to assure the validity of a security policy. Portions of the policy might no longer be applicable, and, as new technologies become available, the emphasis and individual requirements to maintain security can change. Enforcement involves a constant analysis of the results of the audits and the policy. Policies are not bipolar; noncompliance in some instances does not necessarily indicate an incorrect practice. Failures common to large groups of employees or common across related practices should be analyzed to determine whether the mandate is valid and applicable. An organization should also avoid establishing unchanging practices. New security methods and practices should be researched continuously in order to enhance the security of an organization through more efficient and easier-to-use technology.

Documented security policies provide a consistently high degree of security to an organization through their comprehensiveness, consistency, and simplicity of use. They educate users and administrators in secure practices, set an appropriate level of security as necessary for the environment, and provide recourse for the effects of misuse. When creating security policies for your organization, consider the sample guidelines presented here, their focus, and principles—use this knowledge to determine the best and most appropriate policies applicable to your organization.

For more information on some of the topics discussed here, see the following documents.

Password Security

"The Memorability and Security of Passwords—Some Empirical Results." Ross Anderson, Alan Blackwell, Alasdair Grant, and Jianxin Yan.
`http://www.ftp.cl.cam.ac.uk/ftp/users/rja14/tr500.pdf`

Audits and Analysis

"Improving the Security of Your Site by Breaking into It." Dan Farmer.
`http://www.alw.nih.gov/Security/Docs/admin-guide-to-cracking.101.html`

"There Be Dragons." Steven Bellovin.
`http://www.deter.com/unix/papers/dragons_bellovin.pdf`

Site Security Policies

Site Security Handbook. RFC 2196. http://www.ietf.org/rfc/rfc2196.txt?number=2196

Incident Handling

"An Introduction to Incident Handling." Chad L. Cook.
http://online.securityfocus.com/infocus/1184

System Configuration

"Analysis of the Security of Windows NT." Stefan Axelsson and Jonsson Erland.
http://www.ce.chalmers.se/staff/jonsson/nt-part2.pdf

Practical UNIX & Internet Security, Second Edition. Simson Garfinkel and Eugene Spafford. (O'Reilly & Associates) ISBN: 1565921488, 1996.

PART VI

Security and Integrated Services

IN THIS PART

## 26

Secure Application Development, Languages, and Extensions

This chapter covers secure application development, including the design and implementation of Internet applications, systems, and the languages used to create them.

Security and Software

Although software development encompasses a large variety of possible efforts, the need for security is common across them all. Strong security is a continuous process, not a feature that arises from comprehensive and well-thought-out design and development methods and a continuous analysis throughout the life of the application. Although there is no such concept as guaranteed security, the goal is to create software with security in mind and establish a high degree of protection that makes attack and exploitation difficult or unfeasible.

This chapter presents several guidelines that assist in evaluating and bolstering the security of an application or product through the phases of a development cycle. The approach used here differs from common practice. Many sources of information on secure application development focus on the technicalities of the code and implementation, while ignoring other elements in the process. Security in an application comes not only from the code used to create it. It begins with the initial idea for an application and carries through the design and implementation phases to form a cycle of security analysis. Each of these phases depends on the others to provide the highest level of application security needed and possible. This cycle continues throughout the application's lifespan and should be considered with each of its incarnations, enhancements, or modifications. Managers and nontechnical staff who work in a software-development environment need to understand the role of security within their application, the procedures and methods by which security is created, and the issues they might face as a result of weak or strong security. Software developers and engineers need to understand methods to design and write code with security in mind, as well as the security issues that might arise from their efforts.

Application development includes a wide array of software development efforts. Although this chapter focuses primarily on Internet-related applications, the concepts presented are applicable and important to all forms of software development. The discussion covers software applications that run on the desktop computer or server, Web-based applications, operating system issues, and Internet appliances.

Developers achieve security awareness and thoughtfulness through careful implementation and an aversion to pitfalls. Development managers should emphasize development processes and procedures that enforce security requirements. At the end of this discussion, developers and development managers should be able to establish a procedure for secure application development that includes the creation of a security architecture and the ability to examine the design and implementation for relevant security issues.

What Is a Secure Application?

The concept of a secure application might conjure analogies to a battle-hardened, armored tank, ready to respond to all natures of attack and impervious to all but the strongest bombs. Although such tight security might be the goal in some applications, it is likely the exception rather than the rule. Security should be applied and integrated as is appropriate for the specific task or function at hand. An application cannot be made secure by following a checklist of safeguards that, when put together, spits out an armored application. A secure application emphasizes thoughtful analysis, diligent design, and a focused implementation. Its developers consider the security issues of similar applications and analyze innovations for new risk areas while balancing the level of security required by the users of the application. To make this all happen, it is useful to know the effects of insecurity on an application.

NOTE

The term *application* often refers primarily to one particular program or set of programs. The guidelines presented here are useful and applicable to many forms of software development including Internet and system applications and embedded Internet Appliances. The term *application* should therefore be understood to refer to any of these development efforts, as the concepts are applied to them.

The Enemy Within (Your Code)

Common and well-known attacks such as denial of service, buffer overflows, and race conditions can plague applications with poor methods of input validation and data protection. This section provides a brief overview of common vulnerabilities that need consideration when first developing an application.

TIP

Be sure to consider the relevance and effects of the attacks described here when examining an application under development. Also look at similar applications and those with which the new application competes.

Configuration Issues

Security problems with the configuration of an application and the environment in which it runs are very common. Applications often store configuration information in a file or database, write runtime information to other files, and provide multiple services simultaneously. Default configurations—a computer system's operational settings on installation and without any user modification—can be very dangerous. These out-of-the-box configurations exist to help users run the application with the least amount of effort, but can unwittingly leave them open to attack.

The default configuration often enables every option available in the software, to demonstrate its rich feature set. There is a disadvantage to having every option enabled—the user might not understand or even be aware of the enabled options provided. If a vulnerability is discovered, the user is unknowingly at risk. It is not possible to force a user to read and understand documentation about all configuration options; therefore, a responsible developer thinks carefully about which options are enabled for regular operation and which should remain disabled.

Two well-known examples illustrate the dangers of insecure default configurations. The first example is inetd, the Unix Internet Server daemon.

inetd enables users to access a Unix system via protocols such as Telnet, FTP, and remote shell. (Many other services are available through inetd; see the manual page for inetd for more information.) Typical early versions of inetd had a standard configuration that enabled all its services. Various security holes were found in many of these services, making many systems vulnerable to attack, often without the knowledge of administrators.

NOTE

Note that all software comes with insecure default configuration. Xinetd, which is a more secure inetd replacement, ships with no services started by default. Another example is Postfix, a more secure sendmail replacement, which has a very controlled configuration that does not allow the relaying of spam among its defaults.

Another example of insecure default configurations can be found in Web server software.

Apache on Unix and the Internet Information Server (IIS) from Microsoft are two of the most popular Web server applications in use on the Internet. These Web servers come with sample applications that demonstrate various pieces of functionality. In early versions of Apache and Microsoft Internet Information Server (IIS), these samples had numerous vulnerabilities and were installed by default, allowing attackers to compromise the systems. Many users and administrators were not even aware of the existence of these applications or that they were present on their Web servers. These common holes are still present today and part of the many Web server security analyses.

TIP

Carefully document features when creating them and provide information about them in any configuration files.

Race Conditions

As the name indicates, a *race condition* is a window of opportunity in a running application that enables another process or application to exploit the privilege or functionality of the first. Race conditions can occur when complex or multistep procedures run, when an application interacts with other processes or resources, or when a functionality is poorly organized.

Figure 26.1 shows a simple example of a race condition. An application normally runs with the privileges of its user. The application then enters a section of code that increases the normal privileges and modifies a system setting. Upon completion of the modification, the privileges return to normal. Through a weakness in the implementation, a *rogue application* attempts to "win the race" by exploiting the higher privileges. If the program uses Inter-Process Communication (IPC) or temporary files, or takes a long time to perform the operation and does not protect these methods, the rogue application can insert its own commands, which are executed by the application.

NOTE

An operating system typically supports several methods by which different processes or applications can communicate. These methods are known as *Inter-Process Communication (IPC)* methods; they include the use of sockets-based communication, semaphores, pipes, and shared memory.

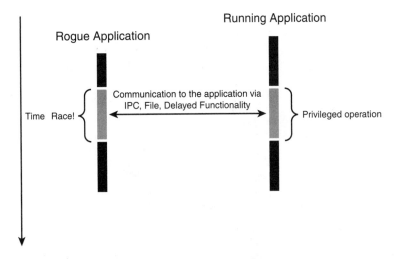

FIGURE 26.1 A race condition: the window of opportunity.

Figure 26.2 demonstrates a race condition with temporary files. In the course of normal execution, the running application makes changes to system settings by creating a temporary file with new settings and then copying that file to the appropriate location. When finished, the running application then deletes the temporary file and continues running. If a window of opportunity exists, during which an attacker can insert his own configuration information into the file after it is created and just prior to its being copied, a race condition is present. This can occur as a result of poorly organized functions, wherein related steps are not grouped logically within the code, or if the temporary file is not properly protected.

The access points of IPC methods such as sockets or shared memory should be initialized with the proper protections, or a rogue application can interact with the application. Good and logically organized code and functionality minimizes the window in which a race condition can occur. Grouping areas of privileged functionality where the code would otherwise repeat multiple privilege increment and decrement calls can do this. Related functionality should also be organized and executed efficiently.

TIP

Before creating a function that requires higher privileges or performs complex interactions with components outside of the application, take a moment to organize the functionality and find an efficient way to write the code. The security of an application is also enhanced by a good design process and code reviews that identify poorly organized code segments.

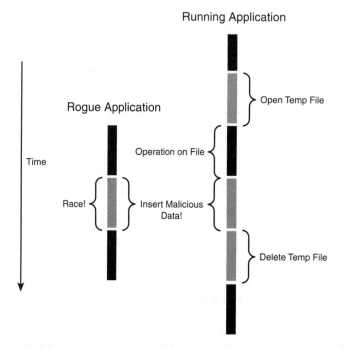

FIGURE 26.2   A temporary file race condition.

Buffer Overflows

Buffer overflows are perhaps the most notorious and widely publicized attacks. These are complex attacks that exploit the fundamental hardware and software capabilities of a system.

For those who are not software developers, a few concepts need explanation. First, it is useful to understand what a *buffer* is. The computer system has a pool of Random Access Memory (RAM) organized into small chunks by the operating system that runs applications. To share this memory among the operating system's many processes and applications, a special memory manager coordinates which chunks of the RAM pool are in use and which are available to run an application. When an application is first run, memory is allocated for the application and all its functions and variables.

As the application runs, more memory can be allocated for new variables and deallocated when no longer in use. A *buffer* is a chunk (or several chunks) of memory used to store a variable. Different buffers can, and often do, exist side-by-side in memory. A buffer that holds a variable can exist next to a piece of memory that holds a function or another application. For example, when you enter your username at a prompt or window, the program has declared a buffer, in which the characters of the name are stored. Figure 26.3 shows a buffer that is used for the username "NAME".

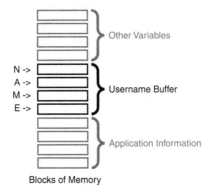

FIGURE 26.3   A buffer that holds the value "NAME".

A buffer overflow occurs when a buffer is too small to accommodate the amount of data provided. The data that does not fit into the buffer will overwrite the next chunks of memory. Herein lies the danger of buffer overflows. The memory that is overwritten with the extra data can be another variable in the running application, a variable for another application, or the application's stack. The *stack* contains application-specific information, such as the physical locations of the application's functions and variables.

This alters the path that the application would normally follow, causing it to use bad data, crash, or execute new functionality. The execution of new functionality is usually the goal of a buffer overflow exploit—whether to provide access to the system or to modify its settings.

When its owner accesses the overwritten memory next, the new data might be invalid, and the application can crash or function improperly. Buffer overflows are exploited by crafting the overflow data into something useful that the machine can understand. This could mean executing another program, causing harm to the system or stealing information.

To better demonstrate this concept, consider the postal machine that scans letters for their destination city. Assume envelope A is destined for New York, NY, and envelope B is destined for Boston, MA. The ZIP code of envelope B has special wet ink that "overflows," overwriting the ZIP code of New York on envelope A with that of Boston when the envelopes are automatically stacked at the postal facility. The postal machine scans envelope A and reads the overwritten ZIP code. The letter is then routed to Boston.

Buffer overflows are often more malicious than mere accidents, so let's assume that a valuable sum of cash is destined for a postal box in New York. The thief, or attacker, knows the exact location of the letter and creates an envelope with runny ink that overwrites the ZIP code on the envelope with the ZIP code for Boston when they are stacked. The attacker rents the Boston postal box with the same number as the original destination in New York and proceeds to steal the money.

A postal machine is only capable of recognizing ZIP codes, no matter from where they come. A computer is capable of executing instructions, no matter from where they come. Therefore, a buffer overflow attack that overwrites the original instructions of an application with new instructions can cause the computer to execute anything an attacker wants.

The exploitation of a buffer overflow in an application is an extremely dangerous problem. Figure 26.4 demonstrates the memory layout of a typical buffer overflow. The application developer declares a buffer that will hold an 8-character username. An attacker tests for an overflow by entering a 10-character name, myusername, at the prompt. The program then starts to copy that name to the previously declared buffer, but the name is 10 letters; the last 2 letters overflow the buffer and crash the program. After confirming that a buffer overflow exists, the attacker crafts a special set of input made of valid machine instructions that executes a malicious program to steal passwords on a system. The attacker then uses this special input set as the input to the username prompt of the affected program, again causing a buffer overflow. Now, the memory is corrupted with these new instructions in such a way that they are executed, causing the malicious program to run and cause harm.

TIP

The solution to the buffer overflow problem is covered later in this chapter, in the section called "Secure Coding Practices."

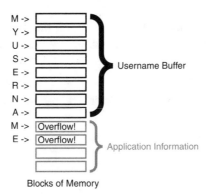

FIGURE 26.4 The memory layout of a buffer overflow.

TIP

For in-depth technical detail on buffer overflows, the following articles are useful resources:

"Compromised—Buffer—Overflows, from Intel to SPARC Version 8" by Mudge, a gifted hacker and VP of @Stake, a top security consulting firm.

`http://www.atstake.com/research/advisories/1996/bufitos.pdf`

"The Tao of Windows Buffer Overflow" by DilDog, another gifted hacker of @Stake.

`http://www.cultdeadcow.com/cDc_files/cDc-351/`

"Smashing the Stack for Fun and Profit" by Aleph1 of SecurityFocus.com, originally issue 49 of the *Phrack* online magazine.

`http://www.shmoo.com/phrack/Phrack49/p49-14`

Data Protection

The scope of data protection is broad—it extends from the internal methods of an application out to the operating system and all the systems to which it connects. This description focuses on data protection within an application and the operating system in which it runs. These concepts can then be extended to interconnected systems.

Applications seldom function completely independently of the underlying operating system and other applications. There are many ways for an application to interact with its operating system. Information is often shared via the previously mentioned IPC mechanisms, and files are a common method by which information is stored, manipulated, or moved within a system.

It is important to remember that, in most cases, the application and its operating system are using the same physical processor and memory—while this might seem obvious, the security ramifications are often forgotten. A developer cannot assume that the memory used by an application is accessible only by that application. The underlying operating system controls access to memory and therefore has access to all memory available—whether used or unused. If an application is using and manipulating information that should be considered secret, it is vital to protect internal data. Important and secret information such as passwords and encryption keys require special handling. Without the proper protection and initialization, exploiting operating system functionality can access this information. Establishing authentication and access control methods can protect data. These mechanisms validate the sender of a message within the system and determine which processes, applications, and systems can access a particular resource.

Temporary Storage

Temporary storage in files is not itself a vulnerability, but it merits discussion, because it exacerbates the problems of data protection and race conditions.

Temporary storage is used when manipulating information, such as application or system configuration files, and when updating other data stored in files. When temporary files are initialized with weak security, an application becomes vulnerable to attacks that allow unexpected information to be inserted into the files. Weak security in temporary files is defined by the permissions that allow or disallow an outsider to access the contents of the file and by the predictability of the filename. An attacker who knows the name of the temporary file prior to its creation already has a jump on the race condition. At the moment when the file is created and initialized, an attacker can attempt to modify it. The race then begins to insert data before the function finishes and removes the file. The results of an exploit vary depending on the use of the temporary storage; typical examples are modification of a system configuration and the alteration of user information and application data.

TIP

When using temporary files, check for their existence during initialization of the routine and set permissions to restrict access only to the application. It is also recommended that the filename be randomized to make it hard for crackers to guess. Finally, remember to delete the temporary file when you are done with it.

Denial of Service

Denial-of-service attacks, which are described in more detail in Chapter 16, "Denial-of-Service Tools," are a common form of attack, and can be initiated from the network or on a local system. These attacks exploit a design's failure to address the negative events in an application. Applications should be developed with an understanding of the functionality they provide and the functionality they do not provide. This enables the developer to build safeguards into the application that protect it from denial of service. These attacks come in several flavors—network bandwidth saturation, system resource utilization, and application flaws.

Network bandwidth saturation results when the entire capacity of a network link is filled with data, preventing new communications from proceeding and slowing down those already in progress. This occurs when the network hardware, which is a specialized computer, is unable to process new network data quickly enough. Therefore, the network hardware is overcome, causing delays in new network traffic or even its complete cessation.

System resource utilization is similar to network bandwidth saturation, except the saturation occurs on the individual system instead of the network wire to which it attaches. System resources—memory, disk storage, processor utilization, and operating system–specific features such as processes and files—all have limits; physical limitations of the hardware naturally reflect on the limitations within the operating system. Examples of physical limitations to a system are the amount of memory and disk storage available and how fast a processor can execute instructions. Examples of operating system–specific limitations that are dependent on the hardware configuration are the number of files and processes that can exist and the number of users who can work simultaneously.

System-based denial of service exploits the confines of these limitations by using all the available resources of the target. These attacks come in many forms. Many operating systems stop functioning properly when all the disk storage space or memory is used. Users can be denied access if the maximum number of users is exceeded. A processor can be completely utilized by endless complex functions, causing all other functions to slow or halt. An application that creates multiple processes can cease to function if the process limits of the system are met.

Developers can be misled into believing that these network and system limits make it impossible to avoid or prevent denial-of-service attacks, but this is not the case. Strong design and implementation of an application can overcome and protect against denial of service and many other forms of attack. There are caveats, however—the nature of the Internet creates situations wherein factors beyond the control of the developer are present. It is impossible to completely eliminate all possibilities for attack, because of the Internet's dependencies on external environments. The goal then becomes to establish an environment that makes it difficult for an attack to succeed. Forethought and analysis in the design and development of an application limit the situations in which an attack succeeds.

To help safeguard against denial of service in networked applications, it can be useful to set high-watermarks within the application that limit and detect abnormally frequent connection attempts, such as 20 connections-per-second for a given service. These abnormalities might be signs of denial of service if an attacker is attempting to starve the resources of the system. Other protections include resource monitoring and limitation that give the application complete control of its execution.

TIP

To protect against denial-of-service attacks, begin to consider where potential vulnerabilities exist in an application. Start early in the design phase and continue the analysis through the completion of the application.

Input and Output Methods

User-supplied or external input is the most obvious and prevalent point of entry for attacking an application. Whether data is coming from a network, from a keyboard connected to the system, or from a user environment, the security of the input method demands careful consideration. These functions are the doorways to the application for many of the aforementioned attacks; they enable the user to alter the path of the running application by providing different inputs. Application design and implementation must have a defined set of criteria for input. This includes the explicit data types and values that are and are not acceptable, the reaction to unacceptable data, and the path of that data through the application.

TIP

Be careful in any application that creates files or accesses the command line based on input. Every operating system has special metacharacters that, if not screened out of the input, can enable the cracker to execute any command she wants on the system. Metacharacters are covered later in this chapter in the section titled "Operating System Interactions."

Application output can also pose a risk when users blindly write data to files, terminals, or devices. It is equally important to validate output before actually committing the data. The conditions that allow for successful output should be defined and documented to provide a level of assurance within the application that any outbound information has been checked. Application output often uses external functionality provided by the operating system or another application; therefore, it is extremely important to provide some protection methods before setting the data out into the wild where it could react poorly with the external elements.

TIP

Criteria for user-supplied input should be defined, and associated functionality should be developed to support its validation. These criteria should outline what is and is not acceptable. Anytime that externally defined data crosses the boundary of an application or module, it should be validated.

A Security Architecture

A security architecture for an application outlines a comprehensive method for the development of highly reliable and secure applications. It establishes a process and a framework by which the security needs of an application are analyzed, defined, and implemented. This section explores in detail several components that constitute a security architecture.

Components of a Security Architecture

A comprehensive security architecture is best achieved through an increasingly granular approach that begins from an external viewpoint and progresses through the details of the implementation. The following components organize the information needed for the creation of an application's security architecture:

- Risk assessment and response

- Security requirements

- Design phase security

- Implementation phase security

Set the Stage for Security

Risk assessment is an important process in the development of any product or application. The creation of an application begins with the spark of an idea. It is likely that this application idea solves a problem or provides new usefulness or innovation that was previously done ineffectively or inefficiently, or not at all, by existing applications. Although analysis is done to determine the shortcomings in function of the older applications, security considerations are often forgotten. The tendency to focus strictly on the functionality an application provides and the benefits to the explicit dilemma it solves increases the potential for security risk. It is extremely important to solve the security problems of an application, as well as the functional problems.

Therefore, the first stage in the creation of an application's security architecture is to document the risks inherent in existing applications that are to be replaced by the new creation. Developers should also note risks related to an application with which the new program will interact. The new application often faces all the security issues that similar applications face, as well as new issues that arise from innovation.

Assessing the security risks of an application requires some diligence on the part of the application designers; if the designers have any level of security experience, the effort to assess risks quickly becomes smaller. The most basic research that identifies the security issues with related applications involves a search through the archives of vendor-specific support issues. The Web sites of these organizations generally have special areas and forums that announce the availability of patches to security problems in their applications. This research gives a sense of the common issues faced by the new application and the functionality it provides. Further research in security-specific forums provides more technical detail regarding the natures of the problems, as well as a broader sense of the security issues related to a specific application area.

As vulnerabilities in the pertinent technical areas are researched, it is important to document them. Creating a list of security risks and vulnerabilities helps establish a scope for the application under development by determining which issues are likely to affect the new development.

The known vulnerabilities of an existing application can provide hints toward the presence or lack of a security architecture in its design. The vulnerabilities can often be categorized as implementation flaws, design flaws, and functional flaws. *Implementation flaws* relate to the actual code used to make the application; they provide only a small amount of insight to the security architecture. Implementation security is discussed in detail later in the chapter. *Design and functional flaws* reflect the thought and effort put into the design of the application. An application with a security architecture highlights and strengthens the functionality by making security awareness an inherent part of it. Shortcomings in design and function leave holes in the thoroughness of functionality, often creating security risks.

Consider the Functionality *Not* Provided

Strong designs recognize the functionality provided, as well as that which is not provided. The most basic level of functionality possible is defining what an application does. This is done under a completely positive view because it outlines only what an application does under the most pristine circumstances. It naively assumes that the world is perfect and that nothing bad will ever happen when the application is running. This means that all inputs will be completely understandable and fit the expected input "mold"—for example, "All usernames will be alphanumeric values of a determined length and no user will, accidentally or otherwise, enter a character that is not either a number or letter." This view also assumes that all network connections would be from known clients, and that these clients would all communicate with the proper protocol—for example, "All clients connecting to the application will adhere to the known messaging sequence required to perform the defined communication." Finally, it assumes that all interaction with the operating system occurs in a sterile environment that the application expects—for example, "Each and every file that is modified always exists and is correctly formatted." Obviously, this is not necessarily the case and cannot be expected. Unfortunately, many applications rarely make it beyond this level of design. A comprehensive design takes into consideration the imperfections in the real world. A design of this nature recognizes that establishing rules and schemes provides reliability.

Considering both positive and negative scenarios for an application's operation is vital when creating it. The negative view defines the reaction to unknown input, invalid syntax and communications, and anomalous conditions that might occur. The application needs to respond properly to events that are not expected or defined. Table 26.1 compares a basic design versus a more comprehensive design and the effects each has on user input, file access, and client connections.

TABLE 26.1   Effects of Basic Versus More Comprehensive Security Design on Application Functions

Application Function	With Basic Design	With Comprehensive Design
User Input	Application receives invalid input and crashes because the non-alphanumeric value is misunderstood.	Application examines the input for invalid values and responds with an error message, indicating a non-alphanumeric value was found.

TABLE 26.1 Continued

Application Function	With Basic Design	With Comprehensive Design
File Access	Application expects to find a database file in the proper format, ready and waiting for access. Instead, an ill-formatted file or a link to another file by that name is opened, data becomes corrupted, and the application crashes.	Application checks for the existence of a named file that is of the appropriate type, as well as the internal format of the file.
Client Connections	Application expects a client to connect with the first message being "hello." If a client connects connects and transmits any other value, the application waits indefinitely, disallowing any other client from connecting, and is no longer functioning.	Application validates the transmission and responds with a warning indicating that the received message was an unexpected value.

The degree to which designers and developers formulate answers to negative results plays a significant factor in the reliability and security of an application. Although it is often difficult and infeasible to explicitly handle every known exception, general rules can easily be created to handle undesired events. These three examples present extremely simple scenarios that might seem unrealistic, but all have occurred more than once in many applications.

Come Here for Guaranteed Security

This discussion would be incomplete without mention of third-party organizations, whether commercial or public domain, that provide security software, development kits, and hardware to enhance the security of applications. Many of these commercial organizations present their products as providing "guaranteed" security.

However, there is no hardware or software substitute for a well-thought-out design. Often, managers, designers, and developers are led to believe that the addition of some complex and expensive security components offered by a commercial security organization provides "guaranteed" security. This is simply untrue; "guaranteed" security is a fallacy. This concept preys on victims who understand security as a feature or component that can be plugged in for immediate security satisfaction. If only one bit of information is gleaned from these pages, let it be the fact that *security is a continuous process*!

Few applications are devoid of security components, but it is not sufficient to simply incorporate the most commonly known components to render a design or implementation secure. The inclusion of security components without consideration for their use does not enhance the security of an application and can, in fact, hinder it. The products offered by security companies are very valuable and useful when used properly, but they cannot guarantee the security of an application. The inclusion of third-party security technologies should be examined for usefulness and value, given the security requirements that are established for the application.

Security Requirements

In conjunction with identifying related security risks known to a specific application or application genre, developers must assess the security requirements for their application. This analysis should arrive at a balanced measurement of the level of security required for an application. It does not have to ponder the extremes of the security spectrum. Given the understanding that true and guaranteed security is nonexistent, protecting against known risks and minimizing the number of successful attacks and their effects is generally an acceptable level of security. Those involved with the development cycle of the application should determine their own "acceptable" security level by examining the known risks, the goals of the application, and the methods used to implement the desired security level.

To arrive at security requirements, managers and developers can find it useful to concentrate on the following commonly known risk areas:

- User authentication and access control

- Data storage of confidential information

- Security in external network communications

- Security of entry points for external applications and the operating system

From these four general areas, application designers and developers can identify a minimal set of important features to analyze. Depending on the functionality of the application, some risk areas are more pertinent than others.

To Secure or Not to Secure

The addition of security to an application affects an application in several ways. It immediately becomes more complex because the code path takes a new turn to accommodate the security methods. The performance of an application might be hindered, especially with the addition of encryption operations. These operations are CPU intensive because of the complex algorithms involved. The efficiency of an application can also be sacrificed if security is applied in areas where it provides few benefits. This can occur if security methods are blindly applied to all components of an application without thought to their requirements. The following sections provide a reasonable starting point to determine a basic level of security requirements.

TIP

It is a good practice to consider the security required for each module or component within an application. Resist the urge to apply blanket security methods across multiple modules or components. Instead, determine the most suitable level of security for each.

Assessing Authentication and Access Control Requirements

User authentication is often handled by the operating system on which the application runs, but several classes of application might need to deal with authentication on its own. Embedded applications, applications that function independently of the operating system, and distributed Web applications often need to accommodate some level of user authentication and access control. Common examples of applications that require these security methods are Internet commerce (e-commerce) applications, wherein users make purchases via a Web site or customer database access. In both cases, the possibility for many different users or groups of users to use the system requires stringent control of accessible data. The applications need methods to allow separate users to access the systems via a login method; they also need restrictions regarding the individual users' respective financial data.

To determine the authentication and access-control requirements, designers should examine the interactions within the application and with the world that surrounds it. This includes the methods by which users access the application—sitting directly at a terminal or accessing from the network are two methods that might require different authentication schemes. An application that is accessed only while sitting at the desktop can effectively be secured via the authentication methods of the operating system on which it runs. Network applications that are accessed by multiple users simultaneously, or through which users access data from common databases, provide strong impetus for access control and authentication. The level of granularity and flexibility of the access control and authentication capabilities provided by the operating system help determine if proprietary methods should be developed. Standalone or embedded applications are often developed from scratch and therefore require their own specialized methods.

Requirements for Data Storage

Data storage reflects the method used to store private and sensitive information. This includes the correct use of the file protection methods of the underlying operating system (such as restricted file permissions) and stronger methods of protecting individual data elements (such as encryption). In many cases, the use of operating system permission methods is sufficient to provide the required degree of security. Encryption can be used to protect extremely sensitive data, such as user credentials and credit information.

The level to which the application needs to store data and the nature of that data drive the requirements for data storage security. The storage of sensitive information is often the gating factor in determining if high security encryption is needed. User credentials, such as passwords, addresses, phone numbers, and financial data, should be considered sensitive and also treated with high security. Configuration information can often be secured sufficiently with standard file permission methods.

When forming the requirements for data storage, designers might be tempted to standardize on one level of security. For instance, if a password is stored in a configuration file along with other nonsensitive information, the temptation might be strong to use encryption on the entire file as a blanket security method. To determine data storage requirements, examine the needs of all components involved. In this example, applying encryption to nonsensitive data might be considered inefficient because of the computational expense of the encryption operations, as well as the lack of granular control of the other information in the file. A single element cannot be accessed easily if the entire file is encrypted. The complexity involved to access other elements is then increased dramatically.

Network and Entry Point Security Requirements

Applications communicate to users, the operating system, and other applications through entry points. These might be on the same machine as the application or across a network; often, they are on both. The methods for providing entry points to the application and support for network communication are often one and the same; therefore, they are grouped together here.

Security of network communications is best addressed by examining the content of the messages being sent. Applications that utilize network communication for informational messaging or passing static data might not require any stronger reliability than the protocol supports. Again, as in the case of Internet commerce, an application that sends and receives sensitive user information likely warrants the addition of a higher security method. Entry points also determine security requirements for applications that communicate in a networked environment.

The entry points to an application require a high level of analysis because they encompass and provide the network communication functionality. Others also interact with the application through the entry points. These functional areas can be protected via a combination of available operating system methods and the defined access control and authentication schemes used within the application. Analysis of the interactions that an application has with the outside world allows the designers to determine the most suitable level of security needed. These interactions and subsequent entry points are categorized as

- Network interaction

- Interaction with other applications

- Interaction with its respective operating system

- User interaction via keyboard and mouse

These categories are well-known functional areas, and designers probably already know if their application interacts in any of these manners. The next step is to consider each area's security.

Network, Application, and System Interactions   Network interaction can be present at several levels. An application can be completely client/server–oriented, for use on remote systems spread across the Internet. The need for security in these applications becomes considerably more complex than it is in standalone applications.

Several dependencies should be discerned. The level to which the developers want to provide security mechanisms in the application should be considered. The designers might decide not to provide any internal security mechanisms. The security of the networked application then relies on the security of the networks on which it runs and communicates; the network topology and firewall determine the maximum level of security that an application can experience. The designer might choose to eschew dependencies and provide the highest degree of security possible within the application. These are the two extremes—most applications fall somewhere in the middle.

Applications can also use network facilities for localized communication that is not destined to go beyond the confines of the system on which it runs. Consideration should be given to the nature of this communication to determine if the implementation creates unnecessary risk.

The need for interaction between applications or with the operating system does not imply a requirement for network communication. Designers should investigate the implementation methods that provide the required functionality. Applications often use sockets-based communication methods to provide these entry points because they are fast and easily implemented. The use of sockets can provide more functionality than is needed, however. Applications that need to communicate only with other applications on the local system or with their own operating systems have many communication methods at their disposal, such as non-Internet sockets and IPC mechanisms.

Commonly, Unix systems use socket communications because of their ease of use and the plethora of documentation. Unix supports several flavors of sockets-based communication, two of which are the popular IP socket and Unix domain sockets.

IP sockets, as the name implies, use the IP protocol for communication, and support remote network communication, which allows local and remote processes to communicate with the application. Many applications that communicate only with processes on a local system and that do not require network communication capabilities use IP sockets as a standard interface. IP sockets are not ideal in this situation because they automatically provide access to local and remote clients.

Domain sockets use an internal Unix protocol for communication and do not support network communication; they do provide a connection-oriented communications channel. Domain sockets have their share of risks if used improperly. Unix domain sockets support the passing of file descriptors as well as informational data. This means that pointers or handles to other parts of the system can be passed from one application to another. This functionality is available only in Unix domain sockets. If this capability is not desired or warranted, diversion from sockets-based communication to another IPC mechanism might be a better choice.

Considering the kind of information sent to and from the application helps define the requirements for its communication method. Designers should evaluate the interaction capabilities of the application before incorporating a standard function. In this example, the application using IP sockets is at risk because it enables remote systems to connect to the application when they should not be allowed. A better design documents the requirement for interaction with only local applications. This comprehensive requirement leads the developer to use something other than IP sockets.

NOTE

For in-depth information about programming with sockets and Inter-Process Communication, see the following well-known books on the subject:

UNIX Network Programming, Volume 1: Networking APIs—Sockets and XTI by W. Richard Stevens. Prentice Hall. ISBN: 013490012X.

UNIX Network Programming, Volume 2: Interprocess Communications by W. Richard Stevens. Prentice Hall. ISBN: 0130810819.

Operating System Interactions   Interaction with the operating system often creates another level of security issues. Many levels of interaction can occur with an operating system—network interaction, Inter-Process Communication, and the manipulation of files have already been mentioned. Two other types of interaction also require attention: The execution of external programs and the use of system and other externally defined calls are common sources of exploitation. Important issues such as permissions, authentication, access control, and input validation should be considered in conjunction with operating system interactions.

Because of their natures, system calls and external applications present a high degree of risk when used improperly. These functions often exist in libraries that are used by many applications simultaneously and that often provide direct access to operating system components and resources. Exploitation of a single application through these functions can affect several applications and the system.

System calls provide access to many general-purpose and system-specific functionalities. They allow an application to interact with specific hardware components as well as kernel-level functionality. The safety of the operating system and components needs to be considered when using system calls. If an application ties together user or network data with the operating system via system calls, designers must minimize exposure to dangerous, unexpected, and improper data.

The execution of external applications is another common, unsecured interaction. Developers often design an application to call upon other applications by various methods. There are several reasons a developer might want to do this, such as to differentiate between functions or to establish environmental control. Calling other applications also allows developers to use existing functionality and to expedite the application's implementation.

There is an inherent danger in calling another program from within an application—the external program can rarely be trusted. The application exists in a dynamic environment where it is possible to modify or replace any program. The problem lies in the methods used to call the application. Unix-based systems often support functions called system() and exec(), which pass the supplied parameters as a string to the execution of the standard Unix shell and subprocess, respectively. The system() call returns to the calling program when complete, but exec() terminates the running program and replaces it with the called program. Windows-based systems have the exec() call that allows the execution of other programs. Unlike Unix, the Windows version of exec() runs the specified program in a subprocess, and the calling function does not terminate. Without input validation, attackers can put shell metacharacters into the input stream, forcing the shell to run possibly harmful commands and parameters. The use of these functions is generally frowned upon, and effort should be made to avoid their use because they allow the execution of untrusted and uncontrolled applications. Alternatively, designers can incorporate the required functionality directly into an application. The use of freely available, open-source software greatly decreases the effort needed to do so.

NOTE

Metacharacters are characters that take on special meaning in a given context. For example, within the standard Unix shell, the semicolon (;) is a command separator, that is, many commands can be put on a single line when a semicolon is between them. The pipe (|) character sends terminal output to whatever follows the pipe, allowing the output from one program to be fed into another.

Many operating systems also allow functionality to run at different privilege levels. Unix has its "root" privileges; Windows has "Administrator" and "SYSTEM" privileges. These special accounts can perform administrative tasks and have more interaction with the operating system and its services than other accounts do. Programs can be written to elevate privilege levels when specialized functionality is needed. An application and the operating system on which it runs can be compromised if privileges are not carefully controlled.

The model of least privilege suggests that an application should run with the minimum set of privileges needed to perform most functions. Functionality that requires higher privileges should be isolated into its own module, however that is defined—as a process, a class, an application, or even another system. Even then, that set of functionality should also run at the least privileged level until those elevated privileges are required. At that time, higher privileges should be obtained, and upon completion of the functionality, privileges should be returned to the minimum level.

Throw Away That Security Blanket

Some application developers choose to forget or ignore security within their applications and put themselves at the mercy of the customer's network or operating system and its security features. Using this blanket security model shuns the responsibility to provide secure applications to the public. The security philosophy advocated in this chapter purports a strong and comprehensive security ideology that assumes nothing about the security of components external to the application. An application should always be as secure as it can be with respect to itself and the external components with which it interacts. The level of follow-through is left to the discretion of the designer or developer, however.

Identification of the Risk Areas

As stated, a good process for application development includes the definition of a strong security architecture. This provides a new level of comprehensiveness that fosters analysis and provides a documented overview of potential security problems, as well as the methods for resolving them. When creating a security architecture for an application, possible attacks can be classified in the following categories:

- Subversion of the application

- Subversion of the system and external applications

- Cessation of functionality

Often, an attacker's goal is to gain access to resources or assume control of an application or the system on which it runs. Short of this, an application can simply be forced to crash, which can also cause the entire system to crash.

Subversion of the application occurs when the attacker causes the application to do something it was not intended to do or to execute some level of unintended functionality. These vulnerabilities are broad in nature and effect. Exploitation of buffer overflows, race conditions, and data input are examples. The effects are limited to the running application.

Subversion of the system and external applications occurs when the exploit affects other running applications or system resources. This can include execution of other applications, such as a shell in Unix, or utilization of a connection to another application using the vulnerabilities outlined here. The effects of the attack are not limited to the running application, and that application is often used as a conduit to other systems, applications, and the operating system.

An application can completely cease to function and crash due to attacks. This is a form of denial of service that targets the limitations of the application rather than the network or operating system. Applications that are well designed and securely coded provide a high level of security and reliability that protects against denial of service.

Security Response

After the risks and requirements are identified, the response to these issues is the logical next step. Identification of potential security issues is not very useful without a known path to protect against those risks. The defense methods become a natural part of the design in this phase of the development cycle.

Knowledge of the various vulnerabilities, interactions, and areas of analysis discussed previously form the basis of a security response. Knowing the relationship of existing vulnerabilities in the target environment and in similar applications establishes the minimum level of security required. Ideally, the new application provides more security than its predecessors and competitors by addressing all the known vulnerabilities and analyzing for new issues. The next steps involve a careful look at all the interactions within and around the application. It's useful to start at the external view and progress inward through the application. To define areas that need higher security, analyze all methods by which the application communicates and interacts with the network, operating system, and other applications. Analysis of the information passed across these channels further clarifies the security requirements.

Security-Aware Designs

The security of an application depends on the comprehensiveness of thought and analysis done during the application's design phase and prior to its actual implementation. The design phase ties together all the requirements and considerations outlined during the early gestational phases of the application idea and provides an explicit implementation path. The concept of security in software development is often ignored during the initial stages and sometimes throughout the life span of a development effort or is viewed as a feature that can simply be added at a later point. Security is not a feature, but an integral part of all phases of a software development cycle. Good security arises from a combination of good processes, good practices, and continuous analysis. The earlier an organization introduces security analysis to the development cycle, the stronger the application will be. This section suggests a process by which the elements of secure application development can be implemented and enforced.

Design Phase Analysis

A comprehensive design provides solutions to the problem addressed by the product and also takes into consideration the effects of the innovation. The security of an application is also created and enhanced by a comprehensive design.

After an organization discards the idea of security as a feature, it becomes apparent that security needs consideration early. Although each organization might have different methods of designing a product or application, the following approach is useful to assure a high level of security in a design. The design phase is analyzed from three viewpoints:

- Global

- Organizational

- Component

The *global viewpoint* is the highest view of the system; it identifies the needs addressed by the application and its feature set. The *organizational viewpoint* highlights the individual components that make up the application. The *component viewpoint* goes to the next level of granularity by examining the explicit details of each module (subsystem, function, and so on) and its implementation. The incremental approach used here allows for a deeper and more comprehensive analysis that also provides an easily understood process flow. This helps managers and developers put the appropriate procedures into place to assure the consideration of security in their application.

The Global Viewpoint

Many applications arise from an unfulfilled need or the inadequacy of current solutions. A good design identifies the following security concerns:

- Security issues related to existing solutions to the problem or the need being solved

- The application's response to those security issues

- The potential security vulnerabilities that exist in the innovations being made

A global analysis provides information that an attacker would otherwise find after the application is released. At this phase, a security architecture should be defined for the application. This architecture formalizes the level of security needed in an application. It helps establish the application's security scope by identifying the relationship of the application to its surroundings and the level of security provided by them. A security architecture also highlights the need for, and amount of, independent security that an application must provide, as well as the features required.

A global analysis and establishment of a security architecture are done via the incremental categorization of the modules, components, interfaces, and methods used in the application. Their location and relationship to each other and their exposure to external applications, users, and interfaces are important points.

The global viewpoint of an application initially presents the proverbial "black box"—the only details known are those seen by outsiders. These external features and functional requirements are then separated into *modules* for security analysis.

Searching vendor advisories, newsgroups, mailing lists, and online forums for disclosed vulnerabilities in competing or similar applications is a good way to learn about some of the major security issues related to the application. It also helps point out ineffective solutions to vulnerabilities found in similar applications.

Case Study Phase I   This hypothetical example is a case study for the development of an Internet commerce application. It will be used throughout the remainder of the chapter to exemplify the guidelines and information presented here. This service allows users to connect from their browsers to make online purchases.

The first level in the design of this application is the definition of its capabilities, independent of the implementation methods used. These features might include the following:

- The selection of an appropriate operating system to host the applications

- Database access for storage of private and public information

- Web serving

- Connectivity of these parts using custom-developed applications

- Connectivity to financial institutions for the transactions

From the global viewpoint, a designer discerns the security features required for each component of these functions.

The database stores private information on many different users, including passwords, credit card numbers, and contact information. To protect this information, the database should have security components that support restrictions to objects and perhaps their encryption.

The Web server should support secure communications with the Secure Sockets Layer (SSL) protocol and some method of interfacing with external applications and the database. This could be via Java servlets and applets or CGI programs.

Network communications are an inherent part of this system. The Web server and database server software probably run on separate machines, hence, a means to secure the network communication between them is required.

The last component to be considered is the actual connection to the organization that authorizes the transactions. This could be a bank or credit card company that authorizes the expenditures by users. Connections are likely accomplished with a modem or other piece of telecommunications equipment that interacts with the financial organization and performs the validation. These connections require high security to avoid access by unauthorized users.

These insights are gleaned from knowledge of the field, analysis of competing products, and familiarity with customer requirements. At this point, diligent research needs to be done to document past and current security vulnerabilities in related products. The resulting list should identify the risk areas that need addressing. Security features missing from the initial requirements list are often identified through this analysis, another of its benefits.

In our Internet commerce example, researchers found the following vulnerabilities in comparable products:

- Databases had no protection schemes, resulting in the exposure of private customer information.

- The Web server had holes that allowed the execution of arbitrary code on the system. The server's default configuration also allowed directory traversal, which allows external users to access many private files and directories on the system.

- The CGI applications used to communicate with the database had vulnerabilities that allowed remote attackers to impersonate other customers.

The research also indicates that data protection, buffer overflows, default configuration, and input validation issues need to be avoided, because these vulnerabilities occurred frequently with similar applications. It also showed that vendors have added security features and patches that will protect against these problems. This makes authentication and access control important requirements, along with network security.

At this point, the designer knows of vulnerabilities associated with the application, the methods by which other organizations respond to them, and a set of important security features that form the basis of a security architecture. The security architecture develops further in the next phase of design.

The Organizational Viewpoint

Security is not an exact science; its needs are specific to each application and environment. Therefore, it is not sufficient to look at security from only the global view. Although an otherwise well-designed application might exist independently of all other applications on the system, the interaction of all components in that application might pose security threats. The organizational viewpoint identifies the individual elements or groups of elements that form the entire application, their functions, and their relationships with each other. An element could be a function, a class, a process, or a set of these elements that are grouped by their relationship to the application.

An application is typically made of several functional modules, such as the user interface, networking or communication components, or data storage and retrieval tools.

Although a module might seem reasonably secure, its relationship with the other components might be executed insecurely. Similar to the analysis of the interactions of the application, organizational level analysis takes the functional requirements and determines the architecture used. The functional requirements allow the designer to identify a set of components and methods that provide the functionality; an analysis of the security between them as they interact yields the safest choices for inclusion with the application.

The incremental identification, organization, and categorization of each component in the application continue in this phase. A logical place to begin—and particularly suspect in terms of security—is the edges of a module. The *edges* are the entry or exit points where data crosses the boundaries between modules. For example, data crosses boundaries between modules during these functions:

- Passing of data as parameters
- Setting global variables
- Manipulating shared memory
- Writing data to files
- Sending data across a communication channel such as the network
- Receiving user input

Case Study Phase II   In the organizational phase of designing the sample Internet commerce application, each application component—the Web server, the database server, and the associated applications—is categorized into its functional module for further analysis.

The database server has a storage component, an authentication and access control component, and a communication component. The Web server has the Web serving component, an external programming model, and secure client communication and secure database communication components. Interactions between these components form a definable path, with several points where security must be strong. Following an interaction between the Web server and the customer, a client Web browser transmits sensitive data to the Web server. This data is then passed to the custom application that interacts with the database and the financial institution. Following the data path through the application, a developer can observe points of vulnerability in the client communication, the Web server application interaction, the communication from the Web server to the database, and the interaction between them.

The security requirements begin to take shape. The application must address these risk areas and provide security in these forms:

- Secure communication to the client Web browser in the form of encrypted network communication, authentication of users, and access control mechanisms on their information

- Safe interaction between the Web browser and the e-commerce application to ensure the safety of the system

- Application integrity of the commerce program

- Secure communications with the database

- Security of database objects

From these requirements, an architecture begins to take shape. The use of SSL on the Web server protects the server-to-browser communications. The application will have its own authentication mechanism that allows clients to sign in safely. Data validation and protection mechanisms will also be implemented in an organized fashion that uses only the minimum required privilege to operate. Functionality will be incorporated into the application for object protection and encryption on the database server. The actual implementation details will be developed in the final component phase.

Pertinent security methods will rise to the surface when the following questions are asked in the organizational phase:

- How will we protect information passed?

- What are the effects if one module passes spurious data to another?

- Have the constraints of the data been defined?

- Is there a preferred method of passing data that lends itself to increased security?

- Which components, applications, and users need access to the data? What kind of access is required—read-only or both read and write capabilities?

The Component Viewpoint

The final viewpoint from which design analysis occurs is the dissection of the individual components within an application. The smallest design and implementation details can introduce obvious and obscure security problems that are difficult to find post-release. Poor implementation can also undo the effort put into the security of a design.

Some of the precautions suggested here fall into what are considered good coding practices and are not necessarily security specific, but they do have an effect on the security of an application.

The security architecture that is defined for an application will mandate that there be a series of checks and balances to which the application must conform. These checks and balances will provide a high degree of assurance that an application acts in a uniform manner in the event of unexpected data or information.

The component view examines each piece that forms a module. (Modules, in turn, form the application.) These components should be analyzed for their individual security features and the interactions with other components within that module. Starting points when examining programmatic issues within a module are

- Return values and exceptions

- Precedence and prerequisites

- Data validation

- Identified response and recovery

- Permissions and privilege

Return values and exceptions are indicators of success or failure within a function. The difference is that a return value always occurs, whereas an exception only happens in the event of failure. Components of an individual module are made of functions, which interoperate and have established relationships that allow the program to perform properly. Developers should also understand what it means when a function fails, and should react appropriately to that failure. A complete understanding of these relationships allows a developer to understand the dependencies between functionalities. Based on these dependencies, components within a module can be organized to enhance reliability and security.

Data is dynamic in any application—it travels between functions and modules, and to separate applications, altering the execution of the initial application as it does so. With the identification of the modules that form an application, and the components that subsequently form those modules, the path of data through an entire application can be traced. The entry points between modules and functions are the pivotal elements that affect the success or failure of the application, therefore, validating data at these points is vital. Working hand-in-hand with validation is a defined response to invalid data and anomalous conditions. Many applications fail to formulate a recovery mechanism in the event of unexpected events; this often results in unstable applications that crash at the earliest sign of imperfect data.

Case Study Phase III   The component phase analysis of our Internet commerce application looks at the individual components used in the application and their security. Entering this stage, designers should have a sense of the complete data path and the relationships between modules. The next granular step establishes the basis for the application's implementation. The goals of this analysis are to determine the privileges of the various components, a sense of organization that will be used during the implementation, and knowledge of how the implementation will occur. Here, previously determined requirements are translated into detailed implementation methods.

Designers choose a Web server and a database server at this point, based on the established requirements. In our example, an Apache Web server was chosen because it can be made to support SSL communications and has a well-documented method to interact with external applications. An Oracle database server was chosen because it provides the flexibility, scalability, and security required in the database, and also because it supports Java-based interaction. Java was chosen as the language and extension for implementing the actual Internet commerce software because it operates with the Web and database servers and supports a strong, configurable security model.

The Web server and database server are then designed by determining the most secure methods for the following components:

- Server default configuration
- Security configuration of the underlying operating system
- Privileges required to interoperate with the Java applications
- Access control components

The commerce software is organized to provide these components:

- Privilege requirements to perform its functions
- The Web server interaction and communication entry points
- User authentication and access control methods
- Session security methods to prevent impersonation of users
- The database server interaction and communication entry points

Based on this analysis and organization, it is determined that the only portion of the system that requires elevated operating system privileges is the commerce application. It also needs an internal set of privilege levels to enforce user access control and authentication. The default configurations enable only the functionality needed for operation of the system, and each operating system is security-hardened with the same minimalist approach.

The commerce application is where the majority of the security components exist. It has the responsibility of validating user credentials, setting permissions on database objects, keeping track of each user session, and having the actual intelligence required to keep the system functioning.

The commerce application needs elevated privileges only when controlling Web and database server startup and shutdown. The most secure method to perform these actions is determined to be a separate controller process that increases its privileges at the time it performs a startup or shutdown action; it then relinquishes its privileges until the next request. The controller process communicates only with the commerce application and uses authenticated messages to initiate the startup or shutdown of the system.

The commerce application will also encrypt private information before storing it in the database to protect user credentials and financial information. In the event of anomalous and error conditions such as invalid input data, user authentication failures, and failed communications, the design calls for a reporting system that can log this information and respond appropriately to the events.

System implementation rises naturally from the continuous analysis provided in the preceding global, organizational, and component analysis phases. The developers use the guides and procedures in place to help them write the code that maintains the high security standard established.

Secure Coding Practices

This section delves into the more technical aspects of security in the code used to implement an application, and provides guidelines to develop an enforcement process for secure implementation. The potential for vulnerabilities in an application is reduced by a strong design, but the implementation of the application seals its fate. Hard work poured into a secure design becomes inconsequential if the implementation is poorly done. It is also important to understand that the inclusion of security-related technologies or design methods does not necessarily imply or guarantee any level of security within an application. The implementation of an application and any security technology used is one of the final components that brings a high level of reliability.

Analysis in the implementation phase is the responsibility of both developers and development managers. Developers are responsible for implementing the design well, whereas managers are responsible for setting forth the process that ensures a good implementation. This can be done via standardized procedures that include documented development and coding standards, design and code reviews, unit testing, and developer training with regard to security in application development. These procedures benefit the developers and applications regardless of which languages are used or the type of application developed.

The most commonly used languages today are the C programming language, Java, and scripting languages such as Perl and the Unix shells. Each of these languages and environments can be used improperly to compromise the security of an application and the system on which it runs. The following demonstrates security issues with these languages in relation to the vulnerabilities outlined earlier in the chapter. However, this section is not a checklist for developers to follow. Instead, the development of a security-focused thought process allows for an arguably stronger coding practice.

Pitfalls by the C

The C programming languages, which include C, C++, and Objective C, are the most commonly used languages and can be dangerous in unsure hands. They provide the developer with the ability to manipulate and access many parts of the system, such as memory, files, and devices. This is a great strength of the C languages, but danger arises when the developer makes mistakes. C provides a high level of access to the underlying operating system, and there are few checks and balances to protect the developer. If the developer mistakenly writes data to the wrong device or memory location, the C program will do whatever the developer writes, regardless of the data or destination.

The first vulnerable area often associated with C is the buffer overflow. The following sample code demonstrates a very basic overflow:

```
char string[10];

strcpy(string, "AAAAAAAAAAAAAAA");   /* 15 "A" characters */
```

Here, 15 "A" characters are copied into the memory area for a variable string, which is declared to be a static 10-character array. The strcpy() function does exactly as directed with no regard for the size of the data being copied or the location to which it goes. A buffer overflow occurs when the 11th element is copied into the memory location, immediately following the location of the 10th element of the variable string. Now apply this principle to any input data that comes from an external source, replacing the string of "A" characters. This allows attackers to control the effects of the overflow.

The strcpy() function is one of several functions in C that do not perform any bounds checking and allow arbitrarily sized buffers to be copied. Other functions to avoid are gets(), strcat(), sprintf(), and the scanf() family of functions. There are updated versions of some of these functions that allow the lengths copied to be specified. These are strncpy(), strncat(), snprintf(), and fgets(). These modified functions copy only up to the number of characters specified by the length parameter. At most, *length* characters are copied from *source* into *destination*:

```
strncpy(destination, source, length);
```

TIP

When using the "n" versions of the string manipulation functions—strncpy(), strncat(), snprintf(), and fgets()—be sure that the length is not larger than the destination string, rather than the source string. The buffer can be overrun if the length value is larger than the size of the destination buffer.

When using pointers to buffers, instead of statically declared buffers, you need to allocate enough memory to store the values being copied. Use the memory manipulation functions, which allow you to specify length.

TIP

When allocating memory for string data, do not forget to add 1 to the total length to accommodate for the NULL terminating character. Without a NULL terminator, the data in memory directly after the last character of the string might be considered part of the string.

These functions are not the only places where buffer overflows occur. Be sure to check that information read, copied, or written to any memory location or assigned to a variable will fit, or that the destination allocated has enough storage space.

TIP

To avoid buffer overflows in your code, be sure to validate input. Check the size of the data and the storage location and use manipulation functions that generate developer-specified amounts of information instead of arbitrarily long chunks of data.

Race conditions add a level of complexity to using C code. Race conditions can be exploited in two aspects of C code creation—sequencing and protection.

Sequencing refers to the order in which events occur in an application. Race conditions can result from sequencing variations between dependent events when no checking is done between the events. This often signifies a shortcoming in any error-checking and validation routines used. If two functions normally run sequentially and the second function assumes that the results of the first are valid, then the possibility for a race condition exists. Elevated privileges, discussed in further detail in the "Operating System Interactions" section earlier in this chapter, are often targets of attack. Organization, combined with sequencing and error checking, minimizes the possibility for race conditions.

This is a bad implementation that creates a race condition:

```
increase_privs();
...
value = special_app_function(); /* requires privileges */

other_unreleted_function(); /* does not require privileges */
other_unreleated_function2(); /* ditto */

special_dependent_function(value); /* requires privileges */
...
exit();
```

Here, a couple of unsafe practices occur. The privileges of the application are elevated early in the application, but not used until later. They are also never relinquished, so most functionality executes with higher-than-needed privilege levels. Finally, the race condition is created through poor organization—dependent functions do not occur near each other. An example that solves these problems is

```
increase_privs();
value = special_app_function; /* requires privileges */
if (!validate_function(value) /* assure the safety of the value */
{
    do_error_processing(value); /* do something intelligent with the error */
}
special_dependent_function(value); /* requires privileges */
decrease_privs(); /* no longer need privileges */

other_unreleted_function(); /* does not require privileges */
other_unreleated_function2(); /* ditto */
```

Note the special validation and error processing routines that are used before passing the value to another function.

TIP

Organize functionality and combine it with validation to ensure that expected information is not compromised between dependent events.

Many race conditions exist as the result of poor temporary file usage. When these files are created, they should be protected against external attack during operation. Unix and Windows allow the developer to set the permission bits and operational flags when creating a file. Permissions should disallow access to anyone but the owner of the process. When creating the file using the open() call, set the O_EXCL and O_CREAT flags, which cause the function to return an error if the file you are attempting to create already exists. Because it is a temporary file, it should not exist prior to the need for it. If the file exists, this is a possible sign of attack. When using these methods, it is also important to check the return values of the functions and to clean up any files in the event of error conditions. The following example shows the syntax to open a file—or create one, if it does not already exist—with permissions that allow only the creator to read, write, and execute it using the S_IRWXU mode macro.

```
open("filename", O_CREAT | O_EXCL | O_WRONLY, S_IRWXU);
```

The call will fail in the event that the file exists already because of the O_EXCL flag. Also, note the unsecure filename. The static naming convention used increases the risk of attack dramatically because one component of the attack is already provided.

Because of the increased presence of temporary file race conditions and the associated insecurities, several operating systems have specific functions to create temporary files in a secure manner. The mkstemp() and mktemp() functions have been written and rewritten to solve the protection issues and the predictability problem discussed in the "Temporary Storage" vulnerability section.

Developers can also use an operating system's built-in file-locking capabilities to control access to the files. These methods control access in the fundamental kernel components.

TIP

When using temporary files, randomize the filenames, set strong permissions, and organize the creation, use, and removal of the files to minimize the possibility of attack.

Another component that increases reliability and can influence the security of an application is the return value. Although it might seem obvious, it is important to stress the necessity of validating return values of functions. Functions often execute serially and rely on the results or data from a previous function. By checking the return value of previous functions, the dependent function is protected from executing with invalid data. Even when the events are not attacks, recovering from anomalous conditions increases the robustness of the application.

This example demonstrates a poor implementation that fails to check return values:

```
n = do_string_check (string, valid_characters); /* function returns an int */
if (n == GOOD_RETURN)
{
    process_string(string);
}
```

Here, the implementation is weak because the negative case, a bad return, is never handled. A better implementation is

```
n = do_string_check(string, valid_characters); /* function returns an int */
if (n != GOOD_RETURN)
{
    special_error_processing_routine(n); /* bad value, do something */
}

process_string(string);
```

The negative return is handled by the error-processing routine, which can exit the program, request a new string, or convert the return value into a valid parameter. If the return value is good, it goes to the process routine.

TIP

The creation of reusable event and error routines provides a standard mechanism by which all applications react to various attacks and issues. Ideas for these routines include common validation methods for string and numeric values, wrapper functions to perform integrity checks, and protection mechanisms that validate variables and memory locations. Always check and process the return value of a function.

The next bit of detail involves the use of sensitive information within the application, including passwords, encryption, or any other private information. As mentioned previously, all program information exists in areas of the common pool of memory that can be subject to reading and modification by external procedures. It is beneficial to clear the memory when the information is no longer in use to avoid revealing information during an attack. The most common and sufficient method to clear data, this is typically referred to as *zeroing out memory*. When stored information is no longer needed, the storage locations should be overwritten with zeros or random data to prevent an attacker from recovering the information via memory or core dumps. This procedure becomes particularly important when encryption is in use. The keys used to encrypt and decrypt messages are the most important pieces of a cryptographic system, and everything possible to protect them needs to be done.

These guidelines exemplify some of the common issues that arise in C-based applications. C is a very popular and powerful language that provides great flexibility to the developer, and care should be taken with its use.

A Perl of an Application

Perl is an interesting beast that combines many of the benefits of a structured programming language, like C, with the flexibility and integration of a Unix shell. Perl allows the developer to create procedures or subroutines, define variables, and utilize applications and commands available with the operating system. These capabilities, and its strength with regular expressions and parsing, give Perl a strong presence in Web applications, system administration, and automation.

Perl programs are not generally susceptible to buffer overflows because of the weakly typed nature of its variables and declarations. Unlike C, wherein variables and memory need to be defined as a particular storage class and memory must be allocated for them, Perl does everything automatically and treats everything as string data. Take the following example:

```
#!/path/to/perl

$one = 1;
$one_s = "1";  # No different than $one
$two = $one + $one_s; # the result is 2, or "2", which are equivalent
```

In C, the variable $one would likely be declared an integer and $one_s, a string. The addition of the two elements would also result in an erroneous value. Perl does not differentiate between the different types, so $two is assigned 2, or "2"—they are equivalent in Perl. The language also does not fall prey to the memory allocation requirements that other languages exhibit. The following example is completely acceptable in Perl:

```
#!/path/to/perl
$var1 = "AAAAA";
$var2 = "BBBB";
$var2 = $var1; # $var2 becomes "AAAAA";
```

$var2 takes on the new value of five "A" characters. All variables are dynamically allocated; there is no concept of preset storage space that could be overflowed.

Perl is susceptible, however, to race conditions and the vulnerabilities associated with the execution of external programs. Care should be given to the sequencing of functions. Input validation is equally important in Perl to prevent the exploitation of external applications. Perl supports the capability to open files, similarly to C and other languages; therefore, the use of temporary files should incorporate appropriate permissions and creation flags.

The use of Perl in Web-based CGI programs is also extremely popular. The greatest risks associated with its use in this environment occur during input validation and execution of external system programs from within. To protect the application, several precautions can be taken. Using the taint-check mechanisms of Perl, any variable set outside of the program will not be passed to any program run by the application. Any variables set by the tainted variable become tainted. Taint-check mode is particularly useful for avoiding vulnerabilities, wherein unchecked user variables are passed surreptitiously to programs called from the Perl application. To initialize version 5 of Perl in taint-check mode, use the following script header:

```
#!/path/to/perl -T # Run in taint-check mode
```

The next precaution is to parse input values to remove metacharacters and unwanted values. This helps protect against attacks that exploit parameter-passing to shells and other applications. The following example shows a simple routine that scans an input string for any metacharacters that might be interpreted by a program:

```
$unclean_input = &get_HTML_forms_response();
if($unclean_input =~ tr/;|`!#$&*()[]{}<>:'"//)
{
    # Print out some HTML here indicating failure
    &do_some_error_reporting();
}
```

In this case, the routine reports an error if a metacharacter is found. Alternative methods replace metacharacters or only continue if no metacharacter is found.

A final precaution is the use of a shell to run other applications. As with the Unix system() call and the Windows exec() call, the system() call in Perl allows the developer to run another application. The exec() call in Perl functions like that call in Unix—the running process is replaced by the program indicated. These functions can be particularly dangerous when used in an environments that allow user input, such as CGI programs or system utilities. If input validation does not occur, the application can be exploited to execute arbitrary programs that can affect the system. The following example demonstrates the insecurities of using system() with nonvalidated input. Assume the user supplied the string username ;/bin/rm -rf / that became assigned to the variable $input:

```
system("ecommerce_app $input");
```

This effectively translates to /bin/sh ecommerce_app username ; /bin/rm -rf /. Assuming that the program is running with privileges, the program will execute a shell to run the e-commerce application; hit the shell semicolon, which is the command separator in a shell; and then run rm -rf, which erases the entire filesystem.

Mi Java Es Su Java

Java is a relatively recent invention in the world of distributed Internet computing. It brings to fruition the concept of platform-independent code. Java works by writing code and compiling it into a special format that is then run on Java Virtual Machines. The Virtual Machine (VM) is platform-specific, but the code that runs on it is not. Java allows Web browsers and remote systems to run more complex and interactive applications. The Web browser accesses a Web site and receives a Java applet from the server. This applet then runs in the Web browser and can communicate with the originating Web server. When introduced, Java transformed static Web pages into dynamic and flowing applications. Since the early days, the use of Java has expanded into many different distributed application areas such as network management, embedded Internet appliances, and other utility functions.

Java is a fine example of a language whose developers considered security in the early design stages. The initial versions of Java had a well-documented security architecture, called the *sandbox*, that prevented the Java applet or application from accessing system resources. As use of Java began to expand, the need arose for access to system resources outside of the sandbox. The first version of the Java Development Kit provided the use of signed applets. The model describes an applet that is digitally signed to verify its creator. When the digital signature is verified, the applet is then trusted by the local system, which allows the applet access to other system resources. This digital signature method involves a fair amount of complex programming to work correctly. It is also important to note that this security model of a digitally signed Java applet is flawed. Anyone can sign an applet. A malicious applet can be signed by the attacker and downloaded by the Web browser. The Web browser effectively verifies that the malicious applet is indeed written by the attacker and then happily executes it, to whatever result is programmed in it.

The current and second iteration of the Java security architecture is much more powerful and flexible than earlier versions. This allows Java to enter many areas of application development previously beyond its capabilities. The new Java security architecture uses easily definable security policies and access control methods that allow an applet or application to access specific resources to varying degrees. In relation to the guidelines presented here, Java designers analyzed the various interactions and vulnerabilities present with distributed Internet applications and arrived at a model that provides high security with extreme flexibility. The use of Java security policies requires a fair amount of reading and understanding that is beyond the scope of this chapter. For complete documentation on Java and its APIs, see http://java.sun.com.

Java also has standard cryptographic libraries. Authentication and security libraries can also be found in Java. This makes it a nice language in which to develop secure applications.

One interesting part of Java is that errors are generally not return codes as we saw with C, but exceptions instead. Most Java exceptions are known as what is called checked exceptions. Even if the programmer wants to ignore an exception, he must still write an error handler, which does nothing. Otherwise, the Java compiler will not compile the program. This system makes it easier to write robust and secure code.

C#/.NET

Microsoft, with its .NET Framework, basically recreated Java, but in a platform-specific and language-neutral way. A variety of languages run on the .NET Framework, but the primary language is C#, which is mostly a Java clone. The Virtual Machine is called the CLR (Common Language Runtime). .NET shares virtually every characteristic with Java.

One area that was changed was in the exception arena. .NET makes all exceptions unchecked, which means the compiler does force the programmer to handle them. This makes it easier for a programmer to be sloppy and forget to check for certain errors in their code.

The Shell Game and Unix

Unix shells form the basis of user interaction with a Unix system. Shells are command-line interpreters that support some level of automation and programming in the form of shell scripts. These scripts are often used to automate system tasks, perform repetitive operations, and run CGI Web applications. As with Perl, areas of potential risk are input validation, race conditions, interaction with external files and programs, and the organization of functionality.

In Unix, a privileged user can run privileged operations, or they can be set to run as a privileged user. There are subtle differences between the two methods. All files in a Unix system, including applications, have a set of attributes that include user and group ownership and a set of permissions flags. Combined, they allow file access to be strictly controlled. A user owns normal applications, and depending on the access permissions, they might be run only by the owner, by a group, or by anyone on the system. The applications inherit the privileges of the user who runs them. An application that requires root privileges can be run by a non-root user, but at those points where higher privileges are required, it will fail. To overcome this and allow normal users to access certain privileged functions, Unix provides the SetUID and SetGID flags. When enabled, they cause the application to run as the owner or group for that application—they set the User ID (UID) of the application to whomever owns it.

Many CGI and system programs require access to system resources and are SetUID root. This applies to compiled programs, such as C programs, and scripts, including Perl and the Unix shells. Experienced Unix users and developers often warn about the dangers of SetUID shell scripts that provide root privileges. As discussed earlier, input validation and race conditions are easily exploited when the script is not protected properly. When running a script as a privileged user, there is no easier way to hand over the keys to the castle than a weak shell script. Such scripts are particularly dangerous when programmed without security measures, because a shell is interactive by nature. Users supply input, and the shell performs a function. Perl has many built-in checks and balances that allow safer SetUID usage.

Internet Appliances

Internet appliances are those systems and devices whose entire purpose is Internet computing. All the design guidelines, programming language considerations, vulnerabilities, and operating paradigms discussed in this chapter are directly relevant to Internet appliances. Internet appliances often use common operating systems, applications, and methods to accomplish their goals. If the application in development follows this path, pay special attention to all the information presented here. Some Internet appliances are developed from scratch, incorporating only newly developed designs and technologies. Assessing security risk for these systems requires extra diligence. It is especially important to integrate security into a design process when starting from scratch.

Summary

Many applications are based on previously created applications and benefit from an established and exercised security architecture. New innovations have no such luxury, therefore it is vital that they begin life with strong security measures. Consideration for security should not end at the completion of the application, system, or product development cycle, however. It is a continuous process that should remain active throughout the lifespan of the application. With every new twist, turn, and feature that the application takes, sincere consideration for its effect on the remainder of the application and the environment in which it runs needs to be examined and understood. Diligence and comprehensiveness throughout the cycle is a necessity—a well-thought design can bolster the security but be undone by poor implementation, and secure code cannot secure a poor design.

The technical details involved with security require a large amount of time, experience, and exposure to grasp. An awareness of security and the ability to analyze from a security perspective allow designers, developers, and their managers to formulate questions and responses that aid the creation of a well-designed, reliable, and secure application. Security is a process, not a feature, that requires a steady but not overwhelming effort. Strive to develop with the model of least privilege necessary to accomplish a given task. Finally, always analyze the ramifications of a design or implementation decision, because there is always a reaction to any action.

27

Wireless Security Auditing

"Friday night is "make-it". After the meeting we slip away into the darkness, the cold night flogging us with a primal urgency. Tonight we hack Dallas.

Crouched in a tricked-out SUV—ebony with tinted windows— the bizarre array of protruding antennas makes us a giant insect. We crawl along the Richardson Telecom Corridor, our faces deathly pallid in the glow of a laptop. It starts immediately, the walls of network security melting around us like ice. Within moments, the largest networks fly open. Nortel—28 access points—all wide open. Driving a little farther, our antenna starts to hum. Fujitsu, Ericsson, Alcatel…hundreds of unsecured portals streaming down our laptop in a torrent. A few are encrypted, albeit weakly, but most are bereft of even a password. And we know that they are ours. And we feel ourselves rising, towering above these buildings of steel and glass, and like gods we look down on them in scorn and pity. And then we enter…"

—from *Windows .NET Server Security Handbook*

Wireless technology and Internet security are two of the fastest growing technology trends, according to a leading information security magazine. However, these two fields have developed upon discrete paths. When *wireless* and *security* finally collided, the results were disastrous. For example, in this chapter, we address wireless local area network (WLAN) security concerns. Specifically, we cover *war driving*, which is the process of auditing wireless networks while mobile. With nascent wireless community networks set to explode, and to potentially usurp the dominion of traditional Internet bandwidth providers, this material becomes crucial.

This is meant to be a practical chapter. We will show you how to choose your equipment, how to set up your test lab, and how to start auditing your wireless networks. In addition, we will briefly introduce how to crack the Wired Equivalent Privacy (WEP) algorithm, which is part of the 802.11 wireless standard.

The information covered in this chapter often shows up in certification exams such as the Wireless Security Expert Certification (WSEC), which is the most difficult, most widely recognized, and most respected wireless security certification in the world. Thus, this material can help you cram for your WSEC exam.

The following sections review the very best hardware used in setting up a typical wireless LAN, including access points, Wireless Network Cards, antennas, and PDAs. We then cover war driving as seen by real experts in the field.

One final point before we begin—remember that all of the techniques in this chapter are available freely on the Web, and are well known to hackers and criminals. We are simply summarizing the information here so that honest administrators will at least have a fighting chance to protect their own networks. So grab your equipment and start legitimately auditing your own network—before someone maliciously does it for you!

Wireless LAN Topology

Wireless Local Area Networks (WLANs) and their topologies differ from those of traditional wired Ethernet networks, but not by much. The premise of WLANs is the same as their hardwired counterparts, with a few minor variations. Let's begin by examining wireless peer networks.

Peer networks, also known as ad-hoc networks, are mostly used in smaller-scale implementations where there are only a few clients in close proximity of each other. This type of network can best be compared with a peer-to-peer network in which there is no central point of management, and all clients are left to themselves to communicate with one another. In a peer topology, clients communicate directly to other clients without any intermediary point. This type of wireless network is most commonly used as an alternative to infrared (IR) when two people want to transfer files between two sources.

Larger corporate environments require additional central control and the capability to manage clients more effectively. This is achieved with an Infrastructure type of topology. When wireless clients are put into Infrastructure mode, they look for a device called an access point and use it to send data to other networked clients. You can think of this access point (AP) as being analogous to a wired network's gateway and hub. The AP receives traffic from multiple clients like a hub, but it also serves as a gateway for the wireless clients to access the wired network beyond. It will also do this in reverse, allowing the wired network to access the wireless one. Some access points even have advanced features such as Network Address Translation (NAT) and basic packet filtering. On a fairly regular basis, an access point will send out a beacon broadcast announcing its presence. Wireless clients then receive these beacons and attempt to connect to the network associated with the access point. Once a client has been authenticated and authorized by the access point, it is the same as the client being given an Ethernet connection to the wired network. Unless other restrictions are in place, the wireless clients will then be able to do everything as if they were directly connected via a cable to the network. An Infrastructure topology does not necessarily indicate a connection to a larger wired network. Quite often, this type of topology is used to allow multiple clients to access common resources on a wireless network without the use of any wired devices.

Wireless networks in Infrastructure mode can be located practically anywhere within a company's regular network topology. However, clients in Peer mode would not have the capability to access the resources of a larger supporting wired network without the use of additional routing resources. In addition, the clients in Peer mode must be located within a close proximity of each other, while the clients using Infrastructure mode are only bound by the constraints of the wired or wireless network that they help comprise.

As a wireless network auditor (or ethical hacker), a good antenna will make your job easier. There are two primary types of antennas used on wireless networks—omni-directional and directional. Omni-directional antennas can receive and transmit from all sides (360 degrees). These are useful when covering a large room, or for providing general coverage. Contrary to popular belief, a true omni-directional antenna is not capable of having any gain. Most antennas sold as omni-directional do not send the radio frequency in all directions. The design of the antenna will null the signal on the Y-axis, and concentrate the power across the X-axis.

Directional antennas take the radio frequency (RF) energy and concentrate it in a specific direction. This can be compared to a naked light bulb versus a flashlight. The light bulb would be similar to the omni-directional antenna, as it gives off light in all directions equally. In contrast, the flashlight (similar to the directional antenna) focuses the light bulb with the help of a reflector, and concentrates it in a single direction. Directional antennas are helpful when you are creating point-to-point wireless links, or when you are trying to reduce the RF signal "bleed" in a specific location.

The following sections will review wireless hardware that we personally recommend. The results are based on testing that we performed for our book, *Maximum Wireless Security* (Sams, 2002). Let's first examine access points, which are a crucial part of WLANs.

Access Points

There are many different manufacturers of access points, and all of them perform essentially the same function. However, there are substantial differences in security and features among the various vendors. For example, some access points are capable of restricting user connections based on the MAC address (unique product identifier) of the Wireless Network Card, while others have the capability to turn off the beacon broadcast, making the access point invisible to hacking programs. Fortunately, advanced security features such as these are becoming more common in SOHO (small office/home office) access points.

In our 2002 field survey of more than 1,300 access points in five cities, Cisco was the leader with 39.7%. Lucent had 19.2%, while Linksys had 17.1%; the remaining 24% were from various other manufacturers. Interestingly, the Linksys access points that are designed for SOHO use are finding their way into the corporate workplace at a rapid pace. This could be because of their low cost, wide availability, the addition of MAC restriction, and the capability to control whether the card broadcasts. However, with the more expensive Cisco AP holding the majority, we can infer that a good deal of money is being spent on the expansion and development of internal, corporate wireless networks. The following section will review APs that we recommend from personal experience.

Linksys WAP11 Access Point

Homepage: http://www.linksys.com

The Linksys WAP11 is a simple but effective low cost/high performance access point. Previously, the widespread use of the WAP11 was held back by its lack of security features. Fortunately, however, this has been resolved. As of firmware version (1.4i.1), the device has several new capabilities, such as the capability to disable the beacon broadcast and to restrict connections based on the client's MAC address.

Administration of the WAP11 requires client-based software and is performed via a USB interface or SNMP over an Ethernet connection (not wireless). Some of the features that were added in the 1.4i.1 firmware require the use of the SNMP interface. However, the settings are only viewable when using a USB interface. When we contacted them, Linksys support was unclear as to why the features are not configurable from both interfaces. They also indicated that this would not be changed in the future. Nevertheless, the administration interface is a joy to navigate and configure in both cases.

The WAP11 features two antennas that can be configured for dedicated sending and receiving. By default, the access point is configured to use each antenna to both send and receive transmissions. Having the capability to configure how the antennas are used can maximize the WAP11's capability to work in almost any environment. The

WAP11 uses a standard (RP-TNC) connector making the default antennas replaceable with higher-gain aftermarket products. This is useful for helping you limit coverage to specific areas, or in directing coverage into a specific area. Please see the section titled "Antennas" later in this chapter for more information on this topic.

Tech Specs

Default SSID:	Linksys
Default IP:	192.168.1.250
Default Channel:	6
Encryption:	40-/128-bit WEP
Clients:	32
Dimensions:	Length: 8.9"
	Width: 5"
	Height: 1.6"
Weight:	12 oz.

NetGear ME102 Access Point

Homepage: http://www.netgear.com

The NetGear ME102 is a fully functional access point packed into a very small package. Measuring only 6.4 inches long, 5.6 inches wide, and 1.1 inches high, it is one of the smallest access points on the market. This makes it perfect for traveling, or for use in any area where space is a consideration. However, do not let the small size fool you. With the 1.4h3 firmware upgrade, the ME102 is capable of 128-bit WEP encryption, point-to-point and point-to-multipoint configurations, and enhanced access point client features with MAC address restriction.

Administration of the ME102 requires client-based software, and is done via a USB interface or SNMP over an Ethernet connection (not wireless). To access and configure the MAC restriction, you must use the SNMP interface. In addition, a statistics page is also available via SNMP that shows various stats for the wireless and Ethernet interfaces on the access point. Another useful feature of the ME102 is the capability to set multiple passwords for the administration interface. This allows an administrator to keep her password a secret while allowing a user to check out the configurations on the access point. While logged in as the user, you are able to browse all configurations, but you are not permitted to change any settings.

In several tests, we found that the ME102 exceeded our expectations in overall functionality and total usability. This access point is very powerful, and is perfect for many situations. Although not quite in the same class as enterprise-level access points, this one will definitely provide you with great value for the money spent.

Tech Specs

Default SSID:	Wireless	
Default IP:	192.168.0.5	
Default Channel:	6	
Encryption:	40-/128-bit WEP	
Clients:	32	
Dimensions:	Length:	6.4"
	Width:	5.6"
	Height:	1.1"
Weight:	0. 076 lb.	

Antennas

Almost everyone uses at least one antenna each day. In fact, the majority of people use antennas for many conveniences in their daily life, whether they realize it or not. Devices such as keyless entry systems, freeway toll passes, satellite TV systems, pagers, cell phones, and wireless networks all require antennas. Very few people that use these antennas can explain how and why they work. Let's take a brief look at antenna technology, and how antennas relate to radio frequency (that is, wireless) networks.

Antennas are merely an extension of a radio transmitter or receiver. As a signal is generated, it is passed from the radio to the antenna to be sent out over the air and received by another antenna and then passed to another radio. The signal that is generated and later transmitted is measured in Hertz (Hz); not the car rental company, but rather a measurement unit of cycles per second. This is better defined as the amount of time it takes a radio wave to complete a full cycle. Imagine that you have a Slinky (a coiled metal spring) on a smooth surface with one end attached to the floor. If you start to move the other end from side to side, you will begin to create waves. These waves represent the radio frequency energy being sent out over the air. By moving your hand side to side at a slow pace, thus creating longer waves, you are creating a low frequency. If you speed up the movement from side to side, making the waves shorter but more frequent, you are generating a higher frequency. Lower frequencies generally have the capability to travel further distances, but are more subject to interference from objects such as building and trees, which block the signal. A higher frequency has a better capability to penetrate buildings and other obstructions, but it has a limited distance.

For example, consider your local FM radio station. If they broadcast their signal on 103.5MHz, this translates to 103,500,000 cycles per second. Their signal can be heard all over your city, even inside buildings and houses, with very little interruption. Meanwhile, an AM radio station two states away is broadcasting on 1320KHz, which translates to 1,320,000 cycles per second. With the correct antenna placed outside you can receive their signal from a longer distance, but with the added difficulty of needing to adjust your antenna.

Antennas are fundamental components to the transmission of radio frequencies. In many situations, a lower power signal transmitted using a good antenna can arrive at its destination with more accuracy than a high-powered signal transmitted using a poor antenna.

Antennas are rated by the amount of gain that they provide. *Gain* is the increase in power you get by using a directional antenna. The overall gain is compared to a theoretical *isotropic antenna*. Isotropic antennas cannot exist in the real world, but they serve as a common point of reference.

A dipole antenna has 2.14-dB gain over a 0-dBi isotropic antenna. So if an antenna gain is given in dBd and not dBi, add 2.15 to it to get the dBi value.

If an antenna's gain is just specified as dB, check with the manufacturer if the rating is dBi or dBd. If they cannot tell you, or simply do not know, save your money and go someplace else.

As stated previously, most antennas are sold with gain measured in dBi, but this is not the only factor to consider when evaluating overall performance. For example, the power input to the antenna plays a major part. Most 802.11b wireless cards transmit 32mW of power. Looking at the conversion chart in Table 27.1, you can see that 32mW (the Po column stands for "Power") is equal to 15dBm. The dBm is calculated by the following equation:

$$dBm = 10 \log (32mW/1)$$

TABLE 27.1   dBm to Power Conversion Chart

dBm	Po	dBm	Po
53	200W	25	320mW
50	100W	24	250mW
49	80W	23	200mW
48	64W	22	160mW
47	50W	21	125mW
46	40W	20	100mW
45	32W	19	80mW
44	25W	18	64mW
43	20W	17	50mW
42	16W	16	40mW
41	12.5W	15	32mW

TABLE 27.1   Continued

dBm	Po	dBm	Po
40	10W	14	25mW
39	8W	13	20mW
38	6.4W	12	16mW
37	5W	11	12.5mW
36	4.0W	10	10mW
35	3.2W	9	8mW
34	2.5W	8	6.4mW
33	2W	7	5mW
32	1.6W	6	4mW
31	1.25W	5	3.2mW
30	1.0W	4	2.5mW
29	800mW	3	2.0mW
28	640mW	2	1.6mW
27	500mW	1	1.25mW
26	400mW	0	1.0mW

Why are these numbers important? Because they allow you to calculate Effective Isotropic Radiated Power (EIRP), also known as Effective Radiated Power (ERP). EIRP is the amount of power that is actually transmitted from the antenna. This information is necessary to help calculate how effective the antenna system is. EIRP also forms the basis of FCC laws regulating maximum output.

For instance, if you know that a typical card is transmitting 15dBm and you want to use, say, a 3-dBi antenna, you can use the following equation to calculate Effective Isotropic Radiated Power (EIRP):

15dBm + 3dBi = 18dBm (64mW) EIRP

The Federal Communication Commission (FCC) currently limits mobile 802.11 stations to 1W or 30dBm EIRP. Fixed stations are given a slight exception to the rule and are allowed to exceed the 1W limitation. When calculating for fixed stations, they are required to subtract 1dB for every 3dB over 6dBi of antenna gain. The following example demonstrates this for a Linksys WAP11 and a 24-dBi antenna:

20dBm + 24dBi = 44dBm or 25W

(44dbM – ((24dBi – 6dB)/3)) = EIRP

(44dBm – (18dBi / 3)) = EIRP

(44dBm – 6dBi) = EIRP

EIRP – 38dBm or 6.4W

In addition to antenna gain and transmitter power, you should also consider the difference in sizes of antennas. Depending on the frequency and type of antenna, there will be a variety of sizes to choose from. The size of the antenna is directly related to the frequency for which it is used. For example, consider a CB radio installed in a car that operates between 26.965MHz (channel 1) and 27.405MHz (channel 40). If you want to have a full wavelength antenna for channel 1, it would need to be 36.491 feet long. This is calculated as follows:

L (in feet) = 984/f (in MHz)

L = 984/26.965MHz

L = 36.491 feet

Now compare that CB antenna to a full wavelength antenna used by a police officer to communicate with his dispatcher on 460.175MHz.

L (in feet) = 984/f (in MHz)

L = 984 / 460.175 MHz

L = 2.142 feet

As you can see, there is a difference of about 34.349 feet between the two antennas. Fortunately for us, wireless 802.11b networks operate in the 2.4GHz or 2400MHz range, thus making the antennas very small.

The following section reviews antennas that are useful to you as a wireless network auditor. These are antennas that we have used and tested, and they come with our strong personal recommendation.

Radome-Enclosed Yagi Antenna: HyperLink HG2415Y

Homepage: `http://www.hyperlinktech.com`

The HG2415Y is a high quality Yagi (directional) antenna with very strong performance. The antenna weighs approximately 1.8 pounds, which makes it lightweight and extremely easy to install. It comes complete with two U-bolt mounting brackets that will allow the antenna to be connected to a mast up to 2 3/8" in diameter.

The antenna is supplied with a 24" pigtail that terminates in a choice of N, TNC, or SMA connectors. The part number that we tested (HG2415Y) corresponds to an antenna terminated in N Female. We used a CA-WL2CABLE1 to connect the antenna to an ORiNOCO PCMCIA card. Our initial tests revealed that while using this antenna, we were able to connect to our test access point from *three times* the distance, on an unamplified signal, using stock antennas on the access point.

This antenna is great for point-to-point links and is built to withstand the forces of Mother Nature. In fact, it is capable of surviving wind speeds of up to 150 miles per hour, so this antenna will perform under extreme conditions. Overall, this antenna is the top of the line, and should be one of your first choices.

Tech Specs

Frequency:	2400–2500MHz
Gain:	14.5 dBi
-3dB Beam Width:	30 degrees
Impedance:	50 Ohm
Max. Input Power:	50 Watts
VSWR:	< 1.5:1 avg.
Weight:	1.8 lb.
Length:	19" long × 3" diameter
Polarization:	Vertical
Wind Survival:	> 150 MPH

NOTE

VSWR is the Voltage Standing Wave Ratio. It represents the ratio of Forward Power to Reverse Power (how much is being put into the antenna versus how much is being reflected back to your radio).

Parabolic Grid Antenna: HyperLink HG2419G

Homepage: `http://www.hyperlinktech.com`

The HyperLink HG2419G is also a very high performance tool. This high-gain, ultra-efficient antenna is extremely well-engineered. The antenna is built from durable, galvanized welded steel, and is coated with a light gray UV powdercoat, making it not only strong but also attractive.

Hyperlink makes three versions of this antenna: a 15-dBi, a 19-dBi (the model we tested for this book), and the granddaddy of them all, a 24-dBi model. In addition to offering high gain, this antenna is also extremely selective. By offering an eight-degree beam on the 24-dBi models, the antenna minimizes interference and maximizes power. As with most directional antennas, this one is best for point-to-point links connecting multiple networks. In our tests with the HG2919G, we were able to connect to our test access point with a solid connection from well over three times the distance, on an unamplified signal, using stock antennas on the access point.

The HG2419G can be mounted to a standard mast up to 2.5" in diameter, and the elevation can be adjusted up to fifteen degrees. This allows you to use it in a wide range of situations and makes it optimal for rooftop mounting. With its capability to select horizontal or vertical wave patterns, high gain ratings, tight beam width, and rugged construction, this antenna is one of the best on the market.

Tech Specs

Frequency:	2400–2500MHz
Gain:	19-dBi
-3dB Beam Width:	17 degrees
Impedance:	50 Ohm
Max. Input Power:	50 Watts
VSWR:	< 1.5:1 avg.
Weight:	3.9 lb.
Length:	16.7" × 23.6"
Polarization:	Vertical or horizontal
Wind Survival:	> 150 MPH

SigMax Omni-Directional: Signull SMISMCO10

Homepage: http://www.signull.com

The SMISMCO10 is an omni-directional antenna designed for medium- to long-range multipoint applications. Standing at less than three feet tall and weighing less than a pound, this antenna packs quite a punch for its size.

Signull Technologies offers three versions, a 10-dBi (the model we tested for this chapter), 8-dBi, and a 5-dBi model. All three of these antennas are perfect for extending the coverage of corporate access points or wireless nodes. They can easily be mounted indoors to provide coverage for a cubical farm, or utilized in a warehouse to help provide coverage for wireless inventory devices. In addition, they are also suitable for outdoor mounting to help provide general coverage in a courtyard or parking lot. While testing the SMISMCO10, we found that it was capable of delivering the high performance that Signull has promised. With its firm construction, light weight, and superior performance, the SMISMCO10 is a useful addition to your wireless LAN.

Tech Specs

Frequency:	2400–2500MHz
Gain:	10-dBi

Beam Width:	360 degrees
Impedance:	50 Ohm
Max. Input Power:	50 Watts
VSWR:	< 1.5:1 avg.
Weight:	0.75 lb.
Width:	7/8"
Length:	38"
Polarization:	Vertical
Wind Survival:	> 100 MPH

SigMax Circular Yagi: Signull SMISMCY12

Homepage: `http://www.signull.com`

This circular Yagi antenna from Signull Technologies is another of our favorites. In addition to great performance ratings, it has a truly stylish design—and isn't style what wireless security is all about? In addition, because the body of the antenna is clear, you can see the internal design. This allows you to also use the antenna as an educational tool.

In our tests, we were able to increase our signal strength dramatically while directing this antenna toward our test access point. Signull Technologies offers this antenna in three models: 8-dBi, 12-dBi (the model we tested for this chapter), and 15-dBi. The 12-dBi antenna we tested seemed to have a sufficient performance boost, but depending on the application, the 15-dBi could be a better option.

Although the antenna's design is attractive with its clear body, long-term exposure to weather may prove to be a problem. This makes the antenna more useful for mounting indoors or under a protective cover. Fortunately, its great looks do not affect its performance—the SMISMCY12 can really perform. This antenna is suitable for creating and linking wireless networks, and you should consider purchasing it.

Tech Specs

Frequency:	2400–2500MHz
Gain:	12-dBi
-3dB Beam Width:	30 degrees
Impedance:	50 Ohm
Max. Input Power:	50 Watts
VSWR:	< 1.5:1 avg.

Weight:	2 lb.
Width:	4″
Length:	23″
Polarization:	Vertical & horizontal
Wind Survival:	> 100 MPH

TechnoLab Log Periodic Yagi

Homepage: `http://www.technolab-inc.com`

This Yagi antenna from TechnoLab is truly one of a kind. Its low profile and small design make it a great indoor directional antenna. In addition, by placing this antenna on the outer perimeter of a building, you can easily create building-to-building links.

Our tests revealed that this little antenna is quite capable of getting the job done. For our tests we connected the Yagi antenna directly to our test access point and attempted to connect to it using a standard ORiNOCO PCMCIA card. We found that the antenna was fairly selective and offered good improvement in signal strength in the desired direction.

We also tested the access point with a combination of one stock antenna and one TechnoLab Yagi antenna, and detected no performance degradation. This is important because there are many instances where an access point will not only be providing remote user connectivity, but also local connectivity to the network. In addition to its small size and light weight, its frequency range will enable you to use it for other applications in addition to wireless networking. Overall, the Yagi from TechnoLab is a useful antenna to add to your wireless office or campus network configuration.

Tech Specs

Frequency:	900–2600MHz
Gain:	12-dBi
-3dB Beam Width:	30 degrees
Impedance:	50 Ohm
Max. Input Power:	10 Watts
VSWR:	< 2:1 avg.
Weight:	1.8 lb.
Wind Survival:	N/A

Wireless Networking Cards

Wireless Network Interface Cards (WNICs) are basic yet essential components of your wireless hardware setup. In this section, we review the ORiNOCO brands alone, as they stand out head and shoulders above any competitors.

ORiNOCO PC Card

Homepage: `http://www.orinocowireless.com`

Hands down, the ORiNOCO wireless PCMCIA cards by Agere Systems are the best on the market. The cards are standard PCMCIA and will fit into one Type II slot on a laptop or portable computer. There are two models of the card, Silver and Gold. The Silver card offers 64-bit WEP protection, whereas the Gold offers 128-bit. Both cards offer connection speeds of up to 11Mbps and are Wi-Fi-compliant, making them compatible with other systems. One of the better features of both the Gold and Silver cards is the capability to connect an external antenna. This capability, while not unique, is fairly uncommon among other manufacturers, and is a crucial feature for wireless auditing and network management. In addition, the cards are widely supported across multiple operating systems such as Mac, Novell, Windows, and Linux.

The ORiNOCO cards can be configured to work in peer-to-peer (ad hoc) or infrastructure modes. Peer-to-peer mode allows you to form a small network in which the cards communicate without the use of an access point. When in infrastructure mode, the card will associate with larger corporate networks that use access points to help relay information onto the wired network.

The Gold and Silver ORiNOCO cards by Agere Systems should be your first choice when outfitting your office. Their solid construction, capability to connect an external antenna, and support for multiple systems make them our favorite.

Handheld Devices

Handheld computing devices, or personal data assistants (PDAs), are rapidly growing in popularity. Along with the growing use of PDAs has come a corresponding growth in the demand for wireless network connectivity, auditing, and management. Consider the advantages of being able to check your email anywhere in your house or office with only a few taps of a stylus—and no boot-up time.

Many companies are already developing high-end productivity applications for the PDA market. For example, the PocketPC (which uses Microsoft's embedded operating system, Windows CE) ships with a Microsoft Terminal Server Client, allowing you to connect to servers virtually anywhere on your network. Medical students are even using PDAs connected to wireless networks to watch surgeries via streaming video. Thus, the potential for growth in this market is tremendous.

Traditionally, the two main competitors in the PDA operating system market have been Palm (using Palm OS) and the PocketPC (using Windows CE).

At the time of this writing, the Palm has not shown much in the way of 802.11b connectivity, but the PocketPC, on the other hand, has shown tremendous capabilities. Many manufacturers are writing PocketPC drivers for their hardware, thus expanding the capabilities of this already very functional product. Just as with desktop or laptop computers, there are many models of hardware that will support and run the PocketPC operating system. Each device is unique and offers its own features and benefits. Features such as increased memory, higher resolution screens, and the capability to work with external hardware such as PCMCIA and compact flash cards are all factors to consider in your purchasing decision.

One device that we have found more than equal to the task is the Compaq iPAQ. When it comes to wireless connectivity and features, iPAQ is the hands-down leader in the PDA market. Companies such as ORiNOCO, Network Associates, and Cisco are aggressively pursuing the iPAQ as a key player in the wireless realm. Vendors are targeting software applications specifically toward the iPAQ and its capability to support a wide range of external hardware devices.

Although not yet as powerful as their desktop forefathers, PDAs are a useful extension to a home or business network. With wider deployment of 802.11b networks and the increase of free public networks, handheld devices will soon be ubiquitous among casual users. In addition, the number of corporate employees telecommuting from their PDAs through Virtual Private Networks (VPNs) is expected to grow rapidly.

Compaq iPAQ

Homepage: `http://www.compaq.com`

The iPAQ from Compaq is the leader among handheld devices with wireless functionality. In fact, the iPAQ is of such a superior quality to its competitors that we do not recommend (or review here) any other PDAs.

Although the base unit is more than adequate, you also have the capability to add expansion packs, or *sleeves*. These sleeves are add-ons that enhance the overall functionality of the iPAQ. There are many different sleeves available on the market today, which allows the iPAQ to make use of everything from PCMCIA and compact flash cards to IBM Micro drives and GPS devices. By using a sleeve, you can take the standard iPAQ and turn it into a wireless workstation. Because many devices use the PCMCIA standard, the PCMCIA sleeve (part number 173396-001) is probably the most functional one to own.

The iPAQ can be used with the PCMCIA sleeve connected and a wireless card inserted into the sleeve. This setup will enable you to connect to various 802.11b networks and perform many functions, such as browsing Web pages (using the built-in version of Internet Explorer) or managing your remote network (using the Terminal Server application). With the addition of software such as NetForce by Ruksun or CENiffer by Epiphan Consulting, you can dramatically increase the overall functionality and usefulness of your iPAQ. Other software developers such as NetStumbler and Network Associates have created products with the iPAQ in mind. With its growing base of hardware and software add-ons, along with the increasing availability of wireless networks, the Compaq iPAQ will be a dominant force well into the future.

Tech Specs

Operating System:	Pocket PC 2002
Processor:	206MHz Intel StrongArm 32-bit RISC
RAM:	32 or 64MB
Display:	TFT liquid crystal display (4,096 colors)
Resolution:	240 × 320
Battery:	Lithium Polymer Rechargeable (950mAh)
Weight:	6.7 oz.
Height:	5.11"
Width:	3.28"
Depth:	0. 62"

Constructing a Wireless Test Lab

Prior to deploying any live wireless equipment in your enterprise, we recommend that you create a lab and test everything. Similarly, a wireless security expert will need a test lab of her own for research and development. A wireless test lab is completely different from your ordinary computer lab. Your wireless lab cannot be confined to a specific space. It needs to be mobile, just like your users will be.

When testing for access point placement in your environment, there are several factors you need to consider. These factors are as follows:

- Coverage area—Where can you get the most coverage without causing interference to other access points?

- Mounting—How will the access point be mounted?

- Network connection—How will the access point connect to the network? This can also be affected by your topology and security setup.

- Power—This may sound simple, but can often become a major dilemma.

Testing for coverage areas and deciding on placement locations can be a bit difficult, as it is difficult to bolt an access point to the ceiling and then constantly move it. Fortunately, we have come up with a better solution. Take a cart similar to those found in libraries and mount a telescoping pole to one of the sides. At the top of the pole, attach a flat piece of wood or plastic (not metal) that is big enough to hold the access point like a "ceiling," perpendicular to the ground. Offset the wood so that the access point can hang down without hitting the cart. Next, attach the access point upside down to the wood or plastic piece on the top of the pole. By raising the pole with the access point on top, you will place the access point at ceiling height and still be able to move it by pushing the cart.

On the cart should be a battery connected to an inverter, giving you a power source in which to plug the access point. By walking the floor with a laptop or PDA, you can test connectivity to the access point. We also recommend that you test not only the area you are attempting to cover, but also the surrounding areas. This will enable you to map wireless coverage that inadvertently "bleeds" beyond your perimeter.

The best type of lab configuration is one that will closely resemble your production environment. In addition, the lab should be flexible enough to allow you to test new products, and allow for future network expansions. Once your test lab is in place, you can start practical wireless security testing for yourself. The following section will introduce wireless attacks from a hacker's perspective. Armed with this knowledge, you will be able to "attack" your own networks as a wireless auditor, before someone else does it for you.

Wireless Attacks

The techniques for wireless attacks are not new. Indeed, they are based on the ancient attacks that have been used on wired networks from time immemorial, with only minor updates. In fact, the goal of attacking a wireless network is usually not to compromise the wireless network itself, but rather to gain a foothold into the wired network within.

Because traditional wired networks have been hardened from repeated attacks for more than thirty years, many are beginning to evolve formidable defenses. For example, a properly configured firewall can provide much security. However, consider what happens when you have an unsecured wireless access point sitting within the firewall—you have just effectively opened a back door right through your firewall. Thus, the proliferation of wireless networks has set the state of information security back more than a decade...almost to the 1980s, when computer systems were wide open to attack via modems and war dialing.

In time, most wireless networks will fall victim to at least one type of wireless attack. These attacks are not limited to just the corporate world, either. One of the largest consumers of wireless networks is the residential customer. These consumers are typically looking for a way to use their broadband connection in any room of the house. Worse, the vast majority of consumers are not aware of security issues. You can now buy access points from the local electronic store for less than $200, but many of these do not have the same security features of the Corporate or Professional models that run $800 and up. With more users installing these low-end access points, both on personal networks and within small businesses, the number of easy targets is growing exponentially.

There are many different models of 802.11b Wireless Network Interface Cards. One thing common to them all is the capability to put them into Infrastructure and Peer-to-Peer Mode. The IEEE defines Infrastructure Mode as Basic Service Set (BSS). It is used to connect a client to an access point on an established network (Figure 27.1). Peer-to-Peer Mode, also known as ad-hoc mode, is known as Independent Basic Service Set (IBSS). This mode is used to connect two or more wireless devices to form a small close range network, much like peer-to-peer networking on wired networks (Figure 27.2).

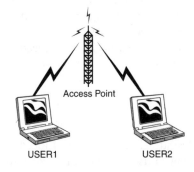

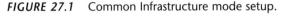

FIGURE 27.1   Common Infrastructure mode setup.

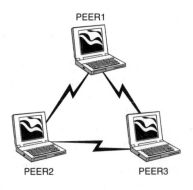

FIGURE 27.2   Common Peer-to-Peer/ad-hoc mode setup.

One of the major disadvantages of this type of wireless network is that there is no central security control; in fact, there is very little security at all. The most difficult part of launching an attack on this type of network is finding one to attack. Because they are informally deployed, they can pop up and disappear overnight. Examples of such networks can be found at conventions and coffee shops, as well as any situation that requires Internet connection sharing (that is, splitting a single Internet connection among several users).

Surveillance

There are several approaches to locating a wireless network. The most basic method is a *surveillance attack*. You can use this technique on the spur of the moment, as it requires no special hardware or preparation. Most significantly, it is difficult, if not impossible, to detect. How is this type of attack launched? You simply observe the environment around you.

Here's an exercise: Whenever you enter a location, whether it's new or very familiar to you, simply open your eyes and search for signs of wireless devices. Also, just because there were not any devices there last week doesn't mean there won't be any today or tomorrow. Table 27.2 gives some suggestions for performing wireless security reconnaissance.

TABLE 27.2 Wireless Security Reconnaissance

Things to Look For	Potential Locations
Antennas	Walls, ceilings, hallways, roofs, windows
Access points	Ceilings, walls, support beams, shelves
Network cable	Traveling up walls or shelves, or across a ceiling
Newly-installed platforms	Walls, hallways and support beams
Devices—Scanners/PDAs	Employees, reception or checkout areas

This might sound basic, but it is still an effective method of reconnaissance. In some cases, you can even find out what type of access point is being used, because many companies place devices in clear view. You can even talk to employees that are using the wireless devices and ask a few simple questions about them. They probably will not be able to give you much usable information, but they might be able to confirm the existence of a wireless network. Be careful when talking to employees and asking questions, as you do not want to tip anybody off to a potential attack.

CAUTION

Even when performing a legitimate security audit of your own network, you still must have prior written permission from your company's management, and you must always obey all local and regional laws.

For example, we took the accompanying pictures (Figures 27.3–27.10) during one such surveillance attack.

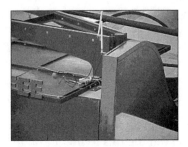

FIGURE 27.3   Antenna and access point found on a surveillance attack.

FIGURE 27.4   Antennas found on a surveillance attack.

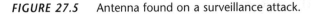

FIGURE 27.5   Antenna found on a surveillance attack.

We took the pictures in Figures 27.3, 27.4, and 27.5 at a nationwide coffee shop chain. In Figure 27.3, you can see a clear shot of the two antennas and the access point. Figures 27.3 and 27.5 demonstrate antenna installations at two different locations. From these pictures, based on our experience we know that they are using an approximately 8-dBi omni-directional antenna for their various installations.

FIGURE 27.6 Access point found on a surveillance attack.

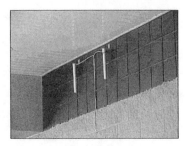

FIGURE 27.7 Antennas found on a surveillance attack.

FIGURE 27.8 Access point found on a surveillance attack.

We took Figure 27.6 at a nationwide discount shoe store chain. All of their locations across the nation are set up with similar configurations. In this picture, you can clearly see the access point, as well as both antennas. Here the company has only chosen to install one 8-dBi antenna and left the other one attached to the access point.

We took Figures 27.7 and 27.8 at a nationwide hardware store chain. The antennas in Figure 27.7 are located outside and are connected to the access point in Figure 27.8 inside. This access point was difficult to miss because of the large orange label that says "AP 10."

FIGURE 27.9   Access point and antennas found on a surveillance attack.

FIGURE 27.10   Access point mount found on a surveillance attack.

Figures 27.9 and 27.10 were taken in a nationwide grocery store chain. You can see in Figure 27.10 the mounting bracket where an access point will be placed; it looks like the antenna is already installed just to the right.

As you can see, the business use of access points is proliferating. APs are routinely found not only in small businesses and homes, but also in large retail chains. However, the fact that you can see a company's access point does not necessarily mean that an attacker will be able to connect to it. He must obtain additional information before he will be able to gain access to the network. In addition, a surveillance attack is not always the best option for discovering a wireless network. Because a surveillance attack is extremely targeted, attackers can go days without seeing anything. In addition, this type of attack is unavailable if an attacker does not have physical access to the premises. Because of this, hackers developed a new method of discovery—war driving.

War Driving

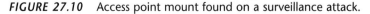

When a surveillance attack is either impossible or too difficult, war driving is an effective alternative. In many situations, war driving follows and adds information to a prior surveillance attack. Conversely, the information obtained from random war driving often leads to a surveillance attack on a discovered location.

The term *war driving* is derived from the 1980s phone hacking tactic known as war dialing. *War dialing* involves dialing all the phone numbers in a given sequence to search for modems. In fact, this method of finding modems is so effective that it's still in use today by many hackers and security professionals. Similarly, war driving, which is in now its infancy, will most likely be used for years to come, both to hack and to help secure wireless networks.

War driving first became popular in 2001. At that point, tools for scanning wireless networks became widely available. The original tools used by war drivers included the basic configuration software that comes with the Wireless Network Interface Card (WNIC). However, this software was not designed with war drivers or security professionals in mind, and thus was not very effective. This created the need for better software. Nevertheless, war drivers have not abandoned the use of WNIC software altogether—in fact, it still serves as a useful complement to modern advanced software.

Why do we need ethical war drivers? Many large corporations have stated that they are not worried about their wireless networks because they would be able to see the attacker in the parking lot and have onsite security pick them up. The problem with this line of thinking is that the wireless networks can, and usually do, extend well past the parking lot. Keep in mind that this is a wireless technology, and unlike standard wired networks, the wireless data packets are not limited by the reach of Cat5 cable. In fact, wireless networks using standard devices and aftermarket antennas have been known to extend over *twenty-five miles*. Knowing this, an attacker can be much farther away than your parking lot and still access your network.

War driving itself does not constitute an attack on the network, and many authorities feel that it does not violate any law. However, this assumption has yet to be tested in the United States court system, and if it ever is, it will be difficult to rule against the war driver.

Specifically, when an attacker (or an honest administrator) is war driving, she is usually on some type of public property, and could even be mobile in some type of car or bus. The software on her computer allows her to capture the beacon frames sent by access points about every 10 milliseconds. Access points use this beacon to broadcast their presence and to detect the presence of other access points in the area. Clients also use the beacon frames to help them determine the available networks in their office. In fact, Microsoft's Windows XP can give you a list of wireless networks using these beacon packets. Thus, war driving *per se* is legal, since the access points are actually reaching out and broadcasting to you, rather than vice versa. You are merely a passive recipient, whether you like it or not.

One of the best-known war driving software packages is called NetStumbler, and it's available free from its kind author Marius Milner at `http://www.netstumbler.com`. NetStumbler examines the beacon frames and then formats them for display.

Significantly, it takes care not to make the raw beacon frames available to the user. The following list shows some of the information that's gathered by NetStumbler and made available based on the beacon frames:

- Basic Service Set ID (BSSID)

  Note: The BSSID (SSID) is a 6-byte hexadecimal number of the access point or base station where the traffic being monitored belongs.

- WEP-enabled or not

- Type of device (AP or peer)

- MAC address of wireless device

- Channel device was heard on

- Signal strength of device

- Longitude and Latitude (if using a GPS)

At no time are actual data frames or any management frames captured or made available to the user of the software. Many access points have the capability to be configured in a stealth mode, thus "disabling the beacon" as one of their options. In reality, the beacon frame is still sent every 10 milliseconds—only the SSID has been removed. If a Network Administrator has done this, NetStumbler will not detect the presence of the network. To review, when using NetStumbler, the following conditions apply:

- A war driver receives a broadcast frame sent by an access point or a peer.

- Only the broadcast frame header is formatted and displayed to the war driver.

- No data or management frames are captured or displayed to the war driver.

Some would question how is this different from wired sniffers that enable you to capture any packets on a network as long as only the header is read. The FCC and the laws regarding the reception of transmitted signals have been amended several times to include new technologies. If you are interested in the legal aspects, make sure to read the Electronic Communications Privacy Act (ECPA). Grove Enterprises Inc has created an easy-to-read, layperson's version called the Listener's Lawbook (http://www.grove-ent.com/LLawbook.html). Prior to starting your career in ethical war driving, make sure you brush up on all the relevant laws in your area.

War driving is typically performed while mobile in cars or buses. One very effective way to war drive a new city is to use public transportation or even a tour bus. Both offer a safe opportunity for you to work the computer and observe what's around you—leaving the driving to someone else. Alternatively, many war drivers are outfitting their vehicles with various setups and antennas to allow for constant war driving (CAUTION: *Not recommended while moving*).

FIGURE 27.11   A vehicle set up for war driving.

These types of setups are becoming more common as mobile electronics are falling in price and becoming popular. The following is a list of items commonly used for war driving:

- Wireless Network Interface Card (Lucent ORiNOCO cards recommended)
- Computer (laptops or PDAs work best)
- Copy of NetStumbler or ORiNOCO NIC software
- Power inverter
- External antenna
- GPS

The last three items are optional, and are not required for war driving. However, we do recommend them for academic researchers, law enforcement, and the military, as they will significantly improve the sensitivity and specificity of your research results.

After obtaining the necessary equipment, a hacker can start searching for wireless networks. You can do this simply by driving the streets of your neighborhood or local business park. Heavily populated metropolitan areas are usually a good place to find several networks. Some of the networks you find might belong to individuals who might be connected to their local DSL or cable modem, whereas others might belong to major corporations. For example, while driving on one normal commute with our equipment inadvertently left on, we found that eight access points—none of which were running encryption—were broadcasting an open invitation to the world. The worst part was that all eight access points were coming from the headquarters of a major financial institution.

To begin war driving using your vender-provided ORiNOCO software, perform the following steps:

1. On a Windows-based computer, install and configure your Lucent WNIC.

2. Launch the ORiNOCO Client Manager (Figure 27.12).

3. From the Actions menu, select Add/Edit Configuration Profile (Figure 27.13).

4. Select the Default profile and click Edit Profile.

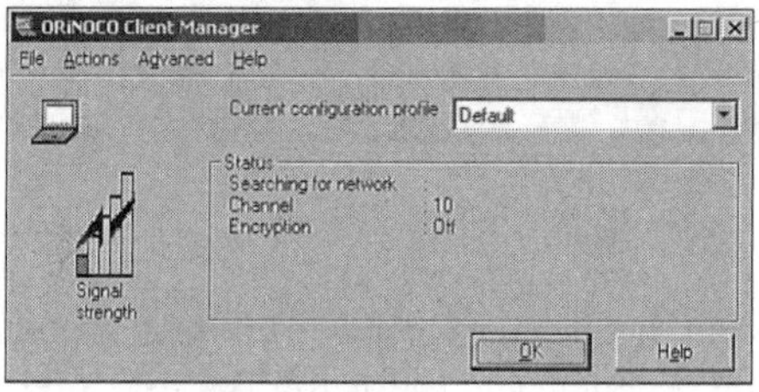

FIGURE 27.12   Configuring ORiNOCO with the Client Manager.

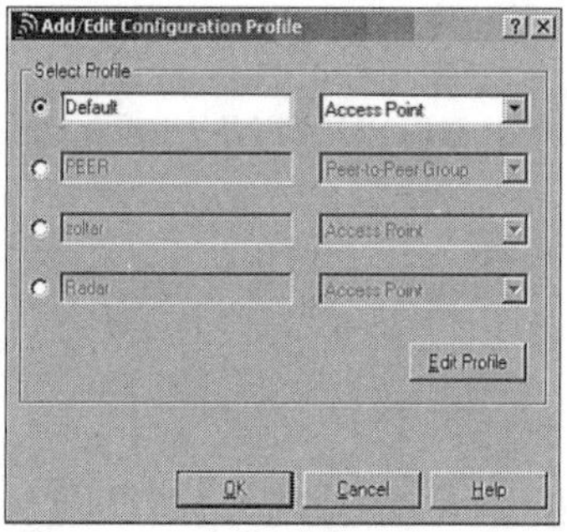

FIGURE 27.13   Editing the Configuration Profile.

5. Set your Network Name (equivalent to the SSID) to ANY. This is a reserved name that tells the WNIC to associate with any SSID (Figure 27.14).

6. Now click on the Admin tab and select Network Assigned MAC Address. This setting allows you to spoof or modify your WNIC's MAC address. This way, when your WNIC registers with an access point, your real MAC address will not be seen. This is also handy if you are attempting to connect to a system

that has restricted access based on the MAC address (please see "Client-to-Client Hacking" later in this chapter for more information). Be creative with your MAC address, as in the example in Figure 27.15 using the MAC address `badf00d4b0b0`.

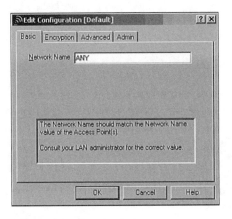

FIGURE 27.14   Configuring the Network Name.

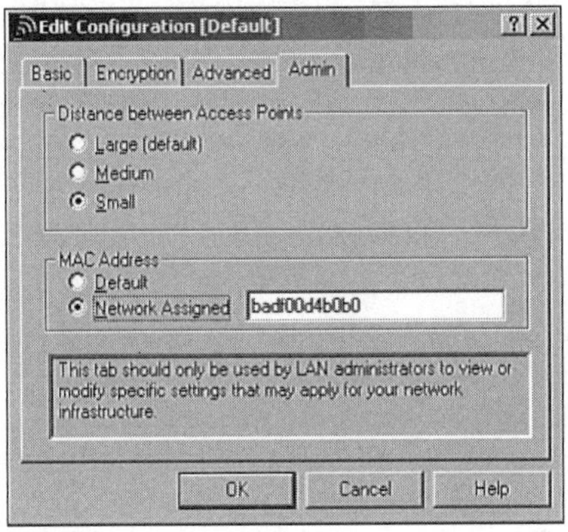

FIGURE 27.15   Entering the MAC address.

With these settings, you will be able to detect the presence of various wireless networks, as demonstrated in Figure 27.16. After you establish an association, you will see the SSID (`zoolander`) and the MAC address of the access point. For more information about the association process, please see the "Client-to-Client Hacking" section later in this chapter.

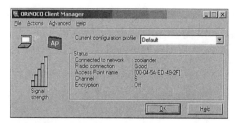

FIGURE 27.16   Detecting the presence of wireless networks.

If a Dynamic Host Configuration Protocol (DHCP) server is running on the access point, or requests are being forwarded onto the wired network, the target network might even assign you a valid IP address! For this to work, your computer must be configured for DHCP for both the IP address and domain name service (DNS) settings. As you will quickly find, the capability to detect and log wireless networks using the ORiNOCO Client Manager is very limited; hence, additional capabilities are necessary. As mentioned previously, NetStumbler is one such product that has more powerful features.

Now let's get NetStumbler up and running:

1. Install and configure your WNIC using the vendor-provided software.

2. From a Windows-based computer, download and install the latest version of NetStumbler from http://www.netstumbler.com.

3. Connect your GPS to your COM port (optional).

4. Launch NetStumbler and click the green Play button at the top of the window.

At this point you can start driving around various residential and business areas. Remember that wireless networks are becoming ubiquitous, so there really is no limit as to where you can search. For example, several national hotel chains have open access points in their lobbies for guests to use. Similarly, national coffee shop chains and airports have Mobile Star access points installed. If you have connected a GPS to your computer, you will also log the location of where you found the access point. Researchers can then output this data to a map, as seen in Figure 27.17, to help track the locations of the networks they have found.

Sometimes larger buildings, such as corporate headquarters, sit so far back on the property and are so large, that even if you are using an external antenna, you will have a difficult time detecting the presence of the networks. In this type of situation, it's nice to have a handheld device such as the Compaq iPAQ with a wireless card in it. Using the iPAQ and a copy of miniStumbler (available from http://www. netstumbler.com), you can put the device in a jacket pocket and enter the building, walking through it floor by floor. As you are walking, miniStumbler is capturing the beacon frames from wireless networks that you might not be able to detect from the street. This is especially effective if you have access to the inside of a specific target office, say for a meeting or interview that you have previously scheduled. This method allows you to conceal the audit, and is a bit less distracting to your staff than walking around with a laptop and an antenna.

FIGURE 27.17   Map of access points found from war driving using GPS data.

Think about the last time you saw somebody on an elevator or in a hallway working on a PDA. Did you guess that he might be war driving, or did you just assume he was checking to see when his next appointment was?

Once you have gathered the information in NetStumber or miniStumbler, you need to analyze and interpret the data you have received. Figure 27.18 is an annotated screenshot of NetStumbler.

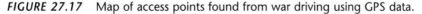

FIGURE 27.18   NetStumbler screenshot.

War driving is performed by all sorts of people. The various war drivers we have met are not the types of people you might expect to be checking out your networks. Most would picture high school kids out on the weekend searching for networks to hack. Granted, these types of people are out there, but the vast majority are older professionals who war drive as part of their legitimate network auditing duties. Over the next few years, more security professionals will add war driving to their regular network maintenance schedule. Unfortunately, more attackers will likewise use this method to detect your wireless network. Thus, it pays to be prepared.

Now that we have found our target wireless network, the actual attack begins.

Client-to-Client Hacking

Clients exist on both wireless and wired networks. A client can range from anything such as a Network Attached Storage (NAS) device, to a printer, or even a server. In a typical ad hoc network, there are no servers or printers—just other individuals' computers. Because the majority of consumer operating systems are Microsoft-based, and because the majority of users do not know to how to secure their computers, there is plenty of room to play here.

For example, an attacker can strike at a laptop that uses a wireless connection. Even though the office has not deployed a wireless connection, a laptop that is connected to the Ethernet could still have its Wireless Network Interface Card installed and configured in PEER mode. Wireless Network Interface Cards running in PEER mode also send out the Probe Request Frames discussed in the war driving section. These Probe Request Frames are sent out at regular intervals in an attempt to connect with another device that has the same SSID. Thus, using a wireless sniffer or NetStumbler, we are able to find wireless devices configured in PEER mode. Figure 27.19 shows a Probe Request Frame that was captured with a wireless sniffer.

This would enable an attacker to connect to the laptop, upon which he could exploit any number of operating system vulnerabilities, thus gaining root access to the laptop. Once an attacker has gained root access to a system, a well-placed Trojan horse or a key logger will enable him to further compromise your various network systems. This type of attack can even take place when the target user is traveling and using her laptop in a hotel lobby or airport, regardless of whether she is actively using her Wireless Network Interface Card.

For a wireless client to send data on a network, the client must create a relationship called an *association* with an access point. During the association process, the client will go through three different states:

1. Unassociated and unauthenticated

2. Unassociated and authenticated

3. Associated and authenticated

```
Flags:          0x00
Status:         0x00
Packet Length: 44
Timestamp:      17:29:13.554563 01/12/1997
Data Rate:      2  1.0 Mbps
Channel:        7  2442 MHz
Signal Level: 90%
802.11 MAC Header
  Version:        0
  Type:           %00  Management
  Subtype:        %0100  Probe Request
  To DS:          0
  From DS:        0
  More Frag.:     0
  Retry:          0
  Power Mgmt:     0
  More Data:      0
  WEP:            0
  Order:          0
  Duration:       0  Microseconds
  Destination:    FF:FF:FF:FF:FF:FF  Broadcast
  Source:         00:A0:F8:8E:E6:3E  SymbolCard
  BSSID:          FF:FF:FF:FF:FF:FF  Broadcast
  Seq. Number:    1891
  Frag. Number:   0
802.11 Management - Probe Request
  Element ID:     0  SSID
  Length:         8
  SSID:           TESTSSID
  Element ID:     1  Supported Rates
  Length:         4
  Supported Rate: 0x02  1.0 Mbps  (Not BSS Basic Rate)
  Supported Rate: 0x04  2.0 Mbps  (Not BSS Basic Rate)
  Supported Rate: 0x0B  5.5 Mbps  (Not BSS Basic Rate)
  Supported Rate: 0x16  11.0 Mbps (Not BSS Basic Rate)
FCS - Frame Check Sequence
  FCS (Calculated): 0x6D823EC4
```

FIGURE 27.19 Probe Request Frame captured with a wireless sniffer.

To begin, a client first has to receive the beacon management frame (packet) from an access point within range. If beacons from more than one access point are received, the client will pick which Basic Service Set to join. For example, the ORiNOCO Client Manager associates with the first BSS heard, but a list of available SSIDs and the capability to switch is available. Those who use Windows XP will be presented with a list of SSIDs, and will be asked to choose what network to join. In addition, the client can broadcast a probe request management frame to any access point.

After an access point has been located, several management frames are exchanged as part of the mutual authentication. There are two standard methods to perform this mutual authentication. The first method is known as *open system authentication*. The majority of access points, especially if left with their default settings, use this method. As the name implies, this is an open system, and all authentication requests are serviced.

The second method is called *shared key authentication*, and it uses a shared secret along with a standard challenge and response. For this to work, the client sends an authentication request management frame stating that it wants to use shared key authentication. When an access point receives the request, it responds to the client by sending an authentication management frame, which contains 128 octets of challenge text. The WEP pseudo-random number generator (PRNG) is used to generate the challenge text with the shared secret and a random initialization vector (IV)[2]. The client then receives the authentication management frame and copies the challenge text into a new frame. A new IV is selected by the client and then included in the frame with the copied challenge text. The entire frame is then WEP-encrypted (using the shared secret) and transmitted to the access point.

When the frame is received, the access point decrypts it and looks at the 32-bit CRC integrity check value (ICV) to verify that it is valid. This is done by comparing the challenge text to that of the first message that was sent. If the text matches, then the authentication is considered successful, but it is only halfway done. At this point, the client and the access point swap roles, and the entire process is repeated. This is done to guarantee mutual authentication. Once completed, the client is considered to be in the second state, Unassociated and Authenticated. Once in this state, a client will send an association request frame to the access point. The access point will respond with an association response frame and send it to the client. When received, the client is then considered to be in the third state, Associated and Authenticated. At this point, the client becomes a PEER and is able to transmit and receive data frames on the network. Figure 27.20 shows the format of an authentication management frame, and Figure 27.21 shows a breakdown of the authentication and association process.

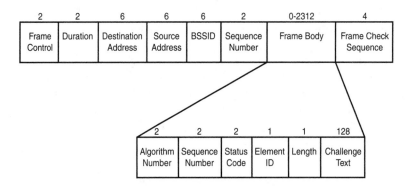

FIGURE 27.20   Authentication management frame.

After your client has been associated and authenticated, you are on the network. However, in most cases, an IP address is required to actually communicate with other clients or servers on the network. Many access points are configured by default to act as a DHCP server. If this is the case, you will be given a valid IP address for that network. If DHCP is not enabled, you will have to assign one to yourself.

Figure 27.22 shows how a typical corporate network might be set up. The firewall offers protection to the internal users and servers, and all wireless devices are inside the firewall. All inbound and outbound Internet traffic is filtered through the firewall. Unfortunately, an attacker that has been associated and authenticated by an access point can suddenly gain access to all internal servers and computers. In addition, the Internet connection can now be exploited to launch an attack on someone else's network.

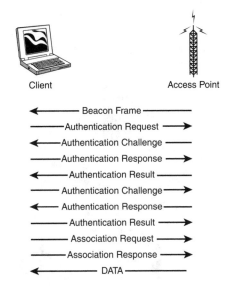

Client   Access Point

←——————— Beacon Frame ———————
———————Authentication Request ———→
←———Authentication Challenge ———
———————Authentication Response ———→
←————— Authentication Result ———
——— Authentication Challenge———→
←——— Authentication Response———
——————— Authentication Result ———→
——————— Association Request ———→
—————Association Response ———→
←——————— DATA ———————

FIGURE 27.21   The Authentication and Association process.

More advanced access points have a feature called Access Control Lists (ACLs). This allows an administrator to pre-define the Ethernet MAC addresses of each client allowed to associate and authenticate. When a client attempts to authenticate, if its MAC address is not contained within the ACL, the client is denied access to the network. As we saw in the war driving section of this chapter, Figure 27.15 showed how it is possible to change the MAC address of our wireless network interface cards. With this functionality, and with a wireless sniffer such as AiroPeek (http://www.wild-packets.com), you can capture a list of MAC addresses that are in use on the network (Figure 27.23). Having gathered this information, you are then able to spoof the Ethernet MAC address of a client listed in the ACL, thus allowing you to associate and authenticate.

After an attacker has been associated and authenticated, his abilities are only limited by your internal network security. For example, suppose you have a network configuration similar to the one in Figure 27.22. This could be your personal home network, or a corporate network with or without all of the components shown. Once the attacker has been associated, his next step will be to gain a valid IP address on the network. Using AiroPeek to sniff wireless frames, the attacker can see a listing of IP addresses currently communicating on the network, and he can get a good idea of how the network IP addressing is configured (Figure 27.24).

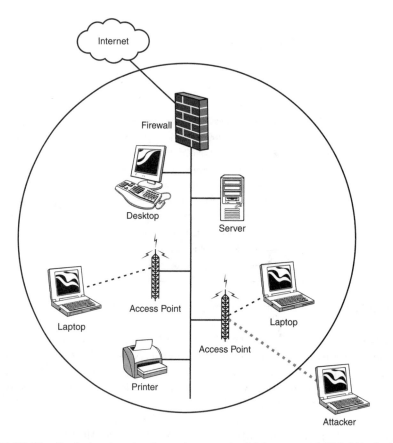

FIGURE 27.22   Typical network setup using standard Ethernet and 802.11b devices.

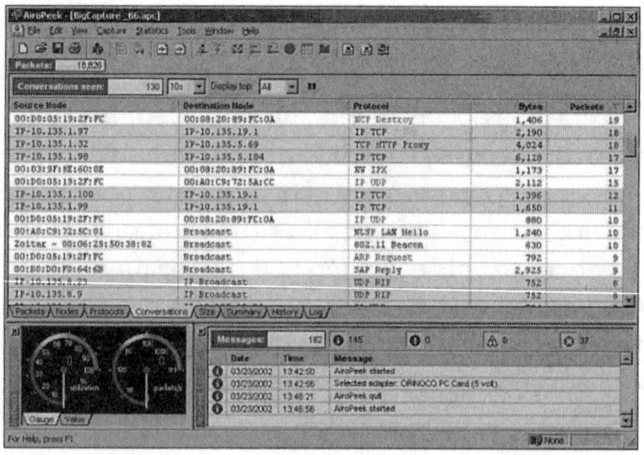

FIGURE 27.23   MAC addresses captured using AiroPeek.

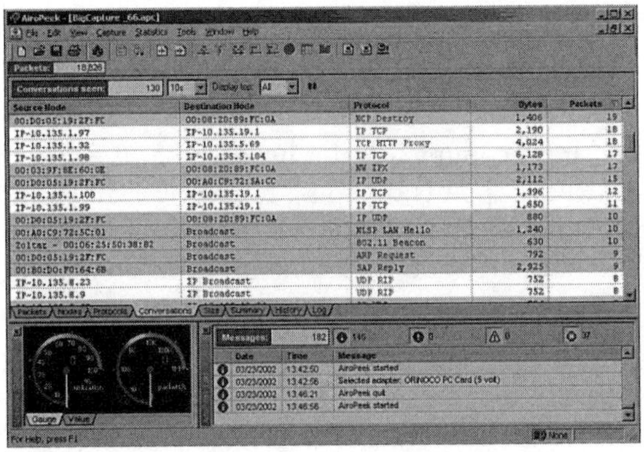

FIGURE 27.24   IP addresses captured using AiroPeek.

Now that the attacker has a valid IP address on your network, it is time for him to find his target and get more information about your setup. The various methods of doing this are no different than those an attacker uses on a standard Ethernet network. Recall when a WNIC associates with an access point, it is as if it is plugging directly into your Ethernet LAN. Hence, general types of information gathering techniques such as port scans and ping sweeps all apply. These various methods will supply the attacker with a list of available resources on your network, such as your printer.

In this example, let's assume the printer has its own built-in TCP spooler and is configurable via a Web interface (a common setup for today's enterprise printers). The attacker finds the printer, and while checking out the Web interface, he spots the capability to put the printer into a test page loop, causing it to print test page after test page. Meanwhile, you are unable to print because the queue is full of these test pages, and your printer is running out of toner quite fast. This is just one example of a fairly harmless yet highly annoying type of attack.

Printer attacks are fairly benign. However, consider how vulnerable this makes your critical data stored on the computers and servers in your network. Consider this paradox: Many companies do not feel it is necessary to protect their internal networks from attacks generated on the inside. Why, then, do they lock their building doors at night, yet not supply every employee with a key?

Rogue Access Points

Rogue access points are those connected to a network without planning or permission from the network administrator. For example, we know one administrator in Dallas who just did his first wireless security scan (war driving) on his eight-building office campus. To his surprise, he found more than thirty access points. Worse, only four of them had authorization to be connected to the network. Needless to say, heads rolled.

Rogue access points are becoming a major headache in the security industry. With the price of low-end access points dropping to just over one hundred dollars, they are becoming ubiquitous. Furthermore, many access points feature settings that make them next to transparent on the actual network, so their presence cannot be easily detected.

Many rogue access points are placed by employees looking for additional freedom to move about at work. The employees simply bring their access points from home and plug them directly into the corporate LAN without authorization from the IT staff. These types of rogue access points can be very dangerous, as most users are not aware of all the security issues with wireless devices, let alone the security issues with the wired network they use each day.

In addition, it is not always well-intentioned employees who deploy rogue access points. Disgruntled employees, or even attackers, can deploy an access point on your network in seconds, and they can then connect to it later that night. In addition, if the access point has DHCP enabled, you now have a rogue DHCP server in addition to a wireless hole in your perimeter.

The following are seven key points to successfully placing a rogue access point:

- Determine what benefit can be gained from placing the access point.

- Plan for the future. Pick a location that will allow you the ability to work on a laptop or PDA without looking suspicious.

- Place the access point in a discreet location that allows for maximum coverage from your connection point.

- Disable the SSID Broadcast (silent mode). This will further complicate the process of detecting the access point, as it will now require a wireless sniffer to detect the rogue access point.

- Disable any management features. Many access points have the ability to send out SNMP traps on both the wired and wireless networks.

- Whenever possible, place the access point behind some type of firewall, thus blocking the MAC address from the LAN and the ARP tables of routers. There are several programs on the market that scan wired networks looking for the MAC addresses of access points.

- Do not get greedy! Leave the access point deployed for short periods of time only. The longer it is deployed, the more likely you are to get caught.

CAUTION

The preceding steps should only be used when experimenting on your own personal test network.

If you already have a wireless network deployed and someone places a rogue access point on your network using your existing SSID, you might have additional problems. This type of access point can extend your network well beyond the bounds of your office. In some cases, the rogue access point can be set up as a link broadcasting your network traffic across town. They can even be made to appear as if they are part of your network, thus causing clients on your network to use them for connectivity. When a client connects to the rogue access point and attempts to access a server, the username and password could be captured and used later to launch an attack on the network.

Jamming (Denial of Service)

Denial-of-service (DoS) attacks, as you learned earlier in this book, are those that prevent the proper use of functions or services. Such attacks can also be extrapolated to wireless networks. To understand this, we must first consider how wireless 802.11b networks operate and upon what frequencies they run.

Effectively attacking (or securing) a wireless network requires a certain level of knowledge about how radio transmitters, frequencies, and wavelengths work and relate to each other. In the United States, the Federal Communication Commission (FCC) governs frequencies and their allocation. Devices such as police radios, garage door openers, cordless phones, GPS receivers, microwave ovens, and cell phones use various frequencies to operate. In fact, millions of such devices are capable of operating simultaneously on the various frequencies of the radio spectrum (see Table 27.3).

TABLE 27.3   The Radio Spectrum as Defined by the FCC

Band Name	Range	Usage
Very Low Frequency (VLF)	10kHz to 30kHz	Cable locating equipment
Low Frequency (LF)	30kHz to 300kHz	Maritime mobile service
Medium Frequency (MF)	300kHz to 3MHz	Avalanche transceivers, aircraft navigation, ham radio
High Frequency (HF)	3MHz to 30MHz	Radio astronomy, Radio telephone, Civil Air Patrol, CB radios
Very High Frequency (VHF)	30MHz to 328.6MHz	Cordless phones, television, RC cars, aircraft/police/business radios

TABLE 27.3   Continued

Band Name	Range	Usage
Ultra High Frequency (UHF)	328.6MHz to 2.9GHz	Police/fire radios, business radios, cellular phones, GPS, paging, wireless networks, cordless phones
Super High Frequency (SHF)	2.9GHz to 30GHz	Terminal doppler weather radar, various satellite communications
Extremely High Frequency (EHF)	30GHz and above	Government radio, astronomy, military, vehicle radar systems, ham radio

Radio waves are very easy to create; in fact, you can demonstrate this right now. The following list illustrates how to create and hear your own radio waves.

Items needed: 9-volt battery, quarter, AM radio

1. Tune the AM radio to a spot between radio stations, so that you hear static.

2. Place the battery near the antenna of the AM radio.

3. Quickly tap the quarter onto the two terminals of the battery, making sure the quarter comes in contact with both terminals simultaneously.

Each time the quarter comes in contact with the battery terminals, it will generate a small radio wave, causing a crackle in the radio.

The circuit you create produces circular waves of electromagnetic interference, perpendicular to the direction of electrical flow.

TABLE 27.4   Frequency and Channel Assignments

CHANNEL	FREQUENCY	CHANNEL	FREQUENCY
1	2.412GHz	8	2.447GHz
2	2.417GHz	9	2.452GHz
3	2.422GHz	10	2.457GHz
4	2.427GHz	11	2.462GHz
5	2.432GHz	12	2.467GHz
6	2.437GHz	13	2.472GHz
7	2.442GHz	14	2.484GHz

When an 802.11b device is sending data, it is not just transmitting on a single frequency. A technology called Direct Sequence Spread Spectrum (DSSS) is used to spread the transmission over multiple frequencies. DSSS is designed to maximize the effectiveness of the radio transmission, while minimizing the potential for interference. In DSSS, a Channel refers to a specific ruleset rather than a particular frequency. These rulesets define how the radio will spread the signal across multiple frequencies, also identified as channels. It is much like having a party at your house at which there are people in eleven different rooms. In each of the eleven rooms, the guests are having a different conversation, and the sound is traveling from room to room. While you are in room one, you can hear the conversations of rooms one, two, three, four, and five. Guests in room six can hear the conversations in rooms two, three, four, five, six, seven, eight, nine, and ten, but they cannot hear anything from room one because of a wall, or *ruleset*. Table 27.5 illustrates the channel layout and shows what can be heard by each channel ruleset. In the entire eleven rulesets, there are only three that do not overlap—CH1, CH6, and CH11.

TABLE 27.5   DSSS Channel Overlap Guide

CH1	CH2	CH3	CH4	CH5	CH6	CH7	CH8	CH9	CH10	CH11
CH1	CH2	CH3	CH4	CH5						
CH1	CH2	CH3	CH4	CH5	CH6					
CH1	CH2	CH3	CH4	CH5	CH6	CH7				
CH1	CH2	CH3	CH4	CH5	CH6	CH7	CH8			
CH1	CH2	CH3	CH4	CH5	CH6	CH7	CH8	CH9		
	CH2	CH3	CH4	CH5	CH6	CH7	CH8	CH9	CH10	
		CH3	CH4	CH5	CH6	CH7	CH8	CH9	CH10	CH11
			CH4	CH5	CH6	CH7	CH8	CH9	CH10	CH11
				CH5	CH6	CH7	CH8	CH9	CH10	CH11
					CH6	CH7	CH8	CH9	CH10	CH11
						CH7	CH8	CH9	CH10	CH11

Conversations governed by ruleset 6 (Channel 6) cannot be heard by a station operating according to ruleset 1 or 11. Thus, in large infrastructure environments, there are really only three rulesets available. For an attacker building some type of jamming device, this is important. Based on the chart in Table 27.5, you can see that by targeting channels 5, 6, and 7, the jammer can cause the maximum amount of interference.

Jamming or causing interference to an 802.11b network can be fairly simple. There are several commercially available devices that that will bring a wireless network to its knees. For example, a Bluetooth-enabled device is one such item that can cause headaches for 802.11b networks. We have found that when a Bluetooth device is located within approximately ten meters of 802.11b devices, the Bluetooth device will cause a jamming type of denial-of-service attack. The same is true of several

2.4GHz cordless phones that are currently available. This is because the 2.4GHz band is becoming widely used and is considered shared, thus allowing all kinds of devices to use it.

The signals generated by these devices can appear to be an 802.11 transmission to other stations on the wireless network, thus causing them to hold their transmissions until the signal has gone, or until you have hung up the cordless phone. The other possibility is that the devices will just cause an increase in RF noise, which could cause the 802.11b devices to switch to a slower data rate. Devices re-send frames over and over again to increase the odds of the other station receiving it. Normally, data is transmitted at 11Mbps when sending one copy of each frame. If it were to drop to 50% efficiency, the device would still be transmitting at 11Mbps, but it would be sending a duplicate of each frame, making the effective speed 5.5Mbps. Thus you will have a significant decrease in network performance because of re-sending duplicate frames. In addition, with a high level of RF noise, you can expect to see an increase in corrupt frames, which also requires a full retransmission of the packet.

Practical WEP Cracking

Unfortunately, WEP is fundamentally flawed, allowing you to crack it. However, even though it is possible to crack WEP encryption, we still highly recommend that you use it on all of your wireless networks. This will thwart the casual drive-by hacker, and it also enables another layer of legal protection that prohibits the cracking of transmitted, encrypted signals. With that in mind, let's look at the practical process of cracking WEP.

The most important tool that you'll need to crack a WEP-encrypted signal is time. The longer you capture data, the more likely you are to receive a frame that will leak a key byte. There is only about a 5% chance, in some cases a 13% chance, of this happening. On average, you will need to receive about 5,000,000 frames to crack a WEP-encrypted signal. To actually capture the encrypted data, you will need a wireless sniffer such as AirSnort (available at `http://airsnort.shmoo.com/`). In addition to the wireless sniffer, you will also need a series of Perl scripts, which are called (appropriately) WEPCRACK. These scripts are available online at the following URL:

`http://sourceforge.net/projects/wepcrack/`

After you have acquired the necessary tools, please refer to the following list for a step-by-step guide to cracking a WEP-encrypted signal.

1. Using your wireless sniffer, capture the WEP encrypted signal. As previously mentioned, you will need to capture about 5,000,000 frames.

2. From a command prompt, execute the `prism-getIV.pl` script using the following syntax:

```
prism-getIV.pl capturefile_name
```

where `capturefile_name` is the name of your capture file from step 1. When a weak IV is found, a file named `IVFile.log` is created for later use.

3. Now that the `IVfile.log` file has been created, you need to run `WEPcrack.pl`. This file will use the `IVfile.log` to look at the IVs and attempt to guess the WEP key.

4. When you run `WEPcrack.pl`, the output is in decimal format. So blow the dust off your favorite decimal-to-hex conversion chart and start converting to hex.

The following shows the decimal-to-hex conversion data.

```
95 = 5F
211 = D3
124 = 7C
211 = D3
232 = E8
27 = 1B
211 = D3
44 = 2C
42 = 2A
53 = 35
47 = 2F
185 = B9
48 = 30
95:211:211:53:185:211:232:44:47:48:124:27:42 (Decimal)
5F:D3:D3:35:B9:D3:E8:2C:2F:30:7C:1B:2A (HEX)
```

5. Take the hex version of the key and enter it into your Client Manager.

Summary

With the recent explosion in the use of 802.11b networks, the state of network security has been set back over a decade. In many cases, the goal of the attacker is not just to connect to and exploit the wireless network, but also to gain free Internet access or a foothold into the wired network beyond. If you are planning to deploy a wireless network, always put security first. In addition, security managers must implement measures to detect and combat rogue access points and unauthorized clients.

There are many 802.11b hardware vendors, and as the popularity of wireless networks increases, there are sure to be more. The products that we have tested and included in this chapter are a tiny selection of the vast array of products on the market. However, each of the products reviewed herein has exceeded our expectations, and you have our personal recommendation on each of them. Of course, each person and network is unique. You should consider specific environment and application requirements when you decide to purchase one product over another.

Wired Equivalent Privacy (WEP) should be used on all deployments of 802.11b networks. This technology, although flawed, will prevent casual interpretation of your network traffic and will help reduce the number of attacks against it. Although it is possible to crack WEP, the amount of time required to do so, combined with the sheer number of easier-to-crack access points that are not running it usually causes an attacker to look elsewhere. However, you should not rely on WEP as your sole measure of security. As always, a traditional, layered approach to security is best.

Wireless attacks can be launched by virtually anyone, from virtually anywhere. From the person next to you in the elevator working on her PDA to the occupants of the car driving next to you at 70 MPH on the freeway, all can be hacking your wireless networks at this very moment. If you do not take the necessary precautions to protect yourself, you might as well just give them a key to your office.

PART VII

References

IN THIS PART

A

Security Bibliography— Further Reading

This appendix is a bibliography on Internet security. Many of these books were released in the last year. Some treat the subject generally, whereas others are more focused, but I recommend all of them as further reading— think of this bibliography as the Internet security dream library.

General Internet Security

Absolute Beginner's Guide to Personal Firewalls. Lee and Ford. Que, 2001. ISBN: 0789726254.

Access Control and Personal Identification Systems. Don M. Bowers. Butterworth-Heinemann, 1998. ISBN: 0750697326.

Advanced Military Cryptography. William F. Friedman. Aegean Park Press, 1996. ISBN: 0894120115.

Applied Cryptography: Protocols, Algorithms, and Source Code in C. Bruce Schneier. John Wiley & Sons, 1995. ISBN: 0471117099.

Applied Java Cryptography. Merlin Hughes. Manning Publications, 1998. ISBN: 1884777635.

AS/400 Security in a Client/Server Environment. Joseph S. Park. John Wiley & Sons, 1995. ISBN: 0471116831.

Audit Trail Administration, UNIX Svr 4.2. Unix Systems Lab. Prentice Hall, 1993. ISBN: 0130668877.

Bandits on the Information Superhighway (What You Need to Know). Daniel J. Barrett. O'Reilly & Associates, 1996. ISBN: 1565921569.

Basic Methods of Cryptography. Jan C. A. van der Lubbe. Cambridge University Press, 1998. ISBN: 0521555590.

Break the Code: Cryptography for Beginners. Bud Johnson and Larry Daste. Dover Publications, 1997. ISBN: 0486291464.

Building in Big Brother: The Cryptographic Policy Debate. Edited by Lance J. Hoffman. Springer Verlag, 1995. ISBN: 0387944419.

Building Internet Firewalls, Second Edition. E. Zwicky, S. Cooper, D. B. Chapman, and D. Russell. O'Reilly & Associates, 2000. ISBN: 1565928717.

Building Secure and Reliable Network Applications. Kenneth P. Birman. Prentice Hall, 1997. ISBN: 0137195842.

Cisco Router Configuration and Troubleshooting. Mark Tripod. New Riders, 2000. ISBN: 0735709998.

Cisco Secure Internet Security Solutions. Andrew Mason and Mark J. Newcomb. Cisco Press, 2001. ISBN: 1587050161.

The Code Book, The Evolution of Secrecy from Mary, Queen of Scots to Quantum Cryptography. Simon Singh. Doubleday, 1999. ISBN: 0385495315.

The Codebreakers: The Comprehensive History of Secret Communication from Ancient Times to the Internet. David Kahn. Scribner, 1996. ISBN: 0684831309.

Codes and Cryptography. Dominic Welsh. Oxford University Press, 1988. ISBN: 0198532873.

Codes Ciphers and Secret Writing. Martin Gardner. Dover Publications, 1984. ISBN: 0486247619.

Computer Crime: A Crimefighter's Handbook. David J. Icove, Karl Icove, and William Vonstorch. O'Reilly & Associates, 1995. ISBN: 1565920864.

Computer Forensics: Incident Response Essentials. Warren G. Kruse II and Jay G. Heiser. Addison-Wesley, 2001. ISBN: 0201707195.

Computer Security. D. W. Roberts. Blenheim Online Publications, 1990. ISBN: 0863531806.

Computer Security and Privacy: An Information Sourcebook. Mark W. Greenia. Lexikon Services, 1998. ISBN: 0944601464.

Computer Security Risk Management. I. C. Palmer and G. A. Potter. Van Nostrand Reinhold, 1990. ISBN: 0442302908.

Computers Ethics & Social Values. Deborah G. Johnson and Helen Nissenbaum. Prentice Hall, 1995. ISBN: 0131031104.

Computers Ethics and Society. M. David Ermann, Mary B. Williams, and Michele S. Shauf. Oxford University Press, 1997. ISBN: 019510756X.

Computers Under Attack: Intruders, Worms, and Viruses. Peter J. Denning. Addison-Wesley, 1990. ISBN: 0201530678.

Course in Cryptography. Marcel Givierge. Aegean Park Press, 1996. ISBN: 089412028X.

Cyber Crime: How to Protect Yourself from Computer Criminals. Laura E. Quarantiello. Tiare Publications, 1996. ISBN: 0936653744.

Cyberpunk Handbook. R. U. Sirius and Bart Nagel. Random House, 1995. ISBN: 0679762302.

Cyberpunk: Outlaws and Hackers on the Computer Frontier. Katie Hafner and John Markoff. Simon & Schuster, 1991. ISBN: 0671683225.

Cyberwars: Espionage on the Internet. Jean Guisnel and Winn Schwartau. Plenum Press, 1997. ISBN: 0306456362.

Crypto: When the Code Rebels Beat the Government—Saving Privacy in the Digital Age. Steven Levy. Viking Press, 2000. ISBN: 0670859508.

Cryptography Decrypted. H. X. Mel, Doris Baker, and Steve Burnett. Addison-Wesley, 2000. ISBN: 0201616475

Cryptography and Secure Communications. Man Young Rhee. McGraw-Hill, 1994. ISBN: 0071125027.

Cryptography, the Science of Secret Writing. Laurence D. Smith. Dover Publications, 1955. ISBN: 048620247X.

Cryptography: Theory and Practice (Discrete Mathematics and Its Applications). Douglas R. Stinson. CRC Publications, 1995. ISBN: 0849385210.

Designing Secure Web-Based Applications for Microsoft Windows 2000. Michael Howard. Microsoft Press, 2000. ISBN: 0735609950.

Digital Copyright Protection. Peter Wayner. AP Professional, 1997. ISBN: 0127887717.

Distributed Programming Paradigms with Cryptography Applications. J. S. Greenfield. Springer Verlag, 1994. ISBN: 354058496X.

E-Commerce Security: Weak Links, Best Defenses. Anup K. Ghosh. John Wiley & Sons, 1998. ISBN: 0471192236.

E-Mail Security: How To Keep Your Electronic Messages Private. Bruce Schneier. John Wiley & Sons, 1995. ISBN: 047105318X.

Elementary Military Cryptography. William F. Friedman. Aegean Park Press, 1996. ISBN: 0894120999.

Encyclopedia of Cryptology. David E. Newton. ABC-Clio Publications, 1997. ISBN: 0874367727.

Enigma: How the German Cipher Was Broken, and How It Was Read by the Allies in WWII. Wladyslaw Kozaczuk. University Publications of America, 1984. ISBN: 0313270074.

Essential Checkpoint Firewall-1: An Installation, Configuration, and Troubleshooting Guide. Daemon D. Welch-Abernathy. Addison-Wesley, 2002. ISBN: 0201699508.

Essential SCO System Administration. Keith Vann. Prentice Hall, 1995. ISBN: 013290859X.

Essential Windows NT System Administration. Aeleen Frisch. O'Reilly & Associates, 1998. ISBN: 1565922743.

Executive Guide to Preventing Information Technology Disasters. Richard Ennals. Springer Verlag, 1996. ISBN: 3540199284.

Fire in the Computer Room, What Now?: Disaster Recovery Preparing for Business Survival. Gregor Neaga, Bruce Winters, and Pat Laufman. Prentice Hall, 1997. ISBN: 0137543913.

Firewalls and Internet Security: Repelling the Wily Hacker. William R. Cheswick and Steven M. Bellovin. Addison-Wesley, 1994. ISBN: 0201633574.

Firewalls Complete. Marcus Goncalves. McGraw-Hill, 1998. ISBN: 0070246459.

Fundamentals of Computer Security Technology. Edward Amoroso. Prentice Hall, 1994. ISBN: 0131089293.

Hackers Beware: The Ultimate Guide to Network Security. Eric Cole. New Riders, 2001. ISBN: 0735710090.

Hack I.T.—Security Through Penetration Testing. T. J. Klevinsky, Scott Laliberte, and Ajay Gupta. Addison-Wesley Professional, 2002. ISBN: 0201719568.

Hack Proofing Sun Solaris 8. Miles, ed., et al. Syngress Media, 2001. ISBN: 192899444X.

Hack Proofing Your Network: Internet Tradecraft. Edited by Syngress Media and Ryan Russell. Syngress Media, 2000. ISBN: 1928994156.

The Hacker Diaries: Confessions of Teenage Hackers. Dan Verton. Osborne McGraw-Hill, 2002. ISBN 0072223642.

Hacking Exposed: Network Security Secrets and Solutions. Joel Scambray, Stuart McClure, and George Kurtz. McGraw-Hill, 2000. ISBN: 0072127481.

Hacking Exposed Windows 2000. Joel Scambray and Stuart McClure. McGraw-Hill, 2001. ISBN: 0072192623.

Handbook of Applied Cryptography. Alfred J. Menezes, Paul C. Van Oorschot, and Scott A. Vanstone. CRC Press, 1996. ISBN: 0849385237.

Have You Locked the Castle Gate? Home and Small Business Computer Security. Brian Shea. Addison-Wesley Professional, 2002. ISBN: 020171955X.

HP-Ux 11.X System Administration. Martin Poniatowski and Marty Poniatowski. Prentice Hall, 1998. ISBN: 0130125156.

HP_UX 11i Security. Chris Wong. Prentice Hall, 2001. ISBN: 0130330620.

HP-Ux System Administration Handbook and Toolkit. Marty Poniatowski. Prentice Hall, 1998. ISBN: 0139055711.

Implementing AS/400 Security. Wayne Madden and Carol Woodbury. Duke Communications, 1998. ISBN: 1882419782.

Incident Response: Investigating Computer Crime. Chris Prosise and Kevin Mandia. McGraw-Hill Professional Publishing, 2001. ISBN: 0072131829.

Information Security: An Integrated Collection of Essays. Marshall D. Abrams, Sushil Jajodia, and Harold J. Podell. Unknown, 1995. ISBN: 0818636629.

Information Security Management Handbook, Fourth Edition. Micki Krause and Harold Tipton. CRC Press, 1999. ISBN: 0849398290

Internet and TCP/IP Network Security: Securing Protocols and Applications. Uday O. Pabrai and Vijay K. Gurbani. McGraw-Hill, 1996. ISBN: 0070482152.

Internet Besieged: Countering Cyberspace Scofflaws. Dorothy E. Denning and Peter J. Denning. Addison-Wesley, 1997. ISBN: 0201308207.

Internet Cryptography. Richard E. Smith. Addison-Wesley, 1997. ISBN: 0201924803.

Internet Firewalls and Network Security. Chris Hare and Karanjit S. Siyan, Ph.D. New Riders, 1996. ISBN: 1562056328.

Internet Security for Your Macintosh. Alan Oppenheimer and Charles Whitaker. Peachpit Press, 2001. ISBN: 0201749696.

Internet Security with Windows NT. Mark Joseph Edwards. Duke Communications, 1997. ISBN: 1882419626.

Internet Site Security. Erik Schetina, Ken Green, and Jacob Carlson. Addison-Wesley Professional, 2002. ISBN 0672323060.

Intranet Firewalls. Scott Fuller and Kevin Pagan. Ventana Communications Group, 1997. ISBN: 1566045061.

Intranet Security: Stories from the Trenches. Linda McCarthy. Prentice Hall, 1997. ISBN: 0138947597.

Introduction to the Analysis of the Data Encryption Standard. Wayne G. Barker. Aegean Park Press, 1989. ISBN: 0894121693.

Introduction to the Public Key Infrastructure for the Internet. Messaoud Benantar. Prentice Hall, 2001. ISBN: 0130609277.

Intrusion Detection. Rebecca Gurley Bace. New Riders, 1999. ISBN: 157801856.

Intrusion Signatures and Analysis. Stephen Northcutt, Karen Frederick, Matt Fearnow, and Mark Cooper. New Riders, 2001. ISBN: 0735710635.

Java Cryptography. Jonathan B. Knudsen. O'Reilly & Associates, 1998. ISBN: 1565924029.

Java Network Security. Dave Durbin, John Owlett, Andrew Yeomans, and Robert S. MacGregor. Prentice Hall, 1998. ISBN: 0137615299.

Java Security. Scott Oakes. O'Reilly & Associates, 1998. ISBN: 1565924037.

Java Security: Managing the Risks. MindQ Publishing, 1997. ISBN: 1575590123.

Linux Firewalls, Second Edition. Robert Ziegler. New Riders, 2001. ISBN: 0735710996.

Linux Security. Ramon J. Hontanon and Craig Hunt. Sybex, 2001. ISBN: 078212741X.

Masters of Deception: The Gang That Ruled Cyberspace. Michele Slatalla and Joshua Quittner. Harper Perennial Library, 1996. ISBN: 0060926945.

Maximum Linux Security, Second Edition. J. Ray and Anonymous. Sams, 2001. ISBN: 0672321343.

Microsoft Windows NT Network Administration Training. Microsoft Educational Services Staff. Microsoft Press, 1997. ISBN: 1572314397.

Netware Security. Doug Bierer and William Steen. New Riders, 1996. ISBN: 1562055453.

Network Intrusion Detection: An Analyst's Handbook, Second Edition. Stephen Northcutt and Judy Novak. New Riders, 2000. ISBN: 0735710082.

Network and Internetwork Security: Principles and Practice. William
Stallings. Prentice Hall, 1995. ISBN: 0024154830.

Network Security in a Mixed Environment. Dan Balckarski. IDG Books, 1998.
ISBN: 0764531522.

NT Network Security. Matthew Strebe, Charles Perkins, and Michael Moncur.
Sybex, 1998. ISBN: 0782120067.

Pcweek Microsoft Windows NT Security: System Administrator's Guide.
Nevin Lambert, Manish Patel, and Steve Sutton. Ziff-Davis, 1997. ISBN: 1562764578.

PKI: Implementing & Managing E-Security. Andrew Nash, Bill Duane,
Derek Brink, and Celia Joseph. Osborne McGraw-Hall, 2001. ISBN: 0072131233.

PC Security and Virus Protection. Pamela Kane. IDG Books, 1994.
ISBN: 1558513906.

***The Personal Internet Security Guidebook: Keeping Hackers and Crackers
Out of Your Home.*** Tim Speed, Juanita Ellis, and Steffano Korper. Academic Press,
2001. ISBN 0126565619.

***Planning for PKI: Best Practices Guide for Deploying Public Key
Infrastructure.*** Russ Housley and Tim Polk. John Wiley & Sons, 2001. ISBN:
0471397024.

Practical Cryptography for Data Internetworks. Edited by William Stallings.
IEEE Computer Society, 1996. ISBN: 0818671408.

Practical Intrusion Detection Handbook. Paul E. Proctor. Prentice Hall, 2000.
ISBN: 0130259608.

Practical UNIX and Internet Security. Simson Garfinkel and Gene Spafford.
O'Reilly & Associates, 1996. ISBN: 1565921488.

Privacy Defended: Protecting Yourself Online. Gary Bahadur, William Chan,
and Chris Weber. Que, 2002. ISBN 078972605X.

The Process of Network Security. Thomas A. Wadlow. Addison-Wesley, 2000.
ISBN: 0201433176.

Protecting Business Information: A Manager's Guide. James A. Schweitzer.
Butterworth-Heinemann, 1995. ISBN: 0750696583.

Protecting Your Digital Privacy! Survival Skills for the Information Age.
Glee Harrah Cady and Pat McGregor. Que, 2001. ISBN: 0789726041.

Protecting Your Web Site with Firewalls. Marcus Goncalves and Vinicius A.
Goncalves. Prentice Hall, 1997. ISBN: 0136282075.

Protecting Yourself Online: The Definitive Resource on Safety Freedom and Privacy in Cyberspace. Robert B. Gelman and Stanton McCandlish. Harper Collins, 1998. ISBN: 0062515128.

Public-Key Cryptography. Arto Salomaa. Springer Verlag, 1996. ISBN: 3540613560.

Risky Business: Protect Your Business from Being Stalked, Conned, Libeled or Blackmailed on the Web. Dan Janal. John Wiley & Sons, 1998. ISBN: 0471197068.

Secrets and Lies. Bruce Schneier. John Wiley & Sons, 2000. ISBN: 0471253111.

Secrets of Making and Breaking Codes. Hamilton Nickels. Citadel Press, 1994. ISBN: 0806515635.

Secure Electronic Commerce: Building the Infrastructure for Digital Signatures and Encryption. Warwick Ford and Michael S. Baum. Prentice Hall, 1997. ISBN: 0134763424.

Secure Electronic Transactions: Introduction and Technical Reference. Larry Loeb. Artech House, 1998. ISBN: 0890069921.

Securing Java: Getting Down to Business with Mobile Code, Second Edition. Gary McGraw and Edward W. Felten. John Wiley & Sons, 1999. ISBN: 047131952X

Securing Windows NT/2000 Servers for the Internet: A Checklist for System Administrators. Stefan Norberg and Deborah Russell. O'Reilly & Associates, 2000. ISBN: 1565927680.

Security Fundamentals for E-Commerce. Vesna Hassler. Artech House, 2002. ISBN: B000066FXJ.

Security, ID Systems, and Locks: The Book on Electronic Access Control. Joel Koniecek and Karen Little. Butterworth-Heinemann, 1997. ISBN: 0750699329.

Security Survival: A Source Book from the Open Group. X Open Guide. Prentice Hall, 1997. ISBN: 0132666286.

Smart Card Security and Applications. Mike Hendry. Artech House, 1997. ISBN: 0890069530.

Solaris 8 Security. Edgar Danielyan. New Riders, 2001. ISBN: 1578702704.

Solaris Security. Peter Gregory. Prentice Hall, 1999. ISBN: 0130960535.

Solaris Security Step by Step. Hal Pomeranz. SANS Institute, 1999. ISBN: 0967299225.

SSH, The Secure Shell: The Definitive Guide. Barrett and Silverman. O'Reilly and Associates, 2001. ISBN: 0596000111.

Technology and Privacy: The New Landscape. Philip E. Agre and Marc Rotenberg. MIT Press, 1997. ISBN: 026201162X.

The Ultimate Computer Security Survey/Book and Disk. James L. Schaub and Ken D. Biery, Butterworth-Heinemann, 1995. ISBN: 0750696923.

The Ultimate Windows 2000 System Administrator's Guide. Robert Williams and Mark Walla. Addison-Wesley, 2000. ISBN: 0201615800.

Understanding Digital Signatures: Establishing Trust over the Internet and Other Networks. Gail L. Grant. McGraw-Hill, 1997. ISBN: 0070125546.

UNIX Installation Security and Integrity. David Ferbrache and Gavin Shearer. Prentice Hall, 1993. ISBN: 0130153893.

UNIX Security. Miller Freeman. Miller Freeman, 1997. ISBN: 0879304715.

Web Commerce Cookbook. Gordon McComb. John Wiley & Sons, 1997. ISBN: 0471196630.

Web Psychos, Stalkers, and Pranksters: How to Protect Yourself in Cyberspace. Michael A. Banks. Coriolis Group, 1997. ISBN: 1576101371.

Web Security & Commerce. Simson Garfinkel and Gene Spafford. O'Reilly & Associates, 1997. ISBN: 1565922697.

Web Security Sourcebook. Avi Rubin, Daniel Geer, and Marcus J. Ranum. John Wiley & Sons, 1997. ISBN: 047118148X.

Web Security: A Step-By-Step Reference Guide. Lincoln D. Stein. Addison-Wesley, 1998. ISBN: 0201634899.

Who Knows: Safeguarding Your Privacy in a Networked World. Ann Cavoukian and Don Tapscott. Random House, 1996. ISBN: 0070633207.

Windows Internet Security. Seth Fogie and Cyrus Peikari. Prentice Hall, 2001. ISBN: 0130428310.

Windows NT Security Guide. Steve A. Sutton. Addison-Wesley, 1996. ISBN: 0201419696.

Windows NT Security Handbook. Tom Sheldon. Osborne McGraw-Hill, 1996. ISBN: 0078822408.

Windows NT Security: A Practical Guide to Securing Windows NT Servers and Workstations. Charles B. Rutstein. McGraw-Hill, 1997. ISBN: 0070578338.

Windows NT Server 4 Security Handbook. Lee Hadfield, Dave Hatter, and Dave Bixler. Que, 1997. ISBN: 078971213X.

Windows 2000 Security Handbook. Cox and Sheldon. McGraw-Hill Professional Publishing, 2000. ISBN: 0072124334.

Wireless Security: Models, Threats, and Solutions. Nichols and Lekkas. McGraw-Hill Professional Publishing, 2001. ISBN: 0071380388.

WWW Security: How to Build a Secure World Wide Web Connection. Robert S. MacGregor, Alberto Aresi, and Andreas Siegert. Prentice Hall, 1996. ISBN: 0136124097.

TCP/IP

Cisco TCP/IP Routing Professional Reference. Chris Lewis. McGraw-Hill, 1997. ISBN: 0070410887.

Demystifying TCP/IP. Paul Schlieve. Wordware Publishing, 1997. ISBN: 1556225393.

Designing TCP/IP Internetworks. Geoff Bennett. John Wiley & Sons, 1997. ISBN: 0471286435.

The Essential Guide to TCP/IP Commands. Martin R. Arick. John Wiley & Sons, 1996. ISBN: 0471125695.

A Guide to the TCP/IP Protocol Suite. Floyd Wilder and Vinton G. Cerf. Artech House, 1993. ISBN: 0890066930.

Hands-On TCP/IP. Paul Simoneau. McGraw-Hill, 1997. ISBN: 0079126405.

High-Speed Networks: TCP/IP and ATM Design Principles. William Stallings. Prentice Hall, 1997. ISBN: 0135259657.

Illustrated TCP/IP. Matthew G. Naugle. John Wiley & Sons, 1998. ISBN: 0471196568.

Implementing IPv6: Migrating to the Next Generation Internet Protocol. Mark A. Miller. IDG Books, 1998. ISBN: 1558515798.

Inside TCP/IP. Karanjit S. Siyan, Ph.D., Nancy Hawkins, and Joern Wettern. New Riders, 1997. ISBN: 1562057146.

Integrating TCP/IP into SNA. Ed Taylor. Wordware Publishing, 1993. ISBN: 1556223404.

Internet Core Protocols: The Definite Guide. Eric A. Hall. O'Reilly & Associates. ISBN: 1565292576.

Internet Cryptography. Richard E. Smith. Addison-Wesley, 1997. ISBN 0201924803.

Internet and TCP/IP Network Security. Uday O. Pabrai and Vijay K. Gurbani. McGraw-Hill, 1996. ISBN: 0070482152.

Internetworking with Netware TCP/IP. Karanjit S. Siyan, Peter Kuo, and Peter Rybaczyk. New Riders, 1996. ISBN: 1562055585.

Internetworking with TCP/IP: Client-Server Programming and Applications. Douglas E. Comer and David L. Stevens. Prentice Hall, 1997. ISBN: 0138487146.

Internetworking with TCP/IP: Principles, Protocols, and Architecture. Douglas E. Comer. Prentice Hall, 1995. ISBN: 0132169878.

An Introduction to TCP/IP. John Davidson. Springer Verlag, 1998. ISBN: 038796651X.

IPNG and the TCP/IP Protocols: Implementing the Next Generation Internet. Stephen Thomas. John Wiley & Sons, 1996. ISBN: 0471130885.

IPv6: The New Internet Protocol. Christian Huitema. Prentice Hall, 1996. ISBN: 013241936X.

Mastering TCP/IP for NT Server. Mark Minasi, Todd Lammle, and Monica Lammle. Sybex, 1997. ISBN: 0782121233.

Networking with Microsoft TCP/IP. Drew Heywood. New Riders, 1997. ISBN: 1562057138.

Novell's Guide to TCP/IP and Intranetware. Drew Heywood. IDG Books, 1997. ISBN: 0764545329.

Sams Teach Yourself TCP/IP in 14 Days. Timothy Parker. Sams, 1996. ISBN: 0672308851.

TCP/IP Administration. Craig Zacker. IDG Books, 1998. ISBN: 0764531581.

TCP/IP and the AS/400. Dan Riehl and Mike Ryan. Duke Communications, 1998. ISBN: 1882419723.

TCP/IP and Related Protocols. Uyless Black. McGraw-Hill, 1995. ISBN: 0070055602.

TCP/IP Applications and Protocols. Walter Goralski. Computer Technology Research Corporation, 1995. ISBN: 1566079519.

TCP/IP Clearly Explained. Pete Loshin. AP Professional, 1997. ISBN: 0124558356.

TCP/IP Complete. Ed Taylor. McGraw-Hill, 1998. ISBN: 0070634009.

TCP/IP for Dummies. Candace Leiden and Marshall Wilensky. IDG Books, 1997. ISBN: 0764500635.

MCSE Exam Notes: TCP/IP for NT Server 4. Gary Govanus. Sybex, 1998. ISBN: 0782123074.

TCP/IP Network Administration. Craig Hunt. Travelers' Tales Inc., 1998. ISBN: 1565923227.

TCP/IP Networking: Architecture, Administration, and Programming. James Martin and Joe Leben. Prentice Hall, 1994. ISBN: 0136422322.

TCP/IP: Running a Successful Network. Kevin Washburn and Jim Evans. Addison-Wesley, 1996. ISBN: 0201877112.

TCP/IP: A Survival Guide. Frank Derfler and Steve Rigney. IDG Books, 1997. ISBN: 1558285644.

TCP/IP Tutorial and Technical Overview. Eamon Murphy, Steve Hayes, and Mathias Enders. Prentice Hall, 1995. ISBN: 0134608585.

TCP/IP Unleashed. Timothy Parker. Sams, 1998. ISBN: 0672311127.

Using TCP/IP. Joern Wettern and Nancy Hawkins. Que, 1997. ISBN: 0789713624.

On NetWare

Bulletproofing Netware: Solving the 175 Most Common Problems Before They Happen. Mark Wilkins, Glenn E. Weadock, and K. Weadock Wilkins. McGraw-Hill, 1997. ISBN: 0070676216.

CNA Study Guide for Intranetware. Michael Moncur and James Chellis. Sybex, 1997. ISBN: 0782120989.

A Guide to NetWare for UNIX. Cathy Gunn. Prentice Hall, 1995. ISBN: 0133007162.

Learning Netware 4.1. Guy Yost and John Preston. Que, 1997. ISBN: 1575760525.

Managing Small Netware 4.11 Networks. Doug Jones. Sybex, 1997. ISBN: 0782119638.

Mastering Netware 5.1. James Gaskin. Sybex, 2000. ISBN: 078212772X.

Netware 4 Made Easy. Taha. Prentice Hall, 1998. ISBN: 0132449633.

NetWare 4.X. John Preston. Que, 1997. ISBN: 1575763826.

NetWare Professional's Toolkit. Gary Araki. Advice Press, 1998. ISBN: 1889671118.

The NetWare to Internet Connection. Morgan Stern. Sybex, 1996. ISBN: 0782117066.

NetWare to Internet Gateways. James E. Gaskin. Prentice Hall, 1996.
ISBN: 0135217741.

NetWare to Windows NT Complete: Integration and Migration. Arnold
Villeneuve and Wayne McKinnon. McGraw-Hill, 1998. ISBN: 0079131719.

NetWare Web Development. Peter Kuo. Sams, 1996. ISBN: 1575211886.

Novell Intranetware Professional Reference. Karanjit Siyan, Joshua Ball, Jason
Ehrhart, and Jim Henderson. New Riders, 1997. ISBN: 1562057294.

Novell's Guide to Creating Intranetware Intranets. Karanjit S. Siyan.
IDG Books, 1997. ISBN: 0764545310.

Novell's Guide to Integrating NetWare and TCP/IP. Drew Heywood.
Novell Press/IDG Books, 1996. ISBN: 1568848188.

Novell's Guide to NetWare LAN Analysis. Dan E. Hakes and Laura Chappell.
Sybex, 1994. ISBN: 0782111432.

Novell's Guide to Performance Tuning Netware. Jeffrey F. Hughes and
Blair W. Thomas. IDG Books, 1998. ISBN: 0764545264.

***Routing in Today's Internetworks: The Routing Protocols of IP, Decnet,
Netware, and Appletalk.*** Mark Dickie. John Wiley & Sons, 1997.
ISBN: 0471286206.

How to Get More Information

This appendix is designed to provide you with some of the sources consulted in this book, as well as sites (or documents) that can assist you in better understanding security.

Establishment Resources

The following list of resources includes articles, papers, and tools. The majority were authored or created by individuals working in security.

Sites on the WWW

The Anonymous Remailer FAQ. This document covers all aspects of anonymous remailing techniques and tools. `http://www.andrebacard.com/remail.html`

BugNet. A site that claims to be "The World's Leading Supplier of Software Bug Fixes." `http://www.bugnet.com`

BugTraq Archives. This is an archive of the popular mailing list, BugTraq, one of the most reliable sources for up-to-date reports on newly found vulnerabilities in Unix (and at times, other operating systems). `http://www.securityfocus.com/`

The Center for Secure Information Systems. This site, affiliated with the Center at George Mason University, has some truly incredible papers. There is much cutting-edge research going on here. The following URL sends you directly to the publications page, but you really should explore the entire site. `http://www.isse.gmu.edu/~csis/publication.html`

The Computer Emergency Response Team (CERT). CERT is an organization that assists sites in responding to network security violations, break-ins, and so forth. This is a great source of information, particularly regarding vulnerabilities. http://www.cert.org

Cryptography Research. A site that publishes much research on cryptography. http://www.cryptography.com/

Department of Defense Password Management Guideline. This is a treatment of password security in classified environments. http://www.alw.nih.gov/Security/FIRST/papers/password/dodpwman.txt

Electronic Frontiers Georgia. This site contains list of tools and sites that can help you maintain your privacy, including privacy tools, anonymous remailers, and Web proxies. http://anon.efga.org

The Evaluated Products List (EPL). This is a list of products that have been evaluated for security ratings based on DoD guidelines. http://www.radium.ncsc.mil/tpep/epl/epl-by-class.html

Forum of Incident Response and Security Teams (FIRST). FIRST is a conglomeration of many organizations undertaking security measures on the Net. This powerful organization is a good starting place to find sources. http://www.first.org/

Information Warfare and Information Security on the Web. This is a comprehensive list of links and other resources concerning information warfare over the Internet. http://www.fas.org/irp/wwwinfo.html

Internet Engineering Task Force (IETF). The IETF is the standards body for the Internet. This includes the security standards as well. http://www.ietf.org

Massachusetts Institute of Technology Distribution Site of Pretty Good Privacy (PGP) for U.S. Residents. PGP provides some of the most powerful, military-grade encryption currently available. http://web.mit.edu/network/pgp.html

NTBugTraq. An NT/2000-specific version of BugTraq. http://ntbugtraq.ntadvice.com/

NTSecurity. A portal for Windows NT/2000 security information. http://www.ntsecurity.com/

Packet Storm Security. A nonprofit organization of security professionals that publishes a huge amount of security information on the Web. http://www.packetstormsecurity.com

A Page Devoted to ATP, the Anti-Tampering Program. In some ways, ATP is similar to Tripwire or Hobgoblin. http://www.ja.net/CERT/Vincenzetti_and_Cotrozzi/ATP_Anti_Tampering_Program.txt

Purdue University COAST Archive. This is one of the more comprehensive security sites, containing many tools and documents of deep interest to the security community. `http://www.cs.purdue.edu//coast/archive`

The Rand Corporation. This site contains security resources of various sorts, as well as engrossing early documents on the Internet's design. `http://www.rand.org/publications/electronic/`

The Risks Forum. This is a moderated digest regarding security and other risks in computing. This great resource is also searchable. With it, you can tap the better security minds on the Net. `http://catless.ncl.ac.uk/Risks`

SANS. The System Administration, Networking and Security Institute is an organization made up of more than 150,000 computer professionals. They provide much security information and training. `http://www.sans.org/`

S/Key Informational Page. This site provides information on S/Key and the use of one-time passwords in authentication. `http://www.ece.nwu.edu/CSEL/skey/skey_eecs.html`

Unix Security. Archive of articles about Unix security. `http://www.itworld.com/nl/unix_sec`

U.S. Department of Energy's Computer Incident Advisory Capability (CIAC). CIAC provides computer security services to employees and contractors of the U.S. Department of Energy, but the site is open to the public as well. There are many tools and documents at this location. `http://www.ciac.org/ciac/`

Virus Bulletin. The Virus Bulletin carries virus news as well as lists of viruses and hoaxes. `http://www.virusbtn.com/`

Wietse Venema's Tools Page. This page, maintained by Wietse Venema (coauthor of SATAN and author of TCP_Wrapper and many other security tools), is filled with papers, tools, and general information. It is a must-visit for any Unix system administrator. `ftp://ftp.porcupine.org/pub/security/index.html`

WordlistsFAQ. This FAQ gives you links to many wordlists on the Internet that are useful in testing the strength of, or cracking, Unix passwords. `http://www.hyphenologist.co.uk/wordlist/wordfaq.htm`

Reports and Publications

General
Authentication and Discretionary Access Control. Paul A. Karger, *Computers & Security*, Number 5, pp. 314–324. 1986.

A Guide to Understanding Discretionary Access Control in Trusted Systems. Technical Report NCSC-TG-003, National Computer Security Center. 1987.

A Model of Atomicity for Multilevel Transactions. 1993 IEEE Computer Society Symposium on Research in Security and Privacy; 1993 May 24; Oakland, California. Barbara T. Blaustein, Sushil Jajodia, Catherine D. McCollum, and LouAnna Notargiacomo (MITRE). USA: IEEE Computer Society Press. 1993. ISBN: 0-8186-3370-0.

Network Security: Protocol Reference Model and the Trusted Computer System Evaluation Criteria. M. D. Abrams and A. B. Jeng. *IEEE Network*, 1(2), pp. 24–33. April 1987.

Java
Microsoft: Vulnerabilities in Internet Explorer. CIAC Bulletin. May 18, 2000. http://www.ciac.org/ciac/bulletins/k-044.shtml

Java Developer's Journal. http://www.javadevelopersjournal.com/java/

Java Security. Sun's official page. http://java.sun.com/security/

Javaworld. Journal. http://www.javaworld.com/

Databases and Security
Access Control: Principles and Practice. R. S. Sandhu and P. Saramati. *IEEE Communications*, pp. 2–10. 1994.

Authorizations in Relational Database Management Systems. E. Bertino, S. Jajodia, and P. Saramati. ACM Conference on Computer and Communications Security, Fairfax, VA pp. 130–139. 1993.

Ensuring Atomicity of Multilevel Transactions. P. Ammann, S. Jajodia, and I. Ray. IEEE Symposium on Research in Security and Privacy. Oakland, CA. pp. 74–84. May 1996. http://www.isse.gmu.edu/~csis/publications/oklnd96-indrksi.ps

An Extended Authorization Model for Relational Databases. E. Bertino, P. Samarati, and S. Jajodia. IEEE Transactions on Knowledge and Data Engineering, Volume 9, Number 1, pp. 85–101. 1997. http://www.isse.gmu.edu/~csis/publications/ieee-97.ps

Honest Databases That Can Keep Secrets. R. S. Sandhu and S. Jajjodia, NCSC. http://www.list.gmu.edu/confrnc/ncsc/ps_ver/b91poly.ps

The Microsoft Internet Security Framework (MISF) Technology for Secure Communication, Access Control, and Commerce. 1997 Microsoft Corporation. http://msdn.microsoft.com/LIBRARY/BACKGRND/HTML/MSDN_MISF.HTM

Multilevel Security for Knowledge Based Systems. Thomas D. Garvey and Teresa F. Lunt. Stanford Research Institute, SRI-CSL-91-01. February 1991.

On Distributed Communications: IX. Security, Secrecy and Tamper-Free Considerations. P. Baran. Technical Report, The Rand Corp. Number RM-376. August 1964.

A Personal View of DBMS Security in Database Security: Status and Prospects. F. Manola. C. E. Landwehr (ed.), Elsevier Science Publishers B.V., North Holland, 1988. GTE Labs. December 1987.

Role-Based Access Controls. D. F. Ferraiolo and R. Kuhn. NIST-NCSC National Computer Security Conference, Baltimore, MD (1993). pp. 554–563.

Trusted Database Management System. NCSC-TG-021. Trusted Database Management System Interpretation. Chief, Technical Guidelines Division. ATTN: C11 National Computer Security Center Ft. George G. Meade, MD 20755-6000. April 1991.

Articles

"Are Your Employees Your Biggest Security Risk?" Mark Joseph Edwards. *Windows IT Security.* December 20, 2000.
http://www.windowsitsecurity.com/Articles/Index.cfm?ArticleID=16445

"DDoS attack targets chat, Linux boxes." Scott Berinato. *EWeek.* September 5, 2000.

"Gartner: Securing Windows Takes 15% Longer than Unix." Marilyn Cohodas. SearchSystemsManagement. April 15, 2002. http://searchsystemsmanagement. techtarget.com/originalContent/0,289142,sid20_gci817194,00.html

"LinuxSecurity.com Speaks with AES Winner." Dave Wreski. LinuxSecurity.com. October 24, 2000. http://www.linuxsecurity.com/feature_stories/interview-aes.html

"MS Admits Planting Secret Password." Ted Bridis. *Wall Street Journal Online.* April 13, 2000. http://zdnet.com.com/2100-11-519911.html?legacy=zdnn

"The Paradox of the Secrecy About Secrecy: The Assumption of a Clear Dichotomy Between Classified and Unclassified Subject Matter." Paul Baran. MEMORANDUM RM-3765-PR; On Distributed Communications: IX Security, Secrecy, and Tamper-Free Considerations. Rand Corporation. August 1964.

"'Security Through Obscurity' Ain't What They Think It Is." Jay Beale. 2000. http://www.bastille-linux.org/jay/obscurity-revisited.html

"Spammer Breaks into AOL Search Engine." Jim Hu. *CNET News.* June 20, 2002. http://news.zdnet.co.uk/story/0,,t269-s2112185,00.html

"Wireless Security Concerns." Tischelle George. *Information Week.* January 3, 2001. http://www.informationweek.com/story/IWK20010103S0006

Tools

Windows
Administrator Assistant Tool Kit.
http://www.aelita.com/Products/AdminAssist.htm

Avatier Password Bouncer. Password Policy Manager.
http://www.avatier.com/products/PasswordBouncer/

Avatier Trusted Enterprise Manager. http://www.avatier.com/products/TEM

BlackICE PC Protection.
http://www.iss.net/products_services/hsoffice_protection/

Bokler Software. Cryptographic Library for Windows. http://www.bokler.com/

Centrally Managed Desktop Security (CMDS). http://www.securitae.com/

Cetus StormWindows. Tools to lock down desktops. http://www.cetussoft.com/

ConfigSafe and RecoverySafe. http://www.imaginelan.com/products.html

Disk Commander. Recovers data from corrupt Windows volumes.
http://www.winternals.com/products/repairandrecovery/diskcommander.asp

DumpEvt. http://www.somarsoft.com/

DECROS Security Card. http://www.decros.com/

Desktop Surveillance. http://www.omniquad.com/

DumpReg. http://www.somarsoft.com/

File Restore. Allows files to be undeleted.
http://www.winternals.com/products/repairandrecovery/filerestore.asp

HDD-Protect. http://www.geocities.com/SiliconValley/Lakes/8753/

Kerio Personal Firewall. http://www.kerio.com/

MailMarshal. http://www.webmarshall.com/

Norton Personal Firewall. http://www.symantec.com/sabu/nis/npf/

NTFSDOS. Access NTFS volumes from DOS.
http://www.winternals.com/products/repairandrecovery/ntfsdospro.asp

Security Expressions. Hardens and locks down computers.
http://www.pedestalsoftware.com/secexp/

Somarsoft DumpAcl. http://www.somarsoft.com/

Somarsoft RegEdit. http://www.somarsoft.com/

Sygate Personal Firewall. `http://soho.sygate.com/products/shield_ov.htm`

Timbuktu Pro. `http://www.netopia.com/en-us/software/products/tb2/index.html`

Tiny Personal Firewall. `http://www.tinysoftware.com/`

WebMarshal. `http://www.webmarshall.com/`

Windows Task-Lock. Password-protect applications. `http://posum.com/`

Windows 2000 Internet Server Security Configuration Tool.
`http://www.microsoft.com/Downloads/Release.asp?ReleaseID=19889`

Windows 2000 Resource Kit.
`http://www.microsoft.com/windows2000/techinfo/reskit/en-us/default.asp`

ZoneAlarm. Personal firewall software. `http://www.zonelabs.com/`

Macintosh Security Tools
Empower. `http://www.magna1.com/`

EtherPeek. `http://www.wildpackets.com/`

InterMapper. `http://www.dartmouth.edu/netsoftware/intermapper/`

KeysOff. `http://www.blueglobe.com/~cliffmcc/products.html`

MacRadius. `http://www.macradius.com/`

Password Key. `http://www.cp3.com/`

Secure-It Locks. `http://secure-it.com/`

Timbuktu Pro. `http://www.netopia.com/en-us/software/products/tb2/index.html`

Password Crackers
Crack. Cracks Unix passwords on Unix platforms.
`http://www.users.dircon.co.uk/~crypto/download/c50-faq.html`

Crack Documentation.
`http://www.parkline.ru/Library/html-KOI/SECURITY/crackfaq.txt`

Distributed Network Attack. Breaks passwords from many applications.
`http://www.accessdata.com/`

Fast ZIP Cracker (FZC). Breaks Zip passwords.
`ftp://utopia.hacktic.nl/pub/crypto/cracking/fzc105.zip`

Guess. Cracks Unix passwords on the DOS platform. This utility is available everywhere. Try the search string `guess.zip`.

John the Ripper. Cracks Unix passwords on various platforms.
`http://www.openwall.com/john/`

Passware Kit. Breaks passwords for Windows and a variety of PC applications.
`http://www.lostpassword.com/`

Word 97 Cracker. Break MS Word passwords. `ftp://ftp.bokler.com/word97cr.zip`

ZipCrack. Cracks the passwords on Zip archives. Try the search string `zipcrk10.zip`.

Scanners and Related Utilities

NetScan Tools. Windows port of many Unix snooping utilities.
`http://www.netscantools.com`

Network Toolbox. Runs on Windows. Has many common Unix snooping utilities
and a port scanner. `http://www.jriver.com/netbox.html`

Nessus. A free extensible security scanner. `http://www.nessus.org`

Nmap. A network discovery tool. `http://www.insecure.org/nmap`

SAINT. High-end vulnerability commercial scanner.
`http://www.wwdsi.com/products/saint_engine.html`

Strobe. Port scanner that runs on Unix.
`http://ftp.cerias.purdue.edu/pub/tools/unix/scanners/strobe/strobe/`

TCP/IP Surveyor. Microsoft platform.
`http://www.winsite.com/info/pc/win95/netutil/wssrv32n.zip/`

WhatRoute. Port of the popular Unix utility Traceroute to Macintosh.
`http://homepages.ihug.co.nz/~bryanc/`

XSCAN. Locates vulnerable X servers. `http://sal.kachinatech.com/E/0/XSCANNER.html`

Mail Bombers

Avalanche. This device is yet another mail-bombing utility. Avalanche is for
Windows. Try the search string `avalanche20.zip`.

Bombtrack. This is a mail-bombing utility for Macintosh.

eXtreme Mail. This utility is a mail bomber for the Windows platform. To obtain
it, try the search string `xmailb1.exe`.

FlameThrower. This is a Macintosh mail-bombing utility.

Homicide. This utility is a mail bomber for the Windows platform. To obtain it, try
the search string `homicide.exe`.

Kaboom. This device is an email bomber. To obtain it, try searching for the string
`kaboom3.exe`.

The UnaBomber. This utility is a mail bomber for the Windows platform. To obtain it, try the search string unabomb.exe.

The Unix MailBomb. This mail-bomb utility by CyBerGoAT works on all Unix platforms. To obtain it, try the search string MailBomb by CyBerGoAT.

The UpYours Mail Bombing Program. To obtain this mail bomber, try searching for the string upyours3.zip.

Intrusion Detectors
Cisco Secure Intrusion Detection System. http://www.cisco.com/

Network Flight Recorder. http://www.nfr.net/

RealSecure. http://www.iss.net

Shadow. http://www.nswc.navy.mil/ISSEC/CID

Snort. http://www.snort.org/

Technical Reports, Government Standards, and Papers

The Rainbow Books and Related Documentation
The Rainbow Books set forth the U.S. government's criteria for the use and certification of trusted systems. The Rainbow Books were written a long time ago, but are still used even today as references by much of the security community.

Computer Security Requirements: Guidance for Applying the DoD TCSEC in Specific Environments *(Light Yellow Book).* June 1985.
http://www.radium.ncsc.mil/tpep/library/rainbow/CSC-STD-003-85.html

DoD Password Management Guideline *(Green Book).* April 1985.
http://www.radium.ncsc.mil/tpep/library/rainbow/CSC-STD-002-85.html

DoD Trusted Computer System Evaluation Criteria *(Orange Book).* December 1985. http://www.radium.ncsc.mil/tpep/library/rainbow/5200.28-STD.html

Glossary of Computer Security Terms *(Teal Green Book).* October 21, 1988.
http://www.radium.ncsc.mil/tpep/library/rainbow/NCSC-TG-004.txt

A Guide to Understanding Audit in Trusted Systems *(Tan Book).* June 1988.
http://www.radium.ncsc.mil/tpep/library/rainbow/NCSC-TG-001-2.html

A Guide to Understanding Configuration Management in Trusted Systems *(Amber Book).* March 1988.
http://www.radium.ncsc.mil/tpep/library/rainbow/NCSC-TG-006.html

A Guide to Understanding Design Documentation in Trusted Systems *(Burgundy Book).* October 1988.
http://www.radium.ncsc.mil/tpep/library/rainbow/NCSC-TG-007.html

A Guide to Understanding Discretionary Access Control in Trusted Systems
(Neon Orange Book). September 1987.
http://www.radium.ncsc.mil/tpep/library/rainbow/NCSC-TG-003.html

A Guide to Understanding Identification and Authentication in Trusted Systems *(Light Blue Book)*. September 1991.
http://www.radium.ncsc.mil/tpep/library/rainbow/NCSC-TG-017.html

A Guide to Understanding Information System Security Officer Responsibilities for Automated Information Systems *(Turquoise Book)*. May 1992. http://www.radium.ncsc.mil/tpep/library/rainbow/NCSC-TG-027.txt

A Guide to Understanding Object Reuse in Trusted Systems *(Light Blue Book)*.
July 1992. http://www.radium.ncsc.mil/tpep/library/rainbow/NCSC-TG-018.html

A Guide to Understanding Security Modeling in Trusted Systems *(Aqua Book)*.
October 1992. http://www.radium.ncsc.mil/tpep/library/rainbow/NCSC-TG-010.txt

A Guide to Understanding Trusted Distribution in Trusted Systems *(Dark Lavender Book)*. December 1988.
http://www.radium.ncsc.mil/tpep/library/rainbow/NCSC-TG-008.html

A Guide to Understanding Trusted Facility Management *(Brown Book)*.
October 1989. http://www.radium.ncsc.mil/tpep/library/rainbow/NCSC-TG-015.html

Guidelines for Formal Verification Systems *(Purple Book)*. April 1989.
http://www.radium.ncsc.mil/tpep/library/rainbow/NCSC-TG-014.html

Guidelines for Writing Trusted Facility Manuals *(Yellow-Green Book)*. October 1992. http://www.radium.ncsc.mil/tpep/library/rainbow/NCSC-TG-016.html

RAMP Program Document *(Pink Book)*. March 1995, Version 2.
http://www.radium.ncsc.mil/tpep/library/rainbow/NCSC-TG-013.2.html

Technical Rational Behind CSC-STD-003-85: Computer Security Requirements—Guidance for Applying the DoD TCSEC in Specific Environments *(Yellow Book)*. June 1985.
http://www.radium.ncsc.mil/tpep/library/rainbow/CSC-STD-004-85.html

Trusted Database Management System Interpretation of the TCSEC *(Purple Book)*. April 1991. http://www.radium.ncsc.mil/tpep/library/rainbow/NCSC-TG-021.html

Trusted Network Interpretation of the TCSEC *(Red Book)*. July 1987.
http://www.radium.ncsc.mil/tpep/library/rainbow/NCSC-TG-005.html

Trusted Product Evaluations: A Guide for Vendors *(Bright Blue Book)*. June 1990. http://www.radium.ncsc.mil/tpep/library/rainbow/NCSC-TG-002.html

Trusted Product Evaluation Questionnaire *(Blue Book)*. May 1992, Version 2.
http://www.radium.ncsc.mil/tpep/library/rainbow/NCSC-TG-019.2.html

Trusted UNIX Working Group (TRUSIX) Rationale for Selecting Access Control List Features for the UNIX System *(Silver Book).* July 1989.
`http://www.radium.ncsc.mil/tpep/library/rainbow/NCSC-TG-020-A.html`

Other Governmental Security Documents and Advisories
"Augmented Encrypted Key Exchange: A Password-Based Protocol Secure Against Dictionary Attacks and Password File Compromise." 1st ACM Conference on Computer and Communications Security, pp. 244–250. ACM Press. November 1993.

Australian Computer Emergency Response Team.
`http://www.auscert.org.au/Information/advisories.html`

"Charon: Kerberos Extensions for Authentication over Secondary Networks." Derek A. Atkins. 1993.
`ftp://coast.cs.purdue.edu/pub/doc/authentication/Derek_Atkins-Charon.ps.Z`

Check Point FireWall-1 Introduction. Checkpoint Technologies Firewall Information. `http://www.checkpoint.com/products/protect/firewall-1.html`

Cisco PIX Firewall. Cisco Systems firewall information.
`http://http://www.cisco.com/warp/public/44/jump/secure.shtml`

"Covert Channels in the TCP/IP Protocol Suite." Craig Rowland. Rotherwick & Psionics Software Systems, Inc. `http://www.firstmonday.dk/issues/issue2_5/rowland/`

"Crack Version 4.1: A Sensible Password Checker for UNIX." A. Muffett. Technical Report, March 1992.

"A Cryptographic File System for UNIX." Matt Blaze. 1st ACM Conference on Computer and Communications Security. pp. 9–16. ACM Press. November 1993.

"Daemons and Dragons UNIX Accounting." Dinah McNutt. *UNIX Review.* 12(8). August 1994.

"Evolution of a Trusted B3 Window System Prototype." J. Epstein, J. McHugh, R. Psacle, C. Martin, D. Rothnie, H. Orman, A. Marmor-Squires, M. Branstad, and B. Danner. In proceedings of the 1992 IEEE Symposium on Security and Privacy, 1992.

"Firewall Application Notes." A good document that starts by describing how to build a firewall. Also addresses application proxies, sendmail in relation to firewalls, and the characteristics of a bastion host. Livingston Enterprises, Inc.
`ftp://coast.cs.purdue.edu/pub/doc/firewalls/Livingston_Firewall_Notes.ps.Z`

"Improving the Security of Your Site by Breaking Into It." Dan Farmer and Wietse Venema. 1995.
`http://www.alw.nih.gov/Security/Docs/admin-guide-to-cracking.101.html`

"Improving X Windows Security." Linda Mui. *UNIX World*. Volume 9, Number 12. December 1992.

"IP v6 Release and Firewalls." Uwe Ellermann. 14th Worldwide Congress on Computer and Communications Security Protection. pp. 341–354. June 1996.

"Keeping Your Site Comfortably Secure: An Introduction to Internet Firewalls." John P. Wack and Lisa J. Carnahan. National Institute of Standards and Technology. February 9, 1995. `http://csrc.nist.gov/publications/nistpubs/800-10/`

"Making Your Setup More Secure." NCSA Tutorial Pages. Much of the information given here applies to Apache.
`http://hoohoo.ncsa.uiuc.edu/docs/tutorials/security.html`

"Network Firewalls." Steven M. Bellovin and William R. Cheswick. IEEECM, 32(9), pp. 50–57. September 1994.

"Packets Found on an Internet." Steven M. Bellovin. Interesting analysis of packets appearing at the application gateway of AT&T. Lambda. August 23, 1993.
`ftp://ftp.research.att.com/dist/smb/packets.ps`

"Password Security: A Case History." Robert Morris and Ken Thompson.
`http://www.alw.nih.gov/Security/FIRST/papers/password/pwstudy.ps`

"Session-Layer Encryption." Matt Blaze and Steve Bellovin. Proceedings of the Usenix Security Workshop, June 1995.

Site Security Handbook. Barbara Fraser. Update and Idraft version, CMU. Draft-ietf-ssh-handbook-03.txt. June 1996.
`http://sunsite.cnlab-switch.ch/ftp/doc/standard/rfc/21xx/2196`

The SSL Protocol. (IDraft) Alan O. Freier and Philip Karlton (Netscape Communications) with Paul C. Kocher.
`http://home.netscape.com/eng/ssl3/ssl-toc.html`

The Sun ONE Security Product Line Overview. Sun Microsystems.
`http://www.sun.com/security/overview.html`

"TCP WRAPPER: Network Monitoring, Access Control, and Booby Traps." Wietse Venema. Proceedings of the Third Usenix UNIX Security Symposium, pp. 85–92, Baltimore, MD. September 1992.
`ftp://ftp.porcupine.org/pub/security/tcp_wrapper.ps.Z`

"There Be Dragons." Steven M. Bellovin. To appear in proceedings of the Third Usenix UNIX Security Symposium, Baltimore, September 1992. AT&T Bell Laboratories, Murray Hill, NJ. August 15, 1992.

"Undetectable Online Password Guessing Attacks." Yun Ding and Patrick Horster. *OSR*. 29(4), pp. 77–86. October 1995.
`http://citeseer.nj.nec.com/ding95undetectable.html`

+X Window System Security. Ben Gross and Baba Buehler. Beckman Institute System Services. Last Apparent Date of Modification: January 11, 1996.

X Through the Firewall, and Other Application Relays. Treese/Wolman. Digital Equipment Corp. Cambridge Research Lab. October 1993.
`ftp://crl.dec.com/pub/DEC/CRL/tech-reports/93.10.ps.Z`

X Security. `http://consult.cern.ch/writeup/security/security_4.html`

Intrusion Detection
"Dragon Claws Its Way to the Top." Greg Shipley and Patrick Mueller. *Network Computing*. August 20, 2001.

"Fraud and Intrusion Detection in Financial Information Systems." S. Stolfo. P. Chan, D. Wei, W. Lee, and A. Prodromidis. 4th ACM Computer and Communications Security Conference, 1997.
`http://www.cs.columbia.edu/~sal/hpapers/acmpaper.ps.gz`

"GrIDS—A Graph-Based Intrusion Detection System for Large Networks." S. Staniford-Chen, S. Cheung, R. Crawford, M. Dilger, J. Frank, J. Hoagland, K. Levitt, C. Wee, R. Yip, and D. Zerkle. The 19th National Information Systems Security Conference. `http://seclab.cs.ucdavis.edu/papers/nissc96.ps`

"Holding Intruders Accountable on the Internet." S. Staniford-Chen and L. T. Heberlein. Proceedings of the 1995 IEEE Symposium on Security and Privacy, Oakland, CA, May 8–10, 1995.
`http://seclab.cs.ucdavis.edu/~stanifor/papers/ieee_conf_94/revision/submitted.ps`

IDS FAQ. SANS Institute. `http://www.sans.org/newlook/resources/IDFAQ/ID_FAQ.htm`

"Intrusion Detection for Network Infrastructures." S. Cheung, K. N. Levitt, and C. Ko. 1995 IEEE Symposium on Security and Privacy, Oakland, CA. May 1995.
`http://seclab.cs.ucdavis.edu/papers/clk95.ps`

"A Methodology for Testing Intrusion Detection Systems." N. F. Puketza, K. Zhang, M. Chung, B. Mukherjee, and R. A. Olsson. *IEEE Transactions on Software Engineering*, Volume 22, Number 10, October 1996.
`http://seclab.cs.ucdavis.edu/papers/tse96.ps`

"NetKuang—A Multi-Host Configuration Vulnerability Checker." D. Zerkle and K. Levitt. Proceedings of the 6th Usenix Security Symposium. San Jose, California. 1996. `http://seclab.cs.ucdavis.edu/papers/zl96.ps`

"Network Intrusion Detection." Biswanath Mukherjee, L. Todd Heberlein, and Karl N. Levitt. IEEE Network, May 1994. `http://seclab.cs.ucdavis.edu/papers/bd96.ps`

"Simulating Concurrent Intrusions for Testing Intrusion Detection Systems: Parallelizing Intrusions." M. Chung, N. Puketza, R. A. Olsson, and B. Mukherjee. Proceedings of the 1995 National Information Systems Security Conference. Baltimore, Maryland. 1995.
`http://seclab.cs.ucdavis.edu/papers/cpo95.ps`

Mailing Lists

The BugTraq List. This list is for posting or discussing bugs in various operating systems, although Unix is the most often discussed. The information here can be quite explicit. If you are looking to learn the fine aspects (and cutting-edge news) of Unix security, this list is for you. Instructions for subscribing can be found at `http://online.securityfocus.com/cgi-bin/sfonline/subscribe.pl`.

Intrusion Detection Systems. This list concentrates on discussions about methods of intrusion or intrusion detection.

> **Target:** `majordomo@uow.edu.au`
>
> **Command:** `subscribe ids` (in body of message)

The NT Security List. This list is devoted to discussing all techniques of security related to the Microsoft Windows NT operating system. Individuals also discuss security aspects of other Microsoft operating systems.

> **Target:** `request-ntsecurity@iss.net`
>
> **Command:** `subscribe ntsecurity` (in body of message)

The NTBugTraq List. This list is for posting or discussing bugs in Windows NT/2000.

> **Target:** `LISTSERV@LISTSERV.NTBUGTRAQ.COM`
>
> **Command:** `SUBSCRIBE NTBUGTRAQ` *firstname lastname*

The Secure HTTP List. This list is devoted to the discussion of S-HTTP and techniques to facilitate this new form of security for WWW transactions.

> **Target:** `shttp-talk-request@OpenMarket.com`
>
> **Command:** `SUBSCRIBE` (in body of message)

The Sneakers List. This list discusses methods of circumventing firewall and general security. This list is reserved for lawful tests and techniques.

> **Target:** `majordomo@CS.YALE.EDU`

> **Command:** `SUBSCRIBE Sneakers` (in body of message)

The WWW Security List. List members discuss all techniques to maintain (or subvert) WWW security (things involving secure methods of HTML, HTTP and CGI).

> **Target:** `www-security-request@nsmx.rutgers.edu`

> **Command:** `SUBSCRIBE www-security` *your_email_address* (in body of message)

Underground Resources

2600 **Magazine.** A magazine that historically focused on phone phracking but has increasingly been following computer hacking. `http://www.2600.com/`

Computer Underground Digest Archives. This is the archive of many of the important publications by the computer underground. `http://www.etext.org/CuD/`

Phrack **Magazine.** A hacker e-zine that has been in existence for many years. There is a great deal of hard-core technical information in it, as well as a fascinating section called Phrack World News, which recounts cracker and hacker activities in recent months. `http://www.phrack.com`

C

Vendor Information and Security Standards

This appendix explains how to obtain security information from particular vendors. It also provides an annotated list of available Internet standards, known as *Request for Comments (RFC)* documents, which address security.

Vendor Security Information

Instead of an out-of-date list of vendor security bulletins, in this section you will learn how to obtain the vendors' current lists of security bulletins and patches.

Any good system administrator will regularly check the security sites of the products he has, or get on their security mailing lists.

Hewlett-Packard

Hewlett-Packard provides a great deal of security information. You must log in to their site to access it. The main page is `http://us-support2.external.hp.com/common/bin/doc.pl/`. Select Technical Knowledge Base after logging in.

You will see search bulletins and patches for HP-UX and MPE. HP-UX is HP's version of Unix. MPE is an old minicomputer operating system from HP. As of the summer of 2002, it appears as though the Compaq information has not been merged in with this site.

On HP's patch page, the best thing to do is pick your series and OS version. Then change the box that says Search by Keyword to Browser Patch List.

For security bulletins, I recommend ignoring the links at the top of the page that only enable you to search the bulletins and instead find the Security Bulletin Archive. At the time of this writing, this link is at the very bottom of the page, in small print.

IBM

Unfortunately, IBM does not seem to have a good single spot for security and security patch information. What security information it has is scattered all over its Web sites.

IBM's main security page is `http://www.ibm.com/security`. This page is focused on security news and products. The Resource Center link on this page will take you to some good information about security.

The main product support page is `http://www.ibm.com/support/us/`. Each product group has its own Web page, and there is little consistency to the information by product. However, if you need security information by product, you should start at this point. The download page here enables you to download security products, but does not focus on security patches.

IBM's Lotus division has a page known as IT Central Security Zone. It is a well-focused page covering security with the Lotus products, and can be found at `http://www.lotus.com/security`.

Linux

Many Linux distributions are available, and this section presents information on security sources for some of the major distributions.

Caldera

Caldera's security advisories page is located at `http://www.calderasystems.com/support/security/`. Caldera appears to have more security advisories than any other Linux distribution. This does not mean that their Linux is any less secure. In fact, the opposite is probably true. Each security advisory tells you the packages you need to download to fix a particular security problem.

Debian

Debian does something unusual among vendors—they provide security alerts from their main Web site. On `http://www.debian.org/security`, you can scroll to the bottom of the page, and the security alerts are right there. Each security alert has links to software that needs to be downloaded to patch your system. A security alert mailing list is available at `http://www.debian.org/MailingLists/subscribe#debian-security-announce`.

Red Hat

Red Hat's setup for security information is as good, if not better, than that of most of the big established companies. The main support page for Red Hat is `http://www.redhat.com/apps/support/`. From this page, you can select your OS version. Under each of the version-specific pages, you will find a link to the security advisories for that version. Each security advisory has links to the new version of software with the bugs fixed.

Red Hat has something you will never see from the major OS vendors. You can search their bug database at `http://bugzilla.redhat.com/bugzilla/` and see the currently open security bugs. From this page, click Query Existing Bug Reports.

You can select a particular product. If you don't, you'll get information on them all. In the status list box, you might want to add additional status information. In the summary field, you might want to type the word **security**. Then click Submit Query and you'll get back a list of bugs.

SuSE

SuSE is a German Linux distribution. The main security page for this Linux distribution is `http://www.suse.com/us/support/security/index.html`. From here, you can find all the security advisories. Each security advisory lists what needs to be downloaded to fix your system.

SuSE has a couple of useful mailing lists. `suse-security@suse.com` is for general security discussion, and you can subscribe by sending email to `suse-security-subscribe@suse.com`. If you just want to get security announcements, send email to `suse-security-announce-subscribe@suse.com`. More lists are documented at `http://www.suse.com/us/support/mailinglists/index.html`.

Microsoft

There are many opinions on whether Microsoft does a good job of keeping on top of security issues. However, one thing you cannot fault it for is a shortage of security information on its Web site. The main security page is `http://www.microsoft.com/security/`.

From the main security page, you will find bulletins, best practices, tools, checklists, and articles. What Microsoft calls bulletins are really documents talking about patches it has out. To find out about other security issues, you need to go to a different part of the Web site—the Knowledge Base.

The Microsoft Knowledge Base is full of information on its products, including security issues. The main search page for the Knowledge Base is `http://search.support.microsoft.com/kb/c.asp?ln=en-us`. Pick the product you want to find security issues for. Many searches will result in security-related articles. I recommend a simple search on just the word "security" to get started. You'll get back all kinds of security articles.

Another useful resource on Microsoft's site is TechNet, available at `http://www.microsoft.com/TechNet`. Whereas Knowledge Base searches a database, TechNet is more article-based, including many articles about security.

Sun Microsystems

Sun Microsystems has a Web site that includes security info called SunSolve (`http://sunsolve.sun.com`). Sun takes security seriously on its site. You will find a link on the main page taking you to the security patch cluster, so you can grab all the security patches for your version of Solaris as one file.

You will also see links to the latest security bulletin, as well as an archive of security bulletins. These are good reading for understanding security issues related to Sun systems and Java.

You can contact Sun with security alerts by emailing `security-alert@sun.com` if you think you have discovered a new security problem. Sun also has a PGP key available on its Web site to encrypt communication. You can find instructions on the Sun site on how to regularly receive the Sun bulletins via email.

RFC Documents Relevant to Security

The following list of security-related RFC documents and their locations is arranged in numerical order from the earliest to the most recently published. All RFCs can be found at `http://www.ietf.org/rfc.html`.

RFC 912. Authentication Service. M. St. Johns. September 1984. Discusses automated authentication of users, for example, in an FTP session.

RFC 931. Authentication Server. M. St. Johns. January 1985. Further discussion on automated authentication of users.

RFC 1004. A Distributed-Protocol Authentication Scheme. D. L. Mills. April 1987. Discusses access control and authentication procedures in distributed environments and services.

RFC 1038. Draft Revised IP Security Option. M. St. Johns. January 1988. Discusses protection of datagrams and classifications of such protection.

RFC 1040. Privacy Enhancement for Internet Electronic Mail: Part I: Message Encipherment and Authentication Procedures. J. Linn. January 1988. Discusses encryption and authentication for electronic mail.

RFC 1108. U.S Department of Defense Security Options for the Internet Protocol. S. Kent. November 1991. Discusses extended security options in the Internet protocol and DoD guidelines.

RFC 1113. Privacy Enhancement for Internet Electronic Mail: Part I: Message Encipherment and Authentication Procedures. J. Linn. August 1989. Supersedes RFC 1040.

RFC 1114. Privacy Enhancement for Internet Electronic Mail: Part II: Certificate-Based Key Management. S. T. Kent and J. Linn. August 1989. Defines privacy enhancement mechanisms for electronic mail.

RFC 1115. Privacy Enhancement for Internet Electronic Mail: Part III: Algorithms, Modes, and Identifiers. J. Linn. August 1989. Technical and informational support to RFCs 1113 and 1114.

RFC 1135. The Helminthiasis of the Internet. J. Reynolds. December 1989. Famous RFC that describes the worm incident of November 1988.

RFC 1170. Public Key Standards and Licenses. R. Fougner. January 1991. Announcement of patents filed on Public Key Partners sublicense for digital signatures.

RFC 1186. The MD4 Message Digest Algorithm. R. Rivest. October 1990. The specification of MD4.

RFC 1244. The Site Security Handbook. P. Holbrook and J. Reynolds. July 1991. Famous RFC that lays out security practices and procedures. This RFC was an authoritative document for a long time. It is still pretty good and applies even today.

RFC 1272. Internet Accounting. C. Mills, D. Hirsh, and G. Ruth. November 1991. Specifies system for accounting—network usage, traffic, and such.

RFC 1281. Guidelines for the Secure Operation of the Internet. R. D. Pethia, S. Crocker, and B. Y. Fraser. November 1991. Celebrated document that sets forth guidelines for security.

RFC 1319. The MD2 Message-Digest Algorithm. B. Kaliski. April 1992. Description of MD2 and how it works.

RFC 1320. The MD4 Message-Digest Algorithm. R. Rivest. April 1992. Description of MD4 and how it works.

RFC 1321. The MD5 Message-Digest Algorithm. R. Rivest. April 1992. Description of MD5 and how it works.

RFC 1334. PPP Authentication Protocols. B. Lloyd and W. Simpson. October 1992. Defines the Password Authentication Protocol and the Challenge-Handshake Authentication Protocol in PPP.

RFC 1352. SNMP Security Protocols. J. Galvin, K. McCloghrie, and J. Davin. July 1992. Simple Network Management Protocol security mechanisms.

RFC 1355. Privacy and Accuracy Issues in Network Information Center Databases. J. Curran and A. Marine. August 1992. Network Information Center operation and administration guidelines.

RFC 1409. Telnet Authentication Option. D. Borman. January 1993. Experimental protocol for Telnet authentication.

RFC 1411. Telnet Authentication: Kerberos Version 4. D. Borman. January 1993. Weaving Kerberos authentication into Telnet.

RFC 1412. Telnet Authentication: SPX. K. Alagappan. January 1993. Experimental protocol for Telnet authentication.

RFC 1413. Identification Protocol. M. St. Johns. February 1993. Introduction and explanation of IDENT protocol.

RFC 1414. Identification MIB. M. St. Johns and M. Rose. February 1993. Specifies MIB for identifying owners of TCP connections.

RFC 1416. Telnet Authentication Option. D. Borman. February 1993. Supersedes RFC 1409.

RFC 1421. Privacy Enhancement for Internet Electronic Mail: Part I: Message Encryption and Authentication Procedures. J. Linn. February 1993. Updates and supersedes RFC 1113.

RFC 1422. Privacy Enhancement for Internet Electronic Mail: Part II: Certificate-Based Key Management. S. T. Kent and J. Linn. February 1993. Updates and supersedes RFC 1114.

RFC 1438. Internet Engineering Task Force Statements Of Boredom (SOBs). L. Chapin and C. Huitema. April 1993. Not really a security-related RFC, but so classic that I simply couldn't leave it out. Check it out for yourself. Clearly, the funniest RFC ever written.

RFC 1446. Security Protocols for Version 2 of the Simple Network Management Protocol. J. Galvin and K. McCloghrie. April 1993. Specifies security protocols for SNMPv2.

RFC 1455. Physical Link Security Type of Service. D. Eastlake. May 1993. Experimental protocol to provide physical link security.

RFC 1457. Security Label Framework for the Internet. R. Housley. May 1993. Presents a label framework for network engineers to adhere to.

RFC 1472. The Definitions of Managed Objects for the Security Protocols of the Point-to-Point Protocol. F. Kastenholz. June 1993. Security protocols on subnetwork interfaces using PPP.

RFC 1492. An Access Control Protocol, Sometimes Called TACACS. C. Finseth. July 1993. Documents the extended TACACS protocol used by the Cisco Systems terminal servers.

RFC 1507. DASS—Distributed Authentication Security Service. C. Kaufman. September 1993. Discusses new proposed methods of authentication in distributed environments.

RFC 1508. Generic Security Service Application Program Interface. J. Linn. September 1993. Specifies a generic security framework for use in source-level porting of applications to different environments.

RFC 1510. The Kerberos Network Authentication Service (V5). J. Kohl and C. Neumann. September 1993. An overview of Kerberos 5.

RFC 1511. Common Authentication Technology Overview. J. Linn. September 1993. Administrative.

RFC 1535. A Security Problem and Proposed Correction with Widely Deployed DNS Software. E. Gavron. October 1993. Discusses flaws in some DNS clients and means of dealing with them.

RFC 1544. The Content-MD5 Header Field. M. Rose. November 1993. Discusses the use of optional header field, Content-MD5, for use with MIME-conformant messages.

RFC 1675. Security Concerns for IPNG. S. Bellovin. August 1994. Bellovin expresses concerns over lack of direct access to source addresses in IPNG.

RFC 1704. On Internet Authentication. N. Haller and R. Atkinson. October 1994. Treats a wide range of Internet authentication procedures and approaches.

RFC 1731. IMAP4 Authentication Mechanisms. J. Myers. December 1994. Internet Message Access Protocol authentication issues.

RFC 1750. Randomness Recommendations for Security. D. Eastlake III, S. Crocker, and J. Schiller. December 1994. Extensive discussion of the difficulties surrounding deriving truly random values for key generation.

RFC 1751. A Convention for Human-Readable 128-Bit Keys. D. McDonald. December 1994. Proposed solutions for using 128-bit keys, which are hard to remember because of their length.

RFC 1760. The S/KEY One-Time Password System. N. Haller. February 1995. Describes Bellcore's S/Key OTP system.

RFC 1810. Report on MD5 Performance. J. Touch. June 1995. Discusses deficiencies of MD5 when viewed against the rates of T1 high-speed networks.

RFC 1824. The Exponential Security System TESS: An Identity-Based Cryptographic Protocol for Authenticated Key-Exchange. H. Danisch. August 1995. Discussion of proposed protocol for key exchange, authentication, and generation of signatures.

RFC 1827. IP Encapsulating Security Payload. R. Atkinson. August 1995. Discusses methods of providing integrity and confidentiality to IP datagrams.

RFC 1828. IP Authentication Using Keyed MD5. P. Metzger and W. Simpson. August 1995. Discusses the use of keyed MD5 with the IP Authentication Header.

RFC 1847. Security Multiparts for MIME: Multipart/Signed and Multipart/Encrypted. J. Galvin, S. Murphy, S. Crocker, and N. Freed. October 1995. Discusses a means of providing security services in MIME body parts.

RFC 1848. MIME Object Security Services. S. Crocker, N. Freed, J. Galvin, and S. Murphy. October 1995. Discusses protocol for applying digital signature and encryption services to MIME objects.

RFC 1852. IP Authentication Using Keyed SHA. P. Metzger and W. Simpson. September 1995. Discusses the use of keys with the Secure Hash Algorithm to ensure datagram integrity.

RFC 1853. IP in IP Tunneling. W. Simpson. October 1995. Discusses methods of using IP payload encapsulation for tunneling with IP.

RFC 1858. Security Considerations for IP Fragment Filtering. G. Ziemba, D. Reed, P. Traina. October 1995. Discusses IP fragment filtering and the dangers inherent in fragmentation attacks.

RFC 1910. User-Based Security Model for SNMPv2. G. Waters. February 1996. Discussion of application of security features to SNMP.

RFC 1928. SOCKS Protocol Version 5. M. Leech. March 1996. Discussion of the SOCKS protocol and its use to secure TCP and UDP traffic.

RFC 1929. Username/Password Authentication for SOCKS V5. M. Leech. March 1996. Discussion of SOCKS authentication.

RFC 1948. Defending Against Sequence Number Attacks. S. Bellovin. May 1996. Discussion of IP spoofing and TCP sequence number guessing attacks.

RFC 1968. The PPP Encryption Control Protocol. G. Meyer. June 1996. Discusses negotiating encryption more than PPP.

RFC 1969. The PPP DES Encryption Protocol. K. Sklower and G. Meyer. June 1996. Discusses utilizing the Data Encryption Standard with PPP.

RFC 1991: PGP Message Exchange Formats. D. Atkins, W. Stallings, and P. Zimmermann. August 1996. Adding PGP to message exchanges.

RFC 2015. MIME Security with Pretty Good Privacy (PGP). M. Elkins. October 1996. Privacy and authentication using the Multipurpose Internet Mail Extensions with PGP.

RFC 2040. The RC5, RC5-CBC, RC5-CBC-Pad, and RC5-CTS Algorithms. R. Baldwin and R. Rivest. October 1996. Defines all four ciphers in great detail.

RFC 2057. Source Directed Access Control on the Internet. S. Bradner. November 1996. Discusses possible avenues of filtering; an answer to the CDA.

RFC 2065. Domain Name System Security Extensions. D. Eastlake III and C. Kaufman. January 1997. Adding more security to the DNS system.

RFC 2069. An Extension to HTTP: Digest Access Authentication. J. Franks, P. Hallam-Baker, J. Hostetler, P. Leach, A. Luotonen, E. Sink, and L. Stewart. January 1997. Advanced authentication for HTTP.

RFC 2084. Considerations for Web Transaction Security. G. Bossert, S. Cooper, and W. Drummond. January 1997. Bringing confidentiality, authentication, and integrity to data sent via HTTP.

RFC 2085. HMAC-MD5 IP Authentication with Replay Prevention. M. Oehler and R. Glenn. February 1997. Keyed-MD5 coupled with the IP Authentication Header.

RFC 2137. Secure Domain Name System Dynamic Update. D. Eastlake, III. April 1997. Describes use of digital signatures in DNS updates to enhance overall security of the DNS system.

RFC 2144. The CAST-128 Encryption Algorithm. C. Adams. May 1997. Description of 128-bit algorithm that can be used in authentication more than network lines.

RFC 2179. Network Security for Trade Shows. A. Gwinn. July 1997. Document that addresses attacks that occur at trade shows and how to avoid them.

RFC 2196. Site Security Handbook. B. Fraser, ed. September 1997. Updates 1244. Yet another version of the already useful document.

RFC 2222. Simple Authentication and Security Layer. J. Myers. October 1997. Describes a method for adding authentication support to connection-based protocols.

RFC 2228. FTP Security Extensions. M. Horowitz and S. Lunt. October 1997. Extending the security capabilities of FTP.

RFC 2230. Key Exchange Delegation Record for the DNS. R. Atkinson. November 1997. Secure DNS and the exchanges made during a session.

RFC 2245. Anonymous SASL Mechanism. C. Newman. November 1997. New methods of authentication in anonymous services without using the now forbidden plaintext passwords traditionally associated with such services.

RFC 2246. The TLS Protocol Version 1.0. T. Dierks. January 1999. Describes a way to use Transport Layer Security to secure communications.

RFC 2268. A Description of the RC2(r) Encryption Algorithm. R. Rivest. January 1998. Describes an encryption algorithm.

RFC 2284. PPP Extensible Authentication Protocol (EAP). L. Blunk and J. Vollbrecht. March 1998. Describes an authentication protocol for PPP.

RFC 2289. A One-Time Password System. N. Haller, C. Metz, P. Nesser, and M. Straw. February 1998. Describes a scheme where passwords are used only once.

RFC 2311. S/MIME Version 2 Message Specification. S. Dusse, P. Hoffman, B. Ramsdell, L. Lundblade, and L. Repka. March 1998.

RFC 2312. S/MIME Version 2 Certificate Handling. S. Dusse, P. Hoffman, B. Ramsdell, and J. Weinstein. March 1998.

RFC 2315. PKCS 7: Cryptographic Message Syntax Version 1.5. B. Kaliski. March 1998. Describes the message format used in PKCS 7.

RFC 2316. Report of the IAB Security Architecture Workshop. S. Bellovin. April 1998. A trip report of a security workshop by the Internet Architecture Board.

RFC 2350. Expectations for Computer Security Incident Response. N. Brownlee and E. Guttman. June 1998. A best practices document dealing with security incidents.

RFC 2356. Sun's SKIP Firewall Traversal for Mobile IP. G. Montenegro and V. Gupta. June 1998. Describes how a device with a mobile IP address acquires access through a SKIP firewall.

RFC 2367. PF_KEY Key Management API, Version 2. D. McDonald, C. Metz, and B. Phan. July 1998. Describes a generic key management API.

RFC 2385. Protection of BGP Sessions via the TCP MD5 Signature Option. A. Heffernan. August 1998. Describes an extension to TCP to secure BGP sessions.

RFC 2401. Security Architecture for the Internet Protocol. S. Kent and R. Atkinson. November 1998. Describes the architectural baseline for IPsec implementations.

RFC 2402. IP Authentication Header. S. Kent and R. Atkinson. November 1998. Describes a mechanism for authentication of IP datagrams.

RFC 2403. The Use of HMAC-MD5-96 within ESP and AH. C. Madson and R. Glenn. November 1998. Describes the combined use of the HMAC and MD5 algorithms as an authentication header in IPsec.

RFC 2404. The Use of HMAC-SHA-1-96 within ESP and AH. C. Madson and R. Glenn. November 1998. Describes the combined use of the HMAC and MD5 algorithms as an authentication header in IPsec.

RFC 2405. The ESP DES-CBC Cipher Algorithm with Explicit IV. C. Madson and N. Doraswamy. November 1998. Describes a confidentiality mechanism for IPsec.

RFC 2406. IP Encapsulating Security Payload (ESP). S. Kent and R. Atkinson. November 1998. Describes the Encapsulating Security Payload of IPsec, which provides security services.

RFC 2407. The Internet IP Security Domain of Interpretation for ISAKMP. D. Piper. November 1998. Describes a mapping from ISAKMP to the Internet security domain.

RFC 2408. Internet Security Association and Key Management Protocol (ISAKMP). D. Maughan, M. Schertler, M. Schneider, and J. Turner. November 1998. Describes a protocol for establishing security associations and keys.

RFC 2409. The Internet Key Exchange (IKE). D. Harkins and D. Carrel. November 1998. Describes a key exchange method for the Internet.

RFC 2410. The NULL Encryption Algorithm and Its Use with IPsec. R. Glenn and S. Kent. November 1998. Describes the way to send data with IPsec without encryption.

RFC 2411. IP Security Document Roadmap. R. Thayer, N. Doraswamy, and R. Glenn. November 1998. Discusses how IPsec-related specifications should be developed.

RFC 2412. The OAKLEY Key Determination Protocol. H. Orman. November 1998. Describes a protocol for parties to agree on a key.

RFC 2419. The PPP DES Encryption Protocol, Version 2 (DESE-bis). K. Sklower and G. Meyer. September 1998. Describes how to use DES encryption more than a PPP link.

RFC 2420. The PPP Triple-DES Encryption Protocol (3DESE). H. Kummert. September 1998. Describes how to use Triple-DES encryption more than a PPP link.

RFC 2433. Microsoft PPP CHAP Extensions. G. Zorn and S. Cobb. October 1998. Describes Microsoft PPP authentication protocol.

RFC 2437. PKCS #1: RSA Cryptography Specifications Version 2.0. B. Kaliski and J. Staddon. October 1998. Makes recommendations of how to implement public-key cryptography based on the RSA algorithm.

RFC 2440. OpenPGP Message Format. J. Callas, L. Donnerhacke, H. Finney, and R. Thayer. November 1998. Describes the message format used by the OpenPGP email system.

RFC 2444. The One-Time-Password SASL Mechanism. C. Newman. October 1998. Describes an authentication mechanism.

RFC 2451. The ESP CBC-Mode Cipher Algorithms. R. Pereira and R. Adams. November 1998. Describes how to use the CBC-Mode Cipher algorithms with IPsec.

RFC 2504. Users' Security Handbook. Guttman, L. Leong, and G. Malkin. February 1999. A security handbook for the end user.

RFC 2510. Internet X.509 Public Key Infrastructure Certificate Management Protocols. C. Adams and S. Farrell. March 1999. Describes the protocols used for certificate management.

RFC 2511. Internet X.509 Certificate Request Message Format. M. Myers, C. Adams, D. Solo, and D. Kemp. March 1999. Describes the *Certificate Request Message Format (CRMF)*, used to convey a request for a certificate to *a Certification Authority (CA)*.

RFC 2521. ICMP Security Failures Messages. P. Karn and W. Simpson. March 1999. Specifies ICMP messages for indicating failures when using IP Security Protocols.

RFC 2522. Photuris: Session-Key Management Protocol. P. Karn and W. Simpson. March 1999. Describes an experimental session-key management protocol.

RFC 2523. Photuris: Extended Schemes and Attributes. P. Karn and W. Simpson. March 1999. Describes extensions to Photuris.

RFC 2527. Internet X.509 Public Key Infrastructure Certificate Policy and Certification Practices Framework. S. Chokhani and W. Ford. March 1999. Presents a framework to be used in writing certificate policies of practices.

RFC 2528. Internet X.509 Public Key Infrastructure Representation of Key Exchange Algorithm (KEA) Keys in Internet X.509 Public Key Infrastructure Certificates. R. Housley and W. Polk. March 1999. Specifies fields to be used in X.509 v3 for KEA keys.

RFC 2535. Domain Name System Security Extensions. D. Eastlake. March 1999. Specifies extensions to DNS that validate data integrity and authentication.

RFC 2536. DSA KEYs and SIGs in the Domain Name System (DNS). D. Eastlake. March 1999. Describes storing Digital Signature Algorithm information in DNS.

RFC 2537. RSA/MD5 KEYs and SIGs in the Domain Name System (DNS). D. Eastlake. March 1999. Describes storing RSA and MD5 information in DNS.

RFC 2538. Storing Certificates in the Domain Name System (DNS). D. Eastlake and O. Gudmundsson. March 1999. Describes how to store digital certificates in DNS.

RFC 2541. DNS Security Operational Considerations. D. Eastlake. March 1999. Describes considerations for the storage of certificates and keys in DNS.

RFC 2548. Microsoft Vendor-specific RADIUS Attributes. G. Zorn. March 1999. Describes RADIUS attributes that apply to Microsoft systems.

RFC 2554. SMTP Service Extension for Authentication. J. Myers. March 1999. Describes an extension to SMTP to handle authentication.

RFC 2559. Internet X.509 Public Key Infrastructure Operational Protocols—LDAPv2. S. Boeyen, T. Howes, and P. Richard. April 1999. Describes a protocol that satisfies some of the requirements in the Internet X.509 PKI system.

RFC 2560. X.509 Internet Public Key Infrastructure Online Certificate Status Protocol—OCSP. M. Myers, R. Ankney, A. Malpani, S. Galperin, and C. Adams. June 1999. Describes a protocol for determining the status of a certificate.

RFC 2574. User-based Security Model (USM) for version 3 of the Simple Network Management Protocol (SNMPv3). U. Blumenthal and B. Wijnen. April 1999. Defines a procedure for providing SNMP message level security.

RFC 2575. View-based Access Control Model (VACM) for the Simple Network Management Protocol (SNMP). B. Wijnen, R. Presuhn, and K. McCloghrie. April 1999. Defines a procedure for controlling access to management information.

RFC 2577. FTP Security Considerations. M. Allman and S. Ostermann. May 1999. Makes recommendations on how system administrators can make FTP more secure at their site.

RFC 2585. Internet X.509 Public Key Infrastructure Operational Protocols: FTP and HTTP. R. Housley and P. Hoffman. May 1999.

RFC 2587. Internet X.509 Public Key Infrastructure LDAPv2 Schema. S. Boeyen, T. Howes, and P. Richard. June 1999. Describes the Schema used in LDAP for PKI.

RFC 2588. IP Multicast and Firewalls. R. Finlayson. May 1999. Discusses issues related to enabling IP multicasts through firewalls.

RFC 2595. Using TLS with IMAP, POP3 and ACAP. C. Newman. June 1999. Describes how to use the TLS protocol, formerly known as SSL, with the various email reading protocols.

RFC 2617. HTTP Authentication: Basic and Digest Access Authentication. J. Franks, P. Hallam-Baker, J. Hostetler, S. Lawrence, P. Leach, A. Luotonen, and L. Stewart. June 1999. Describes how basic and digest authentication works in HTTP.

RFC 2618. RADIUS Authentication Client MIB. B. Aboba and G. Zorn. June 1999. Describes the SNMP MIB used by RADIUS clients for authentication.

RFC 2619. RADIUS Authentication Server MIB. G. Zorn and B. Aboba. June 1999. Describes the SNMP MIB used by RADIUS servers for authentication.

RFC 2630. Cryptographic Message Syntax. R. Housley. June 1999. Describes a syntax used for encrypting, digesting, signing or authenticating messages.

RFC 2631. Diffie-Hellman Key Agreement Method. E. Rescorla. June 1999. Describes how one particular Diffie-Hellman variant works.

RFC 2632. S/MIME Version 3 Certificate Handling. B. Ramsdell, Editor. June 1999. Describes how the S/MIME email encryption standard certificates are handled.

RFC 2633. S/MIME Version 3 Message Specification. B. Ramsdell, Editor. June 1999. Describes the message format for S/MIME email messages.

RFC 2634. Enhanced Security Services for S/MIME. P. Hoffman, Editor. June 1999. Describes security services that can be used with S/MIME.

RFC 2659. Security Extensions For HTML. E. Rescorla and A. Schiffman. August 1999. Describes how to embed S/HTTP negotiation into an HTML document.

RFC 2660. The Secure HyperText Transfer Protocol. E. Rescorla and A. Schiffman. August 1999. Specifies how the secure version of HTTP works.

RFC 2661. Layer Two Tunneling Protocol "L2TP". W. Townsley, A. Valencia, A. Rubens, G. Pall, G. Zorn, and B. Palter. August 1999. Specifies how L2TP, a VPN protocol, works.

RFC 2692. SPKI Requirements. C. Ellison. September 1999. Discusses requirements of the PKI infrastructure.

RFC 2693. SPKI Certificate Theory. C. Ellison, B. Frantz, B. Lampson, R. Rivest, B. Thomas, and T. Ylonen. September 1999. Presents the theory of PKI certificates.

RFC 2695. Authentication Mechanisms for ONC RPC. A. Chiu. September 1999. Describes two authentication mechanisms that can be used by Remote Procedure Call.

RFC 2712. Addition of Kerberos Cipher Suites to Transport Layer Security (TLS). A. Mevinsky and M. Hur. October 1999. Describes how to add Kerberos Ciphering to TLS.

RFC 2716. PPP EAP TLS Authentication Protocol. B. Aboba and D. Simon. October 1999. Explains how to use TLS for PPP authentication.

RFC 2726. PGP Authentication for RIPE Database Updates. J. Zsako. December 1999. Describes how PGP authentication can be used to control updates to the IP address allocation database.

RFC 2743. Generic Security Service Application Program Interface Version 2, Update 1. J. Linn. January 2000. Describes updates to the GSS-API.

RFC 2744. Generic Security Service API Version 2: C-bindings. J. Wray. January 2000. Describes how the C programming language can access GSS-API.

RFC 2747. RSVP Cryptographic Authentication. F. Baker, B. Lindell, and M. Talwar. January 2000. Describes how authentication can be used to protect a resource reservation system.

RFC 2755. Security Negotiation for WebNFS. A. Chiu, M. Eisler, and B. Callaghan. January 2000. Discusses how WebNFS clients can negotiate with servers.

RFC 2759. Microsoft PPP CHAP Extensions, Version 2. G. Zorn. January 2000. Describes the second version of the Microsoft PPP authentication extensions.

RFC 2773. Encryption Using KEA and SKIPJACK. R. Housley, P. Yee, and W. Nace. February 2000. Discusses how encryption is done with the KEA and SKIPJACK algorithms.

RFC 2792. DSA and RSA Key and Signature Encoding for the KeyNote Trust Management System. M. Blaze, J. Ioannidis, and A. Keromytis. March 2000. Discusses key and signature handling in a trust-management system that is Internet-based.

RFC 2808. The SecurID(r) SASL Mechanism. M. Nystrom. April 2000. Describes how the SecurID product can integrate with SASL.

RFC 2809. Implementation of L2TP Compulsory Tunneling via RADIUS. B. Aboba and G. Zorn. April 2000. Discusses implementation issues when using L2TP compulsory tunneling in dial-up networks.

RFC 2817. Upgrading to TLS Within HTTP/1.1. R. Khare and S. Lawrence. May 2000. Describes how a TCP connection can be upgraded to use TLS during a HTTP/1.1 session.

RFC 2818. HTTP Over TLS. E. Rescorla. May 2000. Describes how HTTP runs over TLS.

RFC 2827. Network Ingress Filtering: Defeating Denial of Service Attacks Which Employ IP Source Address Spoofing. P. Ferguson and D. Senie. May 2000. Discusses best practices that can be used to prevent denial-of-service attacks.

RFC 2828. Internet Security Glossary. R. Shirey. May 2000. Provides a glossary of Internet security terms.

RFC 2829. Authentication Methods for LDAP. M. Wahl, H. Alvestrand, J. Hodges, and R. Morgan. May 2000. Discusses methods that can be used for authentication within LDAP.

RFC 2831. Using Digest Authentication as an SASL Mechanism. P. Leach and C. Newman. May 2000. Describes how to use the digest authentication method with SASL.

RFC 2841. IP Authentication using Keyed SHA1 with Interleaved Padding (IP-MAC). P. Metzger and W. Simpson. November 2000. Describes a method to authenticate and ensure integrity of IP datagrams using the Secure Hash Algorithm.

RFC 2845. Secret Key Transaction Authentication for DNS (TSIG). P. Vixie, O. Gudmundsson, D. Eastlake, and B. Wellington. May 2000. Describes how to do transaction-level authentication using one-way hashing and shared secrets.

RFC 2847. LIPKEY—A Low Infrastructure Public Key Mechanism Using SPKM. M. Eisler. June 2000. Describes a way to get a secure channel using GSS-API and the Simple Public Key Mechanism.

RFC 2865. Remote Authentication Dial In User Service (RADIUS). C. Rigney, S. Willens, A. Rubens, and W. Simpson. June 2000. Specifies the authentication mechanism that is used by many sites for dial-up access.

RFC 2876. Use of the KEA and SKIPJACK Algorithms in CMS. J. Pawling. July 2000. Discusses ways to use the Key Exchange Algorithm and SKIPJACK together with the Cryptographic Message Standard.

RFC 2898. PKCS #5: Password-Based Cryptography Specification Version 2.0. B. Kaliski. September 2000. Makes recommendations on how to implement password-based cryptography.

RFC 2930. Secret Key Establishment for DNS (TKEY RR). D. Eastlake III. September 2000. Describes a way to authenticate using DNS queries using DNS resource records.

RFC 2941. Telnet Authentication Option. T. Ts'o, ed., and J. Altman. September 2000. Describes an option that allows Telnet to negotiate whether encryption should be used and if so, which algorithm.

RFC 2942. Telnet Authentication: Kerberos Version 5. T. Ts'o. September 2000. Describes how Kerberos can be used to authenticate Telnet.

RFC 2943. TELNET Authentication Using DSA. R. Housley, T. Horting, and P. Yee. September 2000. Describes how the Digital Signature Algorithm can be used to authenticate Telnet.

RFC 2944. Telnet Authentication: SRP. T. Wu. September 2000. Describes how the Secure Remote Password Protocol can be used to authenticate Telnet.

RFC 2945. The SRP Authentication and Key Exchange System. T. Wu. September 2000. Specifies the Secure Remote Password Protocol.

RFC 2946. Telnet Data Encryption Option. T. Ts'o. September 2000. Describes how Telnet can be used to confidentially encrypt data.

RFC 2947. Telnet Encryption: DES3 64-bit Cipher Feedback. J. Altman. September 2000. Describes how Triple-DES can be used to encrypt a Telnet session.

RFC 2948. Telnet Encryption: DES3 64-bit Output Feedback. J. Altman. September 2000. Describes how Triple-DES in output feedback mode can be used to encrypt a Telnet session.

RFC 2949. Telnet Encryption: CAST-128 64-bit Output Feedback. J. Altman. September 2000. Describes how the CAST-128 encryption algorithm in output feedback mode can be used to encrypt a Telnet session.

RFC 2950. Telnet Encryption: CAST-128 64-bit Cipher Feedback. J. Altman. September 2000. Describes how the CAST-128 encryption algorithm in cipher feedback mode can be used to encrypt a Telnet session.

RFC 2951. TELNET Authentication Using KEA and SKIPJACK. R. Housley, T. Horting, and P. Yee. September 2000. Describes how the Key Exchange Algorithm and SKIPJACK can be used to authenticate a Telnet session.

RFC 2952. Telnet Encryption: DES 64-bit Cipher Feedback. T. Ts'o. September 2000. Describes how DES in cipher feedback mode can be used to encrypt a Telnet session.

RFC 2953. Telnet Encryption: DES 64-bit Output Feedback. T. Ts'o. September 2000. Describes how DES in output feedback mode can be used to encrypt a Telnet session.

RFC 2977. Mobile IP Authentication, Authorization, and Accounting Requirements. S. Glass, T. Hiller, S. Jacobs, and C. Perkins. October 2000. Provides requirements that have to be supported in authentication, authorization, and accounting to provide Mobile IP services.

RFC 2984. Use of the CAST-128 Encryption Algorithm in CMS. C. Adams. October 2000. Describes how to use CAST-128 in the S/MIME Cryptographic Message Syntax.

RFC 2985. PKCS #9: Selected Object Classes and Attribute Types Version 2.0. M. Nystrom and B. Kaliski. November 2000. Provides an object interface and attributes to public-key cryptography and LDAP directories.

RFC 2986. PKCS #10: Certification Request Syntax Specification Version 1.7. M. Nystrom and B. Kaliski. November 2000. Describes the syntax for certification requests.

RFC 3007. Secure Domain Name System (DNS) Dynamic Update. B. Wellington. November 2000. Makes a proposal on how dynamic DNS updates can be made securely.

RFC 3013. Recommended Internet Service Provider Security Services and Procedures. T. Killalea. November 2000. Defines what the IETF thinks ISPs should be doing with respect to security.

RFC 3029. Internet X.509 Public Key Infrastructure Data Validation and Certification Server Protocols. C. Adams, P. Sylvester, M. Zolotarev, and R. Zuccherato. February 2001. Describes the protocols used for digital certificates.

RFC 3039. Internet X.509 Public Key Infrastructure Qualified Certificates Profile. S. Santesson, W. Polk, P. Barzin, and M. Nystrom. January 2001. Describes the format needed for certificates needed for the Europe.

RFC 3078. Microsoft Point-To-Point Encryption (MPPE) Protocol. G. Pall and G. Zorn. March 2001. Explains Microsoft's encryption format for PPP.

RFC 3090. DNS Security Extension Clarification on Zone Status. E. Lewis. March 2001. Revises RFC 2535's definition of a secured zone to be algorithm independent.

RFC 3097. RSVP Cryptographic Authentication—Updated Message Type Value. R. Braden and L. Zhang. April 2001. Updates RFC 2747 to resolve a duplication in message types.

RFC 3110. RSA/SHA-1 SIGs and RSA KEYs in the Domain Name System (DNS). D. Eastlake III. May 2001. Explains how to produce RSA/SHA1 SIG DNS resource records.

RFC 3112. LDAP Authentication Password Schema. K. Zeilenga. May 2001. Defines a schema for user authentication.

RFC 3114. Implementing Company Classification Policy with the S/MIME Security Label. W. Nicolls. May 2002. Discusses how to map company security policies to S/MIME.

RFC 3125. Electronic Signature Policies. J. Ross, D. Pinkas, and N. Pope. September 2001. Defines signature policies used for electronic signatures.

RFC 3126. Electronic Signature Formats for Long Term Electronic Signatures. D. Pinkas, J. Ross, and N. Pope. September 2001. Defines the format of electronic signatures that can remain valid for long periods of time.

RFC 3127. Authentication, Authorization, and Accounting: Protocol Evaluation. D. Mitton, M. St. Johns, S. Barkley, D. Nelson, B. Patil, M. Stevens, and B. Wolff. June 2001. Gives the findings of the AAA WG evaluating protocols against the requirements of RFC 2989.

RFC 3128. Protection Against a Variant of the Tiny Fragment Attack (RFC 1858). I. Miller. June 2001. Updates RFC 1858 to close a gap in its solution to the Tiny Fragment Attack.

RFC 3129. Requirements for Kerberized Internet Negotiation of Keys. M. Thomas. June 2001. Discusses the requirements of Kerberos key negotiation protocool without requiring public keys.

RFC 3130. Notes from the State-Of-The-Technology: DNSSEC. E. Lewis. June 2001. A memo from a DNSSEC status meeting.

RFC 3156. MIME Security with OpenPGP. M. Elkins, D. Del Torto, R. Levien, and T. Roessler. August 2001. Updates RFC 2015 to describe how PGP can be used with MIME.

RFC 3157. Securely Available Credentials—Requirements. A. Arsenault and S. Farrell. August 2001. Describes the requirements needed for Securely Available Credentials (SACRED) protocols.

RFC 3161. Internet X.509 Public Key Infrastructure Time-Stamp Protocol(TSP). C. Adams, P. Cain, D. Pinkas, and R. Zuccherato. August 2001. Defines format of requests for communication with a Time Stamping Authority (TSA).

RFC 3162. RADIUS and IPv6. B. Aboba, G. Zorn, and D. Mitton. August 2001. Specifies how RADIUS should operate more than an IPv6 network.

RFC 3163. ISO/IEC 9798-3 Authentication SASL Mechanism. R. Zuccherato and M. Nystrom. August 2001. Defines an experimental authentication mechanism.

RFC 3183. Domain Security Services using S/MIME. T. Dean and W. Ottaway. October 2001. Explains how S/MIME can be used as a component of Domain Security Services.

RFC 3185. Reuse of CMS Content Encryption Keys. S. Farrell and S. Turner. October 2001. Specifies a method to include a key identifier in a message, so that the key can be re-used for further data.

RFC 3193. Securing L2TP using IPsec. B. Patel, B. Aboba, W. Dixon, G. Zorn, and S. Booth. November 2001. Explains how the L2TP VPN protocol can use IPsec for various services.

RFC 3211. Password-based Encryption for CMS. P. Gutmann. December 2001. Describes a way to encrypt data using passwords.

RFC 3217. Triple-DES and RC2 Key Wrapping. R. Housley. December 2001. Explains key wrap algorithms.

RFC 3218. Preventing the Million Message Attack on Cryptographic Message Syntax. E. Rescorla. January 2002. Gives a strategy for resisting the Million Message Attack.

RFC 3226. DNSSEC and IPv6 A6 aware server/resolver message size requirements. O. Gudmundsson. December 2001. Updates RFC 2535, and RFC 2874 by adding additional requirements.

RFC 3227. Guidelines for Evidence Collection and Archiving. D. Brezinski and T. Killalea. February 2002. An excellent document on how to gather evidence after you have been hacked.

RFC 3244. Microsoft Windows 2000 Kerberos Change Password and Set Password Protocols. M. Swift, J. Trostle, and J. Brezak. February 2002. Documents one of Microsoft's changes to Kerberos.

RFC 3278. Use of Elliptic Curve Cryptography (ECC) Algorithms in Cryptographic Message Syntax (CMS). S. Blake-Wilson, D. Brown, and P. Lambert. April 2002. Discusses how to use ECC algorithm in the CMS.

RFC 3279. Algorithms and Identifiers for the Internet X.509 Public Key Infrastructure Certificate and Certificate Revocation List (CRL) Profile. L. Bassham, W. Polk, and R. Housley. April 2002. Gives algorithm identifiers and encoding formats used with PKI.

RFC 3280. Internet X.509 Public Key Infrastructure Certificate and Certificate Revocation List (CRL) Profile. R. Housley, W. Polk, W. Ford, and D. Solo. April 2002. Gives an overview of the format of X.509 v3 certificates and X.509 v2 certification revocation lists.

RFC 3281. An Internet Attribute Certificate Profile for Authorization. S. Farrell and R. Housley. April 2002. Defines profiles for X.509 Attribute Certificates.

D

What's on the CD-ROM

This appendix lists security tools for various platforms. Most such tools are freeware, shareware, or open source. The rest are commercial products. URLs are included so that you can check to see if there have been any updates since the book was published. If you don't find a product listed in this appendix on the CD-ROM, you can use the provided URL to get more information on it.

.NET Hook

Description: Allows insertion of arbitrary code at the beginning of each function called in a .NET assembly (whether executable or assembly).

URL: http://sourceforge.net/projects/dotnethook/

[Blutch] Network Simulator

Description: Simulates networks. Good for network modeling.

URL: http://sourceforge.net/projects/bns/

AATools

Description: Network diagnostic tools that do just about everything including port scanner, proxy analysis, tracing routes, email address vertification, link analysis, network monitor, process monitoring, and a few other functions. The primary purpose is to get network status and availability information.

URL: http://www.glocksoft.com/aatools.htm

Access Road

Description: Diagram and model your access controls. Very powerful.

URL: http://sourceforge.net/projects/accessroad/

ACID-PHP

Description: PHP-based engine to search and process security incident database in conjunction with Snort.

URL: `http://sourceforge.net/projects/acid-mysql/`

AckCmd

Description: Allows you to get command prompts on remote Windows 2000 systems. Can bypass some firewalls by communicating via ACK packets.

URL: `http://ntsecurity.nu/toolbox/ackcmd/`

Active Ports

Description: A Windows NT/2000/XP tool to monitor TCP/IP port usage, including the applications which own the ports and the IP address connected to it. Useful to detect trojans on your system.

URL: `http://www.protect-me.com/freeware.html`

ActivPack for Windows NT

Description: ActivPack is a Windows RADIUS and TACACS+ authentication server. It suports a variety of devices such as hardware tokens, USB keys, soft tokens, and smart cards.

URL: `http://www.activcard.com/activ/products/infrastructure/activpack_nt/index.html`

Adding SecurID protection to EXE files

Description: Adds SecurID protection to EXE files.

URL: `http://sourceforge.net/projects/sidp/`

Address Lookup

Description: Resolves multiple hostnames or IPs (good for automating checks of who's accessing your site).

URL: `http://sourceforge.net/projects/adlook/`

AdmWin

Description: A set of five tools that make managing Windows NT/2000/XP easier. The tools manage users, groups, active directory, events, and can perform remote management.

URL: `http://www.admwin.com/`

Advanced Security Control (ASC)

Description: Lets Windows administrators control the time of day that users can run certain applications.

URL: http://www.protect-me.com/asc/

AGT

Description: A front end for IP routing tables that allows you to make changes to your firewall quickly.

URL: http://sourceforge.net/projects/agt

Alert Reaction Enemy System ARES LX

Description: Alert Reaction Enemy System is an intrusion detection engine for Linux.

URL: http://sourceforge.net/projects/lxares/

Alfandega

Description: An easy-to-use front end to configure a netfiler firewall.

URL: http://alfandega.sourceforge.net

AMaViS - A Mail Virus Scanner

Description: POSIX-compliant and OS-independent system that grafts virus scanning capabilities to MTAs. Perl required.

URL: http://sourceforge.net/projects/amavis/

Anax Linux Distribution

Description: Live-CD Linux distribution. It's difficult to hack a read-only OS, right?

URL: http://sourceforge.net/projects/anax/

Anti Defacement System

Description: An anti-defacement system for Linux.

URL: http://sourceforge.net/projects/troni-ads/

Antivirus for Linux

Description: Antivirus system for Linux.

URL: http://sourceforge.net/projects/delvirusbr/

antivisor

Description: GUI-based antivirus management system (uses Python).

URL: http://sourceforge.net/projects/antivisor/

apache - mod_antihak

Description: Apache module that kills Nimda and Code Red.

URL: http://sourceforge.net/projects/apantihak/

Apache Intrusion Detection Module

Description: A simple tool to discover intrusion attempts by examining the client requests in real time.

URL: http://yunus.hacettepe.edu.tr/~burak/mod_id/

Apache Web Server Benchmark

Description: AWS Benchmark is for hardening Apache servers.

URL: http://sourceforge.net/projects/apachebenchmark/

Apache-ACEProxy

Description: Perl modules for Apache proxy services.

URL: http://www.cpan.org/authors/id/M/MI/MIYAGAWA/Apache-ACEProxy-0.03.tar.gz

Apache-AntiSpam

Description: Apache Perl module to filter spam from Web pages.

URL: http://www.cpan.org/authors/id/M/MI/MIYAGAWA/Apache-AntiSpam-0.04.tar.gz

Apache-AuthCookie

Description: Perl authentication and authorization via cookies.

URL: http://www.cpan.org/authors/id/M/MS/MSCHOUT/Apache-AuthCookie-3.00.tar.gz

Apache-AuthCookieDBI

Description: An AuthCookie module backed by a DBI database.

URL: http://www.cpan.org/authors/id/C/CR/CROMIS/Apache-AuthCookieDBI-1.18.tar.gz

Apache-AuthCookieDBIRadius

Description: An AuthCookie module backed by a DBI database and an optional Radius server.

URL: `http://www.cpan.org/authors/id/B/BA/BARRACODE/`
`Apache-AuthCookieDBIRadius-1.19.tar.gz`

Apache-AuthCookieLDAP

Description: An AuthCookie module backed by an LDAP server.

URL: `http://www.cpan.org/authors/id/B/BJ/BJORNARDO/`
`Apache-AuthCookieLDAP-0.02.tar.gz`

Apache-AuthCookieURL

Description: Perl authentication and authorization via cookies and URLs.

URL: `http://www.cpan.org/authors/id/H/HA/HANK/Apache-AuthCookieURL-1.003.tar.gz`

Apache-AuthenCache

Description: Authentication caching used in conjunction with Apache.

URL: `http://www.cpan.org/authors/id/J/JB/JBODNAR/Apache-AuthenCache-0.05.tar.gz`

Apache-AuthenLDAP

Description: Apache LDAP Authentication Module.

URL: http://www.cpan.org/authors/id/C/CG/CGILMORE/Apache-AuthenLDAP-0.61.tar.gz

Apache-AuthenN2

Description: Authenticates into the NT and NIS+ domains.

URL: `http://www.cpan.org/authors/id/V/VA/VALERIE/Apache-AuthenN2-0.05.tar.gz`

Apache-AuthenNIS

Description: NIS authentication module.

URL: `http://www.cpan.org/authors/id/D/DE/DEP/Apache-AuthenNIS-0.10.tar.gz`

Apache-AuthenNISPlus

Description: Authenticates into a NIS+ domain.

URL: `http://www.cpan.org/authors/id/V/VA/VALERIE/`
`Apache-AuthenNISPlus-0.06.tar.gz`

Apache-AuthenPasswd

Description: Unix `passwd` file authentication module.

URL: `http://www.cpan.org/authors/id/D/DE/DEP/Apache-AuthenPasswd-0.10.tar.gz`

Apache-AuthenPasswdSrv

Description: Socket-based authenticator handler.

URL: `http://www.cpan.org/authors/id/J/JE/JEFFH/`
`Apache-AuthenPasswdSrv-0.01.tar.gz`

Apache-AuthenRadius

Description: Authentication via a Radius server.

URL: `http://www.cpan.org/authors/id/D/DA/DANIEL/Apache-AuthenRadius-0.3.tar.gz`

Apache-AuthenSmb

Description: NT authentication module.

URL: `http://www.cpan.org/authors/id/PARKER/Apache-AuthenSmb-0.60.tar.gz`

Apache-AuthenURL

Description: Authenticates via another URL.

URL: `http://www.cpan.org/authors/id/JGROENVEL/Apache-AuthenURL-0.8.tar.gz`

Apache-AuthExpire

Description: Provides authentication time limits on `.htaccess`-protected pages.

URL: `http://www.cpan.org/authors/id/J/JJ/JJHORNER/Apache-AuthExpire-0.36.tar.gz`

Apache-AuthLDAP

Description: LDAP access control and authentication module.

URL: `http://www.cpan.org/authors/id/CDONLEY/Apache-AuthLDAP-0.21.tar.gz`

Apache-AuthNetLDAP

Description: Module that uses the Net::LDAP module for user authentication for Apache.

URL: `http://www.cpan.org/authors/id/M/ME/MEWILCOX/Apache-AuthNetLDAP-0.19.tar.gz`

Apache-AuthTicket

Description: Cookie-based access module.

URL: `http://www.cpan.org/authors/id/M/MS/MSCHOUT/Apache-AuthTicket-0.31.tar.gz.`

Apache-AuthzCache

Description: Cache authorization module.

URL: `http://www.cpan.org/authors/id/C/CG/CGILMORE/Apache-AuthzCache-0.06.tar.gz`

Apache-AuthzLDAP

Description: LDAP authorization module.

URL: `http://www.cpan.org/authors/id/C/CG/CGILMORE/Apache-AuthzLDAP-0.61.tar.gz`

Apache-AuthzNIS

Description: NIS group authorization module.

URL: `http://www.cpan.org/authors/id/D/DE/DEP/Apache-AuthzNIS-0.10.tar.gz`

Apache-CodeRed

Description: Responds to CodeRed worm attacks with email warnings.

URL: `http://www.cpan.org/authors/id/R/RE/REUVEN/Apache-CodeRed-1.07.tar.gz`

ApacheCookieEncrypted

Description: Encrypted HTTP cookies.

URL: `http://www.cpan.org/authors/id/J/JK/JKRASNOO/`
`ApacheCookieEncrypted-0.03.tar.gz`

ApacheDBI

Description: Authentication and authorization via Perl's DBI.

URL: `http://www.cpan.org/authors/id/MERGL/ApacheDBI-0.88.tar.gz`

Apache-DBILogConfig

Description: Logs access information in a DBI database.

URL: `http://www.cpan.org/authors/id/J/JB/JBODNAR/Apache-DBILogConfig-0.02.tar.gz`

Apache-DBILogger

Description: Tracks what's being transferred in a DBI database.

URL: `http://www.cpan.org/authors/id/ABH/Apache-DBILogger-0.93.tar.gz`

Apache-DBILogin

Description: Authenticates and authorizes via a DBI connection.

URL: `http://www.cpan.org/authors/id/JGROENVEL/Apache-DBILogin-2.0.tar.gz`

Apache-DebugInfo

Description: Logs various bits of per-request data.

URL: `http://www.cpan.org/authors/id/G/GE/GEOFF/Apache-DebugInfo-0.05.tar.gz`

Apache-DumpHeaders

Description: Watches HTTP transaction via headers.

URL: `http://www.cpan.org/authors/id/ABH/Apache-DumpHeaders-0.93.tar.gz`

Apache-GTopLimit

Description: Limits Apache httpd processes.

URL: `http://www.cpan.org/authors/id/S/ST/STAS/Apache-GTopLimit-0.01.tar.gz`

Apache-Htaccess

Description: Creates and modifies Apache `.htaccess` files.

URL: `http://www.cpan.org/authors/id/BDFOY/Apache-Htaccess-1.2.tar.gz`

Apache-Htgroup

Description: Manages Apache authentication group files.

URL: `http://www.cpan.org/authors/id/RBOW/Apache-Htgroup-1.20.tar.gz`

Apache-Htpasswd

Description: Manages Unix crypt-style password file.

URL: `http://www.cpan.org/authors/id/K/KM/KMELTZ/Apache-Htpasswd-1.5.3.tar.gz`

Apache-Keywords

Description: Stores keywords as a personal profile in a cookie.

URL: http://www.cpan.org/authors/id/M/MA/MAGNUS/Apache-Keywords-0.1.tar.gz

Apache-LogFile

Description: Interface to Apache's logging routines.

URL: http://www.cpan.org/authors/id/DOUGM/Apache-LogFile-0.12.tar.gz

Apache-MimeXML

Description: mod_perl mime encoding sniffer for XML files.

URL: http://www.cpan.org/authors/id/M/MS/MSERGEANT/Apache-MimeXML-0.08.tar.gz

Apache-ParseLog

Description: Parses Apache log files.

URL: http://www.cpan.org/authors/id/A/AK/AKIRA/Apache-ParseLog-1.02.tar.gz

Apache-PHLogin

Description: Authenticates via a PH database.

URL: http://www.cpan.org/authors/id/JGROENVEL/Apache-PHLogin-0.5.tar.gz

Apache-ProxyPass

Description: Implements ProxyPass in Perl.

URL: http://www.cpan.org/authors/id/MJS/Apache-ProxyPass-0.06.tar.gz

Apache-RefererBlock

Description: Blocks requests based upon referrer header.

URL: http://www.cpan.org/authors/id/C/CH/CHOLET/Apache-RefererBlock-0.03.tar.gz

Apache-ReverseProxy

Description: An Apache mod_perl reverse proxy.

URL: http://www.cpan.org/authors/id/CLINTDW/Apache-ReverseProxy-0.06.tar.gz

Apache-RewritingProxy

Description: Proxy that works by rewriting requested documents with no client proxy config needed.

URL: `http://www.cpan.org/authors/id/H/HA/HAGANK/Apache-RewritingProxy-0.7.tar.gz`

Apache-Session

Description: A persistence framework for session data. Many, many fine tools here.

URL: `http://www.cpan.org/authors/id/JBAKER/Apache-Session-1.54.tar.gz`

Apache-Session-Generate-ModUsertrack

Description: Use mod_user_track for session ID generation.

URL: `http://www.cpan.org/authors/id/M/MI/MIYAGAWA/`
`Apache-Session-Generate-ModUsertrack-0.01.tar.gz`

Apache-Traffic

Description: Tracks hits and bytes transferred on a per-user basis.

URL: `http://www.cpan.org/authors/id/MAURICE/Apache-Traffic-1.02.tar.gz`

Apache-Usertrack

Description: Emulates the mod_usertrack apache module.

URL: `http://www.cpan.org/authors/id/ABH/Apache-Usertrack-0.03.tar.gz`

AppShield by Sanctum

Description: Protects applications against cracking attempts.

URL: `http://www.sanctuminc.com/solutions/appshield/index.html`

Argante

Description: Secure Virtual Operating System (VOS) written in C.

URL: `http://sourceforge.net/projects/argante/`

Armed

Description: Linux-based intrusion detection system.

URL: `http://sourceforge.net/projects/armed/`

armor

Description: Hardening module for HP-UX and Solaris.

URL: `http://sourceforge.net/projects/armor/`

ArMyZ Traceroute detector

Description: Linux and Solaris tool for tracing those who trace you via Traceroute.

URL: `http://sourceforge.net/projects/artraced/`

Astaro Security Linux

Description: A Linux distribution with advanced security features such as firewalling, content-filtering, and VPN features.

URL: `http://sourceforge.net/projects/asl/`

Atelier Web Ports Traffic Analyzer

Description: A Windows-based TCP/IP port monitor with maps ports to processes.

URL: `http://www.atelierweb.com/pta/`

Attack and Probe Reporter

Description: Finds scans and attacks based on Linux logs. Researches who to contact at ISPs to stop the attacks.

URL: `http://sourceforge.net/projects/apreporter/`

auth_ip

Description: Provides user authentication by client IP address.

URL: `http://www.troppoavanti.it//modules/mod_auth_ip/mod_auth_ip.html`

auth_ldap

Description: LDAP authentication module.

URL: `http://www.rudedog.org/auth_ldap/`

auth_oracle module

Description: Authentication module for Apache 1.3 -> Oracle8.

URL: `http://www.macomnet.ru/~oskin/mod_auth_oracle.html`

auth_script

Description: Authentication decision by an external CGI or PHP script.

URL: `http://mod-auth-script.sourceforge.net/`

Authen::Prot

Description: Provides access to protected password databases through Unix system calls.

URL: `http://sourceforge.net/projects/authen-prot/`

Authentication (Windows NT Domain Controller)

Description: An Apache for Windows Perl module that does NT Domain Controller/password-based authentication.

URL: `http://recd.hypermart.net/dev`

Automated Security Tools

Description: Provides tools that let network administrators test their network security. For Linux, Solaris, *BSD, and Mac OS X.

URL: `http://sourceforge.net/projects/autosec/`

Automatic Dynamic Firewall

Description: Assists in the deployment of a firewall.

URL: `http://sourceforge.net/projects/dymfirewall/`

Automatic Security

Description: A Linux security scanner that automatically downloads patches.

URL: `http://sourceforge.net/projects/asecurity/`

Autonomous Agents for Intrusion Detection

Description: A powerful intrusion detection system for Unix.

URL: `http://www.cerias.purdue.edu/homes/aafid/`

AVirCap (CodeHunt)

Description: Detects CodeRed and Nimda attacks as well as some others. For Windows.

URL: `http://sourceforge.net/projects/codehunt/`

azAuth

Description: azAuth is a PHP class for authentication.

URL: `http://sourceforge.net/projects/azauth/`

Bandwidth management

Description: Limits bandwidth based on the number of connections.

BANXAD Network Monitoring Analyzer

Description: A combination network monitor, intrusion detector, and file integrity checker.

URL: `http://sourceforge.net/projects/banxad/`

Bash Iptables Script Firewall

Description: An easy-to-use firewall for Linux.

URL: `http://sourceforge.net/projects/bisf/`

BeatLm

Description: BeatLm searches out the password from LM/NTLM authentication information (LanManager and Windows NT challenge/response).

URL: `http://www.securityfriday.com/ToolDownload/BeatLM/beatlm_doc.html`

BLAAST

Description: Scans a machine for vulnerabilities.

URL: `http://sourceforge.net/projects/blaast/`

Blaster Scanner

Description: A TCP port scanner for Linux that does extra security checks.

URL: `http://sourceforge.net/projects/blasterscan/`

B-Level Compliant Linux

Description: A stripped-down version of Linux that attempts to meet the DOS's B-Level security.

URL: `http://sourceforge.net/projects/binux/`

BLISS

Description: A security scanner for Unix.

URL: `http://sourceforge.net/projects/bliss-scanner/`

BrickHouse

Description: Makes using the firewall built into Mac OS X as easy as possible.

URL: `http://personalpages.tds.net/~brian_hill/brickhouse.html`

BrowseList

Description: Retrieves the browse list from any Windows system. This is useful for mapping a Windows network.

URL: `http://ntsecurity.nu/toolbox/browselist/`

Brute Force Binary Tester

Description: BFBTester does proactive security checks of binary programs. BFBTester will perform checks of single- and multiple-argument command-line overflows and environment variable overflows. For Solaris and BSD.

URL: `http://sourceforge.net/projects/bfbtester/`

BruteEX

Description: Tests applications against hacking attempts.

URL: `http://sourceforge.net/projects/bruteex/`

Bruth

Description: Performs remote security assessments and penetration testings.

URL: `http://sourceforge.net/projects/bruth/`

BsdScan

Description: A lightweight port scanner for BSD-derived operating systems.

URL: `http://sourceforge.net/projects/bsdscan/`

bwshare

Description: Bandwidth throttling by client IP address.

URL: `http://www.topology.org/src/bwshare/README.html`

Bypass

Description: An IP forwarding/tunneling tool that can bypass firewalls. For Linux.

URL: http://sourceforge.net/projects/bypass/

cage

Description: Creates a secure chroot environment for running programs on Linux.

URL: http://original.killa.net/infosec/cage/

Camera Monitoring System

Description: Manages video sources such as security cameras, but records only when motion has been detected. For Windows NT/2000.

URL: http://sourceforge.net/projects/videomon/

CDLock

Description: Allows the administrator to set rules on Windows machines regarding how users can use removable storage.

URL: http://www.ntutility.com/cdl/

CECrypt

Description: A file encryption tool for Windows CE.

URL: http://ntsecurity.nu/toolbox/cecrypt/

Cerber

Description: A kernel module for FreeBSD that makes the system more secure.

URL: http://sourceforge.net/projects/cerber/

CGI SUGId

Description: Sets User/Group IDs for CGI execution.

URL: http://www.geocities.com/SiliconValley/Pines/1830/

CGIWrap

Description: A wrapper for sites that allows individual users to post CGI scripts. CGIWrap protects the security of the HTTP server.

URL: http://download.sourceforge.net/cgiwrap/

ChatKiller

Description: ChatKiller is used on Windows to manage running processes.

URL: http://www.macinsoft.bizland.com/win/chatkiller.html

Choom

Description: Web-based administration of Linux firewall tables.

URL: http://sourceforge.net/projects/choom/

Cimtrak WSE

Description: Detects unauthorized changes to an IIS server and restores the original content.

URL: http://www.cimcor.com/ct_wse.htm

cina vb proxy server

Description: Windows-based proxy server.

URL: http://sourceforge.net/projects/cinaproxy/

Class Router

Description: Modifies Cisco router configurations through the Web.

URL: http://sourceforge.net/projects/crouter/

ClearLogs

Description: Clears Windows event logs.

URL: http://ntsecurity.nu/toolbox/clearlogs/

CogniSec Enterprise Firewall

Description: Open source enterprise-level firewall and VPN gateway.

URL: http://sourceforge.net/projects/cognisec-fw/

ColdFusion Module

Description: Interface to the ColdFusion application server.

URL: http://www.allaire.com/

Connection Limitation

Description: This Apache module can limit the number of concurrent connections from one host.

URL: `http://programmer.lib.sjtu.edu.cn/apache/modules.html`

Connection Tracking System

Description: Tracks connections and lets you view them through the Web.

URL: `http://sourceforge.net/projects/conntrack/`

ConnProbe IDS

Description: A distributed intrusion detection system.

URL: `http://sourceforge.net/projects/hack-probe/`

Control Freak: Administrator utility

Description: Monitors activity on a system.

URL: `http://sourceforge.net/projects/control-freak/`

Cookie authentication (MySQL-based)

Description: Compares cookies against the contents of MySQL for authentication.

URL: `http://www.plover.com/~mjd/mac_mysql/`

CopyPwd

Description: A command-line utility that allows Windows accounts to be copied from one computer to another.

URL: `http://www.systemtools.com`

Covalent Antivirus for Apache

Description: McAfee virus scanning engine in an Apache module.

URL: `http://www.covalent.net/products/antivirus/`

Covalent Intrusion Detector

Description: Monitors a site, replaces any defaced content with a notice, and notifies a system administrator.

URL: `http://www.covalent.net/products/intrusiondetector/`

Covalent NetTruss

Description: Tools to set up a network infrastructure quickly.

URL: http://www.covalent.net/products/nettruss/

Covalent Raven SSL

Description: Secures Web transactions with SSL/TLS.

URL: http://www.covalent.net/

cp2fwbuilder

Description: Checkpoint Firewall 1-to-Linux/BSD firewall migration tool.

URL: http://cp2fwbuilder.sourceforge.net/

CPU - Change Password Utility

Description: An LDAP user management tool.

URL: http://sourceforge.net/projects/cpu/

CPU Indicator Screen Saver

Description: A screensaver for Windows that shows CPU utilization.

URL: http://www.protect-me.com/freeware.html

CrackWhore

Description: A Windows security scanner.

URL: http://sourceforge.net/projects/crackwhore/

cryptf

Description: A file encryption tool for Windows.

URL: http://ntsecurity.nu/toolbox/cryptf/

Cryptix SASL Library

Description: A Java implementation of SASL.

URL: http://sourceforge.net/projects/cryptix-sasl/

C-TUN Daemon

Description: Secure tunneling daemon for FreeBSD.

URL: http://sourceforge.net/projects/ctund/

CueCat PAM Module

Description: A PAM (Pluggable Authentication Module) for Linux that uses a CueCat for authentication.

URL: `http://sourceforge.net/projects/pam-cuecat/`

DansGuardian

Description: A Web content filter that currently runs on Linux, FreeBSD, OpenBSD and Solaris. It filters the actual content of pages based on many methods, including phrase matching, PICS filtering, and URL filtering. It does not purely filter based on a banned list of sites like lesser commercial filters.

URL: `http://dansguardian.org/`

DAXFi

Description: DAXFi helps configure firewalls consistently.

URL: `http://daxfi.sourceforge.net/`

DCE Authentication

Description: DCE Authentication/secure DFS module for Apache.

URL: `http://www.intranet.csupomona.edu/~henson/www/projects/mod_auth_dce/`

debian-trusted

Description: A hardened Linux distribution based on debian.

URL: `http://sourceforge.net/projects/debian-trusted/`

demure

Description: A dictionary-based attack tool for POP3, IMAP and FTP.

URL: `http://sourceforge.net/projects/phpbrute-v2b/`

DeSniff

Description: A sniffer detector for Linux.

URL: `http://sourceforge.net/projects/desniff/`

DevilExecuter

Description: Makes Web access more anonymous by using a series of proxies.

URL: `http://sourceforge.net/projects/devilexecuter/`

devsecure

Description: A Web-based log analyzer for OpenBSD, though it can work with most BSD/Linux systems.

URL: `http://sourceforge.net/projects/devsecure/`

DHCP hijack

Description: Hijacks LANs using DHCP.

URL: `http://sourceforge.net/projects/dhcphijack/`

Dial Server and Client

Description: Allows you to remotely control your network gateway from a modem.

URL: `http://sourceforge.net/projects/dialserver/`

Dial-Up Lock Millennium Edition

Description: Allows the administrator to set up per-user security for RAS connections on Windows.

URL: `http://www.winutility.com/dulme/`

Distributed IDS Analysis & Response

Description: Distributed IDS system with a centralized database.

URL: `http://sourceforge.net/projects/distro-ids/`

Distributed Integrity Manager/Client

Description: An integrity-checker for Unix operating systems.

URL: `http://sourceforge.net/projects/daidealus/`

Distributed Secure File System

Description: Serverless, redundant, secure, infinite, nonrevocable filesystem.

URL: `http://sourceforge.net/projects/dsfs/`

DMZS-Biatchux Bootable CD Distro

Description: Bootable CD forensics, virus scanning, recovery, and PenTesting system for Windows and Linux.

URL: `http://sourceforge.net/projects/biatchux/`

DNS Blocker

Description: Allows administrators to filter out and redirect selected inappropriate sites for Linux. This is useful to prevent employees from browsing inappropiate sites at work.

URL: http://sourceforge.net/projects/dns-block/

DoorStop

Description: Firewall for the Mac.

URL: http://www2.opendoor.com/doorstop/

Dr. Steganoctagon

Description: An acoustic steganography application.

URL: http://sourceforge.net/projects/drsteg/

DS NT Authentication Plugin

Description: A Netscape/SunONE LDAP server plugin that performs pass-through authentication to an NT domain controller.

URL: http://sourceforge.net/projects/dsntauth/

DShield IPFW Client

Description: Takes firewall logs and submits them to dshield.net, the distributed intrusion detection system.

URL: http://sourceforge.net/projects/dshield-ipfw/

Dsniff for Win32

Description: Simple password sniffer that can sniff numerous protocols.

URL: http://www.datanerds.net/~mike/dsniff.html

DumpSec, DumpReg, DumpEvt

Description: Products that dump NTFS permissions, user information, event logs, and registry information.

URL: http://www.systemtools.com

E2ECard

Description: An end-to-end architecture to enable universal identification and universal commerce via smart cards.

URL: http://sourceforge.net/projects/e2ecard/

echolot

Description: An ARP packet sniffer for Unix.

URL: `http://sourceforge.net/projects/echolot/`

eJPassword

Description: A simple password generator for the Palm OS.

URL: `http://sourceforge.net/projects/ejpassword/`

Electric Death Ferret

Description: A Perl daemon that sets up accounts and virtual hosting via the Web.

URL: `http://www.guanotronic.com/~serge/EDF/`

Embedded Coyote Linux (Wolverine Firewall and VPN server)

Description: Firewall and VPN server based on Linux.

URL: `http://embedded.coyotelinux.com/wolverine/index.php`

Endoshield

Description: Easy-to-use Linux-based firewall. It is designed for home users who have no knowledge of firewalls.

URL: `http://endoshield.sourceforge.net/`

Enigma Mailer

Description: Allows users to send encrypted email messages to anyone with an email account.

URL: `http://sourceforge.net/projects/enigmailer/`

entren

Description: A packet-matching IDS and traffic analyzer.

URL: `http://sourceforge.net/projects/entren/`

epasswd

Description: An improved Unix passwd program.

URL: `http://sourceforge.net/projects/epasswd/`

EPIC SSL support

Description: SSL support for epic4-2000.

URL: `http://sourceforge.net/projects/epicssl/`

EtherFlood

Description: Floods a network with Ethernet frames with random hardware addresses.

URL: `http://ntsecurity.nu/toolbox/etherflood/`

eTrust Intrusion Detection

Description: An IDS system.

URL: `http://www3.ca.com/Solutions/Product.asp?ID=163`

EMERALD

Description: A comprehensive IDS.

URL: http://www.sdl.sri.com/projects/emerald/

eXistenZ

Description: TripWire 2.3 remote administration for Linux.

URL: `http://sourceforge.net/projects/existenz/`

Extensible User Folder

Description: An authentication system for the Zope Application Server.

URL: `http://sourceforge.net/projects/exuserfolder/`

External Authentication Module

Description: An Apache authentication module that allows the use of external data sources.

URL: `http://www.unixpapa.com/mod_auth_external.html`

Eyeball

Description: Tracks DoS and DDoS attacks.

URL: `http://sourceforge.net/projects/eyeball/`

FakeBO

Description: Logs and emulates common Trojan attacks for Linux.

URL: `http://sourceforge.net/projects/fakebo/`

FakeGINA

Description: Intercepts and captures the communication between Winlogon and the normal GINA.

URL: `http://ntsecurity.nu/toolbox/fakegina/`

Falcon

Description: A free, secure, and OS-independent firewall system.

URL: `http://falcon.naw.de/`

FastSpy Port Scanner

Description: A network port scanner for Windows and Linux.

URL: `http://sourceforge.net/projects/fastspy/`

ferm

Description: A firewall rule parser for Linux.

URL: `http://www.geo.vu.nl/~koka/ferm/ferm.html`

FileManager

Description: A Web-based remote command and directory manager for Linux and Unix.

URL: `http://www.horsburgh.com/h_filemanager.html`

Finger Print Verification System

Description: A library for adding fingerprinting to applications.

URL: `http://fvs.sourceforge.net/index.html`

FireBox

Description: A Web authentication system that uses PHP and MySQL for BSD and Linux.

URL: `http://sourceforge.net/projects/firebox/`

fireflier

Description: A Linux firewall rule building tool.

URL: `http://sourceforge.net/projects/fireflier`

Firepoint Firewall Management Server

Description: Another Linux firewall rule-building tool.

URL: http://sourceforge.net/projects/firepoint/

Firestarter

Description: A firewall solution for Linux.

URL: http://firestarter.sourceforge.net/

Firewall Builder

Description: A GUI-based tool to help build firewall rules.

URL: http://www.fwbuilder.org/

Firewallscript

Description: Parses firewall settings in a configuration file and implements them in a script.

URL: http://my.netfilter.se/

FK

Description: A lightweight firewall toolkit.

URL: http://hairy.beasts.org/fk/

Flow Controller

Description: A Java-based control layer of the MVC design pattern using a servlet and an XML-based flow description.

URL: http://sourceforge.net/projects/flow/

FlySolo

Description: Client-side APIs for an alternative to Microsoft's Passport.

URL: http://sourceforge.net/projects/flysolo/

Foremost

Description: Linux tool for conducting computer forensic examinations.

URL: http://sourceforge.net/projects/foremost/

Fortress Network User Authentication

Description: Tool for managing user accounts.

URL: `http://fortress.s5.com/Solutions/solutions.htm`

Free Agents DIDS

Description: Distributed intrusion detection system for Linux.

URL: `http://sourceforge.net/projects/freeagent/`

FTimes

Description: System-baselining and evidence collection tool for Windows and Linux.

URL: `http://sourceforge.net/projects/ftimes/`

FUZZauth

Description: Pluggable local and network-based authentication system.

URL: `http://sourceforge.net/projects/fuzzauth/`

Fwctl

Description: Easy-to-use Linux packet filtering configuration.

URL: `http://indev.insu.com/Fwctl/#download`

FwGold FW-1 Graphical Log Representation

Description: Graphs a Firewall-1 access log.

URL: `http://sourceforge.net/projects/fwgold/`

fwlogwatch

Description: Firewall log analyzer and real-time attack detector for Unix.

URL: `http://sourceforge.net/projects/fwlogwatch/`

FWM

Description: Manages firewall and routing configuration.

URL: `http://ftp.malikai.net/projects/fwm/`

fwmap

Description: Eases management of firewalls on large networks.

URL: `http://sourceforge.net/projects/fwmap/`

fwwebgui

Description: A replacement for the Checkpoint GUI.

URL: `http://sourceforge.net/projects/fwwebgui/`

GetAcct

Description: Acquires account information on Windows NT/2000 machines.

URL: `http://www.securityfriday.com/ToolDownload/GetAcct/getacct_doc.html`

Ghost Port Scan

Description: Tests firewalls with port scanning and address spoofing.

URL: `http://gps.sourceforge.net/`

GIPTables Firewall

Description: GIPTables Firewall is a free set of shell scripts that help you generate iptables rules for Linux 2.4.*x* and later kernels. It's easy to configure, and at present, designed to run on hosts with one or two network cards. It doesn't require you to install any additional components to make it work with your GNU/Linux system.

URL: `http://www.giptables.org/`

GnoKart Kerberos Utility

Description: A Kerberos authentication utility for Linux.

URL: `http://sourceforge.net/projects/gnokart/`

GNotary Digital Notary

Description: An asynchronous peer-to-peer digital notary service based on email.

URL: `http://sourceforge.net/projects/gnotary/`

GNU Revolutionary Infrastructure

Description: A P2P infrastructure.

URL: `http://sourceforge.net/projects/gnuris/`

GNU userv

Description: A Unix system facility to allow one program to invoke another when only limited trust exists between them. Similar to the well-known sudo.

URL: `http://www.chiark.greenend.org.uk/~ian/userv/`

GnuUsr (New User)

Description: An automated administration tool for Linux that allows remote users to create user accounts in a secure manner.

URL: http://sourceforge.net/projects/gnuusr/

GrabItAll

Description: Spoofs ARP replies to redirect traffic.

URL: http://ntsecurity.nu/toolbox/grabitall/

grsecurity

Description: A Linux 2.4 security system with a ton of features.

URL: http://www.grsecurity.net/download.htm

GSD - Get Service DACL

Description: Gets the DACL (Discretionary Access Control List) of a Windows NT service.

URL: http://ntsecurity.nu/toolbox/gsd/

gShield

Description: A generic iptables firewall script, which allows some configuration, that will work for most people.

URL: http://muse.linuxmafia.org/gshield.html

GTK PassWord Generator

Description: A Linux password generation system.

URL: http://sourceforge.net/projects/gpwg/

Hardware-ID

Description: A Linux module that gives programs a way to forge hardware IDs.

URL: http://sourceforge.net/projects/hardwareid/

Heimdall Linuxconf Firewall

Description: Simple-to-use internet firewall (distributed as part of Linuxconf). Works in the background (as a daemon). Features a Net interface monitor based on a configuration in Linuxconf (done by Web, GUI, client/server or text interface). Linux.

URL: http://sourceforge.net/projects/heimdall/

HFNetNag

Description: Makes tracking the Windows Hot Fixes easy.

URL: `http://sourceforge.net/projects/hfnetnag/`

HLFL (High Level Firewall Language)

Description: A general purpose firewall language that can translate rules into the format needed for various devices.

URL: `http://www.hlfl.org/`

Hoggett

Description: A Web management console for the Snort IDS.

URL: `http://sourceforge.net/projects/hoggett/`

Hotwired Mod_include

Description: Hotwired extensions to mod_include.

URL: `http://www.hotwired.com/webmonkey/99/10/index0a.html`

hping2

Description: Tests firewalls and port scanning via ping.

URL: `http://sourceforge.net/projects/hping2/`

Hsftp

Description: An FTP emulator that uses ssh for secure transport.

URL: `http://la-samhna.de/hsftp/index.html`

httpf

Description: A filtering proxy that improves HTML security by removing potentially dangerous things like Javascript.

URL: `http://sourceforge.net/projects/httpf/`

HTTPush

Description: Audits HTTP and HTTPS security.

URL: `http://sourceforge.net/projects/httpush/`

identd for Windows

Description: An identd (user identification) server for Windows.

URL: http://sourceforge.net/projects/winidentd/

IDMS Firewall

Description: Easy-to-use firewall configuration script with advanced features for Linux.

URL: http://sourceforge.net/projects/idms-firewall/

ImSafe

Description: A Unix-based IDS system.

URL: http://sourceforge.net/projects/imsafe/

Industrial Linux

Description: A secure Linux distribution.

URL: http://sourceforge.net/projects/industriallinux/

inst_auth_module

Description: Apache module for instant password authentication.

URL: http://www.clifford.at/stuff/mod_auth_inst.c

INTACT Change Detection System

Description: Takes snapshots of a system and then later compares against them to detect changes.

URL: http://www.pedestalsoftware.com/intact/index.htm

Integrit File Verification System

Description: Another snapshot and change verification system.

URL: http://sourceforge.net/projects/integrit/

Internet Access Scheduler

Description: Allows a Windows administrator to control which users can access which TCP/IP ports based on the time of day.

URL: http://www.winutility.com/

Intrusion Prevention Module for Apache

Description: Filters Web input to prevent intrusions.

URL: http://sourceforge.net/projects/modsw/

inzider

Description: Lists ports and associated processes for Windows.

URL: http://ntsecurity.nu/toolbox/inzider/

IP Filter

Description: Provides network address translation (NAT) or firewall services for Unix.

URL: http://coombs.anu.edu.au/~avalon/

IP Personality

Description: A Linux kernel patch that pretends it is another OS to defeat tools such as Nmap.

URL: http://sourceforge.net/projects/ippersonality/

IP Sorcery

Description: A BSD/Linux custom packet generator.

URL: http://sourceforge.net/projects/ipsorcery/

IP Tables State

Description: Displays which IP filtering rules on Linux are being used the most.

URL: http://sourceforge.net/projects/iptstate/

ipEye

Description: A TCP port scanner for Windows 2000.

URL: http://ntsecurity.nu/toolbox/ipeye/

IPNetMonitor

Description: Twelve Internet tools for the Macintosh that are useful for network debugging.

URL: http://www.sustworks.com/site/prod_ipmonitor.html

IPNetRouter

Description: Low-cost router for sharing a connection.

URL: http://www.sustworks.com/site/prod_ipr_overview.html

IPNetSentry

Description: Protects a Macintosh from Internet attacks.

URL: `http://www.sustworks.com/site/prod_ipns_overview.html`

iProtect

Description: Apache module to prevent password theft and abuse.

URL: `http://www.digital-concepts.net/cgi-iprotect.html`

IPSecScan

Description: A scanner for IPSec-enabled systems.

URL: `http://ntsecurity.nu/toolbox/ipsecscan/`

iptables

Description: The Linux 2.4.*x*/2.5.*x* firewalling subsystem.

URL: `http://www.iptables.org/`

ipwatch

Description: Dumps network packets on Linux.

URL: `http://sourceforge.net/projects/ipwatch/`

Iridium

Description: A Linux-based firewall geared to protect a LAN from the Internet.

URL: `http://www.karynova.com/iridium/`

Jail Chroot Project

Description: A simple-to-use chroot environment for running programs securely.

URL: `http://www.gsyc.inf.uc3m.es/~assman/jail/configuring/quickguide.html`

Jailinit

Description: Monitors and keeps track of jails and jailproc.

URL: `http://evilcode.net/jailinit/`

James Bond Log

Description: A daemon log watcher for Linux and BSD.

URL: `http://sourceforge.net/projects/bondlog/`

Java API for Role-Based Access Control

Description: A Java API and default implementation for role-based access control.

URL: http://sourceforge.net/projects/rbac/

JAVA/Struts Security Framework

Description: A J2SE 2.3/1.2-compliant security layer that can be integrated into any Struts application.

URL: http://sourceforge.net/projects/jcsf/

JCartera

Description: Stores and protects passwords in a Pocket PC.

URL: http://sourceforge.net/projects/jcartera/

JRSAAce

Description: Converts the RSA Ace/Agent Authentication API 5.0.1 into JAVA API.

URL: http://sourceforge.net/projects/jrsaace/

jWall

Description: Another Linux firewall management tool.

URL: http://sourceforge.net/projects/jwall/

Kerberos Authentication

Description: An Apache Kerberos authentication module.

URL: http://stonecold.unity.ncsu.edu/software/mod_auth_kerb/

Kerberos Module For Apache

Description: Another Apache Kerberos authentication module.

URL: http://sourceforge.net/projects/modauthkerb/

Kerberos Poppassd

Description: A Kerberos password-changing daemon.

URL: http://sourceforge.net/projects/kpoppassd/

Kfirewall

Description: A front end to Linux firewalls, tcpwrappers and IDS systems.

URL: `http://sourceforge.net/projects/kfirewall/`

Kiosk Control library/Module

Description: Disables the mouse and keyboard on Windows machines to use them as Kiosks.

URL: `http://sourceforge.net/projects/kioskcontrol/`

KISS - Kernel Improved Security System

Description: A BSD kernel security tool.

URL: `http://sourceforge.net/projects/kiss-ids/`

kkp NetBIOS Security Tool

Description: A security tool for a NetBIOS vulnerability.

URL: `http://sourceforge.net/projects/kkp/`

klogger

Description: A keystroke logger for Windows NT/2000.

URL: `http://ntsecurity.nu/toolbox/klogger/`

KNet

Description: A network infrastructure for encrypted anonymous distributed P2P communication.

URL: `http://sourceforge.net/projects/knet/`

Knetfilter

Description: A GUI for managing filtering functions in the Linux 2.4 kernel.

URL: `http://expansa.sns.it:8080/knetfilter/`

Komoku

Description: A Linux IDS that relies on an Intel EBSA-285 embedded board.

URL: `http://sourceforge.net/projects/komoku/`

kssl - Kerberized SSL

Description: Apache module and patches to OpenSSL and modssl to support Kerberos authentication for Linux and Solaris.

URL: http://sourceforge.net/projects/kssl/

LanFileWatcher

Description: Extracts files from HTTP and FTP network traffic.

URL: http://sourceforge.net/projects/lanfilewatcher/

LANguard Content Filtering & Anti-Virus

Description: Checks incoming data for viruses and unwanted content, blocking them without blocking other data.

URL: http://www.gfi.com/lanisa/

lcrzo

Description: A C-based network library useful in creating network-based programs.

URL: http://sourceforge.net/projects/lcrzo/

lcrzoex

Description: Extensive toolbox for testing an Ethernet network.

URL: http://sourceforge.net/projects/lcrzoex/

LDAP auth module for Apache

Description: Provides HTTP basic authentication by using LDAP.

URL: http://www.muquit.com/muquit/software/mod_auth_ldap/mod_auth_ldap.html

LEAF "Bering"

Description: A Linux-based firewall.

URL: http://download.sourceforge.net/leaf/

Leviathan Auditor

Description: A penetration testing tool for Windows.

URL: http://sourceforge.net/projects/leviathan/

libconnect

Description: A transparent proxy library.

URL: http://libconnect.sourceforge.net/

Libidmef

Description: An implementation of IDMEF (Intrusion Detection Message Exchange Format) in C.

URL: http://sourceforge.net/projects/libidmef/

libpam-sfs

Description: A Linux Pluggable Authentication Module (PAM) that allows for the mounting of home directories from SFS-enabled (Self-certifying File System) servers.

URL: http://sourceforge.net/projects/libpam-sfs/

LineControl

Description: Runs a server application on a masquerading Linux server.

URL: http://linecontrol.sourceforge.net/

linids

Description: A modular, highly configurable network IDS.

URL: http://sourceforge.net/projects/linids/

Linksys Activity Logger

Description: Captures the logging messages from a Linksys router and stores them in a database.

URL: http://sourceforge.net/projects/linksysactivity/

Linux Access Control LIsts support

Description: Adds full ACLs to the Linux Kernel.

URL: http://sourceforge.net/projects/linux-acl/

Linux Intrusion Detection System

Description: A Linux kernel-based intrusion detection system.

URL: http://sourceforge.net/projects/lids/

Linux packet filtering

Description: Linux packet filter.

URL: http://sourceforge.net/projects/pfilter/

Linux rootkit detector

Description: Detects attacks by rootkits.

URL: http://sourceforge.net/projects/checkps/

Linux Security Auditing Tool

Description: A Linux Security Auditing Tool (LSAT).

URL: http://sourceforge.net/projects/usat/

Linux terminal sniffer

Description: A Linux shell sniffer.

URL: http://sourceforge.net/projects/linsnoop/

LinuxBSM-2

Description: Adds auditing to the Linux kernel.

URL: http://sourceforge.net/projects/linuxbsm2/

ListModules

Description: Lists the modules (EXEs and DLLs) that are loaded into a process.

URL: http://ntsecurity.nu/toolbox/listmodules/

LNS - List NTFS Streams

Description: A tool that searches for NTFS streams.

URL: http://ntsecurity.nu/toolbox/lns/

LnxFire

Description: A Linux firewall tool for the SOHO environment.

URL: http://lnxfire.sourceforge.net/

LockDown Direct

Description: Alters the registry to lock Windows down.

URL: http://sourceforge.net/projects/ldd/

LockOut 4

Description: Keeps unauthorized people from using a Mac.

URL: http://www.mauisoftware.com/

Log-Dispatch

Description: Apache logging module.

URL: http://www.cpan.org/authors/id/D/DR/DROLSKY/Log-Dispatch-1.80.tar.gz

LogHog

Description: Takes proactive actions based on Snort (an IDS) output.

URL: http://sourceforge.net/projects/loghog/

LPRman

Description: Utility that allows remote creation and management of LPR (printer) ports.

URL: http://www.systemtools.com

Lubbock

Description: A Linux distribution based on Linuxcare Bootable Business Card, which is an emergency tool with many uses.

URL: http://sourceforge.net/projects/lubbock/

MacAnalysis

Description: A tool that attempts to hack your servers (Unix and Windows as well as Mac), and tells you what you need to fix.

URL: http://www.macanalysis.com/about.php3

Machine Learning for Anomaly Detection

Description: Detects anomalies for Linux systems.

URL: http://sourceforge.net/projects/madproject/

macMatch

Description: Searches files based on various dates, which can help with a forensic investigation.

URL: http://ntsecurity.nu/toolbox/macmatch/

Mailchecker

Description: Checks email for unsafe content.

URL: http://sourceforge.net/projects/mailchecker/

md5bfcpf

Description: A brute-force MD5 cracker for Linux.

URL: http://sourceforge.net/projects/md5bfcpf/

Mechanical ID

Description: A password and random code generator.

URL: http://sourceforge.net/projects/mecid/

mmtcpfwd

Description: Additions for Linux firewalls, such as a secure TCP/IP port forwarder, a MASQ fake ident, and a FTP passive proxy superserver.

URL: http://mmondor.rubiks.net/software.html

mod_auth_any

Description: Apache mod_auth_style module that allows for arbitrary authentication back ends.

URL: http://www.itlab.musc.edu/~nafees/mod_auth_any.html

mod_access_identd

Description: Mandatory access control based upon RFC 1413 (identd) credentials for Apache.

URL: http://Web.MeepZor.Com/packages/

mod_access_rbl

Description: Controls access via MAPS RBL-style DNS servers for Apache.

URL: http://www.blars.org/mod_access_rbl.html

mod_access_referer

Description: Provides Apache access control based on "Referer" HTTP header content.

URL: http://accessreferer.sourceforge.net/

mod_accessCookie

Description: Apache cookie management module.

URL: `http://unet.univie.ac.at/~a9506264/mod_accessCookie.tgz`

mod_auth_cache

Description: Authentication caching module using authentication from another module.

URL: `http://mod-auth-cache.sourceforge.net`

mod_auth_ldap

Description: Apache LDAP authentication module.

URL: `http://nona.net/software/ldap/`

mod_auth_mysql

Description: Apache MySQL-based authentication.

URL: `http://www.diegonet.com/support/mod_auth_mysql.shtml`

mod_auth_nds

Description: Apache NDS authentication module.

URL: `http://www.users.drew.edu/~pwilson`

mod_auth_notes

Description: Apache Lotus Notes-based authentication.

URL: `http://www.oceangroup.com/download.html`

mod_auth_nt

Description: Apache NT-based authentication for users/groups.

URL: `http://www.kada.lt/alv/apache/mod_auth_nt`

mod_auth_ora7

Description: Apache Oracle 7 authentication module.

URL: `http://ben.reser.org/mod_auth_ora/`

mod_auth_ora8

Description: Apache Oracle 8 authentication module.

URL: `http://ben.reser.org/mod_auth_ora/`

mod_auth_oracle

Description: Authentication module for Apache 1.3 through Oracle8/8i.

URL: `http://oskin.msk.ru/mod_auth_oracle.html`

mod_auth_oracle/win32

Description: Module for authenticating against an Oracle8.*x.x* database. For Apache 1.3.*x* with and without mod_ssl (for Win32 only!).

URL: `http://www.designlab.de/service_support/downloads/downloads/`
`mod_auth_oracle.zip`

mod_auth_pgsql

Description: Authentication module for Apache 1.3 through PostgreSQL.

URL: `http://www.giuseppetanzilli.it/mod_auth_pgsql/`

mod_auth_radius

Description: RADIUS authentication module.

URL: `http://www.freeradius.org/mod_auth_radius/`

mod_auth_rdbm

Description: Apache dbm or db authentication.

URL: `http://www.webthing.com/software/AnyDBM/apache.html`

mod_auth_samba

Description: Samba authentication module for Apache.

URL: `http://www.iki.fi/~jylitalo/apache/mod_auth_samba/`

mod_auth_sys

Description: Basic authentication using system accounts for Apache.

URL: `http://www.ntb.ch/Pubs/mod_auth_sys.c`

mod_auth_tacacs

Description: TACACS+ authentication module for Apache.

URL: `http://sourceforge.net/projects/mod-auth-tacacs/`

mod_auth_tds

Description: TDS authentication (works with MSSQL and SYBASE) for Apache.

URL: http://www.iancharnas.com/projects/mod_auth_tds.html

mod_auth_tkt

Description: Cookie-based authentication module.

URL: http://www.ime.usp.br/~nelio/apache

mod_auth_udp

Description: Forwards Apache auth-requests to an external server with udp-packets.

URL: http://www.rolf-jentsch.de/udpauth/

mod_auth_yp.c

Description: Authenticates Apache usernames/passwords and usernames/groups through NIS (Yellow Pages).

URL: http://www.amtrak.co.uk/ApacheModules/mod_auth_yp.c

mod_authz_ldap

Description: LDAP authorization and certificate verification for Apache.

URL: http://authzldap.othello.ch

mod_bakery

Description: Encrypted Apache cookie access-checking.

URL: http://www.fractal.net/mod_bakery.tm

mod_become

Description: Policy-based application of setuid()/setgid() per HTTP request.

URL: http://www.snert.com/Software/Become/

mod_bol

Description: Sends two WWW-Authenticate headers, one for basic and one for digest.

URL: http://www.berlinonline.de/wissen/computer/linux_tips/os/

mod_fortress

Description: Apache Application IDS and firewall.

URL: `http://www.spunge.org/~io`

mod_hosts_access

Description: Allows you to use the TCPWrapper `hosts.allow` and `hosts.deny` files to configure access to your Apache Web server.

URL: `http://www.klomp.org/mod_hosts_access/`

mod_ip_forwarding

Description: Forwards IP packets between a proxy and a main server.

URL: `http://dev.w3.org/cgi-bin/cvsweb/apache-modules/mod_ip_forwarding/`

mod_ldap.c

Description: LDAP authentication and access rules.

URL: `http://hpwww.ec-lyon.fr/~vincent/apache/mod_ldap.html`

mod_LDAPauth

Description: LDAP authentication module.

URL: `http://allserv.rug.ac.be/~pruyss/mod_LDAPauth/`

mod_limitipconn

Description: Limits the number of simultaneous connections from a single client IP address.

URL: `http://dominia.org/djao/limitipconn.html`

mod_log_mysql

Description: Allows Apache to log access log entries to a MySQL database.

URL: `http://www.grubbybaby.com/mod_log_mysql/`

mod_loopback

Description: Web client debugging tool that echoes everything concerning an HTTP request.

URL: `http://www.snert.com/Software/mod_loopback`

mod_macro

Description: Apache runtime configuration files with macro capability.

URL: `http://www.cri.ensmp.fr/~coelho/mod_macro/`

mod_mya

Description: MySQL basic authentication.

URL: `http://www.fractal.net/mod_mya.tm`

mod_mylog

Description: Logs input into a MySQL database.

URL: `http://www.fractal.net/mod_mylog.tm`

mod_ntlm

Description: NTLM authentication for Apache/Unix.

URL: `http://modntlm.sourceforge.net/`

mod_odbc_auth

Description: ODBC authorization module for Win32 Apache.

URL: `http://www.provox.de`

mod_rpaf

Description: Reverse proxy add forward.

URL: `http://stderr.net/apache/rpaf/`

mod_ssl

Description: Free Apache Interface to SSLeay.

URL: `http://www.modssl.org/`

mod_test

Description: Tests entry for authentication.

URL: `http://modules.apache.org/`

mod_throttle

Description: Limits the bandwidth usage and server load based on policies.

URL: `http://www.snert.com/Software/mod_throttle/`

mod_throttle_access

Description: Limits access on a per-resource basis.

URL: `http://www.fremen.org/apache/mod_throttle_access.html`

mod_ticket

Description: Adds digitally signed tickets at the base of a URL.

URL: `http://germ.semiotek.com/ticket`

mod_tproxt

Description: A module for transparent HTTP proxies.

URL: `http://www.stevek.com/projects/mod_tproxy/`

mod_tracker

Description: Advanced user tracking module.

URL: `http://www.pld.ttu.ee/~indrek/mod_tracker/`

mod_usertrack_proxypass_front and **mod_usertrack_proxy**

Description: A pair of Apache modules to allow the sending of Set-Cookie headers from a fat back end.

URL: `http://steven.haryan.to/mod_usertrack_proxy.shtml`

mod_watch

Description: Watches Web traffic statistics.

URL: `http://www.snert.com/Software/mod_watch/`

mod_z_auth

Description: Authentication using NIS or other methods.

URL: `http://drnick.stuy.edu/~zamansky/projects`

Monitorer

Description: A keystroke logger that can also take screenshots.

URL: `http://www.burning-bytes.com/monitorer.html`

MonMotha's Firewall

Description: Powerful but compact firewall.

URL: http://monmotha.mplug.org/firewall/firewall/2.3/

Mouse Lock

Description: Windows program that locks down the mouse.

URL: http://segobit.virtualave.net/ml.htm

mSQL authentification module

Description: Basic authentication with the mSQL database.

URL: http://www.webweaving.org/mod_auth_msql/

NetBarrier

Description: Personal firewall for the Mac.

URL: http://www.intego.com/home.asp

NetBiosSpy

Description: Watches shared folders on a PC.

URL: http://www.chez.com/vruy/indexUS.htm

NetBSD/i386 Firewall

Description: A firewall solution for permanent Internet connections.

URL: http://www.dubbele.com

netfilter

Description: A firewall for untrusted LANs.

URL: http://hekta.iet.hist.no/netfilter/

NetUsers

Description: A utility to view logged-on users on a specific computer.

URL: http://www.systemtools.com

NetView

Description: Command-line version of Network Neighborhood.

URL: http://www.systemtools.com

NoCase

Description: Non-case sensitive URL mapping for Linux.

URL: http://www.misterblue.com/software/mod_nocase.asp

NorthStar

Description: Tracks and allocates IP addresses in an IP network.

URL: http://www.brownkid.net/NorthStar/

nscopy

Description: A copy command that bypasses security controls.

URL: http://ntsecurity.nu/toolbox/nscopy/

NSS-MySQL

Description: Authenticates Unix groups and users using a MySQL database.

URL: http://savannah.gnu.org/projects/nss-mysql/

OB1

Description: A sample implementation of a B1-rated trusted system.

URL: http://oss.sgi.com/projects/ob1/

OnGuard

Description: Powerful desktop security suite (file, folder, application, and other access controls).

URL: http://www.poweronsoftware.com/products/onguard/

PAM_Auth

Description: Apache authentication against Pluggable Auth Modules (PAM).

URL: http://pam.sourceforge.net/mod_auth_pam/

pam_mount

Description: A PAM module that allows remote volumes to be mounted during login.

URL: http://pam-mount.conectevil.com/

parselog

Description: Perl script to parse and store logs by server and date.

URL: http://www.cs.umn.edu/~bentlema/projects

Password Age

Description: Displays the age of the password for user and computer accounts.

URL: http://www.systemtools.com

PEriscope

Description: A PE file inspection tool.

URL: http://ntsecurity.nu/toolbox/periscope/

PHP Firewall Generator

Description: A firewall generation script.

URL: http://phpfwgen.sourceforge.net/

PipeACL tools

Description: Tools to view and modify Windows ACLs.

URL: http://razor.bindview.com/tools/desc/pipeacltools1.0-readme.html

PMDump

Description: Dumps the memory of a process, which can be useful in a forensic investigation.

URL: http://ntsecurity.nu/toolbox/pmdump/

PortBlocker

Description: Allows you to block the most common types of servers that might be on a system (FTP, HTTP, and so on), but is NOT a firewall.

URL: http://www.analogx.com/contents/download/network/pblock.htm

Posum's Windows Enforcer

Description: Tools for locking down Windows machines for uses such as a computer lab.

URL: http://posum.com/enforcer.html

ProDiscover DFT

Description: Forensic analysis suite.

URL: `http://www.techpathways.com/DesktopDefault.aspx?tabindex=4&tabid=12`

PromiScan

Description: Searches for promiscuous nodes on the network.

URL: `http://www.securityfriday.com/ToolDownload/PromiScan/promiscan_doc.html`

PromiscDetect

Description: Checks the local machine to see whether the network card is in promiscuous mode.

URL: `http://ntsecurity.nu/toolbox/promiscdetect/`

proxyfloppy Linux distribution

Description: A floppy-based Linux that supports three types of Web proxies.

URL: `http://freshmeat.net/projects/proxyfloppy/`

PureSecure

Description: An intrusion detection system.

URL: `http://www.demarc.com/`

RADIUS Authentication module

Description: RADIUS authentication for Apache.

URL: `http://www.wede.de/sw/mod_auth_radius/`

RBA Proxy Filter

Description: An MS Proxy Server plug-in that puts different Web sites in different NT groups for access control.

URL: `http://erwin.richard.net/rbaproxy.htm`

Realm and MD5 Digest-based cookie authentication

Description: Security realms for document tree and fast login for users using MD5-signed cookies.

URL: `http://www.frogdot.org`

Remote Task Manager

Description: Like Windows Task Manager, but can control remote machines.

URL: `http://www.protect-me.com/`

rTables for Linux

Description: A Linux-based firewall solution.

URL: `http://rtables.rebby.com`

runsuid

Description: Runs scripts with another effective user ID/group ID.

URL: `http://www.ftp.uni-erlangen.de/~runsuid/`

ScoopLM

Description: Captures LM/NTLM authentication information (LanManager and Windows NT challenge/response) on the network.

URL: `http://www.securityfriday.com/ToolDownload/ScoopLM/scooplm_doc.html`

Seattle Firewall

Description: A Linux-based dedicated firewall.

URL: `http://seawall.sourceforge.net/`

SecureCopy

Description: Copies files and directories on NTFS files while keeping the security intact.

URL: `http://www.systemtools.com/scopy/`

SecurID Authentication

Description: RSA SecurID authentication for Apache.

URL: `http://www.deny-all.com/mod_securid/`

Share Password Checker

Description: Checks passwords for Windows shares.

URL: `http://www.securityfriday.com/ToolDownload/SPC/spc_doc.html`

SMB Downgrade Attacker

Description: Tries to get people's Windows networking passwords.

URL: `http://ntsecurity.nu/toolbox/downgrade/`

SMBProxy

Description: Authenticates to a Windows NT4/2000 server with only the MD4 hash.

URL: `http://www.cqure.net/tools02.html`

snitch

Description: Converts the asterisks in password fields to plaintext passwords.

URL: `http://ntsecurity.nu/toolbox/snitch/`

Snort

Description: Packet sniffer and logger.

URL: `http://www.snort.org/dl/`

SOAP-Lite-SmartProxy

Description: Redirects and forwards requests.

URL: `http://www.cpan.org/authors/id/D/DY/DYACOB/SOAP-Lite-SmartProxy-0.11.tar.gz`

SOLID Database Authentication

Description: auth_solid provides username/password checking against a SOLID database.

URL: `http://www.synchronis.com/synchronis/html/apache/auth_solid_frame.html`

SQLdict

Description: A dictionary-based password attack tool for SQL Server.

URL: `http://ntsecurity.nu/toolbox/sqldict/`

Squidtaild

Description: A monitoring/managing program for the Squid Web cache server.

URL: `http://trailer.linuxatwork.at/`

StegFS

Description: Steganographic File System for Linux, which encrypts data.

URL: `http://www.mcdonald.org.uk/StegFS/`

SystemTools NTconnect

Description: Creates a login script, allowing commands for NT users.

URL: `http://www.systemtools.com`

SystemTools RenameUser

Description: Renames Windows NT user accounts from the command line.

URL: `http://www.systemtools.com`

The SINUS Firewall

Description: TCP/IP packet filter for Linux.

URL: `http://www.ifi.unizh.ch/ikm/SINUS/firewall/`

theWall

Description: A collection of PicoBSD configuration trees and prebuilt binaries that provide NAT and firewall services for a small network.

URL: `http://thewall.sourceforge.net/`

tini

Description: A simple and very small (3KB) back door for Windows, coded in assembler. It listens at TCP port 7777 and gives anybody who connects a remote command prompt.

URL: `http://ntsecurity.nu/toolbox/tini/`

TrustWALL Toolkit

Description: An inbound proxy that protects your Web site.

URL: `http://www.geocities.com/samngms/twhttpd/`

tsocks

Description: A transparent SOCKS proxying library.

URL: `http://tsocks.sourceforge.net/index.php`

UserPath Module

Description: Provides a different method of mapping user URLs.

URL: http://www.tardis.ed.ac.uk/~sxw/apache/mod_userpath.c

VXE

Description: Protects Unix servers from attacks.

URL: http://www.intes.odessa.ua/vxe/

Win Info

Description: Shows inventory information on your Windows system.

URL: http://www.systemtools.com

Windows Task Lock

Description: Provides a way to password-protect specific applications for Windows.

URL: http://posum.com/tasklock.html

WinDump

Description: Windows version of TCPDump, a network sniffer.

URL: http://windump.polito.it/

Winfingerprint

Description: Provides information about your Windows system.

URL: http://sourceforge.net/projects/winfingerprint/

WinRelay

Description: A TCP/UDP forwarder/redirector.

URL: http://ntsecurity.nu/toolbox/winrelay/

WinSCP

Description: SCP (Secure CoPy) client for Windows using SSH (Secure SHell).

URL: http://winscp.vse.cz/eng/

E

Glossary

$HOME   A shell environment variable that points to your home directory in Unix (typically, /home/*hacker*, where *hacker* is your username). See **environment variable**.

$LOGNAME   A shell environment variable that stores your username. To see your current username/logname in Unix, type `echo $LOGNAME` at a shell prompt. See **environment variable**.

$PATH   A shell environment variable that stores your path in Unix and Windows (or, the list of directories the shell will examine when searching for files). A typical path might look like this: /bin:/usr/bin:/usr/local/bin:/usr/man:/usr/X11R6/bin. Colons separate directories. See **environment variable**.

$REMOTE_ADDR   A Web environment variable that stores the IP address of the remote client browser.

$REMOTE_HOST   A Web environment variable that stores the host name of the remote client.

$REMOTE_IDENT   A Web environment variable that stores the remote user name if supporting RFC 931 identification.

$REMOTE_USER   A Web environment variable that stores the user name used to validate authentication from the remote client. Great for use in password-protected sites.

* (asterisk)   This character matches any series of characters established by the preceding metacharacter's rule.

.awk   This file extension denotes an awk program (Example: count.awk). See **awk**.

.bck   This file extension denotes a backup file.

.c   This file extension denotes a C programming language source file (Example: `menu.c`). See **C**.

.cc   This file extension (denotes a C++ programming language source file (Example: `menu.cc`). See **C++**.

.cgi   This file extension denotes a CGI program source file (Example: `Webcounter.cgi`). Such files probably contain Perl programs, which are also sometimes named with a `.pl` extension. See **Perl**.

.conf   This file extension denotes a configuration file (Example: `access.conf`).

.cpp   This file extension denotes C code (for preprocessing).

.csh   This file extension denotes a C shell program file (Example: `cut.csh`). See **C shell**.

.dat   This file extension denotes a data file that could originate from almost any platform.

.db   This file extension denotes a database file (Example: `users.db`).

.doc   This file extension denotes either a plain text file or a Microsoft Word document.

.gz   This file extension denotes a compressed file (Example: `package.gz`).

.h   This file extension denotes a C programming language header file.

.htaccess   The Apache access file.

.htpasswd   The Apache htpasswd password database (for password-protecting Web sites).

.pl   This file extension denotes a Perl script file. See **Perl**.

.ps   This file extension denotes a postscript file. See **PostScript**.

.py   This file extension denotes a Python program file. See **Python**.

.sh   This file extension denotes a bourne shell script.

.shtml   File extension that denotes that the specified file has within it server-side include (SSI) directives.

.tar   This file extension denotes a tar archive file. See **tar**.

.tcl   This file extension denotes a Tcl program. See **Tcl**.

.tgz   This file extension denotes a compressed tar file (Example: `package.tgz`).

.Z   This file extension denotes a compressed file (Example: `package.tgz`).

;   Use ; to separate shell commands you want to execute sequentially (command1;command2). ; is also used in some programming languages (Perl, C, C++) to end a statement. For example: `printf("This statement ends with a semicolon\n")`;

?   Use ? to match any single character, especially when specifying files or directories. Apache treats ? in a traditional regular expression context; for example, ? will match either zero or one instance of any character.

| Use | to pipe commands or force one command's output to become the input of another. For example, suppose you want to look at logs of the last 10 root logins. Try this: `last root | head -10`. This will grab all recorded logins for root (last root). The resulting output then becomes input for head, which extracts from last's output the most recent 10 logins (`head -10`).

|| || represents a logical OR between two or more expressions. The statement `command1 || command2` tells the shell that if `command1` fails, execute `command2`.

<   Use < to redirect input to a file or process. In various languages, < is also a comparative operator, the "less-than" symbol.

<Limit> (Apache)   The `<Limit>` directive applies access control to the HTTP methods you specify. Methods are ways a client can request a URI (or an operation thereon) from a server.

<VirtualHost> (Apache)   `<VirtualHost>` applies the access control rules you specify to one virtual host. It thus enables you to specify different access control rules to different virtual hosts.

>&   Issuing the >& file combination redirects STDOUT and STDERR to a file (and overwrites that file). See **standard output** and **standard error**.

>   Use > to redirect output to a file. The command `dir > dir-listing.txt` will redirect your directory-listing request (`dir`) to a file (`dir-listing.txt`). Also, in various programming languages, > is a comparative operator, the "greater-than" symbol.

>>   Use >> to redirect and append data to a file. This differs from >. >> appends information, adding text to the end without overwriting it.

3DES   3DES is another way of referring to Triple DES, where DES runs through three levels of encryption. See **DES**.

AAA   Authentication, Authorization, and Accounting.

absolute path   The absolute path is the specified resource's full path, beginning at root. In reference to URLs in scripts, an absolute path is the whole shebang, either on the inside (`/var/http/myhost.com/index.html`) or the outside (`http://www.myhost.com/index.html`), as opposed to a relative path such as `myhost.com/index.html`.

access control list (ACL)   A list wherein you specify what system resources you're allowing users to access (and which users can obtain such access).

ACCESS_CONF (Apache constant)   Access control restrictions inside <Directory> or <Location> directives.

AccessFileName (Apache)   The AccessFileName directive specifies the file that contains Apache's htpasswd access control rules.

Account Policies Snap-in (Windows)   The Account Policies Snap-in lets you set password and account lockout policies.

account policies   In many operating systems, you can establish user logon and password policies. For example, how long is a user's password valid? Should she be allowed to change it?

accreditation   A statement from some authority that your Web site and business practices are secure or lend to security.

Acedirector_request   Exploit for the AceDirector half-closed session vulnerability. Released in 2002.

Active Directory   Microsoft's directory server starting with Windows 2000. It is used for authentication, authorization, and many other purposes.

ActivePerl (Windows)   ActivePerl is Perl for Windows platforms.

address space   The total memory addressable by a machine or program.

address   A hostname or URL on the World Wide Web.

Addusers (Windows)   Lets you add or delete users en masse and works like this: you create a comma-delimited file specifying users, global groups, and local groups (one record per line). Addusers.exe then steps through the file—record-by-record—and adds or deletes the users you specify.

Administrative Tools (Windows)   The Administrative Tools applet leads to applets, controls, applications, and snap-ins that control the majority of your security policies. You reach the Administrative Tools applet by clicking on My Computer → Control Panel → Administrative Tools.

ADSL   Asymmetric Digital Subscriber Line.

Agate.c   Script that exploits the Avirt Gateway 4.2 remote vulnerability. Released in 2002.

AirSnort   A tool for wireless LANs that recovers encryption keys by passively monitoring transmissions, and computing the encryption key when enough packets have been gathered. Works on both 40- and 128-bit encryption. Released in 2002.

AllowOverride (Apache)   Use the `AllowOverride` directive to specify what global access control directives a local `.htaccess` file can override. You specify overrides in either incisive or sweeping fashion.

Anonymous (Apache)   The `Anonymous` directive, included in mod_auth_anon, grants anonymous users access to password-protected areas. Think of `Anonymous` as a second cousin to FTP's anonymous user, where you send your email address (or any arbitrary string) as your password. The difference is that Apache's `Anonymous` directive grants anonymous users access without requiring any password.

Anonymous_Authoritative (Apache)   The `Anonymous_Authoritative` directive, included in mod_auth_anon, when activated, denies access to all but anonymous users or user IDs. Hence, if a user enters any value but a valid anonymous ID, Apache denies access to the specified resource.

Anonymous_LogEmail (Apache)   `Anonymous_LogEmail`, included in mod_auth_anon, when activated, logs passwords that anonymous users provide to error_log. Hence, if users provide their email addresses as passwords, you retain a record of them.

Anonymous_MustGiveEmail (Apache)   The `Anonymous_MustGiveEmail` directive, included in mod_auth_anon, when activated, requires anonymous users to supply their email addresses as passwords.

Anonymous_NoUserID (Apache)   The `Anonymous_NoUserID` directive, included in module mod_auth_anon, when activated, allows users access without supplying a user ID. Hence, when the username/password window pops up, users can simply strike the Enter key or choose OK. Either action is sufficient to obtain the requested URI.

Anonymous_VerifyEmail (Apache)   `Anonymous_VerifyEmail`, included in module mod_auth_anon, when activated, instructs Apache to verify—or try to verify—that visitors supply a valid email address.

Apache-chunked-scanner   Apache Chunked Transfer vulnerability scanner for Windows. Released in 2002.

Apachefun   Script that exploits the Apache chunked-encoding memory corruption vulnerability. Released in 2002.

Apache-nosejob   Script that exploits the FreeBSD, NetBSD, and OpenBSD Apache chunked-encoding memory corruption vulnerability. Released in 2002.

Apache-scalp   Script that exploits the Apache chunked-encoding memory corruption vulnerability. Released in 2002.

Apache-smash   Denial-of-service exploit for the Apache chunked-encoding memory corruption vulnerability. Released in 2002.

apimon (Windows)   apimon watches processes for API calls and page faults. It's an especially useful tool for programmers.

Applequicktimeexploit   Exploit for the QuickTime remote buffer overflow vulnerability. Released in 2002.

applet   A Java program that runs in Web browser environments that contain a Java Virtual Machine. Applets add graphics, animation, and dynamic text to otherwise boring Web pages. Applets can have security implications, however.

AppleTalk Network Device Analyzer (Windows)   The AppleTalk Network Device Analyzer is a discovery and diagnostic tool for AppleTalk networks. Suppose you want to map an AppleTalk network and determine which machines run MacOS and which run W2K. AppleTalk Network Device Analyzer does this and more. For example, you can determine which boxes have attached or shared-out printers.

Application Log (Windows)   Application Log reports application alerts and critical, informational, and warning events (such as device failures, conflicts, crashes, and so on). You reach it through Event Viewer (My Computer → Control Panel → Administrative Tools → Event Viewer).

appsec (Windows)   appsec is a strictly Windows 2000 Server tool and it's a must-have in enterprise environments. It lets you centrally manage which applications users can access. Interestingly, it even whittles this down to the binary's precise location. For example, suppose you restrict access to W2K's solitaire game. sol.exe is located in C:\WINNT\system32 by default. If wily users discover that they can't execute the game from there, they might copy it to another location. Alas, their efforts would be fruitless, because appsec.exe lets you specify the only location from which anyone can execute the file. A pretty nifty tool.

asymmetric cipher   Cipher that employs a public-key/private-key cryptosystem. In such systems, A encrypts a message to B's public key. From that point on, the message can only be decrypted using B's private key.

ATM   Asynchronous Transfer Mode.

attribute   The state of a given file or directory and whether it's readable, hidden, system, or other.

audit policy   Your audit policy establishes what security events you log to file. For example, you can log user logons, policy changes, reboots, and so on. These events can be significant in a security context.

audit trail   Data used to record, track, analyze, and report network activity and the path you take to derive that data from its source. Raw access logs from your Web server are good examples. To polish these, you might use a script that mines the data and formats it cleanly. From there, you can isolate events (for example, requests for a particular file from a particular address) and from this, you can ascertain facts about an attack.

audit   Loosely defined, a systematic analysis of your system or business practices. Its purpose in this context is to ascertain if you maintain best practices. Less loosely defined, a proactive test of your security controls and your server's ability to survive, record, track, analyze, and report attacks.

`auditpol` (Windows)   `auditpol` is a command-line utility for viewing and modifying audit policies, which also lets you do so from within automated scripts. For example, you could create a script to check all W2K machines in your domain to ensure that auditing is enabled in the System, Logon, Object, Privilege, Process, Policy, Sam, Directory, and Account categories. If the script finds that a category's auditing is disabled, it can enable it. By default, `auditpol` prints the current policy settings.

`AuthAuthoritative` (Apache)   The `AuthAuthoritative` directive, included in mod_auth, lets you specify whether Apache can pass authorization procedures to lower-level modules instead of using simple `.htaccess` authentication. (This only works when Apache cannot find a matching user ID and rule for the specified user. In all other cases, Apache proceeds with normal `.htaccess` authentication as specified in your configuration files.)

`AuthDBMAuthoritative` (Apache)   The `AuthDBMAuthoritative` directive, included in mod_auth, lets you specify whether Apache can pass authorization procedures to lower-level modules instead of using simple DMB-based authentication. (This only works when Apache cannot find a matching user ID and rule for the specified user. In all other cases, Apache proceeds with normal DBM authentication as specified in your configuration files.)

`AuthDBMGroupFile`   An Apache directive that stores the location of the DBM file containing the list of user groups for user authentication.

`AuthDBMUserFile`   An Apache directive that stores the location of the DBM file that contains the list of users for user authentication.

`AuthDBUserFile` (Apache)   The `AuthDBUserFile` directive, included in mod_auth, lets you specify the DB file's name. Such files contain username/password pairs for use in DB-based authentication (with `crypt()` passwords).

authenticate   To verify a user's, host's, or session's identity or integrity.

authentication   The process of authenticating a user, host, session, or process.

`AuthGroupFile`   An Apache directive that stores the location of the (text) file that contains the list of user groups for user authentication.

`AuthLDAPAuthoritative` (Apache)   The `AuthLDAPAuthoritative` directive, included in mod_auth, lets you specify whether Apache can pass authorization procedures to lower-level modules instead of using simple LDAP-based authentication. (This only works when Apache cannot find a matching user ID and rule for the specified user. In all other cases, Apache proceeds with normal LDAP authentication as specified in your configuration files).

`AuthName`   An Apache directive that sets the authorization realm's name for directories.

authorization   A user's right to access resources.

`AuthType` (Apache)   The `AuthType` directive, included as a core Apache functionality, lets you specify the user authorization type for the specified directory.

`AuthUserFile`   An Apache directive that sets the name and location of the (text) file containing the list of users and passwords for user authentication.

awk (gawk)   A text-processing and scanning language. Also called gawk (gawk is a free GNU awk variant).

back door   A hidden hole left behind by an intruder or programmer that gives him future access to his victim host.

BackOrifice   A popular cracker tool that allows remote access to a Windows box.

Backstealth   A tool that bypasses outbound restrictions of personal firewalls by embedding an HTTP client in a dll. Released in 2002.

back up   To preserve a file system or files, usually for disaster recovery. Generally, you back up to tape, floppy disk or other, portable media so you can store something safely for later use.

Bed   The Bruteforce Exploit Detector is a Perl script that remotely detects unknown buffer overflow vulnerabilities in FTP, SMTP, and POP daemons. Released in 2002.

`BIG_SECURITY_HOLE` (Apache constant)   Compile-time directive that enables Apache to run as root even after it starts.

biometric access controls   Systems that authenticate users by biological characteristics, such as their face, fingerprints, or retinal pattern.

Blowfish   A 64-bit encryption scheme developed by Bruce Schneier. Blowfish is often used for high-volume, high-speed encryption. (Blowfish is reportedly faster than both DES and IDEA.) To learn more, go to `http://www.counterpane.com/blowfish.html`.

Boegadt   A Unix-based library that attempts to make it easy to write buffer overflow exploits. Released in 2002.

BPSK   Bi-Phase Shift Keying.

BRI   Basic Rate Interface ISDN.

broadcast/broadcasting   Any network message sent to all network interfaces, or the practice of sending such a message.

browmon (Windows)   browmon, short for Browser Monitor, monitors browsers (applications using the Windows Browsing Service) of a given domain. Browmon.exe is useful chiefly in determining whether all browsers in a given domain are operating correctly. It has an alarm function too, so you can address problems immediately and thus avoid those pesky support calls ("Hello? IT? I don't see any computers in my list.")

Browser Client Context Viewer (w3who.dll) (Windows)   A Microsoft-centric diagnostic tool for Web developers and system administrators. It enables you to analyze IIS Web client requests and determine a client's environment variables, the request's associated privileges, and the relevant security identifiers (SIDs). Also catches the client IP, remote host, remote user, and so on.

bug   A bug is a hole, weakness, or flaw in a computer program, typically related to programmer error or sloppiness. See **vulnerability**.

C shell   A Unix command interpreter with C-like syntax.

C   The C programming language.

C++   Object-oriented programming language that resembles C but is, some say, more powerful. C++ relies heavily on inheritable classes.

C4I   Command, Control, Communications, Computers, and Intelligence—an information warfare term.

CA   See **Certificate authority**.

CA-2002-02.aol.icq   Exploit for the ICQ buffer overflow vulnerability. Released in 2002.

cacls (Windows)   cacls displays or modifies file access control lists (ACLs). Using cacls, you can change view or change file permissions such as read, write, and so on. cacls is great for doing this on the fly, within scripts, such as where you need a quick way to grant or restrict a specific user rights on multiple files in disparate directories (perhaps even, if you have Expect installed, located on different machines).

CAP   Carrierless Amplitude Phase Modulation.

CBR   Constant Bit Rate.

cconnect (Windows)   cconnect (the Con-Current Connection Limiter) is an administrative tool for detecting, assigning, and managing concurrent user connections. Some administrators don't fret over concurrent user connections and allow their users free reign. However, beyond security concerns, concurrent user connections can sometimes unacceptably tie up system resources. `Cconnect.exe` simplifies the process of tracking and denying concurrent connections.

Centurion   Centurion checks any CGI script on a remote server for vulnerabilities such as directory traversal bugs, null byte, and incorrect filtering of metacharacters. Released in 2002.

CERT   The Computer Emergency Response Team. CERT assists victims of cracker attacks and provides valuable research to the Internet community at large. Learn more at `http://www.cert.org`.

Certificate authority   Trusted third party that issues security certificates and verifies their authenticity. The most renowned commercial certificate authority is VeriSign.

certification   Either the end result of a successful security evaluation of a product or system, or an academic honor bestowed on one who successfully completes courses (such as MCSE/A+ certification).

checksum   A numeric value composed of the sum (or a finite number) of a file's bits. Checksums can verify file integrity. For example, many network programs use checksums to verify that transmitted data arrives at its destination intact. Typically, network applications generate the checksum at the data's origin and transmit this value to the receiving application. Receiving applications then recalculate the data's checksum. If there's a match, everything went smoothly. If not, the data was damaged in transit, and the applications attempt a resend.

chkdsk (Windows)   chkdsk, an old favorite, reports a disk's current status, including size, utilization, errors, and so on. On NTFS volumes, it also verifies files, indexes, and security settings.

chroot   A restricted environment in which processes run "in prison" so to speak; these cannot access the filesystem at large (outside of the environment you specify).

Cisco677   Perl script that exploits the Cisco 677/678 Telnet overflow denial of service vulnerability. Released in 2002.

Ciscokill   Script that exploits Cisco 2600 routers the spoofed `snmpv1 get` request vulnerability. Released in 2002.

CLASSPATH (Environment, Windows)   The path to your Java classes.

client   Software that interacts with a specific server application. WWW browsers (Netscape Communicator, Internet Explorer, Opera, Mozilla) are WWW clients. Developers design them specifically to interact with Web servers.

client-server model   A networking model wherein one server can distribute data to many clients. The relationship your Web server has to Web clients or browsers is a client-server relationship (Apache being the server, browsers being the clients). In this model, the server generally performs computational services and returns results to the client. Most network applications and protocols are client-server oriented.

Cmaileexp   Script that exploits the CMailServer buffer overflow vulnerability. Released in 2002.

Common Gateway Interface (CGI)   A standard that specifies programming techniques to pass data from Web servers to Web clients. CGI is language-neutral. CGI programs can therefore be written in Perl, C, C++, Python, Visual Basic, BASIC, and shell languages. CGI programs can raise security issues.

comp (Windows)   comp compares two files' contents (similar to Unix's diff).

Concept   Script that exploits the Windows remote command execution vulnerability. Released in 2002.

confidentiality   The principle or policy by which data is sensitive or privileged, and therefore not for general consumption or viewing.

Confuse_router   An ARP cache poisoner that allows you to see traffic in a switched environment such as a cable modem network. Released in 2002.

contingency plan   Procedure or procedures you undertake when an emergency or disaster arises. Example: What if your Web server goes down? What if this occurs on a weekend? Can you get someone to fix it? You must have a contingency plan to handle unforeseen circumstances.

core.c   Apache server source file that contains server core functionalities, including options and commands that control other modules, NCSA backward compatibility, URL handling, and so on.

COTS   Commercial-off-the-shelf.

countermeasure   Any action or technique that minimizes or eliminates a threat.

crack   Any software, procedure, or technique that circumvents security. Less loosely defined, a crack is a Unix-based password cracker called Crack. Also: to breach system security or commercial software registration schemes.

cracker   Someone who unlawfully and with malice breaches system security.

crash   When a system fatally fails and requires a restart.

Crashme.java   Exploit for the Sun JRE denial of service vulnerability. Released in 2002.

CRC   CRC is Cyclic Redundancy Check, an operation to verify data integrity.

cryptography   The science of secret writings. In cryptography, you scramble your writings so they remain unreadable to unauthorized personnel. Theoretically, only authorized users can unravel an encrypted message. However, your encrypted message's ability to evade unauthorized eyes depends on the type and strength of encryption you use.

CustomLog (Apache)   The CustomLog directive, included in mod_log_config, lets you set a log filename, a log format, and a conditional environment variable for logging.

CVE   Common Vulnerabilities and Exposures is a standardized list of vulnerabilities names available at http://www.cve.mitre.org/.

D7-ibm-x   Script that exploits the Informix SE buffer overflow vulnerability. Released in 2002.

DAC (Discretionary Access Control)   DAC provides the means for a central authority to either permit or deny access to all users, and to do so incisively based on time, date, file, directory, or host.

Data Encryption Standard (DES)   IBM Encryption standard originating in 1974 and published in 1977. DES was the U.S. government standard for encrypting nonclassified data.

data integrity   Data integrity refers to the state of files. If files are unchanged and no one has tampered with them, they have integrity. If someone has tampered with them, their integrity is breached or degraded.

data-driven attack   An attack that deploys hidden or encapsulated data designed to flow through a firewall undetected.

Ddk-iis   Script that exploits the Microsoft ASP.NET buffer overflow vulnerability. Includes targets for IIS5 Chinese SP0, SP1, and SP2 and English SP2. Released in 2002.

denial-of-service attack   A condition wherein your server becomes inoperable after an attack. When an attacker undertakes a denial-of-service attack, he seeks to disable your server and thereby deny service to legitimate users.

Dhb   Tool that tries to guess Lotus Domino HTTP passwords. Released in 2002.

dictionary attack   Dictionary or wordlist attacks work like this: Crackers obtain your encrypted passwords and, using the same password algorithm as your system, encrypt many thousands of words. They generally derive the words from dictionaries, hence the name. Their software then compares each newly encrypted word to your encrypted passwords. When a match occurs, that password is deemed cracked.

digest access authentication   A security extension for HTTP that provides only basic, nonencrypted user authentication over the Web. To learn more, please see RFC 2069.

digital certificate   Digital certificates are typically numeric values derived from cryptographic processes, and you or Apache can use these to verify users or hosts.

Dnshijacker   A libnet/libpcap-based packet sniffer and DNS spoofer tool that supports tcpdump style filters that allow you to specifically target victims. Released in 2002.

DoS   See **denial of service**.

Dpathx   Script that exploits the Linux Kernel d_path() Path Truncation vulnerability. Released in 2002.

drivers (Windows)   A program that displays detailed statistics on all currently loaded drivers.

DSS (Digital Signature Standard)   The Digital Signature Algorithm. DSS makes use of the Digital Signature Algorithm, and lets you or Apache identify a message's sender and authenticity. Find DSS specifications in the National Institute of Standards and Technology's (NIST) Federal Information Processing Standard (FIPS) 186: http://www.itl.nist.gov/div897/pubs/fip186.htm.

dumpel (Windows)   dumpel dumps event log data into tab-separated output, which makes it easier to write a program to process the log.

dureg (Windows)   dureg reports on registry space taken and provides a registry tree.

efsinfo (Windows)   efsinfo reports various statistics and status on files encrypted using the Encrypted File System (EFS). For example, efsinfo displays certificate thumbnails, whether files are encrypted, and so on.

Eldre8   Script that exploits the Mozilla malformed email denial of service vulnerability. Released in 2002.

Elfsh   An automated reverse engineering tool for the ELF format that has a sophisticated output with cross references using .got, .ctors, .dtors, .symtab, .dynsym, .dynamic, .rel.* and many others with an integrated hexdump. Released in 2002.

encryption   The process of scrambling data so that it's unreadable by unauthorized parties. In most encryption schemes, you must have a password to reassemble the data into readable form. Encryption enhances privacy and can protect sensitive, confidential, privileged, proprietary, classified, secret, or top secret information.

enumprop (Windows)   enumprop dumps directory service object properties including GUIDs and SIDs.

environment variable   Environment variables are values that denote your default shell, home directory, mail directory, path, username, time zone, and so on. Shells use these variables to determine where to send mail, store your files, find commands, and so on. Many environment variables exist, and generally your operating system sets them automatically when you login.

EPL   Evaluated Products List.

Epop.c   Exploit for the WiredRed e/pop v2.0.3 vulnerability. Released in 2002.

Ethereal   A GTK+-based network protocol analyzer, or sniffer, that lets you capture and interactively browse the contents of network frames. Released in 2002.

Ettercap   A network sniffer/interceptor/logger for switched LANs that uses ARP poisoning and the man-in-the-middle technique to sniff all the connections between two hosts. Released in 2002.

Evelyne   Local root exploit for the Suid application execution vulnerability. Released in 2002.

Event Viewer (Windows)   Event Viewer is a logging utility that reports significant system events, application events, and security events. You reach Event Viewer through the Administrative Tools applet (My Computer → Control Panel → Administrative Tools).

exctrlst (Windows)   exctrlst is the Extensible Counter List, which displays all currently loaded services and applications that report performance statistics. To run exctrlst, run it in from a command prompt.

execute   execute permissions grant users, groups, or others the right to execute the specified file. Also see **read** and **write**.

exetype (Windows)   exetype is a virtual clone of Unix's file utility and reports the specified file's type, its build platform, and where it runs.

Expshell   Script that exploits the UnixWare library function vulnerability. Released in 2002.

Ez2crazy   Perl script that exploits the Ezboard 2000 remote buffer overflow vulnerability. Released in 2002.

Fd_openbsd   Script that exploits the OpenBSD exec C Library Standard I/O File Descriptor Race Condition vulnerability. Released in 2002.

FDDI   Fiber Data Distribution Interface.

filespy (Windows)   filespy lets you watch I/O requests and processes.

filtering   Loosely defined, the process of checking network packets for integrity and security. Filtering is typically an automated process performed by either routers or software. In Apache terms, a system whereby you can specify and send files to or through a filter or program that handles them in a special way.

findgrp (Windows)   findgrp finds group memberships for the specified user.

findstr (Windows)   findstr searches for your specified text string in files or standard output. findstr is similar to Unix' grep and supports regular expressions (and is thus a tad more flexible than find.exe).

firewall   A device (hardware or software) that refuses unauthorized users access to a host or examines each packet's source address or content and performs some predefined operation based on what it finds therein.

Flawfinder   Flawfinder searches through source code for potential security flaws, listing potential security flaws sorted by risk, with the most potentially dangerous flaws shown first. This risk level depends not only on the function, but also on the values of the parameters of the function. Released in 2002.

Fmt_exp   Script that exploits the UnixWare library function vulnerability. Released in 2002.

Food_for_the_poor   Exploit for the KTH eBones Kerberos4 FTP client passive mode heap overflow vulnerability. Released in 2002.

Fragroute   Fragroute intercepts, modifies, and rewrites egress traffic destined for a specified host, implementing most of the attacks described in the "Secure Networks Insertion, Evasion, and Denial of Service: Eluding Network Intrusion Detection" paper of January 1998. Released in 2002.

Freebsdsendmaildos   Script that exploits the sendmail denial of service vulnerability. Released in 2002.

gawk   GNU's awk interpreter (Unix, MSDOS).

getmac (Windows)   getmac gets the localhost's Ethernet layer address.

Getret   Script that exploits the UnixWare library function vulnerability. Released in 2002.

getsid (Windows)   Compares SIDs between primary and backup domain controllers and notifies you of discrepancies. Such discrepancies indicate either foul play, database corruption, or both.

gettype (Windows)   Returns your operating system installation type (Windows 2000 Professional, Windows 2000 Server, NT Workstation, and so on).

global (Windows)   Displays members of global groups on remote servers or domains.

GOBBLES-invite   Script that exploits the IRCIT remote buffer overflow vulnerability. Released in 2002.

Gobbles-own-msn666   Script that exploits the MSN666 remote buffer overflow vulnerability. Released in 2002.

Gps   An advanced port scanner and a firewall rule disclosure tool that uses IP & ARP spoofing, sniffing, stealth scanning, ARP poisoning, IP fragmentation, and other techniques to perform stealthy and untrackable information collection. Released in 2002.

granularity   Degree to which you can incisively apply access controls. The more granularity, the more incisive you can get.

group   A collection of users represented by a value, typically a name, alias, or label. Such values let you specify file or network permissions to many individuals at once. Users belonging to the same group share similar or identical access privileges.

grpcpy (Windows)   Copies usernames from one group on one system to another group on another (or the same) system.

hacker   Someone interested in operating systems, software, security, and networking. Misused by many people to mean cracker.

Hanterm_exp   Script that exploits the Hanterm buffer overflow vulnerability. Released in 2002.

HDSL   High bit-rate digital subscriber line.

heapmon (Windows)   Displays heap information or how data is currently paged into memory. Using Heap Manager (a component service of `ntdll.dll`), you can alter how such data is paged and slice it into chunks smaller than the default page size.

Hl   Exploit for the *Half-Life* server new player flood denial of service vulnerability. Released in 2002.

home   The directory your operating system drops you into when you login. In Unix, it's typically `/home/hacker`, where `hacker` is your username. In Windows, it varies. See **$HOME**.

host table   A record of hostname-network address pairs. Host tables identify the name and location of each host on your network. Your operating system consults this before it begins a data transmission. Think of a host table as an address book.

host   A computer with a network address.

`hosts.equiv`   The trusted remote hosts and users database on some Unix platforms; a file that contains host names and addresses that localhost trusts.

`hosts_access`   A configuration file for tcpd, the TCP Wrapper daemon, that controls what users can access your server.

hosts_options A tcpd configuration file that provides optional extensions for controlling access to your server (an extension to hosts_access).

Hp-sap_evade Perl script that exploits the FreeBSD Process Information Bypass vulnerability. Released in 2002.

HTML (Hypertext Markup Language) A language that tells Web clients how to display data. Hypertext is different than plain text because it's interactive. In a hypertext document, you click or choose any highlighted text or link and the system retrieves the data associated with it.

htpasswd A program for creating and manipulating Apache HTTP-server password files.

HTTP_FORBIDDEN (Apache constant) Denotes HTTP Forbidden status. Indicates that Apache refused to return the requested resource (typically because the client doesn't have authorization).

HTTP_NON_AUTHORITATIVE (Apache constant) Denotes HTTP Non-Authoritative response status. The content came from a third-party source, not its original home server.

HTTP_PROXY_AUTHENTICATION_REQUIRED (Apache constant) Denotes HTTP Proxy Authentication Required status. (Go authenticate yourself at the proxy and come back.)

HTTP_REFERER URL Environment variable that stores the referring document's URL.

httpd An executable file that starts and stops your Apache Web server.

HTTPS HTTP over SSL is an encrypted version of HTTP for secure communications. Also, an Apache variable that specifies whether the server is using HTTPS.

HTTPS_CIPHER The HTTPS_CIPHER environment variable specifies which cipher is being used.

HTTPS_KEYSIZE The HTTPS_KEYSIZE environment variable specifies the session key size.

HTTPS_SECRETKEYSIZE The HTTPS_SECRETKEYSIZE environment variable specifies what secret key size is being used.

HUGE_STRING_LEN (Apache constant) Defines the largest static string buffer Apache supports (same as MAX_STRING_LEN).

Hydra A parallized login hacker that understands FTP, POP3, IMAP, Telnet, HTTP Auth, NNTP, VNC, ICQ, Socks5, PCNFS, samba, Cisco enable, LDAP, and more. Released in 2002.

Hypertext Transfer Protocol (HTTP)   The protocol used to traffic hypertext across the Internet, and the underlying protocol of the WWW.

Ibm-sqlexec   Script that exploits the Informix SE buffer overflow vulnerability. Available in both C and Perl forms. Released in 2002.

Icx   Script that exploits the Icecast buffer overflow vulnerability. Released in 2002.

Icx2   Script that exploits the Icecast v1.3.11 and below remote root vulnerability for Linux/*x*86. Released in 2002.

IdentityCheck (Apache)   The IdentityCheck directive, included as a core feature, enables RFC 1413-style logging of remote user names. This comprises Apache's support of the identification or ident protocol.

Ids-inform   Perl script that exploits the Iimage display system directory disclosure vulnerability. Released in 2002.

Ie.css.txt   Online demonstration exploit for the IE showModalDialog and showModelessDialog vulnerabilities. Released in 2002.

Ie_history.html   Exploit for the Internet Explorer history list vulnerability. Released in 2002.

IEEE   The Institute of Electronic and Electrical Engineering.

IETF   Internet Engineering Task Force.

ifconfig   A Unix tool that diagnoses and configures network interfaces.

IGMP   Internet Group Management Protocol.

Iischeck   Perl script that checks for the Microsoft IIS .HTR heap overflow vulnerability to determine whether the MS02-018 patch has been applied. Released in 2002.

inetd.conf   Internet servers database, a file that lists what services (FTP, TFTP, and so on) your server makes available, and how your server will launch such services when other hosts request them.

Injoin.txt   Exploit URLs for the InJoin directory server vulnerability. Released in 2002.

Innexpl   Script that exploits the multiple InterNetNews vulnerabilities. Released in 2002.

Interbase_gds_drop   Exploit that exploits the Interbase GDS_Lock_MGR and GDS_Drop buffer overflow vulnerabilities. Released in 2002.

Interbase_gds_l   Exploit that exploits the Interbase GDS_Lock_MGR and GDS_Drop buffer overflow vulnerabilities. Released in 2002.

International Data Encryption Algorithm (IDEA)   IDEA is a powerful block-cipher encryption algorithm that operates with a 128-bit key. IDEA encrypts data faster than DES, and is far more secure.

Internet Protocol Security Option (IPSEC)   IP security option used to protect IP datagrams. See RFC 1038 (`ftp://ftp.isi.edu/in-notes/rfc1038.txt`) and RFC 1108 (`ftp://ftp.isi.edu/in-notes/rfc1108.txt`).

interpreter   Generally a command interpreter, a shell, or a program that passes your instructions to the operating system and reports the results. Less generally, a program that reads in and executes special data. Examples: a PostScript interpreter reads postscript data and displays it in documents; a BASIC interpreter runs BASIC code.

intrusion detection   The practice of using automated systems to detect intrusion attempts.

Iosmash   Script that exploits the BSD exec C Library Standard I/O File Descriptor Closure vulnerability. Released in 2002.

IPC   Inter-Process Communication.

Ipchains   A Linux-based firewall administration tool.

ipfwadm   An older Linux-based firewall and accounting administration tool.

ipsecpol (Windows)   ipsecpol views or modifies IPSEC policies, either on a local or remote system, and in this respect, provides the same services as the IPSEC Policy snap-in in the Microsoft Management Console. The key difference is that ipsecpol lets you perform policy changes from inside scripts. This allows you substantial latitude in automating IPSEC policy establishment and disestablishment. (You'll find that many W2K command-line tools exist expressly for this purpose.)

Iptables   A Linux-based firewall administration tool.

Irx_xfsmd   Script that exploits the IRIX rpc.xfsmd remote command execution vulnerability. Released in 2002.

ISO   International Standards Organization.

Java   A popular Sun Microsystems programming language. Learn more at `http://java.sun.com/`.

javareg   Registers Java classes as COM (Component Object Model) components (COM components are interoperable components that work despite being developed on different operating systems or with different programming languages).

JavaScript   Netscape Communications Corporation programming language that runs in Web browser environments. JavaScript has extended functionality, and under certain conditions, can affect local client systems, even reaching beyond a browser environment to the underlying system itself. It therefore can pose security risks in some cases.

job control   Feature that lets you start and stop jobs interactively. See **job**.

job number   A number assigned to a particular job. See **job**.

job   A running process.

Kerberos   Massachusetts Institute of Technology encryption and authentication system that incorporates into network applications, relies on trusted third-party servers for authentication, and armors data against electronic eavesdropping. See RFC 1510.

kerbtray (Windows)   Kerberos Tray reports the tickets you've obtained during the current logon session.

Kernel.keylogger.txt   Paper that describes the basic concepts and techniques used for recording keystroke activity under Linux. Also includes proof of concept. Released in 2002.

kernprof (Windows)   kernprof is the Kernel Profiler, a tool for watching system kernel calls and drawing statistics from the report.

key pair   A key pair consists of two elements—a private key and its corresponding public key in an asymmetric cryptographic system. See **key**.

key   Loosely defined, a unique value derived from an algorithmic process that identifies a process, host, or user. In public key-private-key encryption, users have both public and private keys. They distribute their public key so others can encrypt messages with it. Such a message can only be decrypted with a user's private key. Not even the author of that message can unravel it. Users, therefore, store their private keys securely.

kill_conditions (Apache constant)   Enumeration of how Apache kills processes. Choices are kill_never, kill_always, kill_after_timeout, just_wait, and kill_only_once, or never, with a SIGKILL on pool cleanup, SIGKILL after three seconds, wait forever, or send a SIGTERM and wait, respectively.

klist   klist lists the current sessions Kerberos tickets and lets you delete them.

Kmem_mmap   Exploit for the GRSecurity Linux Kernel Memory Protection vulnerability. Released in 2002.

Lcrzoex   A toolbox for network administrators and network malicious users that contains over 200 functionalities using network library lcrzo. For example, one can use it to sniff, spoof, create clients/servers, create decode and display packets, and so on. Released in 2002.

leakyapp (Windows)   leakyapp lets you run tests to determine how the specified application performs under limited memory constraints. Chiefly, leakyapp is useful in determining whether a particular application (or application set) will fail given a specific memory allocation.

Libfmtb   A library that contains lots of functions for easily exploiting local and remote format string vulnerabilities. Released in 2002.

Libwhisker   A Perl module for performing whisker CGI vulnerability checks. Released in 2002.

Linspy2beta2   Keystroke logger for Linux kernels v2.2 and 2.4 that records TTY activity. Released in 2002.

Linux   An open source Unix flavor that runs on widely disparate hardware architectures.

Lkh   A powerful and documented kernel function-hooking library running on Linux 2.4/x86 that has been explained and had its API described in Phrack #58. Released in 2002.

Local Policies Snap-in (Windows)   The Local Policies Snap-in provides an interface for manipulating audit policies, user rights assignment, and security options. You reach it through My Computer → Control Panel → Administrative Tools → Local Security Settings.

Local Security Settings (Windows)   The Local Security settings utility provides an interface to many security policy tools and settings, including Account Policies, Local Policies, Public Key Policies, and IP Security Policies. You reach it through My Computer → Control Panel → Administrative Tools → Local Security Settings.

local (Windows)   Provides a quick, easy means of identifying users in local groups that have rights on remote domains. Using Perl (or another suitable scripting language), you can use local—in combination with other tools—to build a graphical map of users (and their group memberships) within a cluster of domains.

logevent (Windows)   logevent is one of W2K's cooler utilities. It lets you write directly to the event log from your own scripts (kind of a syslog.h situation expressly for scripts and batch files). For example, you could write a daemon that monitors user directories for specific source files or executables (perhaps a hacking utilities list). When one such file appears, your script could record that to the event log. This would give you evidence of a particular day, hour, and minute that such a tool first appeared on your system. logevent thus provides a means to extend W2K's logging capabilities.

LogFormat (Apache)   The LogFormat directive, available in mod_log_config, lets you specify what data Apache should log and how to format it.

logoff (Windows)   logoff performs a logoff from within a command-line environment. This is useful in automating scripts that perform limited actions and then die. They can log on, perform their assigned tasks, and call logoff, thus eliminating the need for human involvement.

logtime (Windows)   Logs the start and/or finish time of the called program. This is useful from a diagnostic viewpoint, as it tracks the time that a particular process took to complete.

Logwatch211   Script that exploits the LogWatch root compromise vulnerability. Released in 2002.

MAC (Media Access Control)   Layer of the OSI Reference Model.

Matuftp_exploit   Perl script that exploits the Matu FTP client buffer overflow vulnerability. Released in 2002.

Matuftpwin98   Perl script that exploits the Matu FTP server buffer overflow vulnerability. Released in 2002.

MAX_STRING_LEN (Apache constant)   Defines the largest static string buffer Apache supports (same as HUGE_STRING_LEN).

Mayday-linux   Script that exploits the SHOUTCast remote buffer overflow vulnerability. Released in 2002.

MD5   A message digest algorithm that produces a digital fingerprint of specified input. Because such a fingerprint is unique, and it's mathematically difficult to create a duplicate, developers use MD5 to authenticate file and session integrity.

metacharacter   A symbol common to configuration files, shell scripts, Perl scripts, and C source code. Typical metacharacters and metacharacter combinations are ., !, @, #, $, %, ^, &, &&, *, >, >>, <, <<, !=, ==, +=, ?, =, |, ||, and ~.

Mimedefang   A flexible MIME email scanner designed to protect Windows clients from viruses and other harmful executables that work with sendmail 8.11/8.12's milter API and will alter or delete various parts of a MIME message according to a flexible configuration file. Released in 2002.

Mircexploit   Script that exploits the MIRC Nickname Buffer Overflow vulnerability. Released in 2002.

mirroring   Mirroring is the practice of duplicating disk volumes for the purpose of redundancy. Typically you do this across separate drives, or even across separate hosts.

Mnews   Perl script that exploits the MNews remote FreeBSD buffer overflow vulnerability. Released in 2002.

mod_access (Apache)   mod_access provides access control based on client hostname or IP address. mod_access provides this access control through .htaccess files and within <Directory>, <Files>, and <Location> directive blocks.

mod_auth   An Apache access control module that provides user authentication using plain text files.

mod_auth_anon (Apache module)   mod_auth_anon provides anonymous user management, and lets you specify if, how, and where anonymous users gain entry to password-protected directories.

mod_auth_db (Apache module)   mod_auth_db provides user authorization through Berkeley DB (instead of DBM) files.

mod_auth_dbm (Apache module)   mod_auth_dbm provides user authorization through DBM files.

mod_auth_digest (Apache)   mod_auth_digest provides authentication through use of message digest algorithms. Currently, above and beyond Basic-type authentication, Apache supports digest-based cryptographic authentication using MD5. MD5 belongs to a family of one-way hash functions called message digest algorithms, and was originally defined in RFC 1321.

mod_auth_ldap (Apache)   mod_auth_ldap authenticates clients via user entries in a Lightweight Directory Access Protocol (LDAP) directory.

mod_cgi (Apache)   mod_cgi provides Common Gateway Interface program execution. The Common Gateway Interface (CGI) is a standard that specifies how Web servers use external applications to pass dynamic information to Web clients.

mod_cgid   A dynamic content Apache module that provides support for invoking CGI scripts using an external daemon.

mod_isapi   A dynamic content Apache module that provides support for Windows ISAPI Extension support.

mod_ldap   Apache module that offers an LDAP connection pool and shared memory cache.

mod_log_config   A logging-related Apache module that is a user-configurable logging replacement for mod_log_common.

mod_ssl   Apache module that offers Secure Sockets Layer (SSL) and Transport Layer Security (TLS) protocol support.

mod_suexec (Apache)   mod_suexec provides support for running CGI scripts as a specified User and Group. This eliminates many CGI security issues, for it enables you to more incisively control script permissions.

mod_usertrack   A logging-related Apache module that offers user tracking with cookies.

Morpheus   Exploit for the FastTrack P2P Technology Identity Spoofing and Denial of Service vulnerability. Released in 2002.

moveuser (Windows)   Moves a profile's security from one user to another.

mscep.dll (Windows)   Mscep.dll (the Certificate Enrollment Module for Routers) provides an interface through which W2K can easily enroll Cisco routers for IPSec authentication certificates.

Msh3comdos   Script that exploits 3Com 3CDaemon buffer overflow vulnerability. Released in 2002.

mtfcheck (Windows)   Verifies that backup tapes are Microsoft Tape Format-compliant, and can determine whether their data is corrupted. This lets you verify—from an automated script—that your backup was successful.

Nbtenum11   A utility for Windows which can be used to enumerate one single host or an entire class C subnet. This utility can run in two modes: query and attack. Released in 2002.

nbtstat (Windows)   Displays current TCP/IP connections via NetBIOS, local NetBIOS names, sessions, and so on.

Nessus   An up-to-date and full featured remote security scanner for Linux, BSD, Solaris, and some other systems that currently performs over 900 remote security checks. Released in 2002.

net accounts (Windows)   Lets you view or change network user login and password information over a network connection.

net computer (Windows)   Lets you add or delete computers from the specified domain.

net config (Windows)   Lets you view and change your system's configurable services and view statistics.

net file (Windows)   Lets you view the names of files currently open (and unlock files still locked by defunct but persistent processes).

net localgroup (Windows)   Lets you add or modify groups on the local system.

net name (Windows)   Displays the local system's aliases.

net pause (Windows)   Temporarily suspends the specified service. Available services are File Server For Macintosh, LPDSVC, Net Logon, Network DDE, Network DDE DSDM, NTLM Security Support Provider, Remote Access Server, Schedule, Server, Simple TCP/IP Services, and Workstation.

net send (Windows)   Sends messages to other users and computers. This is especially useful to invoke from scripts that warn of a specific condition. To try it, open a command window and type **net send** *computername* **Hello World.**

net session (Windows)   A W2K command that lets you view or kill current client sessions.

net share (Windows)   Lets you view or kill current shares.

net start (Windows)   A W2K command that lets you view or start services.

net stop (Windows)   A W2K command that lets you stop running services.

netclip   netclip is the networked clipboard viewer. Using it, you can view clipboard data residing on a remote machine.

netcons (Windows)   A nifty little GUI tool that displays your current network connections.

Netgear.txt   Perl script that exploits the NetGear RO318 HTTP filter vulnerability. Released in 2002.

netsh (Windows)   The W2K network shell utility, a tool that lets you configure local and remote workstations and servers via script files.

netstat   Command that shows the current TCP/IP connections, and their source addresses.

netsvc (Windows)   Lets you view, display, start, stop, or query network services. A simple query, for example, will list all services, their handles, and their display names.

NetWare   A popular network operating system from Novell.

Network Information System (NIS)   A popular Unix authentication system originally created by Sun Microsystems. Formerly called the Yellow Pages system.

Network Interface Card (NIC)   An Ethernet card.

Nmap   A utility for port scanning large networks. Released in 2002.

Nsat   Network Security Analysis Tool is a fast, stable bulk security scanner designed to audit remote network services and check for versions, security problems, gather information about the servers, the machine, and much more. Released in 2002.

Ntfs-hide   Exploit for the Microsoft Windows NTFS file hiding vulnerability. Released in 2002.

ntrights (Windows)   Lets you grant or revoke user and group rights from a command-line environment. Most commonly, administrators use this to automate the establishment of their preferred rights schemes on new installations. However, you could also use ntrights in IDS scripts (if a user does *x*, revoke his rights).

Obsd-cron   Script that exploits the OpenBSD root compromise vulnerability. Released in 2002.

Ock_mgr   Exploits the Interbase GDS_Lock_MGR and GDS_Drop buffer overflow vulnerabilities. Released in 2002.

oh (Windows)   Reports all the current open windows' handles and therefore bears a vague resemblance to Unix's ps, which shows the numbers and names of current processes.

one-time password   A password generated dynamically during a challenge-response exchange. OTP-enabled systems generate such passwords using a predefined algorithm, but are highly secure, because they're good for the current session only.

Oracle   Database system for large enterprises.

Osshchan   Script that exploits the OpenSSH `channel_lookup()` off by one vulnerability. Released in 2002.

Osxicq   Script that exploits the ICQ for MacOS X denial of service vulnerability. Released in 2002.

owner   User, host, or process with authorization to read, write, or otherwise access a given process, file, directory, user, or host. Generally, you as system administrator assign ownership, although your system may sometimes automatically assign it during an automated task.

Own-screen   Script that exploits the GNU screen braille module buffer overflow vulnerability. Released in 2002.

packets   Data sent over networks is fragmented into manageable chunks called packets, or frames. The protocol used determines their size.

perfmon4 (Windows)   Measures system performance in various areas, including CPU time, interrupt time, user time, and so forth. It graphically and dynamically displays this information in real time.

perfmtr (Windows)   Displays system performance in various areas, including CPU time, interrupt time, user time, and so forth, all in a command-line environment.

Perl   Practical Extraction and Report Language, a programming language suited to network programming, text processing, and CGI.

permcopy (Windows)   Copies share and file permissions from one share to another.

perms (Windows)   Reports the specified users permissions on the specified files.

PGP   Pretty Good Privacy, a public key-private key encryption system that offers high-grade encryption and privacy. Learn more about PGP at `http://web.mit.edu/network/pgp.html`.

Phgrafx   Exploit for the multiple QNX RTOS vulnerabilities. Released in 2002.

Phgrafx-startup   Exploit for the multiple QNX RTOS vulnerabilities. Released in 2002.

Phlocale   Script that exploits the multiple QNX RTOS vulnerabilities. Released in 2002.

Phusion_dos   Exploit for the multiple Phusion Webserver vulnerabilities. Released in 2002.

Phusion_exp   Exploit for the multiple Phusion Webserver vulnerabilities. Released in 2002.

Phusion-get   Exploit for the multiple Phusion Webserver vulnerabilities. Released in 2002.

Phusion-ovrun   Exploit for the multiple Phusion Webserver vulnerabilities. Released in 2002.

Phusion-web   Exploit information for the multiple Phusion Webserver vulnerabilities. Released in 2002.

ping   Tests checks remote hosts to see whether they're alive or reachable, and reports packet loss and other network statistics.

Pkg-installer   Script that exploits the QNX RTOS PKG-Installer buffer overflow vulnerability. Released in 2002.

Pos_expl2   Script that exploits the Posadis m5pre2 local format string vulnerability. Released in 2002.

Ppp-2.4.1+Bf.patch   A patch that adds PPP authentication brute force password guessing support to Linux pppd. Released in 2002.

process   A program or job that is currently running.

Promiscdetect.exe   PromiscDetect for Windows NT 4.0/2000/XP checks whether your network adapter(s) is in promiscuous mode. Released in 2002.

protocol analyzer   Hardware or software that can monitor or intercept network traffic.

ps   A Unix command that lists current processes.

pstat (Windows)   pstat lists all running processes.

PSTN   Public Switched Telephone Network.

Psybnc   Perl script that exploits the PsyBNC oversized passwords denial of service vulnerability. Released in 2002.

ptree (Windows)   Builds and displays the process inheritance tree and lets you kill processes locally or remotely.

pulist (Windows)   Lists all running processes, their PID, and the associated user. In this respect, pulist is very similar to Unix's ps utility, and is useful for monitoring what users are up to.

pUll   Perl script that exploits the SLRNPull spool directory command line parameter buffer overflow vulnerability. Released in 2002.

Python   An object-oriented scripting language that can be used for CGI development.

Qnx-gdb-root   Exploit for the multiple QNX RTOS vulnerabilities. Released in 2002.

qslice (Windows)   A quick-and-dirty process CPU utilization monitor. It graphically demonstrates the CPU usage of each running application.

qtcp (Windows)   Tests a given network connection's quality of service.

RAID (Redundant Array of Inexpensive Disks)   A large amount of connected hard drives that together act as one drive. Helps with data redundancy, backups, performance, and disaster recovery.

Rats   A security auditing utility for C, C++, Python, Perl, and PHP code. Released in 2002.

rcmd (Windows)   The client for the rcmdsvc server, this provides a convenient way to execute commands on remote machines, and functions similarly to Unix's rsh.

rcmdsvc (Windows)   The server for the rcmd client, this is a service that provides a convenient way to execute commands on remote machines, and functions similarly to Unix's rshd.

rcp   Copies the specified file to or from a machine running the rcp server.

read access   When a user, group, or extenal users have read access only, they can read a particular file.

read-only   When a file is read-only, users can read it but not write to it.

reducer (Windows)   Reduces tracelog output to a report on per-thread processes.

regback (Windows)   Lets you back up registry data without backing up to traditional backup media; it instead redirects the data to a file or files. This offers a quick-and-dirty way to perform registry restore (a wise move, because sometimes, registry corruption can block your ability to perform a traditional restore). Also, you can perform registry backups from scripts on the fly.

regdmp (Windows)   Dumps your registry information, such as username and domain membership, local and roam profile settings, group membership, group policies, and so forth, to STDOUT. The report is extensive and lets you view (and perhaps act on) registry information from within scripts (or pipe such information to other programs).

regfind (Windows)   Lets you search the registry from a command-line environment for strings, keys, and such.

regrest (Windows)   Restores registry backup files you created with regback, a tool that writes registry backups to files rather than traditional backup media such as tapes.

Remotefmt-howto.txt   How to Remotely Exploit Format String Bugs tutorial that includes information on guessing the offset, guessing the address of the shellcode in the stack, using format string bugs as debuggers, examples, and so on. Released in 2002.

RFC   Requests for Comments (RFCs) are the working notes and standards of the Internet community. Learn more at `http://www.ietf.org/`.

root   The superuser, or all-powerful administrative account in Unix.

rpcdump (Windows)   A Remote Procedure Call endpoint diagnostic tool that determines whether RPC endpoints are healthy.

RSA   RSA is the Rivest-Shamir-Adleman public key cryptographic algorithm and system.

RSRC_CONF (Apache constant)   Any directive with this bit set can appear in global or server-wide config files.

RSVP   Resource Reservation Protocol.

RTP   Real-Time Transport Protocol.

runext (Windows)   Lets you add a Run option for files you right-click in Explorer (and an options input box to pass parameters). For example, suppose you want to run a script from within Explorer. If the script takes parameters or arguments (and you don't use runext(), you have no way of passing those parameters to the script; Explorer will simply execute it. runext solves this problem.

S/Key   One-time password system that secures connections. In S/Key, passwords never travel over the network, and therefore attackers cannot sniff them. See RFC 1760 for details (`ftp://ftp.isi.edu/in-notes/rfc1760.txt`).

Safemodexploit   Exploit for the PHP MySQL Safe_Mode filesystem circumvention vulnerability. Released in 2002.

Salescart-ex   Script that exploits the SalesCart customer database disclosure vulnerability. Released in 2002.

Sambar.fileparse.txt   Sample URLs for the Sambar server script source Disclosure vulnerability. Released in 2002.

sc (Windows)   A diagnostic tool that lets you start and stop NT Service Controller-driven services from within scripts. Using sc, you can control these services thorough a wide range of commands, including query, start, stop, pause, config, failures, and so forth.

scanreg (Windows)   Lets you scan the registry for arbitrary text strings to find names, keys, and so on.

`scoreboard.c`   Apache server source file that contains scoreboard functions, including those dealing with IPC. Includes `apr.h`, `apr_strings.h`, `apr_portable.h`, `apr_lib.h`, `apr_want.h`, `sys/types.h`, `ap_config.h`, `httpd.h`, `http_log.h`, `http_main.h`, `http_core.h`, `http_config.h`, `ap_mpm.h`, `mpm.h`, `scoreboard.h`, and `apr_shmem.h`.

Screen-stuff.tgz   Exploit for the GNU screen braille module buffer overflow vulnerability. Released in 2002.

Secure Socket Layer (SSL)   A security protocol that enables client/server applications to communicate free of eavesdropping, tampering, or message forgery. SSL is now used for secure electronic Web commerce, and has been renamed TLS.

Security Log (Windows)   Reports security-auditing events (such as object access, logons, and so on). You reach it through Event Viewer (My Computer → Control Panel → Administrative Tools → Event Viewer).

`SECURITY_HOLE_PASS_AUTHORIZATION` (Apache constant)   Passes not just username but password in authentication.

sendmail-flock-sploit   Local exploit for the sendmail denial of service vulnerability. Released in 2002.

Servletexeccrash   Script that exploits the NewAtlanta ServletExec ISAPI 4.1 remote denial of service vulnerability. Released in 2002.

SET   Secured Electronic Transaction. A standard of secure protocols associated with online commerce and credit card transactions. Visa and MasterCard are the chief players in development of the SET protocol. Its ostensible purpose is to make electronic commerce more secure.

shadowing   The practice of isolating encrypted password values so that they're beyond an attacker's reach. The passwords are still usable, but hidden from prying eyes. These often reside in `/etc/shadow` on Unix.

Shared Folders (Windows)   The Shared Folders utility, available through Microsoft Management Console, offers a centralized interface to manage shares, sessions, and open files. You reach it through My Computer → Control Panel → Administrative Tools → Shared Folders.

Show_debug_data   Perl script that exploits the CGIScript.net information Disclosure vulnerability. Released in 2002.

showacls (Windows)   A command-line tool that lets you dump acls for files, folders, and trees to STDOUT, thus offering a means to query and identify user permissions via automated scripts.

showgrps (Windows)   Prints user group memberships to STDOUT.

showmount   A Unix program that displays exported file systems.

showpriv (Windows)   Lets you examine (from STDOUT) a specific group's or user's privileges. For example, you can use it to discover who has backup privileges, who can increase quotas, who can access and manage security logs, and so forth.

Silentlog   A keystroke logging tool that runs under several Windows versions. Released in 2002.

Simpleinitexploit   Script that exploits the SimpleInit inherit file descriptor vulnerability. Released in 2002.

Slrnpull-ex   Perl script that exploits the SLRNPull spool directory command line parameter buffer overflow vulnerability. Released in 2002.

Snexploit   Exploit for a buffer overflow vulnerability in the snes9x Nintendo emulator. Released in 2002.

sniffer   Hardware or software that captures datagrams on a network. Users can deploy sniffers legitimately (to diagnose network problems), or illegitimately (to crack network passwords and subvert security and privacy).

Snscan   A Windows GUI SNMP detection utility that can quickly and accurately identify SNMP-enabled devices on a network. This utility can effectively indicate devices that are potentially vulnerable to SNMP-related security threats. Released in 2002.

source (source code)   Raw uncompiled program code that when compiled (or simply run) will constitute an application or program.

spoofing   Procedure in which a user or host impersonates another user or host to gain unauthorized access to a trusting target.

Sq125x   Exploit for the SquirrelMail theme remote command execution vulnerability. Released in 2002.

SQL (Structured Query Language)   Relational database query language.

Sql_injection_walkthrough.txt   Document that describes SQL injection attack Web applications by submitting raw SQL queries as input. Released in 2002.

Sqlcppx   Script that exploits the Progress sqlcpp local buffer overflow vulnerability. Released in 2002.

Sqlinjectionwhitepaper.pdf   A paper on a technique for exploiting Web applications that uses client-supplied data in SQL queries without stripping illegal characters first. Released in 2002.

srvcheck (Windows)   Reports all server shares and which users have access to them.

srvmgr (Windows)   A GUI tool for managing domains and computers from a central location.

ssh   Secure Shell, a program that encrypts Telnet-like remote sessions.

standard error (STDERR)   Error output from programs. STDERR typically prints directly to your terminal screen in real time. However, you can redirect this output elsewhere.

standard input (STDIN)   Your commands are standard input. Your operating system reads commands (which you express in text) from your terminal and/or keyboard.

standard output (STDOUT)   Output from computer programs. STDOUT usually prints to your terminal in real time, but you can redirect this elsewhere.

su (Windows)   A W2K clone of Unix's classic su. su lets you execute a process under a user ID other than your own. The new process inherits both the environment variables and privileges of the specified user (which could be any valid user in a workgroup or domain).

subinacl (Windows)   Lets administrators transfer user information on files, registry keys, and services from one domain (or workgroup) to another.

sudo   A Unix program that enables system administrators to assign users the power to execute select commands as the superuser.

svcacls (Windows)   The Service ACL Editor lets you use Access Control Lists from a command-line environment (or in scripts) to control user access to services.

svcmon (Windows)   Watches services and emails you when they start or stop.

Symace   Script that exploits the BRU insecure temporary file vulnerability. Released in 2002.

syslogd   A system logging server in Unix that logs system and kernel messages.

sysprep (Windows)   Prepares systems for cloning. You generate one solid W2K installation and then use sysprep to perform automated disk duplication.

System Log (Windows)   Reports system alerts and critical, informational, and warning events (such as service failures, conflicts, and so on). You reach it through Event Viewer (My Computer → Control Panel → Administrative Tools → Event Viewer).

takeown (Windows)   This will obliterate a W2K installation, including system security files that are otherwise undeletable.

Talkspoof   Exploit for the multiple vendor TalkD user validation vulnerability. Released in 2002.

Tcc.tar   TCP Congestion paper and proof-of-concept code for a vulnerability in the TCP protocol that affects several operating systems, allowing remote denial-of-service attacks. Released in 2002.

tcpd   The daemon for TCP Wrapper, which logs (and can allow or deny) Telnet, finger, ftp, and other connections on Unix platforms, and also controls access based on configuration files, such as hosts.allow.

tcpdump   A network-monitoring tool that logs IP packets.

Telnet Server Administration (Windows)   The Telnet Server Administration console application, included in the Microsoft Management Console, offers a central management system for setting your Telnet server options: starting the service, stopping the service, and querying for user sessions. You reach it from My Computer → Control Panel → Administrative Tools → Telnet Server → Administration.

Telozarzo   Script that exploits the Telindus router 10xx and 11xx vulnerability. Released in 2002.

TEMPEST   Transient Electromagnetic Pulse Surveillance Technology. The practice and study of capturing/eavesdropping on electromagnetic signals that emanate from electronic devices. TEMPEST shielding is where a computer system is armored to prevent emissions, and is thus designed to defeat such eavesdropping.

Tgt_v1_x86Lnx   Script that exploits the OpenSSH Kerberos 4 TGT/AFS token buffer overflow vulnerability. Released in 2002.

Tgt-X86linux   Another exploit for the OpenSSH Kerberos 4 TGT/AFS token buffer overflow vulnerability. Released in 2002.

Tnslsnrx   Script that exploits the Oracle 8i TNS listener local buffer overflow vulnerability. Released in 2002.

Tomas   A command-line tool to crack the secret passwords on Cisco routers. Released in 2002.

Tracesex   Perl script that exploits the TrACESroute terminator function format string vulnerability. Released in 2002.

traffic analysis   Traffic analysis is the study of patterns in communication, rather than the communication's actual content. For example, studying when, where, and to whom particular messages are being sent, instead of studying the content of those messages.

TripWire   An add-on file integrity checker.

Trojan horse   A code or application that, unbeknownst to the user, performs surreptitious and unauthorized tasks that can compromise system security.

trusted system   A secure operating system for use in environments where classified information is warehoused.

Ucd-421   Script that exploits the UCD-snmp trap handling vulnerability. Released in 2002.

UID   User ID.

UPS (Uninterruptible Power Supply)   A backup power supply for when your primary power source fails.

User (Apache)   The User directive sets Apache's user ID (UID), or the user under which Apache will answer client requests. Never set this to root. In default installations this value is user nobody.

user ID   Generally, any value by which a user is identified, including their user name. Specifically in relation to multi-user environments, any process ID—typically a numeric value—that identifies a process's owner.

Users and Passwords (Windows)   The Users and Passwords tool lets you manage user passwords, names, and certificates. You reach it via My Computer → Control Panel → Users and Passwords.

usrtogrp (Windows)   Usrtogrp.exe is for adding users to groups on a wholesale basis. It works like this: You first place your desired users in a text file, one per line. Usrtogrp.exe then steps through the file user-by-user and adds the specified users to the domain and group you specify. Usrtogrp.exe is a great solution when you're faced with en masse user migration.

Uw-imap   Script that exploits the Imap4 remote Linux vulnerability. Released in 2002.

VDSL   Very high bit-rate digital subscriber line.

vfi (Windows)   vfi (Visual File Information) displays file characteristics in sufficient detail to constitute a low-grade file integrity assessment tool. You can use it to write scripts that detect subtle changes in your file system (and subsequently warn you of the same, or perhaps take some specified action).

Virtual Private Network (VPN)   A closed, private network and secure circuit over intranet or Internet lines where transitory data is encrypted and passed only between trusted points.

Voodoo2   A library that makes heap overflow exploitation much easier by providing the user with valuable internal data from Doug Lea's malloc implementation. Released in 2002.

Vpnkillient   Script that exploits the VPN client buffer overflow vulnerability. Released in 2002.

vulnerability (hole)   A system weakness (in either hardware or software) that allows intruders to gain unauthorized access or deny service.

War-ftpd-bof   Perl script that exploits the WarFTPd remote buffer overflow vulnerability. Released in 2002.

Webbbsexploit   Perl script that exploits the WebBBS remote command execution vulnerability. Released in 2002.

Wellenreiter   A GTK/Perl program that makes the discovery and auditing of 802.11b wireless networks much easier. Released in 2002.

Wpoison-dev   A tool that attempts to find SQL-injection vulnerabilities on a remote Web document. Released in 2002.

write access   When a user, group, or public users have write access, it means that they have permission and privileges to write to a particular file or directory.

X2   Script that exploits the SSH restricted shell escaping command execution vulnerability. Released in 2002.

Xls_sux   Exploit for the Excel 2002 XML stylesheet arbitrary code execution vulnerability. Released in 2002.

Yahoo-im   Document that describes information regarding the Yahoo! Instant Messenger buffer overflow vulnerability and a how-to explaining the technique used to hijack another IM client. Released in 2002.

Ymxp   Exploit for the Yahoo! Messenger buffer overflow vulnerability for Windows XP Pro. Released in 2002.

Index

**AtStake.com Web site, L0phtCrack pass-
word cracker, 266**

ATT Blitz program (mailbombing), 605

**attack signatures, network-based (NIDS),
233-234**

attackers

  black hats, 178

  script kiddies, 177-178

  white hats, 178

attacks

  blind spoofing, 126

  corporate espionage, 188-189

  credit card theft, 189-190

  DDoS (Distributed Denial of Service),
   181

  DoS (Denial of Service), 181

  external, 385-386

  hacktivists, 182-183

  internal, 183, 385-386

  malicious scripts, transmission of,
   181-182

  motivating factors, 185

    challenge of breaking in, 191

    destruction, 186

    disgruntled employees, 187

    financial gain, 187-190

    knowledge, 190-191

    malicious pranks, 186

    notoriety, 186

    political statements, 187

  non-blind spoofing, 126

  operating system vulnerabilities

    Macintosh OS, 176

    OpenBSD, 175-176

    Windows OS, 176

  persistent dial-up connections, 175

  physical, 385-386

  sequence number type, 125-126

  sniffers

    eliminating, 290-292

    Milnet incident, 283-284

    Solar Sunrise incident, 284

  spoofing, 121

    1644 utility, 129

    ARP, 133-134

    DNS, 134

    document resources, 131

    Hunt utility, 129

    increased occurrence of, 128-129

    ipspoof utility, 130

    Juggernaut utility, 130

    mechanics of, 124-127

    prevention of, 132-133

    rbone utility, 130

    session hijacking, 124

    spoofit utility, 130

    successful indicators, 127

    suitable holes, 127

    synk4.c utility, 131

    targeted services, 128

    Web, 135-136

  targets, 172-174, 183

    corporations, 184

    financial institutions, 185

    government agencies, 184

    home users, 184

    large businesses, 184

    military sites, 184

    small businesses, 184

  TCPWrappers, 451

  theft of intellectual property, 188-189

C

I

How can we make this index more useful? Email us at indexes@samspublishing.com

How can we make this index more useful? Email us at indexes@samspublishing.com

How can we make this index more useful? Email us at indexes@samspublishing.com